Sepher Sapphires:

A Treatise on Gematria

The Magical Language of the Mysteries

Volume 2

Forward by

Chic and Tabatha Cicero

Written by

Wade Coleman

Edited by

Darcy Küntz

Sepher Sapphires: Volume 2 by Wade Coleman.

First Edition, 2001.
Second Edition, 2002.
Third Edition, 2003.
Fourth Edition, 2004.
Fifth Edition, 2005.
Sixth Edition, 2006.
First Renaissance Astrology Press Edition, 2006
Fraternity of the Hidden Light Edition, 2008
Amber Studios Addition, 2019

ISBN: 978-1-7375871-5-6

Acknowledgments

I would like to thank **Kenneth Grant** for his permission to quote liberal sections of his book *Nightside of Eden*. His work on the Tunnels of Set are one of a kind.

I would like to thank **Ordo Templi Orientis** for permission to quote from the *Sepher Sephiroth* by Aleister Crowley.

The material in *True and Invisible Rosicrucian Order* by Paul Foster Case is quoted with Red Wheel / Weiser Publishing permission.

To contact the author, write to this email.

DENDARA_ZODIAC@protonmail.com

Table of Contents

Section 4 – Numbers 400 to 499   7

Section 5 – Numbers 500 to 59   83

Section 6 – Numbers 600 to 699   133

Section 7 – Numbers 700 to 799   177

Section 8 – Numbers 800 to 899   212

Section 9 – Numbers 900 to 999   243

Section 10 – Numbers 1,000+   256

The Appendices

Appendix 1 – Gematria Tables   290

Appendix 2 – The Nature of Numbers   293

Appendix 3 – Theosophic Extensions   296

Appendix 4 – Prime Numbers   297

Appendix 5 – Perfect Numbers   299

Appendix 6 – The Divine Proportion   302

Appendix 7 – Magic Squares   310

Appendix 8 – The Four Worlds   320

Appendix 9 – The Shem ha-Mephorash   322

Appendix 10 – Goetia Demons   330

Appendix 11 – Tunnels of Set   335

Appendix 12 – Names of the Sephiroth   337

Appendix 13 –Tree of Life   338

Appendix 14 –32 Paths of Wisdom I   339

Appendix 15 – 32 Paths of Wisdom II   342

Appendix 16 – Tarot Attributions   389

Appendix 17 – Sound & Color   391

Appendix 18 – Angles of the Sephiroth   399

Biography   404

Section 4

Numbers 400-499

400

I. (2^4 x 5^2)

II. Number of cubits of the porch of Solomon's temple and Holy of Holies.

ת *Tav.* A signature or mark. The actual mark is a cross having four equal arms—the last letter of the Hebrew alphabet. It was written as a cross of equal arms in ancient Hebrew, similar to a plus sign +, and sometimes like the multiplication symbol x. The letter Tav as a cross appears on the breast of the High Priestess in Key 2. The secret of the stone of the wise is also the secret of the cross, which is the end (Tav). This fulfillment or completion is symbolically represented by the 22 letters of the Hebrew alphabet. Note that Tav's direction is center, "the place of holiness in the midst." See 1271 (Greek).

In Ezekiel 9:4 Go throughout the city of Jerusalem and put a mark (Tav, תו) of the foreheads of those who grieve and lament over all the detestable things that are done in it." Those with the Mark were spared from death.

Tav corresponds to the Egyptian Tau. It was a device to measure the Nile's depth and a square for testing right angles. It was a symbol the salvation from death and a signature of eternal life

Representing a signature, this letter implies security, pledge and guarantee. A signature makes a document valid. Thus the letter is the seal and completion of the Great Work. This is an experience that validates our assumption of the Unity of Being. And this is symbolized by the point where the two lines cross, the One Life abode.

Tav represents the point of control at the Center or heart. The heart is here defined as midst, inmost core. The heart of your personal existence is to enter the Palace of the Kingdom. There the One Self is enthroned. There is the central point of authority and rulership, extending boundless influence throughout the Cosmos. This innermost point is in itself No-Thing because it is beyond physical form. The innermost point is the fullness of being. The holy temple stands in the center and is everywhere, as well as in the center of your own being. At this point, when the Great Work is accomplished, and the Father and the Son are in perfect union, and the New Kingdom is established.

The Kingdom [Malkuth] is linked with Yesod by the path of Tav. Tav is the Temple in the midst, as it is written in *Sepher Yetzirah*. The letter Tav the special sign of the Lord and of His Holy Temple. See *C.9*, 89, 430.

Adam is the מלך or King, and his power to rule is the consequence of his utter dependence (Key 12) on what supports him - , which is the center's power corresponding to Tav.

The body is also Tav or the point at the lower end of the 32nd Path on the Tree of Life. In Malkuth, three paths find their completion. They are the 29th Path of the Corporeal Intelligence (Qoph), the 31st Path of Shin (Fire and the Ruach Elohim) and the 32nd Path of Tav (Saturn and of Earth). This is the embodiment or integration of the fire of spirit through the finitizing power of Saturn. Tav that it is "the Temple of Holiness in the midst." Of everybody, whether mineral, vegetable, animal or human, this is true. It is a center or focus for all the powers of Heaven and Earth." See *C.24*, 476.

Key 21 corresponds to Tav. It is a symbol of union. Note that the extension of 6 is 21. The man in Key 6 reaches its full expression (a hermaphrodite) in Key 21. The number 21 is a representation of Binah because 21 reduces to 3. In Key 21, you see delineated a representation of the idea expressed in the word אין, which is both בטן and אמך. This is a great secret with many practical applications." See *C.32*, 67, 713, 61.

I. The letter Tav is the seal of the cosmic administration because it combines the imaginative powers of subconsciousness, Daleth, with the liberating power of change, Nun." [Simple Stories From the Heart, Rabbi Kardia]

II. "This character, as a consonant, belongs to the sibilant sound. In consecrating it to Thoth, the ancient Egyptians, whose name they gave it, regarded it as the universal mind's symbol. As a grammatical sign in the Hebraic tongue, it is that of sympathy and reciprocity; joining, to the abundance of the character ר, to the force of resistance and protection of the character ט, the idea of perfection and necessity which it is the emblem. Although not an article of speech, it often appears at the head of words, thus it was probably used as such in one of the Egyptian dialects, where without a doubt it represented the relation את; in the same manner that the character פ represented the relation פה, פא or פי. [d'Olivet, 1976, pp. 465-466.]

III. "*Tav* (400): Tav is the cosmic resistance to the life-breath which animates it. Without this resistance of Tav (400), life could not come into existence. This resistance to life is that which enables life to produce its prodigiously varied manifest forms." [Suraes, 1992, p. 66.]

הנני יסד בציון אבן *Hinnay, yawsae be-Zion, ehben.* Isaiah 28:16: "Behold, I lay in Zion for a foundation of stone."

כשף *kashawf.* magician. With different pointing: 1. magic, sorcery; 2. to practice magic, mutter incantations, to enchant bewitch, charm. In Jeremiah 27:9, this word is used in the plural. Magic is a two-edge sword-the magician practice it wisely; the sorcerer's incantations bewitch. As a verb: to pay close attention, to listen, to speak softly, to use magic. See 4, 40, 89, 44.

משכיל *maskil.* instruction, erudition; wise person. A wise, prudent skillful person. As a noun, a title of Yesod. Intelligent, wise in Proverbs 10:5: "He who works in summer is a wise man; but he who sleeps in harvest is a son that causes shame." see 80, 350, 355, 979.

פשוטה *peshutah.* Literal sense of the text of the scripture. The "outer garment" of the law. From פשט, straight, plain; simple, flat, level; the direct sense.

שנים *shenaim.* years. With different pointing *shenai*: two, double. Illumination results from the overcoming or balancing all the pairs of opposites. See Key 2, the Uniting Intelligence.

ספרין *sepherin.* (the) books Daniel 7:10: "The Judgement was set, and the books were opened." The books are those inner books of life that are opened during the process of illumination. See 904, 704.

שק *sack.* Sackcloth, bag, sack. Refers to the heart, or blood-sack. See 444.

שעל *shoal.* Handful; the hollow of the hand, the palm, depth of the sea. Grasp or comprehension is attributed to Kaph, which leads one to the knowledge of the great sea, Binah. See 67 & Key 10.

נשים *Nesheim.* Wives. A reference to Tav's path, which connects the king (Tiphareth) to the bride (Malkuth). Genesis 6:2: "That the sons of God saw the daughters of men that they were fair; and they took them, wives, all of which they chose." see 713 and Mark 12:25.

שמין *shemayin.* heavens, heaven. In Daniel 4:11: "The tree grew and was strong, and the height thereof reached unto heaven, and the sight thereof to the end of all the earth." And in Daniel 7:2: "Daniel spoke and said, 'I saw in my vision by night, and behold, the four winds of heaven stirred up the great sea." see 390, 395, 687, 745, 488.

עשל *Ashel.* The 47th name of Shem ha-Mephorash, short form. See 415 & Appendix 10.

קש *qash.* straw, stubble, chaff. Exodus 15:7: "In the greatness of your majesty, you threw down those who opposed you. you unleashed your burning anger; it consumed them like stubble."

כי עירמים that they were naked, literally, the naked ones.

I. Genesis 3:7: "Then the eyes of both of them were opened, and they realized that they were naked; so they sewed fig leaves together and made coverings for themselves." Please note that the actual spelling is כי עירמים [that naked-ones] in the *Interlinear NIV Bible*. [Kohlenberger, 1987, Vol. I, p. 6.]

II. "כי עירמים *that-void-of-light*. Refer to the first verse of this chapter. It is also how the same root ערו, containing the idea of ardor, of a vehement fire, literally and figuratively. Formed from the root אור, which presents the idea of luminous corporeity, it becomes its absolute opposite. The one is a tranquil action; the other, a turbulent passion: here, it is a harmonious movement; there it is a blind, disordered movement. In the above example, the sign of manifestation י has replaced the sign of the mystery of nature. In this way, Moses has wished to show that this terrible mystery was unveiled to the universal man's eyes, Adam. I can go no further in my explanation: the earnest reader must investigate himself, the force, and the Hebrew expressions; I have furnished with all the means. The Samaritan word rendered as עירמים belongs to the root עף, the image of *darkness*, united to the root פש, which develops all ideas of inflation, of vacuity, of vanity. The word עפס, which is formed from it, signifies an *enormous excavation* and a *savage, voracious animal*. [d'Olivet, 1976, pp. 101-102.]

III. F.J. Mayers: "the word [ערום, subtle, 316] which was applied to Nachash [358] is exactly the same word as that which is translated 'naked' when applied to Adam and Aisha [306] when their eyes, Adam and his Aisha became 'aware that their inward light was extinct.' There were 'naked' indeed, but it was something much more important than the nakedness of the body in question. When man first entered the state of life in physical bodies, he would have no more idea of clothes than any other animal, for as far as his physical body is concerned, he is an animal. It was the nakedness of these human' qualities that he became aware of. He had been given faculties for the development of thought, reason and will. Yet, immediately he acts on this own initiative, he discovers that he has absolutely nothing in himself to replace the omniscient wisdom of Elohim, which had hitherto guided all his activities. He acted on his own 'impulse' and found that it was 'blind' and 'without intelligence.' As a 'man,' he was at the 'zero' point of human development. He had qualities far higher than any possessed by the animal world, but he had everything to learn in the use of them. As a man, he was far more helpless than animals. 'Instinct' provided them with everything they needed. To be a man, a man had to replace instinct with thought and reason, and he was a 'baby' in knowledge. An animal knows all it needs to know from the moment it is born. Man has to learn by long and often painful experience; 'wisdom' is always learned through suffering." [The Unknown God, p.187]

IV. The Zohar [I.53A] says: "When Adam sinned, God took from him the armor of the bright and holy letters with which he had been encompassed, and then he and his wife were afraid, perceiving that they had been stripped; so it says, and they know that they were naked. At first, they invested with those glorious crowns, which gave them protection and exemption from death. When they sinned, they were stripped of them, and then they know that death was calling them, that they had been deprived of their exemption, and that they had brought death on themselves and on all the world." (p.168)

V. Swedenobrg adds: "By 'knowing that they were naked' is signified their knowing and acknowledging themselves to be no longer in innocence as before. They are called 'naked' because left to their own; for they who are left to their own, that is, to themselves, have no longer anything of intelligence and wisdom, or of faith, and consequently are 'naked' as to the truth and good, and are therefore in evil." [Arcana Coelestia, pp.92-93]

VI. Nakedness is its lower aspect is "A symbol of a state of ignorance, a lack of ideas and opinions (clothes). As all external states have analogous reference to internal states, this condition is emblematic of an empty state of the soul." In its Higher aspect: 'A symbol of purity, that is, freedom from the limitations and opinions (garments) of the lower nature." [Gaskell, 1981, p. 523.]

Κριος. *Krios*. Ram (Aries). Note that the Greek Upsilon υ (♈) is similar to the sign Aries.

The ram or Aries is the lamb of Gnostic Christianity. Note that the first 2 Greek letters of Ram are equivalent to K.R. (C.R.) in English. This gives a plain intimation that the founder of the Rosicrucian order, Brother C.R., is associated with the lamb. See 220.

"Upsilon, closely resembling in from our letter *Y*; and his letter is the initial of the noun *huios*, meaning 'son.' In Gnostic Christianity, therefore, it was a familiar symbol of the second person of the Trinity, God the Son, viz., Jesus Christ. ... readers familiar with the Pythagorean doctrines would have been struck by the correspondence for the Romans called Upsilon the 'letter of Pythagoras" who is said to have taught that it represented by its two horns the different paths of virtue and vice, the right branch leading to the former and the left to the latter. Thus this letter was the symbol of the way of life, and here we may remind ourselves that God the Son, or Jesus Christ, who is also represented by the letter Upsilon, is reported to have said: "I am the way.:" Finally, alchemist also used the letter to designate their great secret. One text says: "This heavenly dew and its power contained in everything. It is treated by the world with contempt and rejected by it. As it grows, it becomes divided into two branches, white and red, both springing from one root, "Y.""

The text from which this is quoted [Secret Symbols] shows the Pythagorean Y, or Upsilon, with the alchemical symbol for Sulphur above the left-hand branch of the letter, and the symbol for Mercury above the other branch." [Case, 1985, pp. 39-40.]

οινος. *oinos*. Wine (symbol of Life).

Paul Case: "William Jennings Bryan and certain theosophists to the contrary notwithstanding, the New Testament meaning of this word is fermented wine, and not unfermented grape juice.

All doubt about this is removed by the passage in Ephesians 5:18, 'be not drunk with wine.' In the Greek original, the word is precisely the same as the one cited in recording the miracle of changing water into wine.

οξος. *oksos*. Vinegar (symbol of death). The vinegar was given to Jesus on a "reed" while on the cross. See 8.

κοκκος. *kokkos*. A kernel, grain, seed. Spelled κοκκον in Matthew 17:20: "And He [Jesus] says to them [the disciples], 'on account of your little faith, [you were not able to cast out the demon], for indeed I say to you, if you have faith, as a grain of mustard, you might say to this mountain, remove there from here, and it would remove; and nothing would be impossible to you." see 460 (Greek), 1746, 2220, 2276.

401 (prime)

את *eth*. Word used to indicate a direct object; in Golden Dawn usage, essence or spirit. Symbol of God. Ate Thou.

I. "את. The potential sign united to that of sympathy and of reciprocity constitutes a root which develops the relations of things to themselves, their mutual tie, their sameness or selfsameness relative to the universal soul, their very substance. This root differs from the root או in what the former designates as the active existence of being, I, and what the latter designates as the passive or relative existence, *thee*. או is *the subject*; את is *the object*. את that which serves as a *character, type, symbol, sign, mark*, etc." [d'Olivet, 1976, p.300.]

II. "*Et:* If you are now thinking that you have understood the given elements of the problem, you are on the wrong track. You have only the *idea* of it, and the idea is not the thing. The problem, reduced to its essential equation, is *pulsation of life and cosmic resistance*." [Suraes, 1992, p. 79.]

III. "את, means 'the,' 'the very substance of.' Qabalistically it signifies 'the beginning and the end,' and is like the term "Alpha and Omega" used in the Apocalypse. For as Alpha and Omega are respectively the first and last letters of the Greek alphabet, so are Aleph and Tau of the Hebrew. The "two extreme paths" are the crown, Kether, and the kingdom, Malkuth, the first and tenth Sephiroth, the highest and the lowest, Macroprosopus, and the queen. If the reader turns to the introduction, to the Table showing the Sephiroth arranged in three pillars, he will see that Malkuth is, as it were, the antithesis of Kether. Hence, it is said that "Malkuth is Kether after another manner." And this recalls the precept of Hermes in the Smaragdine Tablet: ' That which is below is like that which is above, and that which is above is like that which is below." [Mathers, 1993, p. 96]

שאנן *sha'aenan*. tranquil, quiet, at ease. In Isaiah 33:20: "Look upon Zion, the city of our Solemnities; your eyes shall see Jerusalem a quiet habitation, a tabernacle that shall not be shaken to and fro; whose pegs shall never be removed, neither shall any of its cords be broken." At ease in Isaiah 32:9, Zechariah 1:15 and in Job 12:5: "He that is ready to slip with his feet is as a lamp despised in the thought of him that is at ease."

נשיאם princes. Genesis 17:20.

תא *ta*. and.

אמפרודיס *Amprodias*. Sentenial of the 11th path of Aleph on the inverse Tree of Life.

I. THE 11th path or *Kala* is attributed to Air, and its negative aspect is the demon or shadow known as Amprodias, whose number is 401. 401 is the number of Azoth, which signifies the 'sum and of all conceived as One.' In its negative phase, this essence is conceived as None and is the Void from which manifestation proceeds. The nature of this void is also 401 as תא, the Hebrew word meaning 'out of'; its root is the Egyptian *Ut*, whence uterus, the gate of entrance. It is out of the womb of the *Ain*, via Kether, that manifestation issues.

The sigil of Amprodias exhibits a gaping mouth typical of the uterus, which utters the Word. This Word is the Hidden Light, the symbol of which is the whirling cross or swastika. It is identical with the letter A or *Aleph,* the letter attributed to the 11th path. In the magical grimoire 231, the following verse pertains to this *Kala*:

A is the heart of IA0, dwelleth in ecstasy in the secret place of the thunders. Between Asar and Asi he abideth in joy.

The thunderbolt, or *Dorje*, is the lightning-borne weapon of the Hidden Light that streaks down from the void, reifying as it does so earth or matter. The number 401 is also that of the word ארר, which means 'cursing.' It is the primal curse of the Fire of the Spirit imprisoned in bodily form, described in the Holy Books as 'the Wrong of the Beginning,' the beginning being considered as Kether, through which flash the lightnings of the *Ain* or Eye of the Void.

The inmost significance of this path is summed up in the magical power of the 11th *Kala,* which is divination. This depends upon the divine or supramundane aspect of spirit that rays into the womb and fecundates the virgin earth with Light (intelligence) from beyond the ultimate Pylon (Kether). Divinatory power is the intuitive aspect of intelligence. As such, its course is as unpredictable as the forked lightning, which cleaves the womb of space and manifests as the thunderbolt.

On the magical plane, the divinatory power manifests in the irrational. Thus the greatest masters of Magick traffic constantly with the energies of the 11th *Kala*. The irrational element appears so strongly in magicians using this *Kala* that their work has often not been taken seriously or has been altogether overlooked. H. P. Blavatsky's antics cast such doubt upon the authenticity of her work that few in her time we're able to estimate her at her true worth. The 11th path is that of the Fool who dances on the brink of the abyss, as depicted in tarot trumps ascribed to this path.

Eleven is the number ascribed to the power-zone (Daath) within the abyss. The color attributed to

Daath is Lavender, or Pure Violet, which typifies the color beyond space that vibrates in unison with the *Kala* activated by the evocation of Amprodias. It is the color of the Madman; he that is without the range of normal intelligence. The negation of reason that typifies his state of consciousness is consonant with the positive side of this path ascribed to that part of the soul known as the *Ruach,* or Reason. More correctly, the *Ruach is* the breath of spirit, the whirling seed that impregnates the virgin of space and brings to birth innumerable worlds.

Eleven, being the 'general number of Magick, or Energy tending to change,' the 11th path represents the path of reversal and the point of turning back from the other side of the Tree.

The disease typical of the 11th path is the 'flux,' expressed as unbalanced or 'untimely' discharges of lunar energy in magical terms. It is, therefore, the *Kala* of the Black Moon-Blood. It warns of a leakage of vital fluid, which, on overflowing, forms a residue of unbalanced magical energy. This breeds phantoms that appear in the form of sylphs, elementals associated with air or aether. Like the fairies and sprites of children's' tales, they are depicted as diaphanous and beguiling creatures. The title of the tarot trump ascribed to the eleventh *Kala* is the 'Spirit of Aethyr.' On the hither side of the Tree, this spirit is more resplendently beautiful and luminous than words can describe, but its reverse or reflex is as described above; so also are the bubbles blown by the Fool of the Tarot in his mad career on the edge of the pit. [Grant, 1994, pp. 154-161.]

402

אֵישׁ הָאֱלֹהִים *Ish ha-Elohim.* Man of God; Husband of God (Glory).

שבילין paths; spelled שבילי in Jeremiah 18:15: "Because my people have forgotten me, they have burned incense to vanity, and they have caused them to stumble in their ways from the ancient paths, to walk in paths, in a way not cast up."

מרבע + גוח +גמל Four sided, square + to encompass, compass + camel. This is the familiar Masonic emblem of the compass and square with the letter Gimel at the center. It suggests the mercy of God (Square), which encompasses our desires (compass) and guides the subconscious mind or memory (Gimel). See 312, 17, 73. Gimel is the path of the unit.

בת *bath.* daughter, female, girl, maiden. Suggest Malkuth and Gimel as the sister, or lesser Chokmah (see Key 2). Ezekiel 16:44: "Behold, everyone that listen proverbs shall use this proverb against thee, saying, as is the mother so is her daughter." Subconsciousness or Gimel is amenable to suggestion and manifests the results on the physical plane. With different pointing: liquid measure; belonging to the same party; native, inhabitants of; worthy of (followed by a word describing characteristics or quality); old, aged (followed by a word describing divisions of time); diminutive.

יהוה סלום *IHVH-shalom.* "The Lord is peace." Judges 6:24: "Then Gideon built an altar there unto the Lord, and called it Jehovah-shalom..." Recall that the pair of opposites attributed to Gimel is peace and strife. Unity brings peace to the altar of the soul. Variant spelling. See 396, 376, 26, 962.

שבק to leave, to be left. Daniel 2:44:: "And in the days of these kings shall the God of heaven set up an everlasting kingdom, which shall never be destroyed; and the kingdom shall not be left to other people, but it shall break in pieces and bring to an end all their kingdoms, and it shall stand forever."

403

גת *gath.* wine press.

באת came. See Genesis 16:8.

אבת fathers. See Exodus 12:3.

המשחים the anointed. See Numbers 3:3.

Shows the essential order (4) of the Limitless light (0) expressing itself in the regulation of all things (4).

שקד *shaqad*. Almond. The name refers to the earliness of its flowers and fruit. From the verb *siqod*, which means to a hasten away; to be zealous, to be eager for or intent upon something, to attend carefully. Connected with Kether. The wood is used to make the magical wand. See 43 & Numbers 17.8.

קדש Sanctity, holiness. See 454, 650.

דת *dayth*. royal command, commandment, a law, edict. With different pointing: statute, decree, rule, custom, religion. Represents the outgoing affirmative quality of the primal will of Kether. Combines Daleth (Venus) and Tav (Saturn). The law expresses creative imagination (Daleth) in activities leading to concrete, specialized results (Tav).

יהוה אחד ושמו אחד IHVH *achad ve-shemu achad*. One Lord, and his name one. Zechariah 14:9: "And the Lord shall be king over all the earth: in that day shall thee be one Lord, and his name one."

Zohar I. (p.77) "Two unification are here indicated, on the upper world in its grades, and one of the lower world in its grades. The unification of the upper world is consummated at this point... All grades and all members were gathered there and became in it one without any separation; nor is there any grade in which they are embraced in one unification save this. In it, too, they all mysteriously conceal themselves in one desire. In this grade, the disclosed world is linked with the undisclosed."

405

נשימה *Neshamah*. Divine soul (in Binah). Variant spelling. See 395, 450.

סהרנץ *Saharnatz*. Angel of the 2nd decan of Libra.

שפכה *shawpekaw*. phallus, male member; urethra, urinary canal. From שפכ: to pour out, pour out, pour, shed, spill; empty. In Deuteronomy 23:1: "No one who has been emasculated by crushing or cutting [genital] may enter the assembly of the Lord." Controlled, dedicated use, not celibacy (which atrophies energy), is essential for attainment.

עבדך נזהר בהם *ahbidaykaw nizayhar bawchem*. Your servant is admonished by them. See Psalm 19:11.

406

תו Letter name *Tav*. mark, cross, signature, sign.

In Tav, Saturn's powers (ת) and Venus (ו, Taurus, ruled by Venus) are combined. Since Vav is number 6, it is the letter of Tiphareth (the 6th Sephiroth). The Stone of the Wise changes lead into gold, that is, Saturn into Sun. Not Saturn into Mercury, as many fools imagine. Thus the alchemists say there are two stages at the end of their process, the White Work and the Red. White for the Moon, and Red for the Sun.

The Sphere of the Moon is Yesod, and the Sphere of the Sun is Tiphareth. The White Work transmutes the leaden *Guph* (89) into the Purified Intelligence of Yesod because it shows the alchemist the real basis of his personal life. The work's final stage takes him through his true support up into Tiphareth, where the Red Work is completed in making the transmuting Stone, *Aben* (53).

Sol in action is red, and red is the color of Mars. The completion of the Great Work is in the heart, not in the head. Mercury aids and is, in a sense, one name for the Prima Materia, but the Work is the Sun and Moon's work, and its objectives are to do with Yesod and Tiphareth.

Saturn is the beginning, but the point of departure is Guph. One of the primary doctrines is that of the Microcosm, and not until one understands this, and the real meaning of Malkuth can one begin the work.

The work starts with Saturn and then passes upward through Yesod to Samekh or the fire-trial of Jupiter. In Tarot, you see the lightning or the fire of Jupiter on Key 16 (the Tower), which illuminates the meaning of Peh (Mars).

Remember always that there is but a single power, as The Emerald Tablet states. It is because of this that there is such a kaleidoscopic shifting of meanings within meanings.

All come from One and go back into One. But be warned. Do not be satisfied with words, nor hoard them, magpie-fashion. We are giving you this to **use**. Make sure of our meaning, and then test. There is no other way to arrive at certainty. See *C.11.*

Binah (Sphere of Saturn) is pregnant with the descending influence from Kether through the Path of Beth and impregnated with the influence of Chokmah through the Path of Daleth. Each of which letters end with Tav, and this focuses attention on conjunction, because the word Tav ends with Vav, the grammatical symbol of conjunction, and also because the ancient character for Tav was the joining of two lines to form a cross-like that on the breast of the High Priestess. The horizontal line is feminine, and the vertical is masculine. See C.33.

ת/ו. Saturn (Tav) in Taurus (Vav).

אתה *ahtah.* Thou; you (singular), to thee. Refers to the central reality of Tav, the Self or I AM. Since the את and אתה are equal, the numerical identity may be expressed by the sentence, "thou art the cross." He who grasps this meaning has a key that unlocks all doors-above and below.

דאאת *daath.* knowledge. Variant spelling. See 474, דעת.

ופרסין *upharsin.* divided [Daniel 5:25]. The quotation continues with an explanation: "God has numbered your kingdom and finished it... Thou art weighed in balances and found wanting.

Your kingdom is divided." This indicates an imbalance in disposing intelligence, Key 6.

כשוף *kishshoof.* magic. Sorcery, witchcraft. That which unites us to Tav is magic. That which divides us is sorcery. See 1126.

כשלון *kishshawlon.* a fall [Proverbs 16:18].

יקצרו they reap [Hosea 8:7].

עם הארץ *Am ha-eretz.* people (man) of the earth, an ignoramus, a boor. Through the conscious union of personality with Tav's Administrative Intelligence, the "Man of Earth" is transformed into a conscious vehicle of creative power. The name given by the Pharisees and Sadducees to the "common people" who were the ones, the gospel says, who heard Jesus gladly.

שוק *shoke.* to join closely, to flow, to run; the leg or lower thigh (of man or beast), street, market place, shoulder; one of the equal sides of an isosceles triangle. The meaning "way" or "street" agrees with one meaning of Tav's letter name, Cross-roads. As a verb: *shook,* to run, to flow, to overflow, to cling to, figuratively, to desire, as a noun: street; marketplace, market, desire, longing.

שנוים *shanaim.* repetitions, changes, transformations, alteration. The first word of a specific occult ritual has to do with transforming the "man of earth" into a conscious vehicle of the creative power through the conscious union of personality with Tav's Administrative Intelligence and symbolized by Key 21.

רעה צאן (and Abel became) a shepherd of flocks [Genesis 4:2]. See 280.

רפליפו *Raflifu.* The Sentinel of the 30th Path (Tunnel) of Resh on the Inverse Tree of Life.

I. The 30th tunnel is under the aegis of Raflifu. The *Kala* filtering through this tunnel is of a solar nature. In the infernal tube of Raflifu, this becomes blackened rather like a deep shadow cast in bright sunlight.

The number of Raflifu, 406, is that of the letter *Tau* spelled in full [תו]. The mystical Tau, or Sign of the Cross, became an emblem of the god of the dead because the Cross symbolizes the crossing over from being to non-being. It is the unique emblem of Shaitan, the Chaldean form of Set. The identity of Osiris, the god of the dead, and Set, the Black Sun, is substantiated in the symbol of the *Tau*. 406 is the number of the Hebrew word אתה, meaning 'thou' as in *Do what thou wilt* in the Cult of Thelema. 'Do what thou wilt' is an exhortation to the sun or spirit in the blackness of Amenta, i.e., the subconsciousness. It is an invocation of the True Will and of that spontaneity. [Nightside of Eden]

אתה (*Ateh*) is one aspect of the triple deity AHA, which comprises Ani (I), Hua (Heh), Ateh (Thou); three facets of a deity worshipped in three persons and in three ways: 1) with averted face, 2) with prostration, and 3) with identification. The initials A H A add to 7, the number of the Stellar Goddess whose symbol - in this context - is the glyph of a sexual formula also consisting of three aspects: 1) with an averted face; 2) cunnilinctus (with prostration), and 3) normal coitus (with identification).

The above is substantiated, qabalistically, because Raflifu [406] results from adding the series of numbers from 1-28, which connects it with the lunar cycle.

406 is the number of קוש, meaning a 'bow,' from the Egyptian word *Kesr*, 'an arrow,' the symbol of Sothis the Star of Set. The bow and arrow are among the magical weapons ascribed to this *Kala*. 406 is also the number of שוק, meaning waters, overflow, from the Egyptian *sekh*, liquid; and שקו, 'drink,' from the Egyptian *sheku*, 'drink.' תו (also 406) means 'desire'; and מעצור signifies 'cohibitio,' 'restraint,' 'withholding,' which suggests that a form of Karezza also pertains to this tunnel. These ideas refer to a libation, and the sexual nature of this drink-offering is confirmed by the corresponding text in Liber 231.

Then did the sun appear unclouded, and the mouth of Asi was on the mouth of Asar.

This refers to the twins, Set Horus, embracing and becoming one with the Black Sun (Osiris or Shaitan), the God of the Crossing.

The sigil of Raflifu exhibits the horned trident of Typhon (or Choronzon) flanked on either side by the ax or *neter* sign and surmounted by a black sun in the arms of a crescent moon. The horned trident is the triple deity. The ax is the sign of divinity. It is the cleaving instrument and is therefore of the Goddess, the Cleft One, who is *neter*; that is, she is neither male nor female, but neter (neuter) for she is both male and female in a mystical sense that is inducible. The ax sign is represented by the Arabic figure of 7. Her planetary vehicle is Venus, one of whose names is AHA, whose number also is seven.

The leopard is the animal sacred to this tunnel. The black and gold of its spots symbolize the sun in the darkness of Amenta, or, in magical terms, the sexual gold illuminating the subconsciousness with its lightnings. The hawk is the sun's bird, golden in the upper air where it typifies Horus, black in the abyss where it typifies Set.

The magical *siddhi* connected with the 30th Path is acquiring wealth (gold) and preparing the Red Tincture. This symbolism combines the solar and lunar elements in one alchemical glyph.

The disease typical of this *Kala* of solar energy is depletion. The fetors of swamps and marshes are symbolic of the 'sick' sun in Amenta. The *Qliphoth*, therefore, haunt this tunnel in the form of will o' the wisps or marsh gases that resemble the curious phosphorescences observed by sensitives over the graves of the dead. [Grant, 1994, pp. 245-347.]

ארור *aroor*. cursed be [Genesis 9:25]. The "curse" of labor-serving fellow men is really a blessing for those who understand man's real place in the order of nature.

תבה *Tebah*. Ark (Noah's). Also: a chest, a ship, a sarcophagus. With different pointing: be תבה, *tabah*, "to be bellied, or hollow out." see 971, 1844, 1988, 888, 58, 936.

I. Exodus 2:3,5: "And when she could no longer hide him [Moses], she took for him an ark of bulrushes, and daubed it with slime and pitch, and put the child therein; and she laid in on the stones by the riverbank..." And the daughter of the Pharaoh came down to wash herself at the rivers, and her maidens walked along by the river's side; and when she saw the ark among the stones, she sent her maidens to fetch it."

II. "A symbol of the causal body as a means for the preservation of the individuality and the qualities of the soul, while lower conditions are swept away... the Divine command is given the individuality (Noah) to form a causal-body, and in the higher mental vehicle, several compartments for different functions are to be made. And it is to be limited in this nature within and without. 'Pitch' is a symbol of limitation which provides for the distinguishment of truth... The 'ark' does in a measure correspond with the 'cross,' in that they both indicate the junction between the higher and lower natures." [Gaskell, 1981, pp. 65-66.] see 407, where this word is spelled 37 & תבה (Greek); 432.

III. "תבה, a thebah... It appears to be the Samaritan translator who, rendering this word by...., a vessel, was the first to give rise to all the absurd ideas that this error has brought forth. Never has the Hebrew word, תבה signified a vessel, in the sense of a ship, as it has since been understood; but a vessel in the sense of a thing destined to contain and preserve another. This word, which is found in all the ancient mythologies, merits particular attention. It has so many significations that it is difficult to assign a definite one. On the one hand, the Egyptians' symbolic name to their sacred city, *Theba*, was considered the shelter, the refuge, and the abode of the Gods; that famous city was transported into Greece to a straggling village Beotia, has sufficed to immortalize it. On the other hand, it is a circuit, an orbit, a globe, a land, a coffer, an ark, a world, the solar system, *the universe*, in fact, that one imagined contained in a sort of vessel called בוא (i.e., the fire of magic, especially black magic): for I must recall here the fact that the Egyptians did not give chariots to the sun and moon as did the Greeks. But a sort of round vessel. The vessel of Isis was no other than that *theba*, that famous ark which we are considering; and it must be stated, the very name of Paris... is only the name of the Thebes of Egypt and of Greece, that of Ancient Sybaris, of the Babel of Assyria, translated into the tongue of the Celts. It is the vessel of Isis (Bar-Isis) that mysterious ark, which, in one way or another, carries ever the destinies of the world, of which it is the symbol.

Besides, this word בוא, whose vast meaning could not be exactly rendered by any of those that I know, and which the wisest Egyptians alone were in a position to comprehend, given over to vulgar Hebrew and following the proneness of their own gross ideas, was finally restricted and corrupted to the point of signifying *literally the belly; a leather bottle*; and figuratively, *a magic spirit*, a sort of demon to which the Jews attributed the oracles of their sibyls. But there exist in the Hebraic idiom, and the neighboring idioms form the same source, a mass of expressions, which starting from the same radical principle, show all its importance.

It is first its analog אב, developing the general idea of fructification, of generation, of paternity; then, it is that of will, in אבה; that of love, in אהב: it is all blossoming, in the Syriac... it is every awakening, in the Arabic... all immensity, every unknown place, every inner and profound sentiment, finally, without seeking to link with this root any other signs than the one which enters into the composition of the word תבח, it is the action of being moved in oneself, of returning, of retiring into, of withdrawing to oneself through desire, in the three verbs בב, תובות, and אבות: it is even the name of the Universe, in the compound תבל. One cannot see in all this, either *the coffer* of the Hellenist Κιβωτος or *the chest* of the Latin translator, 'arca.'" [d'Olivet, 1976, pp.191-192.]

אדון כל הארץ *aydon Kawl ha-aretz*. Lord of all the earth. Psalm 97:5: "The hills melted like wax at the presence of the Lord, at the presence of the Lord of the whole earth." see 271, 283, 690, 2208 (Greek), 433 and Joshua 3:13.

שמן טוב *shemen tov*. precious oil. Psalm 133:2: (Unity) "It is like the precious ointment (oil) upon the head, that ran down upon the bread even Aaron's beard: that went down to the skirts of his garments." [Note: Aaron means "lofty" and suggests Kether, the crown; Jordan (above) means 'descending" or "that which flows down." See 256, 264.

אות *aoth*. sign, token, mark, symbol, emblem. The "oil" is a sign of God's blessing, marked upon each forehead of those who have prepared themselves to receive it. With different pointing: Omen, portent; military ensign; letter of the alphabet. See 823.

η κλρονομια. *heh kleronomia*. The inheritance (heritage). In Isaiah 58:14: "Then shall thou delight thyself in the Lord, and I will cause thee to ride upon the high places of the earth, and feed thee with the heritage (i.e., inheritance) of Jacob, your father: for the mouth of the Lord hath spoken it."

Inheritance is the secret wisdom that was transmitted orally in ancient times from mouth to ear. In *Holy Kabbalah* by Waite: "The Secret Doctrine of the Zohar concerning the Holy Shekinah is the Mystery of Sex at its highest, and she is the Mystery of the Oral Law. It is intimated that behind this Mystery, there appears to be an authentic doctrine of knowledge, based on experience." Therefore the central mystery is the mystery of sex. See 700, 1271, Greek.

חת *chath*. broken, terrified, dismayed, fear, dread. 1 Samuel 2:4: "The bows of the warriors are broken, but those who stumbled are armed with strength." And in Job 41:25: "When he [Leviathan] rises up, the mighty are terrified; they retreat before his thrashing."

אהבת *awhabaythaw*. Thou shall love. Leviticus 19:8: "Thou shall not avenge nor bear any grudge against the children of the people, but thou shall love your neighbor as thyself: I am the Lord." This is the 2nd commandment taught by Jesus.

נחשים *nachashim*. sorceries; literally 'serpents." Love has a correlation with the transmutation of the serpent-power. See 358.

שחק *shaykike*. laughter, joy. Psalm 126:2: "Then was our mouth filled with laughter, and our tongue with singing: then said they among the heathen, the Lord has done great things for them." With different pointing *sawchaq*: to laugh, be merry; to moke at, scorn in Job 39:22; 2. *sicheq*: to make merry; jest, play; to mock, deride.

שחק *shaykike*. Fine dust, cloud, heaven; the name of the third heaven. Isaiah 40:15: "Behold, the nations are as a drop of a bucket, and are counted as the small dust of the balance: behold, he takes up the isles as a very little thing."

שחק *shawchaq*. to rub away, to beat fine, pulverize. Exodus 30:36: "And thou shall beat some of it very small, and put of it before the testimony in the tabernacle of the congregation, where I will meet with thee: it shall be unto you most holy."

זאת *zoth*. this. The Zohar [Prologue, 10A, p.43]: "Who is this that comes up (olah) out of the wilderness? The words י (who, 50) and zoth זות (this) denote the separate holiness of the two worlds joined in firm bond and union; and this union is said to be 'olah' (a burnt offering), and so holy of holies. For מי *mi* is holy of holies, and *zoth* through its union with this becomes a burnt offering (olah) which is holy of holies." Rosenroth in K.D.L.C.K. (p.293) says it is Malkuth and calls in *haec*.

409 (prime)

ט *Teth*. Serpent. Letter name Teth. The ancient form of the letter Teth was a crude picture of a tally, in the form of a circle (suggesting the serpent holding its tail in its mouth) enclosing a cross, which was the letter's original form Tav. This is a mathematical symbol of יהוה because every circle equals 22 and every cross 4. As Tav, the cross is a symbol of the Tree of Life, and the Circle is a symbol of the "Power of the Letters." see 9, 380, 358, 1502, 400, 419.

אחת *echath*. She. the feminine form of the word for "One" (13, אחד). The Life-breath, as the divine darkness represented by en, the no-thing, seems to be more feminine than masculine.

ואבן השהם *ve-ehben ha-soham*. and the onyx stone [Genesis 2:12]. This stone is linked to Leo, connect with שט Teth, with Venus and the "nail" (Vav, Key 5). See 345.

אבהתא *abatha*. patriarchs. I.R.Q. Para. 1003: "… reference to the three divisions of the Patriarchs… Abraham, Isaac and Jacob." These are the "fathers" of Israel.

אבות *aboth*. fathers.

הקדש *ha-qadosh*. the holy ones. The 'serpents' who are androgynous are fathers and mothers. See 1010.

קדשה *qedasha*. temple prostitute, harlot. In Genesis 38:21, She was a widow and the son-in-law of Judah, who believed she to be a prostitute and slept with her. As payment, she received his cord and staff and became pregnant with twins—the scarlet women in Set's desert, which gives birth to the twin current.

410

שמע *shema*. hear, sound. Part of the confession of the unity of God. "Hear O Israel, the Lord our God, the Lord is One." With different pointing *shawmah*: 1. to hear; to listen, give heed; to obey; to understand; to infer, deduce. 2. sound, sonority. See 373, 739, 466, 273.

שמע report, fame. See the fame of the brotherhood or *Fama Fraternatas*; meaning, sense; hearing capacity; "he hears." See 1291 (Greek) & Deuteronomy 6:4.

ית *yath*. Chaldee sign for an objective case.

משכן *Mishkan*. Tabernacle.

קדוש *qadesh*. Holy, sacred, Sanctifying [Isaiah 7:3]. Root name of the 3rd path of the Binah. *Qadesh* is an adjective whose root means "to make pure, to set apart, to consecrate." Sanctification is a result of the reorganization of bodies in sleep (Qoph). This is accomplished through desire, embodied in a new creative image (Daleth). One follows the instruction of the inner voice and is guided through the changes. The result is a resurrection into a sanctified body of light through the power of Spiritual Fire (Shin). See 404, 756.

יהושפט *Jehoshaphat*. God has judged. A valley which is the scene for the final judgment. Joel 3:2: "I will also gather all nations, and will bring them down into the valley of Jehoshaphat, and will plead with them there for my people and for my heritage Israel, whom they have scattered among the nations, and parted my land."

I. The alchemical first matter "blooms like a lily standing in the valley of Jehoshaphat" [Secret Symbols].

II. This word has a definite solar significance. Its root is שפט. The first letter is attributed by Qabalists to fire, the second to the fiery planet Mars, and the third to the fiery solar sign Leo." [Great Work lesson 12] Note also that והו (21), the mystic name connected with אהיה (the father) and Tiphareth (the son). See 1210, 478 (Lt), 1812 (Greek).

מצרף *metzareph*. purifying; crucible, melting-pot. Part of the title of a famous qabalistic alchemical treatise. Before one has the "ears to hear" the sacred teaching, one must have purified the interior hearing center, represented by Venus. See 711 and Keys 3 & 5.

דורד *deror*. Flowing, running freely; freedom, liberty; swallow (bird). Suggest the action of the spiritual fire, symbolized by Shin.

משכן *mishekawn*. tabernacle; dwelling-place, habitation. the human body. "The kingdom of spirit is embodied in my flesh." [Pattern on the Trestleboard]. See 446, 889.

שקי butter.

אררט *Ararat*. The mountain where the ark of Noah came to rest. In Genesis 8:4: "And in the seventh month, on the 17th day of the month, the ark rested upon the mountains of Ararat."

"אררט *of-Ararat*... Here is a word which would afford a vast subject for commentary. All peoples who have preserved the memory of the deluge, and nearly all have preserved it, have not failed to relate the name of the alleged mountain upon which rested the mysterious *thebah* [ark], which bore within it the hope of nature and the seed of a new existence. Nicholas of Dams, cited by Josephus, called it Mount *Barris*. This name is not very unlike that *Syraris* or *Sypara*, which Berosus gave to that city of the sun. An Assyrian monarch deposited the world's archives when he knew that the flood's catastrophe was imminent. It is well known that the Greeks called λνκορεος, the *luminous mountain*, the place of Parnassus where Deucalion rested. Still, perhaps it is not generally known that the Americans also had a famous mountain, upon which they declared that the remnants of mankind had taken refuge, and whose name they consecrated by the erection of a temple dedicated to the sun. The name was *Olamgi*. It would certainly be straightforward for me to prove that these names... all have a connection with the course of light...

This word is composed of the two roots רטוא-ר: the first אור is understood: it is light and all ideas which are related to it. The second, רט, formed of the signs of movement proper and resistance,

characterizes a course accompanied, inflected or directed by anything whatsoever. Thence, the Chaldaic verb טורה, *to concur with a thing, to follow it to its source, to direct it*; as light or water, for example; thence, the Hebraic word טיהר, *a channel, a conduit, a promenade*; thence the Syriac word derived meaning *an inflection, a reflection*, etc.

After this explanation, one can feel that the word אררט, does not signify the *mount of malediction* or *of terror*, as has been believed without examination; but indeed that of *the reflected course of light*; which is very different. Besides, it is well to know that the Samaritan translator, the most ancient interpreter of Moses, has not rendered the word אררט, by a proper name of the mount, but Chaladic and Samaritan words סדנא, *axis, wheel, orbit*; and רוב or ריב, *effluence, emanation*: so that it offers a translation quite exact of the sense that I have given to the word אררט: that is to say, instead of signifying *the reflected course of light*, it means *the orbit of luminous effluence*." [d'Olivet, 1976, p.226-227.]

משכן to give a pledge, to take a pledge, seize, levy, (for debt).

411

היכל רצון *hekel rawtzon*. Palace of delight, will, grace, desire. Briatic (heavenly) mansion corresponding to Tiphareth, i.e., the creative place of the central Ego. With different pointing: means will, passion, wish, goodwill, favor, grace, delight. See 1061, 346, 65.

משכנא *mishaykawna*. habitation, dwelling, tabernacle.

סדר זמנים *seder zaymanim*. order of times (ordo seclorum on the great seal). זמן = plan, device; appointed time, title; temple (gram.). With different pointing: prepare, to invite, to say grace after meals in company. See 971.

Rosenroth in K.D.L.C.K. (p.43) gives: *ordo temporum*, and says they are Tiphareth, concerning days and Malkuth with respect of night are contained or understood all times of nature.

אלישע *Elisha*. God of Supplication; God is Salvation. The successor and perpetuator of Elijah's work, by whom he was ordained and anointed to this end. 2 Kings 2:12: "And Elisha saw it [Elijah took up by a whirlwind into heaven], and he cried my father, my father, the chariot of Israel, and the horsemen thereof. And he saw him no more:, and he took hold of his own clothes, and rent them into two pieces."

תהו *tohu*. Desolation, without form. See Genesis 1:1,2; 430, 291, 1152.

I. Paul Case: The formless is the "dwelling-place" of the originating principle. Jeremiah 31:37 refers to מוסי אדץ as being "searched out beneath." Thus תהו is the formless foundation, which is below. By Tarot תהו is Keys 21 + 4 + 5 = 30 > 3 or Key 3, Daleth. Note that Daleth = דלת is 434, the same as bohu spelled in plentitude
(בתי הה וו) התב in plentitude = 406 + 10 + 12 = 428 (בת הה וו) = a precious stone, the gift; scintillating flames (*chashmalim*); And IHVH Elohim formed" [man]; out of darkness; in the midst.

II. "desolation, emptiness, expresses the first root of all good. [Crowley, 1977, p. 43]

שלמיאל *Shelumiel*. Peace of God. Numbers 1:6: "Of Simeon [Gemini, fixation, 466]; *Shelumiel* the son of Zurishaddai [my rock is the almighty, 620]. Angelic guard of the 3rd heaven. [Rf. *Pirke Hechaloth*). [Dictionary of Angels p.272] see. 314, 296.

עפר + אין *ain* + *apar*. no-thing + dust. The no-thing is the primal darkness, the latent state of the supernal triad before manifestation, or living mind. Out of the dust (i.e., particles of solar radiance) of the ground (physical plane) was the essence of humanity (Adam) created by IHVH-Elohim. See 350, 61.

טבת *Tebeth*. Tevet, the 4th Hebrew month, December-January, corresponding roughly to the period when the sun is in Capricorn. See Esther 2:16.

412

בית Letter name *Beth*, meaning house. The house of personality. Made be read be-yath, the accusative or objective case. Thus it is mental concentration directed toward some specific object, that is, receptivity to the Life-power in Kether via the intuitional and form the building of Binah. See 567, 490, 78, 8, 2080.

The 12th Path of Beth links Kether to Binah. The Path of Beth is the path of the Beginning, for, in the 11th Path of Aleph, nothing begins. Nor is there any true beginning in Chokmah; because Chokmah is the mirror of Kether, which has neither beginning nor end. Aleph is the sign of Ruach, which is likewise without beginning or end.

In בית is the initial of בראשית and of *Baruch*, which is a Blessing. Then in בית comes Yod as the second letter, and this stands for the Paternal Wisdom which is before all beginning. Finally is Tav, the letter of Saturn, which completes the tale of 22 Tokens. This can be read that in any beginning, the completion is already present. For the ONE does not know time as men perceive it, and for *Al Shaddai*, the beginning of any outpouring is one with its completion. Understand that the Sabbath of the Eternal never ends. See *C.32*, 713, 52, 61, 400.

ואתה *ve-attah*. and thou. This indicated the true house (Beth) of spirit as the central point of personality (see 406). ואתה contains a reference to the supernal world, indicating that the Shekinah is joined "with Moses." This is the union of the sun with the Moon, "in all-embracing completeness." In Psalm 20:20: And thou, O Lord (ואתה יהוה), the two invocations are, in effect one. That is בית, and יהוה are designations of a single reality.

חדת *khadath*. new, fresh, young (Aramaic) Ezra 6:4: "With three rows of great stones, and a row of new timber." see 312.

יבקש *yebaqqaesh*. will seek out, requires. Ecclesiastes 3:15: "That which has been is now, and that which is to be has already been, and God requires that which is past." "Will seek out" is precisely the essential idea represented in Tarot by the Magician, Key 1. From בקש: to seek, find.

צמר לבן *tzehmer lahban*. white wool. Has a mysterious connection with the white head, a title of Kether. Also, with the white hair of the figure described in Revelation 1:14. "His head and his hairs were white like wool and white as snow, and his eyes were as a flame of fire." The idea is that the influence at work in the 12th Path (Beth) is a direct emanation from Kether.

שמן הטוב *shem ha-tobe*. Precious oil (or ointment). This passage from Psalm 13:2 is familiar to Freemasons, and a perusal of the Psalm will make the inner meaning clear. See 407, 432, 343, 667.

תאוה *tayoh, ta'avah*. longing, desire, wish, the object wished or longed for; appetite, passion; boundary limit; in the Mishnaic, sexual desire. What is desired indicates the definite objective of desire, hence a bound or limit. This is the specific quality associated with the 7th Path on Netzach. It has the limiting characteristic of Saturn (Tav). The mental activity of the 12th Path actually sets limits, selects objectives and established bounds.

413

משכיל + אחד *mahsaykil + achad*. instruction + unity. It is the inner teacher's instruction, which links the created with his creator - I am the nail which joins thee to me. – Book of Tokens, Vav See 400, 13.

תביא you will bring. See Genesis 6:19.

חשקה longs, desires, she is set. See Genesis 34:8.

תאבדו you shall destroy, you destroy. See Numbers 33:52.

משגע mad, crazy, being driven mad. See Deuteronomy 28:34.

414

אין סוף אור *Ain Suph Aur*. Limitless Light. The radiant darkness. Background of the Tree of Life. Three veils of the absolute. Before manifestation, the undifferentiated radiant energy whence all things proceed may be conceived as a limitless ocean of light. A great sea of potential energy is concentrated into the whirling motion, which begins a cycle of manifestation with Kether.

2. The Golden Treatise of Hermes, IV says: "Behold, that which the philosophers have concealed is written with seven letters..." Paul Case: אין סוף אור though written with 9 letters requires only 7 different letters, viz. Aleph Air; Yod, Virgo; Nun Scorpio, Samekh Sagittarius; Vav Taurus; Peh Mars; Resh Sun.

גדר סוף אור *gadar suph sur*. enclosure without limit.

רבה סוף אור *rabah suph aur*. growth without limit.

רז סוף אור *raz suph aur*. mystery without limit.

אזות *Azoth*. An alchemical term for the first matter and the Quintessence. A and Z (Lt), Omega (Greek), and Tav (Hebrew). Initial and final in 3 languages.

אני יהוה אלהי אברהם אביך *Ani Jehovah Elohi Abraham Abika*. I am the God of Abraham your father [Genesis 28:13]. The Limitless Light is the Creative God, the only God. "God is light, and in him, there is no darkness." This declaration occurs in the story of Jacob's dream of the ladder. The ladder represents the Tree of Life.

הגות *haguth*. meditation, thought, musing, whispering. The Limitless Light, identical with the One Creative God, is an active vibration set up by a mental process. The power source of the universe is the meditation of the Universal Mind.

מקור חיים *maqor chaiim*. fountain of lives. In Psalm 36:9: "For with thee is the fountain of lives; in your light, we shall see the light." The Limitless Light or the fountain of lives is the fountain of eternal livingness brought forth all individualized lives. See 974, 1114 (Greek); 346, 419.

Also, in Proverbs 16:22: "Understanding is a fountain of life to those who have it, but the instruction of fools is folly."

משוטטים *mashottim*. goings forth. From the Limitless Light spring all appearances of "going forth," that is, of emanation. See 974, 770.

עין יהוה אל-יראיו *ayin Jehovah al-yeraia*. The eye of Jehovah is on them that fear him. [Psalm 33:18]. Ayin means "fountain, spring," as well as "eye." The preposition *al* may also be translated as "near, within, for." Moreover, the verb translated "fear" actually signifies "to revere," "stand in awe." Thus a better rendering is: The Fountain of Reality (Jehovah, THAT which was, is and will be) is within them who revere that Reality. The intimate and constant availability of the Limitless Light is the Fountain of your life. See 1064.

שחוק *seqhoq*. Mirth, laughing, derision, sport, play. Attributed to the letter Ayin. Equivalent in meaning to the Hindu lila [leela: "play of the gods or cosmic play"] of Brahma. As do all artists, God creates from the exuberance of inner feeling - not only the pretty but also the ugly, not only heroes but also clowns, and he enjoys his cosmic play. See 1784, 708, 358.

נחשון *naashon*. enchanter.

415

שמעה *shemoah*. hearing. The function assigned to Vav, the nail of intuition. See 12, 32, 53, 158, 177, 508.

מעשה *moshah*. work, action, employment, the function assigned to Lamed, the ox-goad. See 74.

הקדוש *ha-qodesh*. The sanctifying; the holy one; i.e., Kether, the ancient of days. As "the sanctifying," it is a title of the 3rd Path of Binah. See 410, 450 (alternate spelling), 765.

ממשדה *memayshala*. dominion, rule, reign. The function attributed to Tav, the mark or signature. Also: government. See 400, 406.

קדישא *qadisha*. holy. From מולא קדישא (*Mezla Qadisha*), the holy influence, from Kether.
I.Z.Q. Para. 673: "What is to be understood by כח יהוה *kach Tetragrammaton*, the power of Tetragrammaton? This is *Mezla Qadisha*, the holy influence, called, even the Concealed with all Concealments. And from the influence that strength and the Light depend." [Mathers, 1993, p. 328] see 493, 54, 620.

קשוט *qishoot*. The forms of truth, the light of truth. With different pointing: 1. *qeshot*: the forms of truth, the light of truth; 2. dress, toilet; ornament, cosmetic.

I.Z.Q. Para. 359: "Who is hidden and not manifested, through those vestments of ornament which are the vestments of truth, QShVT, *Qeshot*, the forms of truth, the lights of truth." [Mathers, 1993, p. 294]

אחות *awchoth*. sister; female relation; companion, mate. i.e., Gimel, Key 2. See 73.

אבראה דבר *abarah dabar*. The voice of the chief seer.

עשליה *Asaliah*. "Just God, who indicates truth." 47th Shem ha-Mephorash. Psalm 104:24: "O Lord, how manifold are your works. In wisdom has thou made them all: the earth is full of your riches." To praise God and to lift ourselves toward him when he sends us illumination. Rules justice and makes known the truth in law-suits; influences men of integrity and those who raise their spirit to the contemplation of things divine. Persons born: endowed with an agreeable character, is fond of acquiring secrets of illumination. Associated with the 5th quinance of

Pisces; Angel by day of the 10 of Cups. See 400 and Appendix 3.

416

המאור צקטן *ha-maor ha-qaton*. the lesser light.

רים עליון *Rom Eleyon*. Height most high, supernal height. A title of Kether. See 620.

קרנינו *qahrayninu*. our horn. Psalm 89:17: "For thou are the glory of their strength: and in your favor, our horn shall be exalted." [Note קרן (350) = horn, figuratively, strength, might power; glory, pride, grandeur; corner point, peak; ray; principal; capital; the damage done by an animal's horn]. Suggest spiritual aspiration. See 1594 (Greek).

אל הערפל *el-ha-aeraphel*. Unto the thick darkness. Exodus 20:21: "And the people stood afar off, and Moses drew near unto the thick darkness where God was." This could be "El [strength, might, power], the thick darkness." see 380, 385, 31.

גבהות *gahbayhuth*. lofty. Isaiah 2:11, 12: "The lofty looks of man shall be humbled, and the haughtiness of men shall be bowed down, and the Lord alone shall be exalted in that day"; "And the Loftiness of man shall be bowed down, and the haughtiness of men shall be made low: and the Lord alone shall be exalted in that day." [Note: "Man" is אדם (45). This word is from גבה gobah, height, altitude, exaltation, grandeur, pride, arrogance, point of illumination.

הרהור *hirayher*. though, meditation; to think, meditate. With different pointing *hahrayhor*: 1. thought, impure thought, what "bows down;" 2. to entertain, impure thoughts;

קדושו *qaydosho*. his holy one. Isaiah 49:7: "Thus says the Lord, the redeemer of Israel, and his holy one, to him whom man despises, to him whom the nation abhorrers, to a servant of rulers, kings shall see and arise, princes shall also worship, because of the Lord that is faithful, and the Holy One of Israel and he shall choose thee." see 991, 578.

יאתה *yeaayteh*. comes. In Job 37:22: "fair-weather" (i.e., gold) comes out of the north with God is terrible majesty." North is the direction of Peh, the Mars or creative word; Gold is linked with the sun.

רעה צאן *ro-eh tzoan*. a shepherd of flocks. Genesis 4:2: "And she [Eve, 19] again, bare his brother Abel (37). and Abel was a keeper of sheep, but Cain (160) was a tiller of the ground." Note that Abel means "a fleeting breath."

417

שכאנום *shakanom*. a title of Tiphareth. See 977.

חבז + הננה יסד בציון אבן *zawbakh + hinnay yawsad be-tzion ehben*. Behold, I lay in Zion for a foundation a stone + to sacrifice. Zion is the holy of holies or adytum, i.e., mercury center in the brain; the stone is the philosopher's stone; sacrifice refers to the white stage, or purification, of the alchemical great work. See 400, 17; 156, 53.

סק + י + או *sahq* + Yod + *ow*. Sack (the heart) + the creative hand, + desire, will, appetite. The heart is the place, in alchemy, where the great work is done; the hand is union, divine touch, the channel of God's will, the power manifested in the reproductive function. Desire, will, appetite are all attributed to Sulphur, or activity (self-consciousness), the 2nd alchemical principle. The motive power in the life-power's self-manifestation is its desire to actualize its own possibilities. See 400, 10, 7.

גן + געול + חר *gahn gawoul + hur*. A garden enclosed + to be white, shining, noble. The garden = 53 = the stone; it is the subconscious cultivation field, as in Key 1. To be white refers to Tiphareth and the central ego. In alchemy, its connection with the sun associates it with the metal gold, which is the most lustrous and is called the noblest metal. See 209, 208.

תיבה *thebah*. Noah's ark. K.D.L.C.K. (p.732) gives *arca*, and says it is Malkuth, whence Noah it is said entered it, i.e., Yesod. Genesis 6:9: "Noah was a righteous man, blameless among the people of his time, and he walked with God."

הדרך + חיים + עץ *etz chaiim* + *ha-derek*. The Tree of Life + the way. The tree is the map of consciousness, a model of the macrocosm in the microcosm. See 228, 229.

זית olive. Genesis sees 8:11.

ביתה her house, her household. See Genesis 39:14.

418

חית Letter name *Cheth*. hedge, field, fence. The Self-limitation of the Life-power.

Scorpio's power, raised by the meditation that unveils Truth, brings about the consciousness that personality is the vehicle, Chariot, the lodge, and the house, temple, or palace of influence.

The vehicle is also a cube, made of stone (אבן, *Aben*, 52). Aben is the verbal symbol of the union Chokmah (2nd Sephiroth) and Tiphareth (6th Sephiroth), or 2 and 6. This union is also shown in IHVH (יהוה) where Chokmah (י) and Tiphareth (ו) are conjoined by the Mother (ה). Note that 2 and 6 add to 8, the value of Cheth.

Note that חית adds to 418, and the reduction of this is 13, leading finally to 4, or Daleth. And Aben is 52 or 13 x 4 or the power of love (13) multiplied by the generation of mental images (4) yields the rider's vehicle in the chariot. And see also that 13 + 4 equals 17, which reduces to 8.

On this, we have given you much. Daleth is the path of union of Ab אב (Chokmah) and Aima אמיא (Binah). Without that union, Binah is אמא, dark and sterile; but after that union, she is אמיא, and brings forth בן, the Son. See *C.13*, 148, 187, 1081, 67, 134 (Lt).

חטאת *khattath*. atonement, a miss, misstep, slip of the foot, sin, sin-offering, punishment. Hence calamity, misfortune. Compare Emerson's Crime and Punishment grow on the same stem. The same word means both "sin" and the sacrifice which atones for it. Derived from a verb חטא meaning "to miss the target, to sin."

Rosenroth says it is the masculine form of the word, חטא is the old serpent [that tempted Eve in Genesis], but חטאת is the impious woman, Lilith. K.D.L.C.K. (p.340)

יתח *Yethech*. to beat, to strike. A reference to the occult teaching that all separate existence is like a punishment in which circumstance after circumstance strikes painful blows. But this painful process ultimately results in union with the originating principle (Charioteer). With that union comes the knowledge that he has endured all the pain that we have suffered; that he had own all our sorrows; that he has been the witness of all our failures to hit the mark; and that he not only assumes all this burden of sorrow and seeming failure but is able, when the great work is finished, to transmute it all into joy. One who is still living on the sense of separateness finds no satisfactory answer to the question 'Why do I suffer? Why do I fall short? Why am I subjected to the blows of adversity?' But one who has overcome separateness and lives in union with the one life never asks these questions, for he neither suffers, falls short, nor receives the buffets of adverse circumstance. Yet such a one knows the answer to questioning the delusion of separateness-he gives this answer freely: 'All this comes because of this delusion of separateness. Unite yourself with the one, and your suffering shall cease.' At every age, this is the unvarying answer. It is the only one that can be given. It is the only one that is true. Many reject it, and in the rejection, continues suffering until pain and failure have taught them the great lesson of utter receptivity, self-sacrifice. [Paul Case, unpublished notes]

את דיג *eth-gid*. With sinew, with tendon, with a penis. את is the grammatical sign in the accusative. As a preposition is a means "with." In

Qabalistic usage, it means "essence." דיג means "a nerve, sinew, tendon, penis. This is the sinew which shrank at the time of Jacob's encounter with the angel. An esoteric reference to the diversion of nerve-currents of the Mars-force, from the lower to the higher centers. See 17.

בית הא *Geth Heh*. House of Heh, House of the Window.

יחת *yechata*. union. The proper name Jahath [1 Chronicles 6:20].

יהוה וישוע *IHVH ve-Yeheshoa*. Tetragrammaton and Jesus. This combination expresses the idea "The Father, and I are One." 418 reduces to *echad* (13), unity.

נוער חסד *nozer chesed*. keeping mercy [Exodus 37:7]. Watchman or preserver of Mercy. See 72, 412.

ות וו *Tav-Vav*. Letter-name of Tav spelled in full. Cross (Tav) and (Vav). The function of Key 21 continued by Key 5, the intuitive teacher. The path of Vav flows from Chokmah into Chesed, thus "keeping mercy." Wisdom or the life-force is the "watchman." see 867, 95, 319, 406.

אבראהאדאברא *abracadabra*. Crowley's spelling. Kenneth Grant says it is the supreme spell or formula of the Great Work.

μηρος. *meros*. thigh. A euphemism for the phallus in the Apocalypse 19:16. Qabalistic ideas associated with Netzach (148) have to do with the activity of the One Life's generative and reproductive powers. See Yarak (710).

419 (prime)

טית Letter name *Teth*. The serpent, foliage. The unity is the strong serpent-power, the Lion of Key 8 and the Fohat of Theosophy. In Thrice-Greatest Hermes (page 89, note 2), the serpent is the form of Hermes (Mercury) in the North.

I. The letter name Teth (419) reduces to 5. Five is Daleth with the paternal Yod, as you see in the character for Heh. In the development of architecture, doors came first, then windows and this is mirrored in the sequence of letters Daleth (door) and Heh (window). Additionally, 419 may be read as 400 and 19. Tav is 400, and 19 is חוה, the Mother, or Aima. Teth is the link between Chesed and Geburah, just as Daleth links Chokmah and Binah. See *C.11*, 9, 409, 1502, 434, 85.

II. Teth is associated with Key 8, Strength. Note that in this Key, our Lady Venus tames her lion. She does not run away from him or kill him. Creative Imagination (Daleth) is the key to taming the lion. Imagination sets man free from the restrictions of sense yet fulfills sensation instead of diminishing or destroying it.

Love linked with purified and perfected sulfur, which the lion symbolizes, is the secret of all spiritual works. The lesser creatures are driven by sense, and they have only glimmerings of love or imagination. Remember that the Red Lion in Alchemy is sulfur purified by knowledge of the office of passion in our lives; for passion purified becomes compassion, purged of the corrosive poison of selfish exclusiveness, and of limitation to the level of mere sensation, which is for the beasts good, but for man slavery.

Saturn, Mars and Jupiter, among the Interior Stars we share with the sub-human kingdoms. They have their place and purpose, but they must be directed by the upper triad of Venus, imagination, Moon, or memory, Mercury, or discrimination in human life. In the Tarot, this is hinted at in many ways, but mainly by the white wand having two similar ends, so too the woman's taming a living lion. This is a clue to the basis of many forms of magical working. One cannot perform magic if you kill or atrophy the lower triad. These are the sources of all potency. To deny or flee from this power makes oneself unfit for the magical path. Take the conditions inherent in the world-process as Saturn. You cannot change their basic nature, but you can transmute them.

To transmute is to bring them across into the field of enlightened understanding. The alchemist is the real subject of the Great Work, and even he does not change his basic nature. How can we since that basic nature is a changeless one? In a single seed lie all the potencies of growth, flower and fruit. These potencies are unfolded as the plant grows, but they were there all the time. So in man's animal nature are potencies that may be unfolded. Their presence is not being apparent. They must be divined by Mercurial insight and Venusian imagination, and this is the actual work of Key 8. See *C.19*, 434, 400, & 90.

III. This process demands unremitting vigilance, the exercises of great patience, and considerable ingenuity. To control the serpent's power is difficult. Not is it enough to become conscious of the obscure sources of our complexes. New outlets for these tremendous forces of subconsciousness must be provided. We cannot afford to let them find expression in their raw, untrained forms. Nothing in the modern psycho-analysis has yet approached the perfection of the inner school's alchemical and magical methods. These methods, of which Tarot study and Qabalah are important parts, the libido's mighty forces may be tamed and transmuted. The accomplishment of this is truly called the great work, and it depends upon the law of consciousness, which Qabalah calls 'the intelligence of the secret of all spiritual activities.' [Paul Case, unpublished notes]

האין סוף אור *ha-Ayin Soph* Aur. The Limitless Light. See 414

המשוטטים *ha-mashottim*. The going forth.

האזות *ha-azoth*. the first matter.

אחדות *achedoth*. unities, uniting. Refers to the 13th path of Gimel. It also means: "The one which is first (אחד) and (ו) last (ת)." This, of course, is what is meant by "Alpha and Omega." Additionally: unity, harmony, solidarity, unanimity. See 424, 532, 108, 13.

אחתי *achdoth*. my sister Song of Solomon 4:12: "A Garden enclosed is my sister, my bride. The garden is אבן, Ehben, the stone. [Case says that this phrase is equivalent to Job 28:2 "copper is molten out of the stone," but it is off by a 6, ו.]

see 53, 126, 661, 30, 216, 1496.

סדם עמרה *Sodom-Gomorrah*. The 2 biblical cities were destroyed by God for their perversity. See 104, 315.

מקור המכה *meqor chokmah*. the fountain of wisdom. Proverbs 18:4: "The words of a man's mouth are like deep waters; and the fountain of wisdom like a flowing brook." see 346, 73, 414.

τὴν γῆν. *tehn gehn*. The earth. Septuagint translation of את הארץ (697) in Genesis 1:28: "And God [Elohim] blessed them said unto them [humanity] 'be fruitful and multiply, and replenish the (essence of) earth." see 697, 11 (Greek), 291, 401.

Δειπνος *deipnos*. a principal meal. "In the lexica, it is quoted as the evening meal, and also as an after-dawn meal. The hermeneutic of the word is said to be 'after which it is needful to labor.' Symbolic meals [as the last supper of Jesus and the 12 apostles] are universal. They usually connote a body of people, co-operating in a certain ideal: their idealistic communion with an exalted being. A personal amendment, continuous service, or the fulfillment of a vow are amongst the sequence of the ceremony. A symbolic meal may be regarded in two aspects:

1. as denoting help received by an approved pupil from exalted instruction and inspiration, friction; that is, Eukcaristia.

2. as implying a consequent obligation to labor for the less advanced; that is, Dei ponein." [Omikron, 1942, p. 253.]

420

רצפים *raytzawphim*. burning coals 1 Kings 19:6: "And he [Elijah] looked, and, behold, there was a cake baked on the coals, and a cruse of water at his head. and he did eat and drink, and laid him down again." (this was his 40 day's sustenance until he came to Horeb, the mount of God). Suggest nourishment is from the divine fire or life-power.

שלמים *shilemim*. perfection, wholeness; peaceable; "peaceableness" Genesis 34:21: "These men are peaceable with us; therefore let them dwell in the land, and trade therein; for the land, behold, it is large enough for them; let us take their daughters to us for wives; and let us give them our daughters." Malkuth is the kingdom, or physical plane, i.e., the land; it is also the daughter and bride. Earthling the divine fire brings completion.

K.D.L.C.K. (p.719) gives: *pacifica* and says this applies to Tiphareth and Malkuth existing in union and maintaining a balance between the extremes of fire and water.

הוית *hawbith*. barrel, jar, cask. Suggest a container for the waters of consciousness, the influx of the divine will (Cheth) into the 'house' (בית) of personality. Rosenroth in K.D.L.C.K. (p.332) gives: *dolium, vas* and says it is Binah. See 412, 8.

תך *tok*. oppression. Translated deceit in Psalm 55:11: "Wickedness is in the midst thereof deceit and guile depart not from her streets." see 900.

421 (prime)

The hypotenuse of a Pythagorean triangle having an altitude of 29 and a base of 420, and an area of 6095.

חזות *chazoth*. Vision, revelation (Chaldaic). See 439.

התבודד *hitboded*. to meditate.

תביט look, you look. See Genesis 19:17.

ותהי and let her be, and let be. See Genesis 24:51.

כשויעיה Angel of 10th house of Capricorn. Godwin's spelling. See 465.

422

The total length of the visible paths on the Tree of Life when the Aleph line is 15 units long.

אריך אנפין *Arik Anpin*. The Greater Countenance, The Vast Countenance, or Macroprosopus. ." A title of Kether is also called: "Ancient of Days" and Ancient of the Ancient Ones." Also, a name for the number 1. Represented in the Qabalah by a man's bearded face turned to show the left eye only, like the Emperor (who faces north). This corresponds to the all-seeing eye of which the new testament states, "If your eye is single, your whole body shall be full of Light." see 580, 1552.

שבעים *shebeyim*. seventy. Numbers 11:25: "and the Lord came down in a cloud, a spoke unto him, and took of the spirit that was upon him, and gave it unto the seventy elders: and it came to pass that when the spirit rested upon them, they prophesied and did not cease." Also, Genesis 4:24: "For if Cain is to be avenged sevenfold, then Lamech seventy and sevenfold."

קו ירוק *kay yaroq*. Rosenroth in K.D.L.C.K. (p.672) calls this *linea* [thread, string, boundary line, plumb line] *flava* [golden-yellow], and says that his name refers to Binah or Tiphareth with respect to Binah.

כתב see Exodus 17:14.

423

עצם הבריאה *etzem ha-briah*. essence of creation, creative force. Refers to Heh, the 15th Path. Signifies the essential nature of the paternal force, which is concentrated primarily in Kether, and then becomes the radiant life force in the Chokmah. The "essence of glory" is really the No-Thing, which is the most abstract conception our minds can form concerning the nature of the ONE BEING, which is the Rootless Root of all manifestation. This No-Thing is what finds expression as *appearance* (the eye), as the Three Supernals (the triangle), and as the radiant energy which is the substance of all things, and, at the same time, the gravitation or weight which holds together the world of name and form (the glory). Another arrangement may be read as היה ברא or היה, Hawyaw, "to be" and ברא, Beraw, "to create." The inner meaning here is that the essential characteristic of being is creativeness. See 203, 20.

אתה תוב *teob attawh*. "You are good" Psalm 119:68: "You are good, and what you do is good; teach us your decrees.

תחיה *tekheawh*. revival, resurrection. From the Hebrew dictionary "resurrection of the dead" תחיה המתים. The "essence of creation" revives and resurrects. See 818, 1313.

אות היא *aoth hia*. the feminine sign. Literal symbol of she; thus "sign she." K.D.L.C.K. (p.66): "And shekinah is called *aoth hia* the feminine sign." Shekinah is the divine presence assigned to Binah. See 67, 419.

תחות *Toth*. Hebrew spelling of the Egyptian god Thoth in Job 38:36, "Who endowed in Thoth with wisdom, or gave understanding to the mind?"

ερημος. *eremos*. Wilderness. Lonely, lone, desert (places). Of persons; lone, solitary, desolate, destitute, helpless. A solitude, desert, wilderness.

424

האחדות *ha-achadoth*. The unities. Meaning: "The (Heh) First (אחד, One) and (Vav) the last (Tav)." Also: "The mother (Heh as Binah) is first (אחד) and last (Tav). Alpha and Omega (Greek). Affirmation of an underlying unity, veiled by the appearance of manifestation. See 108, 532, 419.

חוית *Chayoth*. Living Creatures.

טוטת *Tavtoth*. Lesser angel governing triplicity by night of Taurus. The moon is exalted in Taurus and is expressed in Tarot by Key 2 (Gimel).

תהו בהו *thou bohu*. without form (and) void

[Genesis 1:12]. See 430, 13.

Paul Case: 424 contains Saturn (400), Jupiter (20) and Venus (4). Compare the Fools black outer garment in the Tarot." (424 = 10 = 1= Aleph = Ruach, according to the *Sepher Yetzirah*, and Aleph is assigned to the Fool in the Tarot, whose number is zero, the numerical symbol of thou-bohu, "emptiness of emptiness).

"But we know what a novice would never in the world suspect that the blackness is only a veil hiding the most dazzling whiteness." [D.D. Bryant]

425

נעשה *na'aseh*. Let us make [Genesis 1:26]. Rosenroth in K.D.L.C.K links this word in a discussion of בריאה briah or creation. See 470.

שמיעה *shimidah*. hearing, listening. The faculty of intuition. Variant spelling. See 415, 468.

The prologue of the Zohar [I.p.4] says: "'is heard' points to the sixth day, [of creation], as it is written, 'let us make man,' (namely, him who was destined to say first 'we will do,' and then 'we will hear,' for the expression in our text, na'aseh, 'let us make man' finds its echo in the expression 'na'aseh (we will do) and hear' Exodus 24:7: "And he, [Moses] took the book of the covenant, and read in the audience of the people: and they said, 'all that the Lord has said will we do, and hear.'"

Rosenroth in K.D.L.C.K. (p.723) gives: *auditus*, and says it depends on Geburah receiving Binah.

גור אריה *gur arieh*. a whelp of a lion, lion's whelp. Genesis 49:9: "Judah is a lion's whelp: from the prey, my son, thou art gone up: he stooped down, he couched as a lion, and as an old lion; who shall rouse him up?" Judah is connected with Leo and with alchemical digestion. See 30.

הגזית *ha-gawzith*. the hewn stones. Isaiah 9:10: "The bricks are fallen down, but we will build with hewn stones: the Sycamores are cut down, but we will change them into Cedars." (This text omits the Heh). See 87, 53, 1175.

זאויר אנפין *Zauir Anpin.* The Lesser Countenance; a title of Tiphareth. See 1081.

משיח נגיד *Messiah Nasiyd.* Messiah the Prince. Daniel 9:25: "Know therefore and understand, that from the going forth of the commandment to restore and to build Jerusalem unto Messiah the prince shall be seven weeks and sixty-two weeks: the street shall be built again, and the wall, even in troublous times." see 358, 67.

תהך 8th Shem ha-Mephorash, short form. See 456 & Appendix 10.

426

כי אמ גלה סודו אל עבדיו הנביאים *kiy im-gawlah sodo el-awbadawyou ha-naybiayim.* "But he reveals his counsel (secrets) unto his servants the prophets." Amos 3:7: "Surely the Lord God will do nothing, but he reveals his secret unto his servants the prophets."

אריך דאנפין *Arik Danpin.* The Vast Countenance. a title of Kether. Daleth here is used as a preposition, Aramaic in origin, meaning "of, which." The union of the Hexagram and Hexagon symbolizes the union of Tiphareth with Kether. It is the conjunction of the Personal ego with Yekhidah, the Indivisible Self. See 422, 423, 620.

מושיע *moshyiah.* Savior, deliverer; deliverance. A title of Tiphareth. A noun from the participle of a Hebrew verb meaning "to set free," the same root of Joshua and Jesus. The son (Tiphareth) manifests himself as the deliverer when he set the bride (Shekinah in Malkuth) free. The Liberation is effected by the right knowledge of the true nature of man. See 385, 326, 358.

σπερμα. *sperma.* That which is sown, seed, the seed of germ of anything; of animals, seed (Latin, semen). As a metaphor, seed, offspring, issue, origin, descent, family. See 720 Greek, 50, 64

ερματος. *hermatos.* of, or from Hermes. (Variant spelling, see 353). Latin *mercurius.* Relates to Mercury, Beth (Key 1) and self-consciousness, expressed through attention and concentration. "Not yours, but mine, is the power of attention, of observation, of discovery, of the discerning of sequence in the operation of nature. In all this, and in the power of discrimination, my superior nature works through thee." [Book of Tokens, Beth]
\

αμπελος. *ampelos.* A vine. Christ is the vine, i.e., the real, of which his disciples are the branches. This figure of speech expresses the closest union and communication. In John 15:5: (4), "Abide in me, and I in you. As the branch cannot bear fruit of itself, it abides not in the vine, so neither can you unless you abide in me. (5) I am the vine. You are the branches. he who abides in me, and I in him, he bears much fruit; because severed from me, you can do nothing." see 434, 2663.

427

חסד עלאה דאל + רוח *chesed awlayiah day-el + Ruach.* The supernal mercy of God + life-breath, spirit, imagination. A reference to Chesed or Mercy, the 4th Sephirah and sphere of Jupiter, is assigned to the masters of compassion, or *Chasidim.* They have learned to control and direct the universal mind-stuff's creativity, attributed to imagination, seated in Tiphareth. The central Ego Note that 427 reduces to 4, Daleth's value, or creative imagination]. See 213, 214; 72, 1081.

ויתחבא and hid themselves. See Genesis 3:8.

אותך you, thee. Genesis 17:2.

והתודו and they shall confess if they confess. See Leviticus 26:40.

428

חשמלים *Chasmalim.* Merciful or Benefit Ones. Scintillating Flames. Choir of Angels associated with Chesed, and thus particularly with its expression in Yetzirah. See 378, 282.

אבן חן החשה *eben khan ha shakhud.* A gift is a precious stone; The gift, the stone of the secret wisdom (Qabalah). In Proverbs 17:8: "A precious stone, the Gift (in the eyes of him that has it; Whatsoever he turns, he prospers." This ties in with Chesed, Mercy, benevolence as the source of eternal, unending supply. This supply is rooted in "recovery" or remembering the true place in the scheme of things. It is the gift of the sacred wisdom, the gift of unending, eternal riches and the fulfillment of every need. The secret wisdom is based on Man's conscious union with the ONE, which is the renovating or renewing stone, engraved with a new name, which makes all things new (חדש). See 111, 312, 271, 53.

חידות *hidoth.* hard questions. 1 Kings 10:1: "and when the Queen of Sheba heard of the fame of Solomon concerning the name of the Lord, she came to prove him with hard questions." The Queen of Sheba (372) is connected with Venus and the 7 alchemical metals; Solomon is linked to the Sun or Tiphareth-the higher self, the "nature of the Lord" is the creative word. From: חידה riddle, puzzle.] see 26, 375.

וי-יצר יהוה אלהים *vayi-yetzer IHVH Elohim.* and IHVH Elohim formed. Genesis 2:7: "and the Lord God formed man of the dust of the ground, and breathed into his nostrils the breath of life; and man became a living soul." see 86, 26, 315, 50, 350, 45, 18.

מני חשך *minni khiskek.* out of the darkness. Job 12:12: He discovered deep things out of darkness, and brings out of light the shadow of death. see 1285, 1044.

תו-הה-וו *Tav-Heh-Vav.* The letter name for *tohu*, meaning "without form." Genesis 1:2: And the earth was without form, and void; and darkness was upon the face of the deep. And the spirit of God moved upon the face of the waters. see 411, 328.

אבן שלמה *ehben shelemah.* a perfect weight (stone). Deuteronomy 25:15: "But thou shall have a perfect and just weight, a perfect and just measure thou shall have, that your days may be lengthened in the land which the Lord your God gives thee." Note that שלמה also spells Solomon. See 628.

בתוך *betok.* in the midst, in the middle. Genesis 1:6: "And God said, Let there be a firmament amid the waters, and let it divide the waters from the waters." see 380, 382, 405.

געשכלה *gashikalh.* the breaker of pieces. Qlippoth of Chesed. געש: shaking, quaking, כלה: complete destruction.

429

משפט judgment, equality [Crowley, 1977, p. 45]. See Exodus 23:6.

וחיתה and will live, and she will be spared. See Genesis 12:13.

430

ל/ת Saturn (Tav) in Libra (Lamed).

מספרים *masaparim.* declare, are telling (verb). In Psalm 19: "The heavens declare [are telling] the Glory of God." see 395, 510

The Zohar [Prologue 8a] says the "heavens" are the bridegroom, who enters the bridal canopy. Declare, signifies that they radiate a brilliance like that of a sapphire.. and scintillating from one end of the world to the other. "The heavens declare the Glory of God" as soon as the Bride (10) beholds her spouse (6).

מקדם ימים עולם *miqqedem mimay olahm.* From of old, from everlasting. See 1176 & Micah 5:1.

נפש *Nefesh.* breath. The field of subconscious

mental activity, the animal soul, the Vital Soul in Yesod, is the animating principle shared by a man with the kingdoms of life below the human level (see 448, Nephesh Chai). It builds to manifest the life-power's potencies, via the reproductive process, as ascending scale of bodies, culminating in human organism production. Nun is *Nefesh* represents Scorpio, which governs the reproductive organs of Humanity. Peh represents the Mars forces. Shin stands for spiritual Fire. By understanding the secret of Nephesh and through desire flowing from the Ego in Tiphareth, a man may consciously further his own evolution and enter the 5th Kingdom. See 80, 570, 220.

Above Tav on the Tree stands the Foundation (Yesod), the seat of נפש, Nephesh, and Nephesh, signifying the creative speech's eternal utterance. Its first letter is Nun, which denotes perpetuity, and its second letter is Peh, the sign of the mouth. The third letter is Shin, the symbol of the Holy Spirit. In all 3 letters is one power expressed; because in Nun is the seed-power of Madim (Mars), and Peh is the letter of Mars, and in Shin, the final letter of its letter name Shin (שין) is נ, with which נפש begins. See *C.9*, 89, 463.

With no cessation does the Ruach Elohim's utterance, El Shaddai's might, the source of Life, continues throughout eternity. The Living Soul Nephesh is the vehicle of that utterance. In the letters of Nephesh, for the first relates to Perpetuity, and the second to Utterance, while the third stands in the alphabet for Ruach Elohim, the Fiery Breath of the Eternal Spirit of Life. Shaddai El Chai refers; the Nephesh or the Vital Soul is that same Almighty Everliving One, which centers Itself in all animate forms, and finds its highest expression in the life of man. See *C.27*, 363, 23, 207.

נשף *nahshaf.* to blow, to breathe. Exodus 15:10: "Thou did blow with your wind, the sea covered them: they sank as lead in the mighty waters." This connects with the attribution of the element of Air to Yesod. See Isaiah 40:24.

נשף *nehshef.* Evening twilight, evening; darkness, night; morning twilight, dawn, mist.

ספר מים *Sepher Mem.* Book of Moses. The Rosicrucian "Book M.," also called *ars notaria*, the "art of signatures." To read which the *lux mundi* or "light of the world" is necessary. The Illuminati are recipients, through intuition, of the perfect understanding of the meaning of the cosmic order and can read the "One, only book" from which all secrets are to be learned. See 104, 990.

פרקים *phereqim.* joints, parts, members. The appearances of the separation. See 990.

צדיק יסוד עולם *tzadiq yesod olahm.* righteousness is the foundation of the world. Proverbs 10:25: "As the whirlwind passes, so is the wicked no more: but the righteousness is an everlasting foundation." The full title of Yesod. Sometimes mistranslated as: The righteous man is the foundation of the world. As the sphere of the righteous ones [Chasidim] is in Chesed, this illustrates the occult correspondence between Jupiter (Chesed) and the Moon (Yesod). See 204.

תהו ובהו *tohu va-bohu.* without form and void [Genesis 1:2]. A description of the earth, or "That which is below," in the Biblical creation allegory. The mental image suggested is that of a vast abyss of fluid darkness. The Surangama Sutra states: "The intrinsic nature of space is the real earth-essence." The Lord of Logos is the formative power. [Isaiah 45:7]. Applies particularly to Eretz [ארץ]. See 291, 271, 390, 451.

I. "תהו ובהו, *contingent-potentiality in-a-potentiality-of-being...* If one examines the four original versions, a great difference is found between what they say and what I say. The Samaritan version reads: *distended to incomprehensibility and most rare.* The Chaldaic says ורקניא צדיק: *divided into annihilation and vain.* The Hellenists translate: *invisible and decomposed.* Saint Jerome understands "*inanis et vacua*" *unanimated and vague*, or *unformed and void.* This first error depends upon how they have understood the first word of the Sepher, the famous בראשית. This word, having impressed them neither in its figurative or hieroglyphic sense, has involved all that follows, in the literal and material sense that they have given to it. I pray the reader to give strict attention to this, for upon this depends all the incoherences, all the absurdities with which Moses has been reproached. In fact, if the word בראשית signified simply, in the beginning, in the beginning of time, as it was said, why did not the heavens and the earth, created at that epoch, still exist at that time; why should they have rested an eternity in darkness; why should the light have been made after the heavens and before the sun; can one conceive the heavens without light, light without the sun, an earth invisible, inanimate, vain, formless, if it is material; etc., etc. But what can remedy this? Absolutely nothing but an understanding of the tongue which is translated and seeing that בראשית means not only *in the beginning*, "in principio," but clearly *in principle*; that is to say, not yet in action but in power; as Saint Augustine interpreted it. This is the thought of Moses, profound thought which he expresses admirably by the words והבו צהו, in which he depicts with a master hand that state of a thing, not only in contingent power of being but still contained in another power of being; in short, without form, in germ in a germ. The famous χαος of the Greeks, that *chaos* which the vulgar have also gradually materialized and whose figurative and hieroglyphic signification I could very easily demonstrate. ובהו צהו belong to those words which the sages create in learned tongues and which the vulgar do not comprehend. We know that the sign ה is that of life and that this sign being doubled, formed the essentially living root הה which, by the insertion of the luminous sign, became the verb הוה, to *be-being*. But let express, not existence in action, but only in power, we restrict the verbal root in the sole sign of life and extinguish the luminous sign ו to bring it back to the convertible ו; we shall have only a compressed root wherein the being will be latent and as it were, in germ. This root הו, composed of the sign of life and the link between nothingness and being, expresses marvelously that the incomprehensible state of a thing exists when it exists no more and in the power of existing. It is found in Arabic in which it depicts a desire, a tendency, a vague, indeterminate existence.

Sometimes, it is an unfathomable depth, sometimes a sort of physical death; sometimes an ethereal space.

Moses taking this root and making it rule by the sign of mutual reciprocity ת formed the word תהו through which he expressed a contingent and potential existence contained in another potential existence, בהו; for here he inflects the same root by the mediative article ב.

Thus there is no need of conceiving the earth invisible, decomposed, vague, void, formless, which is absurd or contradictory; but only as existing still in power, in another seed-producing power, which must be developed so that it may be developed." [d'Olivet, 1976, p.29-31.]

II. The Zohar [I:16A, 30A-B] comments: "the earth had been previously. There was snow in the midst of the water, which produced a slime, then a mighty fire beat upon it and produced refuse. So it was transformed and became tohu (chaos), the abode of slime, the nest of refuse and bohu (formlessness), the finer part which was sifted from the tohu and rested on it. The word 'darkness' in the text alludes to the mighty fire. This darkness covered the tohu, namely the refuse, and was buoyed up by it. The 'spirit of God' is a holy spirit that proceeded from חים אלהים (Living God) and this 'was moving over the face of the waters.' When the wind blew, a certain film detached itself from the refuse, like the film which remains on the top of boiling broth, when the froth has been skimmed off two or three times. When tohu has thus been sifted and purified, there issued from it a great and strong wind rending the mountains and breaking in pieces the rocks,' like that which Elijah saw [1 Kings 19:11-12]. Similarly, bohu was sifted, and there was contained in it fire... when what we call 'spirit' was sifted, there was contained in it al still small voice. Tohu is a place that has no color and no form, and the esoteric principle of 'form' does not apply to it. It seems for a moment to have a form, but it has no form when looked at again. Everything has a 'vestment' except this. Bohu, on the other hand, has shape and form, namely, stones immersed in the chasm to tohu, but sometimes emerging from the chasm in which they are sunk, and drawing therefrom sustenance for the world." (pp.66-67).

שפון *shafan*. hidden, to conceal; concealed. Deuteronomy 33:19: "They will summon peoples to the mountain and there offer sacrifices of righteousness; they will feast on the abundance of the seas, on the treasures hidden [ושפוני, and-ones-being-hidden-of] in the sand." With different pointing (פן *saffron*, 435): hidden, concealed. See 599,

תל *tael*. Mound, heap, a hill, lock, curl. The hill of vision "declares" the everlasting truth of the soul's nature. See 830.

רזון בן אלידע *rezon ben elada*. Rezon, the son of Eliada. I Kings 11:23: "And God (אלהים) raised up another adversary unto him, Rezon, the son of Eliada." Eliada signifies "God knows" in the passage cited. Rezon was the adversary of Pharaoh, the symbol of worldly materialism.

Lux Mundi (Lt). The radiance around the head of the Hanged Man.

Ars Notaria (Lt). To have the Ars Notaria is to be able to read in what the Rosicrucian texts call "Book M." In Hebrew, this would be "Sepher Mem," or and the numeration of this is 430, equivalent to Mesaperiym, the verb "declare," used in the 19th Psalm, which says: "The heavens declare the glory of God."

αρθμος. *arithmos*. number. In a sense, all of our finite numbers are synthesized by 9. Also: amount, size, number as a mark of worth, rank.

μονος. *monos*. one, alone. Alone of many.

νομος. *Nomos*. Law. In the Septuagint of Proverbs 13:14: "The law of the wise is a fountain of life, to depart from the snares of death.

"Greek, *nomos*, that which is assigned or apportioned; custom, conventionism; law, ordinance. The Mosaic Law consists of ritualistic observances based upon the action of the forces ruling the material world. It is the law of cause and effect inherent in the elements (or, rather, the *spirits* of the elements) that keeps the soul in bondage in the world of matter. It holds it within the cycle of reincarnation, the mind being attached to the objects of the sense and to the results of actions. From this bondage, the soul can become free only by purification and accepting the 'free gift' of the Logos, when it is reborn in the divine essence and becomes 'the son of a God.' Thus Paulos says (Galatians 4:28): 'We also when we were youngsters. They were enslaved under the elemental-sprits (*stoicheia*) of the Kosmos. But when the fullness of the time came, the God sent forth his Son, born from a woman, born under the law, that he might ransom those under law, so that we might regain the Sonship. And because you are Sons, he sent forth the Breath of his Son into our *hearts*, loudly calling 'Abba, Father!' So that you are no longer a Slave, but a Son, and if a son, also an heir of a God; but at that time indeed, not perceiving a God, you were enslaved by those who by origin are not Gods.'" [Pryse, 1967, pp. 78-79.]

431 (prime)

אשפים *ashpim*. magicians, conjurers; men wise in astrology and music. Daniel 1:20: "And in all matters of wisdom and understanding, that the king enquired to them, he found them ten times better than all the magician's and astrologers that were in all his realm." The work of the *ashpim* was directly connected with the formulation of musical sequences based on astrological calculations. See 991.

נבטריקין *notariqon*. Cabalistic theory of acronyms. This method is used in Rabbinical Hebrew. See 35 (אגלא), 858, 1081.

ת +ל + א *Tav + Lamed + Aleph*. mark, cross + ox-goad + ox. God is the power at the interior center, the place of refuge (Tav); the life-power is also the source of faith (Lamed), and the spirit is what manifests through symbols or abbreviations on the higher planes (Aleph). Note that Tav as "mark" is an abbreviation for something profound. See 400, 30, 1

קרנים + אל *el + qayrawnayim*. God, the strong + horns. The strength of God is the strength of "my servant Moses." משה = 345 = חשם the name, i.e., IHVH, the creative word. Use of this name of power builds the horns of higher spiritual perception, and thus the refuge in the highest. See 400, 31.

א + נפש *nephesh + Aleph*. Breath of life, soul, vital spirit + life-breath, sprit it is (Nun) reproductive power, (Peh) Mars or active energy, (Shin) the transforming power + (Aleph) the free spirit. See 430, 1.

אגורה + גבורה *geburah + aegorawh*. strength + to gather together, accumulate strength is the gathering or accumulating of the life-force; it is what establishes faith. See 215, 216.

432

תבל *taybale, tebel*. The world, the inhabited world. Moist earth [Psalm 24:1]. One of the 7 earths in the diagram of the 4 seas; attributed to Earth of Yesod (and Malkuth). *Tebel* is the equivalent of the title of Key 21. Note the number of Tav (The World, Key 21) is 400 and that it is the 32nd path on the Tree of Life (400+32). With different pointing: 1. *tehbel*. Confusion, violation of the natural order. From Balel בלל, pollution, profanation [Levi 18:23; 20:12]; 2. *tebeil*: spice, seasoning, to spice, to improve. See 291, 50, 365, 105, 302, 337.

בתל *betel*. to separate. An unused root, found in בתולה (448).

אשה אלמנה *aisha alemanah*. A widow woman [1 Kings 17:9 and 10]. The word of the Lord commands Elijah to dwell at Zidon, where a widow woman will sustain him. When he got thee, she was gathering sticks .., "and he called to her and said. fetch me, I pray thee, a little water in a vessel, that I man a drink." The bread and oil she had little of lasted them for many days. See 126, 306.

צללי ערב *tzelelei erev*. Eventide shadows. *Tzelelei* means shadow, shade, shelter, protection. *Erev* means evening, sunset, night, with different vowel points, Arabia (sterility). See 272.

בן עיש *Ben Ayish*. Son of Ayish; Ursa Minor, a constellation. Spelled עש in Job 9:9, 38:32. See 1082.

עלב בן בעור *Bela ben Beor*. Bela, son of Beor. The first King of Edom, associated with Da'ath. See 1082 and Genesis 36:32.

כשמן הטוב *ka-shemen ha-tov*. It is like precious oil. Psalm 133:2: "It is like the precious oil upon the head, that ran down upon the beard, even Aaron's beard: that went down to the skirts of his garments." This is מזלא, Mezla (78), the holy influence or "illumination material." "The oil is the nerve-force (a modification of fohat or kundalini). It is made to energize the 'lamps' (the interior stars or chakras)... using exercises in which counting is essential..." [Book of Tokens: comment on Teth]. [The Kaph, a prefix meaning as, like, about; approximately; while, during] see 407, 412, 390.

433 (prime)

זכות *zakoth*. Merit, privilege, right.

בלאת *Balath*. Goetia demon #13 by day of the 1st decan of Leo. This decan is attributed to the 5 of wands, or Geburah, the seat of volition, in Atziluth, the archetypal world. These are the principles of volition and law. See Appendix 11.

Goetia: "He is a mighty king and terrible. He rides on a pale horse with trumpets and other kinds of musical instruments playing before him. He is very furious at his first appearance, that is, while the Exorcist lays his courage; for to do this, he must hold a hazel wand in his hand, striking it out towards the south and east quarters, make a triangle, without the circle, and then command him into it by the bonds and charges of spirits as hereafter follows… The great king *Beleth* causes all the love that may be, both men and women, until the master exorcist has had his desire fulfilled. He is of the Order of Powers, and he governs 85 Legions of Spirits." [Mathers, 1995, p. 34]

יהוה אדון כל הארץ IHVH *Adon kol ha-aretz*. Tetragrammaton, the Lord of all the earth. Appears without IHVH in Joshua 3:11: "Behold, the ark of the covenant of the Lord of all the earth passes over before you into Jordan." Note that Jordan means "descending" and is linked with the blood-stream; the "earth" refers, in one sense, to the physical body. See 264, 291, 407 and Psalm 97:5; Joshua 3:12.

בתוכה in the same, in her, within her, in the midst. See Genesis 41:48.

ובכתה and she shall cry. See Deuteronomy 21:13.

משפחה family, clan. See Deuteronomy 29:17.

434

דלת Letter name *Daleth*. door (the leaf of the door, not the opening or doorway); page. Corresponding to the path of Luminous Intelligence. See 601.

I. The letter Daleth refers to the activity of the subconsciousness in the generation of mental images. Until this activity is brought under control, it is the case of all strife and contention. Yet from this subconscious activity, we may develop powers that enable us to be numbered among the "people of the almighty" (see below). The root of 434 is 14 x 31. Thirty-one is the divine name אל, strength. Yod (יד, hand) is 14. 434 represents the multiplication of the divine power by the works of the almighty hand. Therefore 434 suggests the process whereby the life-power manifests itself or creates. That power is the generation of mental imagery (Daleth), which enters into the sphere of our experience through the door of subconsciousness. [Paul Case, unpublished notes]

II. Four is the number of Daleth (ד) and Chesed (the 4th Sephiroth). The path of Daleth is the first horizontal path (see Appendix 12) to cross the Tree. Daleth reduces to 11 and then to 2. Likewise, Chokmah (2nd Sephiroth, 73) is numerically equal to the letter-name Gimel (גמל, 73). Two as a letter is Beth. Therefore the value of Beth relates to Chokmah (the 2nd Sephiroth). In the Tarot, the Magician a personification of Wisdom and is also a potential father (*Ab*, 3). Four is 2 x 2, and thus Daleth is the multiplication of Beth by Beth, and even the multiplication of Chokmah by itself is Chesed.

In Daleth are the letters of Venus (Daleth), Libra (Lamed) and Saturn (Tav). Thus we see a strong Venus and Saturnine influence. Daleth is Venus, and her path ends in the Sphere of Saturn, from which the path of Lamed receives an influx through the paths of Cheth and Geburah. In the Tarot, The Empress, Strength, Justice and the World are, but various aspects and manifestations of Daleth, and so is The Star (Aquarius), where the ruling power is Saturn.

Binah is 67 and is the sphere of Saturn. Sixty-seven reduce to 4, or Daleth. Note well the close relation between Saturn and Venus. This is a key to practical knowledge of utmost importance. All this is on the Middle Pillar, and if you do but consider the Sephiroth thereon and their meanings, you should have little difficulty. See *C.11*, 419, 85, 120, 228, 406, 400.

III. This same power, seated in the center, or in the heart, is the cross, and with that cross of Saturn in our Order is the Rose conjoined, and the Rose is the flower of Venus. So in the Tarot, you see Venus and Saturn represented by the same symbols and numbers.

The goad of Lamed to the ignorant is the Devil or Adversary. In the Tarot, The Devil is Key 15 attributed to Capricorn ruled by Saturn. Note that Puritan theologians consider Venus, the goddess of desire was attributed to the Devil. But we must look closer. Fifteen reduces to 6, and Key 6 is The Lovers, which Venus has her dominion. The number 6 is the extension of 3 (1+2+3), and Key 3 is Venus. Thus we see from many points of view the deep connection between Venus and Saturn.

Consider your own physical vehicle. The Saturn center is at the base of the spine, the abode of the secret fire. And Netzach the Sphere of Venus, located near the neck, is a Fiery Sephiroth. In Key 8 Strength, we see Lion's Fiery nature tamed by the cultivated love of Venus.

Among the Interior Stars, the Venus center is to the two above it (Mercury Center), the Saturn center to Mars and Jupiter. The Sun center is midway between these two triads. One Triad is located in the trunk consisting of Saturn, Mars and Jupiter. The second triad is in the head, consisting of Venus, Moon and Mercury. In Alchemy, the object is to transmute lead into gold or Saturn into Sol. But to do this, "you must take Venus and make her into coins." That is manifest (coins) your desires (Venus). We begin with Venus, the Lady of Love, whether that love is celestial or profane, for where love is in any guise, there is our Isis.

Saturn fixes form, Venus foresees new modes of expression. Venus, without Saturn, has no stability and takes flights of fancy from reality. When Venus and Saturn are combined, love divines the true uses of the forms. The perfection of Venus (imagination) is understanding, and this is the Path of Daleth on the Tree, which connects Wisdom (Chokmah) to Understanding (Binah). Imagination sets man free from the restrictions of sense yet fulfills sensation instead of diminishing or destroying it. Thus our Lady Venus in Key 8 tames her lion but does not run away from him or kill him. See *C.19*.

איש מלחמה *Esh milkamah*. Man of War [Exodus 15:3]. The letter-name for Daleth is concealed in this saying, "The Lord is a man of war." A reference to Tetragrammaton. The Book of Tokens says of Daleth: "This is the gateway of life and form. Yet through it come also death and comfort, even as is shown in the numbering of Daleth. For Daleth being 434, it is 11, and 11 is the half, or division of 22, representing the whole circle of creation. Therefore is the door a cause of separation, and of the setting of one

part against another; and for this, it is written that the Lord is a "man of war." See 832.

בית הה וו *bohu* (spelled in full) meaning "chaos," [Genesis 1:2].

את אביך *eth abika*. The essence of your father. The masculine essence (Chaiah) proceeding from Chokmah, in the path of Daleth to Binah. This intimation is that the active principle in the Luminous Intelligence (Daleth) path is actually the masculine "essence" of light. In Tarot, the same thing is suggested, for the Empress (Key 3) is, by implication, the Emperor's wife. Her pregnancy is the consequence of the operation within her of his active power. The ten commandments enjoin us to honor "your father" and mother [Deuteronomy 5:16] see 914, 23, 73.

טל השמים *tal ha-shamaim*. dew of heaven [Genesis 27:28]. Refers to light-the universally diffused radiance, which takes the form of electromagnetic energy. It is granular in structure, falls upon the earth in drops, and the weight of its fall may be measured. See 390, 983, 541.

"For as the dissolution of body and soul is performed in the regenerated gold, where body and soul are separated from one another, and yet remain close together in the same vial, the soul daily refreshing the body from above, and preserving it from final destruction, until a set time: so the decaying and half-dead bodily part of man is not entirely deserted by its soul in the furnace of the Cross, but is refreshed by the spirit form above with heavenly dew, and fed and preserved with Divine nectar." [Waite, 1974, vol. 1, p. 111]

עמישדי A proper name, *Amishaddai*. "People of the Almighty." see Numbers 1:12.

יהוה חשק *ha.shaq IHVH*. The Lord had [affection] a delight. In Deuteronomy 10:15: "Yet the Lord set his affection on your forefathers and loved them, and he chose you, their descendants, above all the nations, as it is today." [Interlinar Bible]

η αμπελος. *heh ampelos*. The vine [John 15:1; Revelations 14:18].

435

I. Σ29 = 435

ה-מקדם מימי עולם *miqqedem mimay olahm*. From everlasting.

המסרים *mesaperiym*. declaration.

הנפש *ha nephesh*. The Animal soul.

הספר מים *Heh Sepher M*. The Book of Moses.

דרכיך יהוה הודיעני *derawkeikaw IHVH hodieniy*. show me the ways, O Lord. Psalm 25:4: "Show me your ways, O Lord: teach me your paths." see 915, 224.

436

שעטנז *sha'ataynez*. woven. In Leviticus 19:19, It refers to a woven mixture of wool and linen. In K.D.L.C.K. (p.505): which happens [also] when the letters שעטנז are transformed to read שטן זע Satan oz, Satan, the strong of the mighty adversary. See 359, 77.

Rosenroth in K.D.L.C.K. (p.723) says this name moreover is understood to be a depraved maid-servant, comprised of an ox and ass and assigned to the cortex or Qlippoth.

בת בבל *Bath Babel*. Daughter of Babylon. Psalm 137:8: "O daughter of Babylon, who are to be destroyed; happy shall he be, that rewards you as you have served us." see 402, 34, 760.

ביתחוי *Bithchauiy*. Lesser angel governing triplicity by day of Scorpio [Crowley, 1977, p. 45].

אפטרופס *Aphatrophas*. tutor, curator; prefectures; administrator, according to Rosenroth in K.D.L.C.K. (p.142) who cites the Zohar.

437

ספר מים + בדא *Sepher Mem + bawdawh*. book M + to form, fashion, to produce something new. To read "Book M," the *lux mundi* or "light of the world" is necessary. The Illuminati are recipients, through intuition, of the perfect understanding of the meaning of the cosmic order and can read the "one, only book" from which all secrets are to be learned. The archetypal phase of the creative process is imagination, inventing a new form of self-expression in the plane of original ideas. See 430, 7.

הנני יסד בציון אבן + הכבוד *hinnay yesad be-Tzion ehben + ha-kobode*. "Behold, I lay in Zion for a foundation a stone" + the glory. Zion is the holy of holies. The stone is the consciousness of union with the source. "The glory" is the mass of potential working power concentrated at the center. The rolled-up scroll or seed idea of the High Priestess, concentrated in the primal will at the beginning of a cycle of the life-power's self-expression. See 400, 37.

אריוא + תהרה *avara + tawhayra*. ether + cleansing, purifying. The ether (Air) comes from light, symbolized by the letter Yod in IHVH, according to the wise of Israel. Receptivity to this ether implies cleansing and purification. See 218, 219.

נדלת great, large ones. See Numbers 13:28.

אלות curses. See Deuteronomy 29:20.

438

ידע שחום *yado schom*. Gates of the shadow of death; the 5th hell, corresponding to Geburah, and to the Muslim sakar [Mem = 600, see 998].

בנפשו with his soul, with life in him. See Genesis 44:30.

בכיתו his weeping, his mourning. See Genesis 50:4.

ותכחד and you have been cut off, and you would be wiped. See Exodus 9:15.

υλη. *Hyle*. wood; a symbol of universal substance. "In the beginning when, according to the testimony of Scripture, God made heaven and earth, there was only *one* Matter, neither wet nor dry, neither earth, nor air, nor fire, nor light, nor darkness, but one single substance, resembling vapor or mist, invisible and impalpable. It was called Hyle, or the first Matter." [Waite, 1974, vol. 1, p. 184]

"It is that one thing which is not dug up from mines, or from the caverns of the earth, like gold, silver, sulfur, salt, etc. But is found in the form which God originally imparted to it. It is formed and manifested by an excessive thickening of the air; as soon as it leaves its body, it is clearly seen, but it vanishes without a trace as soon as it touches the earth, and, as it is never seen again, it must therefore be caught while it is still in the air, as I told you once before. I have called it by various names, but the simplest is perhaps that of 'Hyle' or first principle of all things." [ibid. p.186]

439 (prime)

שפטים *shophetim*. Judges.

הדלת the door. See Key 3, the Empress.

לדתה her confinement, to bear her. See Genesis 38:27.

הלדת birth, to be born. See Genesis 40:20.

אבותיך your fathers. See Genesis 31:3.

לבאות *lebaoth*. Inman: (Josh. 40:32). 'The lioness,' As the lions were emblems of strength, so their females are emblems of salacity [evoking sexual desire].

440

תם *toom*. completeness, perfection, piety, innocence, sincerity, mildness. The ultimate attainment and perfection are found at the center of the Cube of Space. When the soul's eye is single, the whole body is filled with the light of the White Brilliance, and the soul is liberated-set free from the illusions of appearance. Refers to Mem as the 23rd Path of Wisdom. See 441, 510.

חזחזית *chazchazith*. wheeling, circling. Chaldaic word derived from the same root as חזות (Chazoth), signifying vision or revelation. Refers to Beth, the 12th Path is an image (body or substance) of the phase of Gedulah (cosmic memory) or Chesed in Kether-the eternal cycles of the essential memory of itself and its activities and powers. Recall each sephirah is also a tree of 10 sephiroth. It is the source of vision of the eternal cycles of the essential memory of itself and its activities and powers. Ordinary sight is, in a way, memory; we do not "see" anything until we "recognize" it. Insight is the real power at work in the 12th path (the Magician). This is the "source of vision in those who behold apparitions." see 421, 412, 567, 8, 2080.

שכל כללי *Saykel Kelali*. Collective Intelligence. Title of Resh, the 13th Path of Wisdom. Connects the sphere of the intellect (Mercury) with that of the automatic consciousness (Moon). This path has to do with completing the Great Work-the "new creature," evolved from the natural man by the Life-power, working through the human personality's mental, emotional and physical activities. The inner transforming power is the Ego (Christos). The possessor of this path has unusual insight into human nature. He is free from attachment to persons and things, and the pairs of opposites do not disturb his calm poise. His "receptors"-centers in the nervous system, brain and related glands-function differently. He has another kind of vision and is skillful, where most persons are inept. Perfected by the true knowledge of the stars, his personality is enriched-he enjoys fertility instead of sterility. He knows that man is the synthesis of all cosmic activities. Human intelligence gathers the threads of the life-power's self-manifestations and carries it beyond anything that could come into existence apart from himself. See 90, 80, 210, 510, 200.

שמנים *shemonim*. eighty (80); the numerical value of Peh, associated with Mars. In Canticles 6:8: Sixty queens there may be, and eighty concubines, and virgins without number, (9) but my dove, my perfect one, is unique, the only daughter of her mother, the favorite of the one who bore her. The maidens saw her and called her blessed; the queens and concubines phrased her. see 1000.

מת *meth*. Dead. In Psalm 31:12: "A am forgotten by them as though I were dead; I have become like broken pottery."

דלות *Dalluth*. Poverty, penury, destitution. Poverty is a play on the letter name Daleth [434], according to this passage in the Book of Concealed Mystery [I:40, p.60]: "That man [i.e., Jacob] shall say, "I am the Lord's, he descends." That is, that very conception of the word I [אני, 61], which is elsewhere attributed to the supernal mother [Binah], forasmuch as in her agree the three letters of the word אני, Ani, I; namely Aleph is the highest crown; Nun it the understanding itself, in its fifty celebrated gates; Yod is the foundation or knowledge of the father; but in this instance, it is attributed to the lowest grade of the lower mother and now is אדני, Adonai, without the Daleth, or poverty, but filled with the influx, and is אני ani." see 61, 65. The result of "folly": "the wages of sin is death."

חודותו *yakhudotho*. his individuality. From the above gematria, it is clear that individuality is realized through the serpent's power, working with the sun's collective intelligence (Key 19), which completes the personality. This word is derived from יחוד [28], *yirhood*, profession of the unity of God; union, communion; privacy, private meeting. See 2945, 425, 1052.

ליהוה הארץ ומלואה *la-IHVH ha-aretz vu-meloah*. Psalm 24:1: The earth is Tetragrammaton's and the fulness thereof.

תהלת *tawhalaw*. folly, error, sin. The sin of misdirecting the serpent-power (kundalini) to activate the lower centers only.

מכשף *mikashef*. Magician, sorcerer. See 445.

תלי *theli*. the dragon; Satan. See 700.

מרר *marar*. to make bitter, to be embittered. As a noun, gall, bitter herbs, etc. With different pointing: to flow, to run, to ooze out. See 250, 245, 290.

441

אמת *emeth*. Stability (hence, truth.) Refers to Tav, joined with Mem at the center of the Cube of Space. This word suggests the power of Spirit (Aleph), working through the agency of universal substance (Mem) to bring about the dominion of its creation (Tav), which is Man. See 340, 476, 85 Latin.

אמת *atem*. you (masc. plural).

גחלת *gahkheleth*. burning coal, live coal; carbuncle. It is said of the illuminated that they are "coals of fire"- the igniting of the higher brain centers, especially the pineal gland. "Carbuncle" suggests a misfunction of this process, as "the fallen angels."

לריאר *Lariar*. Day demon of the 2nd decan of Leo. This decan is governed by Jupiter, indicating unkindness, intolerance and boorishness, qualities the opposite of which animate the Chasidim (Jupiter) through the Heart (Sun), which Leo represents.

רמרא *Ramra*, Lesser angel governing triplicity by day of Pisces. This suggests that "truth" has something to do with modifying the body cells' perception, bringing spirit down to earth.

אתם *ath-mem*. Essence of water. Also, *Ethem*, the wilderness of Shur [Numbers 33:8] 441 = 9 = Teth, the serpent. See 507, 245, 250, 290, 441, 527.

מאת *meath*. a hundred. Genesis 25:7: "Altogether, a Braham lived a hundred and seventy-five years." For other numerals see 13, 400, 636, 273, 348, 600, 372, 395, 770, 570.

"מאה or מאת, one hundred. The name of this

number indicates an extension produced by the desire to be extended, to be manifested. The root of this word אוה, literally desire, is here governed by the signs of exterior action מ. One finds in Arabic expressing *to extend* and *to dilate*. In nearly all the tongues of Asia, *mah* signifies great." [d'Olivet, 1976, pp. 154-155.]

Of אוה, he writes Determined will: the action of *willing, desiring, tending toward* an object. [p.289]

אילת doe, hind. Proverbs 5:19: "A loving doe, a graceful deer- may her breast satisfy you always, may you ever be captivated by her love."

442

בעל שם *Baal Shem*. "Master of the Name," a Jewish magician.

ארך + יאיר *yaweer + ereck*. he gives light + length, delay, postponement. Illumination comes after the delay caused by the evolutionary process. The real meaning of earth is known. See 221.

אפמי ארץ *afesiay eretz*. Rosenroth gives *termini* [end, limit] *terrae* [that which is dry; hence the earth], and say it is Malkuth in respect to the final conceptions of it, which are Netzach and Hod.

מבקש seek, search, sought. Genesis 37:16.

ונפשו and his soul. Genesis 44:30.

תמו the dead. Numbers 19:11.

ובדלת and into the door. Deuteronomy 15:17.

אפמי ארץ the end of the earth.

βακτηρια. *baktehria*. Staff. Septuagint translation of משענת (860) in Psalm 23:4: "Yea, though I walk through the valley of the shadow of death, I will fear no evil: for thou are with me; your rod and your staff they comfort me." see 860.

443 (prime)

בית אל *Beth el*. House of God [Genesis 28:19]. The name of the place at which Jacob had his dream of the Ladder. See 496.

בתולה *bethulah*. virgin maiden; Virgo. A title of Malkuth. Figuratively, a city. Its root-meaning is "separated one," "to separate." This is precisely the root-meaning of the Greek original for "Hermit." see 10, 145.

In Genesis 24:16: "And the damsel was very beautiful to look upon, a virgin whom no man had known; and she went down to the well and filled her pitcher and came up." Also, in Exodus 22:16: "And if a man entices a virgin who is not betrothed, and lies with her, he shall surely marry her." In Joel 1:8: "Lament like a virgin girded with sackcloth for the husband of her youth." A poetical term for the Jewish nation in Amos 5:2: "The virgin of Israel is fallen, she shall no more rise, she is left lying on the ground, there is none to raise her up."

דרך הרוח *derek ha-ruach*. the way of the spirit. Ecclesiastes 11:5: "As you know not what is the way of the spirit, nor how the bones do grow in the womb of her that is with child: even so you know not the works of God who makes all (things).

גלית *Goliath*. Captivity, bondage. The name of the giant who was slain by David [14, דוד] Has deep occult meaning. In 1 Samuel 17:4: "And there went out a champion out of the camp of the Philistines, named Goliath of Gath, whose height was six cubits and a span." Related to the "dweller of the threshold." See Steiner: Knowledge of Higher Worlds, 123 (Greek).

Paul Case: Note that D. D. Bryant recognizes the inner sensorium corresponding to the five outer senses. Therefore, it seems likely that he speaks of seeing and handling the stone as an interior experience, which, although it is as vividly objective as any physical sense-experience, depends upon the inner faculties. Hence it may be, he speaks of the "unfoldment" of the stone and compares it here to "one perception," which annihilates Goliath (גליות, 449). Here we may recall that in Judges 5:12 occurs the sayings "Awake, awake Deborah (דברה, 217, a bee, from דבר, 212, to arrange or regulate, suggesting the industry of the bee); Awake, Awake, utter a song; arise, Barak (ברק, 302, lighting, brilliancy) and lead your captivity captive, thou son of Abinoam (אבינעם, 179, father, or possessor of Grace.) The words "lead captivity captive" suggest the overcoming of the principle of bondage by itself. Thus although David knocks Goliath down with the stone, he despatches the giant by cutting off his head with Goliath's own sword, which later on, David himself appropriates and uses for his own. Compare also Psalm 68:18: "Thou has ascended on high, thou has held captivity captive. The has received gifts for men, yea, for the rebellious also, that the Lord God might dwell among them." And Ephesians 4:7,8: "But unto every one of us is given grace according to the measure of the gift of Christ. Wherefore he says, when he ascended up on high, he led captivity captive, and gave gifts unto men." The latter shows the same connection between "grace" and the overcoming of bondage, as is suggested by the proper name Abinoam." [Paul Case on The Philosopher's Stone, IX]. See 24 note, 14.

יתגל *yithgal*. was uncovered. Genesis 9:21: "And he [Noah] drank of the wine and was drunken, and he was uncovered within his tent." This, from the story of Noah and the curse of Canaan, has a direct connection with the word Goliath. "What is uncovered" is the gigantic adversary who is overcome by a true vision. The appearances of the physical plane deceive us by seeming to show us all there is to see. The same idea is concealed in the story of the fall. The serpent's subtlety consists of the apparent exposure of truth when the truth is hidden behind the manifestations of name and precede using the physical sense. See 20, 351, 570, 496.

Η Λογος. *ho Logos*. The Word; creative expression. The thought-in-expression. This serves to identify the Hermit with the One Identity, described at the beginning of Saint John's Gospel.

Ιορδανης. *Jordanehs*. The Greek for Jordan (ירדן), "descending." "That which flows down, down it the dead sea." Symbol of the river of manifestation, the stream of Maya, the illusive power of manifestation.

ασμα καινον. *aisma kainon*. A new song. Septuagint translation of שיר חדש (882) in Psalm 149:1: "Praise ye the Lord. Sing unto the Lord a new song, and his praise in the congregation of saints." see 822, 510, 1394.

444

דם שק *dam sack*. blood sack. i.e., the human body.

דמשק *Damascus*, an Old Testament city; work. In alchemy, the Place of the Work is also the Blood-sack, the vessel of Skin containing the liquid "living water," which is also the secret fire. See 400, 53.

In the *Fama* Brother C.R.C., most stop his journeys because of the "feebleness of his body." The place-name Damascus means 'work.' The occult student must have a sound mind and body to perform the Great Work, indicated by Damascus's reference. In Damascus, Brother C.R. gains favor with the Turks [4th root Race Adepts] because of his "skill in medicine." This intimates that that one preparing himself for initiation gains unusual skill in controlling his body's functions. During this period, chastity is necessary, that is, purity in thought, word and deed. If this is neglected, there is a risk that the student could release potent physical and psychical forces that could cause damage to his physical and psychical makeup. See 264, 870 (Greek).

"The body must be cleansed. The mind must be controlled. The bloodstream must be charged with subtle substances from glandular secretions controlled by the subconscious powers called 'Turks' in the Fama. All this must be done in Damascus before one goes to Damcar.

Damascus's work changes the blood chemistry and modifies the structure of certain areas in the brain." [Case, 1985, p. 77.]

צפרדע *tzephardea.* frogs. An animal attributed to Saturn. The 2nd of the ten plagues of Egypt. Exodus 8:2: (1) "Then the Lord said to Moses, 'Go to Pharaoh and say to him, this is what the Lord says: let my people go, so that they may worship me. (2) If you refuse to let them go, I will plague your whole country with frogs."

קדים *makodosh.* sanctuary. Then he brought me back the way of the outer gate of the sanctuary, המקדש, which looks toward the east, קדים, and it was shut." The name of God used here is אדני יהוה [and the Lord] said unto me: "This gate shall be shut, it shall not be opened, neither shall any man enter in by it, for the Lord, the God of Israel (יהוה אלהי ישראל). Has entered in by it; therefore, it shall be shut. As for the prince, being a prince, he shall sit therein to eat bread before the Lord; he shall enter by way of the porch of the gate, and shall go out by way of the same." (Then he brought me the way of the north gate) See Temple of Solomon, in Makey's encyclopedia. The sanctuary, מקדש, was 20 x 40 cubits. Thus its area was 800 square cubits, and the length of the four boundary lines was 120 cubits. Note that the sanctuary area, 800 cubits, equals the porch's combines area and the holy of holies. The alchemical significance has to do with the "place of the work" used to arrive at the "sanctuary." See 120, 470, 864 (Greek), 800, 1025.

חשך אפלא *khoshek-aphilah.* thick darkness. This relates to the place of work, Egypt (subconsciousness), as a place where the alchemical process takes place in obscurity or "thick darkness." see 328, 116, 924, 808, 328.

נפקחו עיניכם *nepekechu eineikem.* (and) your eyes shall be opened. Genesis 3:5: "For God does know that in the day you eat thereof [of the fruit of the Tree of Life], then shall be opened, and you shall be as gods, knowing good and evil." A reference to the awakening of the third eye, the sensorium of inner vision. See 571, 1414.

צו לצו צו לצו *tzaw ka-tzaw tzaw la-tzaw.* precept upon precept, precept upon precept. In the Interlinear Bible, Do and do, do and do. The rest of the verse in Isaiah 28:10 is: "rule on rule, rule on rule; a little here, a little there." The reference is to those who are taught knowledge and made to understand doctrine-that the work begins with "rule on rule, a little here and tittle there." see 484, 928 and Isaiah 28:13.

שכן עד *shoken ad.* who abides forever. Isaiah 57:18: "For thus says the high and lofty one who inhabits eternity (abides forever), whose name is holy, whose abode revive the heart of those who are in pain." see 370.

τε λεια αγαπη. *teleia agape.* Perfect love. 1 John 4:18: "There is no fear in love, but perfect love casts out fear; because fear, has restraint; and he who fears has not been perfected in love." see 620, 93 (Greek).

ο αγρος. *ho agros.* The field. Matthew 13:38: "The field is the world; the good seed are the sons of the kingdom; the tares are the children of the evil one." From a parable of Jesus. R.L. Harrison writes: "It is the world of thought and the senses, where only corruption can reign, being things of the flesh; and where only tares may find a congenial home." [Sr. Paranandas Commentary on St. Matthew, p.118] see 374 (Greek).

ο αργος. *ho argos.* the ship. (From Jason's Argo, 'shining, bright, glistening') With different pointing: the idle, useless; fruitless, unemployed. Indolent, slothful, slow. Inactive in [2 Peter 1:8] "For these things being in you and abounding, they will not permit you to be inactive (αργους) nor unfruitful in the knowledge of our Lord Jesus Christ." see 374 (Greek).

445

מכשפה *mokshepah.* Sorcerer.

הבריאה + אוריה *ha-briah + uriah.* "Light of wisdom" + the creation. The light of wisdom is a compound of אור *aur,* light, with the divine name

יה, attributed to Chokmah; "the creation" refers to Heh, the 15th path as the "essence of creation," and the letters of the word spell הה (Heh insight and Heh foresight) the letter-name Heh, אב *Ab*, father, Yod the Hermit, Resh letter of the sun, see 222, 223.

זחלת *zoheleth*. Serpent. 1 Kings 1:9: "Adonai Jah then sanctified sheep, cattle and fatted calves at the stone of the serpent near En Rogel." see 450, 503.

והדלת and the door. Genesis 19:6.

מתה dead. See Genesis 30:2.

הפשכם a sorceress, one-being-sorceress. See Exodus 22:17.

446

מות *maveth*. death.

פישון *Pishon*. dispersive, overflowing. The first river of Eden in Genesis (associated with Fire), that which compasses the whole land of Havilah where there is gold [Genesis 2:11] It is the activity (Peh) of the divine will (Yod) transforming (Shin) through intuition (Vav) and change (Nun).

Genesis 2:11-12: "A river watering the garden flowed from Eden, and from there it divided; it had four headstreams. The name of the first is Pishon; it winds through the entire land of Havilah (החוילה, 64), where there is gold." Please note that Havilah is 64, Nogah the Sphere of Netzach, associated with fire and *may zahab*, meaning: golden waters. See 64.

"פישון Phishon... this is the root יש, which formed by the signs of manifestation and of relative movement, expresses every idea of reality and of physical substantiality. It is governed by the emphatic sign of speech פ and is terminated by the argumentative syllable. ון, which carries to its highest degree, the extent of every produced being." [d'Olivet, 1976, p.78-79.]

Pishon is closely related to the word *Pîythôwn* (פיתון; "*expansive*"), which derives from the root *pothâh* (פתה); "to *open*," as implying a secret place). *Edom and Eden*, Timothy Scott

קמוש *qimosh*. thorn, thistle, nettle. Isaiah 34:12: "And thorns shall come up in her palaces, nettles and brambles in the fortresses thereof: and it shall be a habitation of dragons, and of court for owls."; Hosea 9:6: "For, lo, they are gone because of destruction: Egypt shall gather them up, Memphis shall bury them: the pleasant places for their silver, nettles shall possess them: thorns shall be in their tabernacles."

קרסולים *qahraysulim*. joints, ankles. Spelled קרסלי in Psalm 18:36: "Thou has enlarged my steps [ankles] under me, that my feet did not slip." Rosenroth in K.D.L.C.K. (p.678) gives: *tali pedum* and says they are Netzach and Hod with respect to Tiphareth.

לבח תו *habel-Tav*. cable-tow. Hebrew version of the English. חבל means cord, rope, and תו is the letter name of Tav, mark, cross, signature, implying salvation. As the 2nd extension of 7, תו may be considered full development of Zain, the Lovers, and the Disposing Intelligence. Mackey says: "The cable-tow is a rope or line for drawing or leading. The word is purely Masonic... in the 2nd and 3rd degrees... The cable-tow is.. supposes to symbolize the covenant by which all Masons are tied, thus reminding us of the passage in Hosea 11:4:: "I draw them with cords of man, with bonds of love.'" [Encyclopedia, p.136]

447

ספריה + יד + יהוה + בדא *seferin + yad Tetragrammaton + bawdawh*. The books + the hand of IHVH + to form, fashion. The books are those inner books of life that are opened during illumination; 'the hand of IHVH' is the one reality's formative power. The archetypal phase of the creative process is imagination, through which the mothers function. 447 reduces to 6, which is the value of Vav or intuition. This formative power is perceived. 6 is also the key of the lovers, attributed to Zain or discrimination. The one reality is divided or cut apart into "that which is below." See 400, 40, 7.

תלי + או *theli + ow*. the dragon + desire, will, appetite. The dragon is the circling, spiraling force in the manifest; the motive power in the life power's self-manifestation is its desire to actualize its own possibilities. See 440, 7.

קבצאל + חוקקוה *kabzeel + chuqqiy*. Gathering of God + the emanating principles. The gathering is the concentration of the limitless light of Kether; the emanating principles are the forces of the paths or branches of the Tree of Life, propelled from Kether by the "mothers." See 223, 224.

אילות *Eloth*. a feminine form of deity, in 1 Kings 9:25: "And three times a year did Solomon offer burnt offerings upon the altar which he built to the Lord, and he burnt incense upon the altar that was before the Lord [Eloth]. So he finishes the house." see 441, 31, 42, 86.

ואמת and truly, and truth, and faithfulness. See Genesis 24:49.

אמות I die, I will die. See Genesis 26:9.

448

מבוקש *meboqash*. Quest, Desirous; hunger, thirst. From a verbal root meaning: emptiness. Has a meaning akin to the English nouns hunger and thirst. Connected with Kaph, the 21st Path. See 886, 100, 194, 178, 20.

חי נפש *nefesh chai*. Breath of Life. The field of subconscious mental activity. See 430, 80, 18.

במות *Bawmoth*. *excelsa* - high places, mountains, altars. The "altar" is nephesh chai, and the "high places" of consciousness are reached through the lamp of the Hermit (Virgo). See Key 9.

מלך משיח *melek mashiah*. King Messiah. The Ego in Tiphareth, which regulates all phases of the great work. It is the origin of the goal and the goal itself. See 90, 358.

הבתולה the virgin, the unmarried. See Leviticus 21:3.

מאהבת from love. See Deuteronomy 7:8.

449 (prime)

תליט *talith*. Cloak [Crowley, 1977, p. 47]. This word does not appear in scripture but is part of the phrase white cloak, תליט לבון, referring to Yesod, the Pure Intelligence. See 536, 80.

d'Olivet writes of the root טל: "The sign of resistance united by contraction to the root אל, symbol of every elevation, composes a root whose object is to express the effect of a thing which raises itself above another thing, covers, veils, or puts it under shelter. That which *cast a shadow*, that which *is projected* from above below; that which *varies, changes, moves* like a shadow: *a veil, a garment* with which one is covered; *a spot* which changes color; *the dew* which forms a veil over plants; *an unweaned lamb* still under the shelter of its mother." [d'Olivet, 1976, p.358.]

כמשפט as manner, ordinance, judgment, as the custom. See Genesis 40:13.

המקדש the sanctuary. See Leviticus 12:4.

450

I. (2x3x3x5x5) or $2 \times 3^2 \times 5^2$

II. 10 x 45, or Adam, (45) multiplied by the ten Sephiroth.

הזחלת *ha-zoheleth*. the serpent [1 Kings 1:9]. Associated with אבן, the stone. This is the serpent power represented by Teth and Key 8. The full expression in the text is אבן הזחלת, Stone of Zoheleth, the stone of the serpent. See 445.

חסף די פחר *kasaf di-pekhar*. potter's clay [Daniel 2:41]. In the text, the clay is mixed with iron in the symbolic image of Nebuchadnezzar's dream.

The physical organism of man and man's body consciousness is one meaning.

מדות *midoth*. Virtues. Refers to the peculiar qualities or properties of man, dependent on his members and organs. Also relates to the various potencies of the Life-power in their latent state, as possibilities in the depths of Binah. Paul Case: מדות *midoth* is a temurah for 3 Sephiroth, חסד Chesed, גבורה Geburah and תפארת Tiphareth, the Egoic Triad. See K.D.L.C.K. (p., 508).

מקודש *maqodesh*. sanctity, holiness. Sanctifying Intelligence of Binah. This a consciousness of Mem perfect dependence upon the Life-power; Qoph, perfect organization of all cell-groups in the physical body; Vav, perfect communion and unquestioning obedience to the inner teacher; Daleth, filled with clear, definite pictures of beautiful consequences flowing from the recognition of the Life-power's true nature; Shin, vivid consciousness of immortality-the fourth dimension. To sanctify is to make pure, clean, and perfect. A saint is one who has surrendered all personal actions to the direction of the Life-power (Mem). He has traversed the road of initiation during the sleep of his physical body (Qoph). He has listened to the voice of the inner teacher (Vav). He has restored the creator to his throne through the generative powers of imagination (Daleth); and completes his work in the perfection and unfoldment of a new vehicle for the Life-power by the refining fire of the Life-breath of the Elohim (Shin). He has mastered control of the serpent-power (Teth). [This is the spelling given in *True and Invisible* p. 281] see 67 (Binah), 756, and 415 for alternate spelling.

שפע *shefah*. abundance, overmeasure, emanation; to flow [Deuteronomy 33:19]. The intelligence of Cheth Connected with water. Shin shows the 4th dimension as the Great sea, Binah. Peh is a symbol of Mezla, the holy influence descending from Kether. Ayin is the way the same power is interpreted as superficial appearances reported by sensation. The noun "influence" suggests the notion of water. The Hebrew *shefah* occurs once in the Old Testament, where it is translated as "abundance." "They shall suck the abundance of the seas." Here the idea of abundance is directly connected with water. In this passage, there is also an occult reference to time because the word for "seas" is ימים, *yomim*, identical in spelling with a noun which signifies "days."

שפע *shefah*. Influence. Part of the Path names of Intelligence of the House of Influence (Cheth) and Intelligence of Mediating Influence (Tiphareth). See 536.

"In Tarot, *Shefah* 'influence' is represented by Keys 20, 16 and 15. Key 20 is a symbol of the 4th dimension, of being above, yet within, all other planes. This key shows the coffins of personal consciousness floating of the great sea of *Binah*, understanding. The 18th Path proceeds from *Binah*, as we go down the Tree of Life, and the same paths lead to Binah on the way of return. Key 16, corresponding to the second letter of *Shefah*, shows the holy influence as a lighting flash, which destroys the tower of false knowledge. Key 15, corresponding to the third letter of *Shefah*, shows how man interprets the operation of this same holy influence when he knows nothing about it except the superficial appearance reported by the physical sense.

Under this last aspect, the Holy influence propounds riddles to us and presents us with problems. Thus the sphinxes of Key 7 and the Devil of Key 15 are related symbols. Both represent incongruous combinations of human and animal elements. They are the types of great magic agent, the force employed in all works of practical occultism." [Case, 1985, p. 272-273.]

לוחות *lookhuth*. "the tables," on which Moses wrote the law. Here is a suggestion that all the powers of man are developments of the Tora. Note that Tora is inscribed on the scroll of the High Priestess, who corresponds to the Moon, ruler of Cancer. Since the manifestation of the Rota is the result of the reactions among the ten Sephiroth. See 897.

פרי עץ *peree etz*. the fruit of the tree. Genesis 1:29: "And God said, behold, I have given you... every tree, in the which, is the fruit of a tree yielding seed; to you, it shall be for meat." The manifestation of the Tora is the result of the reactions among the 10 Sephiroth. Refers to the ripening of the powers of the Tree of Life. See 671, 290, 160, 1260.

פשע *pah.sah, pah.shaw*. sin, transgression trespass; the guilt of transgression punishment. "Missing the Mark." The tower of personality (Peh) is put before the liberty of spiritual realization (Shin). This is the essence of all transgression-the attempt to determine the action of the divine spirit (Shin) by imposing on it forms built up by "personal will" (Peh). With different pointing *pahsha*: to transgress, be in rebellion (verb); to revolt, the rebel; to be unfaithful; to be negligent in guarding a trust. See 100, 1217.

פשע *pahsa*. step, pace, progress. With different pointing: 1. to stride, to make progress; 2. to tread, step, march. When Shin is sounded as "s," it has a more favorable connotation that the Sh sound. See 52, זמה.

קנה חכמה קנה בנה *qenah chokmah qenah binah*. get wisdom; get understanding. Proverbs 4:5: "Get wisdom; get understanding; do not forget my words or swerve from them."

רצון באין גבול *ratzone ain be-gebil*. Unlimited goodwill, Goodwill without limit. The mental state of a saint, a perfect man.

שוכן עד *shoken ad*. dwelling in eternity, abiding eternally. In man, this is the state of having eternal life (inhabitans aeternitatem). See 208.

תן *tan*. Sea-serpent or monster; jackal. Both jackal and dragon refer to the first matter of the alchemical operation. In the Qabalah, *tan* is always the sea monster inhabiting the great sea. It is a symbol of the spiral, whirling force, at work in Binah. See 713.

פארפאחיטאס *Parfaxitas*. The Sentinel of the 27th Path (Tunnel) of Peh on the Inverse Tree of Life.

I. The 27th Tunnel is under the aegis of Parfaxitas, whose number is 450, which is the number of תן, meaning 'Dragon.' It is the root of Leviathan. Tan,

feminine *Tanith*, is that great dragon of the deep that manifests on earth as Babalon, the woman or priestess specially consecrated to the Draconian Current work.

The formula of Parfaxitas comports the assumption of astral animal forms for the reification of atavistic energies. The animals traditionally associated with this ray are the Owl and the Wolf, hence *Le Mystere Lycanthropique*.

The number of Parfaxitas - 450 - is that of כשפים, meaning 'incantations,' 'witchcrafts,' 'sorceries'; and of פשע, 'transgression,' which in this context denotes a crossing over into the astral or spirit world. This is confirmed by the word אתמחא (also 450), 'to be crucified,' which signifies the crossing over from bodily to spiritual awareness. The word אתמחא derives from the Egyptian *makha*, meaning 'balance,' 'level,' or 'crossing,' The sigil of Parfaxitas depicts a Fortress with a door, and two windows (eyes) superposed upon the letters SUE [may be an abbreviation of the name of Crowley's scarlet woman at the time he received this sigil], the number of which is 71, which is the number of LAM The fortress is magically protected by the letters מ ו נ ד ו ס ד (170). The number 71 is that of אליל, which means 'nothing,' 'an apparition' or 'image,' and serves to show the astral or nonphysical nature of the formula of Parfaxitas. It is also the number of חזון, 'vision,' and of אימך, 'your terror'. It is also the number of 'Silence'. On the other hand, 170 is active and is the number of מקל, the 'wand' or *'baculus,'* i.e., the magician's phallus. It is also the number of Nephilim, נפיל meaning 'a giant,' the mythical designation of a god or extraterrestrial being, from the Egyptian word *Nepr*, 'a god'. The two numbers together denote the formula of the 8th degree O.T.O., which involves the Turret of Silence and the Tower of Shaitan (i.e., the wand). In this isolation, it conjures images or visions from the Void.

The path above this tunnel is consecrated to Works of Wrath and Vengeance, which shows the markedly martial nature of the current, which - - is interpreted in the form of primal atavisms in the tunnel beneath it. Furies and

Werewolves haunt its shadows, and the Sword is the magical weapon associated with the deities Mentu, Mars, and Horus, the 'flaming God' who rages 'through the firmament with his fantastic spear.' According to *Liber 231*: 'He smote the towers of wailing; he brake them in pieces in the fire of his anger, so that he alone did escape from the ruin thereof.'

As Scholem has pointed out, the concepts of divine wrath are connected with the purgative current, which in its primary sense is the purgation associated with the feminine cycle. At the time of puberty, the female's bloodshed was the purifying or 'redeeming' water of life. This was the first blood sacrifice as it was also the first sacrament. The bloodshed in battle was a secondary form of this symbolism and pertained to Mars and the Martian Current. In the primary sense of purgation, the expression 'Works of Wrath and Vengeance' should be understood.

Fevers and wounds are the diseases typical of Path 27; also Inflammation, the redness of which is symbolic of the wound of puberty, the first gash being the female cleft with its issue of blood. Hence the Sword as the cleaver or splitter open is symbolic of the vagina and was so interpreted in the primitive astronomical mysteries. This was continued in the symbolism of the sickle attributed to Saturn, the later planetary representative of the primal Goddess in the heavens [Note that the sickle, or sign of Saturn, is a form of the figure 5 - the number of the female as symbolic of Nuit (i.e., the Negative source of all positivity).

The precious stone associated with this 27th *Kala* is the ruby or red stone; the characteristic plants are rue, peppers, and absinthe, all noted for their fiery qualities. [Grant, 1994, pp. 233-236.]

η θαλασσα. he-thalassa. the sea. This is in harmony with the Hebrew conception of Binah as the sea.

תהום *tehom*. the abyss of the waters, great deep [Genesis 1:2]. By this Gematria, the "great deep," or dark abyss of primal water, is identified with the idea of the human race's universal essence. Darkness and evil provide the raw material, which is then formed into light, and then made into good. It also precedes the manifestation of individualized man, yet it is also one with man's essential nature. See *eth ha-adam* (below), 430, 691, 1011, 681; 1273 (Greek).

את האדם *eth ha-adam*. essence of man. Genesis 1:27: "So God created man, in his image" (i.e., essence of man). The "great deep" or dark abyss of primal water is the essence of the human race. See 401, 45, 1011.

יהוה כל עשה *IHVH oseh kole*. IHVH who makes all.

ישמעאל *Ishmael*. "God hears," In Genesis 16:11: "And shall call his name Ishmael; because the Lord has heard your affliction." Abraham's oldest son, by Sarah's maidservant Hagar, the Egyptian. [Hagar means "to flee"] The law of Sinai "which genders to Bondage" is likened to Ishmael by St. Paul [Galatians 4:24]. Like Jesus, Ishmael is the son of another fugitive woman [Case].

מיתא *mithaw*. death. In 1 Corinthians 15:21: "For since by man came death, by man also came the resurrection from the dead." Key 13 or Death is related to the element of water through Scorpio.

אתן *atten*. you, yourselves. The feminine second person, plural pronoun. IHVH is commonly thought of as being masculine. The truth is that God transcends all distinctions of gender. The actual working power, which is the essence of the dark, void abyss, and primordial humanity's essence, is always represented as feminine.

שנאנים *Shinanim*. An angelic choir sometimes associated with Tiphareth and the sphere of the sun. See 1011. Written שנאו in Psalm 68:1: "The chariots of God are twenty thousand, even thousands of angel's [i.e., shin'an]: The Lord is among them, as in Sinai, in the holy place."

"A high class of angels, 'the shinanin of the fire,' adduced from Psalm 68:18 and referred to in 3 Enoch. Myriads of these shinanin descended from heaven to be present at the revelation of Sinai. According to the Zohar [I:18B]: "Myriads of thousands of shin'an are on the chariot of God." Chief of the order is Zadkiel or Sidquiel... 'The 6th sefira, Tifereth (Tiphereth) is represented among the angels of the shinanim, says C.D. Ginsburg in The Essence and the Qabbalah.'" [Davidson, 1971, p. 273.]

κανθαρος. *cantharos*. A wine cup. 1. In classical antiquity, a large drinking cup, having two handles rising above the brim. 2. a fountain or basin in the courtyard before ancient churches, where persons could wash before entering the church. The human body is the cup holding the wine (blood) in which consciousness resides. The laver of purification outside the Hebrew tabernacle was a symbol of the inner purity which must manifest before the dawning of the "light." See 901.

σπορα. *spora*. Sowing; a begetting or children: generation, birth; seed-time; the seed sown; born, seed offspring, issue. In the plural, young ones. See 720 (Greek), 426.

452

ישהוע בן דוד *yeshua ben-dawvid*. Jesus, son of David. [Note: ישע = deliverance, salvation, victory, and דוד = beloved]. See 386, 14, 52.

חמדת *hawmudoth*. One is greatly beloved. Spelled חמדות in Daniel 10:11: "And he said unto me, O Daniel, a man greatly beloved, understand the words that I speak unto thee, and stand upright: for unto thee am I now sent. And when he had spoken this word unto me, I stood trembling." Note that Daniel means "judgment of God." See 54, 95. [probably from חמדה, meaning desire, objects of delight]. See 552.

אפיטרופוש *ephitayropos*. guardian, procurator, administrator. The Lord is the guardian of the desires of the beloved son.

קרקבן *qawrayqebawn*. stomach; crop, craw, maw. The stomach is ruled by Cancer, which is receptivity to the divine will. The path of Cheth connects Binah, the sphere of Saturn, and Geburah, sphere of Mars.

בדמות in the likeness, in the likeness of. See Genesis 5:1.

מבית within. See Genesis 6:14.

453

חיה נפש *Nephesh Chaiah*. Breath of Life. Animal or Vital Soul in Yesod. Life, living creature. See 430, 23, 483.

I. "חיהה נפש soul-of-life. The word נפש, which Moses used to designate, in general, the soul and the animating life of being.

The root form which the word נפש comes, is without doubt material, for there is no word possible, in any tongue possible, whose elements are not material. It is the noun that is the basis of speech. Every time that man wishes to express an intellectual and moral thought, he is obligated to make use of a physical instrument, and to take from elementary nature, material objects which he spiritualizes, and it were, in making them pass, using metaphor or hieroglyphics, from one region into another.

Three distinct roots compose this important word and are worthy of closest attention. The first נף presents the idea of inspiration, an infusion, a movement operated from without, within: it is literally *an inspiring breath*. The second פה, which is only the first reaction, is attached to the idea of expansion, effusion, movement operated from within, without literally *the mouth, the expiring breath, the voice, the speech*, etc. The third, finally אש, characterizes the *principiant principle*. It is *fire*, and that which is igneous, ardent, impassioned, etc.

Such is the hieroglyphic composition of the word נפש Nephesh, the soul, which, formed of the three roots נף פה אש, presents the symbolic image of a thing that the Egyptian priest regarded as belonging to a triple nature. Instructors of Moses saw in נף, the *partie naturante* of the soul, in פה the *partie naturee*, and in אש, the *partie naturelle*. This elementary triad resulted in unity whose immorality they taught, according to all the ancient sages.

Among the Hebrews, נפש signifies *to live* and *breath*; among the Chaldeans, *to grow, to multiply, to fill space*; the Samaritan verb expresses, *to dilate, to develop, to manifest*; the Syriac *to give life, to heal*; the Arabic *to expand, to evaporate*, etc." [d'Olivet, 1976, pp. 51-53.]

II. The breath of life is: "a symbol of the spiritual essence - the divine spark, atma-buddhi, which is immortal... [see Genesis 2:7]. And into this lower mind, or astro-mental body was projected the divine spark, and thence the man (manasic being) became a creature capable of responsible, independent existence." [Gaskell, 1981, p. 126.]

III. The Zohar [I:49A] Comments: "And he breathed into his nostrils the breath of life. The breath of life was enclosed in the earth, made pregnant with it like a female impregnated by the male. So the dust and the breath were joined, and the dust became full of spirits and souls. And the man became a living soul. At this point, he attained his proper form and became a man to support and nourish the living soul." (p.156)

בהמות *Behemoth*. Animal, beast, animality, brutishness, animalism, licentiousness, pointed hippopotamus differently. In Job 40:15: "Behold now Behemoth, which I made with thee; he eats grass as an ox; Lo now his strength is in his loins and his force is in the navel of his belly. He moves his tail like a cedar; the sinews of his stones are wrapped together." A clue connected with the occult force in Geburah.

Behemoth is the word used in I.R.Q: 1104 for the beast which perishes. 1103: "For it is written Psalm: 49:13 'Man (Adam) shall not abide in honor,' that is, Adam, who is more worthy than all honor, shall not abide.. 1104: Wherefore? because if it were thus, I would be like unto the beast (Behemoth) which perish." Note the correspondence to חיה נפש, the animal soul, and השמים כוכבי, the stars of heaven. The animal soul is the personal form of the forces of the stars of heaven. It is the physical life-breath that is related to the force of the sphere of Mars. See 92 (פחד), 142, 98, 496 (Leviathan), 52, 323, 973; 128, 1250 (Greek).

In Job 40:6: "Then answered the Lord unto Jacob out of the whirlwind, and said (14) 'then will I also confess unto thee that your own right hand can save thee.' This verse states that man may become his own savior, affording a key to the allegory which follows (15) "Behold now Behemoth, which I made with thee." Behemoth is no doubt an intensive plural form and means 'a colossal beast'. Behemoth symbolizes the beast in man, the vital energy or solar force manifesting ungoverned in man's lower or animal nature. 'He eats grass as an ox.' The grass here signifies the flesh or carnal nature ('all flesh is grass' - Isaiah 40:6). The ox is an unsexed animal. Hence 'he eats grass as an ox' is equivalent to saying that Behemoth (the vital energy) can, or was intended to, consume man's carnal nature by manifesting unsexed; for regeneration as opposed to ungoverned sex expression or generation. (16) "Lo now, his strength in his loins.' Loins in Hebrew, as in Greek, are used as a euphemism for the organs of generation. His force is in the navel of his belly.' The shining vital energy which is the manifestation of life... is sleeping like a serpent, having three and a half coils. The first stirring or uncoiling of this force before its passage through and energizing the sympathetic system's ganglia manifests in the navel region's abdomen. In chapter 32:18, 19; 8 of the book of Job, the initiate Euhu ascribes this stirring of the vital energy of solar force when speaking under divine inspiration, 'The spirit of my belly constants me, behold, my belly is as wine which has no vent; it is ready to burst like new bottles. I will speak, that I may be refreshed, but there is a spirit in man: and the inspiration of the Almighty gives them understanding.' (18) 'His bones are pipes of copper; his bones are like tubes of iron.' The bones of a behemoth are the network of nerves, which are the solar force channels. Before initiation, these nerves are in the atrophied or, relatively speaking, hardened state typified as copper and iron. In Sanskrit writing, these channels are similarly termed pipes or tubes (nadis). The Uttara Gita states that these nadis 'are like pipes, are hollow and in the space there exist a certain substance, like oil, in which the divine energy reflects."

In the 4th chapter of Zechariah, the word 'pipes' is used in this sense. "And I said, I have looked, and behold a candlestick (the spine) all of gold, with a bowl upon the top of it,' ('the golden bowl is the brain, or accurately speaking the medulla oblongata which is a reservoir of vital force) and his seven lamps thereon, (the seven principle ganglia), and seven pipes to the seven lamps. And I answered again and said unto him, that be these two olive branches which through the two golden pipes empty, the golden oil' (namely, the nerve fluid in which the radiance of the solar force is reflected or manifested)

זולתי *zeulawthi*. beside me. In Isaiah 45:5: "I am the Lord, and there is none else, there is no God beside me: I girded thee, though thou has not known me." see 87, 234, 600, 834.

תמוז *Tammuz*, a Syrian deity, meaning "true son of the deepwater"; the youthful spouse or lover of Ishtar, the great mother goddess, the embodiment of the reproductive energies of nature. Babylonian origin-Tammuz was supposed to die and revive with the seasons of nature like Adonis [Frazer: Golden Bough]. Also: Tammuz, the 4th month of the Jewish calendar (June-July).

Inman: (Ezekiel 8:14). …the identity of this deity with Adonis, Osiris, and Bacchus. The derivation of the word, viz., תמז, tamaz, signifies 'he is powerful, strong, victorious;,' which applies equally to the sun and his mundane symbol. He was bewailed when he began to droop, i.e., after the longest day in the year, after which he daily sank lower and lower, until the winter solstice. The prayers for the dead, compiled in Egypt, B.C.

2250, were 'addressed to Osiris, symbolized by the sun of the west, Tum, or lower world, but understood as the soul of the universe, the uncreated cause of all.' Bunsen's Egypt, vol. 5, pp. 8,9. Possibly the word in question is akin to the Assyrian *tamu*, 'judgment, knowledge.'

עצי גפר *aytzi gopher*. gopherwood In Genesis 6:14: "Make thee [Noah] an ark of Gopherwood; rooms shalt thou make in the ark, and shalt pitch it within and without with pitch." A foot-note in Magil's Linear Bible identifies this as "timbers of cypress." [גפר = "a resinous wood"] Probably some variety of pine or fir. [Standard Bible Dictionary]. See *abiegnus* (Lt).

αμαρτια.. sin. "A condition opposed to, or swaying from, the Truth: that which is apart from the wise and beneficial. An injuring of the Soul: ignorance: disharmony: failure to an ideal." [Omikron, 1942, p. 248.]

454

תמיד *tawmeed*. indefinite extension of time. With different pointing: continuance, extension, constant, always, stretch. In ancient Hebrew, it refers most often to perpetual time. The root of Intelligence of Shin. See 814, 464.

זהראריאל *"Zaharariel-* a title of Tiphareth." [Godwin, 1999, p. 563]

"Zahariel ("brightness") and says this is a great angle mentioned in the words of Jewish mystic writers, specifically the apocalypse of Abraham. In Levi, transcendental Magic, Zahariel is an angel invoked to resist the temptations of the person of the arch-fiend Moloch." [Davidson, 1971, p. 325.]

גדול שמי בגרים *gawdol lshemi ba-goyim*. my name shall be great [is great] among the gentiles. Malachi 1:11: "For from the rising of the sun even unto the going down of the same my name shall be great among the gentiles, and in every place incense shall be offered, unto my name: for my name shall be great among the heathen, says the Lord of Hosts." The "Lord of Hosts" is attributed to Netzach, the sphere of Venus. See 525. In Hebrew, 'nations' is 'goyim' and refers to the gentiles. The 'nations' esoterically are the millions upon millions of cells not directly connected with controlling the body's functions. [The word גוים may be the plural of גו meaning, 'gathering of people; midst, interior; body, back. With different vowel points, within, inside.] see 59.

קדשים *qadawshm*. The holy ones. These are consecrated catamites kept by the priesthood [Crowley, 1977, p. 47]. (Catamite - boy kept for unnatural purposes- Webster). The misuse of desire connected with the power of Venus can make unholy what is holy. See 410.

חמות *hamuth*. walls. Isaiah 49:16: "Behold, I have graven thee upon the palms of my hands; your wall is continually before me." ["your walls" = זומתיך the singular is חומת, wall, city wall. With different pointing: 1. husband's mother; mother-in-law; 2. warmth.

חותם
חותם *hotawm*. seal, signet-ring. In Job 38:19: "The earth takes shape like clay under a seal; its features stand out like those of a garment." Rosenroth in K.D.L.C.K. (p.338): refers to the word as *sigilium* and refers it to Tiphareth. A complicated discussion follows, with other attributions.

455

פוטיפרע *Potiphera*. "He whom Ra Gave." "And Pharaoh called Joseph's name Zaphnath-Paaneah, and he called him to wife Asenath the Daughter of Postiphrah Priest of On [in Egypt]." Paul Case: "It was to a daughter of a priest of On that Joseph (Multiplier) was married. Her name was Asenath (אסנט, 511). She was the daughter of Potiphera (455 = 14, the usual pi-number reoccurring in alchemical names). Thus the father-in-law of Joseph bore the same name as the husband of the women who sought to entice him into adultery. Potiphar and Potiphera are the same in Egyptian. Potiphar, however, is spelled פוטיפר, which omits the Ayin. There is much alchemical significance on both spellings. פוטיפרע is פו =86, אלהים and

reduces to 14; טי (19) = חוה איוב היד = "was black" and reduces to 10; פרע =350 =עפר, The place from which Solomon got his Gold, and reduces to 8. The sum of these 3 reductions (14+19+8) is 32, the number of the Paths on the Tree of Life... Thus the whole word conceals 4 and 55, the quaternary, the decad, and the decad's extension. The extension of 4 is 10, and the extension of 10 is 55. Finally, 455 reduces to 14. The distinctions between these two spellings and their Cabalistic significance should be carefully noted. The key is that by the addition of Ayin, Joseph's owner, who cast him into prison, becomes the priest of the Sun, who is Joseph's father-in-law." [Paul Case on D.D.B. Philosophers Stone, IX, 8]. See 385, 511, 57

מיתה *mithawh*. dying, death penalty of death. Suggest Key 13 - death and change, leading to transformation. See 50, 106, 700.

נתה Nethah. 25th Shem ha-Mephorash, short form. See 470 & Appendix 10.

תנה give. See Genesis 30:26.

כמשפטו according to its fashion, according to his plan. See Exodus 26:30.

456

הה וו תלד *Heh-Vav-Daleth*. Hod, spelled in plenitude. With different pointing: Fig tree in fruit, Mountain of Myrrh, legs, thighs, street, ways. See 15.

כתול *ketol*. Wall of a House. Refers to Tiphareth. K.D.L.C.K. (p.473) says that it is referred to Tiphareth in the Zohar when it is joined to Malkuth *per justum* [i.e., rightly].

תאנה *tehaynaw*. Opportunity and purpose; occasion and design; copulation, a coming together, lust.

As to the word תאנה... to distinguish the sign Tav, the faculty of expressing the continuity of things and their reciprocity. This distinction made, the word אנה has no longer the least difficulty. It is an expression of grief. It is formed from an onomatopoetic root, which depicts the groans, sobs, pain and the annihilation of a person who suffers. This expressive root belongs to all tongues. One finds it united to the Sign Tav on several occasions, especially to express deep, mutual sorrow. Presumably, the fir-tree has received the metaphorical name of תאנה on account of the mournfulness of its foliage, from which latescent tears appear to flow from its fruits. At first, in Hebrew, as in Arabic, only a kind of exclamation as alas! But, transformed into a verb using the convertible sign Vav, it becomes און or אנוה whose meaning is, to be plunged in grief, to cry out with lamentations. Thence תאנה, sorrow, affliction; and finally תאנוה or תאנוה deep and concentrated grief that one share or communicates. [Hebrew Tongue Restored p. 103]

אימתה *amath*. Fear, dread, terror, awe, reverence. According to Rosenroth in K.D.L.C.K. (p.79), this pertains to Geburah. Recall that פחד Pachad [92] fear, is one of the names of Geburah. See 216.

פרצוף *partzuf*. face, person.

קלו ליסרך *kolo leaserekaw*. his voice to instruct thee. In Deuteronomy 4:36: "From heaven he had you hear his voice to discipline you. On earth, he showed you his great fire, and you heard his words from out of the fire." The fire is Shin (Key 20) and Teth (Key 8 = Leo = the Sun). The voice is Vav.

את האדמה *eth ha-adamah*. the ground. In Genesis 2:5: "(The Lord God made) every plant of the field before it was in the earth, and every herb of the field before it grew: for the Lord God had not caused it to rain upon the earth, and there was not a man to till the ground." "Ground" suggests the physical plane. See 296.

כהתאל *Kahathal*. "God, Adorable." 8th Shem ha-Mephorash. 36-40. Genie: ASICAT. March 27, June 7, August 17, October 29, January 9. In Psalm 95:6: "O come, let us worship and bow down: let us kneel before the Lord, our maker."

To obtain the blessing of God or drive away evil spirits. Rules all agricultural production, and principally those necessary to the existence of men and animals. Inspires man and raises him near to God. A person born: loves work, agriculture, the country and the hunt, and has much activity in affairs. Associated with the 2nd quinance (6° -10°) of Virgo; Angel by night of the 8 of Pentacles (Hod of Assiah). See 965, 425 & Appendix 10.

תאנה the fig-tree and fruit [Sepher Sephiroth]. This word is used in Genesis 3:7 and translated "fig" in the New International and Authorized Version. "Then the eyes of both of them [Adam and Eve] were opened, and they realized they were naked, so they sewed fig leaves together, and made coverings, for themselves."

F.J. Meyers comments: "The word thanah translated 'fig' is just the word anah [אנה] with the reciprocal or mutual sign Tav prefixed. Ahinah denotes suffering. In all the Semitic languages, it is an expression of pain, trouble, signing, sobbing. The prefix Tav gives the word the meaning of 'mutual sorrow,' 'sadness shared by others,' when the word 'anah' becomes a verb 'ahnoh' it means 'to be plunged into sorrow, and with the prefix Tav to 'share or communicate some deep sorrow or trouble.'" [The Unknown God, pp.190-191] see 56, 702, 561.

μητηρ. *mehter*. Mother. Refers to Binah, the mother of form and sphere of Saturn. See 656, 744 Greek.

457 (prime)

זתים olives.

אתון *attun*. furnace.

מזבחת Alters. See Numbers 23:1.

דרך עץ החיים The way to the Tree of Life. See Genesis 3:24.

משכיל + און *masaykil* + *own*. enlightened + ability, strength, power, or trouble, sorrow, wickedness. Success in great work depends on the right use of the power symbolized by the "olives"; otherwise, it can have evil results. See 400, 57.

פשע + אבד *pashaw + awbahd*. sin, transgression + to lose oneself, to wander, disperse. Sin is "missing the mark" or activity (Peh), which burns away (Shin) reality and leaves appearances (Ayin). Spirit (Aleph) is lost when it concentrates (Beth) on erroneous desires (Daleth). See 450, 7.

אתנו with us, us. See Genesis 34:9.

נאות we will consent. See Genesis 34:15.

458

ביאת הגואל *biath hasoal*. The coming of the redeemer (messiah). גואל (40) is a title of Yesod. The redeemer is the Sun (i.e., Tiphareth) or Bridegroom.

כבל תו *kebel-Tav*. cable-tow (variant spelling). The cord which binds; the covenant of love. See 446.

שחקים *shechaqim*. Thin garments, cloudy heavens. clouds. The 3rd Heaven corresponding to Netzach, the sphere of Venus or desires and imagination. According to K.D.L.C.K. (p.710), these are *contusores*, called Netzach and Hod, the breakers of manna, i.e., they prepare the influence from Tiphareth to Yesod. Translated heaven in Deuteronomy 33:26: "Therein none like unto the God of Jeshurun, who rides upon the heaven in your help, and in his excellency on the sky." see 1018.

בעב פעור *baal-payoor*. Inman: (Numbers 23:28), signifies 'to open,' also 'to uncover the pudenda,' 'to give oneself up to fornication;' פרא *para*, means 'to cause to bear fruit;' and פרה, *parah*, is to be fruitful. Peor, like פרה, signifies 'a pit or hole,' or rather 'an opening,' 'properly the opening of the maiden's hymen.' It was also the name of a Moabite deity, in whose honor virgins prostituted themselves. [Ancient Faiths, Volume 2, p.471]

see 356.

רוח יהוה דבר בי *ruach IHVH diber-biy*. The spirit of the Lord. spoke by me. 2 Samuel 23:2: "The spirit of the Lord spoke by me, and his word was in my tongue." see 1436.

נחת *nawchath*. coming down. Translating lighting down in Isaiah 30:30: "And the Lord shall cause his glorious voice, to be heard, and shall show the lighting down of his arm with the indignation of his anger [i.e., his descending blows] and with the flame of a devouring fire, with the rainstorm and tempest and hailstones. Spelled ונחת, and-the-coming-down-of in the *Interlinear NIV Bible*.

459

עות בארץ *be-eretz- utz*. in the land Uz. In Job 1:1: "There was a man in the land of Uz, whose name was Job; and that man was perfect and upright, and one that feared God, and eschewed evil." Job means "the greatly afflicted one." see 19, 976.

רזא דעלמא עלאה *raza de-alma illah-ah*. A mystery of the upper world. In Isaac Myer's Qabbalah (p.117): "By the Hebrews the church of Israel was called the mystic bride, but among the early Christians the church of Christ being considered as the true Israel; the ancient prophets may be said to have acted and spoken regarding the 'cosmic mystery,' which in our 'lower' world, is the counterpart of the celestial mystery of Christ and the Christian church in the 'upper.' As the cosmic sanctuary or temple, was a pattern of the heavenly or upper, so a 'cosmic mystery' is a spiritual idea symbolized in the matter-world. The Zohar says 'a mystery of the upper world' [Exodus 90B]... 'on this [1] depend mysteries of above and below.'"

הקדשים holies, the Holy Places. See Exodus 26:33.

נדתה her banishment, her flow. Referring to the menstrual flow in Leviticus 15:24.

המקדיש the sanctifier. See Leviticus 27:15.

460

מלך שלם *Melek Shalem*. King of Salem [Melchizedek]. In Genesis 14:18: "Then Melchizedek King of Salem brought out bread and wine. He was a priest of God most high, and he blessed Abram, saying, 'blessed by Abram by God most high, creator of heaven and earth." see 90, 370, 294, 1500.

יהוה איש מלחמה *Jehovah Ish Milchamah*. the Lord, is a man of war.

ההוא בית אל *ha-hva beth-el*. That place Bethel. In Genesis 28:19: "And he called the name of that place Bethel, but the name of that city was called Luz [almond] at first." This could be read: He (הוא), the house of strength (אל). See 12, 31, 412, 443.

סרר *sawrer*. to be stubborn, refractory, rebellious, intractable; to be bad, evil; to turn away from, slide back. In Hosea 4:16: "For Israel slides back as a backsliding heifer: now the Lord will feed them as a lamb in a large place."

טנתא *tanatha*. According to K.D.L.C.K. (p.371), this word is an abbreviation of the words טעמים (tomim = reasons, motives, accents)' תגין (caps, crowns, diadems); נקורת (nequdoth = points) and אותיות (letters), which denote the underlying concepts of Atziluth, 4 powers of Tetragrammaton.

צללד מירון *Tzallad Miron*. Qlippoth of Gemini. Suggest unbalanced powers of discrimination between self and sub-consciousness.

בני שחץ *beni shachatz*. sons of pride; i.e., of the lion. Poetical of wild animals. In Job 41:34: "He beholds all high things: he is a king over all the sons of pride." see 211, 338, 310, 340, 43, 1702 for other designations of a lion.

נית The 54th name of Shem ha-Mephorash, short form. See 491 & Appendix 10.

ανατολη. *anatoleh*. The east; direction is assigned to Venus and to creative imagination (Daleth) on the Cube of Space. The source of light. Written ανατολας in Septuagint translation of קדם (144) in Genesis 2:8: "Now the Lord God had planted a garden in the east, in Eden; and there he put the man (Adam-humanity] he had formed." Also in Luke 1:78 as 'day-spring': "On account of the tender compassion of our God, by which he has visited us; a day-dawn (ανατολη) from on high;" i.e., the Messiah, who is elsewhere spoken of as light. Note the connection between the seed (Nun), the color red (Mars), Christos, or light source. See 273, 540, 255, 1430 (Greek), 1502, 2295 and Matthew 2:1, 2:9.

κυβικη. *kubo*. cube.

461 (prime)

נצץ אריך *nawtzatz + ayrikay*. to glitter, bloom or flower + grow big. The increase of spirit blooms in Malkuth, the Resplendent Intelligence and flower of the Tree of Life. See 230, 231.

איתן *aithan*. Given in K.D.L.C.K. (p.86) as *horrios, rigidus, robustus, validus, asper* meaning "rough, stiff or hard, or hardwood, strong or powerful, harsh." He says these names apply to Geburah and cites Deuteronomy 21:4: (Take a heifer) "And lead her down to a valley that has not been plowed or planted and where there is a flowing stream. There in the valley, they are to break the heifer neck."

ותוכל and you have prevailed [overcome]. See Genesis 32:29.

נאותה let us consent. See Genesis 34:23.

וכלות and frail with longing, the ones worn out. See Deuteronomy 28:32.

γυνη. *gyne*. Woman. "women. Or womb-man. Symbolically an unfoldment that receives and enfolds within itself the generative principles of all growing things. Or, in another sense, *andris*-that which has been generated from the members of the [sleeping] *aner*[159], who is an Outbreathing of Divinity. The word *gyne* is connected in meaning with the word *Ge* [Earth] and *Gennain*, To Generate. Regarded as the enfoldment from which, in time, greater phases [of Consciousness] are unfolded, the *Gyne* is the *Zoe*, the Mother of Increase-of-Being. The word often connotes the potential fruit-giving Earth [*Ploutos* or *Panspermia*]: also the Human Race which, in its aionian travail, eventually begets a numerous Spiritual Offspring: also the Human Soul which, under the Creative Plan, gives Birth to the SON [fruit of God]. The state of continual transformation in Nature, for the sake of Fruition, is the Travail, or the 'Order of Women.' In the Pythagorean schools and others, the word *gyne* implied a certain age or stage." [Omikron, 1942, pp. 252-253.] See *nymphe* (998).

462

נתיב *nawthb*. A path, road, a way [Job 18:10; Psalm 78:50]. This noun includes the idea of action or method. The ruling principle is the beginning of a methodical process, the initial point whence proceeds a line, or course of conduct, behavior or performance. See 467.

מצות יהוה *mitzvath IHVH*. The commandments of Jehovah. In Psalm 19:8: "The statutes of the Lord are right, rejoicing the heart; The commandment of the Lord is pure enlightening the eyes." Note the connection between the eyes and the next entry below. [מצוה command, commandment, precept; meritorious deed, religious action.]

באר לחי ראי *beer-lahai-roi*. Well of the living and seeing one, Well of the Living One, my seer. In Genesis 16:14: " So she [Hagar] called the name of the Lord that spoke unto her, thou God sees me; for she said, have I also here looked after him that sees me? (14) wherefore the well was called beer-lahai-roi; behold it is between Kadesh [holy] and Bered [hail]."

I. The Zohar [135B] says: "The 'well' is none other but the Shekinah; 'the living one' is an allusion to the righteous one who lives in the two worlds, that is, who lives above, in the higher world, and who also lives in the lower world, which exists and is illuminated through him, just as the moon is only illuminated when she looks at

the sun. Thus the well of existence literally emanates from the 'living one' whom it sees, and when it looks at him, it is filled with living waters."

II. "The identity of numeration between this 'well' which the Zohar explains as representing the sum total of existence, emanating from the righteous one, or the supreme unity, and 'the commandments of Jehovah' points to an underlying identity of meaning. This is fairly obvious, for it is one of the Qabalah fundamentals that the universe is commanded into manifestation through God's word. Thus it follows that whatever is manifested is the visual presentation of the divine intention. Observe that the well of existence is also the well of vision and that the Psalmist asserts that the commandments of Jehovah enlighten the eyes. So, too, the *Fama* conceals its central mystery in this vault's symbolism, a symbolism addressed to the eyes. And elsewhere, defining the qualifications of a true Rosicrucian, the Confessio declares: 'Truly, to whom it is permitted to behold, read, and thenceforth teach himself those great characters which the Lord God hath inscribed upon the world's mechanism, and which he repeats through the mutation of empires, such a one is already ours, though yet unknown to himself.' Remember, too, that this number 462 is that which represents the total area of the vault, which the *Fama* describes as a compendium of the universe." [Case, 1985, pp. 119-120.]

עד כי יבא שילה *ad ki yaba Shiloh*. until Shiloh come; as long as men come to Shiloh. Genesis 49:10: "The scepter shall not depart from Judah, nor a law-giver from between his feet until Shiloh come..." see 358.

קמוע רום *phofundum celsitudinis*; depth-height, exaction. See 216, 236.

463 (prime)

ג-ס-ת *Gimel-Samekh-Tav*. A reference to the Paths or "length" on the Middle pillar.

The wand the Fool carries over his shoulder is 463 lines long. This is a reference to the middle pillar because the letters of that pillar are Gimel (3), Samekh (60) and Tav (400). The Fool picture gives a clue to the magical significance of the middle pillar and its practical application. 463 reduces to 13 and finally to 4, the number of Daleth. The secret of all works is a secret of the Empress. The Tarot shows her secret plainly when it is placed on the Tree of Life. The secret of the Empress is then seen to be the mystery of Da'ath. In Da'ath, all the secret places are filled. The practical work is one of creative imagination that directs the serpent's power.

Additionally, the letter Nun (the Imaginative Intelligence) represents this power, as does the letter Teth. All magic is fundamentally in the Will but only becomes operative and effective only through imagination. However, no imagination is either pure (and therefore potent) without understanding what the Qabalists call love.

The word Love is used sparingly because it has so many contradictory connotations. And this "true love" is represented on the Tree of Life by Binah, the Divine Mother. Note that the 14th Path of Daleth (The Empress) joins Binah to Chokmah. Look closely, for this is the secret of the Stone of the Wise. The Emerald Tablet gives another hint when it says: "All things have their birth from One." Even chairs and tables are born not made, but few see this, which is why there are only a few true magicians. But when countenance beholds countenance, when Kallah and Ben are united, when the returning current of the White Brilliance flashes upward through the middle pillar into and beyond the veil of the No-Thing which is the primal בטן, then is the Great Work completed, for then is conceived the Heavenly *Adam* (45) of whom our Brother and Father C.R. is a symbol. See *C.20*, 124, 4, 474, 61, 220.

נשמה חיים *Neshamah chaiim*. The breath of life. In Genesis 2:7: "And the Lord God formed man of the dust of the ground and breathed into his nostrils the breath of life, and man became a living soul." Note that in this passage it is written נשמת. נשמה is the feminine singular for breath; vital spirt, life; spirit, soul, living creature. See 395.

תחנה *taykhinah*. mercy, favor, grace; supplication, prayer. [תחן prayer, supplicated] mercy suggests Chesed, the link between the supernal triad (through Binah to Ruach, of the 6 Sephiroth from Chesed to Yesod. This linkage is by "grace" through prayer, i.e., meditation, and employs the divine volition through the "breath of life."

תגין *tagin*. caps, crown, diadems. Receptors of the supernal influence from Kether, symbols of attainment and dominion. See 460.

זכוכית *zekokith*. crystal, glass. The "Adytum," or holy of holies in an adept brain, is a crystal receptor of the higher worlds.

מטה השקד *matten ha-shaqad*. a rod of almond. The "rod" is connected with divine will, flowing through the spine in the microcosm; "almond" is connected with Kether [מטה stick, rod, staff; branch; tribe support. With different pointing: bed, couch, litter; bier]. See 54, 404.

באתין *Bathin*. Goetia demon #18 by day of the 3rd decan of Virgo, ruled by Venus. This corresponds to the 10 of Pentacles. See 1113.

Goetia: "He is a mighty and strong duke, and appears like a strong man with the tail of a serpent, sitting upon a pale-colored [horse]. He knows the virtues of herbs and precious stones and can transport men suddenly from one country to another. He rules over 30 Legions of Spirits." [Mathers, 1995, p. 36]

חרא צדיקים *erech tzadiquim*. The path of the just. A term used to describe the middle pillar of the Tree of Life. This is the way of attainment to the higher consciousness, and it is achieved by being in harmony with the divine will or Justice. See 85, 95, 89, 73, 120, 406.

The Middle Pillar is Kether, Tiphareth, Yesod and Malkuth. Above Yesod is the path of Samekh, descending from Tiphareth who is King (Melek, מלך) and the seat of Ruach (רוח). Above the King, Ben (בן), the son, extends upwards the 13th Path of Gimel, The Uniting Intelligence, which descends from the Kether, The Crown. From Kether to Malkuth descends one unbroken path, though it has 3 parts, Gimel, Samekh and Tav. This is the Erech Tzadiqim, the path of the just, is the Middle Pillar. Thus the power of the Indivisible One in Kether descends through the Uniting Intelligence into Tiphareth. Below Tiphareth descends the Path of Samekh (סמך), which carries the power of Tiphareth to Yesod. The path of the just is the path of union (Gimel) and support (Samekh), and it ends in that center, which is the abode of the Most High. This is *Guph* does the power of the Crown stand centered.

Note that Gimel and Samekh's paths are both blue and that Tav is blue-violet. It is as if the blue of Samekh, after passing through Yesod, had become tinged with the violet of that Sephirah. See *C.9*.

All the horizontal paths are feminine, even though the path of Peh is related to Mars, and the ruling power in the path of Teth is the Sun. In the Tarot, Samekh is sometimes represented as Diana, so there is a lunar influence in this path. סמך (Samekh) is 120, and this reduces to 3, that is, Gimel. But the paths of Samekh and Gimel are vertical or masculine so that in the three crossings, male and female powers are conjoined at the point of crossing. This is the clue to the secret.

Note that horizontal and vertical paths cross three times on the Tree of Life. Venus (Daleth) and the Moon (Gimel) cross just below Kether and mark the location of Da'ath. Gimel (the Moon) and Teth (Leo, ruled by the Sun) cross just above Tiphareth. Samekh (Sagittarius, ruled by Jupiter) crosses Peh (Mars) midway between Tiphareth and Yesod. Note these carefully, and mark well also the close relation between Saturn and Venus. Here are the keys to practical knowledge of utmost importance. All this is on the Middle Pillar, and if you do but consider the Sephiroth thereon and their meanings, you should have little difficulty. See *C.11*.

On the Tree, the quickest way from Malkuth to Kether is up the middle pillar. At the first step upward, attention is focused, not too obtrusively

perhaps, on Da'ath. Da'ath is the union of *Ab* (אב) and Aima (אמיא), pictured in the Tarot by the Empress. The straight and narrow path is up the middle pillar. It is made of Saturn's 32nd Path, and in Malkuth Guph, then in Yesod Mars. Note that Yesod (יסוד) is 80 ad is equivalent to Peh (פ, Mars). Thus Yesod and the reciprocal 27th Path of Peh (the Active or Exciting Intelligence) are two aspects of the same thing. The reciprocal Path of Peh crosses the 25th Path of Samekh. Samekh means Tent-peg or prop, which has the same basic meaning as Yesod the Foundation.

Additionally is a hieroglyph of a serpent with its tail in its mouth (symbol of eternity) and is the same as the Magicians girdle in Key 1. A serpent's power feeding on itself symbolizes an increase in potency by being magically directed. In magic, this involves the change from temporal to eternal expression. This is so subtle but note well.

Samekh is attributed to Sagittarius, ruled by Jupiter and refers to the Interior Star located near the solar-plexus. Note that Key 14, Samekh is just below the Sphere of the sun, with the Path of Teth (Leo, ruled by the Sun) above it. Note also that the Path of Peh is above Yesod. Between the heart symbolized by Tiphareth and Teth and the head in Kether runs the Path of Gimel. All these centers are part of the subconscious functioning of the High Priestess or the Moon. As one rises through the middle pillar after the heart center, the next crossing point is Daleth (Venus center near the throat) and Gimel (Moon center near pituitary body). Above this, the path of Gimel continues, and note that in Key 2, only the uppermost part of the picture shows plain Moon symbolism. This is her crown, and it corresponds to the portion of the Path of Gimel above the point where the Path of Daleth crosses it.

Now we have located on the 6 of the Interior Stars on the Tree of Life. Mercury is the 7th and highest, and this is Kether. Descending from Kether are the Paths of the Magician and the Fool. The first is Mercury (the Magician) and is the Fool in reality because the Fool is the higher aspect of what the Magician typifies. In astrology, Uranus is considered a higher octave of Mercury. Then, on the middle pillar is the Path from the Bride

(Malkuth) to the Crown. If you have ears to hear is hidden knowledge. For even the Crown is but the center of manifestation.

το θελημα. *to thelema*. The will. Matthew 7:21: "Not everyone who says to me, 'Master, Master,' will enter into the kingdom of heavens; but he who performs the will of the father of mine in the heavens."

εντολη. *entoleh*. The precept. John 15:12: "This is my commandment that you love each other as I loved you."

αποταγη. *apotageh*. Renunciation. A favorite mystery word with the gnostics, who appear to have well understood the necessity of the connection between γνωσις (gnosis) and αποταγη κοσμου (the renunciation of the world). See 1263 & Apostolic Gnosis, p.118.

464

בדגת הים *bi-degath ha-yawm*. over fish of the sea. Genesis 1:28: "(and have dominion) over the fish of the sea. The "fish" is the power of Nun. It is the reproductive power that transforms man into the new image via intense, sustained desire. The end result of man's dominion over this power is his perpetual intelligence of unity with his creator. See 1024.

תמידי *temidi*. steady, continuous, perpetual. Name of the 31st Path associated with Tarot Key 20, Judgement and the Hebrew letter Shin (ש). As a state of consciousness, *temidi* refers to a level of development where there is a moment by moment, remembering without cessation of the eternal truths that are only facts. Temidi is derived from דימת, *tawmid*, meaning: "continuance; daily offering in the temple." In ancient Hebrew refers to perceptual time. See 300, 369, 454, 814.

"The 31st path is called the Perpetual Intelligence because it rules the movements of the sun and moon according to their constitution, and perfects all the powers of all the revolutions of the zodiac, and the arrangement (or, form) of their judgments." The word "forms" is the plural of תורה (301), written תורות (702). This is a reference to archetypal forms. "Their Judgements" or "their laws" is *Mishpatiham* (משפטיהם, 484). The Judgement pictured in this Key is the last stage of a Law's operation, which completes the soul's return to its Divine Source.

Shin is the 3rd of the three Mother letters attributed to Fire. The 31st Path of Shin (Perpetual Intelligence) is a fiery path and the Ruach Elohim's path. In this connection, note that Shin (ש) and Ruach Elohim (the Life-Breath of the Gods, רוח אלהים) are both 300. Thus Fire and Spirit are one.

Temidi means perpetual and is the perfection of the handiwork of the Eternal. The first two letters, Tav and Mem (תמ) spell *thum* (or *toom*), which is perfection; the second two spell Yod יד, meaning hand; and the last is the letter (י) which represents Kether and Chokmah. The Fire of Spirit is the root of Fire (ש) attributed to Chokmah, and this is that Consuming Fire is God Himself. The Fire of Mind divides itself into the appearance of duality, and its descent into manifestation brings forth bodies. Being Eternal, it is also Superior, and thus it is written that it regulates the motions of Shamash (Sun, Tiphareth) and Lebanah (Moon, Yesod). Therefore may you know that the 31st Path has to do with regulating the powers of Ruach and Nephesh.

The 31st Path joins Hod (Splendor, Mercury) to the Kingdom (Malkuth). And it is said that the Great Work is with the Sun and Moon, performed by the aid of Mercury. The work of the 31st Path is that of the woman (the Moon) and the man (the Sun), and from this work comes forth the child, which is the new creature. This is a work of embodiment, and not without its proper body, the Perpetual Intelligence may manifest. Although it is flesh and blood, it is different from the one that came forth at your birth. It is a body incorruptible, though the seed of it is sown in corruption. It is a Perpetual body transmuted from the ordinary body that comes through the gate of birth.

Without the aid of Mercury, this transmutation

may not be affected, for this body takes one out of the flux and reflux of birth and death, and truly is it a work of art wherein the powers of Sun and Moon, or Ruach and Nephesh, are conjoined in full perfection. This is accomplished by the working of a power descending through the Paths on the side of Binah on the Tree of Life. All Paths on the side of Binah have their beginning in the Path of Beth, which is Mercury or Kokab. Every individual will face a crisis where they are released from the delusion of separate personality and from the shackles of times, seasons and places. This does not come in the lesser wheelings of nature, the cycle of normal evolution. It always has its beginning in an influx from above.

At the beginning of the return path, it appears that our own will and purpose are seeking release, but this is not so. The fire consumes what it will. The Breath of Spirit blows where it wants. And there is no law of man to perceive how this operation is governed. Its work is without beginning or end. Never does it fail in anything small or great. Yet is there in it no trace of what man means by plan, law, or design. Freely it works, and thus it is written of the Sephiroth that they are "belimah," which means "something not to be expressed, and something altogether free from bonds or encirclement of any kind." Waste, not their strength in trying to comprehend this. Know if you may, but grasp it you can not. See C.43, 814.

The man and the woman are shown in the tarot key "Judgment" are the alchemical King and Queen. The woman is more identified with Yesod than Malkuth. In a sense, any lunar symbol is related to Yesod, and any solar symbol to Tiphareth. What is pictured in this Key (belonging to the Path of Shin) indicates a special aspect of the relation between Tiphareth and Yesod, or Ruach and Nephesh, and is the outcome of that relationship between the sun and moon, which is symbolized by the child. This general principle has many practical applications in self-unfoldment.

The 31st Path has to do with the alchemical Sun and Moon as they work in the hidden laboratory and the secret vessels. This application has many ramifications. It applies to the work of those who conduct the experiment alone, but it also applies to those who undertake the joint operation. Although few can do the latter because it requires rigorous training and unusual circumstances. Do not expect us to give you formulas for any of these operations. The text contains the principle behind all practice variations, and if you combine it with the study of the Key, you will learn what you require. Though it may be that for each of you, the instruction you receive from within, in response to the stimulus afforded by the Text and the symbolism of the Key, will differ for each of you. It will almost certainly turn out to be incommunicable so that you cannot share your knowledge with one another at the level of verbal expression.

This is one of the most obscure Paths. Consider what has been said about *Thum* תם, and יד, and the letter Yod. The letter Yod is connected with the Hermit. And תם is 440, which reduces to 8, the value of Cheth. Cheth is Key 7 (The Chariot), this may be taken as representing this part of יד. תמיד is 14 and is a veil for *Zahab* (זהב) and alchemical gold. Fourteen reduces 5, and this is its essence. These two letters can be represented by Heh (the Emperor). Therefore we have Key 7 for תם, Key 4 for יד, and Key 9 for the final Yod. Add these Keys (7 + 4 + 9 = 20) and the result is the first matter. This is shown by Key 20, Shin and the 31st Path. He also said the same thing of the Devil; see if you can discover the connection. See *C.44*, 440, 8, 14.

360 (Shin, שין) + 160 (Ayin, עין) = 420, which reduces to 6 (Tiphareth & ו, the Hierophant) 6 (The Lovers) + 15 (The Devil) + 20 (Judgment) = 41 which reduces to 5 (Heh, the Emperor).

The extension of 5 (1+2+3+4+5) is 15 (the Devil). Key 5 is the Hierophant assigned the letter Vav, and Intuition is fully expressed in Key 15 (the Devil). The Devil and Hierophant (Key 5) added are: 15 + 5 = 20

The extension of 15 is 120, the number of "thick darkness" or "and darkness" (ועלטה). 120 reduces to 3, which is the Divine Mother.

The extension of 20 is 210, the number of depths (Psalm 130:1, מעמקים) and הרה pregnant. Note also that 210 reduces to 3.

η μητηρ. *heh-mehter*. The mother. Note that the woman in Key 20 is the active one of the 2 adult figures. In John 2:1: "And on the third day there was a marriage feast in Cana of Galilee, and the mother of Jesus was there."

Ναξαρετ. *Naksaret*. Nazareth. Nazareth. This place-name is from the Hebrew נצר, *Netzer*, which means "a sprout, a shoot, a branch." It is used in Isaiah 11:1: "And there shall come forth a rod out of Jesse, and a branch shall grow out of his roots." see 301, 360, 300, 173, 741.

465

I. Σ30 = 465. The mystic number of the 30th path of Resh.

מלך שלמה *Melekh Shelomoh*. King Solomon. One of the three original master masons, connected with Tiphareth and the Sun. the result of divine union is King Solomon's temple building. 1 Kings 4:1: "So King Solomon was king over all Israel." Israel means "He shall rule as God." see 541, 90, 375, 1378, 273; 620, 2769 (Greek).

כשניעיה *Kashenyayah*. Angel of 10th astrological house [Capricorn]." [Godwin, 1999, p. 564] Spelled with a ו instead of a נ in *777* Table IV, Column CXLII.

הכלית the kidneys. See Exodus 29:13.

השמעים them that heard, the ones hearing. See Leviticus 24:14.

466

גלגלת *Gulgoleth*. the skull, head. The place where Jesus underwent crucifixion. See 478, 301 Greek, 186.

יהוה בחכמה יסד ארץ *IHVH be-chokmah yawsad-*

eretz. Tetragrammaton, by (or in) wisdom, hath founded the earth [Proverbs 3:19]. The material world (Malkuth) has its actual substance (Yesod-foundation) from the radiant energy of Chokmah. This energy of *Ab*, the father, is what performs the alchemical operations described under this number. See 536, 1276.

יוד וו תלד The letter name *Yod* spelled in plenitude. Yod is the paternal hand of creation, pictured in this word. It suggests that the functions of the inner hearing and creative imagination must be employed to conclude the work begun by the "father," whose lantern sheds light on the return path.

כליות *kilyoth*. kidneys, reins, loins; testicles. kelyoth is the plural of the noun keli, כלי, meaning any utensil, but especially arms, or weapons of war, so that the idea is basically related to זין, Zain, the sword. Thus one girds up his loins to prepare for battle. When very little was known of anatomy, both urine and semen were secreted by the kidneys, and in later Hebrew, *kilyoth* sometimes means the testicles. Thus the word refers physically to the primary sources of bodily power and vigor.

Furthermore, the Hebrews shared the belief of all the ancient world: The lions and reins were the lower mind's seat, called *phrehn* in Greek. The Greek noun, the Latin *renes*, signifying kidneys, was derived and *renes*, passed into English as reins. In this sense, *kilyoth* means "inward parts, mind, the seat of desires, affections and passions." Here we see the relation between fixed, cardinal air (Libra), governing the kidneys-equilibrium, and mutable air (Gemini) - discrimination. K.D.L.C.K. (p.478) says *renes* relate to Netzach and Hod. See 658 Greek.

עולם היצירה *Olahm ha-Yetzirah*. World of Formation. In Qabalah, the plane of the Life-power's activity next above, and within, the physical plane. The physical plane is the world of making or a world of manifested forms. The World of Formation or astral plane (Vav in IHVH) must be controlled and directed by the reins and discrimination to effect a change in the "skull." The angelic kingdom, attributed to this plane, is of great use here. See 536, 315, 1026.

מתוך from out of. See Deuteronomy 5:22.

שמעון *Simeone.* hearing; a tribe of Israel corresponding to Zain and Gemini. In Genesis 49:5 (a reference to Simeon and Levi), "Ruthless weapons are their daggers." This obviously refers to the meaning of the letter name Zain. See 513, 497, 67, 273, 739.

Simeon also means: to hear; to listen, give heed, to obey; to understand, to infer, deduce. From שמע *shema*, the confession of the unity of God; calling together; hearing capacity. This is the inner hearing which Vav the Hierophant represents. Jesus called Simon (Peter) "Hearing, son of the dove" (bar-Jonah). The "dove" is Venus. Hearing (Vav) precedes discrimination (Zain). See 420.

נוית *Nuit*, Hebrew transliteration of the name of the Egyptian sky Goddess.

סתו *sethav.* autumn; "winter" in Canticles 2:11: "For the winter is past, the rain is over and gone."

467 (prime)

נתיבה *nethibah, netivah.* a path, road, way (feminine form). See 462.

וימתהו and he slew him, so he killed him. See Genesis 38:7.

ויתמהו and they marveled. See Genesis 43:33.

וימררהו and they dealt bitterly with him, and they attacked him. See Genesis 49:23.

468

חתמך your signet, your seal. See Genesis 38:18.

חללת you defiled. See Genesis 49:4.

חכמת wise, skilled. See Exodus 35:25.

η κυβικη. *ho kubos.* the cube.

469

בר אורין *bar-auriyawm.* scholar; erudite. It is noteworthy that the *Fama Fraternatas*, which described C.R.'s vault as a compendium of universal wisdom, was addressed to the "erudite of Europe." [בר pure, clear, clean; learned. אורין scholarship.]

שיא חמסים *aish haymasim.* the violent man. The same "consuming fire" when misdirected, becomes anger, rather than learned meditation. See 315.

חשוקיהם "warmly desired thing" [קושח = thing desired; beloved. חם = warmth, heat]. Either wisdom or passion; the higher vs., the lower nature. K.D.L.C.K. (p.366) gives *ligaturae, illarum, trabeationes* [hooks and bands]. He cites Exodus 27:10,11: (the courtyard for the tabernacle) "With twenty bronze bases and with silver hooks and bands on the posts. (11) the north side shall also be a hundred cubits long and is to have curtains, with twenty posts and twenty bronze bases. And with silver hooks and bands on the posts." He says this name applies to Netzach and Hod because they are joined together and united by Jachin and Boaz's pillars.

ותבונה and understanding and ability. See Exodus 36:1.

μαθησις. *mathesis.* The mental discipline of Greeks.

ποιημασιν. *poimaemasin.* Things which have been made [Romans 1:20]. See 510

470

עת *eth.* time, season; appointed time, due season; destiny, fate; occurrence, occasion. The Book of

Tokens (Cheth) says: "And because nothing can prevail against me, Even the worst of sinners shall come in their appointed time, to liberation. See Ecclesiastes 9:11.

שכל דמיוני *Saykel Damyoni.* Imaginative Intelligence, Intelligence of Resemblance. Title of Nun, the 24th Path and Key 13, Death, the sign Scorpio which rules sex and death. Nun means "to sprout, to grow." As the "fish," it implies continuous growth through the reproductive powers of imagination.

I. The possessor of this path may "speak learnedly on all subjects" to realize all created beings' similarity. This path modifies the blood, and its secret has to do with the blood's valuable occult properties. The fear of death (the will-to-live) is eradicated through concentration and meditation. Practical occult word tends to put out the fires of false desire. The will-to-live ceases when one finds within the fountain of limitless life and lives it to the full. Then death is understood as being truly beneficent. Certain brain cells are developed to give a memory record of out of the body experiences. There is an increasing command of the physical plane's subtle forces to enable the adept at establishing a perfect state of balance between those activities that tear down the body and those which build it up. Dissolution of form is a fundamental tendency of the cosmic process. All things change. Existence is a stream, a series of waves, an eternal movement. See 120, 106, 44, 68, 50.

II. The 24th Path of the Imaginative Intelligence is the link between the Ego (Tiphareth) and the desire nature (Netzach). It shows the means to control the great magical agent. All magic is accomplished by the mind's power of generating mental images. Mastery of our nerve currents is achieved by mental imagery by formulating the pattern of the deathless solar body, which is symbolized by the rising sun in the background of Key 13 (Death). The Bible states that Death is swallowed up in Victory. Note that the 24th Path of Nun leads from Netzach (Victory) to Tiphareth (Beauty), the deathless solar body's location.

III. The Path of Nun is the first manifestation of the dynamic or projective aspect of Tiphareth as contrasted with the receptive aspects (the Paths of Gimel, Yod and Lamed). Imaginative Intelligence is the primary activity of beauty works through imagination and brings about new expression forms. This involves the passing away of old forms replaced by those that imagination calls into existence. The passing away of old forms is shown in Key 13 (Death) by the harvest gather by the reaper. The result is the perfection of Netzach. The transformative power of Beauty (Tiphareth) brings the final victory (Netzach).

IV. "I am the Intelligence of Imagination, creating an expanded, liberated life by my power of true vision." [Meditations on the Paths of Wisdom]

המלך שלמה *ha-Melek Shelomoh.* "King Solomon," "(The) King of Peace." Engraved on Zinc (Jupiter) ring of a magical wand. Solomon is the "king" or adept connected with the Sun or heart center. The Ego in Tiphareth establishes completeness, wholeness, perfection, and harmony (shalom = peace) through the direction of Nun's power. See 1010, 375, 404.

דור דורוד *devir devirim.* A cycle of cycles, eternity. "A magician should work as if he had eternity in which to complete his operation." [Eliphas Levi] Consciousness of eternity is accomplished by overcoming death. It is also aided by a knowledge of the cycles of Kaph, the path of Jupiter, connecting the sphere of Jupiter with the sphere of Venus on the Tree (Chesed and Netzach). See 1010, 1480.

נעשה אדם *nahesey adam.* In Genesis 1:26: Let us make man" (in our image, after our likeness; and let them have dominion over the fish of the sea.

כליתי *keliothai.* "(for thou has made) my reins..." [Psalm 139:13]. The faculty of balance or equilibrium (Libra, kidneys). See 466.

נכת *nakath.* precious things [2 Kings 20:13]. The reins and the reproductive organs, both governed by Mars (the adrenals over the kidneys), are indeed "precious things," for with them does the great work succeed. [נכחה is the spelling, also in Isaiah 39:2].

אמך כגפן בדמך על מים Your mother was like a vine in your blood. See Ezekiel 19:10.

עשק *esek*. strife. Name of the well, from a spring of springing [living] water dug by Isaac's servants in Genesis 26:20. The "water" of life or consciousness brings peace or strife depending on its balanced use. Man is "made" through subconsciousness. See Key 2, the High Priestess.

מקדש יהוה *mikedash IHVH*. The sanctuary of Tetragrammaton. The human body, especially the Mercury center (adytum) in the brain, and the Egoic or heart center. See 444.

עמר נקי *omer naquio*. pure wool. A reference to the beard of Macroprosopus (Kether) and the lamb's wool (Aries, Mars) must be purified before it can become the redeemer.

נתהיה *Nithahiah*. The 25th Shem ha-Mephorash. "God who gives wisdom." For the acquisition of wisdom and the discovery of the truth of hidden mysteries. Governs occult sciences. Gives revelations in dreams, particularly to those born of the day over which he presides. Influences those who practice the magic of the sages. Negative influence: black magic.

I. The angle of the 1st decan and 1st quinance of Sagittarius; Angel by day of the 8 of wands, which corresponds to Hod of Atziluth, and the 1st decan of Sagittarius. See Appendix 10.

II. A variant form of this name is Nilaihah. Davidson says: "Ambelain in *La Kabalah Pratique* list Niliahah as a poet-angel of the order of Dominations. He is invoked by pronouncing any of the divine names along with the 1st verse of Psalm 9. He is in charge of occult sciences, delivers prophecies in rhyme, and exercises influence over wise men who love peace and solitude." [Davidson, 1971, p. 207.]

המוריה הר *ha-Moriah har*. Mount Moriah. Moriah means: seen of Jah. Thus Mount Moriah signifies The hill of the divine vision. Jah (IH) is the divine name of Chokmah, the root of fire. The Tejas Tattva is the subtle principle of sight attributed to fire. The "temple" is erected on a foundation of fire. The temple, which was nearing completion when Hiram Abiff was murdered, was built on Mount Moriah. See 15, 72, 273, 255.

The name Moriah appears in Genesis 22:2: "And he [God] said 'take your only son Isaac, whom you love, and go to the land of Moriah; and offer him there for a burnt offering upon one of the mountains which I will tell you of.'"

אלף שין *Aleph-Shin*. The spelling of *Esh*, fire, in abundance. See 301.

אויר מרוח *Eveer merauch*. Wind from Life-Breath. The elementary Air, of Spirit. Part of Rauch, the cosmic Life-breath. "On the harp of ten thousand strings, the wind of the spirit moves ever" [Book of Tokens, Malkuth]. The life-breath is the doer and the actor in human bodies and brings about the subtle senses' development. See 214, 217.

היכלות *hekawloth*. palaces, temple. The human body is the temple or palace of the highest, who looks out the window (Heh) of our eyes when we have the vision to see.

The Zohar [I:65A, p.213] says: "The upward striving thought is... illuminated by a light undisclosed and unknowable even to that thought. That unknowable light of thought impinges on the light of the detached fragment which radiates from the unknowable and undisclosed, so that they are fused into one light, from which are formed nine palaces (hekaloth). These palaces are neither lights nor spirits nor souls. Neither is there anyone who can grasp them. The longing of the nine illuminations, which are all centered in the thought - the latter being indeed counted as one of them - is to purse these palaces at the time when they are stationed in the thought. However, they are not (even then) grasped or known, nor are they attained by the mind's highest effort or the thought. All the mysteries of faith are contained in those palaces, and all those lights which proceed from the mystic supreme thought are called en-soph (limitless)."

אדרירון "The mighty one sings"; a title of Tiphareth. See 1131.

נכאת *niekoth.* spices, aromatic powder. See Genesis 37:25.

האבן הזאת *ha-ehben hazzoth.* "pillar stone" or "foundation stone." In Genesis 28:22: "And this stone, which I have set up for a pillar, shall be God's house: and of all that you shall give me I will surely give a tenth unto you." The Zohar [I:72A, p.243] adds: "That stone... was the foundation stone out of which the world evolved and on which "the temple was built..." Jacob instituted the evening prayer, and it was about this prayer, which he instituted for the first time as a proper method of propitiation, that he said in his own praise, 'and this stone which I had put for a pillar,' as up to that time no one had erected one like it. This is implied in the expression, 'and he put it as a *matsebah* (erection, upstanding) [מצבה = קבלח], implying that he set up again something which had been prostrate. He also 'poured oil on its head,' thus doing more than anyone else to restore it." see 137, 768.

ο καθαρος. *ho katharos.* The clean pure, spotless, unsoiled (of garments); clear, open, free; in the moral sense with clean hands, pure, free from offense; pure bright, clear, hence genuine, true; perfect, complete, effective. Paul Case: i.e., "pure intellect."

472

ויעש אלהים *va-ya-as Elohim.* and God made.

שכל דמיוני + ב *saykel diamyoniy + Beth.* Intelligence of Resemblance (Nun) + Beth house. Concentration (Beth) on the proper use of reproductive power (Nun) makes the Son (בן).

One is seen as the transparent agent (Beth) for change (Nun) by the Life-power. See 470, 2.

צפוני + הר אל *zayphooni + Ale-har.* "My secret place" + "the mountain of God." The "secret place" is the "mountain of God,"; i.e., in Zion, and thus it is connected with the "secret." See 236.

בעת in time. See Genesis 21:22.

כתבים written. See Exodus 31:18.

בכיתם you have wept. See Numbers 11:18.

ושמענו and we will hear. Spelled without the ו in Deuteronomy 5:24.

473

גולגלתא Skull. See 466.

אבתיכם your fathers. See Genesis 48:21.

תגע touch, she touches. See Leviticus 5:2.

επισκοπη. *epskipeh.* "visitations," i.e., the act of being visited or inspected; in the New Testament spoken of God, who is said to visit men for good. See Luke 19:44: (43) and 1 Peter 2:20. This word also means the duty of visiting, inspecting, i.e., charge, office or overseership, "the charge" in Acts 1:20 and 666.

474

דעת *Da'ath.* "Knowledge"; mind, reason. The invisible Sephirah of the Tree of Life. Associated with generation and conception, as the idea of night. (Biblical: "And Adam knew his wife, and she conceived.") Title of the invisible point connecting Chokmah and Binah, seated in the "abyss" at the junction of Gimel and Daleth's paths. Signifies insight. One of the four occult maxims (to know, to will, dare, and be silent). Daleth, the door, true magical knowledge opens a door from the outer world of effects and appearances, leading inward to the realm of causes. It is based on creative imagination and is an interior illumination. Ayin, the eye, one sees, with the inner eye and perceives reality's true perception in all things with the outer sense of sight. Tav, the mark, one experiences the unity of life. See 346, 131, 70, 581, 345, 503, 84 and K.D.L.C.K. (p.252).

I. Daath pertains to knowledge gained by direct personal experience. Located between the 3 Supernals (Kether, Chokmah, and Binah) and the crossing of the Paths of Gimel and Daleth. It represents the division between two levels of being and can be thought of as the Sephirah of Becoming; It is the aspect of consciousness experienced as "relation."

In the construction of the Tree of Life, Da'ath is the point at which the circles corresponding to Atziluth (Archetypal Plane) and Yetzirah (Formative Plane) meet. Knowledge is the link between the archetypal (initiating) and the formative (synthesis) planes. Da'ath is 474, which reduces to 15 and then to 6. Six is Vav, the Tetragrammaton letter (IHVH) letter assigned to Yetzirah, which proceeds from Da'ath. Moreover, the number 474 yields 112 (4 x 7 x 4), and 112 reduces to 4. The extension of 4 (1+2+3+4) is 10. Ten is Yod, the letter assigned to Atziluth. The enumeration of Da'ath conceals the idea that it is related to Atziluth and Yetzirah.

Da'ath is the exact center of the Path of Gimel (Key 2, the High Priestess). The Qabalist knowledge is midway between the pillars of light and darkness, which sits the High Priestess. Nothing could be planer. (See meditation of Daleth and notes, Book of Tokens.)

No magical rite is effective unless it is the formal expression of the operator's vision. The purpose of all ceremonial is to establish an unbroken flow of knowledge. Do not confuse knowledge with information. Da'ath is knowledge. By attributions to these 3 letters Venus (Daleth), Mars (Peh) and Saturn (Ayin), we can understand the work. Remember that planets are interior stars and alchemical metals. From an astrological perspective, Ayin is Capricorn ruled by Saturn, Mars is exalted (sublimated) in Capricorn, and Venus is the esoteric ruler of Capricorn.

Capricorn is the sign associated with the Redeemer's birth, and in the Tarot is the Devil, which is a symbol for the First Matter. Hence, when we read that Da'ath the secret places shall be lead, we must be slow if we suppose this knowledge is learned from written or spoken words.

Mars is action, and Saturn is manifestation. Specific actions are indicated, and if you ask for further light from within, you may discover why Capricorn is related to the 26th Path of Renewing Intelligence. Be on guard here. Do not look for symbolic meanings. Look for specific forms of action, and while you do so, remember that the text is concerned with Guph. See C.24.

I. William Gray considers the residence of Daath, the Abyss, to be fought with danger, for to fall into it is to never retrieve one's sanity. The Abyss itself acts as a filter between the Divine triad and the rest of the Sephiroth and: ...all the horrors, loathsomeness, abominations and evils that would be unthinkable in association with God...are swallowed up by the Abyss, where they exist in a state of utterly insane chaos pending some ultimate disposal.

II. "When the fall had occurred, and the Sephira Malkuth had been cut off from the Tree by the folds of the dragon, there was added unto the Tree Daath, the Knowledge, as the 11th Sephira, to preserve intact the ten-ness of the Sephiroth. Showing how by that very eating of the Fruit of the Tree of Knowledge of Good and Evil should come the Saving of Mankind, for Daath is the priceless gift of Knowledge and Intellect whereby comes Salvation. Wherefore also is 11 the Key Number of the Great Savior's Name (יהשוה = 326 = 11) - Allan Bennett

III. Proverbs 3:19-20: "By wisdom (בחכמה) God (יהוה) established the earth (ארץ), with Understanding he established the heavens, and with his knowledge, the depths (chaos) (תהומות, 857) were broken up." Through Daath (Knowledge), the creative power of the Elohim (emanating from Binah) begins to manifest something from the chaotic nothing. In Qabbala, depths are often referred to as the Womb or *Ani* in Hebrew. This word is simply a rearrangement of the word *Ain* or Nothingness and, therefore, would have the same numerical value (61).

IV. The name given by qabalists to this Gate of the Gulf is Daath. In occult tradition, it is the place at which the eight-headed dragon of the deep disappeared behind the Tree when it scaled it in an unsuccessful attempt to strike at the very heart of the Godhead (i.e., Kether). The word Daath instantly suggests the name of that other gateway that opens upon the void of personal extinction, i.e., Death. These terms, Daath and Death, do indeed have a mystical affinity. It is no refutation of this fact that the words are in different languages, for the salient elements of both words Daath are qabalistically equivalent to the number 474. One of the meanings of Daath is Knowledge. It is called 'the *sephira* that is not a *sephira.'* In one aspect, it is the child of Chokmah. It is also the Eighth Head of the Stooping Dragon, raised up when the Tree of Life was shattered, and Macroprosopus set a flaming sword against Microprosopus. By permutation Doth (Daath) equates with עתד, meaning a 'ram' or a 'he-goat'; it is also the number of the Greek word duo, meaning 'two.' The double is the *eidolon*, doll, or shadow, glyphed by the ancient Egyptians by the *Tat* which is equivalent to Doth. Daath is also the Home of Choronzon, the Guardian of the Gate of the Abyss. Gathering together these various meanings, we see that the Knowledge of Daath, or Death, is of the nature of the secret of Duality represented by the shadow or magical double whereby man overcomes death and enters at the gate of Daath to explore the Abode of Choronzon, the Desert of Set.

As Chokmah and Binah's child, Daath is attributed to Uranus, which indicates this 'knowledge' highly explosive nature. As Chokmah, Neptune is a form of Hadit, and Saturn, as Binah, is a form of Nuit. This knowledge, therefore, is the knowledge of Life which, Life also, knowledge of Death, and, as such, it suggests the sexual nature of its formula.

Daath was described by the qabalists as the false

sephira because it had no place in the scheme of numbers from one to ten, no place that is in the dimension represented by the front or obverse of the Tree. In consequence, it was considered to be the eleventh *sephira*. Eleven is the number of magick, of 'energy tending to change,' which is the precise formula of the Operation of Daath and the reason for its association with death as the supreme type of change.

In the Tantric scheme of *chakras* or microcosmic powerzones, Daath is attributed to the Zone of the Word, the Visuddha or, throat-center. This center represents speech, but the Word in its occult sense of the True Voice may be uttered only by a Magus, whose natural provenance is the second sephira, Chokmah. The II (two) and the 11 (eleven) thus meet in Daath, the sphere of knowledge, for knowledge, is possible only where duality (two; *duo*) prevails. These two - subject and object -unite, and their union causes change, which is magick's formula. Union occurs in consciousness, where the act is reflected as in a mirror, and the act opens the gate through which the Will (Hadit) is projected. Its image appears in the mirror-world at the back of the Tree and in reverse, for in that dimension, time flows backward, and man reverts to an ape. Therefore, the cynocephalus was chosen as a magical symbol of the Word by the ancient Egyptians who attributed it to the moon-god, Thoth. The name of this god is equivalent to Daath. The reflection of the sun (human consciousness) in the waters of the abyss is thus symbolized by Thoth, and his cynocephalus as the man and his dog are reflected in the moon. [Grant, 1994, pp. 8-10.]

עדת *edeth.* testimony (within the ark). Psalm 122:4: "unto the testimony of Israel, to give thanks unto the name of the Lord." This word is intimately connected with the center of the Mars-force. The "ark" is the human body.

חכמות *chakemoth.* wisdom (plural). Knowledge and wisdom are closely related.

עתד *oethed.* to prepare, make ready—a prerequisite of knowledge.

עתד *othad.* a ram, a he-goat; a prepared sacrifice. The ram is Aries, a symbol of the Mars-force, sublimated or sacrificed to knowledge by preparation.

אחתי כלה *echothi kallah.* my sister (my) bride. Song of Solomon 4:12: "A garden enclosed is my sister, my bride: a spring shut up, a fountain sealed." The "garden" is the perfect state of being, which is also the stone. See 53.

זה היום עשה יהוה *zeh-tayom yasha IHVH.* "This is the day which the Lord has made" [Psalm 118:24].

475

כהבת *koheneth.* Priestess; suggest the High Priestess in Key 2, a symbol of cosmic memory, linking Tiphareth the central Ego, and Kether the One Self of the Tree of Life. See 75.

כהנת priesthood. Numbers 25:13.

ולשפטים and judges. 1 Chronicles 26:29.

קרקעה *Karka*; a town of the southern border of Judah. Recall that Judah is connected with Leo and thus with the sun. Joshua 15:3: (and their south border) ."... went up to Adar and fetched a compass to Karka."

עתה now. See Genesis 19:9.

אבותינו our fathers. See Genesis 47:3.

גויתנו our bodies. See Genesis 47:18.

גבעת hills. See Genesis 49:26.

המשקל the weight. Ezra 8:34.

העת the time

וגנותי I will defend. 2 Kings 19:34.

יללתה it's howling. See Isaiah 15:8.

יתהלל let him boast. I Kings 20:11

רברבנוהו his nobles (Lords). Daniel 6:18.

תוגיון You will torment. Job 19:2.

hoc universi compendium unis mihi sepuchrum feci (Lt). "I have made this sepulcher as a single compendium of the universe." The inscription engraved on a circular altar, covered with a plate of Brass (copper), was found in the tomb of brother C.R.'s vault in the Rosicrucian allegory (*Fama*). This statement indicated that the symbolism of the vault is both macrocosmic and microcosmic. The pyramid, Solomon's temple, and Noah's ark are also macrocosmic and microcosmic symbols. See 87, 122, 76, 150 Latin, 106, 37, 23, 24.

476

שכל נעבד *Saykel Ne'evad* (neobed). Serving (or Administrative) Intelligence. 32nd Path of Tav. Connects the automatic consciousness (Yesod, Moon) to the field of sensation and embodiment (Earth, Malkuth). The power of this path is the full development of the 17th Path of Zain. Concentration and discrimination are used to make sharp distinctions between conscious and subconscious functions, necessary to establish balance in the personality. The possessor of this path directs the inner planetary forces through the central indwelling presence. He perceives the whole universe to be continuous with and inseparable from his body. The ego is seen as working as the servant to all human life, and as such, is the greatest of all. He has centered himself in the cosmic heart through practice. He knows that every slightest thought, word and action is part of the administration of cosmic law. He shares in the Life-power's dominion over all things. Other meanings of *neobed* are: be tilled, be cultivated, worshiped; to be dressed, be tanned (of hides); from עוד to be worked, be made to serve, and work, deed. See 126, 406, 400, 331, 340.

כל מעשיו *kawl-maesawiv.* all his works. Psalm 103:22: "Bless IHVH, all his works in all places of his dominion..." Tav is Saturn, to which is attributed the pair of opposites <u>dominion</u> and slavery.

מלקוש *malekeosh.* the latter rain (vernal rain); spring rain. Figuratively eloquence. In Proverbs 16:15: "In the light of the king's countenance is life, and his favor is as a cloud of the latter rain." The King's countenance is to Microprosopus, which is names מלך melek. "favor" is רצון rawtzon or will. The dominion of the divine will produce the eloquence of serving; here, the greatest of all becomes the servant of all. See 346, 352, 1453.

בית דין house of Justice; judicial consistory; a courthouse; court of law. When the law of God is obeyed, then the Lord is in his holy temple (house), the abode of regenerated human personality. See 412, 64, 1126.

Rosenroth in K.D.L.C.K. (p. 197) gives: *domus judici, curia, consistorium iudiciaie,* and said by him to refer to Malkuth. In the Zohar, the Rabbi Shimeon Ben Johai calls it shekinah, which contains a triumvirate of the animal bodies-the face of a lion, the face of a bull and the face of an eagle.

ביתחון *Baythchan.* Angel Lord of the triplicity in the sign Scorpio by day. See 1126.

צלילימירון *Tzelilimiron.* The Clangers, Qlippoth of Gemini.

This reflects unbalanced discrimination. The letters of this name suggest the perverted power of meditation (Tzaddi) alternating between action (Lamed) and influencing will-force (Yod) for personal ends, reversing mental substance (Mem) and creating (Yod) the degeneration of solar force at odds with its purpose (Resh) by the psychic voices of disunity (Vav), frozen in a cycle of reproductive error (Nun). See 1126.

d'Olivet writes of the root צל': This root, composed of the final sign united to the directive sign, characterizes a thing whose effect is spread afar. This thing expresses either noise, or shadow passing through air and void; or void itself containing darkness: thence, צל every *noise* that is striking, clear, piercing like brass; every *shadow* carried, projected a great distance into space; every obscure *depth,* whose bottom is unknown: metaphorically, *a screaming voice;* any kind of object extending overhead and making a shade as *a canopy, dias, covering, roof, veil;* every deep, obscure place, *a cavern.* In its primitive sense, the Arabic word characterizes the state of that which grows dark being corrupted, imitating the darkness of shadow, which lengthens, gains, as a shadow, etc. According to the onomatopoetic sense, it is a prolonged sound, a cry which invokes succor, a prayer, etc. That which is prolonged indefinitely wanders or disappears, etc." [d'Olivet, 1976, pp. 434-435.]

477

שכל מוטבע *Sekhel Motba.* Natural Intelligence. Title of Tzaddi, the 28th Path. Connects the desire nature (Venus, Netzach) to the automatic consciousness (Moon, Yesod). Only meditation can plant the seed of the word in the heart. Then the seed grows and bears fruit. Human personality is the instrument that nature devises and perfects to express the Life-power's knowledge of its own nature and its possibilities. The key to success in meditation is to overcome distractions and forgetfulness by faithful practice. The possessor of this path is filled with the spirit of wisdom and counsel. He is the agency through which the natural process of an unbroken flow of consciousness in a particular object is expressed. Nothing but good then results from his thought and action. He shares in the cosmic activity and knows the exact situation at any moment to be the right and necessary one. *Motba* is derived from the root יבע which, as a verb, means "to press in, to impress, to sink." "Nature" is the meaning of rabbinical writing. The implication is that nature is like the "impression" made on wax by a signet ring. See 127, 81, 103, 203, 222, 104, 127.

זרע צדוק *zero zadok.* the seek of Zadok. In Ezekiel 43:19: "And thou shall give to the priest the Levites that be of the seed of Zadok... a young bullock for a sin offering." Zadok means "righteous" and was one of the two chief priests in the Davidic sanctuary in Jerusalem (abode of peace). The "seed" is Yod, assigned to Kether and Chokmah, in the divine name IHVH. The "bullock" is Taurus, represented by Key 5, the Hierophant or intuition. When Vav is "sacrificed," Zadok becomes צדק Tzedek or Jupiter, the sphere of Chesed. Here we see the influx of the "seed," represented by Uranus's path (super-consciousness) into Chokmah and thence through the path of Taurus to Chesed. The Chasidim or the merciful ones are possessors of the path of Tzaddi because of the occult connection between Jupiter and Moon, and they give "efficacious councils."

מכון הר ציון *mawkon har-Tzion*. the habitation of Mount Zion. The "pillar of three colors," or one of the 4 angels in the Garden of Eden. Zohar II: *vayehi*, (p.310): "Using this pillar it [the soul] ascends to the great righteousness, in which are Zion and Jerusalem. If it is worthy to ascend further, happiness is its portion and lot to become attached to the king's body. If it is not worthy to ascend further. Then 'he that is left in Zion, and he that remains in Jerusalem shall be called holy." see 156, 586, 116.

μετανοια. *metanoia*. Repentance; after-thought; change of mind on reflection. Has a special meaning about New Testament writings. The Gnostic inference is that repentance is really a renewal of the mind, in this instance, through the exercise of meditation. This brings "completion" to the great work of regenerated personality.

εκδικησις. *ekdikehsis*. Vengeance. Romans 12:19: "Dearly beloved, avenge not yourselves, but rather give place unto wrath: for it is written, 'vengeance is mine; I will repay, says the Lord.'" Refers to another biblical passage, Proverbs 24:29: "Say not, I will do so to him as he has done to me: I will render to the man according to his work." There is no vengeance in love, and the compensation is shalom. See 370, 190.

זעיר אנפין *Zauir Anpin*. Lesser Countenance. Microprosopus. A title of Tiphareth. The complete Lesser Countenance is composed of the Sephiroth from 4 to 9, and all are aspects of Ruach, the human spirit.

בלילות *be-liloth*. by night [Psalm 134:1].

גולגולת *gulgoleth*. the skull (as round), cranium. Hebrew original of Golgotha, or calvary (Calvaria, cranium). The "Place of the Skull" is the mystical crucifixion, and the right understanding of this detail is of utmost importance in practical work. See 466.

מבקשי יהוה *mi-baqashiy IHVH*. who seek the Lord. Isaiah 51:1: "Listen to me, you're who pursue righteousness and who seek the Lord: Look to the rock from which you were cut and to the quarry from which you were hewn;" The "rock" is the stone (53). The stone is found in the skull (above) on the physical plane.

ויחל נח איש האדמה *vayachel Noah aish ha-adamah*. Noah, a man of the soil, proceeded (to plant a vineyard) [Genesis 9:20].

כתובים *Haglographia*, the third part of the Bible. [From Greek sacred, holy and to write, or written by inspiration]. The last of the Old Testament's three Jewish divisions, or that portion not in the prophets' law. [Webster]. The "inspiring word" is here related to the "search for IHVH," to "Noah, Man of the Ground," and to the center or adytum in the "skull," which is created "by night." See 1038.

מחלת *Mahalath*, daughter of Ishmael; with of Esau. In Genesis 28:9: "So he [Esau] went to Ishmael and married Mahalath, the sister of Nebaloth and daughter of Ishmael son of Abraham, in addition to the wives he already had." Later Mahalath was considered a major demon, the mother of Agrath, and the angel of prostitution.

Sanguinalis animala rosa Hierichuntis

Spiritualis (Lt). Animal blood, spiritual Rose of Jericho. Part of the Latin motto in a diagram on page 13 of Secret Symbols. See 958. The whole Latin passage of which it is the first sentence adds to 958, the value of Jesus in Greek, written with the usual definite article.

479 (prime)

בורא רע *borae rah*. I create evil. Isaiah 45:7. רע not only means evil but pointed רע means "friend, companion; thought, purpose and aim." With Heh added this word רעה means: to feed, graze a flock; figuratively to lead, guide, direct (as a shepherd). See 270, 485.

טכנת *tokhnoth*. mills, hand mills. Perhaps like the "Mills of the Gods." To grind wholly but slowly, this suggests that the Lord's ways may appear to be evil, but perfect justice is the ultimate purpose of the divine plan. "Evil" does exist, however. See 270.

האל בית אל *ha-El Beth-EL*. The God of Bethel [Genesis 31:13]. See 560.

הדעת *ha-da'ath*. The knowledge. See 474, 581, 293.

החכמות *ha-chokmoth*. the wisdom; of the wise. Feminine plural, or collective. See 73.

טוחנות *tuhanoth*. masses [Crowley, 1977, p. 48]. d'Olivet writes of "תוח: Action of *placing in safety, guaranteeing, covering, inlaying: a covering, an inlay, a coat of plaster*, etc." [d'Olivet, 1976, p.357.] The last three letters suggest the plural form.

480

לילית *Lilith*. Adam's First wife. Qlippoth of Malkuth, the queen or physical plane. See 773.

I. "Queen of the Night, Queen of Demons, wife of Samael, wife of Asmodai, first wife of Adam. Arch-demon corresponding to Yesod." [Godwin, 1999, p. 565]

II. "In Jewish tradition, where she originated, Lilith is a female demon, an enemy of infants, bride of the evil angel Sammael (Satan). She predates Eve, had marital relations with Adam... According to Rabbi Eleazar (The Book of Adam and Eve), Lilith bore Adam every day with 100 children. The Zohar (Leviticus 19A) describes Lilith as 'a hot fiery female who first cohabited with man,' but, when Eve was created, 'flew to the cities of the sea coast,' where she is 'still trying to ensnare mankind'... In the Cabala, she is the demon of Friday and is represented as a naked woman whose body terminates in a serpent's tail... Lilith is drawn from the Lili, female demonic spirits in Mesopotamian demonology, and Ardat Lili. The Rabbis read Lilith into scripture as the 1st temptress, as Adam's demon wife, and as the mother of Cain.. in Talmudic lore and the Cabala (The Zohar), most demons are mortal. Still, Lilith and two other notorious female spirits of evil (Naamah and Agrat Bat Mahlat) will 'continue to exist and plague man until the Messianic day, when God will finally extradite uncleanliness and evil from the face of the earth...' Lilith and Sammael are said to have 'emanated from beneath the throne of divine glory, the legs of which were somewhat shaken by their [joint] activity.'.. Lilith went by a score of names, 17 of which she revealed to Elijah when she was forced to do so by the Old Testament prophet." [Davidson, 1971, pp. 174-175.]

III. Lalita (Sanskrit): the sexual aspect of shakti or power. The original symbol of the concept was not the woman, but the sow, known in ancient Egypt as Rerit. The great sow or sower became the Lalita of the Indian and the Lilith of Chaldean lore, where she appears as the Queen of Night and the prototype of the succubus or sexual vampire. Adam's first wife was the astral image of desire that became the type of the *succuba*. She represents the visions of unsatisfied desire reflected into consciousness as the vivid and voluptuous imagery manifested in the flesh as Eve (woman). [Grant, 1994, pp. 269-270.]

IV. Inman: "This name occurs but once in the Old

Testament, and is then associated with wild beasts and satyrs. In our authorized version, the word is rendered 'screech owl.' the context, and the termination of the word itself, indicate that Lilith is of the feminine gender and associated with 'satyrs.' The Lilith of the Rabbins is a specter, under the form of a beautiful woman, well attired, who follows children, in particular, to kill them. Lilith was Adam's first wife, with whom he procreated demons. She stands by the side of women in child-bed to kill the infants. The amulet inscribed on the bed, or worn by child-bearing Hebrew women, is אדם חוה חוץ לילית, 'Adam, Eve, get out Lilith.' [Inman, 1942, Vol. 2., pp. 212-213]

תלמוד *Talmud*. Teaching.

כל נפש *kawl-nephesh*. all living. In Genesis 1:21: "And God (Elohim) created great whales, and every living creature that moves, which the waters brought forth abundantly, after their kind, and every winged fowl after his kind: and God saw that it was good."

היכל הקודש *haikal ha-qadosh*. The palace of holiness, or holy temple. In *Sepher Yetzirah* 4:4: "And the Holy Palace precisely in the center, and it supports them all." [Kaplan, 1997, p. 163] (i.e., the 6 dimensions: height, depth, east, west, south, north). See 586, 282, 65, 404.

אבני תוהו *abeni tohu*. stones of emptiness; *lapides inanitatis* in K.D.L.C.K. (p.21) pertains to Chesed. Suggest a lack of memory, as Chesed is associated with Jupiter and cosmic memory. See 411, 53.

עית *Aiath*; Malkuth, 42-fold name in Yetzirah [Crowley, 1977, p. 48].

I. Isaiah 10:28: "He comes to Aiath..." (באול עית), Malkuth in Yetzirah, the formative world.

II. According to Westcott, this is one of three names for "bird" in alchemy, which generally means sublimations. *Aesch Mezareph*: A beast with 4 wings like a bird was given power over the lion and bear that he may extract their gluten or

blood. [Westcott, 1997, p. 25] see 156, 315, 376.

סטרא אחרא *sitayraw ahchayraw*. Evil power, demonry, adverse influence, evil side, the devil's domain. Literally, "the other side" [Aramaic].

תף *tof*. a hand-drum or tambourine called the timbrel; also bezel-the part of a setting that receives and holds a gem. See 1200 and Job 21:12.

פת *path*. bit, morsel [of bread] in Genesis 18:5. Note that פתה means, to be open; to be simple, foolish, enticed, deceived; with different pointing: to seduce; to persuade, entice.

I. "*poth*: opening; pudenda." [Godwin, 1999, p. 566].

II. "Suggests that which enables doors to be open and shut [Daleth = door]. But the *path* is also translated 'secret parts,' i.e., yoni, and here was are close to a very carefully guarded doctrine of Qabalah." [Paul Case, The Flaming Cube: Light of the Chaldees, p.4]

481

אדירירון *Adiryaron*. The Mighty One Sings. A title of Tiphareth. [Godwin. 1999, p. 499.]

I. Also known as Adir, Adriron. The angelic chief of "The Might of God" [i.e., Michael]; also a name for God. Adiririon is invoked as an amulet against the evil eye. He is said to be a guard stationed at one of the halls or palaces of the 1st heaven. In Sepher Raziel, Adiririon is a "trusty healing-God, in whose hands are the heavenly and earthly households." [Dictionary of Angels, p.7] see 1131.

טבעת *tabaoth annulus*. a circuit of the sun, cycle of time. [Crowley, 1977, p. 48]. Rosenroth in K.D.L.C.K. (p.367) says it is the conception of Malkuth in Chokmah; its symbol is a ring of betrothal.

επισκοπεια. *episkopeia*. overseership. [επι, over + σκοπη, watchtower; επισοπη, an overseeing, office of overseer or bishop; a visitation, or punishment].

η επισκοπη. *heh episkipeh*. "The Lord's visitation" 1 Peter 2:12: "Having your conduct upright among the gentiles, so that in what they may speak against you as evil-doers, from the good works which they behold, they may glorify God in a day of inspection.: This is the act of being visited or inspected for good, i.e., the care and oversight of the Lord. See 1480.

η γενεσις. *heh genesis*. The beginning, origin, source, birth, race, descent; generation, procreation, nativity. Matthew 1:18: Now the nativity of the Christ Jesus was thus: Mary his mother had been pledged to Joseph; but before they were united, she was discovered to be pregnant by the holy spirit." See Luke 1:14, James 1:23 and 532, 709 and 1550.

μαγνηια καθολικη. *magnesia katholikeh*. Greek form of Latin *magnesia catholica*, universal magnet, the alchemical first matter. In *The Hermetic Museum*, it is said of the matter of the stone that writers "also call it the universal magnesia, or the seed of the world, from which all other objects take their origin." [Waite, 1974, vol. 1, p. 77] see 129 (Lt), 1766 (Greek).

τρια μεγεθη. *tria megetheh*. three dimensions.

Ιαου. *IAOU*. The name of Tetragrammaton, Notice the similarity to God IAO's name, used in the Phoenician mysteries. This is definitely a Gnostic derivation from the Alexandrian brotherhood.

αρτοι. *artoi*. "loaves," i.e., bread; part of the temptation of Jesus by the Devil in Matthew 4:3: "Then the tempter approaching him, said; 'if you be a son of God, command that these stones become loaves." see 671 (Greek); 1964, 370, 4884, 710, 1059, 1219.

482

γη επιλησμενη. *geh epilelehsmeneh*. "land of oblivion" or "land of forgetfulness." Septuagint translation of ארץ נשיה (656) in Psalm 88:12: "Are your wonders known in the place of darkness, or your righteous deeds in the land of oblivion?" see 656.

לבנת to build. See Genesis 11:8.

משבצים enclosed, ones being mounted. Referring to the breastplate of the high priest. See Exodus 28:20.

ובדעת and in knowledge. See Exodus 31:3.

לבנת white. White ones. See Leviticus 13:38.

483

מזלות *Mazloth*. Constellations; the Sphere of the Zodiac. Singular form מזל is the root of Mezla, the force proceeding from Kether is identified with planetary influences. See 73 (Chokmah) and 23 (chaiah).

Chokmah is called מזלות *Masloth*, the Sphere of the Zodiac (fixed stars), because the One Self knows itself as light. *Masloth* means "highways" and refers to the order and arrangement of the constellations. All events in the universe are related, including those of our own lives. No event occurs by itself. Because Chokmah is the Sphere of the Zodiac, wisdom includes knowledge of astronomical relationships and the connection between the heavenly order and men's affairs. The more we learn concerning the various influences in our environment, the more intelligently we may direct the course of our lives. The more we realize that all manifestation is orderly, the less shall we be victims of Fate.

In a sense, *masloth* represents what is called in the Bible the "kingdom of heaven," literally, "kingdom of the skies." The motion represented in this order of the heavens is precisely the absolute, or whirling, motion which has its first manifestation in Kether. This whirling motion is the animating principle of all life, including humanity. It expresses itself in conscious activity and in subconscious activity also. Therefore, Chokmah (Wisdom) is the perfect self-knowledge that a Limitless Life must possess, which is essentially a principle of pure consciousness.

לא תחמד *lo tha-chemod*. "Thou shall not covet." The last of 10 commandments revealed to Moses by God, in Exodus 20:17.

נושא עון *neusha ayon*. Given as *ferens iniquitatem* (difficult wild beast?) [Crowley, 1977, p. 48].

תועבה an abomination. Genesis 43:32.

484

I. (2^2x11^2)

משפטיהם *mishpatiham*. their judgments; their laws. Refers to Shin, the 31st Path. The "revolutions of the zodiac" influenced by this path are the cycles of successive incarnation. The form of "their judgments" is a veiled reference to completing the incarnation cycle by the resurrection from what Saint Paul calls "The body of this death" in Romans 7:24. This is the "natural body," the body of sin, dominated by Nephesh, the vital soul and not yet perfected by the Ego. See 814, 464.

לתהו והבל *le-tohu ve-hebel*. for naught and in vain. In Isaiah 49:4: "Then I said, I have labored in vain, I have spent my strength for naught and in vain: yet surely my judgment is with the Lord, and my work with my God."

עתיד *eytheid*. ready, prepared; future. Future time to come [Sepher Yetzirah 1:2]. Shin is located on the pillar of severity, attributed to the future (feminine). The masculine pillar of mercy is equated with the past.

קו לקו קו לקו *qav la-qav qav la-qav*. line upon line, line upon line or line by line, line by line. Isaiah 28:10, 13: "To whom shall one teach knowledge [דעת]. For it is precept by precept, precept by precept, line by line, line by line." Resurrection is a step-by-step process. See 474.

חצר עינון *Hazar-Enan*. The enclosure of the fountains. Numbers 34:9: "And the goings out of it shall be at Hazar-Enan." This was a point of departure on the ideal north-east border of Canaan near Dan. It has alchemical significance. (Ayin = fountain). See 54, 190, 830, 1134, 993.

אור זרע *aur zerao*. light is a seed. The Zohar [IV 167A, B p.77] Comments: ."..there is first light, then water, is a firmament formed amid the waters. Similar is the formation of a man at his birth. First, he is 'seed,' which is light; it carries light to all the body's organs. That 'seed' which is light, sheds itself abroad and becomes 'water,' which in its moisture penetrates to all parts of the body; in which body, when it has taken shape, the diffusion of water is solidified and is called 'firmament.'" see 718 (a light is sown to the righteous), 207, 277.

Θεου. *Theou*. God.

485

תהלים *tehillim*. Psalms; i.e., songs of Joy. Name for the book of Psalms at a later period. Spelled תהלות hymns, praises in Psalm 22:3: "But thou are holy, O thou that inhabits the praises of Israel." see 1045.

התלים *haethulim*. Mockers, mockeries. Job 17:2: "Are there not mockers with me? And does not my eye continue in their provocation?"

כהני המשנה *kohaeni ha-mishayneh*. the priest of the second order. In 2 Kings 23:4: "And the king commanded Hilkiah, the high priest, and the priest of the second order, to bring forth out of the temple of the Lord all the vessels that were made for Baal, and for the Grove, and for all the host of heaven: and he burned them without Jerusalem in the fields of Kidron, and carried the ashes of them unto Bether." see 400.

בת נלים *bath-galim*. daughter of Galim. In Isaiah 10:30: "Lift up your voice, O daughter of Galim: cause it to be heard unto Laish, O poor Anathoth." Galim means "stone-heaps" and is a place in Benjamin (162, Sagittarius, incineration). Laish (lion) was the original name of the city Dan (54, Scorpio, putrefaction) in the extreme north of Israel. Anathoth is a name connected with the Semitic goddess Anat, also called *filia scaturiginium*, "daughter of a spring of bubbling water."

מן השמים *min ha-shamaim*. from the heavens. Genesis 19:24: "Then the Lord (IHVH) caused to rain upon Sodom and Gomorrah brimstone and fire from את (essence of) IHVH (the Lord) out of the heavens." see 104, 315, 401.

דנתאל Goetia demon #71 by night of the 2nd decan of Pisces. See Appendix 11.

Goetia: "He is a duke great and mighty, appearing in the form of a man with many countenances, all men's and women's faces; and he has a book in his right hand. His office is to teach all arts and sciences unto any, and to declare the secret counsels of anyone; for he knows the thoughts of all men and women, he can cause love, and show the similitude of any person, and show the same by vision, let them be in what part of the world they will. He governs 36 Legions of Spirits." [Mathers, 1995, p. 65]

להמית to slay, to kill. See Genesis 18:25.

התיכן the middle, the center. See Exodus 26:28.

העדות the testimony. Exodus 26:33.

המזלגת the flesh-hooks, the meat forks. See Exodus 38:3.

ο αληθης ανηρ. *ho alethes aner*. The man of truth. See 1455, 2910, 2758, 3395 & Apostolic Gnosis, p.126.

486

I. (2 x 3 x 3 x 3 x 3 x 3) or 2 x 3^5

יסודות *yesodoth*. foundations. Plural of Yesod, to which is attributed the reproductive activities of both Microcosm and Macrocosm. Refers to Daleth's 14th Path, the "Instructor in the Secret Foundations of holiness and perfection." see 703, 564, 80, 434.

תיכון *tikon*. inner, central, middle. The name in Hebrew of the Mediterranean sea, less the definite article Heh. There is a connection between the great interior sea (Binah) and the lunar sephirah, Yesod, located on the tree's central or middle pillar. See 541, 546.

מצה פרוסה *matzoh perusaw*. unleavened bread (agymum fractum). Taken by the Israelites in their flight from Egypt over the Red Sea. The Christ child is born in the "house of bread" (Beth-lechem). See 490.

Rosenroth in K.D.L.C.K. (p.546) refers to Malkuth's phrase because it is fermented and purified by her husband [i.e., Tiphareth].

שין יוד נון *Shin-Yod-Nun*. The letter Shin, spelled in full. The power of transformation (Shin) through the agency of divine will (Yod) produces perpetual change (Nun). Resurrection has to do with Fire, with bread and with the inner "sea."

יהוה בחכפה ימד ארץ *IHVH be-kachfeh yamad eretz*. "IHVH in the power of his mouth (fertilizes, founds) the earth." A name of God.

עוית *ovuioth*. a King of Edom. Suggest unbalanced force in the automatic pattern-world (Subconsciousness as Yesod) through wrongly directed desire (Daleth).

"*Avith*- a City of Edom; the city of King Hadad." [Godwin. 1999, p. 566.] see Genesis 36:35.

תומם *teomim*. twins, a variant spelling of תאומים, the Hebrew name for the sign Gemini. Genesis 25:24: "And when her days to be delivered were fulfilled, behold there were twins in her [Rebetah's] womb." see 1046.

סכות *sukkot*. Tabernacles. Leviticus 23:34: "Speak to the children of Israel, saying, 'the 15th day of this 7th month shall be the feast of tabernacles for seven days unto the Lord." The tabernacle was a pavilion or booth, and the festival was one of thanksgiving for the harvest. This is a feminine word, corresponding to the pillar of Boaz. Richardson's Monitor of Freemasonry says: "Master: where were they cast? Senior warden: on the banks of the river Jordan, in the clay ground between Succoth and Zaradath, where King Solomon order these, and all other holy vessels to be cast." see 79, 699.

לא תגנב *lo-thi-genov*. thou shall not steal. The 8th of 10 commandments revealed to Moses by God, in Exodus 20:15.

נהתאל *Nahathel*. The angle of the 8 of Pentacles [Crowley, 1977, p. 49]. This corresponds to Hod, sphere of Mercury, in Assiah, the physical plane, and in astrology to the first decan of Virgo.

Πετρα. *petra*. rock. "As a symbol, the word *petra* is used in an antiphrastic sense that, relying on an alleged composition of the word, suggests a rapid rising to a great height. Hence it is a synonym for the Narrow Way, the Way of the Mystic: or, for the few in their evolution, have passed the Narrow Gate. The Khristos, the Anointed in Godhood, is its Goal. It may be remembered that Demeter when seeking the *Kore* [maiden, 198], sat on a "Reverend Rock" (agelastos petra)." [Omikron, 1942, p. 262.]

487 (prime)

תואמם double, ones being double. See Exodus 36:29.

לזנת to go astray, she turns. See Leviticus 20:6.

והבדלתם and you shall separate, so you distinguish. See Leviticus 20:25.

488

מתחיל beginner.

חלב הבתולה *chawlawb haw-baythlawh*. milk of the virgin; virgin's milk. A name of the alchemical first matter. Recall that the Rosicrucian fraters were "of vowed virginity." Note that 488 reduces to 2, the high priestess, a virgin, "whose purity naught can defile." [Book of Tokens, Gimel]. This is Beth's value, the Magician. When he impregnates the high priestess, she becomes Daleth, the empress, the open the door to life and form. See 570, 40, 443.

דמו בנפשו the life of every creature is in the blood. Note that this life is the Nephesh (430). See Leviticus 17:14.

תעבודו *tobudu*. you shall worship. The great work is aided by reverence.

תאומיאל *Thaumiel*. Twins (Double) of God, Qlippoth of Kether. "The doubles of God, said to be two-headed and so named because they pretend to be equal to the supreme crown. This is properly the title of the adverse sephirah corresponding to Kether" [Waite: Doctrine and Literature of the Qabalah]. The negative use of two is seen here to be a source of division.

צבא השמים The host of the heaven, i.e., celestial bodies. In Deuteronomy 4:19: "And lest you lift up your eyes to heaven, and when you see the sun, the moon and the stars, even all the host of heaven, should be driven to worship them, and serve them, which the Lord your God has divided to all nations under the whole heaven." see 390, 745, 687, 395.

פתח door. The entrance of. See Genesis 18:1.

בתוככם in the midst of you, among you. See Genesis 23:9.

חלמתי I have dreamed. See Genesis 37:6.

489

רוח רעה *ruach raah.* evil spirit.

משלם גמול *mushaylawm gimul.* repaying, returning favors [גמול = dealing; recompense, desert, benefit; משלם = complete, perfect]. thus: perfect payment, recompense. The pearl is payment for completion or peace.

תפדה you shall redeem. See Exodus 13:13.

אדמדמת reddish. See Leviticus 13:19.

כמשפטם according to their ordinance, as specified of them. See Numbers 29:6.

490

בית לחם *Beth-lechem.* House of bread; Bethlehem. The Birthplace of Jesus (reality liberates). This corresponds to the Virgo area of the human body, where food assimilation is carried out. Also sheds light on the real meaning of the dogma of Jesus' Virgin Birth. See 412, 78, 686, 1050.

יפת *Japheth.* Expansion; One of Noah's 3 sons. Refers to the diffusion of energy through innumerable forms. See 936.

"יפת Japeth. This name holds a medium between *Shem* and *Ham* and partakes of their good or evil qualities without having them in itself. It signifies, in a generic sense, material extent, indefinite space: in a more restricted sense, latitude. The root פת, from which it comes, contains every idea of expansion, of a facility to extend, to allow itself to be penetrated; every solution, every divisibility, every simplification. It is governed by the sign of potential manifestation י, which adds to its force and universalizes it.

Let us compare the three sons of Adam diligently with those of *Noah.* The first production of Adam, after his fall, is *Kain* [160]; the second *Habel* [37]; the third, *Sheth* [700]. Moses, for

very strong reasons, inverted the order of similitudes of the productions of Noah. *Shem* [340], whom he names the first, in this instance, corresponds with *Habel*, whom he has named second in the other; *Ham*, whom he names second, corresponds with *Kain*, whom he has named first; *Japheth*, who correspond with *Sheth* preserves with him the same rank.

It is without a doubt very difficult to know what Moses was concealed under the symbolic names of *Kain*, *Habel* and *Sheth*: but if one wishes to admit that this may be the three constituent principles of the being called Adam, that is to say, the developed, or decomposed triad of the collective unity, he will soon perceive that the symbolic names of *Ham*, *Shem* and *Japheth*, are the constituted principles of the being called *Noah* and that these cosmogonic personages are related one to the other, in the same manner as the effect is related to its cause." [d'Olivet, 1976, pp. 171-173.]

תץ *tetz.* refers to the 42-fold name of Binah, in Yetzirah, the formative world. As a formation, it is תצורה (tetzurawh). The formative power of the great mother is the agent of the perfect "rock." See 42.

טוב אתה ומטוב *tob-attah vu-metib.* "thou are good, and does good (teach me your statutes)" [Psalm 119:68]. The creative power is always working toward good results.

מתן *matawn.* Gift. In Genesis 34:12: "Ask me never so much dowry and gift, and I will give according to you shall say unto me." With different pointing: 1. present, offering. The gift of the Life-power is freely given to those who work to extend its expression in ways of goodness; 2. *moten*: loin-place of desire and carrier of the "new-birth"; 3. *mawtan*: to become soft-connected with the assimilation of food. See 1140.

סלת *soleth.* fine meal, flour. Used in see Ezekiel 16:13. The passage refers to Jerusalem, the "abode of peace." It is the vision of the perfected man, who has become the Christ-child.

נפשכם your mind, soul, your will. See Genesis 23:8.

מולדתי my birthplace, own relatives. See Genesis 24:4.

יפת beautiful, sleek [cows]. See Genesis 41:4.

מררים bitter herbs. See Exodus 12:8.

491 (prime)

שכל נאמן *Sekhel Ne'eman.* Faithful Intelligence. 22nd path of Lamed. Joins the seat of volition with the Central Ego. This "pranic force" partakes of spiritual power, whose urge is toward increase and is related to the reproductive drive. All work is attributed to this path, including the Great Work-whose secret is equilibrium. The possessor of this path is mentally and emotionally poised, and the result of his work established balance in his surroundings. He uses intelligence to discover the positive opposites of negative mental states and "overcomes evil with good." He is free from fear and thus inspires no fear. He masters wild beasts in his environment because he has subdued their counter-part-the coiled serpent power-in his own nature. He is an unobstructed channel for the one free will, which established the undeviating Justice of universal law. See 67, 74, 141, 1141.

לחת אבן *luchoth ehben.* tables of stone. In Exodus 31:18: "And he gave unto Moses when he had made an end of communing with him upon Mount Sinai, two tables of testimony, tables of stone, written with the finger of God." Refers to the law of God, which is engraved on every action (Lamed) of man, as an agent of divine volition (Geburah). See 642 (Greek).

היסודות *ha-yesodoth.* the elements; the foundations. [Hebrew lexicon]. Refers to Daleth, or Venus, the ruler of Libra, to which Lamed is attributed. Creative imagination governs the actions and establishes poise. See 486.

ניתאל *Nithael.* "King of the Heavens." 54th Shem ha-Mephorash. 266 ° -270 °. CHÉNON. May 12, July 23, October 3, December 14, February 24. 5:40-6:00 PM. Psalm 103:19: "The Lord has perpetuated his throne in the heavens, and his kingdom rules overall." To obtain the mercy of God and for long life. Rules emperors, kings, princes, and all civil and ecclesiastical dignitaries. It controls legitimate dynasties and the stability of empires. It gives a long and peaceful reign to princes and protects those who wish to be maintained through their employments—a person born: guises himself by his virtues and merits his prince's confidence. Associated with Aries' 6th quinance; Angel by night of the 4 of Wands [Chesed of Atziluth]. See 965, 460 & Appendix 10.

אמנת *omeneth.* nurse; a name of בינה Binah [67], root of water. Literally "she who rears up," a foster mother. In Lamentations 4:5: "They that did feed delicately are desolate in the streets: they that were reared up [i.e., nursed] in scarlet embrace dunghills." see 497.

492

צבת *zibeth.* handful. Name of the Philosophers' stone, which Lamech says contains "the first elements, and the final colors of minerals, or spirit, soul, and body, joined into one." *Zibeth* refers to the letter Yod (Hand), the sign of Virgo and Key 9. The Virgo region transmutes an ordinary human being into an adept. See 80, 112.

צור עולמים *tsore olahmim.* Everlasting Rock. Everlasting Strength [Isaiah 26:4]. See 301, 490.

בת-מלך *bath-melek.* the king's daughter. Psalm 45:13: "The king's daughter is all glorious within (the palace): her clothing is of wrought gold." The king is the Ego in Tiphareth: his daughter is Kallah, the Qabalistic bride or Malkuth. The glory is the divine radiance; the temple is the inner sanctum. "Gold" refers to the solar force. In alchemy, when the inner glory shines like gold, the great work is completed. See 972, 3101 (Greek).

את יהוה אלהיך *Eth Jehovah Elohekah.* the Lord, your Lord.

בצאת as was departing, at the end [death]. See Genesis 35:18.

לזנות to go astray, to prostitute. See Leviticus 20:5.

התנחל have inherited. See Numbers 32:18.

דרך כוכב מיעקב *dawrahk kokab mi-yahayqob.* there shall step forth a star out of Jacob. Numbers 24:17: "I shall see him, but not now: I shall behold him, not nigh: there shall come a star out of Jacob, and a scepter shall rise out of Israel, and shall smite the corners of Moab, and destroy all the children of Sheth." The commentary on this is Matthew 2:2: "star in the east: saying where is he that is born king of the Jews? for we have seen his star in the east, and are come to worship him." see 17, 8, 224, 48, 182, 541, 1430 (Greek).

תפוח *tappuah.* apple. The apple is connected with the serpent-power, with Mars and knowledge [i.e., the fruit of good and evil]. Canticles 7:8, 8:5: "I said, I will go up to the palm tree, I will take hold of the boughs thereof: now also your breasts shall be as clusters of the vine, and the smell of your nose like apples." "Who is this that comes up from the wilderness, leaning upon the beloved? I raised thee up under the apple tree: there your mother brought thee forth: there, she brought thee forth that bare thee." see 418, 95, 474, 906, 858.

כובע הישועה *kobah ha-yeshua.* Helmet of deliverance; *galea salutis,* according to Rosenroth in K.D.L.C.K. (p.472) who says some refer this name to Ain-Suph others to Tiphareth, others to Malkuth. It is the foundation, being on the crown of the head.

ידעתי I know. Genesis 4:9.

צפרדעים the frog. Exodus 8:2.

תמימה *temimah.* perfect [Psalm 19:7]. Refers to "The law of the Lord." Suggests limitation (Tav), reflection (מים, waters) and definition (Heh). May be represented by Keys 21, 12, 5, whose numbers added are 38, reduces to 11, the number of Justice, which relates to the perfect Law of IHVH. See 1032, 490.

Psalm 19:7: "The law of the Lord is perfect [תמימה], reviving the soul. The statues of the Lord are trustworthy, making wise the simple."

עפר מן האדמה *aphar min ha-aedemhuh.* dust of [from] the ground. Genesis 2:7: "And the Lord God formed man of the dust of the ground and breathed into his nostrils the breath of life, and man became a living soul." The law of the Lord is to make man in his own image. See 350, 90, 50.

דמות אדם *daymuth adam.* the likeness of a man. Rosenroth in K.D.L.C.K. (p.251) gives *similtudo hominis,* who says that it is Malkuth because, in it, Tetragrammaton is perfected. See 450.

ויהי בשלם סוכו *va-yehi be-shaleh sukkoh.* and in Salem also is his tabernacle. In Psalm 76:2: "And in Salem also is his tabernacle and his dwelling-place in Zion. See 1055, 489, 1049, 370, 376, 156.

I. Σ31 = 496. The mystic number of the 31st Path of Shin. The third perfect number (see Appendix).

מלכות *Malkuth.* Kingdom. The Resplendent Intelligence of the 10th center on the Tree of Life. The physical universe. From the root מלך, King. Manifestation or expression of power to rule, derived from the Ego or Christos in Tiphareth. The point at which all the influences which descend from Kether finally converge, and the point from which, on the way of return, man's consciousness begins its ascent to liberation and illumination. The fruit of the tree, which holds the seeds of new manifestations. The physical plane, the seat of גוף (Guph), the physical body. Known also as כלה (Kallah), the Bride, and תורה (Torah), the Law. To attain the Kingdom is to regularly listen to the Hierophant's voice (Vav) and put this knowledge into action through Tav, the Administrative Intelligence, which is Cosmic Consciousness-a permanent state of mind. The consciousness of Zelator, in Rosicrucian initiation. See 89, 90, 543, 1006, 55, 31, 564, 95, 570, 1026, 656, 676.

Malkuth is 496, and this is a perfect number. The idea of perfection is combined with the other ideas associated with 10 in the name of the last Sephirah (Malkuth). Because the sum of 4, 9 and 6 is 19, the number of חוה (Eve), the Bride and Mother, and the reduction of 19 is 10. The Kingdom is perfect. Nothing needs to be added or anything subtracted. As the *Sepher Yetzirah* says: "Ten, and not nine; ten, and not eleven." See *C.13* & 52.

496 is the sum of the numbers from 0 to 31. This implies the complete extension of the powers represented by אל, the divine name attributed to Chesed, the 4th Sephiroth (אל is 31, which reduces to 4). Ten is the numerical extension of 4. Thus the name of the 10th Sephirah is the numerical extension of the name of God attributed to the 4th Sephiroth. 31 is also the number of לא, lo, not, or no-thing, Malkuth is the full manifestation of the divine strength which is itself no-thing.

In Malkuth is the power of our Lord and King מלך אדני, *Adonai Melek*. Malkuth is also כלה (Kallah) the Bride, and מלכה (Malkah) the Queen. So the *Guph* (89), the embodied Kingdom, is the King himself and the Queen, his Bride. *Adonai Melek* is 155, and also נאמן דוד, the faithful friend, for our Lord King is our friend. Here is a mystery, the Kingdom, King, Substance, that is Guph, Queen and Bride are all but ONE, and the ONE is ALL because כלה can be read as הכל (Hakal) the ALL.

Heh-Malkah is המלך, the King, and the King is Tiphareth, and Tiphareth תפארת is 1081. And 1081 reduces to (the seed) 10, which is both

Malkuth and Yod.

Malkuth is the synthesis of all the Sephiroth, and that *Guph* (89) must be understood not only as of the human body but also as the substance from which all bodies are formed. This substance is One, though it is given a masculine Divine name *Adonai Melek*, and two feminine titles, *Kallah* and *Malkah*. See *C.26*, 155, 55, 95, 89.

שקוץ *shiqqootz*. disgusting, filthy, an abomination, an idol [the detestable thing] in Daniel 12:11. Referring to Malkuth, the sphere of physical sensation that is apparently separated from the Sephiroth above Malkuth is the lowest and most external Sephirah. When man's consciousness is fixed on Malkuth, he is an idolater to exclude higher, more interior objects of perception. For in Malkuth are but the projected images of inner states of being; and to worship the image, to trust in appearances, is idolatry.

לויתן *Leviathan*. The dark serpent, Dragon, the great serpent of the darkness, of the deep-the Great Devourer. Used as a symbol for Egypt [Psalm 74:14, Isaiah 27:1]. In these two passages, Leviathan is a symbol of a symbol. Egypt represents the darkness of the physical plane and the earth as the great grave swallows generation after generation of human bodies. He symbolizes the Cosmic Antagonist; he is the physical plane as it appears to the ignorant. Yet when we understand this plane, the Dark Antagonist is seen to be the perfect order of the Kingdom. Without spiritual understanding and knowledge that there are realities beyond the physical plane, Malkuth, the sphere of the physical sensation behind the elemental forces, is interpreted too grossly. When a personality is extremely receptive to others' thoughts and errors, this misinterpretation can lead to the self-undoing. Properly understood, the dark antagonist is seen to be the perfect order or kingdom. In India, Capricorn (Ayin) is Makara (Dragon or sea-monster), closely related to Leviathan. In Sanskrit, its literal meaning is "five-handed" or "five-sided," related to the pentagram, one of the symbols for Mars (Exalted in Capricorn, where the world-savior is born). Related to Tiamat of Babylonian mythology. In

Hebrew folk-lore, Leviathan was supposed to be the cause of eclipses of the sun and moon by throwing its fold around them [Job 41:1]. See 708, 358, 130, 854.

I. Leviathan is the sea monster in Job: "Can you draw out Leviathan with a hook?" The letter Tzaddi is the fish-hook and is associated with meditation, and the sea is Binah, the great ocean of the universal subconsciousness. Leviathan is the great ocean of power of subconsciousness. Thus this passage can be interpreted as, "Can you draw out the power of Malkuth by the power of meditation?"

את המים *eth hamem*. essence of the waters.

את המלך *eth ha-melek*. essence of the king.

צרור *tzeror*. a small bundle; a little stone, pebble; package, bag, pouch. *Tzeror* refers to the kingdom's powers are concentrated in a small point, the center of each man's experience. Malkuth is in Kether and Kether in Malkuth, or that the kingdom or manifestation of the Life-power is present in the primal will, and the primal will is present in the kingdom. The *small point* (554) is one of the names for Kether, represents the same though as *Tzeror*, a small bundle. It is an indication that the object of the practical occultist quest is the central reality of his personality, which is identical to the Primal Will (Kether). It is the greatest of the great, yet it is also the smallest of the small. It is the cause of all activity, and yet it is perpetually at rest. It expands throughout infinity yet is also focused on a single point.

צרור *tzahroor*. bound up, tied; preserved; pebble. The physical plane must be understood as the plane wherein forces from higher levels are bound up or preserved in physical form.

אבן בית אל *Ehben Beth-el*. The stone of God's House. This is the stone described in the story of Jacob's dream (Genesis 28:11, 19). Tradition identifies it with the stone in the British coronation chair, now in Westminster abbey. Beth-el is the "house of the Lord." The

consciousness of the Lord's house is aware of the indwelling presence in physical forms. Note that Jacob named the place of his dream אל ההואבית which may be surmised as being "He, the house of El." It is translated "that" in the Jewish translation. Yet הוא is a name of God (Kether). See 443, 460.

הדם הוא הנפש *ha-dam hu ha-nefesh*. blood is the life [Deuteronomy 12:23]. Note that in this passage נפש is the same animal consciousness, which has its special seat in Yesod. This passage goes on to say, ".. thou shall pour it [blood] upon the earth as water." The water of consciousness is working to raise lower forms to higher. There are important alchemical considerations: i.e., occult properties of the blood. See 44 and 430.

חזות לילה *chahzooth layelah*. night vision, night revelation. חזות also means covenant.

כר עור *kar or*. Lambskin. A Mason's apron is lambskin. See 220 and Key 18.

שלום יהיה לכם *sholam yehiyeh lah-kam*. You will have peace [Jeremiah 4:10]. Peace (shalom) comes when "the kingdom of spirit is embodied in my flesh" (and blood).

ותמים *ve-thummin*. and perfections. The affirmation of the perfect cosmic order, proceeding from the divine self-impartation or beneficence represented by Chesed or Jupiter, manifested in Malkuth.

μονογενης. monogenohs. one-begotten; alone-born. Closely refers to Jesus. See 888.

Pater, filius, spiritus sanctus, divina natura, Deus (Lt). Father, Son, Holy Spirit, Divine Nature, God [Secret Symbols page 30]. These words are brought together as the text explaining a diagram. This diagram is a radiant, golden circle enclosing a down-pointing equilateral triangle. Inside the triangle is written the word *Deus*. Above the triangle, in the circle, are the words *Divina Natura*. Outside the circle, the three points of the triangle are the words: *Pater*, at the left upper point, *filius*, at the right upper point, and *spiritua sanctus* at the lower point.

תאומים *teomim*. Twins; Gemini. It connects the tribe of Simeon, not only because in Genesis 49:5 Simeon and Levi are coupled together, but also because the Talmud says the standard of Simeon bore a picture of the city Shechem. This was a Rebus, referring to the basic meaning of the word שכם, "shoulders," or "shoulder-blades." According to astrology, Gemini governs the shoulders.

I. Genesis 38:27: "And it came to pass in the time of her travail, that, behold, twins were in her womb."

II. The twins, ascribed to זין, are the "two apples" of the 7th confirmation of the beard of Macroprospus. Zain connects בינה to תפארת and 67, בינה = זין. The 2 apples equal מים חיים = תפוחי מקור, which add to 504, the value of דרש, "to seek." The two apples are the fountain of the Water of Life. They are correctly described as twins. דין, Din and דני, Doni, are the twin Intelligences. See 64.

III. I.R.Q. Para. 238: "Tradition: A most secret thing is this disposition of the beard. The secret is it and hidden; hidden, yet not hidden; concealed, yet not concealed in its dispositions; known, yet unknown."

IV. I.R.Q. Para. 408: "The 7th conformation is that wherein the hair is wanting, and there appear two apples in the circles of fragrance, fair and beautiful of aspect."

אמונת *omonath*. trade, handicraft (later Hebrew). Gemini rules the hands and is connected with manual dexterity.

Rosenroth in K.D.L.C.K. (p.123) links this word to Binah when it has the meaning of firmness (*firmitatis*) and with Malkuth when it pertains to faith (*fides*). He also translates it as truth (*veritas*).

מלאכתו *melaketo*. His work Genesis 2:2: "and he rested on the 7th day from all his work which he had made." The connection between work and hands should be apparent; this the work of discrimination [Gemini, Key 6] and the "hand" is also Yod. See 466, 513, 67.

אומנת *aomanth*. Nurse or *nutrix*, according to Rosenroth in K.D.L.C.K. (p.57), who links this word to אמנת, which as the same meaning. It is applied to Malkuth because it makes all things grow, and also the Binah as Naomi was thus called by Ruth, for Naomi is Binah as Ruth is in Malkuth. See 491.

איש בן אדם מלך *Ish Ben-Adam Melek*. Man, Son of Man, King. The Divine Soul, Neshamah, and Ruach are not two, but ONE, Man, Son of MAN, King and this is the royal Presence we call "The Dweller in the Heart." This perfect law has two fundamental precepts: 1. Thou shall love the Lord your God with all your heart, and with all your mind, and with all your strength; 2. Thou shall love your neighbor as thyself. As your SELF, as the ONE EGO dwelling "among" us because that ONE EGO also dwells "within" us.

בית אלהים *Beth Elohim*. House of God.

היכל זכות *Hekel Zakoth*. Palace of Merit, purity, innocence, justice. Briatic palace (heaven) of Geburah. The creative plane for divine will-Geburah is the sphere of Mars, here expressed in its essential purity and perfect Justice. This is the basis of the pillar of fire and secret to attainment [Corresponds with the 5 of Cups]. See 65.

אמרו צדיק כי טוב *emayu tzaddik ki-tov*. Say of the righteous one that he is good (i.e., that it shall be well with him). Isaiah 3:10: "Say of the righteous, that it shall be well with him: for they shall eat the fruit of their doings." The "righteous" one dwells in the house of God, for he has eaten of the fruit, which is the "pillar of fire," in the microcosm. The Zohar [I:30B, p.116] comments: "These three letters [טוב tov, good, i.e., Teth representing the ninth grade, wisdom, Vav, the heaves, and Beth, the two worlds] were afterward combined to signify 'the righteous one (Zaddik) of the world," as it is written, 'say of the righteous one that he is good' because the supernal radiance is contained therein."

שבילי עולם *shebily olahm*. paths of old, ancient paths. In Jeremiah 18:15: "Yet my people have forsaken me and have burned incense to vanity and have stumbled in their ways, and have departed from the ancient paths to walk in a way which was not trodden." see 362.

יפתח *Jephthah*. "He [God] opens"; one of the major (8th) judges of Israel. See Judges 12:7.

499 (prime)

צבאות *tzabaoth*. Armies (hence, multiplicity). With different pointing: busy, arduous, 'hosts.' See Leviticus 20:9.

תליא אהבים *cerva amorum*. A loving doe. In Proverbs 5:19: "A loving doe, a graceful dear-may her breasts satisfy you always, may you ever be captivated by her loved." K.D.L.C.K. (p.77) links this phrase to Malkuth when the glorious horns of Hod are placed above it.

הצפרדעים the frogs. See Exodus 7:29.

περγαμος. *Peregamos*. A celebrated city of Asia Minor, famous for its library. Connected as one of the 7 churches or congregations of Asia (השיה, the physical plane) with the inner planetary center of Jupiter. Spelled περγαμω (1029) in Revelation 2:12: "And by the messenger of the congregation in Pergamos write: "These things say the who has the sharp two-edged broad sword; (13) I know here thou dwells-where the throne of the adversary is; and yet to you firmly retains my name; and thou did not deny my faith even in the days in which Antipas was my witness, my faithful one, who was killed among you, where the adversary dwells."

I. "Pergamos stands for the manipuraka chakra, the solar plexus, which is the chief center of the sympathetic nervous system, and the seat of the eputhumetic nature-the Dragon, or Satanas, the Adversary of the Logos... 'Such then, is the nature of the liver, such its function and place, as said, formed fro the sake of second-sight.' This, of course, is the faculty of the mantis, or individual gifted with 'second-sight'; and this is also the 'witness Antipas,' who has inded been shail by those who have lost even this psychic function of the liver, as well as the intuition of the intellectual nature. ANTI-ΠA-E is simply mantis disguised by having its initial M converted into ΠA (pa) and anagrammatically transposed. To solve the puzzle, it is only necessary to combine the letters π and A, forming IAI, which when inverted makes a passable M-and incidentally shows why 'eminent scholars' have failed to find a satisfactory Greek derivation for the word or any historical record of the supposed 'Martyr.'" [Pryse, 1965, pp. 101-102.]

Recall that חסד Chesed, the sphere of Jupiter, is the cosmic Moon or memory and that Kaph, the Hebrew letter of Jupiter, is assigned to the liver and the solar plexus, the center of psychic activity. See 1029 (Greek), 20, 100, 72, 194, 555 (Greek); 980, 798, 1105, 570, 1096, 151 (Greek).

Section 5

Numbers 500 - 599

500

I. (4 x 5 x 5 x 5) or 2^2 x 5^3

II. ך Final Kaph. See 20.

נתן *Nathan*. to give.

פרו ורון *peru u-renu*. be fruitful and multiply.

שר *sar*. master, prince, head, chief, noble, ruler, official, captain, general, prefect. Isaiah 9:6: "For unto us a child is born, unto us a son is given: and the government shall be upon his shoulder: and his name shall be called Wonderful, counselor, the mighty God, the everlasting father, the prince of peace." With different pointing *shor*, *shar*: navel, navel-string (seat of the Mars force); health, strength. See 576, 911 (Greek), 4000, 376.

תנים *tannim*. whale (Ezekiel 32:2); jackals, wild beasts.

יהוה דעת *yehaueh daath*. shows knowledge (Psalm 19:2).

כפת *kawfath*. to tie, bind, to fetter. Alchemical gold is fettered in the heart until its liberation, with different pointing *kopeth*: block of wood; lump of dough.

תימן *Teman* "which is on the right hand"; an important district, apparently in the north part of Edom in Ezekiel 25:13. "This is what the Sovereign Lord says: 'I will stretch out my hand against Edom and kill its men and their animals. I will lay it waste, and from Teman to Dedan, they will fall by the sword. Recall that Edom [51] signifies unbalanced force. A Duke of Edom [Crowley, 1977, p. 49]; Godwin associates with Hod. See Genesis 36:11.

כתף back. Zechariah 7:11: "But they refused to pay attention; stubbornly they turned their backs and stopped up their ears." With different pointing *kitawph*: to carry on the shoulder; *kahtawph*: porter.

שלקע *Shalicu*. The Sentinel of the 31st Path (Tunnel) of Shin on the Inverse Tree of Life.

I. The 31st tunnel is under the dominion of Shalicu. The triple tongue of flame (*shin*, ש) is attributed to Path 31, and this is reflected into the abyss in the form of the inverted trident of Chozzar (a form of Choronzon and an emblem of Atlantean magick). This is the path of Evocation and Pyromancy *via* the secret fire-tongue that manifests in the tunnel of Shalicu in the form of Choronzon. As it is written in the grimoire, the Pyramid was built to complete the Initiation.

The number of Shalicu is 500, which is the number of שר, meaning 'Prince, SORAH, 'principal,' from the Egyptian *Ser*, 'chief' or 'head,' whence the English 'sir.' Shalicu is the prince of the Qliphoth in his form of the archdevil Choronzon who reigns within this tunnel and who conveys the most secret *Kala*, which is known as The Aeon. This *Kala* flows from the power-zone of Mercury to that of the earth. Therefore, this tunnel is of prime importance in that it extends to earth the Choronzonic vibrations of Daath, via Mercury.

תנן, 'to extend,' also has the number 500. The attribution is confirmed by תנים, meaning 'wild beasts of the desert.' תנים approximates to the Egyptian word *tenemi*, which means 'make to recoil.' The residents of this tunnel are the ravenous beasts of the Desert of Set, and they repulse all efforts to gain access to the pylon of Daath. 500 is also the number of מתני, 'the loins,' which has affinities with the Sanskrit word *maithuna*, signifying 'coupling,' 'sexual congress.' תנים
The fire of this path is the fire of Set, which is the sexual heat typified by the beasts that lurk on the threshold of Daath before the Veil of the Abyss. The Pyre or Pyramid, and the Fire, are identical; hence the pyramid is a symbol of Set and the Star Sothis.

The gods attributed to the 31st *Kala* are Vulcan and Pluto, twin aspects of Hades (its fiery and dark aspects). Pluto is a form of the Cerberus or dog-headed beast that guards the Gates of the Abyss.

The sigil of Shalicu shows the tomb or plaque of Christain Rosencreutz that announces the fact of death, judgment, and resurrection. These comprise the threefold formula of Crossing the Abyss via the crucifixion or passage from life to death. The idea of judgment denotes the purgation and refinement of the gross body (the mummy) and its preparation for the crossing over to Amenta. This is adumbrated in the alchemical formula of the Black Dragon, which symbolizes the appearance of the First Matter (Being) in its corrupt or unregenerate state (ego) before its projection as the Ultimate *Kala* (medicine).

The magical *siddhi* of Path 31 is Transformation, Invisibility, or Disappearance; the disappearance of the world of appearances (interpreted in terms of objective existence, is the transformation of the gross body into its ethereal essence).

The typical disease ascribed to Path 31 is Fever, which is associated with heat or fire and culminates in the tunnel of Shalicu as Death and/or Full Insanity.

The Last judgment was the title given to the Tarot Trump, which showed the dead rising from their tombs. The symbolism of this trump, revised per New Aeon doctrine, is now entitled *The Aeon*, and it is in the form of the Child that the resurrected spirit arises from the darkness of Amenta. However, the great mystery is that this child is feminine: the daughter, not the son. She is shadowed forth in the imagery of the fabulous bird, ציצ״ש, which denotes the feathered or fledged bird (i.e., the pubescent female), the bird of qabalistic legend. Its number is 500. It is the ultimate symbol of the Aeon of Maat as adumbrated in the Dark Doctrine of *Ma Ayon*.

The 31st Path is divided between Fire and Spirit's powers, and the 32nd and final path are divided between the powers of Earth and Saturn. In the 31st tunnel, Fire and Spirit's powers resume the Fire Snake formula, Spirit/Matter in the macrocosm and Choronzon/Woman in the microcosm. In other words, the essential forces of darkness (matter) are activated in the macrocosm by the element of Spirit. In the microcosm, they manifest in the woman who embodies the Fire Snake [i.e., the Beast's initiated Priestess, Shugal-Choronzon].

To this *Kala* 31, the Red Poppy, Hibiscus, or China Rose, are attributed, for these flowers are symbolic of the Scarlet Woman -- Babalon - who incarnates the cosmic energies of the Fire-Snake. These are symbolized by the Fire Opal, which exudes as a precious stone from her vulva, and by the Pyramid of Set, the cosmic phallic flame that consumes it utterly with its triple fire-tongue. [Grant, 1994, pp. 248-252.]

εαδυα *enduna*. Vestments. In Matthew 28:3: "And his appearance was like lightning, and his vestments white as snow." And in Matthew 22:11, 12: "Now the king having entered to view the guest, saw there a man not clothed with a wedding garment; and he says to him, 'Friend, how camest thou here, not having a wedding garment? And he was struck speechless." The garment is the body of light, the 'vestments' of the angel. See 2698, 1014, 1549 and Matthew 3:4.

ο αριθμος. *ho arithmos*. The numbers. Acts 4:4: "But many of those having heard the word believed; and the number of the men became about 5,000. See 666 and Acts 6:7, Romans 9:27 and Revelation 15:2.

Μανασσον. *Manasseh*. "Causing to forget." Septuagint translation of מנשה (395) in Genesis 49:20. Connected with Aquarius and with alchemical dissolution.

אשר *Asher*. A tribe of Israel, associated with Libra and alchemical sublimation [Genesis 49:20]. With different pointing: straight, level, prosperous, happy, blessed. Sublimation involves the elevation or exaltation of undesirable natural trends or impulses, by education or conscious effort, into some more desirable type of behavior or activity. It includes eliminating the mental picture of future action, every detail not wished to see realized, whatever wastes power. Libra governs the kidneys-organs of elimination, which maintain the chemical balance of the blood. Breath control is also essential to the work of sublimation. See 570, 331, 95, 30, 54.

אשר *esher*. as a pronoun and conjunction: who, which, that, as for regarding. Translated "that" in Exodus 3:14: "I am that I am."

The Zohar says (I, p.155) "The truth is that Heh (Binah) is called אשרה, Ashera (Venus) after the name of its spouse *esher*." Thus אשר refers to Yod or אב, which is חכמה.

אשר *eyshar*. to be guided. Note the root idea of the word למד Lamed, which means "ox-goad" and "to teach." Pronounced *ishsheyr*, this word means: loan, guide, to be lead, to walk straight; to set right, strengthen, to confirm, verify; to be made happy, to praise. See Book of Tokens, Lamed.

אשר *eisher*. relative pronoun (without distinction of number or gender). With different pointing: the name of the cedar tree. The feminine אשרה means happiness, happy, and is the Biblical name of the Phoenician Goddess of Fortune (Syrian עשתרת [1 Kings 11:5], Ashtoreth or Astarte, who is Venus. Compare with Jacob's blessing in Genesis 49:20: "Out of Asher his bread shall be fat, and he shall yield royal dainties." מעדנים (dainties) is derived from עדן Eden (see Key 3). Sustenance, alimentation (about the roundness of a well-fed body). In the same text, fat is שמן oily, olive oil, and the occult meaning of this also relates to Venus, to whom the olive was sacred. See the dove and olive branch in the story of Noah. "Royal dainties" is equal to 214, the number of רוח, Ruach or Air, the Libra element ruled by Venus.

שאר *shawar*. to remain, be left. With different pointing *sheawr*: remnant; rest, remainder. Isaiah 10:21, 22: "The remnant shall return, even the remnant of Jacob, unto the might God. For though your people Israel be as the sand of the sea, yet a remnant of them shall return: the consumption decreed shall overflow with righteousness." See Isaiah 4:3 and Daniel 7:7.

שאר *sheayer*. flesh, the body; blood relation, kinsman. True alchemy is the embodiment of spirit (Shin) as Mercury (Aleph = Uranus, a higher octave of Mercury) into the blood, which regenerates the heart (Resh). See Leviticus 18:6.

שאר *seore*. leaven, yeast; fermentation, swelling sustenance, alimentation (about the well-fed body's roundness). Compare the Jacobs blessing: "out of Asher-his bread shall be fat, and he shall yield royal dainties." Remember that corn, wine and oil are directly associated with weighing and measuring the third seal's symbolism, according to Revelation 6:6. "And I heard a voice amid the 4 beasts say, a measure of wheat for a penny, and three measures of barley for a penny; and see thou hurt not the oil and the wine." Fermentation is Capricorn, where Mars is exalted (see notes on Nun, the night house of Mars in the Book of Tokens). Nun means "to sprout," like yeast. Also, with different vowel points: to be hot, to ferment. See Exodus 12:15.

אל גנת אגוז *el-ginnath agoz*. the garden of nuts [Song of Solomon 6:11]. According to the Zohar, this refers to Yesod, "seed principle," which is the clue to the inner meaning. See 1125.

עיר הכר *or ha-car*. skin of a lamb.

קו השמים *qav ha-shamayin*. The rule of heaven.

ראש *rosh*. head; chief, principal. With different pointing: beginning, choicest, best, division, company.

רצון הקדום *Rawtzone ha-qahdome*. the Primal Will.

שין הקדום *shane ha-olayl*. urine of the infant or urine of the babe. This is Raymond Lully's name for the alchemical first matter. Note that שין are the letters of the element Fire, or Shin (360). Lully spells it also נער שין הנער. It also means "boy, lad, youth; servant, retainer; scattering, scattered one. See the "boy" pictured in Key 20 (Shin). Here is another translation might be: "fire of the boy" or "infant fire" see 148, 74, 141, 631 685, 320.

שכינה עילאה *Shekinah Ilahah*. The Superior Shekinah. A name applied by Qabalist to Binah.

תמונה *temunah*. appearance, form; image, likeness, shape.

החכמה תחיה *ha-chokmah techayeah*. wisdom gives life. In Ecclesiastes 7:12: "For wisdom is a defense, and money is a defense: but the excellency of knowledge is, that wisdom gives life to them that have it." Wisdom is the Life-force, Chaiah in Chokmah. See 23, 78.

אתנים *athenim*. strong, robust (ones). Those in whom the life-force has sprouted as divine volition (Geburah, sphere of Mars). They are regulated by balance. See K.D.L.C.K. (p., 178).

שאר *Sar*. Goetia demon #70 by night of the 1st decan of Pisces. See 259 & Appendix 11.

Goetia: "He is a mighty prince, and powerful, under AMAYMON, King of the East. He appears in the form of a beautiful man, riding upon a winged horse. His office is to go and come, and to bring abundance to things to pass on a sudden, and to carry or re-carry anything whither thou would have it to go, or whence thou would have it from. He can pass over the whole earth in the twinkling of an eye. He gives a true relation of sorts of theft, treasure hid, and many other things. He is of an indifferent good nature and is willing to do anything which the Exorcist desires. He governs 26 Legions of Spirits." [Mathers, 1995,

p. 65]

דצך עדש באחב *detzak adhash beachab*. The 10 plagues of Egypt;: a Notariqon, formed by taking the first letter of each word. See פגן plague. See 981.

אך *ak*. but, only, surely, indeed, again, once more [Kaph = 500, see 21]

γραμματεια. *grammateia*. lettering, use of letters.

Ιασπις. *Jaspis*. A precious stone; jasper. The first foundation of the holy city. See Revelations 21:19.

ο ανομος. *Ho anomos*. The lawless one.

ο πλανος. *ho planos*. The deceiver, anti-Christ [John 2:7].

το παν. *to pan*. The all, the whole. This is the neuter of πας all (Latin *omnia*). Neuter implies a combination of male and female principles, thus relating the balance represented by Lamed and Libra to the whole picture. See 46 (Lt)

502

בתק *bawtahq*. to cut asunder, to thrust through. In Ezekiel 16:40: "They shall also bring up a company against thee, and they shall stone thee with stones, and thrust thee through [ובתקוך] with their swords." Note that 502 reduces to 7, the value of Zain, the sword of discrimination. See 7, 67.

בשר *biser*. to bear or bring good tidings. Isaiah 40:27: "The first shall say to Zion, behold, behold them: and I will give to Jerusalem one that brings good tidings."

בשר *bawsar*. flesh, meat; kindred; pulp of fruit. In 1 Chronicles 11:1: "Then all Israel gathered themselves to David unto Hebron, saying, behold, we are your bone and your flesh." Also, in Genesis 2:21: "So the Lord God caused a deep sleep to fall upon Adam, and he slept, and he took one of his ribs and closed up the place with flesh in its stead." see 14, 685, 783.

I. This word is related to the alchemical metal Iron. *Aesch Mezareph*: "And this is that mystical thing, which is written in Daniel 7:5: "And behold another Beast, a second like unto a Bear, stood on its one side, and it had three ribs standing out in his mouth, between his teeth; and thus they said unto it, 'Arise, eat much flesh.'" The Meaning is that to constitute the Metallic Kingdom, in the second place, Iron is to be taken; in whose Mouth or Opening (which comes to pass in an Earthen Vessel) a three-fold Scoria is thrust out, from within its whitish Nature.

Let him eat *batsar*, i.e. Flesh, whose lesser Number is 7 [502 = 5 + 2 = 7], that is Puk [פוך, 106 = 7], that is Stibium [i.e. antimony], whose lesser number is like manner 7.

And indeed much Flesh, because the proportion of this, is greater than of that; and indeed such a proportion as Puk, that is 106, bears to Barzel 239; such shall be the proportions of Iron to Antimony [i.e., three must be nearly two and a half times as much antinomy as iron].

But understand the *Flesh of the Lion*, which is the first Animal; whose *Eagles Wings*, and so much as is very Volatile in him, shall be *drawn out*, and it shall be *lifted up*, and by purifying be separated from its *Earth* or Scoria: And it will stand *on its Feet*; that is, shall be its Consistency, in a Cone; *like a Man* erect and with a shining Countenance; like Moses. For Enos [אנש] and Moses [מושה] in full writing by Gematria each give 351. And the Heart of Iron [for the heart Leb [לב] and Iron Barzel [ברזל, 239] in their least number both give 5], (Mineral), i.e., the Tiphareth of Man Mineral shall be given to." [Westcott, 1997, p. 24]

II. "And YAHWEH Elohim caused a profound and sympathetic sleep to fall upon Adam (universal man), and he slept; and He broke from the unity, one of his involutions (exterior envelope, feminine principle) and shaped with

form and corporeal beauty, its original inferiority (weakness). [d'Olivet, 1976, p. 315.]

He comments בשר, *shape and corporal-beauty...* The word בשר also demands all of our attention... The Hellenist translators, always restricted to the material meaning, have rendered it by σαρε [361], a common word that Saint Jerome has copied in 'caro,' the flesh. Now שר or שור is a Hebraic root which contains in itself all ideas of movement toward consistency, corporeity, elementary form and physical force, as is sufficiently denoted by the signs of which it is composed. The sign of interior activity ב governs this same root, and constitutes the verb בשור which always signifies *to inform; to announce a thing, to bring glad tidings*; as is proved by the Arabic which adds to this signification, that of showing a pleasant physiognomy, and of pleasing by its beauty. If בשר designates the flesh, among the vulgar, it has been only by a shocking abuse and a continuation of that unfortunate inclination that the Jews had of restricting and materializing everything. It signified first, *form, configuration, exterior appearance, corporeal beauty, animal substance*. The Chaldeans deduced from it all ideas relative to exterior forms, ideas more or less agreeable according to the point of view under which they considered these forms. Thus, for example, they understood by the nominal בסר the action of informing, announcing, evangelizing, preaching, scrutinizing, disdaining, scorning etc." [ibid., pp. 89-90.]

III. The Zohar [I:28A, 48B] comments: "The words 'and the Lord God built the side,' can also be applied to Moses, insofar as he is built from the side of Chesed (kindness). 'And Moses both were combined. This time bone of my bone and flesh of my flesh. This is said of the shekinah, the betrothed maiden, by the central column, as though to say, 'I know that this is bone of my bone and flesh of my flesh; so this of a surety shall be called woman, from the supernal realm, which his mother, for she was taken from the realm of the father, which is Yod.' And as with the central column, so with Moses below. At that time, every Israelite will find his twin soul... (p.108). And the Lord God built (*vayiven*) the side he had taken from the man, etc. Said Rabbi Simeon: 'It is written, 'God understands the way thereof, and he knows the place thereof' [Job 28:23]. This verse may be taken in many ways. One is that the word 'understood' (hevin) has the same sense as vayiven in the second chapter of Genesis. Hence the 'side' here is the oral law, which forms a 'way' as it is written 'who makes a way in the sea' [Isaiah 43:16]. Similarly, 'place' here can be interpreted as written law, a source of knowledge. The double name 'Lord God' is used to show that it competed in all details. Hence it is called both Chokmah (wisdom) and Binah (understanding). 'The side' (zela) is the unclear mirror, as it is written 'they rejoiced at my halting (be-zal) and gathered together' [Psalm 35:15]. 'Which he took from the man': because the oral law issued from the written Torah, into a woman: to be linked with the flame of the left side, because the Torah was given from the side of Geburah. Further, Ishah (woman) may be analyzed into אשה (Fire of Heh), signifying the union of the two." (pp.153-154).

שבר *shawbahr*. to break, destroy, tear down, mangle, quench. Isaiah 42:3: "A bruised reed shall he not break, and a flickering lamp he shall not extinguish; he shall truly bring forth judgment." And in Psalm 69:20: "O thou, hear my broken heart and bind it; I looked for some to take pity, but there was none, and for comforters, but I found none."

בך *be-kaw*. in thee, with thee. Kaph = 500. See 22.

503 (prime)

בית האלהים *Beth-ha-Elohim*. The House of God [Elohim]. An ancient title of Key 16. Beth (בית) is the 12th Path descending from Kether to Binah. ha-Elohim adds to 91, the number of אמן (Amen). The word Elohim itself is the divine name attributed to Binah. In 1 Corinthians 6:19, the Tower of Key 16 may be regarded as a symbol for the human body. It is made of clay bricks, and the Hebrew for brick is *Levanah* (Moon, 87), designated to Yesod (80), associated with the reproductive organs of the Grand Man (Tree of Life). See 91, 899, 412.

רגש *rawgash*. to rage, to be violent; to come together, to assemble (as a mob). This last meaning, though it applies more particularly to an angry, or even riotous assemblage, is closely related to the Greek original for our word "church, " for ekklesia means "an assembly, a congregation." Perhaps the connection is even closer than appears at first, for the history of religion makes it only too clear that churches have on many occasions been scenes of violence and of unseemly exuberance of the mob spirit. The underlying quality of group consciousness is emotional unity-mob spirit can erupt into violence as well as harmony. See 294.

אבן הזחלת *ehben ha-zoheleth*. stone of the serpent.

גרש *gawrash*. from a primitive root meaning: to drive out from a possession; especially to expatriate or divorce, drive away, thrust out [Strong's Bible dictionary], cast out; to expel, to put forth fruit. Directly related to the Mars-force attributed to Key 16 and the letter Peh. It is the active principle in reproduction (Mars presides over the fertility of the fields and herds "to put forth fruit," and lighting was supposed to make fields fertile.) As a noun: "a fruit, a product of the earth, produce." Gimel is the letter of the Moon, Resh of the Sun and Shin the Hindu Prana, the alchemical Fire and Quintessence. It symbolizes that most precious fruit, the stone of the Wise (אבן), compounded by the moon, sun and Fire from elements composing the Earth. "the cup of Stolistes" [Crowley, 1977, p. 50]. See 703.

שגר *sheger*. what is brought forth, increase (of cattle). See Exodus 13:12 and Deuteronomy 7:13.

ותוצא and brought forth, "and-she [the land]-produced." In Genesis 1:12: "The land produces vegetation: plants bearing seed according to their kinds and trees bearing fruit with seed in it according to their kinds. And God saw that it was good."

and-it-did-shoot-out.... It is the verb אויץ, *to come forth, to proceed, to be born*, used according to the executive form, in future tense made past by the convertible sign. I beg the reader to observe here again this hieroglyphic expression. God speaks in the future, and his expression repeated, is turned suddenly to the past. Let us examine this important verb. The first which offers itself is the sign צ, expressing every terminative movement, every conclusion, every end. Its proper and natural place is at the end of words: thence the roots אצ or הצ, in Arabic containing every idea of corporeal bounds and limits, of repressing and concluding force, or term. But if, instead of terminating the words, the sign begins them; then, far from arresting the forms, it pushes them, the contrary, toward the goal of which it is itself the symbol: thence, the opposed roots צא, in Syriac and Arabic, whose idea is, leaving the bounds, breaking the shackles of the body, coming outside, being born. From this last root, verbalized by the initial adjunction י, the verb which is the subject of this note is derived. It signifies *to appear, to come outside by a movement of propagation*, as is demonstrated unquestionable, by the substantive nouns which are derived therefrom, ציא *a son*, and צאצא *a numerous progeny*." [d'Olivet, 1976, pp. 43-44.]

504

דרש *dehrash, dawrash*. To seek or ask for; consult, inquire of. 2 Chronicles 17:4: "After the Lord God of his father did he seek, and walked in his commandments, and not after the doings of Israel." With different pointing: to ask for, demand, require, to seek with care, care for, be concerned, to seek with the application, study, follow, practice; to expound, explain, interpret; to teach, lecture, preach.

שדר *shedar*. to exert oneself, to strive. Daniel 6:14: "Then the king, when he heard these words, was very much grieved, and made up his mind to deliver Daniel; and he strove (labored) till the going down of the sun to deliver him."

יהיה דעת *yehaueh da'ath*. reveals or displays forth knowledge. Psalm 19:2: "Day after day, they pour forth speech; night after night, they display knowledge." This is directly associated with Peh,

the mouth as the organ of Speech. Note that "Night" is the name for darkness -Binah, the mother. The womb of night brings froth the day. The night is associated with generation and reproduction, and the Hebrew word da'ath is known to mean what the Bible intimates when it says, "And Adam know his wife, and she conceived." see 84, 474, 683, 688, 475, 1163.

מקור מים חיים *mahqohr mem chaiim*. Source (or fountain) of the waters of life. Referring to the name *Pau*, פעב, ("brightness," 156) as the alchemical king's city, Tiphareth. *Aesch Mezareph*: "Nor will you err, if you shall attribute to it another special name, for it may be called Mekor Mayim Chaiim, that is, a Fountain of Living Water. For, from this Water, the King is enlivened, that he may give Life to all Metals and Living Things." [Westcott, 1997, p. 40]

ולילה בעמוד אש "and by night in a pillar of fire. Exodus 13:21: "And the Lord went before them by day in a pillar of cloud, to guide them on their way; and by night in a pillar of fire, to give them light, so that they could travel by day or night." see 498, 130.

תפיחי *tehpukhiy*. apples; an apple tree.

505

The sum of any row, column or diagonal of a 10 x 10 magic square. See Appendix 8.

שרה *Sarah*. Princess, noble lady; Sarah, wife of Abraham ("Father of many nations, of a multitude"). She is called the "mother" of the true Israel in Isaiah 51:2: "Look unto Abraham, your father, and unto Sarah, that bare you: for I called him alone, and blessed him, and increased him." Genesis 11:29: "and Abram and Nahor took them wives: the name of Abram's wife was Sarai..." Rosenroth in K.D.L.C.K. (p.725) says, "*Principissa* is Malkuth when she is united with her husband Chesed; for Abraham was the husband of Sarah."

שרה *shawrah*. to let loose, to send forth, set free;

to soak, steep in water, with different pointing *sherah*: chain, bracelet.

את חניכו *eth haeniykawyu*. his trained servants, trained men. Genesis 14:14: "And when Abram heard that his relative had been taken captive, he called out the 318 trained men born in his household and went in pursuit as far as Dan" Case says חניך (a trained person, apprentice) means "initiated." See 88, 94, 2308.

רשה *rasha*. to be able; to have left. The consequence of initiation.

506

אשרה *Asherah*. happiness; Canaanite goddess; sacred tree or pole. Asherah is translated "grove" in the authorized version of the Old Testament. It is the name of a Goddess worshiped under the form of a pillar. In later Judaism identified with Ashtoreth, or Astarte, the Semitic equivalent of Venus. This establishes a link with other attributions of the 16th Path, particularly with the sign Taurus, ruled by Venus. The Zohar connects *Asherah* with Binah; it is clear that Key 5 in Tarot is a symbol of the manifestation of the Divine Understanding-intuition's power is attributed to Binah.

I. "*Asherah*- Phoenician goddess of prosperity." [Godwin. 1999, p. 569.] see 12, 158, 331.

II. "The truth is that Heh (Binah the Mother) is called הרשא Ashera, after the name of its spouse אשר, Asher." The Zohar [I, p.55]

III. Case: "It was in the wilderness of Shur that the Lord showed a certain tree to Moses that made the bitter waters of a well sweet. At the same well in the wilderness of Shur, according to Genesis 16:7, the Angel of the Lord found Hagar (הגר, fugitive) the Egyptian wife of Abraham." see 245, 208, 441.

שור *shor*. ox, bull; In later Hebrew Taurus. This agrees with the Talmudic assertion that the standard of Ephraim was a Bullock (331). There is a correlation between this sign and the sense of hearing. With different pointing: *shoor*: to look, regard, behold; to lie in wait, lurk; to journey, travel. As a masculine noun, same pointing, wall, watcher.

ושר The 32nd Shem ha-Mephorash, short form. See 521 & Appendix 10.

פרצופים *partzuphim*. persons. Faces.

כפות *kapoth*. The palms of the hands, the handle of anything; palm-branches, as curved. This word's singular form is spelled with the same letters, Kaph and Peh, which spell a word meaning rock or stone, כף, Kafe. This word is the origin of the name Kephas or Cephas, given to Peter, and in the later Hebrew, כפות had almost the exact sound of Kephas. Note here that Kaph (כף), as a letter, represents the cycles of recurrent activity (Key 10). It is upon an intuitive knowledge of these cycles that ageless wisdom largely depends.

Furthermore, it is an ancient belief that every man's unique place in the world cycles may be read from his palms' lines. He, whose grasp of eternal principles is strong, can stand firm as a rock. See 1196, 729.

507

בעלי השמים *Daali ha-shamaim*. Masters of the heavens, astrologers. A term used to describe the Illuminati or adepts-those "new creatures" who have become masters of their own interior stars is a consequence of the meditation symbolized in Key 17. They have linked themselves with the Ego in Tiphareth, which reflects the self in Kether. See 1067.

שכל מופלא *Sekel Mopla*. Admirable or Wonderful Intelligence [Isaiah 9:6]. Title of Kether. On all planes is the contraction of power (Kaph), at a point of condensation (Tav), which, about the stages of manifestation, becomes a point of radiation (Resh). Created beings cannot attain the essential reality of this "Primary Glory" because that reality transcends everyone of the limitations that characterize "created beings." It projects itself simultaneously through the Paths of Aleph (superconscious), Beth (selfconscious) and Gimel (subconscious). It is present in human personality as Yekhidah, The Self (in Atziluth), as the "seed atom," continuous throughout in the whole series of incarnations (in Briah), as the "thousand-petaled Lotus" within the etheric-astral vehicle surrounding the physical body (in Yetzirah), and as the pineal gland or "third eye" (in Assiah). See 157, 620, 1032, 876, 579, 21, 32, 78, 483, 111.

"It is the Admirable Intelligence, without beginning, without end, imparting understanding; itself beyond comprehension." [Meditations of the Paths of Wisdom].

זך *Zakh*. pure, clear, transparent, innocent. See 27.

באור פני מלך חיים *be-aor penne melek chaiim*. "in the light of the King's countenance is life" [Proverbs 16:15]. The king is Tiphareth, the light is Kether. The verse concludes: "and his favor is as a cloud of the latter rain." The "rain" is the solar radiance, falling in drops, or Yods.

שאור *sheor*. that which causes ferment; yeast, leaven (alternate spelling, see 501). The "light" is the ferment or leaven, which works to increase its influence in manifested forms. See 455, 656, 148, 889 and Matthew 12:33.

עמודי שבעה *ammudi shibeaw*. seven pillars. The seven pillars of wisdom [Proverbs 9:1]. These are also the 7 interior "stars." See 585, 1986 (Greek).

אשור *Asshur*. Assyria. In Genesis 2:14: "The third river of the Tigris; it runs along the east side of *Asshur*. And the fourth river is the Euphrates."

508

הרגש *ha-regash*. sensible or disposing, feeling, sentiment. The adjective ha-regash is from a noun signifying feeling or sensation. Stenring translates the title of this path as "Sensible or Disposing Intelligence." The adjective ha-regash is derived from a verbal root meaning to rage, to be violently agitated. One can see the connection between the letter-name Zain, sword, and the notion of violent activity. Zain's intelligence (sword), The 17th path of wisdom, linking Binah and Tiphareth on the Tree. Heh, "the" stands for the Mars-force which rules Aries, represented by the Emperor, and Heh of IHVH is particularly assigned to Binah. Binah particularizes, sets up distinction, limitations and boundaries, and is the field of specialization. Resh is attributed to the sun and to regeneration (Key 19). Gimel is the letter of the Moon. Shin represents the element Fire and Spirit of God (Key 20 - the Perpetual Intelligence). It is the Quintessence, symbolized by the 8-spoked wheel. Thus הרגש may be read as "The (Heh) Sun (Resh), Moon (Gimel) and Fire (Shin)," or alchemical as "The (Heh) Gold (Resh), Silver (Gimel) and the Quintessence (Shin)." see 858, 513.

שכל נצחי *Sekhel Nitzchi*. Triumphant or Eternal Intelligence. Title of Vav, the 16th Path of Wisdom. Connects the Life-force of Chokmah with the source of cosmic memory in Chesed, gives awareness of Victorious quality to the Life-power because of its freedom from time limitations. Associated with faculty of Intuition. The proper use of recollection may consciously unite personal memory with that of the Life-power. The message of the inner voice has to do with the mystery of the divine radiance, termed "Glory." See 32, 158, 12, 177, 53, 122.

Vav joins Wisdom (Chokmah) to Mercy (Chesed). When creatures begin to exist, mercy becomes active. This is the passage of wisdom, Chokmah, into the self-impartation of the divine spirit through the self-contemplation of its limitless possibilities as an eternal spirit of life.

"I am the eternal intelligence, triumphing overall changes of name and form, sowing all problems of substance in justice, love and truth." [Meditations of the Paths of Wisdom].

כל נפש החיה *kawl-nephesh ha-chaiah*. all the living creatures. Genesis 1:21: "And God created... every living creature that moves... and... saw that it was Good." The "glory" of divine creativity disposes all living creatures towards the highest good.

חך *chek.* to taste; the throat, palate, mouth as an organ of speech. [Kaph = 500, see 28].

שחר *Shachar.* Dawn.

חרש carpenter, craftsman. Isaiah 44:13: "The carpenter measures with a line and makes an outline with a marker; he roughs it out with chisels and marks it with compasses. He shapes it in the form of man, of man in all his glory, that it may dwell in a shrine."

509 (prime)

הדך *hadak.* to break down or overturn, cast down. [Kaph = 500, see 29].

חורם + מריה *khuram + moriah.* khuram, the personification of the Christos + "seen of Yah." The "land of Moriah" is the place Abraham was directed to take his son Isaac from the sacrifice. See 254, 255.

שטר *setayr.* writer, scribe, hence: administrator, ruler, overseer. Said of the ant, in Proverbs 6:7: "Though having no harvest and no ruler over her, neither anyone to guide her." With different pointing: 1. officer, leader; magistrate in Deuteronomy 16:18: "You shall appoint to yourselves judges and scribes in all your cities, which the Lord your God gives you, throughout your tribes; and they shall judge the people with just judgment." 2. *saytahr.* Side. as part of a vision in Daniel 7:5: "And the second beast was like a bear, and it stood upon one side, and it had three ribs in its mouth between its teeth; and they said thus to it, 'arise, devour much flesh.'"

שרוג *serug.* the 'son of Rev' in Genesis 11:22.

Of the root שר: That which liberates, *opens, brings out, emits, produces*; as the *navel, a field*, etc.; שרר (intens). That which is *solid, firm, resisting*, like *a wall, breast-plate, chain*; that which is *strong, vigorous*, as *a bull*; that which is *dominating, powerful*, as *a king, a prince*; that

which is *formidable*, as *a rival, an enemy*, etc. [d'Olivet, 1976, p. 464.]

לדעתה to know her, to lie with her. See Genesis 38:26.

חרשא *Harsha.* Bible Name meaning Magician. See Ezra 2:52.

ואשבר and I have broken. See Leviticus 26:13.

510

אב ואם בן ובת *ab ve-am ben ve-bath.* Father and Mother, Son and Daughter. The Father is Chokmah (2), the Mother is Binah (3), the Son is Tiphareth (6), the Daughter is Malkuth (10). Note that the number 510 reduces to six, assigned to Tiphareth, the Sphere of the Sun.

דקות *daqquth.* thinness, fineness, subtlety, nicety. The primal radiance is subtle and hard to distinguish. Associated with the 4th Path Chesed (Mercy), the sphere of Jupiter.

"The emphasis here is one the receptivity of *Chesed*, a grade allocated to *Chesed* would therefore be distinguished by this quality of receptivity. The spiritual power exercises by an Exempt Adept are received *from above.* He is a center for the radiation of these powers. The agency whereby he broadcast them is called דקות, *dakkooth*, literally 'smallness, thinness, fineness." This agency, we are told, itself emanates from the supreme crown, that is from *Kether*...

The Exempt Adept uses this subtle emanation somewhat as a speaker in a broadcasting station that uses the electric current. The energy employed comes from a higher source, as do the powers that are radiated.

In this connection, it is noteworthy that the noun *dakkooth* has the numeral value of 510, which is also the value of the Hebrew letter name ריש, Resh, corresponding in astrology to the sun Tarot Key 19. *Dakkooth*, subtlety, is a technical name for a force used in practical occultism, and that force is actually a form of solar radiation. The word is from the root דק, *dakh*, 'fine, slender, lean.' The same word means 'dust.' In modern Hebrew, it signifies 'minute, infinitesimal.' Try to get a mental picture from these hints. Remember that the thing we are discussing is an actual reality. Metaphysically it is the radiant energy of *Kether*, represented in Key 0, The Fool, the White sun. But this is not merely metaphysical. It is a real force, properly designated by a Hebrew term signifying 'dust' because it is the fine-grained cosmic 'dust' that eventually takes form in all things. Greater Adept's work is concerned with his control of the subtle something which is substance and energy at one and the same time." [Case, 1985, p. 254.] see 104, 178, 528.

דרוש *deroosh*. figurative sense; to examine, inquire, the metaphorical sense of the scriptures—thesis, dissertation, lecture, sermon. K.D.L.C.K. (p.12) gives *sensus allegoricus*.

ירש *jeresh*. to seize, lay hold of, take possession of.

ריש Letter name *Resh*. Countenance, head, face; beginning, commencement. See 440

דרשו *dereshu*. and seek. From the root רשו meaning: to tread or frequent, to follow (for pursuit or search), by implication, to seek or ask, especially to worship. Inquire [Strong's Bible Dictionary] see 1329, 366.

ישר *yeshir*. to go straight, right, upright, to make smooth, make or lead straight, direct; to esteem, right, approve; to be pleasing, agreeable. See 541, 566, 732.

שיר *shiyr*. song, poem, hymn, singing, enchantment, mantra yoga. With different pointing: *shiahr*: remnant remainder, relic. A suggestion of the correlation between sound and light. The vibration of the eternal radiance makes Plato's "music of the spheres." The true sense of sacred texts is in their allegorical meaning, and the secret is of mentally controlled vibration. See 1394.

שרי *Sarai, sawray*. princess. First name of

Abraham's wife. Genesis 11:29: "The name of Abram's wife was Sarai." See 505, 302 (Greek), 753.

שכל קיים *Saykel Qayam*. Stable intelligence. 23rd path of Mem, joining the sphere of Mars (Will) to Mercury (Intellect). The secret of stability is the "Great Reversal," toward the source of all at the center. This Path is the "Power of Permanence" related to Rhythmic controlled vibration. It presupposes the 17th Path (Zain) work, liberating subconsciousness from wrong self-conscious interpretations of appearance. The possessor of this Path gets the Pentagram right side up, and then the "demon" vanishes. Thus he possesses the *Ars Notaria,* which gives the true universal science-the Art of reading the signs and characters with God has inscribed in every Kingdom of Nature. The seer is filled with the "Light of the World." Control of the serpent-power through concentration definitely limits the associative powers of subconsciousness. This intention is continually recollected at first, but isolation or union with the SELF is the result. See 160, 440, 184, 45, 104, 430, 90, 250, 640, 53, 1070, 40.

תנין *tanniyn*. serpent, crocodile, dragon, whale, sea monster. In Genesis 1:21: "And God created great whales..." Exodus 7:9: "take your rod, and cast it before Pharaoh, and it shall become a serpent." Isaiah 51:9: "Awake, awake, put on strength, O arm of the Lord; awake as in the ancient days, in the generations of old. Art thou not it that hath... wounded the dragon." Ezekiel 29:3: "Thus said the Lord God, I am against thee, Pharaoh, king of Egypt, the great dragon that lies amid his rivers, which has said, my river is mine own, and I have made it for myself." Job 7:12: "Am I the sea, or the monster of the deep, that you put me under guard?" A symbol of the cosmic vibratory radiance, the serpent power. See 358, 409, 1160, 975 (Greek).

תפל *tafel, tawfale*. slime, unseasoned, tasteless, untempered mortar. As a figure of speech, *taphel* means "folly; licentiousness; uncontrolled desire." In Job 6:6: "Can that which is unsavory be eaten without salt...?" Originally signified something vicious or slimy. Employed figuratively means "frivolity." Refers to the avoidance of physical impurity as preparation for initiation. And in Ezekiel 13:11: "Say unto them which daub it with untempered mortar, that it [the wall] shall fall: there shall be an overflowing shower; and you, O great hailstones, shall fall; and a stormy wind shall rend it." This has significance in Freemasonry. There is a hint of the same notion in some versions of Key 19.

תימני *Temani*. One of the sons of Asshur in 1 Chronicles 4:6 and the land of King Husham of Edom in Genesis 36:34.

קדנש ליהוה *qadnash le-IHVH*. holiness to the Lord.

θυρα. *thura*. Door, the entrance of passage into any place; an epithet of Christ. John 10:7,9: (7) "Then said Jesus again, 'indeed, I truly say to you, I am the door of the sheep. (8) All who come before me are thieves and robbers, but the sheep heard them not. (9) I am the door; if anyone comes in by me, he shall be saved, and shall come in, and go out, and find pasture." see 3010, 1480 (Greek).

Κρονος *Kronos* (Greek). The god Cronus (Saturnus in Latin). *Kronos* was the son of *Uranos* and of *Gaia* (Earth). He was the Husband of *Rhea* and the father of *Zeus*. His age was the Golden age. Inman: …was always spoken of as an old God or the father of the Gods. We conceive that he was one of the Phoenician gods and introduced by them into Greece, as it was only in later times that he became identified with Χρονος, *Chronos*, or Time. If so, it is probable that the name was קרניש, karanis. The etymons for this might be קרן, *karan,* 'to point upwards,' 'to emit rays,' 'to shin,' and קרן, *keren*, 'a horn,' 'might,' 'power,' 'a king': כרן *caran*, 'to knot together,' 'to unite,' for the root of the first syllable of the word, and for the second שי, *is*, or איש השע, and in *kran-is*, 'the mighty being,' may be seen a juxtaposition of the ideas of the Sun, the phallus, and antiquity. [Ancient Faiths, VII, p.197-198]

νθξ. *nux*. Night; goddess of night. The Greek Dictionary gives night, gloom, darkness, murkiness; the night of death, i.e., death itself; the netherworld. And, as a proper noun, the Goddess of Night, Daughter of Chaos. The Romans called her Nox.

ποιηματα. *poihmata*. Things which have been made [Romans 1:20]. The things which have been made reveal the invisibles.

511

אסנת *Asenath*, "dedicated to Neith"; wife of Joseph and daughter of Potipherah, Priest of On.

Paul Case: "From Joseph's union with Asenath come Ephraim and Manasseh, the Tribes of Israel corresponding to Taurus and Gemini's signs respectively. The sign Taurus rules the throat; Gemini rules the Lungs. Symbolically, Taurus is the sign of Sol and Luna's junction, while Gemini signifies the two pillars. Here is much for development. Kabbalistically, Ephraim is the Letter Vav, and Manasseh is the letter Zain. The corresponding numbers are 6 and 7, which digits are combined in 67, the number of Binah, while their addition is 13, represented by 4 as the least number. The ideas corresponding to these numbers throw light on the alchemical process. All this maze of symbols, numbers, and attributions must be carefully traced out. The results will shed light upon may alchemical problems." [PFC of D.D. Bryant's Philosopher's Stone, IX, 8]. See 331, 395, 270 (Greek), 455, 57, 385, 156.

רישא *Risha*. head. Title of Kether. Note this word contains the word אשר, the tribe of Israel connected with alchemical sublimation. See 501, 820. It may also be read Ash = Fire (301) + Resh (Sun) + Yod, Virgo or the solar fire expressed through alchemical distillation. See 570.

שורה *shurawh*. row, line; rule of conduct; wall; custom. In K.D.L.C.K. (p.463), "But in the breast (heart) the *shurawh* (rule of conduct) is called Jeshurun by our judges." Jeshurun "up-right one" is a poetical name of Israel ("He shall rule as God"). See 566.

סתימא *saythimawh.* concealed; cover, closing, stopping up. The Greater Holy Assembly (p. 62) "The supernal head [Kether] is the holiest ancient one, the concealed with all concealments."

איך *ayek.* how? how is that? [Kaph = 500, see 31]

הוך *huk.* to go, to bring. See 31.

גקבות *gayqebuth.* femininity; female genitals; female sex, feminine gender; dull side of the tool. Receptivity of the great song is a feminine quality; Qabalah means reception. See Key 2, The High Priestess. [From גקדה tunnel, passage, orifice.]

512

I. (2⁸)

דבקות *deybequth.* adhesiveness, attachment; communion with God; devoutness. From דבא, soldering; attachment, appendage, paste, putty]. See 106.

Rosenroth in K.D.L.C.K. (p.245) says they are chiefly attributed to "fathers" and "mothers" from the marks of their sequence, descending the tree as mercies and severities are the supernal parents of its body. He refers to the word נפל (160).

שחדר *Shakhadar.* Angel of the 3ʳᵈ decan of Libra. This decan is ruled by Mercury and suggests qualities of logic, perceptive, and impartial. Alert watchfulness of actual conditions is combined with the Venusian quality of imagination. The third decan of Libra is also represented by the 4 of Swords or Chesed, sphere of memory, in Yetzirah, the formative world. The constructive use of memory, beneficence and the ability to partake of eternal supply is related to human discriminatory activity. It is the power of suggestion, self-conscious attention to a particular idea, which acts upon the formative substance to bring these ideas into an active expression. The expansiveness of Jupiter, without bounds, would negate or destroy form and detail. Its positive expression brings rest from sorrow,

yet after and through it; relief from anxiety, rest after illness and quietness. Its negative aspect is inharmony, unsettled conditions, disorder and lose.

במתיכם your high places. Leviticus 26:30.

513

אביך *abika.* your father. [Kaph = 500].

הנני יסד בציון אבן בחן *hinni yissad be-zion ahben ehben bokhan.* "Behold, I lay in Zion for a foundation a stone, a tried stone" [Isaiah 28:16]. One of the great key-texts of ageless wisdom. The foundation stone אבן is laid "in Zion," because the basis of all the prophet had in mind is man's intimate communion with the inner teacher, who is the Hierophant of Key 5, and the Angel of Key 6. See 53, 156, בציון (158).

יוצר אור *yotzer aur.* "I form the light" [Isaiah 45:7] I Form the light, indicates the world of formation. The light is formed from preexistent darkness. "and evening and the morning were the first days"; "in the beginning, God created... [i.e., cut apart. See disposing]... and darkness was upon the face of the deep." "And God said, 'Let there be light." [Genesis 1:2,3,5] The FORMATIVE power is the WORD. The same passage in Isaiah also says, "I create evil."

אש זרה *aysh zawrah.* strange fire. In Leviticus 10:1: "And they put in them (their fire pans) fire, and they put upon it incense, and they offered before Tetragrammaton strange fire." This is the consecrated fire of formation, Shin, which is specialized in the nerve currents as the serpent power, or kundalini.

בשורה *besorah.* tidings, good news, gospel. In the Septuagint, this is translated as "Gospel."

ההרגש *ha-hargashah.* of feeling, of sensation, of disposing. The intelligence of Zain. Derived from a root meaning "to be violently agitated, to rage tumultuously." The idea of violence is in direct relation to the basic meaning of Zain, the sword. See 858, 508.

פמן שמן *palegay shamen*. rivers of oil. In Job 29:6: "And the rock poured out rivers of oil." see 67, 466, 497.

נסגדול היה שם *nesgadal chaiah shom*. "A great miracle happened there!" the acrostic נ-ג-ה-ש (nah-gah-ha-ish) was placed in the spinning dridle at the Chanukah festival. One letter was put on each of four wings on top, corresponding to the 4 worlds and Cherubim. Nun = Death; To experience wisdom means true knowledge of Life and Death. Gimel = Moon; One then automatically expresses the Law through Love and peace. Heh = Emperor; The coming of the Messiah is the coming of the King. Shin = Judgement; When awakening comes, it brings eternal life.

514

שחיר *shihor*. black, charred, sootiness, dingy, melancholy. Jeremiah 2:18: "And now what have you to do in the way of Egypt, to drink the waters of Shimor?..." The waters of Shimor have to do with illusion. See 564.

שכל מעמיד *Saykel Maamid*. Constituting Intelligence. 15th Path of Heh and attributed to Aries, ruled by Mars. The dominant power in this path is the Mars-force, the active generative power in nature. It links the radiant energy of the fixed stars or suns (Chaiah in Chokmah) with the Central Self (Ego in Tiphareth) with distributes it to all human personalities. All personal experience of vision is a particular expression of the cosmic power-to-see. To the degree that things are seen as they really are, the personality is a channel for original creative power. See 164, 10, 423, 200, 223, 219, 380.

ידך *yadawk*. your hand. Psalm 138:7: "Though I walk amid trouble, thou will revive me: thou shall stretch forth your hand against the wrath of mine enemies, and your right hand shall save me." Yod is assigned to Chokmah, Yah (15), the father.

From which emanate the path of Heh, the Emperor, the Constituting Intelligence. See 750 (Greek).

אחד ראש *achad rosh*. one principle, one head. God, the father, is the head of the one creative principle. See 2945, 425, 926, 440, 1052, 1065.

הללו אל בקדשו *hallew-al be-qadesho*. "Praise God in his sanctuary (praise him in the firmament of his power" [Psalm 150:1]. The "sanctuary" includes a vision of the whole.

חקות statue, laws. The feminine singular of חקה enactment, ordinance, statute, law, custom, constitution. The masculine is חק with the additional meaning of "prescribed task; prescribed due; prescribed limit or boundary. The emperor is the law-giver (Key 4) and prescribes the boundary of his domain. In K.D.L.C.K. (p.213), the text refers to Leviticus 18:4: "You shall do my judgments and keep mine ordinances, to wake therein..." And says that the masculine and feminine forms mentioned here refer to El-Chai (The Almighty) and Adonai (Lord) and to oral laws (heaven) and written laws (earth).

נחלת יהוה *nahaelath IHVH*. heritage of the Lord. Psalm 127:3: "Lo, children are a heritage of the Lord; the fruit of the womb is a reward." The Zohar [II:188A, pp.217-218] comments: ".."..the phrase 'heritage of the Lord' is an allusion to the 'bundle of souls in the world to come, and the passage indicates that it is children that make a man worthy of that heritage of the Lord. Hence happy is the man who is blessed with them and who trains them in the ways of the Torah."

515

נחלה בלי מצרים *nachayla beli mitzraim*. Possession without want (tribulation, distress, straightness). The Hebrew translates "possession without distress." The word *mitzriam* means Egypt [From מצר distress, straits; boundary; narrow pass]. To possess is to rejoice in freedom from oppression. Rosenroth in K.D.L.C.K. (p.569) says this phrase alludes to Binah.

תפלה *tiphaylaw*. unsavourness, unseemliness, impropriety, folly. From תפל tasteless, unseasoned; plaster, whitewash, untempered mortar. Folly is the oppression of man; it is the "second" beast, tamed by prayer and meditation. See 510, 859.

תפלה *tepilhuh*. phylactery; parchment inscribed with a scriptural text. Worn by Jews on the forehead and left arm near the heart; *tefillah*, the prayer of the *amidah*.

In Jewish antiquity, the parchment was enclosed within a small leather case, which was fastened with straps on the forehead just above and between the eyes and left arm. The 4 passages written on the phylactery were Exodus 13:2, 9, 10, 16: (2) "Sanctify unto me all the firstborn, whatsoever opens the womb among the children of Israel, both of man and of the beast: it is mine; (9) and it shall be a sign unto thee upon your head, and for a memorial between then eyes, that the Lord's law may be in your mouth: for with a strong hand has the Lord brought thee out of Egypt; (10) thou shall therefore keep this ordinance in his season from year to year; (16), And it will be like a sign on your hand and a symbol on your forehead that the Lord brought us out of Egypt with his mighty hand."

And Deuteronomy 6:4, 9; 11:13-22: (4) "Hear O Israel: the Lord our God is one God." (9) "Write them on the door frames of your houses and on your gates." (13) "So if you faithfully obey the commands, I am giving you today-to love the Lord your God and to serve him with all your heart and with all your soul. (14) then I will send rain on your land in its season, both autumn and spring rains, so that you may gather in your grain, new wine and oil. (15) I will provide grass in the fields for your cattle, and you will eat and be satisfied. (16) Be careful, or you will be enticed to turn away and worship other gods and bow down to them. (17) Then the Lord's anger will burn against you, and he will shut the heavens so that it will not rain and the ground will yield no produce, and you will soon perish from the good land the Lord is giving to you. (18) Fix these words of mine in your hearts and minds; tie them as symbols on your hands and bind them on your foreheads. (19) Teach them to our children, talking about them when you sit at home and when you walk along the road, when you lie down and when you get up. (20) Write them on the door frames of our houses and on your gates, (21) so that your days and the days of your children may be many in the land that the Lord swore to give your forefathers, as many as the days that the heavens are above the earth. (22) If you carefully observe all these commands, I am giving you to follow-to love the Lord your God, to walk in all his ways and to hold fast to him-(23) then the Lord will drive out all these nations before you, and you will dispossess nations larger and stronger than you."

The custom was founded on a literal interpretation of Exodus 13:16 and Deuteronomy 6:8: "Do what is right and good in the Lord's sight so that it may go well with you and you may go in and take over the good land that the Lord promised on oath to your forefathers." Among the primitive Christians, this was a case in which they enclosed the relics of the dead. Any charm, spell, or amulet is worn as a preservative form danger or disease—[Greek phy-lak-terion, from phylassein, to defend or guard – Webster].

Rosenroth in K.D.L.C.K. (p.738) says that this is a name for Malkuth because it assembles all the sephiroth within it.

שוטר *shoter*. official, officer; policeman; minister, minister of influence. The destiny of man is to be a minister or mediator for the divine influence. Rosenroth in K.D.L.C.K. (p.707) says that when Malkuth is the thong of the whip falling on the godless, Tiphareth is the helper or aid which strikes. Suggests the testing of the holy guardian angel in Key 14 via the path of Samekh.

παρθενος. *Parthenos*. Virgin. See 456, 744 Greek.

516

פרצופין *pharaytzophin*. personae; masks. Suggest personalities of humanity, which are, but masks form the indwelling higher self. From פרצוף. Mace, visage, front.

Rosenroth in K.D.L.C.K. (p.649) says these masks are representations of the divine grades under the analogy of human figures, some of which are Arik Anpin, father and mother (Chokmah and Binah) and Seir Anpin [Tiphareth].

מלכותך *malaykuthaykaw*. the kingdom (a kingdom for all ages). Those who have strength and knowledge possess the kingdom. As Jesus said, "Your kingdom come, your will be done, on earth as it is in heaven." Esther 3:8: ."..there is a certain people scattered abroad and dispersed among the people in all the provinces of your kingdom, and their laws are diverse from all people..." see 496 (Malkuth).

תמוע *Timnah*; a duke of Edom, associated with Da'ath [474]." [Godwin. 1999, p. 308.] Edom [51] signifies unbalanced force. See 1 Chronicles 1:51.

וכלכלתי and I will sustain [provide]. See Genesis 45:11.

שירו sing. See Exodus 15:21.

לכסתו to cover it. See Exodus 26:13.

כתפיו his shoulders. See Exodus 28:12.

צויתי I command, I am commanded. See Leviticus 8:31.

517

פלאות *pehlaoth. occult*; "hidden" or "concealed," according to Rosenroth in K.D.L.C.K. (p.644) says that this name refers to Tiphareth since it truly ascends beneath the secret place of Da'ath.

See 1081, 474.

קו תהו *qav-tohu*. line of chaos. The Zohar [Prologue, 11B, pp.48-49] comments: "'And the earth was chaos and confusion (*tohu va-bohu*), and darkness was upon the face of the abyss.' This is an allusion to the four kinds of punishment which are meted out to the wicked: tohu (chaos) alludes to strangulation, as it is written: 'a line of (tohu) chaos' [Isaiah 34:11], meaning a measuring cord." see 76.

ארימירון *Arimiron*. Qliphoth of Taurus. Misuse of the qualities of determination, practicality, duty. The Moon, which is exalted in Taurus the focus of negative astral entities. Recall that Taurus is fixed earth. For a variant spelling, see 321.

518

לפתח at the door. Genesis 4:7.

כחצת about midnight. Exodus 11:4.

οι ΚΛΗΤΟΙ *hoi kletoi*. The elect. Romans 1:6,7: "Among whom you are also the elect (invited) ones of Jesus Christ; to all who are in Rome, the beloved of God called (elected) saints; favor and peace to you from God our Father, and the Lord Jesus Christ." Matthew 20:16: "For many are called (elected), but few chosen"; Romans 8:28: "And we know that all things work together for good to those who love God, to those being invited (elected) according to a purpose." see 438 (Greek), 540.

ου ...μη. ou...meh. (Greek). Not. Acts 4:20: "For we are not able, what we saw and heard, not to speak."

ο λογος εν ιδεα. *ho logos en idea*. The idea word; living perfect word. Refers to Christ, or the second person of the trinity. See 1850. Adds to 2368.

οικησις. *oikehsis*. A dwelling place; a house, dwelling; the act of dwelling. See 111, 370, 333 (Greek).

η θυρα. *heh thura*. The gate.

Benedictus Dominus Deus Noster Qui Dedit Nobis Signum. "Blessed be our Lord God who gave us this sign." A Rosicrucian phrase is exchanged by two Fraters and appears written on a cross on one of the Secret Symbols' plates. See 94, 85, 45, 82, 43, 41, 53, 75, 246 Latin.

519

ברבטוש *Barbatos*. Goetia demon #8 by day of the 2nd decan of Gemini. According to the *Aurum Solis*, a demon of the 3rd quinance of Libra. This decan is assigned to the 9 of Swords. This represents the operation of Yesod, the automatic pattern-world of the Moon, in Yetzirah, the world of mental formation. See Appendix 11.

I. *Goetia*: "He giveth understanding of the singing of birds, and of the voices of other creatures, such as the barking of Dogs. He breakout the Hidden reassures open that have been laid by the enchantments of Magicians. He is of the order of virtues, of which some part he retaineth still; and he knows all things Past, and to Come, and conciliates Friends and those that be in Power." [Mathers, 1995, p. 31]

II. "An angel formerly of the order of virtues. In Hell… he is a great duke, ruling over 30 legions of spirits. He 'giveth understanding of the song of birds, knows the past and can foretell the future.' He may be invoked in magical rites, and he will appear gladly, but only when the sun is in the sign of Sagittarius." [Davidson, 1971, p. 70.] see *Book of Ceremonial Magic* (p.198).

520

כשר *kosher*. ritually clean, wholesome. With different pointing *kawsher*: legitium; to be right, fit, to succeed, prosper.

כשר *kisher*. to prepare, make fit, make proper. In Esther 8:5: "If it pleases the king, she said, 'and if he regards me with favor and thinks it the right thing to do, and if he is pleased with me, let an order be written...'" And in Ecclesiastes 11:6: "Sow your seed in the morning, and at evening let not your hands be idle, for you do not know which will succeed, whether this or that, or whether both will do equally well."

מתניך *mawthayneikaw*. your loins. In Jeremiah 1:17: "Thou, therefore, gird up your loins, and arise, and speak unto them all that I command thee: be not dismayed at their faces, lest I confound thee before them." This has to do with the Mars-force's transmutation, seated within the "loins," ruled by Sagittarius. This implies the probation and testing by the Holy Guardian Angel via the process of alchemical incineration. See 162, 1890 (Greek).

כרש *Koresh*. Cyrus, king of Persia. See Ezra 1:2. See 586, 30; 790 (Greek). In Isaiah 45:1: Cyrus is called למשיחו, " to his anointed" "This is what the Lord says to his anointed, to Cyrus, whose right hand I take hold of to subdue nations before him and to strip kings of their armor, to open doors before him so that gates will not be shut." see 358.

תען *thah'an*. let sing (speak, proclaim). In Psalm 119:172: "My tongue shall speak of your word: for all your commandments are righteousness." As a masculine noun (medieval), fasting, fast-day.

דמעות *dimayoth*. tears. In Psalm 80:5: "Thou feeds them with the bread of tears, and gives them tears to drink in great measure." note that דם spells blood. See 44, 78.

521 (prime)

יהונתן *Yehonathan*. Jonathan. "God is the Giver." Beloved and loyal friend of David and son of Saul in the Biblical Allegory in 1 Samuel 14:6: "and Jonathan said to the young man that bare his armor, come, and let us go over unto the garrison of these uncircumcised: it may be that the Lord will work for us: For there is no restraint to the Lord to save by many or by few." Because 521 reduces to 8, Jonathan is a symbol of alchemical Mercury.

ושריה *Vasariah*. "God the just." 32nd Shem ha-Mephorash. 156º -160º. Psalm 23:4: "For the word of the Lord (IHVH) is upright; and all his work is done in faithfulness (truth)." Rules justice; influences through the nobility, jurists, magistrates and advocates. A person born: good memory, speaks with faculty and is amiable, spiritual and modest. Associated with the 2nd quinance of Capricorn, Angel by night of the 2 of Pentacles (Chokmah of Assiah). See 506, 965 & Appendix 10.

מחשוף הלבן *mahashue ha-leben. nudatio* [bare] *candoris* [shining white]. Rosenroth in K.D.L.C.K. (p.527) attributes this phrase to Kether, the highest crown because the light is manifested therefrom. In the Zohar, however, Tiphareth is so-called because it too manifests light.

פתאם suddenly. See Numbers 6:9.

522

יחד + פרו ורבו *yawchud + phayru uraybu*. unity to be united, joined + be fruitful and multiply. The unity of the sons of God or 'thousands of angels' leads to the admonition "be fruitful and multiply." It is expanding spiritual growth of divinity or spirit in matter or the manifest. See 500, 22.

רש + אחוה + ב *sawr + achaevah + Beth*. prince, noble, ruler + fraternity, brotherhood + house. The prince of peace, who is the ruler in our heart of hearts, is also the center of the mystic brotherhood, which is at once within and above its transparent house of personality. See 500, 20, 2.

ברכש substance, with possession. See Genesis 15:14.

בנתיכם your daughters. See Genesis 34:9.

בשרך your flesh. See Genesis 40:19.

במכסת according to the number, by number of. See Exodus 12:4.

523 (prime)

כהנת הגדול *Koheneth ha-Gadhol*. High Priestess; the title of Tarot Key 2, attributed to Gimel, i.e., universal subconscious memory.

חיה + פרו ורבו *phayru uraybu + chaiah*. be fruitful and multiply + the life-force. It is the characteristic of light to extend itself through all its centers of manifested life. The life-force is centered in Chokmah, the father. See 500, 23.

תימן + ג + חזה *teimawn + Gimel + khawzawh*. south + camel + the have a vision of. South is the direction of the sun or Tiphareth; Gimel is the Uniting Intelligence linking the universal Self in Kether with the Ego in Tiphareth; the prophet's vision is in truth a recollection of that which seems to belong to the past. See 500, 20, 3.

בתוך המים *be-toke ma-mayim*. amid the waters. Genesis 1:6: "And Elohim said, 'Let there be a firmament amid the waters, and let it divide the waters from the waters.'" See 90, 95.

"בתוך המים, in-*the-center of-the-waters*... In examining the roots and the figurative and hieroglyphic sense, this is to say *in the sympathetic and central point of universal passivity*, which agrees perfectly with a rarifying and dilating force such as Moses understood. But the Hellenist, having considered it proper to change this intelligible force into a sentient solidity, have been led to change all the rest. The word מבדל [slacking, a loosening], which is obviously a continued facultative, according to the excitative form, expressing the action of making a separation exists among diverse natures, they have changed into a substantive, and have seen only a separation produced by a kind of wall that they have created. The Arabic verb attached to the same root as the Hebrew בדל expresses a mutation of nature or a place." [d'Olivet, 1976, p. 37.]

נתחכמה, let us deal wisely [shrewdly]. See Exodus 1:10.

כשר + ד *kisher* + *Daleth*. to prepare, make fit, make proper + door. Before the fruit is produced, the field must be prepared. This is done through the open door of creative imagination, as a result of sustained desire. See 520, 4.

כתף + ויד + בב *kawtef* + *dehyo* + *babah*. Arm of a vine + fluid darkness + a well, vein. Jesus said: 'I am the vine, you are the branches.'. The "darkness" represents the Mars-force's operation at subconsciousness levels; the "well" is the receptacle for this force, energizing the vein or the blood-stream. This produces the grapes, or fruit of the vine. See 500, 20, 4.

שדרך *Shadrach*. The name was given to Hananiah, one of Daniel's companions at the court of Babylon. See Daniel 1:7.

שיחור *Shiyhor*. Hebrew name of the Nile river (from שחר), in allusion to its turbid waters. Isaiah 23:3: "and by great waters, the seed of *Shihor*, the harvest of the river, is her revenue; and she is a mart of nations." And Jeremiah 2:18: "And now, why is it you go in the way of Egypt (i.e., make an alliance and adapt its policy), to drink the waters of Shihor?..." Also designation of the southern limit of Palestine." Joshua 13:3: "From Shihor, which is before Egypt..."

525

יהוה צבאות *Jehovah Tzabaoth*. Jehovah (Lord) of Hosts. In Psalm 24:10: "Who is the King of Glory? The Lord of Hosts He [הוא] is the King of Glory." The Divine Name attributed to Netzach, with fire, and to the South. Tzabaoth is from a root meaning: to go forth to war, to assemble, to mass. The Hosts massed in the Heavens and on Earth are manifold expressions of love. Purified and perfected desire is transmuted into love. It is the attractive force that maintains the order of the Universe and is the driving power behind every form of desire. To some degree, this name corresponds to the central figure of Tarot Key 7,

a warrior riding in a chariot. See Isaiah 45:13, 1813 Greek.

זרע אברהם *Zerah Abraham*. Seed of Abraham (2 Chronicles 20:7). Abraham means "Father of Multitude." The patriarch is the biblical personification of reproductive power. "Seed" designates the force, which is basic in occult practice. The seed is the Word, and the Word is the sword of the Spirit. The Word is love, and love gives the victory (Netzach). The universe is even now the manifestation of a power that is always victorious. In the passage cited, Abraham appears as a friend of God. This is a link with one basic meaning of the seventh Sephirah. See 148, 710, 64, 519, 1085.

חכמת המבטא *chokmath ha-mebita*. rhetoric. One of the 7 liberal arts. It is an art of speech. This connects with Key 7 in the Tarot, as Cancer is attributed to Speech. Note also that the first path proceeding from Netzach is that of Peh, the mouth as the organ of speech. Speech gives victory over the "seed."

דניאל רב חרטיא *Daniel Rab Chartiah*. Daniel, Master of the Magicians. (חרט, magic, to engrave; חרטם, Magician) The original text calls Daniel Rab Chariomia "Master of the Astrologers." "That which is translated 'astrologer' would be more accurately rendered 'enchanter,' for it signifies a person skilled in the correlation of the various kinds of vibration through the use of sound. This science and art of controlling all modes of vibration through certain uses of sounds is akin to what the Hindus call mantra-yoga, and it is closely allied to astrology." [Paul Case, in the Article "Daniel Master of Magicians"] Desire of Mastery of "speech" aids illumination. See 217, 257, 609, 1102.

526

אבראכאלא *abrakala*. "Original form of Abracadabra." [Godwin. 1999, p. 569.] see 418 for Crowley's formula.

דו פרצופין *du-paraytzophin*. the two faces. King and Queen or Tiphareth and Malkuth. "The 'king' and the 'queen' commonly also called the 'two faces' דו פרצופין (du partsufin), form together with a pair whose task is to pour forth constantly upon the world new grace, and through their union to continue the work of the creation. But the mutual love that impels them to this work burst forth in two ways and produces fruits of two kinds. Sometimes it comes from above, going from the husband to the wife, and from there to the entire universe; that is to say, existence and life, starting from the intelligible world's depths, tend to multiply more and more in the objects of nature. Sometimes, on the contrary, it comes from below, going from the wife to the husband, from the real world to the ideal world, from earth to heaven, and brings back to the bosom of God the beings capable of demanding their return." [Franck: The Kabbalah pp.168-169]

כורש *Koresh*. Cyrus, king of Persia. As spelled in Isaiah 44:28: "Who says of Cyrus, He is my shepherd and will accomplish all that I please; he will say of Jerusalem, Let it be rebuilt." see 520, 540 (korshid), 950, 956.

שתוך *Siroc*; a shoe-latchet. In American Freemasonic lodges, it is a significant word in the Mark Mason degree. (It is the name of the true grip of a Mark Master Mason, meaning "mark well"). Possibly a veiled reference to its metathesis, כורש, Cyprus. In Mackey's Encyclopedia: "It.... refers to the declaration of Abraham [248] to Melchizedek [294], that of the goods which had been captured he would 'not take from a thread even to a shoe-latchet,' that is, nothing even of the slightest value."

שפיפון *shaypifon*. horned adder. Minus the Vav in Genesis 49:17: "Dan shall be a serpent by the way, an adder in the path, that bites the horse-heels so that his rider shall fall backward." A symbol of the Egyptian royal serpent stands for Scorpio's and is associated with Dan's Tribe (דן). See 54.

משקוף *masheqof*. superluminal. Rosenroth in K.D.L.C.K. (p.558) attributes this word to Yesod and cites Exodus 12:7: "Then they are to take some of the blood and put it on the tops and sides of the door-frames of the houses where they eat the lambs." He says that sometimes Yesod is raised above Netzach and Hod as a door-post.

527

זמה זמה עזא רחמה עזיה *zammah zammah ozzah rachamah ozai*. Thought thought, the power of the womb of the strength of Yah. See 2467.

מטבעות *matbeoth*. coins; corresponds to pentacles suit of the Tarot minor arcana, and to Assiah, the world of Action or physical plane.

חכמה אמת אהבה *chokmah emeth ahebah*. wisdom, truth, love. Suggest Father (Chokmah), Mother (Truth = Tav = Binah, sphere of Saturn and intuition, which revels truth) and son (love = Sun = heart = Tiphareth). See 73, 441, 13, 1081.

פליאות *payliawth*. wonderful, miraculous, mysterious; wondrous. Spelled מפלאות in Job 37:16: "Does thou now the balancing of the clouds, the wondrous works of him which are perfect in knowledge?" see 126, 111.

אלמנות widows. See Exodus 22:23.

הורישו he has driven out. See Numbers 32:21.

528

I. Σ32 = 528. The mystic number of the 32nd Path of Tav.

שכל קבוע *Sekhel Qavua*. Measuring, Cohesive, Receptacular, Arresting, Receiving, Settled, or Constant Intelligence of the 4th Path of Chesed. "It is so-called because from thence is the origin of all beneficent power of the subtle emanations of the most abstract essences which emanate one from another by the power of the Primordial Emanation." These are powers of Chokmah, powers of the universal light-force, which is also the life-force of mankind. These beneficent powers emanate from one another by the power of the Primordial Emanation, Kether. They are abstract essences because they are subdivisions or specializations of the life-force, like waves in an ocean, or currents within it, though not really separate from the sea's whole expanse & depth. This path's possessor is linked to the cosmic seat of memory, where the "Laws of Nature" are rooted. His actions express goodwill and compassion. See 178, 72.

"It is the Cohesive Intelligence receiving that which comes from above and measuring all power to those who wait below." [Meditations on the Path of Wisdom]

העגנת *Hogenth. Haagenti.* Goetia demon #48 by night of the 3rd decan of Cancer. In the Tarot minor arcana, this decan is assigned to the 4 of Cups. This represents Chesed, or cosmic memory, in Briah, the creative world. See Appendix 11.

Goetia: "He is a president, appearing in the form of a mighty bull with griffin's wings. This is at first, but after, at the command of the Exorcist, he puts on human shape. His office makes men wise, instructs them in divers things, transmutes all metals into gold, and changes wine into water and water into wine. He governs 33 Legions of Spirits." [Mathers, 1995, p. 53]

מפתח *maftayakh.* key. This is the key to the knowledge of immortality as well as the key of the House of David, "And that house is the temple, not made with hands, eternal in the heavens.

Note that 525 is the summation of the numbers from 1 to 32 (Σ32 = 528). Indicating that 528 is the full manifestation of the 32 Paths of Wisdom as shown on the Tree of Life. This is the key of the House of David, [מפתח ביט דוד, 954] that that house is the Temple not made with hands, eternal in the heavens. See 954, 273 (Greek).

תצלח shall prosper. See Numbers 14:41.

529

I. (23²)

יעלו בתהו *Yelu Battohun.* They go to nothing. See Job 6:18.

תמעיט you shall diminish [decrease]. See Leviticus 25:16.

והחריש he will be silent, but he says nothing. See Numbers 30:5.

אויביך your enemies. Judges 5:27.

מידתעה the he-goats. In Genesis 31:10: In breeding season, I once had a dream in which I looked up and saw that the male goats mating with the flock were streaked, speckled or spotted. See 580 (satyr, goat).

הידעתם know you? Genesis 29:5. The root of this word is דעת (474), meaning: knowledge, mind, reason. The "invisible" Sephirah of the Tree of Life. Associated with generation and conception, and the idea of night. (Biblical: "And Adam knew his wife, and she conceived.")

נטעת you did plant. Deuteronomy 6:11. How do you create a new cycle? In silence and darkness, by understanding that which must diminish, it is nothing. See 1329, 401, 256.

שיטרי Goetia demon #12 by day of the 3rd decan of Cancer. See Appendix 11.

Goetia: "He is a great prince and appears at first with a leopard's head and the wings of a griffin, but after the command of the Master of the Exorcism, he puts on a human shape, and that very beautiful. He enflames men with woman's love and women with men's love and causes them to show themselves naked it be desired. He governs 60 legions of Spirits."

530

אתה עמדי *attawh immawdiy.* thou is with me. Psalm 23:4: "Yea, though I walk through the valley of the shadow of death, I will fear no evil:

for thou are with me; your rod and your staff they comfort me."

כנסת *kaymeseth*. congregation, assembly. With different pointing: gathering, storage; synod; community. See 55, 156, 586.

כ = bride connects with כנסת = church, i.e., the church, ecclesia Israel, and brings us back to that place called mystically Zion and Jerusalem, in which the divine is communicated to man..." [Waite, 1993, p. 219]

חבתלת *khaebatzeleth*. the rose. Isaiah 35:1: "The wilderness and the solitary place shall be glad for them, and the desert shall rejoice, and blossom as the rose." [Also: crocus, lily (lexicon)]

קלת *qalath*. voices. With different pointing: 1. receptacle under the millstone (to receive flour dust); 2. women's work-basket. See 130.

תקל *tawqahl*. weighted. Daniel 5:27: "Tekel; thou art weighed in the balances and found wanting" [suggest Libra]. A word of the writing on the wall [numbered, numbered, weighed and measured] at Belshazzar's feast. See 30, 74, 158.

עינת springs. Exodus 15:27.

531

לאשר steward. Genesis 43:16: "When Joseph saw Benjamin with them, he said to the steward of the house..."

לראש the head. Genesis 49:26: "Your father's blessing are greater than the blessing of the ancient mountains, then the bounty of the age-old hills. Let all these rest on the head of Joseph, on the brow of the prince among his brothers."

ותענה and she dealt harshly, then she mistreated her. Genesis 16:6: "Your servant is in your hands," Abram said." Do with her whatever you think best." Then Sarai mistreated Hagar; so she fled from her."

532

אבן החכמות *eheben ha-chokmoth*. stone of the wise.

הדעת אבן *eheben ha-da'ath*. Stone of knowledge.

מנהיג האחדות *menahig ha-achadoth*. Driver of Unities (literally); The Uniting Intelligence, Conductive Intelligence of Unity, Conducting the (powers) of the unities, Leading to Unity. The 13th path of the letter Gimel. "The perfection of the truths of spiritual unities." The noun *menahig*, "driver," is from the verb מנהג, *minhag*, "to drive" (as a chariot). This word conveys a reference to the whole meaning of the Tree of Life because the study of the Tree and its relations is often termed "The Work of the Chariot." see 108, 424, 419, 882.

The Path of Gimel is the link between God (Kether) and Man (Tiphareth), centered through the pituitary body (Moon Center). This path's work is related to alchemical sublimation and the completion of which is the philosopher's stone by divesting the serpent-power (astral light) of all appearances of manyness. See Appendix 12.

חמה החכמות *Khammaw ha-Chokmath*. Sun of Wisdom.

חמה הדעת *Khammaw ha-Da'ath*. Sun of knowledge. The son in Tiphareth has perfect knowledge of union with the self in Kether. See 474.

יהוה הוא וחלתו *IHVH hu nakhalatho*. Tetragrammaton is their inheritance [Deuteronomy 18:2]. The Lord unites with the light of the vast countenance in Kether, igniting the powers of memory.

מחל תמית *lekhem tawmid*. perpetual bread. The bread is never absent from its table in the temple and the tabernacle. There were always 12 loaves representing the 12 tribes and the 12 zodiacal influences (signs). *Mezla*, influence, which represents the active power flowing through all 32 paths of Wisdom, is numerically 78, which is also the value of Lechem, bread. The "influence" is the real support of human existence, our true staff of life.

αλφα. *Alpha.* The Greek spelling of Alpha in plentitude. The first letter of the alphabet also meaning first. Transliteration of the Hebrew Aleph, the Ox. See 111.

533

טבל וילון שמים *tebel (tabal) viyalon shamaim.* "Immersed (baptized) in the door of heaven." Veil of the Firmament; the First Heaven corresponding to Yesod of Malkuth. *Tebel* טבל means to dip, immerse, to make produce subject of priestly dues. With different pointing: to dip (into salt, vinegar, etc.) to season; to baptize. *Viyalon* וילון means door, curtain; door-curtain. See 395.

מלך בלהות *melek balawhoth.* King of Terrors. Job 18:14: "His confidence shall be rooted out of his tabernacle, and it shall bring him to the King of Terrors."

להתנחם to be comforted. See Genesis 37:35.

מגפתי my plagues. See Exodus 9:14.

η αγκυρα. heh agkura. the anchor.

534

I. 3-4-5 triangle

3 = vertical = Osiris = אב = Father
4 = the horizontal = Isis = אימא = Mother
5 = the hypotenuse = Horus = בן = son.

The area is 6, the perimeter 12. The angle of base and hypotenuse is 37, the value of הבל *Abel* (transitory breath). The angle of hypotenuse and perpendicular is 53, the number of *Ehben* אבן, stone. The angle of perpendicular and horizontal is 90, the value of מים, water and Tzaddi [צ], fishhook. Note that the constant relation between

perpendicular and base is expressed by 90 or Tzaddi, which, according to the Zohar, consists of Nun surmounted by Yod, representing together the male and female principles. 90 is also the value of יכין Jakin ("firm one"), of סוד הווג the mystery of sex, a technical name of Qabalah, of מים, water.

The relation between Isis and Hours, the ascending hypotenuse, or son, is expressed by 37, which as *abel* transitoriness, or continual change of form and state, but as יחידה [Yekhidah. I AM, The Supreme Self] reminds us of the unchanging self, the indivisible one, persisting throughout forms. This transitory character is in contrast to the stability and solidity of *Ehben* [53] stone (which forms a root meaning "to build"), and this "stone" is the "head of the corner." Note that 53 is also ακακια, acacia, guilelessness, from α-κακος, without evil, unknowing of ill.

חורם מלך צור *Khurum melek Tzor.* Hiram, King of Tyre.

לדרש to inquire. See Genesis 25:22.

בינותינו between us. See Genesis 26:28.

דלקת hotly pursued, you hunted. See Genesis 31:36.

ευρηκα. Eureka. I have found it! Attributed to Pythagoras when he discovered the properties of the right-angled triangle. The Word is a formula for the construction of this triangle. Eureka is 534. The right triangle ratio is the base is 4 units, the hypotenuse 5 units and the side vertical line 3 units. See 758.

535

הלך *hawlak.* to go, depart, disappear; traveler. With different pointing *hawlak:* 1. to walk, to go; to walk about, to proceed; to depart, go away; to pass away, disappear; 2. traveler, flowing. The divine traveler is Aleph, the spirit or eternal fool, who passes through one cycle of evolution and apparently departs to begin another. See 55, 111.

מרכבה + חסר *merkabah + khoser.* chariot, vehicle plus want, lack, poverty. The personality is the vehicle through which divine creativity functions. Its use or misuse brings wealth or poverty. See 267, 268.

קהלת *qoheleth.* preacher, teacher; a surname of King Solomon. The first word of Ecclesiastes' book: "The words of the teacher (preacher), Son of David, King of Jerusalem."

להעלת to light, to burn [for a lamp, נר] see Exodus 27:20.

הלינתם have murmured [grumbled]. See Numbers 14:29.

עניתה you have afflicted her, you dishonored her. See Deuteronomy 21:14.

και ειπευο θεος. *kai heipen ho Theos.* "And God said"; the creative Word or powers which brought forth the universe. Septuagint translation of אלהים ויאמר (343) in Genesis 1:3: "and God (Elohim) said 'let there be light,' and there was light." see 343, 86, 284 (Greek), 3218.

536

מסלות *masloth.* Highways, roads. The Sphere of the Zodiac is attributed to Chokmah. It indicates whatever the life-force may be in itself, it is also identified with the radiant energy streaming from suns or stars. The life-force, which is the power of formation, is the same force that pours itself from innumerable suns. Our sun's energy and the energy of radiations from the cosmos directly affect human vitality. Used in connection with the courses of the stars and the affairs of men in Judges 5:20: "The stars in their courses fought against Sisera." "The same word is used figuratively in Proverb 16:17: "The highway (Masloth) of the upright is to depart from evil." This heavenly order is a manifestation of the power of gravitation and the radiant energy of electromagnetism. Because Chokmah is the Sphere of the Fixed Stars, Chokmah is the greater whole, including the special Sphere of the Sun, Tiphareth, since the sun is one of the stars. See 23.

חכמת המדידה *chakmath ha-medidah.* geometry. The measurement of spatial relations is basic in practical occultism. This is linked to its source in the stars [Post-Talmudic]. See 124.

מקום ספיר *maqom-saphir.* place of sapphires. Job 28:6: "The stones of it are the place of sapphires, and it has dust of gold." In the passage," the stones of it" is אבניה, which breaks down into יה אבן, ehben Yah. As Yah, is the special Divine Name attributed to Chokmah, and אבן expresses the union of the Father with the Son, or the union of Chokmah with Tiphareth, אנהיב, is a verbal symbol for that union. Chokmah, as the sphere of the fixed stars, is the greater whole that includes the special sphere of the sun, or Tiphareth, since the sun is one of the fixed stars. See 68.

בית עדן *Beth-Eden.* House of Eden. In Amos 1:5: "I will... cut off... him that holds the scepter of the House of Eden..." A mystical reference to the garden mentioned in the Bible as being the first abode of humanity.

עולם העשיה *Olahm ha-Assiah.* The World of Action (Assiah), or the Material World. The commentary on this is the statement in Proverbs 3:19: יהוה בחכמה יסד ארץ, Jehovah be-chokmah yasad eretz, Jehovah by (or, in) Wisdom hath founded the earth. What is indicated is that what we think of as the material world has its actual substance, or basis, in the radiant energy of Chokmah. Our personal life force is one form of that energy, and the physical things surrounding us are another form of the same energy. Assiah, or the world of action, is also called the world of shells. This refers to the world of matter made up of the grosser elements of the other three worlds. It is also the abode of the evil spirits or "shells" called Qlippoth, the material shells.

שיר יהוה *shiyr-Jehovah.* Song of Jehovah [2 Chron. 29:27; Psalm 137:4]. All manifestation is vibration. The universe is the "Song of Jehovah." see 270.

טלית לבנה *tallayth lebanah*. a white cloak. Intimating Yesod, the purifying Intelligence. See 777.

שכל נסיוני *Sekhel Nisyoni*. The intelligence of Probation, Tentative Intelligence, Intelligence of Temptation or Trial. The 25th Path of Samekh. Connects the Egoic body (Sun) with the vital soul and its astral body (Moon). The Work of this path is testing of those in whom is active the spirit of Mercy (The "compassionate"-(Chasidim). To devote oneself wholly to receiving instruction from the One-Self and minister to Humanity's welfare is necessary. The instruction received must be tested in the fires of experience. One must practice directing the mental stream always in the way desired it should progress. The spirit test daily that we may interpret our experiences as cosmic events and personal activities. Right recollectedness provides a clear pattern via the suggestion that one never can do anything of himself. Eternal being manifests themselves in the special functions of temporal existence. It is the true foundation of personal attainment. See 176, 666, 120, 800 60, 310, 216, 162, 166, 260.

The path of the Intelligence of Probation, attributed to Samekh (ס), follows the path of Imaginative Intelligence (24th Path) because it signifies testing the ideas and innovations suggested by the Imagination. It joins Beauty (Tiphareth) to Foundation (Yesod) because only by experiments, trials and tests can the harmony of Tiphareth become actualized in the established certainty implied by the term foundation. Yesod (Foundation) is the propagative sephirah, and this is a clue to many problems.

"I am the Intelligence of Probation, proving all knowledge in the fires of experience." [Meditations on the Paths of Wisdom]

שפע נבדל *Shepa Neobedal*. Mediating Influence. The 6th Path of Tiphareth. *Shepa* שפע also means emanation. It is so-called because it is the abundance of the increase of archetypal influence and because it is the influence over the grafted shoots of the extended unities themselves [Yetzartic Text]. Neobedal is from the ancient

Hebrew word עבר, Abad, "to work, prepare, make, serve." It is used throughout the Bible in a great variety of shades of meaning. Tiphareth stands between what is above and what is below. The whole process whereby powers from above are concentrated in Tiphareth and diffused to planes below is what is meant by "Light in Extension." see 86, 1081, 548, 640, 214.

מצות *metzivath*. commandments, precepts [Jeremiah 35:18]. That is legislation, in direct correspondence with Key 11, Justice (Lamed). With different vowel points: strife, contention.

פיתום *paytom, pehtom*. A magician; necromancer, conjurer, ventriloquist. [neo-Hebrew, Greek] The false magicians shall be tried by fire, in the meditating influence. Then darkness shall be dispelled, and they will walk the highways of righteousness, singing the Lord's song.

למען שמו *he-maon shemo*. for his name's sake. Psalm 23:3: "He restores my soul: he leads me in the paths of righteousness for his name's sake." see 349, 885.

537

אצילות *Atziluth*. Nobility; the Divine or Archetypal World. Rosenroth in K.D.L.C.K. (p.146) gives *emanatio*, a system of emanating.

פטר רחם *pheter-rechem*. the firstborn. In Exodus 13:12: "You are to give over to the Lord the first [פטר] offspring of every womb [רחם]..." The above quotation is listed in the Hebrew Lexicon, as meaning: "opening of the womb, first-born" פטר = opening, firstling, first-born. Rosenroth in K.D.L.C.K. (p.644) gives *apertio uteri* and links it to Malkuth. See 587, 248, 289.

חוט השדרה *khoot ha-shidayraw*. spinal cord; back-bone. Conveyer of the life-force's nerve-currents through the planes of consciousness to Kether, the crown, in Atziluth. [חוט = thread, cord, line; sinew]. Rosenroth in K.D.L.C.K. (p.335) gives: *medulla spinalis* and says it is the middle line Tiphareth, for it collects and sends out the influx to all parts of the tree. See 23.

המצות the sacred stones. See 2 Kings 18:4.

והמופת And the wonder. See Deut. 13:3.

והמסכות and the cast images. See 2 Chron. 34:3.

ומצאת then you will find. See Deut. 4:29.

להתיצב to present self. See Job 1:6.

538

צ/ד Daleth/Tzaddi, Venus (Daleth) in Aquarius (Tzaddi).

בת קול *Bath Kol*. Daughter of the Voice; (inner voice). Mackey writes: "The Jews say that the Holy Spirit spoke to the Israelites in the days of the tabernacle through the *urim* and *thummim*, and under the first temple of the prophets, and under the second by the *bath kol*, an inferior divine intimation to the oracular voice proceeding from the mercy-seat, as a daughter is supposed to be inferior to the Mother." [Encyclopedia of Freemasonry, p.953]

המנהיג האחדות Ha-*Menahig Ha-Achadoth*. The Driver of the Unities. 13th Path of Gimel. See 531.

אין ברוחו רמיה *ayin beruacho remiyah*. In his spirit, there is no guile [Psalm 32:2]. Quoted by Jesus about Nathanael in John 1:47. Nathanael means "Gift of El," which relates to Chesed, whose divine name is El (אל). The indwelling spirit has masks of, veils-it is impersonal בת קול, *Bath Kol*, Divine Voice. Literally, "daughter of the Voice." Refers to the 'still, small voice' of intuition, which speaks from the inner center, when one has ears to hear (the Hierophant).

η νοτικη αλθεα. *he-noetike aletheia*. The truth is perceived by direct cognition.

νοησις. *Noesis*. Knowing. Direct cognition of truth by the lucid mind, apart from any reasoning reason.

חכמה ואמת ואהבה *chokmah ve-emeth ve-ahebah*. Wisdom and truth and love. "Jesus Christ is that wisdom, truth and love. He as wisdom is the principle of reason and the source of the purest intelligence. Like love, he is the principle of morality, the true and pure incentive of the will. Love and wisdom beget the spirit of truth; this light illuminates us and makes supernatural things objective to us." [Cloud Upon the Sanctuary, p.4] see 888, 1480, 2368 (Greek), 73, 441, 13, 527, 533.

תלקט you shall gather. See Leviticus 19:9.

נפדתה she redeemed. See Leviticus 19:20.

540

שמר *sawmer*. kept, observe. [Genesis 37:11]. Keeper or guard in Canticles 3:3: "The watchmen [השמרים, the-men-watching] found me as they made their rounds in the city. have you seen the one my heart loves." see 546, 1087, 545.

יה יהוה צבאות *IHVH Yah Tzebaoth*. The Lord of hosts, or IHVH of Hosts. The Zohar [III: 146B, pp.15-16] says: "The celestial chief of whom we have spoken is an angel sent forth by the holy one, blessed be he. He is Lord over many celestial hosts. He wreathes crowns for his Lord, and this is the significance of his name, Akathriel (God-crowning): for he prepares crowns from the graven and inscribed name יה יהוה צבאות." see 525.

הוא חייך *hia hayekaw*. she is your life. Proverbs 4:13: "Take fast hold of instruction, let her not go; keep her, for she is your life." see 12, 18.

רמש *remes*. Creeping thing.

מתנים the loins. Deuteronomy 33:11.

οι εκλεκτοι *hoi eklektoi*. The elite, the chosen. See Colossians 3:12, 220, 518.

διδασκαλος. *didaskalos*. A teacher, instructor, master. In Romans 2:20: "An instructor of the simple, a teacher of babes; having the form of knowledge and truth in the law." Written διδασκαλε in John 1:38: "And Jesus turning, and seeing them following, says to them, 'What do you seek?' and then said to him 'Rabbi (teacher), where you dwell?'" see 1850, 185 (Greek); 212 (Hebrew).

541 (prime)

אילך *akilak*. farther, further. With different pointing *alika*: to thee, towards thee. [Kaph = 500, see 61].

אמך *ammeka*. your mother. See 61.

הלוך *hawlok, hillook*. walking, motion. See 61, 50.

ישראל *Israel*.

1. Paul Case: "Israel. This name, which occurs so often in the text, merits consideration. In Hebrew, it is spelled ישראל, and its number is 541. This is a prime number, that is, indivisible so that it suggests solidarity and impregnability. The digits composing it are 5, the number of Severity, 4 the number of Mercy, and 1, the Crown's number, in the ten sephiroth scheme. Thus it refers to all three pillars on the Tree of Life... The sum of the digits in 541 is 10, and this is the number of Malkuth, the kingdom, and the number of the letter Yod, which Qabalists regard as the basis of the whole alphabet. Thus the name ישראל sums up the whole Qabalistic scheme of the Tree of Life. It means 'he will rule as God.' The promise embodied in this name should be kept in mind because Qabalist's study and practice's main object is 'to restore the creator to his throne.' As a symbolic name, Israel designates those chosen ones, of whatever race or creed, who are destined to regain the divine command of circumstance which is the birthright of all humanity." [From the original typewritten manuscript, Book of Tokens, commentary of Aleph, 1924]

2. The Zohar [I:27B, p.106] Adds, "Adam [45], who is Israel, is closely linked with the Torah, of which it is said, 'It is a Tree of Life to those who take hold of it'; this tree is the Matron, the Sephirah Malkuth (kingship), through their connection with which Israel is called 'sons of kings.'" "Note this identification of humanity (אדם) with Israel (ישראל). See 45.

לחת אבנים *lukoth aebawnim*. tables of stone. The two tablets on which the law of God was carried by Moses. See 53, 546, 642 (Greek), Exodus 39:1,4 & Deuteronomy 5:22.

ים התיכון *yawm ha-thikon*. the Mediterranean sea. See 87, 380, 486, 546, 870 (Greek) & Genesis 2:9.

This is the sea that Brother C.R. sailed to come to Fez (as the Arabians directed him) in the allegory of the Fama *Fraternitatis*. This city is at the western end of the sea, in contrast to Cyprus (Venus, associated with the east), where the transmutation's first work occurred. Fez is also at the other end of the sea from Egypt. Recall that the sea is in the microcosm. This is the key to the allegory. In the 1500s, Fez was the intellectual center of the world. Therefore Fez corresponds to the intellectual powers associated with Mercury. Please note the intellectual center in man is in his head, and the Turkish headdress, the fez, was named after the city.

אשמר *eshaymor*. I might observe. In Psalm 119:101: "I have refrained my feet from every evil way, that I might keep your word." דברך "your word" refers to the path of Peh. See 226.

התונן *hithaylonen*. to dwell, abide; to seek shelter, take refuge.

542

עולם מושכל *Olam Mevshekal*. Intellectual World.

יהוה אלה ודעת IHVH Eloah ve'da'ath. see 548.

וישכרו became intoxicated, so they drank. See Genesis 43:34.

אהיה אשר אהיה *Eheyeh Ahser Eheyeh*. I AM THAT I AM [Exodus 3:14]. Also, "Existence of Existences," A title of Kether. The Central Self, Yekhidah in Kether. The only two prophets in the Bible who attained this degree were Moses and Jesus. See 55, 1006, 496, 21, 37.

בעל אמת *Baal Emeth*. Lord of Truth. A title given to Philosophus (4=7, Netzach) in Rosicrucian initiation. Note that בעל means lord, possessor, owner, proprietor; husband; the Canaanite God Baal. With different pointing: it means to rule over, be married, have sexual intercourse. See 102, 441.

בעבר הירדן *bayawbar ha-yaredden*. Beyond (over) Jordan. ירדן Jordan means "that which flows down." Down to the Dead Sea. Symbol of the river of manifestation, flowing down to death. "I am that I am (אהיה אשר יהוה) is beyond Jordan, because it is that which is beyond and above the stream. "Difficult to crossover," the stream of Maya, the illusive power of manifestation. Note that עבר means to pass, pass over or through, cross, go through, traverse; to pass along, pass by, sweep by, overtake; to be passed, be over; go on, proceed, travel; to pass beyond, pass away, emigrate; to overflow, overstep, transgress.

שמגר *Shamgar*. The 4th judge of Israel, who smote 600 Philistines and delivered Israel. In Judges 3:31: "After Emud came *Shamgar* son of Anath, who struck 600 Philistines with an ox-goad. He too saved Israel." see Anath (520).

קדמת on the east, east of. See Genesis: 2:14.

נפתחו were opened, they were opened. See Genesis 7:11.

צמחות sprouting forth. See Genesis 41:6.

נחלתנו our inheritance. See Numbers 32:19.

משרה *misayraw*. government; dominion, rule; appointment, office, position. In Isaiah 9:6: "For unto us a child is born, unto us, a son is given: and the government shall be upon his shoulder: and his name shall be called Wonderful, Counselor, The Mighty God, The Everlasting Father, The Prince of Peace. Of the increase of his government and peace there shall be no end, upon the throne of David, and upon his kingdom, to order it, and to establish it with judgment and with justice from henceforth even forever. The zeal of the Lord of Hosts will perform this." see 525, 550.

בשם אל יהוה עולם *be-shem IHVH El olahm*. On the name of Tetragrammaton, El everlasting. In Genesis 21:33: "And Abraham planted a grove in Beersheba, and called there on the name of the Lord, The Everlasting God." Beersheba means "well of the seven"; Abraham means "father of many nations."

הרמש creeping thing, the one crawling. See Genesis 1:26.

אבעבעת blisters, fester. See Exodus 9:9.

התפלל pray. See Numbers 21:7.

רישא דלא *Risha Dela*. The Head Which is Not; a title of Kether.

פיתון *pithon*. Inman: "(1 Chron. 8:35). Furst translates this name "a harmless one," from פות, *puth*; this word signifies the female pudenda. We may, with greater probability, derive it from פתה, *pathah*, and ון, *on*, "On parts asunder, open, or expands." The name is borne by a grandson of Meribbaal, a son of Jonathan, David's friend, and one of these brothers is named Melech. It is possible that the word comes from Greek πυθων, *python*, the great serpent; but it is just as likely that the Greek came from the Phoenician. the serpent was an emblem because it could erect and distend itself; it was also considered to be very wise, and to give oracles; and פתה, various pointed, signifies 'he expands,' 'cleaves asunder,' and 'he decides, or judges.'" [Ancient Faiths, VII, pp.497-498]

לחת האבנים *luchoth haw-ebawnim*. the tables of stone. In Deuteronomy 9:11: "And it came to pass at the end of forty days and forty nights, that the Lord gave me the two tables of stone, even the tables of the covenant." see 552.

מתוק *mawthoq*. sweet, pleasant. In Judges 14:14: "And he said unto them, out of the eater came forth meat, and out the strong came forth sweetness. And they could not in three days expound the riddle." Refers to the riddle of Samson.

שומר *shomer*. watchman, keeper, guard, as in שומר ישראל, (God) keeper of Israel. See 1087, 545, 541, 540.

שמור *shimmur*. custom; guarding, care, watching; removal of lees of wine, straining. Rosenroth in K.D.L.C.K. (p.721) connects this word with Malkuth because it is the custodian of all other sephiroth, receiving their influence.

הים התיכון *ha-yom ha-tikon*. the Mediterranean sea. [תיכון = inner, central, middle]. The Mediterranean is that inner, central, middle sea which brother C.R. crossed from Egypt to Fez. See 486, 540.

עלמות *olamuth*. eternity. With different pointing: 1. *awlaymuth*: youthfulness; strength, vigor; 2. *aelmwmoth*: a musical term. Musical harmony and strength are associated with the ability to experience eternity.

שרהיאל *Sharhiel*. Lesser assistant angel of Aries. Aries is ruled by Mars, which is connected with youthfulness, strength, and vigor.

547 (prime)

חכמת ההגיון logic. Literally, "the wisdom of meditation." הגון, meditation = 74 = intention, device; logic, one of the 7 liberal arts. With different pointing: gentle murmur, solemn sound. Meditation is the device through which we are guided to divine intention. This develops the capacity for logic. Logic is the result of the receptivity to wisdom. See 74, 73.

משזר twined, woven, being twisted. See Exodus 26:1.

548

יהוה תעדו הולא *hakaymoth ha-higgawyon*. "That which was, is and will be, strength and knowledge." The Lord of Knowledge. The Divine Name is attributed to Tiphareth and the 6 of Wands. The Ego center's highest function in man is to be aware that humanity's essence is the Universal Life of the Father-Mother at the level of self-consciousness.

Dion Fortune writes, "The God-name of this sphere is Aloah va Daath, which associates it intimately with the invisible sephirah that comes between it and Kether. This sephirah... may best be understood as apprehension, the dawning of consciousness. We may interpret the phrase 'Tetragrammaton Aloah va Daath' as 'God made manifest in the sphere of mind'... it is here that the initiated adept functions when in the higher consciousness. and it is by... an understanding of the significance of the name of Aloah va Daath that he opens up the higher consciousness." [The Mystical Qabalah, pp.206-207]. See 1080, 26, 36, 474 for other divine names of the sephiroth see also 37, 166, 26, 86, 31, 297, 525, 585, 363, 155.

אני יהוה עשה כל אלה *Ani Tetragrammaton asah kal-elleh*. I, Tetragrammaton, do all these things [Isaiah 45:7]. This is the secret of union with the Central Ego. All work is accomplished by the power of the Universal Self. The secret of Karma or union by work or action. "The Father works, and I work."

בית יוד נון הה *Binah* spelled in full. Understanding. A consciousness that the One Reality is both strength and the very principle of knowledge is the perfect manifestation of the Divine Understanding. Tiphareth is the result of the finitizing power of Binah.

כי חולת אהבה אני *keiy-khavolath ahebah ani.* For I am sick of love; I am love-sick [Song of Solomon 2:5]. The desire for light and the lack of it are both aspects of the One Reality. See 1081, 45, 90, 52, 536, 548, 640, 214.

בעריון *Beayriron.* Qlippoth of Aries. "The herd." Suggesting a misuse of the Mars-force, or divine strength. See 1198.

עביריון *Obiriron.* Qlippoth of Libra, suggesting a lack of balance and harmony exemplified in the sephirah of beauty-Tiphareth. The meaning is "the clayish ones"; clay suggests impermanence; in the Old Testament refers to the plastic material molded by God into Man. God is the potter. Likewise, the "House of Clay" [Job 4:19]. עב [72] is darkness, i.e., the darkness of ignorance veiling the light of truth. According to Kenneth Grant, it is also the serpent, the negative or feminine aspect of אוד, which is the magic light itself. Lack of balance regarding the directive action of the serpent power, which Lamed represents, is also unresponsiveness to the ox-goad of divine volition. See 1198.

שחרם *Shakherim.* the dawning-ones. See 3321.

Υριηλ. *Uriel.* The angel Uriel. Archangel of Light, also called Lucifer, "Light-Bearer." see 248, 251.

η κρισις *heh krisis.* The crisis, the judgment, the condemnation. Romans 8:33: "In his humiliation, his judgment was taken away; and who will tell of his generation? Because his life is taken from the earth."

αδελψη *adelpheh.* A sister, born of the same parents in Luke 10:39, 40. A female friend, esteemed and beloved as a sister, in Matthew 13:50 and 1 Corinthians 7:15.

549

מורגש *morawgash.* exciting, active; moral. The 27th Path of Peh. From a verbal root meaning "to be noisy, to be tumultuous, to rage." Used in the term עולם מורגש, Olahm Murgash, Moral World, to describe the powers of the 4th, 5th, and 6th Sephiroth.

מורגש *muregawsh.* threshing-sled, threshing roller. Compare this with the symbol of the skeleton-reaper in Key 13 (Mars as Nun or Scorpio).

יהושע בן נון *Yeoshua ben-Nun.* Joshua, son of Nun. The successor of Moses. The name יהושע is the original name of "Jesus."

רוח סערה *rauch seahrah.* Whirlwind; wind storm. It comes out of the north and is described as a great cloud and a fire infolding itself. In Ezekiel 1:4: "There came from the North a violent gale, accompanied by a great cloud, with fire flashing through it, while out of the midst of it gleamed something with a luster like that of shining metal." The Hebrew translation gives Electrum for metal, חשמל, Khashmal, meaning: shining substance, electrum, fairy, angel; modern meaning: electricity. The word translated "brightness" is נגה, Nogah (a short spelling of נוגה) meaning: shining, brightness; morning-light; the planet Venus. What is indicated is that the motive-power of Mars brings "gold" (the Christos) from the north (direction of Peh) when Venus or the power of desire brings the Sun and Moon centers into balance, with the aid of Mercury. The is a profound alchemical statement. Electrum is Latin for Amber, also an ancient alloy of Gold and Silver. See 85, 226, 876, 95, 878.

נשר *nasher*. eagle.

שרטיאל *Sharatiel*. angel of Leo.

שבט ברזל *shebet barayze*. a rod of Iron. In Psalm 2:9: "thou shall break them with a rod of iron; thou shall dash them as pieces like a potter's vessel." see 1230 (Greek).

שרים *sawrim*. princes. In Psalm 45:16: "Instead of your fathers shall be your children, whom thou may make princes in all the earth. Rosenroth in K.D.L.C.K. (p.725) says the Zohar refers this word to Chokmah and Binah because they are the first of many grades of Atziluth. See 898, 500.

שמיר *shawmir*. diamond; adamant, flint; a fabulous worm that cuts. [Canon pp. 171-173] "Before the operations commenced [on the construction of the temple], Solomon asked the rabbis, 'how shall I accomplish this, without using tools of Iron? "And they, remembering of an insect, which had existed since the creation of the world, whose powers were such as the hardest substances could not resist, repelled 'there is the shameer, with which Moses cut the precious stones of the Ephod." Solomon asked, "And what does the wild cock do with the shameer?' To which the demon [Ashmedia] replied 'he takes it to a barren rocky mountain, and utilizing it he cleaves the mountain asunder, into the cleft of which, formed into a valley, he drops the seeds of various plants and trees, and thus the place becomes clothed with verdure and fit for habitation.' This the shammer." In Ezekiel 3:7: "As an adamant (diamond) harder than flint have I made your forehead, fear them not, neither be dismayed..." see 970.

מיך The 42nd name of Shem ha-Mephorash, short form. See 70, 101 (Michael). Kaph = 500

אנך *Anakh*. Plumbline. See Amos 7:7-8.

נשאר is left (remains). See Genesis 47:18.

נאקת groaning. See Exodus 6:5.

תקומה stand. See Leviticus 26:37.

קנאת jealousies. See Numbers 5:15.

המארשה the betrothed, being pledged. See Deuteronomy 22:25.

שקוציהם their detestable things, detestable images of them. See Deuteronomy 29:16.

חמדת ימים *khemidawth yawmim*. desire of days. ימים means days, seas, times, and refers to the influence or abundance of water, which is the mind-stuff carrying the life-force, as in Deuteronomy 33:19: "...for they shall suck of the abundance of the seas, and of the treasure hid in the sand." see 100.

מבשרי *mibesawri*. in my flesh. In Job 19:26: "And though after my skin worms destroy this body, yet in my flesh shall I see God." [the Jewish translation is "without my flesh shall I see God." The prefix Mem is the short form of מן, Mem meaning from, of; being that, since; more than. See 615.

תלמיד חכם *talemid khawkam*. disciple of wisdom; scholar, student. The disciple's task is to purify and prepare according to the cosmic law, represented by stone tables. Then he will be ready for the influx of wisdom, which is the life-power.

Σαταν. *Satan*. Satan. See 1042 Greek, 364, 69 Latin and Matthew 4:10.

שיר גדול *shiry gawdo*. great song. "You can stand upright now, firm as a rock amid the turmoil obeying the warrior who is thyself and your king. Unconcerned in the battle save to do his bidding, having no longer any care as to the result of the battle; for one thing only is important, that the warrior shall win, and you know he is incapable of defeat; standing thus, cool and awakened, use the hearing you have acquired by pain and by the destruction of pain. Only fragments of the great song come to your ears while yet you are but man. If you listen to it, remember it faithful, so that none which has reached you is lost, and endeavor to learn from it the meaning of the mystery surrounding you. In time you will need no teacher. For as the individual has the voice, so has that in which the individual exists. Life itself has speech and is never silent, and its utterance is not, as you that are deaf may suppose, a cry: it is a song. Learn from it that you are part of the harmony; learn from it to obey the laws of the harmony." [Light on the Path II:8] Note the correspondence between dragon and shir (510), the serpent of vibration in Key 10, the Wheel. "The straight, or true sense of sacred texts in their allegorical meaning, and the secret of that meaning is the secret of mentally controlled vibration." shir means song, enchantment, mantra yoga. See 510, 386.

תנין גדול *thannin gawdol*. great dragon. Has to do with the serpent-power, symbolized by the letter Teth. See 418, 450, 358.

נקדה פשוט *Nequdah Peshut*. the Simple Point, the small point. A title of Kether and the number one. See 620, 747.

ערז ערז *zorea zara*. bearing seed.

בחכמה יבנה בית *be-chokmah yebawneah bayth*. In Proverbs 24:3: "with wisdom the house is built." Chokmah, the cosmic father, carries the seed of life (Chaiah, the Life-force) to build the house of human personality. According to the Zohar,

Chokmah here refers to Abraham (the father of Israel). See 2307, 2392, 1007, 831.

מלכות האבן *malkuth ha-ehben*. kingdom of stone. Referred to in the prophecy of Daniel. "The stone kingdom... is a system of government democratic in outer form. The units of its body-politic, the persons from whose consent this government derives its powers, have come to a realization of the identity of the I AM in man with its heavenly source, the identity implies in the junction of the letters which spell father and son in the one word, ehben, stone." [Daniel Master of Magicians]

כתם אופז *ketem ah-Uphaz*. fine gold of Uphaz. In Daniel 10:5: "Then I lifted up my eyes, and looked, and behold, a certain man clothed in linen, whose loins were girded with fine gold of Uphaz." This refers to Tiphareth and the angel in Key 14. Uphaz is related to the word Mophaz, "pure" in 1 Kings 10:18 and Ophir, the land where fine gold was obtained. Gold is assigned to Tiphareth.

מרחוש *Marchosh. Marchosias*. Goetia demon #35 by day of the 2nd decan of Pisces. This decan is assigned to the 6 of Cups. This represents Tiphareth, sphere of the Central Ego, in the world of Briah, the plane of mental images and creative thinking. See Appendix 11.

I. "An angel who, before he fell, belonged to the Order of Dominations. In hell, where he now serves, Marchosias is a mighty marquis. When invoked, he manifests in the form of a wolf or an ox, with griffin wings, and serpents tail... he confided to Solomon that he 'hopes to return to the seventh throne after 1,200 years.'" [Davidson, 1971, p. 183.]

II. *Goetia*: "He is a great and mighty marquis, appearing at first in the form of a wolf having griffin's wings, and a serpent's tail, and vomiting fire out of his mouth. But after a time, at the command of the exorcist, he puts on the shape of a man. And he is a strong fighter. He was of the Order of Dominations. He governs 30 legions of Spirits." [Mathers, 1995, p. 46]

555

The Height of the Washington D.C. obelisk in feet.

הקדמות *ha-qadmuth*. The primordial. Hod's reference is the perfect intelligence called "treasure" or "dwelling-place of the primordial" in the text of the 32 paths. Every advance toward a greater perfection is a utilization, development and unveiling of the primordial treasure. See 15, 1431.

עפתה *aefawthawh*. obscurity; darkness. Job 10:22: "A land of darkness, as darkness itself; and of the shadow of death, without any order, and where the light is as darkness." The path of Peh descends out of the "darkness" of the north, bringing Uriel, "Light of God," to the darkness of the cell-consciousness of the physical body. The darkness or obscurity of ignorance cannot see the origin of light, "The light shines in the darkness, but the darkness comprehends it not."

אלף בית יוד וו A:B:I:V: *Aleph-Beth-Yod-Vav*. Abiff, written in full. Hiram Abiff is the Masonic personification of the Christos. See 19, 258, 290.

הנשר *ha-nasher*. the eagle. "It is a stone and not a stone, viz. the eagle [Scorpio] stone. The substance has in its womb a stone, and when it is dissolved, the water that was coagulated in it burst forth; thus, the stone is the extracted sprit of our indestructible body. [Case: viz. the incorruptible body sown in the corruption of the natural body]. It contains mercury, liquid water, in its body, or fixed earth, which retains its nature. This explanation is sufficiently plain." [Waite, 1974, vol. 1, p. 211] see 550.

εν υμιν. *en humin*. Among you, in you. In James 3:13; among us (literally in us) in John 1:14; "In you" in Colossians 1:27.

διακρισις. *diakrisis*. A discerning clearly, a distinguishing; a judging of, estimation; discrimination. Spelled διακρισιν in Hebrews 5:14: "but the solid food is for adults-for those possessing faculties habitually exercised for the discrimination both of good and evil." Plural διακρισες in 1 Corinthians 12:10 and Romans 14:1.

556

תקון *tiqqun*. restoration.

אגב + נשר *agab* + *nesher*. utilizing, through, + eagle. Liberation is accomplished utilizing the Mars force, which the eagle represents. This force is transmuted into the "noble fire, the princely light." see 550, 6.

גרגשים *Girgashim*. "Girgashites" Genesis 10:16: (And Canaan begat) "And the Jebusite and the Amorite, and the *Girgashites*."

"And (that of) the Jebusite (inward crushing), and (that of) the Amorite (outward wringing), and (that of) Girgashite (continuous gyratory movement)." [d'Olivet, 1976, p. 344.]

He comments ואת הגרגשי and-that-of-the-Girgashites… The two distinct roots of which this word is composed, are גר, which designates all gyratory movement executed upon itself, all chewing, all continued action; and גש, which expresses the effect of things which are brought together, which touch, which contract; so that the meaning attached to the word גרגש, appears to be a sort of chewing over and over, of doing over again or rumination, of continued contractive labor. [ibid., pp. 287-288.]

ראשנה foremost, first, front. See Genesis 33:2.

תעוף flies, she flies. See Deuteronomy 4:17.

557 (prime)

ראשון *rashun*. the first, former, primary. A title of Kether. In Exodus 12:2: the first month, "This month is to be for the first month," the beginning of the First Passover.

ספר הזהר *Sepher ha-Zohar*. The Book of Splendor. Qabalistic text. See 340.

וסופתה the whirlwind, literally: and-to-whirl. What is sown by the wind, i.e., Ruach רוח. See 1500 and Hosea 8:7.

558

שיר הגדול *shiyir ha-gawdol*. the great song. "Only fragments of the great song come to your ears while yet you are but man. But if you listen to it, remember it faithful, so that none which has reached you is lost, and endeavor to learn from it the meaning of the mystery which surrounds you. In time you will need no teacher. For as the individual has no voice, so has that in which the individual exists. Life itself has speech and is never silent. And its utterance is not, as you that are deaf may suppose, a cry: it is a song. Learn from it that you are part of the Harmony; learn from it to obey the laws of the harmony." [Light on the Path II:8] see 553.

תקבנו curse them. See Numbers 23:25.

559

נקדה פשוטה *nequdah peshut*. the Simple Point, a smooth point. A title of Kether. See 554, 747.

בראשון in the first. Genesis 8:13.

εγεντο σιγη *egeneto sigh*. There came to be silence. In Revelations 8:1: "And when he opened the seventh seal, there was silence in the heaven about half an hour." The 7th seal or planet is the Mercury center, and the experience is that of cosmic consciousness.

"The seventh seal is the *Sahasrara chakra*, which corresponds to Leo's sign, the sole domicile of the Sun. This *chakra*, the conarium or pineal body, is the 'third eye' of the seer-that, and much more. It is the focal point of all the nervous system forces and of the aura; here they come to an equilibrium, and here reigns the mystic silence." [Pryse, 1965, pp. 134-135.]

560

פשוט נקודה *Nequdah Peshut*. The Simple Point. A title of Kether, the crown of primal will. Variant spelling. See 559.

"The only conceivable beginning is an act of intention, or the Life-power's turning toward a point within itself at which to begin. At this stage of the creative process, there are neither psychical nor physical objects. They come later. There is only the first point, the center of the field within itself, selected by the Life-power as its operation theater. Consequently, Qabalists give to Kether the number 1, the additional titles *Nequdah Peshuit*, The Simple Point... from this simple beginning all things have their origin." [Tree of Life Lesson 9] נקודה means: point, dot; punctuation; phonology (grammar); פשוט simple, straight, flat, level; the plain.

נקדות *nayqudoth*. points, studs; spangles Canticles 1:11: "We will make thee circlets of gold, with studs of silver." These are the Gold and Silver of alchemy. See 921.

תמנע *timna*. restraint. That calms the serpents and brings illumination from the "still waters." (Capricorn = Ayin), bringing an abundance of gold and silver. A Duke of Edom [Crowley, 1977, p. 52].

דרושים *dayrushim*. lectures, discourses. Thesis, dissertations, homilies, and sermons attempt to implant the seeds of direct knowledge into the lower mind.

דעת אלהים *Da'ath Elohim*. Knowledge of God (the Elohim, or creative powers). See 86, 474.

מכשר *mekeshar*. Sorceress. The letters of this word suggest a reversal of mental substance (Mem), flowing into the personality (Cheth), to subvert the spiritual fire (Shin) for purposes of hindering the regenerative force of others (Resh).

I. "The root אך, image of every restriction, every contraction, united to the sign of exterior and passive action, constitutes a root whence spring the ideas of attenuation, weakening, softening of a hard thing: its liquefaction; its submission. מך That which is *attenuated, debilitated, weakened; distilled; humiliated*. [d'Olivet, 1976, p. 390.]

II. שר It is the sign of relative movement which is united simply to that of movement proper, their results form this abstract mingling of the circular line with the straight line, an idea of a solution, opening, liberation; as if a closed circle was opened; as if a chain were slackened: if one considers this same sign of relative movement, being united by contraction to the elementary root אר, then it partakes of the diverse expressions of this root and develops ideas of strength, domination, power, which result from the elementary principle; if finally, one sees in the root אר the root שו, one discovers directed according to just and upright laws; thence, according to the first signification; שר That which liberates, opens, brings out, emits, produces. [ibid., p. 463-464.]

ου μν. *hou min*. Nothing.

561

I. Σ33 = 561

עלה תאנה *aeleh thanem*. "fig-leaves"; so rendered in Genesis 3:7: "Then the eyes of both of them [Adam and Eve] were opened, and they realized they were naked, so they sewed fig leaves together and made coverings for themselves."

I. "And the eyes of them both were opened, and they know that they were void of light (of virtue, sterile and unveiled in their dark principle), and they brought forth a shadowy covering, veiled of sadness and mourning, and they made themselves pilgrims 'cloaks'." [d'Olivet, 1976, p. 318.]

He comments: עלה signifies neither a leaf, nor leaves, but a shadowy elevation, a veil; a canopy, a thing elevated above another to cover and protect it. It is also *an elevation, an extension, a height*. The root על develops all these ideas. As to the word תאנה, it is a little difficult to explain. The

sign ת is used as the faculty of expressing the continuity of things and their reciprocity. This distinction is made. The word אנה expresses grief. It is formed of an onomatopoetic root, which depicts the groans, sobs, pain and the *anhelation* of a person who suffers. United to the sign ת to especially express deep, mutual sorrow. Presumably, the fig-tree was received the metaphorical name of תאנה on account of the mournfulness of its foliage, from which lactescent tears appear to flow from its fruits. [ibid., p.103]

II. The Zohar [I:53B] comments: "And they sewed fig leaves together. As explained elsewhere, this means that they learned all kinds of enchantments and magic and clung to worldly knowledge, as has been said. At that moment, the stature of man was diminished by a hundred cubits. thus a separation took place (of man from God), a man was brought to judgment, and the earth was cursed, all as we have explained." (p. 169).

עתניאל *Athnial*. Othniel, son of Kenaz, a hero in Israel and one of its judges. See Judges 3:11.

562

ראשונה *rashunah*. the Primary (or first) point.

לא תנאף *lo thi-ne'aph*. Thou shalt not commit adultery [Exodus 20:14]. The comment on this is in the New Testament in Matthew 5:27, 28: "You have heard that it was said, 'thou shall not commit adultery; but I say to you, that every man gazing at a woman to cherish impure desire, has already committed lewdness [i.e., adultery] with her in his heart." see 1282; 1440 (Greek); 31.

יהוה שמך לעולם *IHVH shamay sheemk le-olahm*. Tetragrammaton your name endures forever. In Psalm 135:13: "Your name, O Lord, endures forever; and your memorial, O Lord, throughout all generations." see 146, 340.

יהוה אלהיך *IHVH Elohekaw*. The Lord your God. Deuteronomy 15:4: "Save when there shall be no poor among you; of the Lord shall greatly bless thee in the land which the Lord your God gives for an inheritance to possess it." see 82, 26. [Kaph = 500]

הראשון the first. See Genesis 25:25.

ואשריהם their Asherim. See Deuteronomy 7:5.

563 (prime)

ג + תמנע *Gimel + timna*. camel + restraint. The Uniting Intelligence, through universal memory, symbolizes travel, communication and change. The restless mind must be restrained from excesses to assimilate only the pure nourishment of the divine. See 560, 3.

כפת + כבוד אל *kawphath + kaybod-El*. to tie, bind, fetter + the glory of God. Alchemical Gold, until its liberation, is fettered by the mind through ignorance and lack of concentration. See 500, 63.

564

אבן הראשא *eheben ha-roshah*. the head-stone. In Zechariah 4:7: "Who art thou, O great mountain? Before Zerubbabel thou shall become a plain: and he shall bring forth the headstone thereof with shoutings, crying, Grace, grace unto it." Zerubbabel means 'offspring of Babel" or "the grief of Babel" and is recognized as the rebuilder of Jerusalem and the temple after the Babylonian exile [Standard Bible Dictionary]. The pinnacle stone of a pyramid. *Lapis Capitalis*, (133). The passage cited is a very important one. Some have thought the headstone was the arch's keystone, but actually, it is the pinnacle of a pyramid, the capstone that is at once a determinant and the building's completion. The pinnacle stone of a pyramid is itself a scale model of the whole pyramid's proportions. See 1214, 1276 (Greek), 53, 241, 801.

ויהי האדם לנפש חיה *vayehi ha-adam le-nefesh chaiah*. And man became a living soul [Genesis 2:7]. A reference to the physical body of a man.

See 1124.

I. I.R.Q. Para. 941: "And the Adam was formed into a living Nephesh [soul] so that it (*the physical Nephesh form*) might be attached to himself (otherwise, so that it might be developed in him), and that he might form himself into similar conformations (That is into conformations similar to those of the supernal man.); and that he might project himself in that Neshamah from the path into the path (That is, into forms, conditions, and qualities analogous to the Sephiroth), even unto the end and completion of all the paths." [Mathers, 1993, p. 228]

חלם יסודות *Kholem Yesodoth*. Breaker of the Foundations. The Sphere of the Elements; the part of the material world corresponding to Malkuth. The field in which the fundamental unity of cosmic substance appears to be broken up. The verb חלם, *khahalam*, means primarily "to bind," and by indirect reference to how one is bound by the conditions of a dream while the latter continues, is also the Hebrew for "to dream." The other translation, "breaker," seems to reference the separative power active in Malkuth. The four elements attributed to Malkuth are not things in the universe but mental concepts. At the same time, they are the subtle principles of sight (Fire), taste (Water), touch (Air), and smell (Earth). See 496, 31, 55, 80, 95, 471.

מי שחור *Mae Shihor*. Water of Shihor [Jeremiah 2:18]. שחור means dinginess, sootiness, black, charred, melancholy. Thus the "Waters of Shihor" refers to illusion. One may see by their connection with the passage cited, with the "Way of Egypt." Egypt symbolizes the sphere of sensation associated with Malkuth, and the "Waters of Dinginess" is sense impressions that conceal reality, as cloudy water hides what it contains.

חנוך *Enoch*. Initiated. With different vowel points *Innok*, meaning: inauguration, consecration, training, dedication. [Genesis 4:17]. (Kaph = 500, see 84].

Ἡ Πημη *Heh Phemem* (Greek). The Report

(*Fama*). The Greek dictionary is defined as 1. a Voice from heaven; a prophetic voice; an oracle, an augury; 2. a speech, saying, song. 3. A common saying, an old tradition, legend. 4. like the Latin *Fama*, a rumor, report. 5. a message. The *Fama Fraternitatis* is a book which the Rosicrucians themselves declare to be a veiled, allegorical expression. Just as the Bible has been misinterpreted by those who take it literally, so has the Fama brought nothing but confusion to the minds of those who take it at its face value, as the story of an actual man who founded a German secret society. See 20.

The numeric value of the 4 mottos around the altar in the vault of C.R. [170+113+155+126 = 564].

Nequaquam Vacuum (Lt). Nowhere a vacuum. The sign Leo. The element Fire. See 170.

Legis Jugum (Lt). The yoke of the law. The eagle, Scorpio; element Water. See 113.

Libertas Evangelii (Lt). Liberty of the Gospels. Man, Aquarius, the element Air. See 155.

Dei Gloria Intacta (Lt). The untouchable glory of God. Taurus, the Bull. Earth. See 126.

565

כי ביה יהוה צור עולמים *ki be-Yah IHVH tzur olahmim.* For in Yah Tetragrammaton, rock [strength] everlasting. In Isaiah 26:4: "Trust in the Lord forever: for in the Lord Jehovah is everlasting strength [צור]." see 26, 196, 146.

שליט ברוח *shalliati ba-rauch.* who has power over the spirit. Ecclesiastes 8:8: "There is no man that has power over the spirit to retain the spirit; neither has he power in the day of death: and there is no discharge in that war; neither shall wickedness deliver those that are given to it." see 214.

עד קצה הארץ *ad-qaytzeh ha-aretz.* unto the ends of the earth. In Psalm 46:9: "He makes wars to cease unto the ends of the earth; he breaks the bow, and cuts the spear in sunder; he burns the chariot in the fire." see 3205 (Greek).

566

ישרון *Jeshurrun.* The upright one, a valley, a plain. The symbolic name of Israel. Occurs 4 times in the Old Testament [Deuteronomy 32:15; 33:5; 33:26 and Isaiah 44:2. Upright, Just (see note 732). By Qabalistic exegesis ישר (mas) uprightness represents the male or "upright one" conjoined with (the conjunction being Vav) Nun, which represents the female because Nun (50) is the numerical symbol of the 50 gates of Binah בינה. See 511.

צלמות *tzalmaeth.* shadow of death, deep shadow, great darkness. "The 2ⁿᵈ Hell, corresponding to Hod." [Godwin. 1999, p. 575.] Paul Case attributed this to the Hell of Netzach. One of the seven infernal mansions, depicted in the diagram of the 4 seas. Psalm 23:4: "Yea, thou I walk through the valley of the shadow of death, I will fear no evil for thou art with me; your rod and your staff they comfort me." see 337, 57, 911, 99, 1026, 108, 291.

נקודות *nequdoth.* points, dots. Refers to the points of manifestation, originating as Kether. See 160, 165.

תיקון *tiqon, tikkun.* restitution, restoration, reintegration. The goal of the personality of the aspirant. See 1216.

סמך וו דלת *samekh-vav-daleth.* Sod, "a secret," spelled in plentitude. This refers to the secret knowledge of Jeshurun, which overcomes the "shadow of death." It is the mystery of renewal and regeneration. See 70, 80, 96.

חמדת כל הגוים *chemedath kahl-ha-goyim.* The desire of all nations, the choicest things of all nations. In Haggai 2:7: "And I will shake all nations, and the desire of all nations shall come: and I will fill this house with glory, says the Lord of Hosts." Paul Case adds: "nations" is "goyim" and refers to the gentiles. The nations esoterically are the millions upon millions of cells not directly concerned with controlling the body's functions. See 59, 412, 32, 100, Key 18.

משיח בן ייסף *mashiah ben-Joseph*. Messiah, son of Joseph. Joseph, meaning "multiplier," is related to Pisces and the seed ideas alchemical multiplication that the Christos resides eternally in the heart. See 1936, 259, 358, 53, 156, 424, 1074.

חכמות כוכבים *chawkaymuth kokawbim*. wisdom of the stars; i.e., astrology. Note that Chokmah, wisdom, is the sphere of the Zodiac. [Note short spelling of chokmoth to fit this number]. See 48, 98, 474.

567

I. (3 x 3 x 3 x 3 x 7) or 7 x 3^4

אסוך *awsook*. vessel, flask, cup, pot for holding anointing oil. Refers to Yesod as the receptacle of influences flowing down from above. See 87. [Kaph = 500]

שכל בהיר *Saykel Bahir*. The intelligence of Transparency or Light. The 12th Path of Beth. The active principle is the Limitless Light concentrated in Kether. This path serves as a transparent medium for the passage of that Light, and its activity is penetrative, specializing and particularizing. The agency of self-consciousness carries this power from above, through and into a field prepared to receive it below (subconsciousness). The adjective בהיר is closely related to the word אור, *aur*, light. Here we must bear in mind that Beth is used in Hebrew as the preposition <u>in</u> and <u>into</u>. See 217, 412, 8, 2080.

"I am the Transparent Intelligence, penetrating all veils of ignorance with the light of life eternal." [Meditations on the Paths of Wisdom]

ראשוני *reashoni*. First-born. First, primary, original. The primary impulse born into the form-building sphere of Binah is the attention to the flow of images in Kether, symbolized by the uplifted wand of The Magician, centered in the path of Beth.

568

הנחש הקדמון *ha-nachash ha-qadaymon*. the primordial serpent; the original serpent, seducer of Eve. See 358.

במצולת into the depths. See Exodus 15:5.

תעצוו you be grieved, you be distressed. See Genesis 45:5.

569 (prime)

עמק השדים *emeq ha-siddim*. the valley of Siddim. Siddim means "plains"; this is the name of the plains afterward occupied by the Dead Sea. In Genesis 14:3: "All these [kings] were joined together in the valley of Siddim, which is the salt sea. See 354.

קטנתי I am not worthy. See Genesis 32:11.

ευλογιαν. *eulogian*. Blessing. Septuagint translation of ברכת "blessings" (622) in Genesis 28:4: "And give you the blessing of Abraham, to you, and to your seed with you; that you may inherit the land wherein you are a stranger, which God gave to Abraham." see 622.

570

נפתלי Tribe of *Naphtali*. My wrestling. Genesis 49:21: "Naphtali is a hind, let loose: he gives goodly words." "Goodly words" is the attribute of Naphtali in Jacob's blessing. Connected with the letter Yod, the sign Virgo, the Intelligence of Will, the function of coition, the sense of touch, the direction north-below, Key 9, The Hermit, and alchemical distillation, the 6th stage of the Great Work. Distillation separates volatile essences of solar energy from intestinal chyle by acts of self-consciousness attention. It is the assimilation of "liquid gold." By this process, the adept charges his blood-stream and nervous system with a superabundance of liquid "Yods."

He exerts this rule in selecting what he eats and drinks and in the conscious control of breathing. The direction assigned to Yod and distillation is a combination of North (Key 16) and below (Key 2) corresponding to the Mars center and the Moon center, or pituitary body. Psychologically, it is impossible to recognize the One Identity pictured as the hermit until false separateness structures are broken down and united to the subconscious field pictured by the High Priestess. When one knows, he can make a specific suggestion that assimilation of the subtle essence can be increased, the use of positive affirmations combined with visual imagery. See 501, 54, 162, 830, 395, 30, 95, 331, 443, 20, 7, 351, 466, 46.

Inman: "…From these considerations, we come to the conclusion that Naphtali is a variant of some Egyptian name resembling that which the LXX translates ΝεΦθαλειμ. Or, taking *Neptoah* for 'the vulva,' we may presume that the addition of אלי, eli, would be abbreviated into *neptohli*, *naphtali*, or *napthali*, which would be equivalent to "The Yoni is my God," = "I worship the celestial Virgin." [Inman, 1942, Vol. 2., p. 368]

כספית *Kasepith*. Quicksilver, Mercury. A reference to the first matter of the stone.

למך *Lamech*. Powerful. According to Masonic tradition, the name of the biblical patriarch was the father of that ancient craft. See Genesis 4:18]. [Kaph = 500, see 90]

מלך *Melek*. King, ruler, to administer. A name for Tiphareth, as the set of the higher Ego or Christos. The essential spirit of Man (Adam) is the dominant power in creation. See 90.

רעש *ra'ash*. quaking, shaking, quivering, earthquake, commotion. From the verb meaning: to quake, shake, to storm, rage. In Jeremiah 47:3: "At the noise of the stamping of the hoofs of his strong horses, at the rushing of his chariots, and at the rumbling of his wheels, the fathers shall not look back to their children for feebleness of hands." Rosenroth in K.D.L.C.K. (p.691) says that רעש (earthquake) with an allusion to רשע wickedness is that impiety, which seduces and

moves the earth, and in a moment loses all sense of justice and balance. See Nahum 3:2.

רשע *raesha*. wickedness, viciousness, injustice, wrong, guilt; wicked men. Psalm 5:5: "The foolish shall not stand in sight: thou has all worker of iniquity." With different pointing: *rawshaw*. wicked man; villain, sinner, guilt, a wrongful claimant in Job 20:29: ""This is a portion of a wicked man from God, and the heritage appointed unto him by God."

שכל טהור *Saykel Tahoor*. Purified or Pure Intelligence. The 9th path of Yesod. Tahoor means clean, so-called because it "Purifies the essence of the Sephiroth, proves and preserves their images and prevents them from loss by their union with itself." Teth is the lion that is tamed, not killed by the wreath of roses. Heh is related to man's power of directing circumstance through the use of foresight. Vav represents the Self, which reveals the secret wisdom of the forces concentrated in Yesod. Resh is the early stages of man's awareness of becoming a "new creature"- the child-like fusion of Self and subconsciousness centered in the Ego. Man makes himself a member of the 5th kingdom by utilizing the tremendous surplus of reproductive power. Here the fitness of every personality is tested and tried. They who are called and chosen are they whose organisms are ready for the work. See 220, 80, 430, 160.

"It is the Clear Intelligence, purifying all numerations and preserving the integrity of their images." [Meditations on the Paths of Wisdom]

שער *sha'ar*. Gate, entrance; market; a meeting place, measure, estimate, estimation, proportion. In later Hebrew, a title page of a book. A title of Malkuth in Judges 16:3. See Amos 5:12.

עשר the number ten; wealth. The 10th Sephirah, the Kingdom of Earth.

עשר *asar*, *essar*. ten. "This is to say, *the congregation of power proper, of elementary motive force*. This meaning result forms the two contracted roots שר עש. By the first, עש, is understood, every formation by aggregation; thence, the verb הועש *to make*; by the second, שר, every motive principle; thence the verb שור to direct, to govern. [d'Olivet, 1976, p. 154.] For other numerals see 13, 400, 636, 273, 348, 600, 372, 395, 770, 441.

Of עש: Every idea of conformation by aggregation of parts, or in consequence of an intelligent movement, combination or plan formed in advance by the will; thence, a *work, a composition; a creation, a fiction, labor* of any sort, *a thing*; action of *doing* in general. [ibid., p. 422.] See 560 for his notes on שר.

ערש *eres*. couch, bed, sarcophagus [Deuteronomy 3:11]. Rosenroth in K.D.L.C.K. (p.634) refers to this word as *lectus*, couch, marriage-bed; (dining or funeral couch), and says it is Malkuth, being the metathesis of עשר, ten, because it [Malkuth] stands under the decade or 10 Sephiroth. With different pointing *oras*: to bind, to roof.

יסך *yawsak*. to pour. See 90.

עשר *awsare*. to tithe; take a tenth part of. As an intransitive verb, "to make rich, become rich."

ויטע יהוה אלהים גן בעדן מקדם Now the Lord God had planted a garden in the east, in Eden" [Genesis 2:8]. The divine seed is planted in the physical body (the garden) to bring delight (Eden) and enlightenment (eastward). This is accomplished through alchemical distillation. See 53, 124.

רישין *reshin*. heads.

רשמר *reshin*. To guard. See Genesis 3:24.

ο θρονος. *ho thronos*. The throne; seat, chair of state, judge's chair, teacher.

οι υιοι. *hoi huioi*. The sons. In Matthew 13:38: "The field is the world; the Good seed are the sons of the Kingdom..."

Visita Interiora Terrae Rectificando Invenies Occultum Lapidem. Visit the earth's interior; by rectifying, you shall find the hidden stone [Secret Symbols page 17]. The earth is *Guph* [89], the body attributed to Malkuth. We find the stone with the body. When we "visit the interior of the earth," we find that the moving spirit which animates the organism is what we term "I, Myself." see 150, 57, 94, 164, 160, 73, 99, 61, 88, 96 Latin, 54.

571 (prime)

מלאך *Maleak*. messenger, angel, one sent. Applied also to a certain type of human personality who is a messenger of the higher self. See 133 (Greek) [Kaph = 500, see 91]

Spelled מלאך in the Hebrew of 2 Kings 1:3: "But the angel of the Lord said unto Elijah the Tishbite, go up to meet the messengers [מלאכי, messengers-of]of the king of Samaria, and ask them, 'Is it because there is no God in Israel that ou is going off to consult Ball-Zebub, the god of Ekron?"

מתקלא *metheqela*. balance. From תקל tekel Daniel 5:27: "You have been weighed on the scales and found wanting." Suggest weighing. (Note תקל = to weigh). Thus, it leads to the whole series of ideas represented by Libra and those described in the Book of the Dead's judgment scenes. According to Mathers, *metheqela* applies "To the two opposite natures in each triad of the Sephiroth, their equilibrium forming the third Sephirah in each trinity." In other words: 1 is the equilibrium of 2 and 3, which are in balance, 6 is the equilibrium of 4 and 5; 9 and 10 are equilibriums of 7 and 8 [9 interiorly, 10 exteriorly].

הקללות the curses. See Deuteronomy 28:15.

υιος. son.

572

חסדך *khesed-ka.* your loving kindness. Psalm 138:2: "I will worship toward your holy temple, and praise your name for your loving-kindness and for your truth: for thou has magnified your word above all your name." What the ignorant fear, the wise interpret correctly as the loving-kindness or Chesed. [Kaph = 500, see 92]

יהוה אלהיך *Jehovah Elohekah.* Lord, your God. See 92.

מתקבל *mitheqabal.* active. The Lord God is touching his people, hiding the waters of consciousness with the "stone" of unity. It is the reversal (Mem) of limitation (Tav) which multiples (Qoph) the concentration of Light (Beth) and teaches the perfect law of balance (Lamed).

פורפור *Phurayfur.* Goetia demon #34 by day of the 1st decan of Pisces. This decan corresponds to the 8 of Cups, or the activity of Hod, sphere of self-conscious activity in Briah, the creative world. See Appendix 11.

Goetia: "He is a great and might earl, appearing in the form of a hart with a fiery tail. He never speaks truth unless he is compelled… he will take upon himself the form of an angel. Being bidden, he speaks with a hoarse voice. Also, he will wittingly urge love between man and women. He can raise lightnings and thunders, blasts, and great tempestuous storms. And he gives true answers both of tings secret and divine if commanded. He rules over 26 legions of Spirits."

חכמות כוכבים *chawkaymuth kokawbim.* wisdom of the stars; i.e., astrology. Note that Chokmah, wisdom, is the sphere of the Zodiac. [Note short spelling of chokmoth to fit this number]. See 48, 98, 474, 566 (variant spelling).

573 (prime)

בראשיכם heads over you set them over you. Deuteronomy 1:13: "Choose some wise, understanding and respected men from each of your tribes, and I will set them over you [בראשיכם, as-heads-of-you]."

574

קול ורוח ודבור *qol ve-ruach ve-dabur.* voice and breath (spirit) and word. As spelled in *Sefer Yetzirah* 1:9. See 568.

ירחשון *yerakhshon.* Has a general meaning of "movement." In Sepher Dtzenioutha 19 (pp.83, 87): "It is written, Genesis 1:20 'Let the waters bring forth the reptile of a living soul (חיה living creature, 23]. Another explanation; 'Let the waters bring forth abundantly.' In this place, in the Chaldee paraphrase, it is said ירחשון, which has a general meaning of the movement. As if it should be said: 'When his lips by moving themselves, and murmuring, produced the words, like a prayer from a righteous heart and pure mind, the water produced the living soul.' (the meaning is concerning the act of generation life)." Note that ירח is the Moon, as a wanderer, to wander.

מקל שקד *mawel shawqed.* A rod of an almond tree. In Jeremiah 1:11: "Moreover, the word of the Lord came unto me, saying, 'Jeremiah, what sees thou? And I said, "I see a rod of an almond tree.'" Note that the almond wood was used to make the magical wand, connected with Mercury, or attention and concentration. [שקד = to wake, be watchful; to watch, keep watch, keep guard; to be studious, be zealous, be industrious; שקד diligence, sedulity]. See 404, 170.

575

ויאמר אלהים יהי אור *vayomer Elohim yehi aur.* "And the Elohim said, 'Let there be light.'"

עשרה *asarah.* ten (10). See 570.

יצר הרע *yawtzer-ha-roa.* Impulse to evil, the evil tempter. In The Zohar (I. p.76): "The ef'eh (adder) bears off-spring from the nachash (serpent) after seven year's gestation. Herein is the mystery of the seven names borne by the Gehinnom as well as by the 'evil tempter' (yetzer-hara), and from this source, impurity has been propagated in many grades throughout the universe." What redeems is a force, improperly understood, which pollutes. See 358.

אר כשדים *aur Kasaydim*. Light of the Chaldees. This is the "astral light" or universal radiance from the stars. See אור (207), 251, 581, 571.

הקרח הנורא *ha-qerach ha-noraw*. the terrible ice; the awe-inspiring (revered, wonderful) ice. Ezekiel 1:22: "And the likeness of the firmament upon the heads of the living creature was as the color of the terrible crystal, stretched forth over their heads above." [קרח = ice]. Ice and crystal suggest a lens of consciousness or Mercury.

באר שבע *Beer-sheba*; well of the seven. In Genesis 21:14: "And Abraham rose up early in the morning, and took bread, and a bottle of water, and gave it unto Habar, putting it on her shoulder, and the child, and sent her away: and she departed, and wandered in the wilderness of Beersheba." See Genesis 21:31, 33 and 2 Samuel 21:7. באר means well, pit; with different pointing: to make plain, distinct, explain, elucidate. שבע seven, seven-fold; seven times, many times; with different pointing: 1. to swear; 2. to do something seven times. See 203, 373, 248.

העשר riches. See Genesis 31:16.

הרשע the wicked, the guilty. See Deuteronomy 25:1.

המפתים the wonders. See Exodus 4:21.

576

I. (24x24) or 2^6 x 3^2

מקלות *maqqeloth*. wands.

סור מרע *sur meraw*. depart from evil. Psalms 37:27: "Depart from evil, and do good, and dwell for evermore.." Job 28:28: "and unto man he said, behold, the fear of the Lord, that is wisdom, and to depart from evil is understanding." The word "fear" can be rendered more accurately, "reverence." understanding is בינה. See 643, 917, 1953 (Greek).

שעור *sheur*. measure, magnitude, size, lesson. The measure of a man is the measure of his wisdom and understanding. See 626.

שוער *shoer*. gate-keeper, porter; a metathesis of שעור. See 2 Kings 7:10.

ושלום צדק *tzedque ve-shalom*. righteousness and peace. In Psalm 85:10: "Mercy and truth are met together, and righteousness and peace have kissed each other." see 194, 376, 73, 441, 995 (Greek).

ογγελος αληθειας. *angelos alethelas*. angel of truth.

αετος. *hetos*. An eagle. Written αετψ in Revelations 4:7: "And the first living-one resembled a lion, and the second living-one resembled an ox, and the third living-one having the face of a man, and the fourth living-one was like to a flying eagle." Connected with Scorpio and the regenerative force. See 550, and Revelations 8:13 & 12:14.

πνευμα. *Pneuma*. Breath, Life, Spirit. The psychical nature includes the ordinary elements of personality, self-consciousness and subconsciousness. Connected with the Hebrew Ruach [214]. See 69 Latin.

577 (prime)

פרו ורבו + ע + בדא *phayr uraybu + Ayin + bawdah*. Be fruitful and multiply + Ayin, the "eye" + to form, fashion, to produce something new. The fruitfulness is the idea of renewal (Ayin is the Renewing Intelligence). Ayin is attributed to Capricorn, in which Mars is exalted. The archetypal phase of the creative process is imagination, inventing a new form of self-expression. The archetypal world is the plane of original ideas. "as above, so below." see 500, 70, 7.

עז + שר *sawr + oz.* prince, noble, ruler + strength, power might. עז is related to Capricorn and thus gives foundational power to מזלא Mezla, the influence from Kether. This builds the ruler or son, which is Tiphareth. See 500, 77, 78.

רחף + פטר *richef + pawtar.* to flutter, hover + to break through, to liberate; first-born. The spirit "hovers over the face of the waters" (of consciousness), and the result of this brooding is the liberation of the first-born son of God. See 288, 289.

ευα γγελιον. *euaggelion.* Goodness, glad tidings, gospels. Matthew 9:35: "And Jesus went through all the cities and villages, teaching in their synagogues, and announcing the glad tidings of the kingdom, and curing every disease and every malady."

578

בצעתיו and it grieved, and he hurt. See Genesis 6:6.

ותבקע and did split, cleave asunder, that she was split. See Numbers 16:31.

חפצת delight, you are pleased. See Deuteronomy 21:14.

579

טרף + מרים *tawraph + miriam.* to tear to pieces, to seize forcibly, mix, confuse + rebellion, perversity, antagonism. Their meanings are mental states having close association with strong but unfulfilled desires. Christian tradition gives the virgin, who is also the holy mother (Binah, the "superior" mother, in contrast to Malkuth, the "inferior" mother), the same name as the Magdalene, Mary, who was forgiven because she loved much. See 289, 290.

חצות לילה *chatozoth lailah.* midnight. *media nox,* or "middle night." According to K.D.L.C.K. (p.361) says that in the Zohar Malkuth is called *medietas,* the middle or mean, because it partakes of the other parts of the tree; Geburah is called *nox* or night because at the time it rigorously judges; compassion coming after the middle of the night; others attribute this name to Tiphareth, for other reasons.

תענוגים *thonugim.* Sons of Adam [Crowley, 1977, p. 53]. Of the root: "תע: That which is false, illusory, vain; that which has an only appearance, semblance. For the root תן: Every idea of substance added, of corporeity increasing more and more; an extension, an enlargement, largess, in a restricted sense, *a gift.* The action of *giving; an offering,* a present: that which is *liberal, generous.*" [d'Olivet, 1976, pp. 469-470.] Both meanings have to do with the uses of human consciousness.

580

עתיק *ahthiq.* old, ancient, antique. IN Daniel 7:9, 13: "I beheld till the thrones were cast down, and the ancient of days did sit, whose raiment was as white as snow, and the hair of his head like the pure wool: his throne was like the fiery flame, and his wheels as burning fire." (13) "In my vision at night I looked, and there before me was one like a son of man, coming with the clouds of heaven. He approached the Ancient of Days and was led into his presence." Refers to Kether. With different pointing: eminent, choice. See 620, 647, 696.

גיא צלמות *gey tzalmaveth.* Valley of the Shadow of Death. Psalm 23:4: "Yea, though I walk through (Beth) the valley of the shadow of death, I will fear no evil: for thou art with me; your rod and your staff they comfort me." *Tzalmaveth* is explained by Paul Case as being the "Hell of Netzach." The Hebrew Lexicon gives deep shadow, great darkness, hell (literally 'shadow of death'). Paul Case also lists this word as one of the 7 Infernal Mansion. See 566, 3826 (Greek).

שעיר *sair, sawyir.* satyr, a goat-shaped demon; hairy one; he-goat; hairy, bulk, thin shower

125

(plural). Isaiah 34:14: "The wild beast of the desert shall also meet with the wild beast of the island, and the satyr shall cry to his fellow; the screech owl also shall rest there, and find for herself a place of rest." With different pointing: scapegoat, shaggy. In Leviticus 16:22: "And the goat [השעיר] shall bear upon him all their iniquities into a solitary land; and he [Aaron, "lofty"] shall let go the goat, את השעיר, in the wilderness." see 1329, 401, 256.

עשיר *yawshir*. rich, rich man. The man who has sublimated the Mars-force. Note that the goat is a symbol of Capricorn, in which Mars is exalted.

לנך *Nelak*. The 21st Shem ha-Mephorash, short-form. [Kaph = 500, see 131]

שרף *Seraph*. Fiery Serpent [Numbers 21:8]. Ruler of Fire; one of the Seraphim. In Numbers 21:8, "The Lord said to Moses, Make a snake (seraph) and put it up on a pole; anyone who is bitten can look at it and live."

פרש *peresh*. Dung. An alchemical term, a blind for Seraph, by transposing the letters. See 711.

פך *pakh*. flask, bottle. See 1 Samuel 10:1. [Kaph = 500, see 100].

פרי + רמים *phayriy + remim*. fruit, off-spring, product, result + unicorns. The fruit of consecration is the "one-horned" or spiritual illumination-the Mercury center or third eye. Note that the "horn" can be made to play music. See 290.

αλληλουια. *Alleluia*. Hallelujah; from Hebrew הללויה praise Jah (Jehovah)! Revelation 19:1: "After these things I heard a loud voice as a great crowd in heaven, saying 'Hallelujah! the salvation and the glory and the power of our God." see 86 and Revelation 19:3, 4, 6.

"Here, the main action of the drama is resumed: the chorus, which is the seventh and last, is a tribute of victory following the attainment by the conqueror of the spiritual rebirth. The chorus is chanted by all the microcosmic universe's powers, the enthroned Logos being the chorus leader. The word hallelujah, which is not found elsewhere in the New Testament, is here chanted four times." [Pryse, 1965, p. 168.]

581

עתיקא *ahthiq*. The Ancient One, ancient of. The Kabbalah Unveiled (page 23), it is spelled עתיקא. See 580 for Biblical spelling.

אור כשדים *Ur Kasdim*. Light of the Chaldees (astrology). In the Old Testament, Kasdim was blind for astrology. See 848, 291, 352, 126, 201, 713, 406, 400, 251, 575 & Genesis 11:31.

בעל הדעת *Bal ha-Daath*. Master (Lord) of Knowledge. The name is attributed to the Rosicrucian Grade of Theoricus (Yesod). One who has acquired the necessary knowledge relative to the hidden forces and processes of Yesod. All attributions of Da'ath are on the Middle Pillar and include Tiphareth as well. Da'ath is a feminine noun and connotes copulation, with consequent giving of birth. As a transitive verb, it means: to know, consider, to care for, to have sexual intercourse with; to know-how be skillful. With different pointing: knowledge, mind, reason. See 80, 474, 479, 84.

פוטי פרע כהן אן *Poti-phera kohen On*. Potiphera, priest of On. The father-in-law of Joseph. Genesis 41:45: "And Pharaoh called Joseph's name Zaphinath-paanea, and he gave him to wife Asenath, the daughter of Potiphera priest of On."

Potiphera and Potiphar (whose wife attempted to seduce Joseph) are identical names. Their Egyptian name means, "He whom Ra Gave." (Ra is the Egyptian sun-god). So the inner significance of "Potiphera" is "Light." "On" is the city of Heliopolis, of Beth-shemesh (1052), the house of the sun. And "Asenath," the wife of Joseph, is the Hebrew for Isis-Neith. [In Egyptian mythology, Isis and Neith are more or less blended or confused. Isis is a Moon Goddess and fertility deity. Neith, armed with bow and arrows, is like Artemis of the Grecian mythology, a lunar-deity. This shows that the hidden knowledge here indicated has to do with "Light" and particularly with those subconscious manifestations which reflect those higher light-sources represented on the Tree of Life as the three Supernals. See 302, 126, 120, 850 (Greek).

הראש כהן Cohen ha-rosh. Chief priest [2 Kings 25:18].

שעורה shorah. barley.

מקלי את ayth-maqeu. my staff. Zech 11:11:. "And I took my staff, even beauty, and cut it asunder, that I might break my covenant which I had made with all the people." The staff here is called "graciousness" in the Jewish translation. In the A.V., it is called "beauty." see 1142.

ולשמרה vu-leshawmerah. (to till it) "And to guard it." Genesis 2:15: "And the Lord God took the man, and put him into the garden of Eden to dress it and to keep it." The purpose of man is to spiritualize the physical plane through the right knowledge. The "garden of delight" is the human body. See 124.

582

במשמר in the ward (prison), in the custody of. See Genesis 40:3.

מבשרם of their flesh. See Leviticus 11:8.

מקבילת opposite, parallel, opposing. See Exodus 26:5.

תעוננו soothsaying, you practice sorcery. See Leviticus 19:26.

583

טמירין דטמירא Temira De-Temirin. The Concealed of the Concealed, a title of Kether. See 620 and Kabbalah Unveiled (p.23).

מסתגף misetageyf. a hermit; literally, "a hidden body." Both these refer to Key 9, which pictures the Concealed One as the solitary Watcher on high. [גף = body, מסת = hidden]

עשר אחד achad awsawr. eleven. Connected with the 11th path of wisdom, Aleph, the Fiery Intelligence, and with Lamed, depicted in Justice, the 11th Tarot Key. In Genesis 37:9: "Then he [Joseph] has another dream, and he told it to his brothers. "Listen, he said, "I had another dream, and this time the sun and moon and eleven stars were bowing down to me.'" see Exodus 26:8.

אבימלך Abimelek. "my father is king"; A Philistine King of Gerar, a locality near Gaza. Genesis 20:2: "And there (Gerar) Abraham said of his wife Sara, 'she is my sister.' Then Abimelek King of Gerar sent for Sarah and took her."

החיים שרי Shawiyr hachaiim. A song of life.

Κυβαλιον. Kybalion. a coined word: Qabalah + Cybele. A book of Hermetic philosophy.

Paul Case: "KYBALION... is a coined word of Greek derivation, chosen because, by sound, it suggests both "Qabalah" and "Cybele." The latter is the name of the Asiatic "mother of the gods," corresponding to Rhea, the earth-goddess who was the wife of Saturn, and the mother of Vesta, Juno, Neptune, Pluto and Jupiter. In Tarot, she is represented by the Empress, by the woman in Key 8, taming a lion, by Justice and by the kneeling water-bearer of Key 17. Although she is primarily a symbol for Venus, the Empress also corresponds to most of the mother goddesses of ancient mythology. [The Kabalion]

2. Written in Greek letters, the numerical value of KYBALION is 583. This is 11 x 53, and since 53 in alchemy is referable both to [אבן], ehben, stone, and to [חמה], khammaw, sun, while 11 (as Tarot shows) has to do with equilibration, there is more than a hint here that KYBALION has to do with the Great Work of equilibrating the powers of the Spiritual Sun, to produce the Stone of the Wise.

ויתעצבו and they were grieved. See Genesis 34:7.

תלחצנו and shall oppress him. See Exodus 22:20.

תפקד you shall number [count]. See Numbers 1:49.

585

I. $12^2 + 21^2$ or $144 + 441$. Represents the fullest manifestation and the perfect expression of Kether mathematically.

אלהים צבאות *Elohim Tzabaoth*. God of Armies, Creative Powers of Hosts. The Divine Name attributed to Hod, the 8 of Wands and associated with self-conscious human intellect, represents the fullest manifestation and the perfect expression of Kether mathematically. This, in essence, is the purpose of human self-consciousness. This purpose is seen to be the perfect expression of the powers of the One I AM. The feminine aspect of the divine being, descending from Binah. Tzabaoth (armies) indicates the diversity and apparent subdivision of these powers when they find expression in human life through "host" personalities. Thus, personal intellect in Hod is the expression and temporal manifestation of the eternal creativity of the divine soul. See 15, 370, 720.

The first word in this two-part name is that assigned to the third Sephirah, just as the first word in יהוה צבאות, Jehovah Tzabaoth, is the extended form of יה, *Jah*, the name assigned to Chokmah. Jah and Jehovah express the masculine aspect of the Divine Being. Elohim is the Qabalistic designation for the feminine. For Netzach, the seventh Sephirah, though it is called the Sphere of Venus, is nonetheless a male Sephirah; while Hod, the Sphere of Mercury, has its place on the feminine side of the Tree.

השרף *ha-seraph*. The fiery serpent, fiery angels. The serpent is one symbol for Mercury or Hermes. When the self-conscious powers of man are misunderstood and misdirected toward separateness, then they express the evil connotation of Mercury as the slanderer of man to himself. That is why the Mercury symbol is on the belly of the Devil in Key 15. The name of the order of Angels assigned to Geburah. Spelled נחש in Genesis and שרף in Numbers 21:8, where Moses made a "serpent of Brass." see 580, 358, 630.

לחוף אנית le-*khop ahnith*. for a haven of ships. Said of Zebulon in Genesis 49:13: "Zebulon shall dwell at the haven of the sea, and he shall be for a haven of ships..." Zebulon means "habitation" or "home" and is the tribe corresponding to Cancer, a watery sign. Cancer, the 4th sign, corresponds to the 4th house of the horoscope, referred to home, and to the "end of the matter," that is, to "coming into port." It also corresponds to Alchemical separation. See 95, 1305

עמודי שבעה החכמה *ammudi shibeaw he-chokmah*. The seven pillars of wisdom. Development of the intimation given in Proverbs 9:11: "Wisdom has built her house, she has hewn out her seven pillars." see 512, 507.

פרשה *parahshaw*. Sum [Esther 4:7], declaration [Esther 10:2]. With different pointing: exact statement; branching off, sea voyage; crossing the ocean, section of scripture. Relates to Zebulon, with the aid of Mercury.

תקיעה *tequiaw*. horn blast; Blowing of Shofar, pledging (by striking hands). Suggest Key 20. See 586 and K.D.L.C.K. (p. 386).

השעיר *ha-sawir, ha-saweer*. The goat. See 580 and Leviticus 16:22 Capricorn (fermentation) is the "scape-goat" when the Shofar is blown on the day of atonement. Refers to the path of Ayin and to Key 15, the devil and to apparent obstacles. See 580.

586

The 16 invisible paths' total length is when the Aleph line equals 15 (length of line between

Kether and Chokmah).

The Middle Pillar is the greatest secret of the Tree, and its central point, Tiphareth, is the heart of the secret. Tiphareth (תפארת), the 6th Sephirah is 1081, which reduces to 10 then 1, or both Kether (1) and Malkuth (10). Thus 1, 6 and 10 are all essentially the same.

Also on the Middle Pillar is Yesod (יסוד), whose number is 80. Yesod spelled in plentitude is יוד סמך וו דלת adds to 586, which reduces to 19 to 10 then 1.

Nineteen is our mother Eve (19, of חוה), Malkuth is 10, and Kether is 1. The whole idea is of the manifestation of Unity in the Kingdom; and the center, which is the Son, is also מלך & אדם. See C.13, 45, & 90.

פוך Pook. Antimony, stibium; first matter. See 106.

ירושלם Jerusalem. (older spelling) "abode of peace," or "founded in peace." see 596.

In the Fama, Brother C.R. begins his journey with his intended destination Jerusalem. The desire to visit Jerusalem symbolizes the longing for contentment, the desire for rest from strife caused by the struggle with the pair of opposites in the physical plane. This is the primary motivation for our new initiates. Please note that in the Fama, our Brother C.R. had a change in plans.

When the Fama was written, the last crusade was abandoned approximately 100 years ago. Jerusalem was a place of pilgrimage to the holy sepulcher. Thus a pilgrimage to Jerusalem was a reverence for the dead forms of the past. When an aspirant begins his quest for truth, they usually begin their search by revisiting old worn-out forms that provide comfort in times past. See 111, P.A.L.

יוד סמך וו דלת Yesod. Basis, Foundation, spelt in full.

Yesod is the Sphere of the Moon, and the Moon in the Tarot is Key 2, attributed to the letter Gimel and the Uniting Intelligence. The intelligence assigned to Yesod is טהור which means pure. Man enjoys a special privilege of multiplying the astral radiance by subtle means which transcend physical generation. Please note that an attitude of repudiation of physical generation is an error that will thwart any effort at the direction of the astral power to finer and higher uses. Never condemn the normal functions of life, or consider them to be unclean. What is taught and practiced is sublimation - , not a repudiation. The astral is not evil, nor is it to be feared. It is the plane that is the basis of our physical existence, and that basis is Light and Life. See C.27.

פרוש parush. abstinent person, hermit [Case]. With different pointing: 1. abstemious, saintly, pure; pharisee; 2. explanation; commentary. One who knows the "secret" of purifying Yesod eventually becomes a saint.

שופר Shofar. war-trumpet. In Exodus 19:16: "And it came to pass on the third day in the morning, that there were thunders and lighting, and a thick cloud appeared on the mountain and the sound of the trumpet exceedingly loud; so that all the people that were in the camp trembled." And in Job 39:24: "He gallops with rage that makes the ground tremble, nor does he fear the sound of the trumpet." see Key 20 and 585.

מתוך הסנה mayttok haseneh. out of the midst of a thorn-bush. In Exodus 3:2: "and the angel of the Lord [יהוה] appeared unto him [Moses] in a flame of fire out of the midst of a bush: and he looked, and, behold, the bush burned with fire, and was not consumed."

587 (prime)

פוראש Purash. Goetia demon #31 by day of the 1st decan of Aquarius. This decan corresponds to the 5 of Swords, or the Operation of Geburah, the will-force in Yetzirah, the formative world. See Appendix 11.

Goetia: "He is a mighty president and appears in

the form of a strong man in human shape. He can understand how men may know the virtues of all herbs and precious stones. He teaches the arts of logic and ethics in all their parts. If desired, he makes men invisible [Invincible?], live long, and be eloquent. He can discover treasures and recover things lost. He rules over 29 Legions of Spirits." [Mathers, 1995, p. 42]

ואשרף and I burnt. See Deuteronomy 9:21.

והמופתים and the wonders. See Deuteronomy 34:11.

588

יהוה אלהי לא עזר לבן אלמנה *IHVH Elohay lo-etzer leben-alaymanah*. O Lord, my God, is there no help for the widow's son? Mackey says: "In ancient craft Masonry ["window's son"] was the title applied to Hiram, the architect of the temple, because he is said to have been I Kings 7:14: 'A widow's son, of the tribe of Naphtali." As the wife of Hiram remained a widow after her son was murdered, the Masons, who regarded themselves as the descendants of Hiram, call themselves 'sons of the widow.'" [Encyclopedia of Free Masonry, p.881] [Lo, help = הן עורת, 732; the no-thing the help = אין עורת] see 1018, 1002.

בר ישוע *Bar-Jesus*. Acts 13:6: "And when they had gone through the isle unto Paphos, they found a certain sorcerer, a false prophet, a Jew, whose name was Bar-Jesus."

589

כבוד ראשון *Kabode Rashun*. First Splendor, Primal Glory. A title of Kether. It is the light of the Primordial Intelligence-a conscious, living, radiant energy, possessing weight or mass, and the force of Gravitation. See 78, 438, 32, 557, 620.

שער הגיא Gate of the Valley. See Nehemiah 2:13.

590

שרץ *sharatz*. to bring forth abundantly With different pointing *sheretz*: Creeping thing, moving creature.

טורו + אפרוח *epheruh + patoor*. young bird + open blossom. Both are metaphors of the "new creature," which is multiplied throughout the body cells. "Open blossom" is an epithet for the Sephiroth Malkuth, meaning "free." See 295.

צלעת *tzaleotha*. ribs. In Genesis 2:21: "so the Lord God caused the man to fall into a deep sleep; and while he was sleeping, he took one of the man's ribs and closed up the place with flesh."

1. See 502 for Fabre D'Olivet's translation of this verse.

He comments: "ומצלעתי, of-the-involutions-of-him... In a word wherein forms are formed so many different images, one cannot choose an idea more petty and more material than that which the Hellenists have rendered by the word a rib. The root צל are those of a shadow, an object extending above, shadowing, a canopy, a curtain, a screen hanging, roof, etc.

What is the meaning of the root עה. Is it not that which is attached to all the curving all circumferential form, to all exterior superficies of things..."

Therefore the word צלע signifies exactly an envelope, an exterior covering, a protecting shelter. This is what the facultative צולע proves, to be enclosing, covering, enveloping: This word which is derived from the root על, characterizes a thing raised to serve as covering, canopy, etc." [d'Olivet, 1976, pp. 88-89.]

591

נאקתם their groaning. See Exodus 2:24.

592

שכל מצוחצח *Sekhel Metzochtzoch*. Scintillating or

Fiery Intelligence. The 11th Path of Aleph. From a root meaning: brightness, clearness, splendor. The channel for the first outpouring from Kether, the concentrated brilliance of the Limitless Light.

Scintillating or Fiery is a root word meaning brightness, clearness, splendor. The 11th path is the channel for the 1st outpouring from Kether, the concentrated white brilliance of the Limitless Light.

"I am the Scintillating Intelligence, veiling with the fire of Spirit, the causes superior from the causes inferior." [Meditations on the 32 Paths of Wisdom].

פעולות *pehulloth*. activities.

Θεοτης. *Theotes*. Godhead.

η εκκλησια η πασα. The Whole Church.

αγιοτης. *Hagiotes*. Holiness.

η αληθινη μαθησις. *heh alethine mathesis*. The true teaching.

593 (prime)

בא + שפיר *baw + shafir*. coming, future; to go out and in + beautiful, fair, right, well good. The Life-power manifests in every event and condition throughout the cycles of evolution. Inside the hedge of safety, which is also a wall of limitation (i.e., Cheth). This appears to be in the future. But the beautiful and good results are always in the eternal now. See 590, 3.

רמון + אלהים גבור *rimon + Elohim gibbor*. Pomegranate + the Creative Powers of Strength. The fruit of the pomegranate, having many seeds, is a symbol of seed-though, as in Key 2. (Note the lunar crescents in Key 7). "Strength" is the name of Key 8, assigned to Teth. Strength is the result of the creative powers working on seed-thoughts. See 296, 297, 86, 211.

594

ישוע בן יוסף *Yeshua ben-Yoseph*. Jesus, son of Joseph. "Jesus is the liberator, and his self-conscious centers upon the idea of releasing men from bondage and death." [From Day to Day 3/12/1916] The son is the special designation of Tiphareth and name of the "secret nature" of Yetzirah, the formative world. Joseph means: "multiplier" and refers to the alchemical doctrine that the stone has multiplication powers. Usually, Joseph is attributed to Yesod as the generative power of Tiphareth. See 386, 52, 156.

והארץ הדם רגלי *ve ha-aretz haedom ragelawi*. and the earth is my footstool. Isaiah 66:1: "This is what the Lord says: Heaven is my throne, and the earth is my footstool. Where is the house you will build for me? Where will my resting place be? see 1080, 486, 759.

פקדתי I remembered I watched. See Exodus 3:16.

595

שפיר + אבב *shahfir + awbab*. beautiful, fair, right, good + to blossom, to shine, to yield fruit. The result of the union of darkness and light is always beautiful and good; it is the shining fruit of opposites' harmony. The first reduction of 595 is 19, the Key of the Sun, the second of Key 10 or Kaph, the grasp of cycles of manifestation, and the final reduction is 1 or Beth, the Magician (Key 1). 1 is also the value of Aleph or spirit. See 590, 5.

אופיר + אמן אור *amen aur + opir*. amen our light + "fine gold" or "red" (meaning sulfur). Amen means to be firm, faithful, to support. Ophir is a place where gold was brought to Solomon. "Gold is the sun of illumination. Note that Sulphur is connected with Peh and Gold with Resh. See 297, 298.

השרץ the reptile, the creeper. See Leviticus 11:31.

התפקדו they were numbered [counted]. See Numbers 1:47.

κεντρον. *kentron*. Center, pierce; sting, prickle.

596

שמרון *Shomron*. Samaria, capital of Israel.

ירושלים *Ierusalaim*. Jerusalem, the "abode of peace." The holy city of Israel. Later spelling from Hebrew Lexicon. See 1010, 586, 370.

ותפעם he was troubled. See Genesis 41:8.

קעות ends, extremities, ends off. See Exodus 25:18.

597

אפקיות *Ierusalaim*. horizontals. Another word for balances or scales, in later Hebrew. It is connected with Libra, rhythm and ritual. In Masonic symbolism, a clue to the meaning of "horizontals" is the position of the beam of a balance when the weights in the pans are equilibrated (alchemical sublimation, 501). From אפקי horizon, level. See 191 and מאזנים (148).

ויתאפק and he refrained himself. See Genesis 43:31.

σιδηρεος. *sidereos*. Iron; made of iron. The metal of Mars. See 239, 792.

598

דלת + מים + למד Lamed (ox-goad) + Mem (seas or waters) + Daleth (door). Lamed, "to teach, instruct" spelled in plentitude. The letter-name implies that instruction is the goad from levels above and within. Working within the water or mental substance to alter the desire natures that its images are in harmony with positive forms of creation. The correspondence should also noted in the gematria as indicted that instruction is the fruit of 'our iniquities," עונותינו. See 74, 90, 434.

צחקת you did laugh. Genesis 18:15.

599 (prime)

אנחמך I comfort you, I console you. See Isaiah 51:19.

המספחות The veils see Isaiah 62:6.

הפקדתי I posted [watchmen]. See Ezekiel 13:18.

Section 6

Numbers 600 - 699

600

I. (3 x 5 x 5 x 8) or 2^3 x 3 x 5^2

II. ם Final Mem. See 40.

זולתי אין אלהים *zulahthiy ain Elohim*. Beside me (there is) no God, no God beside me. Isaiah 45:5: "I am the Lord, and there is none else, there is no God beside me." The realization of the adept, "of myself I do nothing," is the direct consequence of his perception that God is One.

טהור ערפל *tawhore arawfel*. the pure darkness. The obscurity of the universal subconscious plane of life activity, represented by Yesod. (The path of Samekh connects Yesod with Tiphareth).

ירם קרן *yawrem qeren*. He lifted up a horn (for his people) [Psalm 148:14]. See 1186.

מינקת *meynehqeth*. Nurse [Genesis 35:8]. Deborah, Rebecca's nurse. The word is translated in Greek as a name for the pentad, which equals sound. See 1240 Greek, Plutarch, On the Generation of the Soul.

מינקת *menaqqiyth*. bowl for libations, sprinkling vessel [Exodus 25:29]. In all versions of Key 14, such a bowl or vessel is a prominent feature of the design.

מסך to mix (liquids). The angel in Key 14 pours the water from the vase. With different pointing: *mawsawk*. Curtain, screen. The path of Key 14 screens the initiating from the Ego or Higher Self-they must first be purified in Yesod. this is the veil, or paroketh, screening the Holy of Holies in the temple. [Kaph = 500, see 120].

מצפץ מצפץ Temurah for יהוה יהוה. A qabalistic cipher for Tetragrammaton Tetragrammaton (IHVH IHVH), the first 2 names of Mercy's 13 categories. In Exodus 34:6: "And the Lord passed by before him [Moses] and proclaimed, the Lord, the Lord God, merciful and gracious, long-suffering, and abundant in goodness and truth." If the Hebrew alphabet is inverted, Mem is in place of Yod, Tzaddi in the place of Heh and Peh in place of Vav. In its explanation of Genesis 1:16, the Zohar says the "two great lights" symbolize the "full name" IHVH ALHIM, Tetragrammaton Elohim. "Through him, the name of the whole was called *Matzpatz Matzpatz*, the two highest names in the 13 categories of Mercy." see 6, 60.

פליאות חכמה *peliyahoth Chokmah*. hidden (admirable) Wisdom. (From פליאה, miracle, marvel, wonderful deed).

סמך Letter name *Samekh*. Tent peg, to prop, support, hold. Connects Tiphareth to Yesod on the Tree of Life. What is pictured under one aspect of Key 13 manifests also in the activities of Key 14-the skeleton reaper and the angel is one. See 120.

קרש *qeresh*. board, plank. As a Mishnaic or Talmudic word, Unicorn. With different pointing: 1. *qawrash*: to become solid, congeal, contract. From a root meaning to split off, to cut apart. Exodus 26:15: "And thou shall make the boards [i.e., split boards] for the tabernacle of shittim wood standing up; 2. *qahshar*: to bind, to tie, to bind with cords (as the hanged man), to plot, conspire. With different pointing: 3. *qushshar*: to be strong, be vigorous; 4. *qehsher:* alliance, in both good and bad sense, plot, conspiracy, a band of conspirators; knot, band, loop; protuberance, joint; problem. See 103, 190 (Lt).

שש *shesh*. six; white marble, linen, white stone. Among the ancients, a cloth of exceedingly fine texture. Related to the white linen robes and white stones in the apocalypse in Revelations 3:17, 4:4. When one is in continual union with the central point, he has the state of purity symbolized by the robe and a new name. Its peculiar revelation is always ineffable. It is incommunicable because there are no words or other symbols whereby it may be expressed. As a masculine noun, same pointing, white marble. See 6, 60, 186, 162, 800, and Genesis 41:42 & Proverbs 31:24 and Song of Solomon 5:15.

שש *six*. "The root שו contains all ideas of equality, of equilibrium, of fitness, or proportion in things. United to the sign of relative duration ש to form this number's name, it becomes the symbol of every proportional and relative measure. It is quite well known that the number *six* is applied to particular, to the circle's measure, and in general, to all proportional measures. One finds in the feminine, ששה, and the Chaldaic read שת: which is not unlike the name of the number *two* [400]; furthermore, between these there exist great analogies, since *six* is to *three*, what *two* is to *one*; and since we have seen that *three* [636] represented a sort of unity." [d'Olivet, 1976, p. 153.] For other numerals see 13, 400, 636, 273, 348, 372, 395, 770, 570, 441.

ציצית *tzeytzeyth*. lock, forelock, tassel, fringe. From ציצה: blossom, flower. Refers to the white stone, the opened center in the head that receives God's glory and is adorned with a fringe.

Η Θεοτης. *Heh Theotes*. The Godhead, divine nature. The divine nature and perfection. The cosmos is of one substance with Godhead.

κοσμος. *kosmos*. Order, arrangement (of the Universe). The intelligible world or order of all things includes the intelligible word or reason (Logos). 1. order. 2. good order, good behavior, decency. 3. a set form or order: of states, government. 4.the mode or fashion of a thing. an ornament, decoration, dress, raiment. 5. an honor, credit.

This word is used in two opposite senses in the New Testament. This first is akin to the philosophical meaning, as found in the Pythagorean and Platonic texts. As a designation for "this world" and the present order of things, it stands for the false system with its conventions and erroneous standards that man sets up because of his ignorance (see John 14:17). A tabernacle of Moses, a cubical room was a symbol of this cosmic order. See 128, 670, 2670, 2541, 2516, 2219, 1850, 1517, 849.

I. James Pryse: "Greek, kosmos. The world's primary meaning is 'good order,' and it is applied to anything having definite form or arrangement, from an ornament or a fashion in a dress to the whole manifested universe. Chaos, or rather the primary matter it contains (*hyle*, unwrought material) becomes, though the formative power of the Logos, the kosmos or objective universe, each department of which is also a Kosmos or world in itself; hence the word applies to the suns and planets in space, to this earth, to humanity in general, and to the individual man. [The Magical Message According to Ioannes, p.75]

II. "World. An ordered condition, one of beauty, proportion, cultivation. Also, a constituted union, an order, or fellowship. Also, a leader, a general, who has been trained and developed. The use of this word to indicate the 'World' as an antithesis to the 'Spirit' has obscured its real meaning." [Omikron, 1942, pp. 257-258.]

χ *Chi*. Greek letter with the value of 600. It appears in Pythagorean, Gnostic, and other forms of symbolism (St. Andrew's Cross) in Christianity. It stands for Christ, as the foundation and support (Samekh) of personal existence and of the world order represented by κοσμος.

601 (prime)

אם *am*. womb, origin, mother. Refers to Binah, the Great Mother, symbolized by the Empress in the Tarot. See 41 and Key 3, #41. [Mem = 600]

שכל מאיר *Sekhel Mier*. Luminous Intelligence. The 14th Path of Daleth. First of the reciprocal path of the Tree, Joining Chokmah to Binah. Derives its luminosity from the Illuminating Intelligence of Chokmah. It is the Mysteries (Institutrix Arcanorum) Establisher because it is "the path of the hidden things of not-existent creation, the pattern forming power of creative imagination which shapes mind-stuff into form. The subconscious mental activity behind physical cell function was related to reproduction, impressed on the Jupiter center's cells. It may be used consciously to rejuvenate the body into the fifth kingdom. A master of this path can also influence the health of others via spiritual healing. On the cosmic level, this activity is the generation, multiplication, and development of the paternal see (Chaiah in Chokmah) and its expression in mental imagery. See 358, 378, 70, 71, 486, 703, 67, 73, 257 (Lt), 434, 4.

Beauty (Tiphareth) being established, the 14th Path, Daleth, unites Wisdom (Chokmah) and Understanding (Binah). The central point where Daleth crosses Gimel (13th Path) is Da'ath (דעת, 474). Da'ath means knowledge, and all knowledge has its root in the divine contemplation of the perfect primal beauty.

"This path is said to be 'the instructor of arcana' - that is, the establisher of things shut up because Daleth represents not the doorway, but the *valve* of the door, the bar to the entrance. Daleth's 14th path is also termed the 'foundation of holiness,' or more accurately, the 'holy foundations.' The word translated *foundations* are יסודות, *Yesodoth*, the plural being in the feminine form. Here is a very plain intimation that by Venus and Copper, alchemy refers to the feminine basis of manifestation, which is recognized throughout the various versions of the ageless wisdom. Described in plural because in what is so designated is the root of the bewildering diversity of forms, which does, indeed, act as a barrier to the aspirant's entrance into the secret place where the great treasure is hidden at the center. It is the same as what Krishna, in the *Bhagavad-Gita,* calls my mysterious power difficult to cross over. To pass this barrier, to open the door, is to clear the way to what the *Chaldean Oracles* call 'the adytum of God-nourished silence' [*Fama*].

The combined power of memory and intuition, the table and the nail, bring with them the stone of conscious union with the Higher Self, and thus the door of liberation is revealed. This is the door that leads to an understanding of the mathematical and psychological principles at work in constructing the universe. Thus, the Fama says that the brethren gained access to such a treasure of knowledge through this door as would serve for the complete restoration of all the arts and sciences. [Case, 1985, p. 109-110.]

2. I am the Luminous Intelligence, enlightening my entire experience with the Wisdom of the Ages. [Meditations on the Paths of Wisdom]

תאר *tawar*. to mark a boundary, describe, compress, go round. With different pointing: 1. to mark out, delineate, trace out; to give a fine appearance to; to compass, go round; 2. outline, form, figure, shape; aspect, vestige; title, degree. These are all meanings associated with the function of creative imagination. In Joshua 18:14: "And the border [of the tribe of Benjamin] was drawn and compassed, and turned about to the west side..."

הפעילות *hapeyelooth*. the activities. Refers to Teth's activities, the serpent-power controlled and directed by acts of creative imagination. See 600.

תאר curse, you curse. See Exodus 22:27.

602

אור פשוט *Aur Pashot*. Simplest Light, a title of Kether. See 620, 207.

בשעריך within your gates. See Deuteronomy 26:12.

מן בנות דן *men-benith Dan*. of the daughter of Dan [2 Chronicles 2:14]. Said of Hiram-Abiff, The son of a woman of Dan's daughters. Dan is the tribe attributed to Scorpio and alchemical putrefaction. Before the brightness of the light of heaven may be seen, there must be darkness and death of the old pattern of separation.

בתר *bawthar*. to divide. In Genesis 15:10: "And he took unto him all these, and divided them in the midst..."

קצוות *qetzaoth*. boundaries. Ends. Rosenroth in K.D.L.C.K. (p.677) says *extremitates* and cites as examples מב, the written name of God, קו, cord, measuring line and דעת Da'ath knowledge. Written קצות in Psalm 65:9: "You visit the ends of the earth and water it, you greatly enrich it with the river of God, which is full of water: you prepare them grain when you have so provided for it."

תגר *tiger*. To haggle; the basis of the name תגריון (869) tagirron, The Hagglers, the title of the Qlippoth of Tiphareth, the contending forces of disunity and hate. See 869.

גם *gam*. together, also. In Psalm 133:1: "How good and pleasant it is when brothers live together in unity." Mem = 600, see 43, 65.

Paul Case: The tradition of Freemasonry preserves this Psalm... 'together in unity' is יחד-גם = 65 = אדני... The dwelling together of brethren, as a family, or בית, is suggested.

שלהבירון *Shalhebiron*. The Flaming Ones, Qlippoth of Leo. The letters of this name suggest the power of spiritual fire [Shin] employed in actions for the direction of personality [Lamed], to constitute selfish vision (Heh), and to concentrate the force (Beth) to obstruct divine will (Yod), using the regenerative solar force (Resh) in immoral and false teaching (Vav) of reproductive practices (Nun).

I. The order of Qlippoth ascribed to this tunnel is the Shalchbiron of the flaming; the flames that lick the cauldron of the Sabbath in which the lion-serpent are seethed... the occult use of the serpent's tongue was well-known to the ancients. [Grant, 1994, p. 204.]

בארת pits, wells. See Genesis 14:10.

דם *dam*. Blood. Formed from the second two letters of Adam. It is from the blood that the substance used in the great work is derived. Mem = 600, see 44.

אגרת *Agrath*. a Queen of Demons.

דרך מצרים *Derek mitzraim*. The way of Egypt. See 224, 380 and Jeremiah 2:18.

לרכב בשמי *lawrokeb bishaymi*. to the rider in the heavens. In Psalm 68:33: "To him, that rides upon the heavens of heavens, which were of old; lo, he does send out his voice, and that a mighty voice."

רכב means charioteer, driver; With different pointing: chariot, upper millstone, drawn for grafting. See 574.

בכל לבבך *bay-kawl-layeawkekaw*. with all your heart. In Deuteronomy 30:2: When you and your children return to the Lord your God and obey him with all your heart and with all your soul... Kaph = 500, see 124, 32, 50.

מזריע זרע *mezerio zerao*. yielding seed. In Genesis 1:11: "And God [Elohim] said, Let the land produce vegetation: seed-bearing plants and trees on the land that bear fruit with seed in it, according to their various kinds."

εγετο σιγη. *egeneto sigh*. "There came to be silence." Revelation 8:1: "And when he opened the seventh seal, there was silence in the heaven about half an hour." The 7th seal or planet is the Mercury center, and the experience is that of cosmic consciousness: see 559.

אדם *Adam*. Man. Paul Case notes *Adam = gebereth*. With different pointing: the color red. Mem = 600, see 45.

הם they (masculine). See 45.

גברת *gebereth*. mistress, sovereign lady; enclosure, wall. In Isaiah 47:5, 7: Sit in silence, go into darkness, daughter of the Babylonians; no more will you be called the queen of kingdoms.. you said, 'I will continue forever-the, the eternal queen! But you did not consider these things or reflect on what might happen.' The queen suggests one of the names of Malkuth, the physical plane, i.e., the seat of the lower shekinah. See 496, K.D.L.C.K. (p.226).

ושפני טמוני חול *vu-shayphnnei temunei chol*. and the hidden treasures of the sand. Deuteronomy 33:19" "They shall call the people unto the mountain; there they shall offer sacrifices of righteousness: for they shall suck of the abundance of the seas, and of treasures hid in the sand." see 114 (טמוני, secret knowledge, counsel), 756, 44.

ששה six. In Genesis 30:20: "Then Leah said, 'God has presented me with a precious gift. This time my husband will treat me with honor because I have born him six sons.' So she named him Zebulun [honor]. This is the number of the hexagram, the cross of six squares and Tiphareth. See 600.

ארפכשד *Arphaxad*, Arpachshad; the third son of Shem and the second in line of descent from Shem to Abraham. Translated by Fabre D'Olivet as "restorer of providential nature." Note that the 2nd half of the name is the singular form of Chasidim. See 340 and Genesis 10:22.

Fabre D'Olivet divides this word (ארפ כשד) and comments: "*and Arpa-cheshad*… The two words that I separate here are joined in the original, but this conjunction appears to have been a copyist's mistake. The first word, ארפ, comes from the root רף, which develops all ideas of mediative remedial, restorative, curative cause. United to the sign of stability and power Aleph, it has formed that name, famous in all the ancient mythologies, written ΟρΦευς by the Greeks, and by us, *Orpheus*. The second word, כשד, nearly as famous, since it was the favorite epithet of the Chaldeans, is derived from the root שד, applied to providential powers, to productive nature. Thence the name given to God himself, שדי, *Providence*. In this instance, this root שד is inflected by the assimilative article כ. [d'Olivet, 1976, pp. 292-293.]

τελος. *Telos*. End accomplished; completed state. In Revelation 22:13: I am the Alpha and Omega, the first and the last, the beginning and the end. The end, the final lot, ultimate fate, in Romans 6:21. Of a declaration, prophecy-an end, accomplishment, fulfillment, in Luke 22:37. An end, final purpose that all parts tend and all terminate; the chief point in 1 Timothy 1:5. See 1776 (Greek), 2146, 2627, 1235, 3747 and Romans 10:4, 1 Corinthians 15:24, Mark 3:26.

606

קשיר *qishur*. nexus, ligature, binding, tying, contraction. With different pointing *qawshoor*: tied together, joined. Spelled קשירה in Proverbs 22:15: "Foolishness is bound in the heart of a child, but the rod of correction shall drive it far from him." With different pointing: obligation; impotence due to magic. See קשר.

אחיזת עינים *aechizath einaim*. Hocus-pocus. Jugglery; delusion by optical deception. This relates to the appearance symbolized by Ayin and by Key 15. See 70, 130.

רות *Ruth*; companion; ancestress of King David of Israel. In Ruth 1:15: And Ruth said, 'entreat me not to leave thee, or to return from following after thee: for whither thou goes, I will go; and where thou lodges, I will lodge: your people shall be my people, and your God my God. With different pointing: a turtle-dove.

פעלת יהוה *peulluth IHVH*. works of Tetragrammaton. In Psalm 29:5: "The voice of the Lord breaks the cedars, yet the Lord breaks the cedars of Lebanon." The works are connected with the voice. The voice is in the heart. See 136, 138, 612.

תור *tor*. turtle-dove. Canticles 2:12: "Flowers appear on the earth; the season of singing has come, the cooing of the turtle-dove is heard in our land." The dove is יונה, associated with Venus and passion. See 71.

עצמות bones. See Exodus 13:19.

607 (prime)

ארתו *Erato*. Greek muse of lyric and love poetry.

ותרא and she saw. See Genesis 3:6.

ראות see, to see. See Exodus 10:28.

זרת a span. See Exodus 28:16.

בהרת a bright spot. See Leviticus 13:2.

חם *Ham*. Warmth, heat; Noah's son. Mem = 600, see 48 and Genesis 9:18.

שכל מזהיר *Sekhel Mazohir*. Illuminating or Radiant Intelligence. The 2nd path of Chokmah. See 73.

אבן הנשר *ehben haw-nesher*. eagle stone. [Glory of the World, p.211] Note that הנשר of the eagle is 555, equal to the land of Jordan.

בבא בתרא *bawba bathayra*. the last gate or third gate. K.D.L.C.K. (p.184) says that this is a Talmudic book title cited in the Zohar (III:92). See 5.

תרח *Terah*. Father of Abraham. See Genesis 11:16

חתר *chawthar*. entreaty, begging for forgiveness. Rosenroth in K.D.L.C.K. (p.640) says that this word is related to עתר (*depreoatus*-begging forgiveness, deprecating, entreating) and cites Genesis 25:21: "And Isaac entreated the Lord for his wife because she was barren: and the Lord was entreated of him, and Rebekah his wife conceived." He says it is because it explains the Sephiroth, so long as they emanate from Kether. After all, מזל (Mazel-constellation) is its influence.

Written חתר נא meaning: dig now! in Ezekiel 8:8: (7) "Then he brought me to the entrance to the court. I looked, and I saw a hole in the wall. (8) He said to me, 'son of man, now dig into the wall.' So I dug into the wall and saw a doorway there."

וארבת and the windows, and the floodgates of. See Genesis 7:11.

אחרת another. See Genesis 26:21.

רדתה fall, be subdued, to fall her. See Deuteronomy 20:20.

תרדה you shall rule. See Leviticus 25:43.

האדם *ha-Adam*. Archetypal idea of Man, the first man. See Genesis 2:25. Mem = 600, see 50.

ימינך *yeminehkah*. your right hand. See 130.

עמך *immekah*. with thee. See Psalm 36:9, Kaph = 500, see 130.

ים *yam*. the sea; one of the titles of Binah, the great reservoir of substance from which forms are specialized, i.e., the radiant darkness of limitless light. Mem = 600, see 50.

אתרוג *ethayrog*. citrus, one of the 4 plants used on the feast of the tabernacles. With different pointing: citron, lime, lust and desire. K.D.L.C.K. (p.178) says: ...it is Malkuth, and it is a symbol of the heart, which denotes Shekhinah [the divine presence]. See 613.

מעשר *maeser*. tithe; a tenth (offering). See Deuteronomy 26:12.

אגורת *aegorath*. Small coins, pennies. From אגורה, something gathered, to gather together, accumulate. Refers to the unity of all life. See 215.

כרמי שלי *karemi shellay*. my own vineyard. See 260 and Canticles 1:6.

ירת *Yereth*. The 27th name of Shem ha-Mephorash, short form. See 641 & Appendix 10.

טאמפיעת *Temphioth*. The Sentential of the 19th Path (tunnel) on the Inverse Tree of Life.

I. Tunnel 19 is sentinelled by the demon Temphioth, whose number is 610. The predominant influence is that of the lion-serpent, Teth, a glyph of the spermatozoon, shown in the sigil in the shape of four vesicas depending on a serpentine form attached to a beast's head.

The number 610 is that of אתרוג, meaning 'lust' and 'desire.' This is in accord with the Tarot Trump entitled Lust relevant to the Path above this tunnel. The trump shows a woman mounted upon a leonine beast with seven heads: 'The head of an Angel: the head of a Saint: the head of a Poet: the head of an Adulterous Woman: the head of a Man of Valor: the head of a Satyr: and the head of a Lion-Serpent.

Another form of 610 is חברת which means 'coupling point,' 'place of a junction,' and it is in the tunnel of Temphioth that the magical coupling of the woman and the beast occurs. On the 19th path, the lioness Sekhet is the vehicle of Leo's force, which she represents as the torrid summer sun at its zenith, this being typical of sexual heat. *Liber 231* declares:

Also came forth mother Earth [Isis] with her lion, even Sekhet, the lady of Asi. This means that Sekhet is the sexual heat of Isis, the force that overcomes 'evil.' It is shown by her bridling the Beast whereon she rides.

This path's magical siddhi is Training Wild Beasts, with the woman dominant, bridling and directing the unconscious passions. The magical formula of this *Kala* is thus *Io Mega Therion* (the Great Wild Beast). In the tunnel of Temphioth, this formula is reflected as unbridled lust symbolized by the Black Cat of the Sabbatic Mysteries.

Whereas the 19th path is the lion's place, the tunnel thereof is that of the serpent. The serpents that writhe in the cauldron of the witches at the sabbath of Set are depicted in Frieda Harris's design of the Atu entitled Lust [note that the word ZOON (197) means 'Beast']. Its number is 11, the number of magick or 'energy tending to change.' In the African and Voodoo systems, this is the place of the serpent deities. The phenomenon of lightning, symbolic of the serpent's flickering tongue, also pertains to the tunnel of Temphioth, and the sudden spasm of orgasm that it represents is the mudra or 'magical gesture' of the Cult of the Spermatozoon. A stroke (syncope) is the typical disease of this path.

The Order of Qliphoth ascribed to this tunnel is the *Shalchbiron* or The Flaming; the flames that lick the cauldron of the Sabbath in which the lion-serpents are seethed.

The supreme symbol of the tunnel is the goddess Qatesh, seen in vision (by its Adepts) as a radiantly beautiful, naked woman mounted upon a lion. In her right hand, she holds flowers in her left a serpent. A full moon resting in a crescent is the form of her headdress. These symbols indicate the lunar current in its active phase. [Grant, 1994, pp. 202-204.]

611

תורה *Torah*. The law, precept, statute. The Kingdom is seen as the result of the Life-power's perfect memory of the orderly sequence of self-expression. The Zohar [IV:166B, p.74] comments: The Torah is a light which kindles that lamp (i.e., the mishnah] from the side of primordial light, which is of the right hand because the Torah has given from the right hand [Deuteronomy 33:2], although the left was included in it to attain perfect harmony. This light is included in the 207 [אור = light = 207 = סוף אין, the boundless) worlds which are concealed in the region of light, and is spread throughout all of them. These worlds are under the hidden supernal throne. There are 310 [310 = יש = מטרונה matrona) of them: 207 belong to the right hand and 103 [אבנים, stones = 103 = הוא האלהים He is God] to the left hand. These are the worlds which are always prepared by the holy one for the righteous, and from them spread treasures of precious things, which are stored away for the delight of the righteous in the world to come.

אשיש *awshish*. glass bottle, flagon; a pressed raisin cake. The bottle suggests the alchemical vase of art, where transmutation of fear into wisdom takes place as putrefaction. This is the law of the fountain of life, which frees from death. It is the operation of Spirit (Aleph) to transform (Shin), the divine will (Yod), which transfigures through fire (Shin). See 50, 106, 700, 1017 and Key 13.

אדום *Edom*. Red (variant spelling). Land S.E. of

Palestine, a name given to Israel. Note that red is the color of blood, the carrier of consciousness, and Mars. Mem = 600, see 51, 45, 342.

אים *Em*. Goetia Demon by day of the 2nd decan of Scorpio. See 51.

612

שכל מזהיר *Seykel Mazohir*. Illuminating Intelligence. The 2nd Path of Chokmah. The light of Chokmah is the original light of Kether, the source of illumination for all below it on the Tree of Life. It is the Kether of Briah or Crown of Creation. It is the body of the letter Yod at the beginning of the divine name IHVH. The initial active point of the Life-power's self-manifestation (Kether) expanded into the power of conscious life, which begins all creation cycles, great and small. See 73 (Chokmah), 642, 536, 15, 23.

It is the Illuminating Intelligence, the crown of creation, the splendor of the supreme unity. [Meditations on the Paths of Wisdom]

ברית *berith*. covenant; treaty, an oath of fidelity. Ezekiel 20:37: "and I will bring you unto the bond of the covenant. Refers to the covenant made between God and Abraham and between God and Moses regarding spiritual Israel. Also, the day demon of the 1st decan of Capricorn. This decan is ruled by Saturn and indicates fearfulness and caution regarding one's personal covenant to live when materiality inhibits spiritual vision. With different pointing: alkali, soap, lye. The purified shall be bound to light. See 638, 68 (Greek), 700, 618 and Psalm 25:14.

אדון האור והחשך *aydon ha-aor ve-ha-khoshek*. Lord of the light and of the darkness. Part of the gnostic adoration. See 61, 207, 328, 616.

פעלות יהוה *peolooth IHVH*. The work of Tetragrammaton. It is to spread the light and to illuminate the darkness. See 606.

בים *Bim*. Beam. Goetia demon by day of the 2nd decan of Sagittarius. Mem = 600, see 52.

ברית Goetia demon #28 by day of the 1st decan of Capricorn. See Appendix 11.

Goetia: "He is might, great, and terrible duke. He has two other names given… He appears to form a soldier with red clothing, riding upon a red horse and having a crown of gold upon his head. He gives true answers, past, present, and to come… He can turn all metals into gold. He can give dignities and can confirm them unto man. He speaks with a very clear and subtle voice. He is a great liar and not to be trusted unto. He governs 26 Legions of Spirits." [Mathers, 1995, p. 40]

יבם *yabam*. brother-in-law. With different pointing: *Yebem*. 70th Shem ha-Mephorash, short form. See 52, 67 & Appendix 10.

Ζευς. *Zeus*. Greek God, associated with the planet Jupiter.

613 (Prime)

The number of bones in the human body.

אבים *Aebiyawm*. Father of the sea. Mem = 600, see 53, 50, 3, 52, 73, 434, 4, 474.

משה רבינו *moshe rabbinu*. Moses, our Rabbi. Moses is מ = Water, ש = Fire, ה = vision or 345 = tranquility, inner peace = the name, i.e. IHVH. Rabbi means master, lord, teacher. The name of the Lord is the teacher who brings inner peace. See 345.

בראתי I have created. See Genesis 6:7.

גרתי I have sojourned, I strayed. See Genesis 32:5.

הברות the pits. See Genesis 37:20.

חום *khoom*. burned swarthy, black, brown. See 54.

תריד you shall break loose, you grow restless. See Genesis 27:40.

האחרת the next. See Genesis 17:21.

אדם מלך *Adam Melek*. King Adam. This the One Ego or Higher Self, also called the Stone, seated in Tiphareth. To attain union with King Adam is to become the Stone. Our purpose is to provide an adequate personal vehicle through which the Central Ego or Adam the King may express itself. Final Kaph = 500. See 45, 90, 570, 135, 1081, 53.

הדום *haedom, ha-dom*. a footstool; a stool resting-place for the feet. Malkuth is the only Sephirah referred to as the element earth. Mem = 600, see 55.

לשרפה burn thoroughly, with fire. See Genesis 11:3.

נכספתה you longed (desire). See Genesis 31:30

יום *yom*. day, the manifest. With different pointing: to be warm or bright. Mem = 600, see 56.

עתיק יומין *Atik Yomin*. The Ancient of Days; a title of Kether. See 620 (Kether) 696, 1266, 1290, 1346, 1746.

Greater Holy Assembly [IRQ 1:22]: For neither does the world remain firm, except through secrecy. And if in worldly affairs there be so great need of secrecy, how much more in the things of the most secret of secrets, and in the meditation of the Ancient of Days, which matter is not even revealed unto the highest of the angels.

IRQ 6:64: Nevertheless, the [brain] membrane is opened from below. And this is that which we have said: among the signatures of the letters is תו Tav; nevertheless, he impresses it as the sign of the Ancient of Days, from whom depends the perfection of knowledge, because he is perfect on every side, and what is said: an old one, his knowledge is hidden, and his brain is hidden and tranquil. And that membrane has an outlet from ze'ir an-peen and therefore this brain is spread and goes out to 32 ways. This is that which is written: 'And a river went forth from Eden.' [pp.368-369]

חרבות *charavoth*. swords. In Isaiah 21:15: "They flee from the drawn swords, from the bent bow and from the heat of battle. Written חרכותם in Isaiah 2:4 concerning the Lord [IHVH]: "He will judge between the nations and will settle disputes from many peoples. They will beat their swords into plowshares and their spears into pruning hooks. Nation will not take up sword against nation, nor will they train for war anymore."

ממסלותם *mimaysilotham*. in their courses. In Judges 5:20: "They fought from heaven; the stars in their courses fought against Sisera. The word literally means 'highways, paths." see 1176, 231, 48, 98.

יתרו *Yethayro*. Jethro. "his excellence"; "He abounds, excels, is superior," "He is prominent" [Inman]. Father-in-law of Moses. A priest and head of a tribe of Midian among whom Moses found asylum on his flight from Egypt. Exodus 2:21: And Moses was content to dwell with the man: and he [Jethro] gave Moses Zipporah his daughter. Note that Midian means "the seed of Dan." see 104, 54, 50, 345 and Exodus 18:1

תירו *Tihro*. The Pentateuch. The first 5 books of the Bible, also called the law of Moses. Note that this word is a metathesis of Jethro.

שימירון Shimiron. Qlippoth of Pisces. This sign's unbalanced or negative qualities are a negative medium for obsessing entities, single-hearted evolution to the intolerant and bigotry in religion and politics; spiritual pride; alcoholism, drug addiction, hopelessness. The remedy is to recognize the fact of utter dependence of personality upon life itself and to express oneself in works of charity and altruistic service to one's neighbor.

617 (prime)

דגים *dagim*. fishes; Pisces, the 12th sign of the zodiac, attributed to Qoph, the corporeal or body-building intelligence, and to sleep. Mem = 600, see 57.

את דברי *eth-daybawri*. the essence of my word. See 401, 206 and 1 Kings 6:12.

אים *iyoom*. threat, warning; terror, fright; formidable, terrible. The mighty acts and essence of the Lord are formidable and terrifying to the ignorant. See 57.

תיראו you shall fear. Deuteronomy 13:5.

רהבית *Rahbith*. A King of Edom. Edom denotes unbalanced force. אדם means "red" and suggests Mars. It is spelled with the same letters as Adam, generic humanity. *Adam* is spirit (Aleph) in the blood (*dam*, 44). See 45, 44.

רישא עלאה *resha illawtha*. the supernal head. A title of Kether, the crown of primal will. See 620, 511, 200, 106.

618

ריבות *riboth*. contentions, strife, quarrels, controversies. See Deuteronomy 17:8.

דאגים *dagim*. fishes (variant spelling). Attributed to Pisces and Qoph the corporeal or bodybuilding intelligence. The covenants of the God of Israel is the wisdom embodied in the child after all inner controversy has ceased. See 57, 617, 100.

ביתור *Bethor*. Olympic planetary spirit of Jupiter. The letters of the angel's name suggest concentration (Beth) carry out the divine will

(Yod) at the center of manifestation (Tav), linking itself (Vav) to solar radiance (Resh), forever expansive and beneficent.

"One of the 7 supreme angels ruling the 196 provinces in which heaven is divided. Bethor rules 42 Olympic regions and commands kings, princes, dukes, etc., and 'governs all things ascribed to (the planet) Jupiter.' To do Bethor's bidding, there are, also, 29,000 legions of spirits." [Davidson, 1971, p. 75.]

חית כף מים הה *Chokmah*; spelled in full. Chokmah is the wisdom of the sphere of the zodiac. See 73, 418, 100, 90, 10.

619 (prime)

אחרית *ahaerith*. The end (of space, time); future; latter end; result; posterity. In Isaiah 46:10: "Declaring the end from the beginning, and from ancient times the things that are not yet done, saying, My counsel shall stand, and I will do all my pleasure." see 743 and Deuteronomy 11:12.

הרוחת the spirits. Numbers 16:22.

Δοξα Θεου. *doksa theou*. The glory of God. Septuagint translation of כבד אלהים (112) in Proverbs 25:2. It is the glory of God to conceal a matter; to search out a matter is the glory of kings. The kings are those alchemists involved in the great work of personality transmutation. See 135.

620

כתר *Kether*. The Crown, of Primal Will. The alchemical Mercury or first principle, or sattva guna, the "illumination material," or substance of enlightenment. Alchemical "first matter." See 21, 111,149 Latin, 1032, 157, 352, 507, 364, 602, 397, 736, 837, 583.

I. As a verb, it is used in Psalm 22:12 to mean "beset me round." Paul Case cites Psalm 142:7: "Shall encompass me about" (others shall crown, i.e., glorify, themselves with me). Also, Proverbs

14:18: וערומים יכתרו דעת, "but the prudent are crowned with knowledge." In Judges 20:43: כתרו to besiege. Habakkuk 1:4: "compass about."

II. In Job 36:2: כתר לי "bear with me." Also means: to surround; to wait, tarry; to crown. See 833, 557, 588, 727, 1238, 1225, 996, 696, 721, 559, 733, 391, 422, 616, 1239, 617.

III. Kether is the focus of Cosmic Consciousness, and its first manifestation is Light. The Ain, which is its source, is not Darkness but Absence of Light, and therefore the true essence of Light. Kether is the infinitesimal point in space-time at which Absence of Light becomes its Presence by turning the Void (Ain) inside out. Kether, and the resulting Tree of Life, may be conceived as the interior of the Void manifesting in Space, which is the menstruum, of Light. [Grant, 1994, p. 24.]

דורית dorith. generations (special spelling). From the root דור, a revolution of time, an age, an eon. The supernal is the origin of all generations.

צפנת zafenath. thou has laid up, savior. In Psalm 31:19, it is a reference to accumulated treasures of goodness. The verb expresses activity, accumulation, addition, multiplication. This correlates with the Ace of Swords' idea to focus on the Limitless Light's accumulated energy. It is a point at which diffused energy is concentrated to set up the whirling motion, which is the basis of all forms. Part of a name given to Joseph. Hebrew transliteration of an Egyptian meaning savior and refers to the salvation of the Egyptians from famine. The name given to Joseph (פענח צפנת, Zaphenath-paneam) means Salvator Mundi or Savior of the World. Joseph signifies addition or multiplication. See 156.

To hide, to conceal relates to the fact that the innermost will is hidden. צפנת is related to the word צפון north, and it is said: "gold comes from the north." see 226.

שערים shawrim. gates, doors. The gates are the various points of entrance whereby the Limitless Light projects Itself into manifestation. Kether includes the potency of all these gates (whether

50, (Binah) or 231). Thus its action in Yetzirah denotes the beginning of the formative process and the totality of its expression through the other aspects depicted by the rest of the suit of Swords. See 231, 1180.

עשירם Pluto.

נתיב nathib. a path, road or way (of progress).

חכמה בינה ודעת Chokmah, Binah, Da'ath. Wisdom, Understanding and Knowledge. The first descending triad. The first two are the Sephiroth numbered 2 and 3, and Da'ath, Knowledge, is said to be Chokmah and Binah's union. Thus Da'ath is a sort of reflection of Kether, and Kether is here shown as that which, in itself, is the potency of wisdom, understanding and knowledge. For Kether is the seed of the Tree of Life, and whatever emanates from the crown is in the Crown before emanating therefrom.

משפר Mishpar. The angle of the 3rd (Venus) decan of Virgo.

כרת karath. to cut off, to make a covenant [Psalm 105:9]. The covenant which we made with Abraham. This alludes to the cutting of victims offered for sacrifice when a covenant is made. Related to Kether, because the basic motion is separation from unity into a point.

שדי צורי Zuri Shaddai. Rock of the Almighty.

רשעים rawshawim. wicked men [Psalm 1:1 and 4]. See 12, 21, 37, 157, 1032, 501.

עשרים esrim. twenty, the value of Kaph, attributed to Jupiter. See 1180.

רוחות ruachoth. winds; breezes, airs, spirits, souls, minds. In Psalm 104:4: "He makes winds his messengers [angels], flames of fire his servants."

ששך shashak. Temurah of בבל, Babel. In Jeremiah 25:26, 51:41: "And all the kings of the north, far and near, one with another, and all the kingdoms of the world, which are upon the face of the earth: and the king of Sheshach shall drink after them. (I took the cup at the Lord's hand, and made all the nations to drink) How is Sheshach taken! And how is the praise of the whole earth surprised! How is Babylon become an astonishment among the nations!" see 34.

שדה איש *ish saweh.* a man of the field, i.e., one living in the open country. In Genesis 25:27: "And the boys grew: and Esau was a cunning [skillful] hunter, a man of the field; and Jacob was a plain man, dwelling in tents." see 309, 376, 182.

μιτος. *mitos.* Thread (a thread of the warp). A euphemism for Semen, as the link between one generation and the next. Related to the Hindu word sutratma, thread-soul.

τελειος. *teleios.* Complete, ripe, matured, perfect. Used in Matthew 5:45 in the sense of full maturity. Relative perfection is meant-including the notion of mental maturity. To arrive psychologically at Kether is to reach the highest point in Human attainment.

θυσια. *thysia.* Offering, a sacrifice; the act and rite of sacrificing; as an expiation for sin. In Hebrews 10:26: "For if we should voluntary sin after having received the knowledge of the truth, there is no longer a sacrifice for sins." see 1924, 1628, 2294, 2360, 1620, 2257.

621

היום *ha-yom.* This day. See 61.

ראיתי have I seen, I found. See Genesis 7:1.

תיראי fear. See Genesis 21:17.

באחרית in the end, the last, in coming off. See Genesis 49:1.

622

בדרתיו in his generation. See Genesis 6:9.

בריתי my covenant. See Genesis 6:18.

ברכת blessing. See Genesis 28:4.

αιματος. *haimatos.* Streams of blood.

623

רוח צקדש *Rauch ha-Qodesh.* Holy Spirit.

יגרתי I was in dread of, I feared. See Deuteronomy 9:19.

624

עין תפוה *en-Tappuah.* foundation of the apple [Joshua 17:7] A place-name. The land of Tappuah belonged to Manasseh, the border between the land of Manasseh and Ephraim. "In metaphorical usage, a fountain is the emblem of any source of spiritual blessing, whether issuing in cleansing or in refreshment and revival... preeminently, however, God is the fountain of life, i.e., the source of all good. Hence the knowledge of God is also a fountain of life." [Standard Bible Dictionary]. This relates to Ayin (70, 130). The apple is connected with the serpent-power, with Mars and with knowledge. See 331, 395, 474, 494, 418.

חירות *kiruth.* liberty. The liberation of the spirit is part of the great work.

הגוים *ha-goyim.* the nations, gentiles. Mem = 600, see 64.

נחשירון *Nachashiron.* Qlippoth of Sagittarius. "The snaky ones." Suggest unbalanced force, resulting in negative qualities of material ambition, self-deceived and cruelty blunt, stuffily over-conventual. Connected with Samekh and Key 14, the test and trials of the Holy Guardian angel can overcome these tendencies, as the soul is purified.

I. "In the African pantheon, Aidowedo-the rainbow goddess-is a cognate deity. Her coming is likened to the lightning flash. This is the Sagittarian influence manifesting in the form of the female current. 'Her fetish is a large serpent that appears only when it wants to drink. It then rests its tail on the ground and trusts its mouth into the water. It is said that he who finds the excrement of this serpent is rich forever.'" [Grant, 1994, p. 227.] see 1274.

625

I. (25x25) or 25^2 or 5^4

נתיבה *nathibah*. path, road, way (feminine).

הרי אררט the mountain of Ararat. Ararat means "burst up into light," from אור light and רט to boil up. The Ark of Noah is a symbol of salvation, which can rest on the mountain of light. See 58.

626

קליפות *Qlippoth*. Shells, material shells. Order of evil demons. Literally "Shells of the dead." The negative and outworn thought-forms whose patterns enslave the ignorant and seek to survive by feeding like parasites on their deluded victims. See 131, 208, 8, 777.

I. The plural form of *qlipha*, meaning 'a harlot' or 'strange woman'; terms which signify 'otherness.' The shadowy world of shells or reflections. Each sephira of the Tree of Life has its corresponding *qlipha*, which reflects the energy it represents, and these averse power-zones - or *Qliphoth* - form the Tree of Death. [Grant, 1994, pp. 275-276.]

עשרון the tenth portion. In Exodus 29:40: "And with the one [sacrificial] lamb a tenth deal of flour..." [spelled, ועשרן] The number 10 refers to Malkuth, the physical plane where the Lamb of God, the Christos or Higher Self in Tiphareth is sacrificed or slain by the Qlipphotic forces. See Numbers 15:4.

שעורים *sherurim*. measures, sizes, magnitudes; proportions, standards; measure, limits. These all depend on how they are used-if in ignorance. They can represent and define evil tendencies;

they can define the measure of good in an enlightened context. See 576.

רכות weak [eyes]. See Genesis 29:17.

וכרת and cut down. See Deuteronomy 20:20.

627

חוג הארץ + שטה *choog ha-artz* + *shittiah*. circle of the earth + acacia. The earth is the physical plane or condensation in the heavens; the actual substance of which the "House of God" is made is actually the omnipotent power or energy of the almighty. The Acacia is a symbol of immortality, and its wood was used to make the tabernacle and its furniture. See 313, 314, 291.

628

ברכות benedictions.

חיים *chayim, chaiim*. life, the living ones; sustenance, maintenance. Mem = 600, see 68.

אלף או ריש *Aleph Vav Resh*. אור *aur*, light, spelled in full, with Vav spelled או instead of וו. See 111, 12, 510, 207.

גן נעול אחתי a garden enclosed is my sister. See Song of Solomon 4:12.

נון וו שיר *Nun-Vav-Resh*. נור *nour*, fire, spelled in full, with Vav as וו. See 106, 12, 510, 256.

נון צדי חית *Nun-Tzaddi-Cheth*. נצח, *Netzach*, victory, spelled in full. See 106, 104, 418, 148.

אדני שמעה בקולי *Adonai shemeawh be-qoli*. Lord, hear my voice. Psalm 130:2: "Lord, hear my voice: let your ears be attentive to the voice of my supplications."

אבן שלמה וצדק *ehben shaylemawh vaw-tzedeq*. A stone perfect and just. Deuteronomy 25:15: "But thou shall have a perfect and just weight, a perfect and just measure shall thou have: that my days may be lengthened in the land which the Lord your God gives thee."

בכרתו his birthright. See Genesis 25:33.

629

הדך + זולתי אין אלהים *zeulawthi ain Elohim + hawdak*. no God beside me + break down, overturn, cast down. The realization of the unity of God and man breaks down all barriers of separation. See 600, 29.

גאה + שערים *shayawrim + gaw'ah*. gates, doors + to rise, grow, be exalted, lifted up. "Lift up your gates, ye everlasting doors, and the king of glory shall come in," says the Psalmist. The gates are the various points of entrance whereby limitless light projects itself into manifestation. The trumpet-calls lifts up the vibratory activity of consciousness into a realization of union with the divine." see 620, 9.

שדי + בר הבנים *rab ha-bonim + shaddai*. the almighty + master of the builders. Divinity is the creator of all; the almighty is associated with Malkuth, physical manifestation, and Shekhinah, the divine presence. See 314, 315.

אחריתו my end. See Numbers 23:10.

ער ונגע time & chance. See Ecclesiastes 9:11.

630

I. Σ35 = 630

שרפים *Seraphim*. Fiery Serpents, Fiery Angels. The Choir of Angels is associated with Geburah (and Kether of Briah). Represents the purifying activity of the Divine Will. The Mars force is often symbolized by a serpent and refers to the reproductive energy utilized in the regeneration of personality. See 585.

צפנתי *Tzafanathi*. I have laid up [Psalm 119:11]. The word is from a root, *Tzafan* צפן, to hide, conceal, preserve, treasure, and keep in store. As it functions in Yetzirah, the fiery Mars force is the basis for the patterns that serve as a storehouse for wisdom. It is also the basis of the patterns which express the cosmic order of nature. These patterns *conceal* the true nature of the force they express. See 44, 661, 1335.

שעירם *Seirim*. Hairy ones; he-goats; demons. Connected with Capricorn and unpurified force. See 1190.

שלש *shawlash*. three, the number-name. Suggest Yetzirah, the 3rd of the 4 Qabalistic worlds. See 889, 1379, 1969 (Greek); 636.

רוחא קדישא *ruacha qaddeshaw*. The holy spirit. The Seraphim express the holy spirit for the Mars-force. Key 20 or Shin represents the Holy Spirit as Fire, transforming the personality into an agent of the divine will. See 624.

שמע בקול עבדו *sha.meh be-kol ab'de.u*. That obeys the voice of his servant. In Isaiah 50:10: "Who is among you that fears the Lord, that obeys the voice of his servant, that walks in darkness, and has no light? Let him trust in the name of the Lord and stay upon his God." His servant = חסיד Chassid or saint; one of the Hassidim rules Gemini: and suggest that purification of the Mars-force must be a self-conscious activity.

631 (prime)

חפץ המבקש *khayfetz ha-meboqash*. Desirous quest, inclination to seek; the intelligence of the 21st path of Kaph. See 636.

פעלות אדם *payuloth Adam*. the works of man. In Psalm 17:4, "Concerning the works of men, by the word of your lips, I have kept me from the paths of the destroyer." (written with Prefix lamed). See 612, 3450 (Greek).

השער ליהוה *ha-sha'ar li-IHVH*. The gate of Tetragrammaton. In Psalm 118:20: "The gate of the Lord, into which the righteous shall enter." see 570, 26; 2296 (Greek).

θανατος. Death. See 446, 50, 106, 700 and Hebrews 2:9, Revelations 21:4.

I. In 1 Corinthians 15:21: "For since by a man, *came* death, by a man, also, *came* the resurrection of the dead," and in 15:54 "And when this perishable will have put on the imperishable, and this mortal will have put on immortality, then will come about the saying that is written, '*Death is swallowed up* in victory.'"

II. "This word appears to equate the moral condition, and *apothanatos* is such a noun in use, would signify the quitting of the mortal condition. The Immortals mortals. The Immortals were the *Athanatoi*-those apart from the fate of mortals. The verb *apothneskein* means literally, to strive to get away from the mortal state (*thnesis*): *apothanein* - to pass from mortality. The word analysis seems to be a synonym for [*apo*]*thanatos*." [Omikron, 1942, pp. 255.]

632

בלטשאצר *Belteshazzar*. "Protect his life." In Daniel 1:7: "Unto whom the prince of eunuchs gave names: for he gave unto Daniel the name of *Belteshazzar*..." The Babylonian name of the prophet Daniel. See Daniel 4:18.

בית כר *Bayth-kar*. "House of the Lamb." In 1 Samuel 7:11: "And the men of Israel went out of Mizeph, and pursued the Philistines, and smote them until they came under Beth-car." This shows that the "house" or temple established by KR (C.R.) is intended. A man's family is his house, in Hebrew, as in English. From this "house" is transferred to an organization, company, fraternity. Thus House of the Lamb = House of C.R. See 220, 412.

עולם יסודות *Olam Yesodoth*. Literally, The World of Foundations. A title of Malkuth, the Sphere of the Elements. It is part of the material world. See 1192, 486, 146.

צפנתי + ב *tzawfanethi* + *beth*. I have laid up (your word in my heart) + house. The house of personality contains the word of God. Note that 2, Beth's value is also the number of Key 2 or Gimel, the High Priestess, connected with the Moon or memory. It is the memory that recalls us to unity (Gimel = the Uniting Intelligence). See 630, 2.

שער הדגים (632) Gate of the Fishes. See Nehemiah 2:13

בכרתי my birthright. See Genesis 27:36.

ברכתי my blessing, my gift. See Genesis 27:36.

633

אביכם abikem. your father. See 73

וזכרת and you shall remember. See Deuteronomy 5:15.

זכר ונקבה בראם *zakar ve-neqebah berawm*. He created them male and female. In Genesis 5:2: "Male and female he created them; at the time they were created, he blessed them and called them humanity [אדם]." see 390, 45.

634

חורם מלך צר *Khuram Melek-tzor*. Hiram, King of Tyre. The literal translation is "Hiram, King of the Rock" [2 Chronicles 2:3]. The "rock" is one of God's occult symbols as the Life-source or origin of physical existence. Associated with the west and the setting sun in Freemasonry. The officer who represents him is charged with preserving harmony and seeing that the builders receive the wages. Thus Hiram is a symbol of the completion of work and of fulfillment. See 640.

נחוש יצוק ואבן Copper is molten out [being smelted] of stone [ore]. Job 28:2: "Iron is taken out of the earth, and brass (copper) is molten out of the stone."

לרדת to go down. See Genesis 44:26.

הילל בן שחר *Helel ben-Shachar*. Morning Star; Son of the Dawn; Lucifer. In Isaiah 14:12: "O morning-star, son of the dawn! You have been cast down to earth, you who once laid low the nations [גוים, 59]!" Note that the authorized version translates "morning star" as Lucifer ("Light-bearer"). It is connected with Venus, or desire through creative imagination. The A.V. also reads, "Which did weaken the nations." The nations, esoterically, are the millions of unspecialized body-cells who are "brought to light" in the process of regeneration. See 75, 52, 508, 59, 1285.

השרפים

סיפרשה the burned, fiery. See Numbers 17:4 & 21:6.

שלשה *shelshah*. number three. Connected with Key 3, Daleth on Venus. Referring to the menorah or lampstand of the holy tabernacle. See 636 and Genesis 6:10.

להם la-hem. Unto them. See 75.

אלף דלת מים *Aleph-Daleth-Mem*. The letters of אדם, Adam, or generic Humanity in plentitude. A title of Tiphareth. See 1081, 45.

636

החפץ המבוקש, *ha khayfetz ha meboqash*. "the inclination to seek." The 21st Path of Kaph. It is called the Path of Desirous Quest. Man's quest for abundance is expressed as the seeking of that which is within (Chesed). So-called "because it receives the divine influence, which it distributes as a blessing to all modes of being." see 986, 183, 892, 2203 (Greek).

ואבו איש צרי *ve-abiv ish-Tzori*. and his father was a man of Tyre (Rock) [1 Kings 7:14]. Refers to the parentage of Hiram Abiff, the hero of freemasonry. Hiram's father is further described as being חרש נחשת *khoresh nekhosheth*, a worker in brass. Brass is the symbolic metal of Venus, creative imagination, so he, a "worker in brass,"

excels in creative imagination. (note that there is a correspondence between צר, rock, and אבן, the stone which is 53, the key number of 636. See 1266, 611, 133, 1596.

ויהי ערב ויהי בקר *va-yihi-ereb va-yehi-beker*. Literally, "and it was evening, and it was morning" (one day). [Genesis 1:5]. See 2309 (Greek)

זהור האחדת *Zeyhoor ha-Achedeth*. Splendor of Unity. A title of Chokmah [Yetziratic text], which is the goal from Chesed, through the path of Vav, of those who seek. See 218, 413.

מלכות עלם *Malkuth Olam*. Everlasting kingdom. In Daniel 7:27, "And the kingdom and dominion, and the greatness of the kingdom under the whole heaven, shall be given to the people of the saints of the most high, whose kingdom is an everlasting kingdom, and all dominions [order of archangels] shall serve and obey him." Refers to the same kingdom concerning which Gabriel is reported by Luke to have told Mary. See 496, 736, 1196; 1400 (Greek).

צדיק אתא יהוה *Tzaddi Attah IHVH*. Just (Righteous) are you, God (Tetragrammaton). See 406, 204, 26.

צדיק ונושע *tzaddiq ve-noshah*. He is just and having salvation [Zechariah 9:9]. Interpreted in the New Testament as a prophecy of Jesus Triumphal entry into Jerusalem. צדיק, Tzaddiq, just, is from the root, צדק, righteousness, particularly related to the 21st Path because it is also Jupiter. True Justice is based on comprehension, Kaph, כף. The Mercy of God is that he freely gives his own wise understanding to all who make knowledge of the divine order their primary object of the desirous quest. They who seek always find. The true masters are always masters of compassion, constituting the great circle of dominion, pictured in Key 10 as the Wheel of Fortune. "Behold the King comes unto thee, he is triumphant and victorious, lowly and riding upon an ass." see 2203 (Greek)

ראש פנה *rosh pinnah*. head of the corner or chief

corner-stone (Hebrew translation); viz. the pinnacle stone of the pyramid. In Psalm 118:22: "The stone which the builders refused becomes the headstone of the corner." "The stone which the builders refused" (273), equivalent to אביו הורם, Hiram Abiff, and referring to Christ in the New Testament. The "rejected stone" refers to man's words when those words express Desirous Quest's intelligence (i.e., true science). These are the best evidence. Hence Jesus said, "Believe me for the very work's sake." He promised that those who followed his method should not only equal but even surpass his own works of power. They who pursue his way of liberation must be doers, not merely hearers and talkers, of such is the everlasting Kingdom. See 135.

פעלות האדם *pehulloth ha-adam*. the works of man, the deeds of man. The suggestion here is that when man's works are rightly performed, they will constitute an everlasting Kingdom. Relates to the letter Kaph and to its basic meaning, grasp. See 631, 1196, 3450 (Greek).

צפרירון *Tzapheriron*. Qlippoth of Virgo. Implies a misuse of the Mercury or energy of attention on superficial, earthly, i.e., material things in the quest for enlightenment. Truth is found within.

I. The letters of this name suggest a misdirection of the power of meditation (Tzaddi), focusing on the destructive force of Mars (Peh) for the personal use of the solar regenerative force (Resh) and thus a perversion of the divine will in creative acts (Yod), diverting the radiant energy of the sun (Resh) in obedience to false teachings (Vav) and linking oneself to endless cycles of reproductive error (Nun).

II. "Narcissus, the flower attributed to this tunnel, yields a key to the nature of the formula of sexual magick associated with it, which in its dark aspect reflects karezza as a sterile, spending of magical force. This is confirmed by the letter Yod being regarded as sacred to Yamatu [connected with the Egyptian Set or Typhon]. Yod means a 'hand,' and to this tunnel, ascribed the order of Qlippoth known as the Tzaphiriron, meaning 'the scratchers.' This light or secret seed, concealed

within the body, suggest the idea of invisibility, and this is the magical Siddha attributed to this ray, as also is Parthenogenesis [virgin birth-C.F. the Virgo-virgin symbolizes] the work of the black brothers thus belongs naturally in the tunnel of Yamatu where the seed, spilled in a sterile act, renders the body bereft of light and therefore 'invisible.' It was the object of the new light sent to retain the light within, thus defying death and achieving immortality in the flesh... to be trapped in this tunnel is to suffer the death in the life of petrifaction. The typical disease is paralysis, and the inclusion of all anaphrodisiacs among the list of vegetable drugs ascribed to this ray again suggest the anti-vital nature of its sterilizing influence." [Grant, 1994, pp. 209-210.] see 1286.

בתוך הבאר *be-tovha habbar*. amid the pit. [2 Samuel 23:20, Zohar 1, p.26] ."..He went down also and slew a lion amid a pit..." Note that "in the midst" is בתוך, which may be read "in your Tav," and תו Tav is the mist or center of the Cube of Space, according to the *Sepher Yetzirah*. The quest for the Stone is "in the midst" of all things.

שלוש *shalosh*. the number 3. "This word is formed from the two contracted roots של שול, as opposed in their significations as in the arrangement of their characters. By the first של, is understood every extraction or subtraction: by the second שול, on the contrary, every amalgamation, every kneading together. The name of number *three* presents, therefore, under a new form, the opposed ideas contained in *one* and *two*; that is, the extraction, consequence of the division, becomes a kind of relative unity. This new unity is represented in a great many words under the idea of peace, welfare, perfection, eternal happiness, etc." [d'Olivet, 1976, pp. 152-153.] For other numerals, see 13, 400, 273, 348, 600, 272, 395, 770, 570, 441.

637

אולם *ulam*. vestibule of the temple Mem = 600, see 77.

פורנאש *Phuranash*. Goetia demon #30 by day of

149

the 3rd decan of Capricorn. This decan corresponds to the 4 of Pentacles, which symbolizes Chesed's influence, the sphere of Jupiter in Assiah, the material world.

Goetia: "He s a mighty and great Marquis and appears in the form of a great sea-monster. He teaches and makes men wonderfully knowing in the art of rhetoric. He causes men to have a good name and to have the knowledge and understanding of tongues. He makes one beloved of his foes as well as friends. He governs 29 Legions of Spirits, partly of the Order of Thrones, and part of that of Angels." [Mathers, 1995, p. 42]

שאלוש *Shaulsh*. Goetia demon #19 by day of the 1st decan of Libra. This decan corresponds to the operation of Chokmah, in Yetzirah, or the order of the universe as it expresses through man, the microcosm.

Goetia: "He is a great and mighty duke, and appears in the form of a gallant soldier riding on a crocodile, with a ducal crown on his head, but peaceably. He causes the love of women to men, and men to women; and governs 30 Legions of Spirits." [Mathers, 1995, p. 36]

לראות to see, gaze. Genesis 2:19.

κριτης. *kretehs*. Judge; one who sits to dispense justice. Septuagint translation of דין (64). In 1 Samuel 24:16: "May the Lord be our judge (κριτην) and decide between us. May he consider my cause and uphold it; may he vindicate me by delivering me from your hands." see 1257 and 2 Timothy 4:8.

638

חלם *kholem*. breaker; to bind, see visions. Mem = 600, see 78, 486, 564.

לחם *lekhem*. bread, food; a feast. The Tree of Life, which is the support and sustenance of man. Note that Beth-lechem, "house of bread" where Christos is born, is the Virgo region in the body. See 78.

קדם ידעתי *qedem yawdaithi*. I have knowledge of old. Psalm 119:152] "Concerning your testimonies, I have known of old that thou has founded them forever." This section of the Psalm is under the heading of Qoph (100, 259). This refers to knowledge brought over from a time before the writer's incarnation. See 144, 494, 474.

639

עץ הדעת *Etz ha-Daath*. Tree of Knowledge. The life-power directs the serpent-fire's heat toward the goal symbolized by the white stone. This is accomplished by eating the fruit of the Tree of Knowledge. Notice that 639 reduces to 18 (Qoph, Pisces), then to 9, Teth's value. See 600, 30, 9.

צפנתי + בבה *tzawphanethi + bawbah*. I have laid up + cavity, something hollowed out, the apple of the eye. As it functions in Yetzirah, the formative world, the fiery Mars-force is the basis for the patterns that serve as a storehouse for wisdom. This is laid up in the cavity of the heart. See 630, 9.

סרטן + נער *sahraytawn + na'ar*. crab + boy. The adept protects and isolates himself from his environment's illusions by using magical speech (sound vibration correlated with imagery). By this means, he builds an indestructible body of light. The boy is the result-the awakened Ego-consciousness turning inward and eastward to Yekhidah in Kether. See 319, 320.

עשרים ואחד *esrim ve-echad*. twenty-one, 21. Key 21 is The World, attributed to Tav (400, 713), Saturn and the Administrative Intelligence at the center of the Cube of space. See 476; 1199.

640

שמש *Shemesh*. The Sun. In Alchemy, the sun is gold. With different vowel points: battlement; servant, virile member. Also: *shimmashe*. To minister, officiate, to serve; to perform marital duty (verb).

תמר to rise up straight (like a palm tree). With different pointing *Tamar*: ancestries of David (a palm tree).

חורם מלך צור *Khurum Melek-Tzor*. Hiram, King of Tyre. The word Tzor (Tyre) is spelled defectively in the Hebrew text, צר, that is, the Vav is omitted, and the O-sound is supplied by placing the dot over Tzaddi. See 634, 1081, 45, 52, 90, 311, 478, 536, 548, 214, 465, 273, 1378 and 2 Chronicles 2:3.

כוס תנחהמים *kos tanchumim*. cup of consolation, which is the same as the cup in Psalm 23, "my cup runs over." See 1200, 1434 and Key 2, 3.

שילש *shalish*. one third, name of measure, musical instrument; middle finger; arbitrator; triangle. Tiphareth is the third projection from Kether, Chokmah being first and Binah second. A hint that the rulership that is implied by calling the sixth path Melek, King, is based on measurement.

A Triangle, i.e., musical instrument in 1 Samuel 18:6. In K.D.L.C.K. (p.719) relates this to triplicates or thirds into which the Tree of Life is divided: the first third is assigned to Chokmah, Binah, and Da'ath; the middle third to Gedulah, Geburah and Tiphareth, the last third to Netzach, Hod and Yesod. See 680.

דביר קרשך *Debir Qadeshkah*. the Holy Sanctuary. In Psalm 28:2: "Hear the voice of my supplications, when I cry unto thee, when I lift up my hands toward your holy oracle." see 975 (Greek).

עיניך *inehkah*. your eyes. See 160.

עתיקין *Atiqin*. Ancient Ones. This refers to the Ancient of Days. See 510, 250, 90, 53, 200, 702, 1290.

פניך *pahnehkah*. your face; your presence. See 160.

צפייתן *tzephiyathan*. their appearance. Refers to the appearance of the 10 Sephiroth, comparing it

to a flash of lighting [Sepher Yetzirah 1:6]. See 1290.

תיכאראח *Characith*. The Sentinel on the 18th Path (tunnel) of Cheth on the Inverse Tree of Life.

I. The 18th Path is under the aegis of Cancer. Its tunnel is sentinelled by Characith whose number is 640. Cancer is the astro-glyph of the Holy Graal, and 640 is the number of כוס תנחומים, the Cup of Consolation; and that which consoles the Adept on the Path of Cheth is the Graal of Our Lady. Such is this Chalice's nature, which yields both ecstasy and magical immortality, that its *Kalas* is highly addictive. Should the Adept linger overlong in this tunnel, the addiction becomes obsessive, and he runs the risk of becoming a vampire, draining cup after cup of the hellbroth distilled by the Great Harlot, the Mother of Abominations, who yields eagerly to the dark desires of those who are drunk on the wine of her fornications.

The magical formula of this *Kala* is cunnilinctus, which, if it exceeds the proper limits, leads to the death [by depletion] of the partner and the magician himself. The Order of Qliphoth inhabiting the tunnel of Characith is therefore known as the *Shichiririon*, 'the Black.'

The letter *cheth* (8) is ascribed to path 18, and, significantly, the positive reflection of the negative *Qliphoth* assumes the form of Krishna [meaning, the Black One] the Charioteer. Apollo the Charioteer is also attributed to this path. The 'Lord of the Triumph of Light' is reflected into the tunnel as the Black Sun of Tiphareth, the Child of the Waters of the Abyss that swirl in the Grail of Babylon.

The number of Characith, 640, is also that of שמש the Sphere of the Sun, which equates with ממסך, meaning 'a drink offering,' and תמר the 'palm of the hand' and a 'palm tree.' The dates of the palm tree are connected with the phenomena of menstruation.

The sigil of Characith shows a downward-facing mummy overshadowed by a camel-headed entity that issues from its feet. This image is as it was concealed in the name Characith, for 640 is the number of מפלצת, a 'horrible idol.' The camel is the ship of the desert. Its symbolism has been explained in connection with the 13th tunnel, which crosses the abyss *via* the Priestess of the Silver Star path. The camel is also attributed to the 18th path, where it functions like a beast of burden. The crab, turtle, and whale are also included because this path is under the aegis of Cancer, a watery influence representing the most vital element in astro-magical workings.

The *siddhis* associated with this *Kala* are Bewitchments and the Power of Casting Enchantments.

The Cup and the Furnace are the appropriate magical weapons. In the vegetable kingdom's symbolism, the watercress is attributed to this *Kala* because the combination of heat and moisture, fire and water, typifies the cup's contents containing the goddess's fiery dew. The appropriate verse from *Liber 231* declares He rides upon the chariot of eternity; the white and the black are harnessed to his car. Therefore he reflects the Fool and the sevenfold veil.

This implies the orderly ruling of diverse forces. The white and the black are the two suns of the upper and lower horizon, the height and the depth, the infernal Furnace of Amenta and the supernal Sun of the frontal Tree (Tiphereth). The solar force (Heru-Ra-Ha) is here implied, for the white and the black are Ra-Hoor-Khuit and Hoor-Paar-Kraat and whose initials of these gods total 640 [הפך + רהך + הרה], the number of Characith. The sevenfold veil is that of the Seven Stars' Goddess, who is translucent in her luminosity. 'He' [i.e., Asar (Osiris), the dead] reflects the Fool, that is, the Hidden Light that is 'A' between I and 0 (Isis and Osiris). 'A' is Apophis, the God Set in his Ophidian form. He is the Light that imbues the graal of the goddess drained by the Adept. [Grant, 1994, pp. 198-201.]

βασιλεια ειρηνης. *basileia eirenes.* Kingdom of peace. Basileia also means a queen, a princess. Note that in Hebrew, this would be "Kingdom of Solomon." The basic idea is that of balance or equilibrium. See 375.

641 (prime)

מארת *meoroth.* lights, luminaries. [Genesis 1:14-16]

I. "תורומא, sensible lights... This is the root אור light, determined into form by the plastic sign מ. The Divine Verb is always expressing itself in the future, and the accomplishment of the will of the Being of beings, following likewise in the convertible future, the creation always remains in power, according to the meaning of the initial word בראשית. This is why the word מארת is deprived of the luminous sign not only in the singular but also in the plural." [d'Olivet, 1976, p. 44-45.]

ירתאל *Ierathal.* "God who punishes the wicked." 27th Shem ha-Mephorash; 131° - 135°. HÉP, Jupiter. April 5, June 26, September 6, November 17, January 28. 8:40-9:00 AM. Psalm 140:1] "Deliver me, O Lord, from the evil man: preserve me from the violent man." Confound the wicked and the calumniators, and for being delivered from our enemies. Protects against those who provoke us and attack us unjustly through the propagation of light, civilization and liberty. Person Born: Loves justice, the sciences and art, and distinguish themselves in literature. See 965 & Appendix 10.

Associated with the 3rd quinance [10° -15°] of Sagittarius; Angle by day of the 9 of Wands. The 9 of Wands corresponds to Yesod, the sphere of the Moon or subconscious patterns, in Atziluth, the archetypal world of ideas. The letters of the angel's name suggest the power of divine will (Yod) acting through solar regenerative force (Resh) to construct and limit (Tav) the unbridled freedom and license, amoral in itself (Aleph) of those who work and act contrary to cosmic law (Lamed).

Yesod is associated with the astral plane and with the generative facility in nature. Its essence is essentially clean. As the automatic consciousness seat responds to whatever is sent down to it from the self-conscious level (This is indicated by the angle being assigned to "day" or self-conscious mentation). Therefore one of its attributes is impressionability. The 9 of Wands as Yesod in the world of principles (Wands) is seen as the principle behind the One Self's reproductive power. No matter upon what plane they are expressing, the reproductive functions are not evil potencies in themselves. When the reflection from Tiphareth is distorted, as in an imperfect mirror image, the reflection will not mirror its source's perfection. Key 14 (Sagittarius) shows the Ego as the Holy Guardian Angel tempering and modifying the vital soul, pictured as the pool at the angel's feet. It is through the 24th Path of Samekh that the direct influence of Tiphareth is brought to Yesod. See 60, 120, 80.

אמרת purple. This is the color of Yesod, the foundation or firmament. See 80, 233 (Greek).

MDCCLXXVI + annutt coeptis + novus ordo seclorum + E pluribus unum (Lt). 1776 + He hath prospered our Undertaking + a new order of the ages + one out of many. The three mottos on the Great Seal of the U.S. date the American Declaration of Independence. See 99, 150, 220. 172.

642

זהור האחדות *Zhir Ha-achadoth*. Splendor of Unities. A title of Chokmah as the 2nd Path. Indicates the general aspect of this quality of unity, using the plural form brings to mind that Unity (אחד) is by no means empty and abstract. It a unity of Unities, a fullness rather than an emptiness. See 72, 73, 536, 15, 23.

להאיר לע הארץ *le-haair el-haeretz*. To give light upon the earth. In Genesis 1:15: "And let them be for lights in the firmament of the heaven to give light upon the earth..." Refers to the sun and moon. Proper direction of the solar (surya) and lunar (rayi) currents of the life-breath leads to balanced operations of self and subconsciousness, as pictured in Key 6, and this gives light (illumination) on the earth-the physical body.

פורשון *Purson*. Goetia demon #20 by day of the 2nd decan of Libra. The lion, serpent and bear are obvious allusions to the Mars-force and to its use or abuse. See 1292 & Appendix 11.

I. "Before he fell, Purson was an angel of the order of virtues and partly also of the order of thrones... Purson is now a king in the nether regions with 22 legions of spirits to do his bidding. His appearance is that of a man with a lion's face, carrying a viper in his hand and astride a bear. He knows the past and future and can discover hidden treasure." [Davidson, 1971, p. 230.]

II. *Goetia*: "...a great king. As a man with a lion's face, his appearance is comely, carrying a cruel viper in his hand and riding upon a bear. Going before him are many trumpets sounding. He knows all things hidden and can discover treasure and tell all things past, present, and come. He can take a body, either human or Aerial, and answers truly of all earthly things, both secret and divine, and the creation of the world. He brings forth good familiars, and under his government, there be 22 legions of Spirits, partly of the Order of Virtues and partly of the Order of Thrones." [Mathers, 1995, p. 37]

643 (prime)

סור מרע בינה *sur mah.rah Binah*. To depart from evil is understanding. In Job 28:28: "And unto man he said, behold, the fear of the Lord, that is wisdom; and to depart from evil is understanding." Paul Case: To depart from evil is Binah." to depart means to turn aside. See 270, 67.

וזכרתי and I will remember. See Genesis 9:15.

644

אדדא זוטא קדישא *Idra Zuta Qadisha*. Lesser Holy Assembly.

Εμμανουηλ. *emmanouel*. Immanuel.

645

המם *hawman*. to rout, confuse, to drive, impel. See 85.

מהרת you hastened, you were quick. See Genesis 27:20.

משרקה *Masreqah*. Masrekah, the home of King Samiah, who once ruled over Edom. Note that Edom suggests unbalanced force. See Genesis 36:36.

עין התנין Well of the Serpent (or Crocodile, or Jackal). Nehemiah 2:13.

646

אלהים *Elohim*. Strengths, creative name of God. Mem = 600, see 86.

מום *moom*. blemish, defect, spot, stain. Mum, "blemish," name of the 72nd Shem ha-Mephorash, short form with different pointing. See 86, 101 & Appendix 10.

לוים *Levim*. Levites, the class of priest among the Jews. See 86.

משוש *mishoosh*. touching, feeling. With different pointing: mishayosh. Groper, slow walker. See 1383.

יה יהוה אדם *Yah IHVH Adam*. the father, the creative word and making or humanity. [IRQ:778] "Rabbi Eliezar arose, and commenced and said, Psalm 108:5 "I called upon Yah in my distress; Yah heard me at the lodge. Tetragrammaton is on my side, I will not fear, what can man do unto Me? Tetragrammaton takes my part with them that help me, and I shall see my desire upon mine enemies. It is better to trust in Tetragrammaton than to put any confidence in man [Adam]. It is better to trust in Tetragrammaton than to put any confidence in princes."

השמש the sun. See Genesis 15:12.

המארת the lights. Genesis 1:16.

מצלעתיו of his ribs. Genesis 2:21.

647 (prime)

זמם *zahmam*. to think, plot, devise, plan. Mem =600, see 87.

ותאמר and she said. See Genesis 3:2.

648

I. (8x9x9) or 2^3 x 3^4

חמש five (5). *five*. "This word expressed a movement of contraction and of apprehension, as that which result from the five fingers of the hand grasping a thing, pressing tightly and warming it. Its root is double. חם, the first, designates the effect of the second, מש, that is to say, the former depicts the general envelopment, the heat which results and the effect of the contractive movement impressed by the latter." [d'Olivet, 1976, p. 153.] For other numerals, see 13, 400, 636, 273, 600, 372, 395, 770, 570, 441.

נר למשיחי *ner le-meshichi*. a lamp for mine anointed. In Psalm 132:17: "There will I make a horn to shoot up (bud) unto David: there I have ordered (ordained) a lamp for mine anointed." In the middle ages, משיחי means Christian (messianic). The horn of David is the principle of power, and the lamp, the principle of illumination. See 250, 358.

חורם אביו + שלמה *Churum Abiv + Shelomoh*. Hiram Abiff + Solomon. The architect and builder of the temple of God and the King, representing the Sun. See 273, 375.

עץ חיים תאוה באה *etz chaiim tauah bah*. Desire fulfilled is a Tree of Life. In Proverbs 13:12: "Hope deferred makes the heart sick: but when the desire comes, it is a Tree of Life." see 160, 68.

כבכרתו his birthright. Genesis 43:33.

כברכתו, according to his blessing. Genesis 49:28.

η παυαγαθια Θεοε. *heh panagathia. Theou.* The holy God. See 484.

ηρεμια Θεου. *heremia Theou.* The quiet God.

Μαρ ιαμ μητηρ. *Mariam methehr.* Mary, the mother. See 192, 456.

649

לטים *lataim.* enchantments, illusions. Incarnate life veils consciousness through the illusion of separation. Mem = 600, see 89, 883 (Greek).

תרדמה trance, deep sleep. See Genesis 2:21.

I. "תרדמה *a-sympathetic-slumber...* This is a kind of lethargy or somnambulism that takes possession of the sentient faculties and suspends them. The hieroglyphic composition of the Hebrew word is remarkable. It can cause strange reflections anent certain modern discoveries. The two contracted roots דר רם, express the first, that which extends and takes possession by a proper movement; the other that which is similar, homogeneous and conformable to universal nature. The sign of mutual reciprocity ת and the emphatic article ה are here a the beginning and the end to increase this mysterious word's energy.

After analyzing this word, one cannot fail to recognize that extraordinary condition, which the moderns have given the name of magnetic sleep, *somnambulism*, and which one might perhaps designate, as in Hebrew, *sympathetic sleep*. I must moreover state that the Hellenists who say εκστασις, *a trance* is not so far from the truth as Saint Jerome who merely says 'soporem' *a deep sleep*. [d'Olivet, 1976, pp. 87-88.]

II. "*(a)* The so-called sleep of Adam is a marvelous event, the reflected action of which is seen in the sleep of the newborn child. Compared to every other species where the newborn animal is automatically set into motion by accumulated knowledge, the human being is born to learn; and his *not knowing* [i.e., freedom from the animal instinct and influence of the accumulation of the past.] is in proportion to his evolutionary development and tends to create the greatest possible intensity of life.

(b) Adam's consciousness is now freed. It leaves him and plunges into *Tardamah* (deep sleep). This schema is *Tav-Raysh* (400.200) and *Damah,* the feminine of blood. *Tav* (400) is the total resistance of life's physical support (the universe), and *Raysh is* the total organic process of universal life. We can translate that "deep sleep" symbolically by saying that Adam's blood is mated with the highest power of cosmic energy in it. Then, into this now pregnant flesh, a double life is projected. The extraction of a rib has no connection with the cabalistic meaning of the text. The schema for rib is a shadow to which is added 70: it is the opening of all possible possibilities for man." [Suraes, 1992, p. 113.]

תפקחנה and were opened. Genesis 3:7.

האדרא זוטא קדישא *Ha Idra Zuta Qadisha.* The Lesser Holy Assembly. Name of One of the 3 books in The Kabbalah Unveiled by Mathers. It is also abbreviated I.Z.Q.

אתאוריאל *Ithuriel.* Discovery of God. Ithuriel is formed from two words. The first, *ayt*, את, is used to denote the direct object in a sentence (the sign of the accusative). For example, in the sentence "John ate food," food is the direct object. Figuratively speaking, *ayt* points, reveals or marks the direct object. The other meaning of *ayt*, is a mattock, a versatile hand tool used to dig and chop. It has a long handle with an ax blade on one side and a pick on the other. It is a farming implement that can be converted to a weapon of war. In this connection, Mars is the god that presides over warfare and is the fields' protector. The next 3 letters form the word אור, *ur*, which means light, the brightness of flames, and is a metaphor suggesting to reveal what is hidden. Therefore the name of this angel means to reveal through light.

דומם *domam*. a great silence, still, silent, dumb in silence. Mem = 600, see 90.

ימם *yamin*. hot springs [Genesis 36:24]. See 90.

מים Letter Name *Mem*, meaning: waters. (mute, dark mirror). Alchemical water, microcosmically, is the cosmic fire specialized in the nerve currents and chemistry of the blood see 90.

נתר *nawthar*. to tremble, to fall off (as the foliage or fruit of a tree). With different pointing *nitar*: to be torn loose, be released. Related to the hanged man-in some versions, he holds behind him a bag, from which fall objects not very clearly drawn. Possibly coins symbolizing visible works or accomplishments.

נתר *nether*. natron, a mineral alkali, either sodium nitrate or potassium nitrate, combined with oil to make soap. Together with various spices and Bitumen, the Egyptian Niter was an important ingredient of the mixture used for embalming mummies. Niter is associated both with cleansing or purification and with preservation. In alchemy, the "sun" of Tiphareth concocts niter, which is a stage of preparation of "Salt." It is a process of vitalizing the dead forms of sensation and infusing them with seminal or reproductive powers. This happens by correctly perceiving the inner principles of anything. Niter is more pure and more lasting than the forms it is derived from. See 160.

מדבר קדש *midebbar kadesh*. the wilderness of Kadesh. In Psalm 29:8: "The voice of the Lord shakes the wilderness; the Lord shakes the wilderness of Kadesh." "Wilderness" also means mouth, speech (Peh) and Kadesh, with different points, means sanctity, holiness; to cleanse, purify. To wash hands and feet before a sacred act, to prepare the water of purification. Note that דבר is "word," and Mem maybe "from" or "from the holy word." The Lord cleanses and sanctifies with proper use of speech. See 246, 404.

נרת lamps. Exodus 39:37.

לשעירם *daemonibus hirsutis*. To the hairy deities.

"These were types of Set as gods of generation. Nuit says, 'My incense is of resinous wood & gums; there is *no blood* therein: because of my hair the trees of Eternity.' Massey notes, 'There is a particular kind of hairy goat known on the monuments as the Serau... In Egypt's language, says Herodotus, both a goat and the god Pan are called Mendes.' i.e., the serau were sacred to Set, the Egyptian form of Pan." [Grant, 1994, p. 118.]

651

האלהים *ha-Elohim*. The Creative Powers (of God). Mem = 600, see 91.

מי יעלה לנו השמימה Who shall go up for us to the heavens?

תמורה *Termurah*. Permutation and substitution of letters. Hebrew cryptology.

שטולוש *Shatulosh*. Goetia demon #36 by day of the 3rd decan of Pisces. See Appendix 11.

I. The 3rd decan is attributed to the 10 of Cups or the power of Malkuth, the physical plane, in Briah, the creative world. This corresponds to the influence between experience in the world and creative thoughts and images.

II. *Goetia*: "He is a great and powerful prince, appearing in the shape of a mighty raven at first before the exorcist; but after he takes the image of a man. He teaches the art of astronomy and the virtues of herbs and precious stones. He governs 26 Legions of Spirits." [Mathers, 1995, p. 47]

τελεσται. *telestai*. Mysterious, "mystic rites." from τελετη, a making perfect: initiation in the mysteries, the celebration of mysteries.

ναυς. *Naus*. Ship. Applied to a ship by the Greeks gives it a cosmic meaning... "The church was called a ship since the temple was designed as an image of the universe." [Canon, p.73] ο παρθενογνης. *ho parthenogenehs*. The virgin-born; an epithet of Jesus. Related to the phrase "Logos of virginity." See 1480. Adds to 2368, the value of Jesus Christ. See 888, 2368, 570.

652

כצל ימינו על הארץ *katzel yawmenu Al ha-eretz*. He has made the earth by his powers.

רבתים *rebbothim*. two myriads. In Psalm 68:17: "The chariots of God are two myriads [22,000], even thousands of angels: the Lord is among them, as in Sinai, in the Holy Place."

οι γιγαντες. *hoi gigantes*. The mighty men. Septuagint translation of הנפילים (785) in Genesis 6:4: "There were giants on the earth in those days, and also afterward when the sons of God went to the daughters of men and had children by them. they became the might men of old, men of renown." see 785.

653 (prime)

מאורות *meorith*. Lights, luminaries; light-holes. Written without second Vav in Genesis 1:14: "Then Elohim said, 'Let there be lights in the firmament of the heaven to separate the day from the night, and let them be for signs, and for seasons, and for days, and years. variant (defective) spelling. See 647, 666.

תגרן *Tageran*. The Haggler; one of the Qlippoth of Tiphareth (תנרירון). As a demon, it represents the contending force that seeks to disrupt harmony. See 1303; 1519, 869, 666.

יכנא יהוה אלהיך *anokiy IHVH Eloheka*. I am the Lord your God. in Exodus 20:2: "I am the Lord your God, who brought you out of Egypt, out of the land of slavery." These words are the preface to the ten commandments. Kaph = 500, see 173.

654

בוא השמש *bo ha-shamesh*. going down of the sun; sunset.

מדים *Madim*. Mars; "powers of vehement strength." Mem = 600, see 94. 95, 655.

זלברהית *Zalbarhith*. Lord of triplicity by night for Leo. The name suggests the power of discrimination (Zain), which is guided by the one teacher (Lamed) into concentration (Beth) of solar regenerative force (Resh) to constitute (Heh) a rational use of divine will (Yod) in dedicated service in the limitation of the material world (Tav).

655

מאדים *Madim*. Mars, Powers of vehement strength. The masculine plural of מאד, Meode, "strength, might," and adverb: very, exceedingly. Mem = 600, see 95.

המים *ha-Mem*. the waters. See 95.

ספר יצירה *Sepher Yetzirah*. The Book of Formation, or one of the principal Qabalistic texts. Attributed to Abraham. It treats the cosmogony as symbolized by the 32 Paths of Wisdom: the 10 Sephiroth (numbers) and the alphabet's 22 letters. The term path is used to signify a sphere or hieroglyphic set of ideas.

שהם יקר *Soham Yaqar*. the precious onyx [Job 28:16]. See 80, 85, 549, 226, 876, 345.

היכל עצם שמים *hekel etzem shamaim*. Palace of the body of heaven; heavenly mansion corresponding to Netzach (Victory), sphere of Venus on the Tree of Life. See 4775, 65, 200, 390, 148.

הקדוש ברוך הוא *ha-Qadosh Barukh Hu*. The Holy One, blessed be He. An ancient Hebrew blessing.

משם רעה *mishahm roeh*. because of the shepherd.

In Genesis 49:24: "But his [Joseph's] bow remained steady, his strong arms stayed limber, because of the Shepherd, the Rock of Israel."

כי קרוב אליך הדבר מאד *kei-qarob alika ha-dabar medde*. the word is very near you. In Deuteronomy 30:14: No, the word is very near you; it is in your mouth and n your heart so you may obey it." see 1633, 978, 308, 206, 61.

656

I. A pentagram between two hexagrams (6-5-6). Geometrical figures of initiation.

מתנוצע *Mathnaztzo*. Resplendent. The intelligence of Malkuth. This represents the idea that man is the mediator and adaptor, set between the infinite and eternal cosmic past and the infinite and eternal cosmic future, from the verb *nawtzatz* נצץ to glitter, to bloom, to flower. Malkuth is often called the flower of the Tree. It may also be understood as the "Blossoming Intelligence." see 65 (Adonai) 495 (Malkuth), 1006, 1026, 230, 496, 570, 656 and Appendix 12.

תנור *thanoor*. Furnace. The symbol of the human body. Origin of the alchemical term Athanor, defined as "a self-feeding, digesting furnace, wherein the fire burns at an even heat." Its fire is the fire of life, and this is the fire which the Zealator or alchemist's assistant, keeps burning. With different pointing: an oven (Aramaic תנורא, Septuagint κλιβαυος). In Leviticus 2:4: ."" an oblation of a meat offering, baked in an oven..." Observe that נור (Aramaic for fire) + Tav (Saturn). See 662, 85 (Lt).

שושן *shoshan*. rose (the lexicon gives "lily"). In Canticles 2:1: "I am the rose of Sharon and the lily of the valleys" This word is used in the feminine plural, שושנת [1056]. The rose is a symbol of the human soul, or air and of aspiration. See 661, 1617, 1071.

ששון *sahsone*. delight, joy; exultation, rejoicing. From Hebrew lexicon" "oil of joy" סמן ששון. This oil is used for anointing on the joyous occasion.

ארץ נשיה *ertz neshyaiam*. land of forgetfulness. In Psalm 88:12: "Shall your wonders be known in the dark? And your righteousness in the land of forgetfulness." Paul Case credits נשיה [365] to "Earth of Tiphareth." It is also "pasture land, on the Seven Earths." See 291, 482 (Greek), 658.

גילי מאד בת ציון *geliy meod bath Tzion*. rejoice greatly, daughter of Zion [Zechariah 9:9]. This verse refers to the king coming: "He is just and having salvation" (i.e., Tiphareth). Note that "rejoice"; גילי is 53, the value of אבן. See 53, 45, 402, 156.

Μεσσιας. *Messias*. The Anointed. A title of Jesus. See 644, 1768, 1480, 1408, 1844, 888, 358, 2183, 2220.

αλευρον. *aleuron*. Meal. In Matthew 13:33: "The kingdom of heaven is like unto leaven, which a woman took, and hid in three measures of meal, till the whole was leavened." The "meal" is leavened in the "furnace." See 148, 507, 889, 1919 (Greek).

657

זלברחית *Zelbarachith*. An angel of Leo. This connects with the heart, the Sun and Tiphareth, which is the "location" of the order of Melchizedek.

אדם בן *Ben Adam*. Son of man [Psalm 8:4]. Refers to man as the means whereby the divine grace becomes manifest through a correct understanding of the desire nature. Mem = 600, see 97, 747, 1307, 2198 (Greek).

שבט סופר the pen of the writer (i.e., scribe). Judges 5:14: "And Barak's works are known in Malek; after you marched Benjamin with affection for you; out of Machir came forth a seer, and out of Zebulun those who write with the pen of a scribe." Zebulun is attributed to Cancer, associated with Cheth and speech; שבט also means rod, scepter, tribe, race. See 311, 95.

נזרת *Nazareth*, the city in which Jesus grew up

[Variant synthetic spelling, see 740]. Part of the I.N.R.I. formula. See 340, 270, 1147, 1231, 1236 (Hebrew); 2573 (Greek), 46 (Lt).

ותרודיאל *Uthrodiel*. Angel of the 3rd decan of Scorpio. This decan is ruled by the Moon and denotes the qualities: subtle and abrupt... there is the ability to be quick and responsive to the thoughts and feelings of others. The 3rd decan of Scorpio also corresponds with the 7 of Cups, or the operation of the desire nature in the creative world (Netzach in Briah). When well-dignified, this influence can lead to a possible victory, but the person may be too indolent to take advantage of commanding circumstance opportunities. Success may be gained but not followed up; there is a necessity for choosing only the highest objectives.

658

וברכתיך and I will bless you. See Genesis 26:24.

תרבון may increase, you may increase. See Deuteronomy 6:3.

תחרים you shall destroy. See Deuteronomy 7:2.

φρην. *phren.* The seat of the lower mind; reins.

659 (prime)

η ναυς. *heh naus.* the ship. "The church was called a ship since the temple was designed as an image of the universe." [Canon, p.73] see 651.

660

שתר *sawther.* (verb) to hide, to veil, to cover, to conceal. The root of Nesether (נסתר), Intelligence of Netzach. This path's powers are hidden from the eye of sense and beheld by the eye of faith. See 710, 1060.

ימים *yawmim.* days, seas, times. Mem = 600, see 100.

כלים *kaylim.* vases, utensils; weapons. See 100.

סם *sahm.* spice; drug; poison. Plural סמים, "sweet spices" in Exodus 30:34: "And the Lord said to Moses, "Take sweet spices; stacte, onychia and galbanum; sweet spices with pure incense; of each shall be thereby equal weight; (35) and you shall make it a perfume..."

"The circumferential sign being universalized by the collective sign מ, becomes the symbol of the olfactory sphere, of every fragrant influence given to the air: thence, every kind of *aromatic.* The Arabic root characterizes that which is penetrated with force, whether good or evil. In the modern idiom, the verb signifies *to bore*, a hole, *to pierce.*" [d'Olivet, 1976, pp. 409-410.] see 100.

שגג ומשגה *segeg ve-masayggeh.* Deceived and deceiver. In Job 12:16: "To him belong strength and victory; both deceived, and the deceiver are his (the Lord's)." see 306, 311.

תינר is Given without comment in *Sepher Sephiroth* [Crowley, 1977, p. 56]. The letters of this word suggest the power of contraction or limitation (Tav) of divine will (Yod) through reproductive force (Nun) and solar regenerative energy (Resh).

"תה [analogous of תי]. A root analogous to the root תא [Every idea of determination, designation, definition]; but whose expression, more moral, characterizes the influential and sympathetic reason of things. Arabic signifies literally *to be led astray*, lost in empty space. By the compound word *a vain thing*; by the verb... a thing which is liquefied.

Of the root נר: The root אור, united by contraction to the sign of produced existence, constitutes a root whose purpose is to characterize that which propagates light, literally as well as figuratively: thence, *a lamp, a beacon, a torch: a sage, a guide*; that which *enlightens, shines*, is *radiant*: metaphorically, *a public festivity, an extreme gladness.*" [d'Olivet, 1976, pp. 404, 467.]

קול תחנוני *qol takaenuni*. the voice of my supplications. In Psalm 130:2: "Lord, hear my voice: let your ears be attentive to the voice of my supplications." see 4006 (Greek).

עץ קץ *ayth qaytz*. The time of the end. Note: קץ in the Hebrew lexicon is given as meaning "the time of redemption, the Messianic age."

ניציצית *Nitzizith*. Sparks. The Hebrew lexicon gives the feminine plural as ניציצת these are the divine sparks, or Yods of radiant solar energy manifest as light but hidden in their essence from the eyes of the profane. When fully evolved, these sparks become the "sons and daughters of the most high," i.e., human souls.

Rosenroth in K.D.L.C.K. (pp.571-578) gives *scintillae*, and in a long discourse of 26 sections, goes into great detail on its various attributions. He relates them, among other things, to the Briatic "lights" and shows their grades of descending influence, in an elaborate table, as aspects of Tetragrammaton.

קשוין *kesheron*. connection; zones, members, knots. IRQ:999: "In the first arm (otherwise in the holy arm) [of Microprosopus] these members (or divisions) are bound together." From shoulder to elbow, there are three natural divisions in the arm, from elbow to wrist and from wrists to the fingers' tips. The word קשוין, here translated as "members," means, properly speaking, "zones." Here we may infer that this gematria suggests that the hidden zones of the "sparks" in the holy mountain are to lighted by the delivery of the "seed of the righteous."

שלל *shawlahl*. spoil, booty. In Joshua 22:8: "And he spoke to them, saying 'return to your tents with much riches… divide the spoil of your enemies with your brothers." Also poetical for captives, i.e., for the necks of them that take the spoil. In Judges 5:30: "Are they not finding and dividing the spoils: a girl or two for each man, colorful garments as plunder for Sisera, colorful garments embroidered, highly embroidered garments for my neck-all this is plunder?" Also: gain, profit in Proverbs 31:11: "The heart of her husband does not safely trust in her so that he shall have no lack of gain."

εκλεκτοις. *elektois*. Chosen. Septuagint translation of בחיר in Psalm 89:3: "You said "I have made a covenant with my chosen one, I have sworn to David my servant, (4) I will establish your line forever and make your throne firm through all generations." In this instance the "throne" alludes to the Mercury center; David means beloved. See 14, 499, 220, 540 (Greek). The chosen one has been re-generated.

661 (prime)

אמרתך *emrawthaka*. your word. Psalm 119:11.

אסם *awsam*. a granary or storehouse. Mem = 600, see 101.

בלהטיהם *belahatahem*. By their secret arts, by their enchantments [Exodus 7:11]. See 101.

חלל ידו נחש ברח *kellah yado nachash beruach*. his hand has formed the crooked serpent [Job 26:13]. In the Jewish translation, it is "the hand has pierce the crooked serpent." This is in direct correspondence with the letter-name טית, Teth. Yod, the creative hand forms this energy in various ways and pierces its lower expressions to be used in new ones' birth. See 418, 358, 20, 1885.

סוד הפעלות *sod ha-pehulloth*. Secret works. Designates the 19th Path of Teth. "The 19th path is called the intelligence of the Secret of all Spiritual Activities. It is called because of its influence from the supreme blessing and the supernal glory (blessing and glory refer to Chesed). See 667, 1502.

שושנה *shoshannah*. a lily (white); a lily ornament, a rose (late use). With different pointing: a lily ornament in architecture, a tubular trumpet (from its shape). Many Qabalists translate this as rose and refer it to Malkuth. This influence may be traced in several Rosicrucian texts. The Zohar [Vol. 1, page 3] says, *Shoshannah* symbolizes the community of Israel. It is also a symbol of the cup of benediction. See 656.

Rosenroth in K.D.L.C.K. (p.708) says this word, in the feminine gender is Malkuth since it contains red and white colors, which indicate stimulations from the right and left sides [i.e., the pillars of Mercy and Severity on the Tree]; and that in the Zohar section *beresheth* speaks of the rose having 13 leaves or petals. This refers to Malkuth having 13 kinds of mercy because its splendors [i.e., The Resplendent Intelligence] are said to be a rose.

תורה האדם *torah ha-adam*. the law of Adam (Humanity), the manner of Humanity, the coming generations of men. In 2 Samuel 7:19: "And this was yet a small thing in the sight, O Lord God; but thou has also spoken of your servant's house for a great while to come. And is this the manner of man, O Lord God?" The American translators render it "the coming generations of men" to agree with the context. It has to do with humanity's law, which is the secret of works, which gives the foresight suggested by the Bible passage.

כי לקח אתו אלהים *ki-lawqah otho Elohim*. for Elohim took him. In Genesis 5:24: "And Enoch walked with the Elohim, and was not, for Elohim took him." see 84, 1831.

662

את הנור *eth ha-nour*. Essence of Fire, Athanor. An alchemical term referring to the human body and its finer counterparts (subtle bodies). Described as "A self-feeding, digestive furnace, in which an equable heat is maintained." Symbolized by the figure of the pentagram. See 256, 301, 656, 401.

"Take counsel: be not so careful of the fire of the athanor as your internal fire. Seek it in the house of Aries [i.e., the head or brain, particularity the sight center = Heh], and draw it from the depths of Saturn (i.e., the basal center = Muladhara chakra = Tav); let Mercury be the interval, and

your signal the doves of Diana [Venus center]." [Atwood, 1918, p. 283]

מלאך האלהים angel or messenger of God (the Creative Powers); King of the Gods. The inheritance of those who have learned to rule as sons and daughters of the most high. Kaph = 500, see 182.

בסתר in secret. See Deuteronomy 27:15.

Corona Dei (Lt). Crown of the Lord. Rosenroth in K.D.L.C.K. (p.86) says it is the name of God which Rabbi Moses says refers to Malkuth, and that is this, says Rabbi Ishmael, which is blessed and the fount of blessings. For Rosenroth, it also refers to Briah as signifying all forms and manifestations born [i.e., imaged] from the crown of the Lord.

663

I. The square of the first 7 prime numbers: $1^2 + 3^2 + 5^2 + 7^2 + 11^2 + 13^2 + 17^2 = 663$

II. Length of the Staff that the Fool carries related to the Middle Pillar of the Tree of Life. That is the path of Gimel [3]+ Samekh [60] + Tav [400] = 463.

בנאים *Bonaim*. builders, masons. A name used by the Essenes. True builders share the one secret doctrine, which is practical and has much to do with the stars' occult doctrine. Mem = 600, see 103, 108, 1379 (Greek).

הכוכבים *ha-kokabim*. the stars. Mem = 600, see 103, 1777 (Greek), 48.

הוא האלהים *Hu ha-Elohim*. He is God [The Elohim]. Mem = 600, see 103, 1994 (Greek).

אבנים *awbaynayim*. stones. Plural of *ehben* [53], the Stone. See 103, 53, Genesis 31:46 and 1 Kings 5:17.

היקוד + אור צורי יהוה *ha-yeqod + IHVH tzuri aor.* Tetragrammaton my rock + the burning light. The rock is the Stone, which burns with the light of illuminated consciousness. See 332.

סדם *Sodom*; "burning, conflagration." The Biblical city was destroyed by God because of its perversity. Mem = 600, see 104, 50, 106, 700, 385 (Greek).

נחום *Nacham*. Nahum, "comfort"; one of the minor prophets. See 104.

ורחמתי and I will show mercy. See Exodus 33:19.

תהרגנו you shall kill. See Deuteronomy 13:10.

פתה עינים *poawtah einayim*. The eye-opener. In The Zohar (1:4): "Rabbi Eleazar opened his discourse with the text: 'Lift up your eyes on high and see: who has created these?' (Isaiah 40:26) "Lift up your eyes on height,' to which place? To that place to which all eyes are turned, to wit, petah enaim (eye-opener). [פתה socket, female pudenda; With different pointing: 1. to be open; to be simple, be foolish; to be deceived; 2. to be seduced. פתה = 485 = "out of the heavens"; עינים = 180 = קף Qoph, "back of the head." See 100, 259, 130, 70.

כורש מלכאדי בבל *koresh makekaw di dawber.* Cyrus, King of Babylon. In Ezra 5:13: "But in the first year of Cyrus, the King of Babylon the same King Cyrus made a decree to build this house of God." see 526, 90, 34, 950, 956.

הסתר hide. See Deuteronomy 31:18.

סתרה protection. See Deuteronomy 32:38.

בית הרחם the womb [Crowley, 1977, p. 57].

I. $(15^2 + 2^2)$

II. $\Sigma 36 = 666$.

The total of the numbers in the sun's magic square and the value of the sun's magic line. A solar number representing man as a center of solar activity and referring specifically to Tiphareth.

In Revelations (Apocalypse), it is the number of the Beast. It is a cryptic reference to the Roman Empire and to Caesar Nero. Caesar's symbol was a solar disk, and the essential spirit of Roman imperialism was a crass, materialistic exaltation of physical force. It is the number of the sum of the cells in the magic square of Tiphareth, and therefore an indication of the misuse of the charismatic power associated with Tiphareth for selfish means.

אלהיכם *Elohikam*. Your God [Amos 5:26]. It is the value of God's "secret place" mentioned in Psalm 18:11 (He made darkness his hiding place). Mem = 600, see 106.

סתרו *sithru*. His secret place, his covering. In Psalm 18:11: "He made darkness his secret [i.e., hiding] place; his pavilion round about him were dark waters and thick clouds of the skies." The material world veils spiritual truth. See 994.

אסתהר *Ishtar*. The planet Venus (Aramaic), and the goddess Ishtar. Remember that בן *Ben*, the son, and אימא *Aima*, the mother, are both the number 52.

השלך על יהוה יהבך והוא כלדיכל Cast your burden upon Jehovah and He will sustain you (Psalm 55:22). See 1554.

יהי מארת *yehi meoroth*. Let there be lights (stars). See Genesis 1:14.

סורת Sorath. The Spirit of the Sun. The radiant physical energy is the source of all personal activity. The outer vesture of the spiritual sun.

שמש יהוה Sun of Jehovah (Tiphareth). "He had assumed divinity and used solar symbols." [Revelations 13:16]

שם יהשוה Shemesh-Jehovah. The Name Jesus, Qabalistic spelling. It signifies The idea (name or word) that the nature of Reality is to liberate. See 326, 340, 1226.

Paul Case: "You shall know the truth, and the truth will set you free," in Jesus' words. "Reality sets us free," this is the true secret of the power of the name of Jesus. Because to that meaning, all that is said of this name is true, all that has been claimed for it is true, even the claim that no other name given among men has the power to deliver us. [The Name of Names]

נתן להם האלהים Nahthan le-hem ha-Elohim. God gave them.

נרון קסר Neron Qaesar. Nero Caesar [Hebrew spelling of a Latin name]. The 'beast' mentioned in the Apocalypse Revelations 13:18: "Here is wisdom. Let him that has understanding count the number of the beast: for it is the number of a man, and his number is 666." Nero was the "beast" because he had assumed divinity and used solar symbols (Apollo). A cryptic reference to the Spirit of Roman imperialism-materialistic exaltation of physical force has lasted until the present. See 1316.

רומיית Ayron ha-qodesh. A Rabbinical term designating the Latin language. The dominance of Rome through pagan sun-worship, symbolized by the beast (the Emperor), was the logical outcome of the materialistic belief.

טסרו you shall turn aside. Deuteronomy 5:29.

ארון הקדש The Holy Ark (on which the tables of the law were written). See 257

עממו סתן Ommo-Saittan. Ommo-Satan, the 'evil triad' of Satan-Apohras, Typhon, Besz, attributed to Yesod, sphere of the Moon of the Tree of Life. "Stoop not down into the darkly-splendid world,' says the Chaldean Oracles. ."..It is termed the place of the evil one, the slayer of Osiris [i.e., the sun]. He is the tempter, accuser and punisher of the brethren. He is frequently represented in Egypt with the head of a water-dragon, a lion or leopard body, and the hindquarters of a water-horse. He is the administrator of the evil triad. The members are Apophraz, the stooping dragon; Satan-Typhon, the slayer of Osiris; Besz, the brutal power of the demoniac force." [The Secret Rituals of the Golden Dawn, pp. 52-53]

האדומים ha-Edomim. The Edomites; i.e., those who ruled the kingdoms of unbalanced forces. See 106.

עשה ארץ He has made the earth. In Jeremiah 51:15, 10:12: "He has made the earth by his power, he has established the world by his wisdom, and has stretched out the heaven by his understanding." see 702, 652, 1476.

נשימירום Nashimiron. "Malignant women" or "the Snaky"; Qlippoth of Pisces. See 1316.

λογος αγαπης. Logos agapes. Word of love.

ευπορια. euporia. Material wealth, materialism, gold [Acts 19:25]. Used in a context that identifies it with revenues derived from idolatry. A quotation from the mouth of the Ephesian Silversmith, Demetrius. Implies Materialism. In classical Greek: 1. facility in moving; facility in doing. 2. readiness of supply; means, resources. 3. plenty, store, wealth. 4. revenues derived from idolatry. See 160.

η φρην. ηeh phren. Lower Mind. From a root meaning: "to rein in, to curb." In the plural, the midriff or the muscle parts the heart and lungs from the lower viscera. In Homer, both in singular and plural, the heart, mind, understanding, reason. Thus it relates to Tiphareth, the seat of the Ego-sense, derived from Kether. See 538, 597 (Greek); 1105 (Greek); 200, 1081, 53, 640.

Ο Σεραπις. Ho Seraphs. Serapis. Egyptian god Apis, the element of Earth, the animal nature of man. The worship of Apis, in connection with that of Isis, was spread over the Roman world at the beginning of the Christian era. Apis was a copy of the "Golden Calf."

παραδοσις *pharadoisis*. Traditions. Traditions of men, as opposed to the ordinances of God. They limit human freedom by imposing standards of behavior, having no foundation in things' real nature. 1. a handing down of traditions. 2. a giving up, surrender. 3. the transmission, or handing down, of legends. "The passing on, during personal intercourse, of a master's teaching and methods to his accepted pupils. The word usually implies that which is unwritten: and also an inner knowledge privileged to the suitable few." [Omikron, 1942, p. 261.]

τειταν. *Teitan*. Sol, Phoebus.

απολλυμεθα. *Apollumentha*. we perish. [Matthew 8:25] . "Lord, save us, we perish."

ο σπειρας. *ho speiras*. The sower of tares. Referred to in Matthew 13:39: (38) "The field is the world; the good seed are the sons of the kingdom; the darnel (tares) are the sons of the evil one; (39) That enemy who sowed them is the adversary; the harvest is the end of the age, and the reapers are the messengers."

Vicarius Filii Dei (Lt) Vicar of the Son of God. Note that Filii, son, is the number 43.

D.C.; L.X.; V.I (Lt). Sum of the only 6 numerical letters the Romans used.

Ecce Bestia Magna (Lt). Here is the Great Beast.

667

שמן למאור *shemen le-mawaur*. "oil for lighting." The lamps are the interior starts or chakras. The oil is the nerve force, a modification of Kundalini (which is the esoteric "coiled fiery power" or astral light). The oil is made to energize the lamps through an exercise in which counting is essential because they include rhythmic breathing, rhythmic intonation of divine names, etc. See

412, 390, 207.

סוד הפעולות *Sod Ha-Pehooluth*. Secret of all spiritual activities. The 19th Path of Teth. See 1502, 206, 409, 380, 358, 661.

הוא גלא עמיקתא *Hua galah omikatha*. He reveals the depths (the unfathomable things) for those who know the secret of the lighting of the oil. See 38.

Θειος λογος. Divine logos.

668

בונים *Bonim*. Builders. Mem = 600, see 108.

גיהנם *Gehenna*. One of the 7 infernal Mansions. Sheol (Hades) subdivision into a cavern separated by a wall or chasm, occupied by the departed unjust. Mem = 600, see 108.

שם יהוה אקרא *Shem IHVH ehqayarah*. I will proclaim (publish) the name of Tetragrammaton [Deuteronomy 32:3]. The name lights up all areas of darkness and ignorance symbolized by Gehenna. See 345, 26, 340.

סחרת *sokereth*. *negotiatrix*, i.e., a female who manages or conducts a matter requiring skill or consideration, such as an obstacle or test of strength. With different pointing: trader, trafficker. Gesenius has "a stone used (with marble) in paving." In Esther 1:6: "the beds were of gold and silver, upon a pavement of red, and blue and white and black, marble." The higher self (Samekh) negotiates the soul to victory (Cheth) over evil through test and trial, conducting it to rebirth (Resh), and this is the dominion (Tav) of the Stone, which is composed of memory (blue-Chesed), volition (red-Geburah), unity (white-Kether), and embodiment (black-Malkuth).

זרע ושממה *zero ve-shammah*. fruitfulness and sterility. The pairs of opposites attributed to Resh. Illustrates the sun's effects on land. Sun + Water = זרע; Sun - Water = שממה.

עץ ברוש *etz berosh*. Fir or Cyprus wood. In Isaiah 55:13: "Instead of the thorn shall come up the Fir-tree, and instead of the brier shall come up the Myrtle tree: and it shall be to the Lord for a name, for an everlasting sign that shall not be cut off." ברוש, cypress, fir was used in Egypt for the mummy cases which have endured for over 1100 years. The Cypress is said to have never grown in the holy land. See 72, Abiegnus, 811.

669

בגד + סתר *sither + beged*. to hide, veil, cover, conceal + a cloak, covering, garment. Beneath the garment of outward forms is veiled the secret of Venus. סתר is the root of נסתר, the Hidden or Occult Intelligence of *Netzach* [148], the sphere of Venus. It is the higher self (Samekh) in limitation (Tav) to produce the regeneration of the soul (Resh). See 660, 9.

הר סיני + הבונים הדביר *ha-bonaim ha-debir + har Sinai*. The builders of the Adytum + Mount Sinai. Those who are building the organ of illumination are obeying the divine desire and will reach the mountain of attainment. See 335, 334, 323, 324.

אחרנית backward. See Genesis 9:23.

ותסגר and was shut up. See Numbers 12:15.

670

עם *Am*. nation, populace, kinsman. With different pointing: *im*. With, together with, by, close to, near. Mem = 600, see 110.

נשימירין *Nashimirin*. Qlippoth of Pisces. It can lead to despondency, lack of self-confidence, religious fervor united to bigotry and separateness, and psychic obsession with receptivity to this level. Alternate spelling. See 666.

רעת wickedness. See Genesis 6:5.

671

The sum of any row, column or diagonal of an 11 x 11 magic square. See Appendix 8.

אלף תלד נון יוד *Adonai*. spelt in full. Divine name of Malkuth. See 65, 55, 95.

Adonai (see 67) written in full is 671, which is also the value of תרעא the gate, one of the names for Malkuth. Malkuth is the Bride, and to her is assigned the name Adonai. But this name always is combined with *Melek*, which is assigned to Tiphareth the Son. Thus the quest assigned to one grade has to do with Son's union (Tiphareth) with the Bride (Malkuth). The Bride is the breaker of the foundations (*Cholom Yesodoth*, 798), and to her, the body, Guph (89), is attributed. The Son is the Central Self, not the indivisible Yekidah in Kether, but the Ego in Tiphareth. The hidden knowledge is in Yesod because, in Yesod, the Bride and the Son are combined. Thus in the grade, the aspirant seeks but has not attained the knowledge. That is the דעת, Da'ath, which is that of which it is written: "In Da'ath shall all the secret places be filled." The secret places are in Yesod. You must know from where you come, and until you recognize this, you cannot discover the knowledge you aspire.

We may endeavor to follow the Path of Good, but can we define what is "good." Or we may, if we have sufficient audacity, follow the Path of Evil. But same ignorance can turn us back because the will to "evil" can be degraded by some unintentional invasion of good. At the beginning of the path, the aspirant does not know what is good or evil. Most people usually have very strong convictions at too good or evil, but this has little foundation. Thus in the grade which concerns itself with the passage from Malkuth to Yesod, through the Path of Tav, one learns that the name of Adonai spelled in full is the same as one of the names of Malkuth. This is to make clear that the keys to the hidden knowledge are already in our possession. One clue is the echoing answer, "I come from between the two pillars." This is a fact, which many who aspire to occult knowledge find it convenient to forget. See *C.20*.

א-ע-מ *Aleph-Ayin-Mem* A.O.M. Variant of the Hindu Pranava Aum and of α = beginning, μ = middle and Ω = end. Said to be a veil for the wheel of the Law, ROTA. Mem = 600, see 111, 851.

ארת מצרים *Ertez Mizaim*. Land of Egypt. This confirms what has been said of Malkuth and its relations to "Egypt." In Deuteronomy 15:15: "And thou shall remember that thou was a bondman in the land of Egypt, and the Lord your God redeemed thee."

בכל הר קדשי *be-kawl-har qahdeshi*. In all my holy mountain. In Isaiah 65:25: "The Wolf and Lamb will feed together, and the lion and will eat straw like an ox, but dust will be the serpent's food. They will neither harm nor destroy on all my holy mountain." see 3804 (Greek).

גבורתכם *geburathekem*. your strength. In Isaiah 30:15: "This is what the Lord, God the Holy One of Israel, says: In returning to Me and resting in Me you shall be saved: in quietness and in (trusting) confidence shall be your strength..." see 1231.

ובאבנים *vo-ba-ehbanim*. and in (vessels of) stone. With different pointing: *vo-baehbanim*. Spirits (of Daath). See 111.

סאים *seim*. a dry measure for grain (1/3 of an epha). See 111.

פרי עושה *osah periy*. bearing (producing, making) fruit. See 290, 160, 450.

רעתא *Rota* (Lt). Wheel. The cosmic wheel of manifestation, Malkuth. The hidden name of the Tarot. See 48 (Lt).

תארע *Taro*. The "wheel" of Tarot speaks the law of Hathor (mother nature) in this Latin phrase: Rota Taro Orat Tora Ator. See 48 (Lt).

תערא *Torah*. The Law, as that given to Moses by God. As alternate spelling is not found in scripture. See 611.

תרעא *Throa*. The Gate (Aramaic title of Malkuth). It is the gate for the influx of spirit, manifesting into name and form, and originating in the higher 'gate' or 50 gates of Binah, the mother through the door of Daleth.

נפית אפים *nepith apim*. "fallen on their faces."

אסתיר I will hide.

גבורתכם *Geburathekem*. Literally your strength. The intelligence of Da'ath, according to Soror A.L. See Isaiah 30:15.

לפקערציאץ *Lafcursiax*. The Sentinel of the 22nd Path (Tunnel) of Lamed on the Inverse Tree of Life.

I. The 22nd Ray appears behind the Tree in the tunnel guarded by Lafcursiax, whose number is 671. 671 is of major importance in the traditional qabalah, for it is the number of the Law (תערא), the Gate (תרעא), the Wheel or *Chakra* (תארע), and the Goddess of Love (אתער, or Hator). It is also the number of Adonai, the Holy Guardian Angel, spelled in full. These ideas combined adumbrate the formula of this path, for when the *chakra* of the goddess is subject to the law or rule of 671 (i.e., Lafcursiax), the Gate of the Abyss is thrown open.

Adonai is a glyph of the Sun; the word is usually translated as the 'Lord,' but beneath the path, Adonai becomes Aidoneus, a form of Had [Hades], the Lord of Hell. The name Aidoneus means invisible or Unseen; in the present context, Adonai's invisible form may be evoked by the formula of Lafcursiax. The demon's left hand is in the form of a *yod* enclosed in a circle from which falls obliquely a sword or long-armed cross. The scales symbolize the constellation Libra which rules Path 22. Its reflection in the abyss is tilted by Lafcursiax, whose tunnel runs oblique to this path. It represents a blasphemy against that 'adjustment,' which is the formula of this Path. 'Adjustment' is also the title of the Tarot trump ascribed to it. That which in *manifestation* is a pathway of justice and Equilibrium (תערא,

166

Law) is based upon the oblique pathway symbolized by the falling cross or sword.

The Egyptian deity attributed to Path 22 is Maat. It is easy to recognize in the tunnel of Lafcursiax the distortion of Maat's symbols: the balance, the feather, the sword, etc.

The Cross of Equilibrium is awry and the Scales upset; the 'Ruler of the Balance' has been put down as the Lord of the Abyss opens the gate of the Dark Goddess and brings forth fantastic beings that haunt this tunnel in the form of ravenous birds with the faces of women who snatch away the souls of the living from their mortal clay. Hence the name of the Order of Qliphoth reigning with Lafcursiax is *A'abirion*, meaning 'The Clayey,' for their talons drip with the ribbons of flesh (or mortal clay) that their ravening rips from the souls of the living.

Aidoneus or Hades is a form of the Plutonian Current that rules the Abyss. The magical *siddhi* associated with this tunnel is the ability to balance upon the treacherous and funambulatory way that leads from the negative to the positive in the realm of creative chaos. In other words, it enables the magician to spin a web across the gulf of the Abyss, thus constructing a tenuous and perilous bridge between nonbeing and being.

Understandably, the animal sacred to this formula is the spider, and the precision and symmetry of this Path are exemplified by the ideas of Truth and justice (Maat). [Grant, 1994, pp. 211-215.]

αρτος. *Artos*. Bread [John 6:35]. This word should be carefully considered in connection with the rest of this section. In the relation between "bread" and "bearing fruit," the discerning student should find food for thought for the explanation of "our daily bread" in the Lord's prayer. See parable of the loaves and fishes in the Bible [Matthew 14:17, 15:24], and 78, 181, 450, 581, 741, 1995, 1071, 1443, 3254.

παραδεισος. *paradeisos*. Paradise; A park or pleasure ground. Used in the Septuagint for the Garden of Eden.

672

יהוה אלהים *Jehovah Elohim*. the special Divine Name of Binah, the third Sephirah. Mem = 600, see 112.

אדם בינה *Binah Adam*. "The understanding of Adam." see 112, 67, 45.

תוסרו you will be corrected. See Leviticus 26:23.

בבל צבי ממלכות *bawbel tzaybi mamaylawkoth*. "Babylon, the glory of the kingdoms." In Isaiah 13:19: "And Babylon, the glory of Kingdom, the beauty of the Chaldee's excellency, shall be as when God overthrow Sodom and Gomorrah." see 638, 496, 104, 315.

חידות מני קדם *hidoth minni-qedem*. dark saying of old. In Proverbs 1:6: "To understand a proverb, and the interpretation; the words of the wise, and their dark sayings." [חידה = riddle, puzzle; קדם from ancient times; מני God of destiny]. See 140.

כבד אלהים *kebode Elohim*. glory of God. כבד has the connotation of weight and gravitation, as well as "glory." See 32, 112, 619 (Greek) and Proverbs 25:12.

673 (prime)

בארץ מצרים *Beraytz Metzraim*. In the land of Egypt [Deuteronomy 34:11]. See 380.

אמת יהוה דבר *Dahbar IHVH emeth*. Word of God is truth. See 52.

הבונים *ha-bonaim*. the builders. This is a reference to the Messiah or Christos. See 113, 1389 (Greek).

ארבעת four. See Numbers 7:7.

וזכרתם and remember. See Numbers 15:39.

προβατον. *prosaton*. Sheep. While a probationer,

the occult aspirant is the sheep who must listen to the inner instruction of the Master. This will bring him through the pitfalls of subconsciousness (Egypt).

λιγυριον. *ligyrion*. Ligure; a kind of precious stone, perhaps the jacinth [opal]. Listed in the Septuagint of Exodus 28:19 and 39:12 as the 7th stone in the breastplate of the Jewish high priest: see 370 (םשל); 491 (Greek).

674

לדרתם throughout their generations. See Genesis 17:7.

675

I. (5 x 5 x 27) or 5^2 x 3^3

זהב שחוט + חשכי *chawsheki + kahab shawhut*. my darkness + fine and drawn gold. Out of the darkness of the waters of creation shall the fashioning of the heavenly sun (gold) take place. See 337, 338.

נכרתה let us cut (make). See Genesis 31:44.

הסירת the pots. See Exodus 38:3.

676

I. (26 x 26) or 26^2 or 2^2 x 13^2

מתנוצץ *Mathnutzetz*. Resplendent, dazzling. The 10th Path of Malkuth. See 656, 1026, 230, 496, 570.

גלגלים *galgalim*. whirlings, whirling motion. Gilgulim is a term for the sum total of the manifestations of the cosmic forces beginning in Kether. The Path of Malkuth in any world is always a receptacle for the total forces and activities expressed by that word. Mem = 600, see 116, 1032.

ערות *erath*. Nakedness; shame, ignominy [Genesis 9:22]. The external genitals of either sex. Refers to the "nakedness" of Noah or the Hidden potencies of undifferentiated substance. In its various Hebrew meanings, this word is one of the most important parts of this gematria. See 936, 58, 48.

קהל ישראל *Qehal Israel*. Congregation of Israel. In Deuteronomy 31:30: "And Moses spoke in the ears of all the congregation of Israel the words of this song until they were ended." These are companies or assembly of those who rule as God. See 312, 441.

רעות *raooth*. thought, stirring, feeding upon, reflection; feminine companion; pursuit, striving (feminine noun). The masculine noun means friendship, companion, comradeship. Malkuth is the feminine counterpart of Kether, feeding upon the thought of the primal will. As the bride, she has overcome the obstacles of "nakedness," bringing friendship.

תמים פעלו *tawmim pawalo*. His work is perfect. In Deuteronomy 32:4: "He is the rock, his work is perfect: for all his ways are judgment: a God of truth and without iniquity, just and right is He."

עתור *Othur*. Lesser angle governing triplicity by day of Aquarius. The bride in Malkuth is also the kneeling woman in Key 17, the key of Meditation and revelation of truth. This "nakedness" is without shame. Saturn and Uranus rule Aquarius, suggesting that unveiled truth brings the dominion of Key 21 and the spirit of adventure in Key 0.

Λαμεχ. *Lamech*. "Powerful." The Greek transliteration of Lamech, the Father of Noah, and the traditional founder of Masonry. Alchemical Water is related to things having to do with creation and construction-with, the building of form. See 90.

Iesus Christus; Amor Meus Crucifex; Fides, Spec, Charitas; Via, Bita, Veritas (Lt). Jesus Christ; my crucified love (or love crucified me): Note the identity of the values of these two phrases (174); Faith, Hope, Charity (167); Way, Life, Truth (161) [Secret Symbols page 52]. Written on a diagram of a cross surmounting two upright triangles, Faith, Hope, Charity is the immediate supports of the cross (*Iesus Christus + Amor Meus crucifex*); and they rest on a foundation identified by the words Way, Life and Truth.

677 (prime)

תבערה *tabayeraw*. burning, conflagration. Suggest the consequence of the Lord toward the ignorant-not being receptive, they are consumed by their own errors.

זרעת mighty, arms. See Deuteronomy 33:27.

678

ערבות *Arabhoth*. Plains; the 7th Heaven corresponding to the 3 Supernals. Assiatic ("plains") Heaven if the 1st palace corresponds to the 3 supernal sephiroth: Kether, Chokmah and Binah. Rosenroth in K.D.L.C.K. (p.634) calls this word *planitles coeli* and says that it refers to Yesod in the Zohar. Also that Tiphareth is called ערבות in combination, because Geburah and Gedulah (Chesed) are mixed or combined in it, thus in Yesod, Netzach and Hod are combined because they are the powers of Gedulah and Geburah.

בירנית Fortress. 2 Chron. 17:12.

בערות Burning Ones. The Holy Living Creatures (האופנים, Ophinam, Wheels) in Ezekiel 1:13.

ברעות troubles. Psalms 88:4.

עברות rage, furies. Job 40:11.

רחמתיך I will show you compassion to you. Is. 60:10.

תבערו you light, kindle, "you will not light any fire throughout your home on the Sabbath.

תעברו you cross (pass) over. Genesis 18:5.

תרעבו you will go hungry. Isiah 65:13.

את הכרבים *eth-ha-kerubim*. the cherubim. In Genesis 3:24: "So he drove out the man; and he placed at the east of the Garden of Eden Cherubims, and a flaming sword which turns every way, to keep the way of the Tree of Life." see 277, 401.

אדם בליאל *Adam Belial*. wicked men. Arch-demon corresponding to Chokmah. Belial means unprofitable or wicked; thus, "wicked man." Mem = 600, see 118.

חמש טושיה *Chamish Tushiyah*. Quintessence; the alchemical fifth essence or spirit. See 348.

679

תגרעו shall diminish. See Exodus 5:8.

ולחשך קרא לילה and the darkness he called Night. See Genesis 1:5.

חעם The 38th Shem ha-Mephorash, short form. Mem = 600. See 118.

680

בערבות In the sky (heaven or wilderness).

רוחניות *ruachnioth*. Spiritual. Part of the title of Teth's intelligence, Key 8 (strength), the secret of all spiritual activities. See 685, 1702.

כנים *kinnim*. vermin. See 120.

פרת *Phrath*. Euphrates, a river of Eden (associated with Earth) [Genesis 2:14].

I. "הוא פרת, *that-is the-fecundating-cause...* The Euphrates is הוא פרת, *that which fecundates...* הוא is a masculine pronoun which governs the nominal pronoun פרת, *the action of fecundating*. [d'Olivet, 1976, pp. 81-82.]. For Euphrates, see 1514 (Greek).

II. "A symbol of the physical plane, including the etheric." [Gaskell, 1981, p. 254.]

III. The fourth river is the Euphrates, *Perâth* (פרח; "to *break* forth"; "*rushing*"). We might compare this with the word *pôrâth* (פרה), which is the same as the primitive root *pârâh* פרה); "to *bear fruit*"; to be, or cause to be). An interesting connection is suggested here, for *pârâh* derives from *par* (פר), which means "a *bullock*," where the bullock, like the ox, is a universal and common symbol of *prima materia*. Moreover, *Strong's Dictionary* suggests that this itself comes from the idea of either "*breaking* forth in wild strength" or, perhaps, from the image of "*dividing* the hoof," and this from *pârar* (פרר; "to *break* up"). Again, *pâras* (פרש), which differs to *pârar* by the shift from the final *resh* to a final *shin*, also means "to *break* apart" in the sense of "to *disperse*," which returns us to the symbolism of the first river, Pishon. – *Edom and Eden*, Timothy Scott

פתר *pawthar*. to explain, interpret. In Genesis 41:15: "And Pharaoh said unto Joseph. I have dreamed a dream, and there is not that can interpret it. (16) And Joseph answered Pharaoh, saying, it is not in me: God shall give Pharaoh an answer of peace." see 370.

תפר *tawfar*. to sew, to sew together; to stitch, mend, With different pointing: *tepher*. Seam, stitch. In Genesis 3:7: "And the eyes of them both were opened, and they now that they were naked; and they sewed fig leaves together, and made themselves aprons." In Job 16:15: "I have sewed sackcloth upon my skin, and defiled my horn in the dust." see 350, 281.

תרף *teraf*. the sustainer. Metathesis of the preceding three words. God is what sustains, interprets, binds together and makes fruitful the life of mankind. With different pointing: *toreph*. The essential parts of a document, the variable particulars of a document as distinguished from the fixed formula; nakedness. See 730.

שלשים *shelshim*. "thirty" (30); the value of

Lamed, the ox-goad, which teaches and instructs through equilibrated action. The numbers of men slain by Samson at Ashkelon ("weighing place," 487) in Judges 14:19: "And the spirit of the Lord came upon him, and he went down to Ashkelon, and he seized thirty of their men, and he slowed them and took their garments, and gave them to those who had interpreted his riddle. And his anger was kindled, and he went up to his father's house." The riddle is: What is sweeter than honey and stronger than a lion? Answer: a heifer (i.e., little Aleph). Recall that ox-goad Lamed is that which incites the Ox, Aleph into Action. See 74, 1240; 852 (Greek). Kindling anger and rise of Mars force into the Mercury center.

שלשים *shawlishim*. three-fold, three times; "excellent things" (from the signification of 3) in Proverbs 22:20: "Have I not written to you excellent things in councils and knowledge." see 640, 650.

υιος *huios*. Son (reference to Jesus).

681

אפרת *Ephrath* or *Ephratah*; "hamlets" or "heifers" [Inman]. The second wife of Caleb (52) and the mother of Hur (214), the ancestor of Bethlehem. In Micah 5:2: "But thou, Bethlehem Ephratah, though thou be little among the thousands of Judah, yet out of thee shall he come forth unto me that is to be ruler in Israel; whose goings forth have been from old, from everlasting." see 490, 919, 541.

תרועה joyful noise; battle-cry; the sound (of a trumpet). Joshua 6:5: "When you hear them sound a long blast on the trumpets, have all the people give a loud shout; then the wall of the city will collapse, and the people will go up, every man straight in." With different pointing: battle-cry; a blast of trumpet or shofar; teruah, a succession of tremulous notes of the shofar.

להורתם that you may teach [instruct] them. See Exodus 24:12.

ממארת malignant. See Leviticus 13:51.

ערותה her nakedness. See Leviticus 18:7.

הרעות the evils. Deuteronomy 31:17.

682

חסדים *Chasidim*. Merciful or Beneficent ones. See 122.

ירק עשב *yereq esev*. Green herb.

מרכבה מעשה *ma'aeseh merkawbah*. The work of the Chariot. The Chariot [the personality] work is transforming the vehicle into a suitable instrument for the Life-power. The study of the Tree of Life. "Then I, Enoch, replied to him, concerning everything I am desirous of instruction, but particularly concerning this tree." [Enoch]

ערבית *Arebith*. of the evening, of the west. On the Cube of Space, the western face is attributed to Jupiter and Kaph, the manifestation direction. In the Zohar, it refers to Yesod. As Tiphareth is called ערבית (678), because Gedulah (Chesed) and Geburah are mingled within it, in Yesod are mingled Netzach and Hod, which are the powers of Gedulah and Geburah. K.D.L.C.K. (p.634) calls it the "plains of heaven." With different pointing: evening time, evening prayer, as an adverb, Raven-like. See 272.

אל האלהים *el ha-Elohim*. "unto the Elohim"; unto God." Mem = 600, see 122.

ערותו his nakedness. See Leviticus 20:17.

ברעתי in my wretchedness, to ruin of me. See Numbers 11:15.

683 (prime)

עולם אצילו *Olam Atziluth*. The World of Nobility, the Divine or Archetypal World. The reception of

metaphysical truth from above is possible because the archetypal world is really within. See 36, 252, 315, 154, 224, 314, 29.

דעת יחוה ללילה לילה *lilah lilailah yikhaveh-da'ath*. night unto night shows Knowledge [Psalm 19:2]. Much of the work of transfiguration is accomplished during sleep of the physical body. We are never out of touch with the one source whence every wise man who ever lived has drawn his treasures of the hidden knowledge. See 475, 1163, 689, 503.

קבלה עיונית *Qabalah evneith*. speculative Qabalah. The metaphysical tradition.

ולמקוה המים קרא ימים *vu-lemekaiah qarah yawmim*. Genesis 1:10: "And the collection of the waters he called [named] seas." Binah is the "Great Sea" of elemental waters, the archetypal womb of life. See 67.

Ex Deo nascimur, in Jesu morimur, per Spiritum Sanctum reviscimus. From God, we are born, in Jesus, we die, through the Holy Spirit we live again. This appears at the end of the Latin *Elogium*, which the *Fama Fraternitatis* quotes from Book T.

684

וייצר יהוה + שלהבה *va-yetzer IHVH + shilihebah*. and Tetragrammaton formed" + a blase, flame. Illumination is the reception of the divine flame of light in the Adytum which God has formed. See 342.

תרדף you shall follow, purse. See Deuteronomy 16:20.

685

הרוחניות *ha-ruachniyuth*. the spiritual. Part of the title of the 19th path of wisdom, attributed to Teth; "The Intelligence of the Secret of All Spiritual Activities." see 680, 1702.

שין הנער *sheyin haw-no'ar*. Urine of the babe. Raymond Lully's name for the first matter. נער also means boy, lad, youth; servant, retainer; scattering, scattered one. שין Shin is the letter-name symbolizing the element Fire; another translation might be "Fire of the Boy." In Key 20, the boy is the regenerated consciousness. See 320, 360, 501.

איפת צדק *eiphah tzedeq*. a just ephah. Leviticus 19:36: "Just balances, just weights, a just ephah, and a just hin, shall you have: I am the Lord you God, which brought you out of the land of Egypt." see 257, 302, 259, 194.

אני אלהי כל בשר I am the Lord, the God of all mankind (flesh) [Jeremiah 32:27] see 61, 26, 46, 50, 502.

686

I. (2 x 7 x 7 x 7) or 2 x 7³

זרע הקדש *zerao ha-dodesh*. the holy seed. In Ezra 9:2: "for they have taken of their daughters for themselves, and for their sons: so that the holy seed have mingled themselves with the people of those lands: yea, the hand of the princes and rulers has been chief in this trespass." see 681, 277, 404.

ויעתר and he entreated, and he answered prayer. See Genesis 25:21.

פרות cows. See Genesis 32:16.

687

I. The numbers of days of the sidereal revolution of Mars around the Sun.

בדא + פרת *bawdah + pharath*. to form, fashion, produce something new + fructifying, i.e., the blood-stream. The new image bears fruit in the chemical composition of the blood. See 680, 7.

זכרתני remember me. See Genesis 40:14.

מזמרת of the choice fruits, from best produced of. See Genesis 43:11.

688

באחרית יומיא in days to come. See Daniel 2:28.

נעשה אדם בצלמנו *naaseh adham be-tzelmenu*. Let us make man in our image.

פרחת breaking out. See Leviticus 13:42.

ויתעבת he was filled with wrath, and he was angry. See Deuteronomy 3:26.

689

יבוסים *Yebusim*. Jebusites; from a "son of Canaan"; the ancient inhabitants of Jerusalem and the neighborhood, in early Palestine.

פטרת that opens, the first [of the womb]. See Numbers 8:16.

690

מנרת *menorath*. the candlestick, lampstand (variant spelling). In Exodus 25:31: "And thou shall make a candlestick [מנרת, lampstand-of] of pure gold: of beaten work shall the candlestick be made: his shaft, and his branches, his bowls, his knops, and his flowers, shall be of the same." The "lampstand" is the spinal cord, containing the "lamps" or interior stars. See 301, 14, 1141 (Greek).

תמרים *tomerim*. palm trees. Ezekiel 15:27: "Then they came to Elim [אילמה, palm-trees-86], where there were 12 springs and 70 palm trees, and they camped there near the water. Note that *Ayin* [70] means: spring fountain. Note that *Elim* is a Metathesis of *Elohim*. See 86.

סלם *sullawm*. a ladder; specifically the ladder mentioned in Jacob's dream. Mem = 600, see 130.

נמם *Nemem*. "God praiseworthy." 57th name of

Shem ha-Mephorash, short form. Mem = 600, see 130, 145.

יריעת curtains. See Exodus 26:1.

691 (prime)

ותרפה *Euterpe*. Greek muse of music.

תרופה *terufawh*. healing, remedy, medicine. Resh precedes Vav, indicating that the limitations of sense-life (Tav) need to be regenerated by the heart (Resh) before true intuition (Vav) can break down the structure of ignorance concerning the use of Mars (Peh) and lead to clear vision (Heh) or the elixir of the wise, the universal medicine.

אש שמים *esh shawmayim*. Fire of heaven. An old name for Key 16. The heavens are Fire (Shin) plus water (מים). See 395, 300, 90, 301, 98.

מקוד ישראל *maqud Israel*. The reservoir of Israel, i.e., IHVH Israel, refers to those who gain dominion over the elements of personality. The word for reservoir appears in Isaiah 22:11: "You also made a ditch between the two walls for the water of the old pool, but you have not looked unto the maker thereof, neither had respect unto him that fashioned it long ago." see 541, 346, 887.

Πατμος. *Patmos*. Pathos, a small island of the Aegean sea, where the apostle John was banished in Revelation 1:9.

"Serene patience is one of the indispensable qualifications of the aspirant for spiritual knowledge, and so is the 'ruling' or dominance of the higher intellect, the nous (Iesous), over the lower faculties. The ordeal (thipsis) is that of initiation, now begun. Through the awakening noetic perception (the 'evidence of Iesus') and the increasing light form, the Logos-the whitening of the dawn of the new life-the aspirant becomes isolated. In the drear loneness of one who has forever abandoned the illusions of sensuous existence but has not seen the sunrise of the spirit, he dwells as it were, on an island, apart from his fellow-men. Then through his introspection comes the message of the Great Breath, and in the sacred trance, he attains his first *autopsia*, beholding the apparition of his own Logos." [Pryse, 1965, p. 88.]

692

את זרע דוד *eth-zerao Dawvid*. the (essence of the) seed of David. In Jeremiah 33:22: "As the host of heaven cannot be numbered, neither the sand of the sea measured: so will I multiply the seed of David my servant, and the Levites that minister unto me." see 401, 277, 14, 1215 (Greek) and 1 Kings 11:39.

רביעית *rebi'ith*. fourth; one quarter; a liquid measure; a square block; Wednesday; a musical instrument. See Leviticus 19:24 and Numbers 15:5.

חסידים *Haesidim*. Chasidim; godly men, saints, Merciful or beneficent ones. Those who have attained the consciousness of Chesed and also known as Master of Compassion. Mem = 600, see 132, 269, 72, 194.

ακρατο. *akratos*. Unmixed, unpolluted. Spoken of the wine of God's wrath, as strong and intoxicating in Revelations 14:10.

693

גפרית *Gafrith*. Sulfur. The alchemical principle, composed of 1. Gimel: the Moon-Silver; 2. Peh: Mars-iron; 3. Resh: Sun-gold; 4. Yod: the operation of Mercury in Virgo; 5. Tav: Saturn-Lead. These correspond to the body's parts actively concerned in the Great Work, fundamental in human personality activities. *Gaphrith* is one of the names of the Red Stone, which is also called האדם אבן and אדם, and also called brimstone. See 700, 7, 73, 738, 1000, 158, 1298, 1436 (Greek). See also 76, 372, 961, 287, 98; 144 (Lt).האדם

I. Pernety says in the *Great Art* (p.186) that this Red Stone is also termed phison, i.e., pison (פישון = 446). Pishon is the first river of Eden (associated with Fire), which compasses the whole land of Havilah where there is gold.

II. In the *Aesch Mezareph* or Purifying Fire, *gophreeth* is spelled גופריתא Gophritha and given the value 700.) The text says: "In the science of minerals the principle is referred to Binah, to the left because of its color... you must dig up this sulfur; and it is to be dug up out of the water, that you may have fire obtained from water."

"Gophrith is Sulfur; in the Science of Minerals this Principle is referred to Binah, to the left because of its Color; and to left also, Gold is wont to be referred; and Charutz [304, חרוץ], a kind of Gold, is also referred to Binah, and Binah, and is 7 in its lesser Number agrees with that of Gophritha [700, גופריתא]. [Westcott, 1997, p. 44]

Therefore the Gold of Natural Wisdom ought to be Charutz, dug out, or the like not excocted. And this is that Sulphur, which hath a fiery Color, and is penetrating and changing to impure Earths; to wit, Sulphur with Salt, Deuteronomy, 29:23. Sulfur with Fire, rained down upon the Wicked, that is the impure Metals, Psalm 2:6.

You must dig up this Sulphur; and it is to be dug out of the Water, that you mayest have Fire obtained from Water. 'And if your Ways be right before the Lord, your Iron shall swim upon the Water," 2 Kings, 6:6. "Go your way then to the River Jordan with Elisha"; see v. 4. "But who shall declare the Geburah of the Lord?" Psalm 106:2.

Many seek other Sulfurs, and he that hath entered the 'House of the Paths' shall understand them, Proverbs, 8:2. The Sulfurs of Gold and Iron, the Extraction, are taught by many, and easy; Gold, Iron and Brass. Gold, Iron, Copper and Antimony gathered together after Fulmination by Vinegar, out of the lixivium, changed into a Red Oil with a moist Hydrargyrum – do tinge Silver. For from Proverbs 21:20, we know there is a Treasure to be desired and also an Oil to be found in the dwelling of a Man of Wisdom." [ibid]

694

אליצורי + אפריון *elitzuri + aphireyon*. my God, my rock + canopy, chariot. The God within dwells in the chariot of personality; that receptacle must be purified by the test and trials of experience. Then the secrets of the rock are revealed. See 347.

695

שמרי הסף *semayrei hassaf*. keepers of the door. In 2 Kings 23:4: "And the King commanded Hilkiah, the high priest, and the priests of the second-order, and the keepers of the door…" The "door" is Daleth or creative imagination, and it is also Venus or the power of desire. [סף = lentil, sill, threshold]. See 434, 896.

מורגש עולם *Olam Morgash*. Moral World

היריעת the curtains. See Exodus 26:2.

התמרים the palm trees. See Deuteronomy 34:3.

696

יאתה זהך מצפון *matzafon zhub yathan*. Gold comes from the North [Job 37:22]. Enlightenment has its origin in the hidden sources of power, which terrify the ignorant.

הארץ שמני *shemeni ha-eretz*. Oiliness of the Earth [Genesis 27:28]. In Secret Symbols [p.48], the alchemical first matter is comprised of the "Dew of Heaven" and "the oiliness of the Earth." A metaphor for "fertile fields"-the active power of reproduction, is the driving force expressed in the evolution of forms from lower to higher expression levels. The "oiliness of the earth," then is human flesh and those incarnating the forces of heaven, and expressing these forces in the "word made flesh," dwelling within us. See 434, 1757 (Greek).

ויקרא אלהים לאור יום *vayekera Elohim la-aur yom*. And God called the light Day [Genesis 1:5].

The day is manifest. All manifestation is the phenomenal expression of the powers of light. See 740, 2775 (Greek).

צורת *tsoreth*. Form, design. In Ezekiel 43:11: "And if they are ashamed of all that they have done, show them the form of the house..." All forms, whatever, are forms of light. From root צור (tsoor) rock, meaning: to press, to confine, to render compact. The form is the result of the compression or condensation of energy, which is Light. See 296.

אש השמים *Esh ha-Shamaim*. Fire of Heaven. The cosmic Life-force pictured in Key 16. See 899, 434.

לא יהיה לך אלהים אחרים על פני *lo yieyeh-leka Elohim acherim al-pana*. Thou shall have no other gods before me. The Zohar: "Thou shall have no other gods before me (literally, before my face). Said Rabbi Isaac: "This prohibition of 'other gods' does not include the Shekinah; 'before my face' does not include the 'face of the king' (The sephiroth), in which the holy king manifest himself, and which are his name and identical with him. That they are his name is shown by the verse: "I am IHVH, that is my name' [Isaiah 42:8]. Thus he and his name are one. Blessed be his name forever and ever." [pp.260-261]

אל אלהי הרוחת *El Elohay ha-rauth*. The God of Spirits. Numbers 16:22: "And they fell on their faces, and said 'O God, the God of the spirits of all flesh, shall one man sin, and will you be angry with all the congregation." The Zohar [I:17A, p.71]: "Unity was retained in the central pillar from that surplus of light which was in it. The central pillar was complete in itself and made peace on all sides. Additional light was left to it from above and from all sides through the universal joy in it. From that additional joy came forth the foundation of worlds, which was also called *misaf* (additional). From this issue, all the lower powers and spirits and holy souls alluded to in the expression 'Lord of Hosts' (IHVH Tzabaoth) and 'God the god of Spirits' [Numbers 10:22]."

עתיק יומין *awthiqa yomin*. the ancient of days: A title of God. In Daniel 7:13: "I saw in the night visions, and, behold, one like the son of man came with the clouds of heaven, and came to the Ancient of Days." This title is often attributed to Kether. The "Ancient of Days" symbolizes a bearded man shown in profile as in Key 4, the Emperor. See 647, 1395, 1233, 996, 581, 599, 620, 733, 391, 422.

שמשון *Samson*. Inman: (Judges 13:24), or Shimshon. "On is the Sun,' or 'Shemesh is On.'

697

תארע יהוה *Jehovah TARO*. Letters on the Wheel on Key 10.

את הארץ *Armanoth*. "(and fill) the [essence of] Earth Genesis 1:28: "And God blessed them (Humanity) and said unto them, be fruitful, and multiply, and replenish the earth." see 40, 291.

ארמנות her citadels; walled cities, Rosenroth in K.D.L.C.K. (p.156) refers to this word as *castellum* [castle] *munitae* [fortified] and refers to the Zohar where Psalm 48:3 is cited: "God is in her citadels [בארמנוריה, in-citadels-of-her]; he has shown himself to be her fortress. He suggests that Netzach and Hod are called fortresses with respect to Malkuth. Because they gather the influence as by analogy the masculine testicles, from justice [Geburah], from whence they are transmitted to the female uterus [i.e., Yesod] when they are full (as "walled cities"). See also Psalm 48:13.

תרצח shall kill, murder. preceded by not [לא]. One of the 10 commandments. See Exodus 20:13.

תבצרו you shall gather them, you harvest. See Leviticus 25:11.

ובצרת and fortified, and walls. See Deuteronomy 9:1.

תחרימם you shall destroy. See Deuteronomy 20:17.

פליאות חכמה + נביאי יהוה *nebiyi IHVH* + *pelioth chokmah*. The prophets of IHVH + hidden (or admirable) wisdom. The prophets are those possessing the "wisdom of the stars." see 600, 99.

אדד + צ +מ *Mem* + *Tzaddi* + *adad*. water, seas + fish-hook + to endure, last continue. Mem is the interior center experience with the suspended mind; Tzaddi is the meditation whereby the wise attain to conscious union with the Life-power via the water, the "mute, dark mirror." This brings the enduring consciousness of eternity. See 600, 90, 9.

צדק במענלי + שכל *saykel* + *bemayegelay tzedek*. intelligence, insight, awareness + "in paths of righteousness." Intelligence designates both awareness and the ability to make practical use of insight. The practical use is the fulfillment of the righteous and of the path which leads to righteousness. See 349, 350.

צרדתה *Tzaradatha*. Zaradatha, "to pierce, to puncture." This corresponds to a masculine word to Jakin, the right-hand pillar. Richardson's *Monitor of Freemasonry* (p.26): "Master: where were they cast? Senior Warden: on the banks of the river Jordan (264), in the clay (28) ground between Succoth (486) and *Zaradatha*, where King Solomon ordered these, and all other holy vessels to be cast." Refers specifically to one of

two large globes or hollow balls on each column. See 90.

וחפרתה and you shall dig. See Deuteronomy 23:14.

Section 7

Numbers 700-799

700

I. (5 x 5 x 5 x7) or 7 x 5³

II. ן Final Nun. "fish." See 50.

כפרת *Kapporeth*. cover or lid to the Ark. Mercy seat [Exodus 25:17, 30:8, 3:7]. These are all double letters and follow the same order as in the Hebrew alphabet. Kaph: (Jupiter, west, tin), Peh (Mars, Iron, and north), Resh (Sun, South, and Gold) and Tav (Saturn, Center, Lead) and the interior stars. From the root word כפר [300]: to atone, make atonement; procure forgiveness.

The *Kapporeth* conceals the ark's contents, and the paroketh (veil of the Holy of Holies, see below) hides the ark. Therefore both words indicate occultation, secrecy and mystery. The four metals indicated by the Hebrew letters above indicate the human body's chakra and nerve centers. The combined activity of these forces creates normal human consciousness (the 4 centers below the throat). Yet these are the same forces use by the initiates of open the higher vision, which enables man to comprehend the true meaning of the mystery of his own nature.

Howard Severance: "The lid of the ark, or mercy-seat over which appeared the 'glory of God' was also know as the 'expiatory,' in reference to the custom of the high-priest once a year to enter the most holy place and sprinkle the lid of the ark with the blood of an expiatory or sacrificial victim whereby he had atonement for the 'sins of the people.' As this was the most solemn and significant act of the Hebrew ritual, it is natural that a reference to it should be involved in the name which the covering of the ark acquired. By a comparison of the text in which the word occurs, it will be seen that there would, in fact, have been a little occasion to name the cover of the ark separately from the ark itself, but for this important ceremonial." [Bible Encyclopedia]

מלכים *Melakin*. Kings; angels of Tiphareth in Assiah and of Netzach in Briah. Mem = 600, see 140.

מסרת *massoreth*. a band or bond (covenant). This suggests limitations. See 612 and Ezekiel 20:37.

רך roke. tenderness, delicacy; gentle, bland. Name of R.C. See 220.

מסתר *mistawr*. a hiding-place, place of ambush (lying in wait); secret. Isaiah 45:3: "I will give you the treasures of darkness, riches stored in secret places, so that you may know that I am the Lord, the God of Israel, who summons you by name."

פרכת *pahroketh*. Curtain, veil. Literally "she that separates"; the veil or curtain between the Holy of Holies and the outer sanctuary in the temple. One of the technical terms in certain Rosicrucian mysteries. Describes the 4 lower personality sephiroth (Netzach, Hod, Yesod and Malkuth) or 1st order, from the Egoic triad (Tiphareth, Geburah, Chesed) or 2nd order. (Made of the same letters כפרת but in a different order-Mars, Sun, Jupiter and Saturn).

שרר *sarar*. to have dominion, to rule, to be a prince. With different pointing: 1. *sharar*. To twist, to twist together, to be firm, hard, tough, especially in a bad sense, and hence to afflict. 2. *shorer*: the umbilical cord.

שת *shath*. Foundation, basis, a pillar, noise, tumult. Pernety gives this as one name for the Quicksilver of the Sages at the white stage. Also *Seth*. The 3rd son of Adam, meaning "replace" or "compensation." Chaldean for the number 6. See Genesis 4:25, Daniel 3:1, Ezra 6:15 and The Zohar I [p. 174].

Seth is formed from the last two letters of the alphabet and symbolizes an end. It is also a beginning because the name symbolized the reincarnation of the spirit which had been lost. In Genesis 4:25: God hath replaced, שת, for me another seed instead of Abel.

I. "שת *Sheth*. This root composed of the signs of relative and reciprocal movement, indicates the place toward which things irresistibility incline, and the things themselves which incline toward this place: thence, *the depths, the foundations*, literally as well as figuratively; *the place* where *the sea* is gathered; *the seas* itself; every kind of *depth*, every kind of *beverage*.

The Arabic has retained only a portion of the radical sense, in that which concerns the movement of water, the separation of this fluid into drops, its distillation, dispersion." [d'Olivet, 1976, p. 465.]

II. שת Sheth... This name's significance is of the utmost importance for those seeking to penetrate the essence of things. This name, as mysterious as those of *Kain* and *Habel*, could never be translated exactly. All that I can do is to furnish the means necessary for unveiling the hieroglyphic depth. First, let us examine the root. The two signs that compose it are ש, a sign of relative duration and movement, reciprocity, mutual tendency, and the liaison of things, ת. United by the universal, convertible sign, they form the verbal root שות, which is related to every action of placing, disposing, setting, founding. As a noun, the root שת signifies *foundation* and depicts the good, the bad, the highest, and the lowest things. It can also signify every kind of beverage, and provides the verb שתוה *to drink*; because it is water, which, by its determined movement, always indicates the deepest place, that upon which is placed the foundation.

"שת express the foundation of things and the element which inclines to it, but it also serves to designate the number *two*, in its feminine acceptation, and in Chaldaic, the number *six*. The name of *Sheth*, or *Seth*, presents itself, like those of *Kain* and *Habel*, under two acceptations wholly opposed. We have seen in treating of the latter two that if *Kain* was the emblem of force and power, he was also that of rage and usurpation; we have seen that if one considered *Habel* as the emblem of thought and the universal soul, he was also regarded as that of nothingness and of absolute void: now, Sheth is the object of

contrast no less striking. The Hebrews have represented him as the type of a chosen family; the historian Josephus has attributed to him the erection of those famous columns, upon which was carved the history of mankind and the principles of universal morals; certain oriental peoples and particularly those who make profession of Sabaeanism, have revered him as a prophet; indeed many of the Gnostics called themselves *Sethians*: but is known, on the other hand, that the Egyptian confusing him with *Typhon*, called his *the violent, the destructor*, and gave him the odious surnames of *Bubon* and of *Smou*: it is also known that the Arabs considering him as the genius of evil, called him *Shathan*, by adding to his primitive name שת the augmentative final ון. This terrible name, given to the infernal adversary, *Satan*, in passing into the Hebraic tongue with the poems of *Job*, has brought there all the unfavorable ideas which the Arabs and the Egyptians attached to the name *Seth, Sath* or *Soth*, without harming, nevertheless, the posterity of this same *Sheth*, whom the Hebrews have continued to regard as the one from whom men, in general, and their patriarch, in particular, drew their origin. [d'Olivet, 1976, pp. 146-147.]

תליסר *thalisar*. thirteen (13). An Aramaic word in the Zohar wherever the number 13 is mentioned. Its first 3 letters spell תלי, Theli, the Dragon; the last 2 סר, Sar, mean: rebellious, heavy, sad, sullen. Compare with Key 13 and its various meanings, and bear in mind that *thalisar*, like 700, is the equivalent of Final Nun. See 7, 70, 175, 440, 260. [Sep. Dz. 2:3,5]

תלי סר theili sar. Rebellious, sullen dragon.

גופריתא *Gophritha*. Sulfur. The alchemical principle attributed to Chokmah is spelled in *Aesch Mezareph*. See 693.

חכמה + כחמה + מסלות + אב + יה *Chokmah + kachmah + masloth + Ab + Jah*. Chokmah + its power of formation + the "highways of the stars" + the father + the divine name Jah, all attributed to Chokmah. See 73, 536, 3, 15.

ערלת *arelah*. foreskins. In Deuteronomy 10:16:

"Circumcise therefore the foreskins of your hearts."

ערכתי *araketti*. I have ordained, set up. In Psalm 132:17: "Here I will make the horn grow for David and set up a lamp for my anointed one. See 648, 1348.

XP Chi-Rho. Greek monogram for Christ. Please note the similarity between these letters and initials for Brother C.R. in the *Fama*. In Egyptian, these letters spell Khoor, Horus. Note that the greek letter Chi is a cross, and Rho is derived from the Hebrew letter Resh (ר), meaning head. Thus they form a skull and crossbones. Note also that Chi-rho sounds like the word Cairo, a city next to the Giza Plateau. See 220 & *True and Invisible Rosicrucian Order* [p.43].

ακροατης. *akroatems*. A hearer. One who hears but does not regard. In James 1:23 (22), "But obey the message; be doers of the word, and not merely listeners to it, betraying yourselves [into deception by reasoning contrary to the Truth]. (23) for if anyone only listens to the word without obeying it and being a doer of it, he is like a man who looks carefully at his [own] natural face in a mirror; (24) For he thoughtfully observes himself, the goes off and promptly forgets what he was like." see Romans 2:13.

701 (prime)

אן *On*. An Egyptian god and The city of the "sun," Heliopolis in the Bible. See Genesis 41:45.

אן *an*. where? Written אנה in Psalm 139:7: "Where shall I go from your spirit? Or where shall I flee from your presence?"

והגה שלשה *ve-hinneh shelshah*. "And behold, three..." the first words of Genesis 18:2, describing Abraham's confrontation with 3 men represent God.

אלו מיכאל גבריאל וראפאל *Elu Michael Gabriel ve-Raphael*. "These are Michael, Gabriel, and Raphael." This tells who the 3 men were (see above).

הרצון שכל *Sekhel ha-Ratzon*. The intelligence of Will. The 20th Path of Yod carries the influence of Mercy (Chesed) into Beauty (Tiphareth). Key 9, The Hermit, shows beneficence's masculine expression (Chesed) through Yod (the letter of the father, Chokmah). See 346, 107, 20, 351 & Appendix 12.

The "Will" power we feel is the surge of the Light-force through the bloodstream, nerve and tissue, which is the inner light of the Hermit's Lantern. The true magical will is perfect obedience. It takes us from intellectual recognition of the central Ego's true nature (Tiphareth) to perfect identification with cosmic memory (Chesed). This is accomplished through meditation and listening with complete attention to the instruction of the inner voice.

"I am the Intelligence of Will, knowing the way, the truth and the light." [Meditations on the Paths of Wisdom]

מלאכים *malakim*. angels; messengers. See 141.

בשם עזרנו יהוה *etzerenu be-shem IHVH*. our help is in the name of Tetragrammaton. In Psalm 124:8: "Our help is in the name of the Lord, who made heaven and earth." see 2607, 1101 (Greek).

תפרא *tekayrah*. kinswoman. In Proverbs 7:4: "Say unto wisdom, thou art my sister; and call understanding your kinswoman." The word or name calls forth understanding, i.e., Binah, the "kinswoman" through Da'ath or direct knowledge.

נפילת אפים *Nephitith Apihm*. A slipping or falling down in the act. Rosenroth in K.D.L.C.K. (p.589) calls this phrase *prolapus in fariem* and refers to the Zohar. אפים also means "anger."

ארך *Ereck*. a City in Ancient Babylonia, founded by Nimrod, and a center for Ishtar's worship, the Semitic Venus. Elsewhere this is referred to as a city in Ephraim's vicinity, the tribe associated with Taurus, ruled by Venus. See Mem = 600, 221.

Υιος Δαβιδ. *Hulos Dabid.* Son of David, i.e., Jesus. See 680, 21 (Greek).

702

בן *ben.* Son. See 52.

מחמדים *makhaymaddim.* desires, delights, precious things. Mem = 600, see 142.

פחדים *pekhawdim.* loins, thighs, testicles. Mem = 600, see 142.

צורות *tzuroth.* Forms. Refers to archetypal or prototypical forms, centered in the Self in Kether. See 301, 464.

שבת *Sabbath.* Day of rest. Cessation from work; dwelling place; seat, sitting; indemnity for loss of in Exodus 21:19. Name of a tractate of the Talmud. *Sabbath,* the archetypal creation, is divided into periods or cycles or rest and work. This is the divine pattern or plan. Rosenroth in K.D.L.C.K. (p.703) says it divides between Yesod and Malkuth, i.e., Saturn's Path. See 1460, 713, 1837.

Translated "ceased" in Joshua 5;12, "to rest" in Exodus 31:17: "It [the Sabbath] is a sign between the children of Israel and me forever; for in six days the Lord made heaven and earth and the seas and all that is therein, and on the seventh day he ceased from work and rested." And "lost time" in Exodus 21:19: "If he rises again and walks in the street with his staff, then the one who struck him shall be acquitted, except that he shall pay for the loss of his time [שבתו]and the physician's fee."

ויתפרו *va-yathpheru.* and they sewed. In Genesis 3:7: "Then the eyes of both of them [Adam and Eve] were opened, and they realized they were naked, so they sewed fig leaves together and made coverings for themselves."

I. וויתפר *and-they-yielded-forth...* In this instance, the Hellenist have obviously and with deliberate purpose, exaggerated the vulgar sense, to thicken more and more the veil which they had resolved to throw over the Sepher, for it is evident that the verb תופר, used here according to the reflexive form, signifies, *to produce, to bring forth, to fecundate,* and not *to sew.* I do not see how they dared to take this ridiculous expression and still less why Saint Jerome agreed with them. Here are their verbal translation [Chaldaic]. "And-they-condensed a-condensation (a thick veil), the elevation of sorrow-mutual-and-of-mourning." [And the Hebraic version]

וחטיטו טרפי להון תאנין And-they-excited-profoundly in-them a-trouble (a confusion obscure) of sorrow-mutual-and-of-mourning." One can see nothing in them that can excuse the extravagant Greek and Latin phrase: they sewed fig-leaves! [Hebrew Tongue Restored pp. 102-103]

II. F.J. Mayers: "'The sewed': Hebrew, 'va-ithepherou.' This is the reflexive form of the verb 'pharaoth,' 'to produce,' 'to bring forth,' 'to give birth to.' The word's root is 'phr,' which denotes 'fertility' or 'productiveness,' as, for instance, in 'phari,' 'fruits.' It is impossible to justify the word 'sewed' as the translation, even in a figurative sense." [The Unknown God, p.170]

רבך *ravak.* to be mixed, mingled; to dip, soak (into oil). See 222.

ברך *barakh.* to kneel, bless. Mem = 500, see 222.

בלעם *bielam.* Balaam; a stranger. With different pointing: *Balam.* Goetia demon by night of the 3rd decan of Leo. Mem = 600, see 142.

ועתיק וימין and Ancient of Days. A title of Kether. In Daniel 7:9: "As I looked, thrones were set in place, and the Ancient of Days took his seat. His clothing was as white as snow. The hair of his head was white like wool. His throne was flaming with fire, and its wheels were all ablaze."

Σ37 = 703, the complete expression of the power of יחדה, Yekhidah.

אבן *eben*. stone. See 53.

רזי יסודות *Raziy yesodoth*. secret foundations. Refers to the 14th Path of Daleth as the instructor in the secret foundations of holiness and perfection. See 486, 601, 80, 378.

גן *gan*. garden. Both *eben* and *gan* are emphasized by the symbols of Key 3, *eben* by the great stone on which the Empress sits, and to by the garden, which is the scene of the picture. Both are symbols of the Great Work and of the power which is controlled and transmuted in alchemy. This is the power of Yesod, reproductive energy. It is shaped, moreover, by acts of creative imagination. See 124, 45, 53.

אברך *abreach*. tender father translated "bow the knee" in Genesis 41:43. The legendary "father R.C.," founder of the Rosicrucian Order. Kaph = 500, see 223.

אוצרות *aotzoroth*. treasure; storehouse, granary; treasury. The treasure of seed-thoughts; the granary from the empress; garden.

מסגרת *mesegereth*. strong-hold; border, rim; the which encloses. Frame. This the cubic Stone.

ואת הארץ *veath ha-eretz*. and the earth. In Genesis 1:1: "In the beginning, the Elohim cut apart the heavens and the earth." The physical place is to be made into the garden. See 401, 291.

אלף למד חית מים הה *Aleph-Lamed-Cheth-Mem-Heh*. Aleph-Lamed-Cheth-Mem-Heh. אלחמה or alchemy, written in full. See 84.

סאתאריאל *Satarial*. "Concealment of God." Qlippoth of Binah. The "adverse" Sephirah "who hides the face of mercy." Called Sheiriel in supplement to the Zohar. This implies an imbalance in creative imagination, which conceals God's light, i.e., physical plane illusion appearances.

Χανααν. *Canaan*. Canaan; the ancient name of Judea or Palestine, the Hebrew כנען (190). In Acts 7:11: "And a famine came upon all the land of Egypt and Canaan, and great distress; and our fathers found no provisions." See also Acts 13:19.

ο αγιος Ισραηλ. *ho agios Israel*. The holy one of Israel.

I. (11 x 64) or 11 x 2^6

דן *Dan*. Judge, a tribe of Israel associated with Scorpio. Nun = 700, See 54, 50, 106, 700.

לדרתיכם throughout your generations. See Genesis 17:12.

דרך *derek*. way, path, manner of life; occasionally a metaphor for worship. Kaph = 500, see 224.

קדם *qedem*. front; east, ancient times; anterior. With different pointing *qadem*: before, the east; ancient things. Mem = 600, see 144.

נתדוריגאל *Nethdorigael*. Lesser angel governing triplicity by night of Pisces. Pisces have to do with alchemical multiplication; the sign is connected with the Hebrew letter Qoph, associated with body cells' organization during sleep, i.e., at night. The name of this angel suggest reproductive power (Nun), limiting its expression (Tav) in acts of creative imagination through desire (Daleth) and intuitive guidance (Vav), linking itself to solar regeneration force (Resh) by the aid of divine will (Yod) working through subconscious patterns (Gimel); the spiritual force (Aleph) is goaded into balanced action within (Lamed). See 259, 180.

באבן *be-ehben.* with (or in) a stone. Nun = 700, see 55, 53.

הן *hen.* Lo!; whether, if. "Behold" in Genesis 4:14. See 55.

הקם *Hadem.* "God who erected the universe." The 16th name of the Shem ha-Mephorash, short form. Mem = 600, see 145.

טל אורת טלך *tal aroth talleka.* "your dew as the dew of lights." In Isaiah 26:19: Your dead shall live, my dead bodies shall arise-awake and sing, you that dwell in the dust-for your dew as the dew of light, and the earth shall bring to light the shades." see 39.

מיתריהם their cords [ropes]. Exodus 35:18.

הפרכת the veil [curtain]. See Exodus 26:33.

שער העין Gate of the Fountain. Nehemiah 2:13.

706

דברך *debahrekah.* your word. Mem = 600, see 226.

עולם *Olam.* Hidden times, time immemorial; antiquity; universe, eternity, the world. Signify primarily "hidden times, times long past," the world or universe. Indicates the whole cycle of manifestation as a space-time continuum. Mem = 600, see 146.

כפתור *kahpaythor* Capital of pillar; knob, button. In Amos 9:1: "I saw the Lord standing upon the altar: and he said, smite the lintel [Capital] of the door…" Rosenroth in K.D.L.C.K. (p.485) says that this refers to Yesod, the 'Mercy-seat," seeing that it is above the "ark" which is Malkuth of the Tree. He quotes Exodus 25:17: "Make an atonement cover (mercy-seat) [כפרת, atonement-cover]of pure gold-two and a half cubits long and a cubit and a half wide."

שמחה אור שמחה *aor olahm* + *simekhaw.* everlasting light + joy, gladness, mirth; a joyful occasion, festivity. The "blood of the grape" is the everlasting light, and its reception is a time of joy.

וצרתי and I will be an adversary, and I will oppose it. See Exodus 23:22.

וסרתם and you turn aside. See Deuteronomy 11:16.

Σαυλος. Saulos. Saul, name of the apostle, who before his conversion, persecuted Christians. In Acts 9:1: "And Saul, yet breathing out threatening and slaughter against the disciples of the Lord, went unto the High Priest." D.D. Bryant says that both this Saul and the Saul of the Old Testament who fought the Philistines is Sol, the Sun. The two stories bear many resemblance points, and mystically interpreted, they will be the same story in a different setting.

Paul Case: More likely [than that Paul is but a paraphrase of the Greek Apollo, God of the Sun] that "Paul" has the exoteric sense of "littleness" in contrast to the greatness implied in the kingly name Saul; and the esoteric sense of Mikros, small, implied in Paul's evident realization of the truth that man is a microcosm. [Case of D.D. Bryant]. See 331, 340 Greek, 337, 781.

707

און *On,* the city of the "Sun" or Heliopolis in Egypt. Variant spelling, Nun = 700, see 57, 51, 701.

בהן *bohen.* thumb, big toe. Nun = 700, see 57.

דגן *sawgawn.* corn, grain. Nun = 700, see 57.

און *own.* strength, power; manly vigor; wealth, riches; grief. With different pointing: 1. *awen.* Trouble, sorrow; wickedness; 2. Idolatry. Nun = 700, see 57.

און *Avnas.* Night demon #58 of the 1st decan of Scorpio of the *Goetia* [Mathers, 1995, p. 11]. See 57 & Appendix 11.

זן *zan*. species, kind, sort. Nun = 700, see 57.

אבדן *awbedawn*. abadon; destruction, perdition. One of the 7 infernal mansions. See 57.

הבן *hawben*. comprehend. With different pointing: ebony. See 57.

אשתו his wife [Eve]. See Genesis 3:20.

שבתה rest, she rested. See Leviticus 26:35.

708

אהיה יה יהוה אלהים *Eheyeh Yah Jehovah Elohim*. A divine name of God, comprising I Am, the father, IHVH, the creative powers, attributed to the supernal triad, which is the source of renewal. See 148.

בני אלהים *Beniy Elohim*. Sons of God, Sons of the Elohim. The angelic choir associated with Hod in Assiah (the physical plane) and Briah (the creative plane). Mem = 600, see 148.

חן *khane*. grace, precious, favor; gracefulness, charm. With different pointing *khen*: Notariqon for נסתרה חכמה (788). "Secret Wisdom" (Qabalah). Nun = 700. See 58.

מאזנים *moznaim*. balances, scales; the sign of Libra. Renewal through equilibration. See 148.

שכל מחודש *Sekhel Mechudash*. Renovating or Renewing Intelligence. The 26th Path of Ayin. It is the link between imagination (Sun) and Intellect (Mercury). This path overcomes conflict between an inner feeling of competence and outer appearance that "material" forces work against oneself. By experiment, he learns that confident expectation forms patterns realized in physical forms and that nothing fights against him but his own ignorance and clumsiness. The adversary is the master of the game. As we play with him, he develops our intellectual skills to plan, foresight and judgment. Thus nature is forced to "make us free at our pleasure." The Life-power is the great renewer, forever making all things new. The principle of limitation (Saturn), at the center of the Cube of Space-the "Temple of Holiness in the midst"-changes our slavery into dominion. Development of conscious comprehension of daily experience's meaning requires facing problems, transforming apparent evils into evident goods. The Devil is seen as the Ego in disguise, performing the Great Work upon one's personality. See 358, 130, 496, 414.

I. The path of Ayin is perhaps the most difficult to understand of all the paths. The Renewing Intelligence completes the dynamic expression of Beauty by uniting it to Splendor. Ayin is assigned to Key 15, the Devil, and associated with the sign Capricorn and the planet Saturn. Saturn is limitation, and therefore the Renewing Intelligence is the source of limitation, bondage and incompleteness for human consciousness. Our sense of bondage comes from our intuitive knowledge that freedom is the essential self of humanity. When we consider our small personal achievements, the One Self's essential perfection seems far from ideal. People personify this ideal as an externalized deity. And it's opposite, to which they attributed limitation of all kinds, they personify as a hostile and malignant agency, the devil. It is our sense of bondage and limitation that drives humanity to seek freedom. Ultimately thus leads to the splendor, which is the consequence of the strict justice of Geburah.

II. "I am the Renewing Intelligence, destroying apparent limitations that the law may be fulfilled." [Meditations of the Paths of Wisdom]

ברוך *barukh*. blessed. See 228.

מלאך הברית *malakh ha-berith*. the angel [messenger] of the covenant. In Malachi 3:1: "Behold, I will send my messenger, and he shall prepare the way before me: and the Lord, whom you seek, shall suddenly come to his temple, even the messenger of the covenant, whom you delight in: behold, he shall come, says the Lord of Hosts." The "angel" is Key 15, the Devil, in disguise. See 1188.

שחת *shachath*. pit, pitfall; grave; former; perdition, to spoil, ruin, destroy; to corrupt, pervert. Translated as "destroyed" in Genesis 13:10. According to IRQ, it is called "by burning, kindled a fire." Often the path of liberation is full of the pitfalls of hell [i.e., Key 15]. Translated "pit" in Job 9:31: "Yet shall you plunge me in the pit, and my own clothes shall abhor me." "Grave" in Ezekiel 28:8: "they shall bring you down to the grave, and you shall die the deaths of those that are slain amid the seas." "Pitfall" in Proverbs 26:27: "He who digs a pit will fall in, and he who rolls a stone, it will return to him." "Destroyed" in Genesis 13:10: "And Lot lifted up his eyes, and behold all the plain of Jordan, that it was well and watered everywhere, before the Lord destroyed Sodom and Gomorrah, even as the garden of the Lord, like the land of Egypt, as you come into Zoar." See 911, 715.

בית צור *beth-zur*. house of the rock [Joshua 15:58]. The meaning of beth-zur depends on the significance of צור, which distinctly relates to יהוה. See 296.

שבות *shebuth*. exile, prisoners; figuratively: a former state of prosperity, captive, captivity. [Strong's Bible Dictionary]

χλοη. *chole*. ripeness. "The word suggests that which has been produced from below in the operations of nature: the high mark of development: great productiveness. a synonym is *phloe*, which implies great generative power. In the following, the word *ichthys* (fish) is to be understood symbolically." [Omikron, 1942, pp. 264-265.]

709 (prime)

באורך *be-aorekaw*. in your light. Psalm 36:9: "For with you is the fountain of life; in your light, we see the light." "Your Light" is represented by the seven doubles corresponding to the lights of the candlestick in the tabernacle. See 692.

οι ευθεις. *hoi eutheis*. The upright. Septuagint translation of ישרים [560] in Psalm 49:14: "Like sheep, they [the foolish] are laid in the grave; death shall feed on them, and the upright shall have dominion over them in the morning, and

their beauty shall consume in the grave from their dwelling." see 560.

710

נסתר *Nisetar*. hidden, occult, mysterious, concealed. With different pointing: to hide oneself; to be hidden, concealed; to be demolished, destroyed. From the verb סתר, to hide, to veil, to cover, to conceal. Part of the path name of Netzach. The "brilliant splendor of all the intellectual power which are beheld by the eye of understanding and the thought of faith." These forces' operation opens the "eye of understanding, the awakening of an organ in the human brain. See 1060, 148.

ירך *yarak*. the thigh, but used as a euphemism for the phallus. The Hebrew lexicon gives: thigh, lion, side, flank; base; leg of a letter. Kaph = 500, see 230.

בחן *bakhan*. to test or try; trial. A tried (stone) in Isaiah 28:16. Nun = 700, see 60, 708.

קים *qayam*. Stable, enduring, lasting, living. Variant spelling, see 160.

יקרת *yekaerath*. costly. In Isaiah 28:16: "a cost [precious] corner-stone." From יקר precious, costly, dear; rare, scarce; heavy, weighty; glorious, splendid. The prize of testing. See 310.

מערת *maarath*. waste. Form מער nakedness, pudenda (a source of "waste") With different pointing: 1. cave, cavern (the hidden source); 2. a bare, open space (which occult knowledge brings into the open).

אדם עלה *Adam elah*. celestial Adam. The heavenly man is the secret pattern upon which the wisdom of the microcosm is inscribed. Mem = 600, see 151, 156, 150.

עמם *Amem*. The 52nd name of the Shem ha-Mephorash, short form. Mem = 600, see 150.

πιστον. *piston*. Faithful, true, trustworthy.

πνευμα αγιον. *Pneuma agion.* Holy Spirit, Holy Ghost [John 20:22]. The Greek text uses these words without the article, just as they are written in the passage cited. See 576, 134, 660.

θυρας. *thuras.* Door. In John 10:1,2: "He who comes in by the door is the shepherd of the sheep."

711

אדין *Adon.* master, lord, possessor. See 61.

אני *Ani.* I, myself. First-person, singular pronoun. See 61.

בטן *beten.* belly, stomach, womb, the inmost part. See 61.

הון *hone.* wealth, riches, substance. See 61.

אש מצרף *peresh ha-soos.* a refiners fire [Malachi 3:2]. This is the alchemical fire used for sublimation. See 1431.

פרש הסוס *dung of the horse.* Found in alchemical texts, in connection with the fire used for sublimation. After the first matter has been properly enclosed in the philosopher's egg, it is buried for a certain amount of time in a heap of horse manure. Actual heat, just about what is generated by the chemical activity in a dung-heap, is required to perform the Great Work. The source of heat is indicated by transposing the letters of פרש, *peresh,* to make שרף, *sahrahf* or Seraph, fiery serpent. It is the kundalini or serpent fire. The word סוס is a blind for אפילה *aphilah,* darkness (126). The "horse's dung" is the serpent fire working in darkness, and this darkness (which conceals the operation of the fire) is that of physical embodiment. See 126, 580, 1059, 192.

אין *Ain.* Nothing, No-thing. First veil of the absolute. See 61.

זאגן *Zagan.* Goetia demon by night of the 1st decan of Sagittarius. See 61.

712

בין *bin.* to understand, discern, know, perceive, to distinguish, separate mentally-part of the discrimination which characterizes illumination. See 62.

שבתי *Shabbathai.* The planet Saturn. Binah, sphere of Saturn, is connected to Chokmah, the Illumination Intelligence by the Path of Daleth, the Luminous Intelligence. A light goes into form via creative imagination. Also, the personal name of a Levite in Ezra 10:15. See 713 for alternate spelling.

שבית *shebith.* captivity. See Numbers 21:29 and Ezekiel 16:53. See 317, 312, 708.

713

שבתאי *Sabbathai.* Rest, Saturn relates to the 7th day of rest. Binah is the sphere of Saturn. "Rest" is one of the New Testament promises to those who repent. Rest comes when one finds the point of equilibrium at the interior center. See 67, 496, 42, 450.

I. Through the Sphere of Saturn, the Holy Mezla descends into the World of Formation, entering the field of Microprosopus (Tiphareth) from *Aima* (52). *Aima* is the Throne of Life, and the Gate through which the Power of the Supernal Triad rushes down into the six Sephiroth (Chesed to Yesod) that constitute *Ben* [52] the Son. Yet from *Ben* (Tiphareth) to *Kallah* (Malkuth), the channel of descent is also the letter of Saturn, and this letter stands in the Holy Temple in the midst. See *C.28.*

II. Sabbathai is rest, and there is a great mystery in rest. The Eternal was not tired after his work, because what can exhaust the endless? Thus Jesus, who came into perfect union with *Ab* [3], said the Sabbath was made for man, not man for the Sabbath. Man needs rest to restore his powers, but not the Eternal. The completion of creation is itself the Sabbath. When the *Kabode Ale* (Glory of God) finds full manifestation in the world of things and creatures, the new manifested forms themselves reveal, and at the same time conceal, the presence and power of the Eternal. The rest of the true Sabbath is the outer seeming of the ceaseless flow of the Holy Influence.

The first two letters of Sabbathai are the mother letter Shin, the sign of the Ruach Elohim's consuming fire, and Beth, a sign of the Eternal's dwelling place in the Eternal Beginning. Because creation begins anew with every moment of man's time. Is not the womb of אימא ever-virgin? The third letter is Tav, the sacred sign of union and completion. This completion is not an end because Tav is followed by the Aleph, which is the sign of Spirit before all beginnings and after all completions. The word is finished with Yod, the sacred seed of all letters, which begins the Holy Name יהוה, and is the special sign for Chokmah.

To know God, one must be still. In the stillness is but the veil for the abiding Presence of the Living God. Shabbathai is 713, which is the Holy name אל *Al* multiplied by חיה, Chaiah, which is the Life-force of all beings welling out from God Himself. In Chokmah, is Chaiah centered, and Chaiah is the power of אב the Father. Chiah is 23 when *Al* (31) is multiplied by it produces Shabbathai (rest). *Al* is Chesed's special name, and Shabbathai is thus made known as being the full manifestation of God's loving-kindness through the working of His living wisdom.

A stone appears to be at rest; its main characteristic is called *Tamas*, or inertia. Thus the completion of any cycle of creative activity brings forth something concrete. Manifested things, in general, have this quality of inertia, or apparent inactivity or rest. This is the mystery of Shabbathai, this appearance of absolute quiescence, a semblance of darkness, to which the color of Binah and Saturn are assigned the color black. Rest is not cessation, but Chesed's complete expression through the Divine Life Force Chiah's operation. That is the essence of all

the numeral references.

In Greek, the words "the power" η δεναμις (see below) and its number is 713. The **power** is the **inertia**. The darkness is that which comes into manifestation as Light. Do not confuse the manifested Light with its hidden Source. See *C.29*.

III. In *Aima* (Binah) is the sphere of *Shabbathai* and is the same number as תשובה (Teshubah, see below). The power of Shabbathai is expressed in the return of seasons and in the conversion of the Ruach in Adam. Teshubah is also assigned to Malkuth because the Kingdom partakes of the quality of Shabbathai, which completes manifestation by rest. Note that Binah is the sphere of Shabbathai, and Malkuth is completed by the letter Tav (32nd Path connecting Yesod to Malkuth), to which Shabbathai also pertains. Malkuth depends on the Tree from the Path of Tav. Tav is the Temple of the Holiness in the Midst, and that Midst is a central point of perfect rest. By repentance, and when that return is completed, there is rest also. The sinner's minds find rest from strife, which is found in the Palace in the Midst.

Rest is one with the perfect work of creation. All unrest is incompletion. By way of return, completion comes to the Sons of Adam to become the Sons of the Elohim. Note that the בני האלהים, *Beni Ha Elohim* is 713, if you take the final Mem as 600. Those who have followed a path of return to the Father's Palace in the Midst. They have always been the Sons of God, but in the whirling forth is this forgotten, to be brought once more into mind when the work of the Chariot is consummated.

Consider the emphasis on Saturn and rest. Rest, as the result of completion, takes the operator into the Palace of the King. Thus the title of one of the great alchemical writings is "The Open Entrance to the Closed Palace of the King." One of the aspects of the Palace is in the Midst is Binah on the Tree of Life. While another is Malkuth, and to both of these, *Teshubah* refers. Here is a plain condensed statement, and perhaps even cryptic to minds unused to turns of phrase and thought. Yet it is perfectly open, and what makes it so is the Beni Ha Elohim's reference. The Sons of the Elohim are an order of Angels attributed to Hod and the grade of Practicus. The Chariot's work is to transmute the substance of fallen Adam back into its original splendor as the Chariot of the Most High. The transmutation begins with Saturn, though it is a work of the Sun and the Moon, and the radical moisture is the water of the sea of Binah. A Rosicrucian text speaks of the mingling of the dew of Heaven with the oiliness of the earth. This has the same meaning as what the eastern mysteries speak: the Sun and Moon must be conjoined to make the nectar. See *C.30*.

IV. The active Tribes are 11, not 12 because the Sons of Aaron are Levites, separate from the rest. Seven is the number of the Sabbath and of rest, and 17 is טוב, which signifies "goodness," and 7 x 11 x 17 is 1309. This is the secret number of Shabbathai because when the letter names of Shin, Beth, Tav, Aleph and Yod are spelled in full, they add to 1309, as does Teshubah.

Special emphasis was placed on the Tribes and signs. This has to do with a method that converts Sons of Adam into Sons of the Elohim, and makes them Angels in Heaven, for Heaven is here, and an Angel is a herald of the Divine Self. Thus the בני האלהים belong to Hod, the Sphere of Mercury, and all magical practice is intended to make the Magician truly an Angel. See *C.31*.

תשובה *teshubah*. answer, reply; return to God (Noun). As a verb: to return (to a place); to return (in time), to recur; to return to former ways, to repent. Refers to the return of the seasons through the power of Sabbathai, which gives us our ordinary time sense. It also expresses the idea of converting the One Force (as expressed in Ruach) through Adam, man. This conversion has to do with a radical interior change that converts ordinary genus homo into "more than man" and is seen as the purpose behind all alchemical practices. Pertains to Binah and to Malkuth. Sanctification is the result of following the way of return. The parable of the prodigal son is the comment. It is the power of Shabbathai to restrict, concrete and limit that holds and preserves wisdom and love in substance so that it can be continuously reapplied. See 1200.

בני האלהים *Beni ha-Elohim*. Sons of the Elohim. Mem = 600, see 153.

עגלים *egalim*. calves. Mem = 600, see 153.

דגון *Dagon*. A fish-god of the Philistines. Nun = 700, see 63.

אבדון *abaddon*. destruction; the angel of the bottomless pit. Nun = 700, see 63, 57.

η δυναμις. *he dunamis*. The power, strength, force. The power is the inertia, the darkness that comes into manifestation as light. [See the English word "Dynamite" derived from Dunamis]. "Your is the Kingdom, the power..." (ve-Geburah). The essential power, the true nature and efficacy of anything. In the New Testament, it often refers to the divine power. In the Greek dictionary, Dunamis is defined thus: 1. strength, might, power ability; 2. a force for war, forces; 3. a quantity; 4. the force of a word, meaning; 5. a faculty, power; 6. worth, value.

714

דין *Deen*. Justice, the highest name for the 5th Sephirah, Geburah. See 64.

הגון *hahgun*. Worthy, respectable, suitable. See 64.

אתון נורא *attun nura*. fiery furnace.

והאבן *ve-ha-ehben*. "and this stone" see Genesis 28:22 & 64.

לחם ויין *lekhem va-yahyin*. bread & wine. The bread symbolizes the Life-power as a substance. The wine is the same as the "blood of the grape"; and is the animating energy. Mem = 600, see 154.

עולם הבא *olahm ha-bah*. the world to come, the future world. According to some, it means the same as גן עדן *Gan Eden*, the Garden of Eden. It is called 'the world to come' in relation to the idea that man in his dream of separation must consider his restoration to the paradisiacal state as in the future, or "to come." "The world to come" is the "new heaven and earth" Mem = 600, see 154.

715

נסתרה *nesethrah*. secret. The plural form, נסתרות means mysteries, hidden things. נסתר means: hidden; mysterious, occult; mysticism. See 710, 788.

אדמת נכר *adimath nekawr*. a foreign (strange) land. In Psalm 137:4: "How shall we sing the Lord's song in a strange land?" see 270.
Paul Case: "The Lord's song (verse 4) is שרי יהוה = 536 = the world of making, Assiah, the material world עולם העשיה. "In a strange land" is נכר אדמה לע = 419= טית [Note: the Biblical test gives אדמת = 445; thus the phrase = 815, which see. That actual value here is given by Case is 420, but the discussion is most pertinent, nevertheless]. The 'strange land' is the field of appearances produced by the serpent's power, pictured in Key 8 as the lion. When we are 'in' that land, we are deceived by the appearances of separateness. This כנר strange = רע [evil] which is created [Isaiah 45:7]. It is the - or darkness. Yet אדמה נכר, strange land = 319 = life forever עולם חיים על. For a continuation of the discussion see note in 270.

קטורת *qitoroth*. perfumed, fumigated, censed. Spelled נקטרת in Canticles 3:6: "Who is that comes out of the wilderness like pillars of smoke, perfumed with myrrh and frankincense, with all powders of the merchant."

צח ואדום *tzach ve-awdom*. white and ruddy. In Canticles 5:10: "My beloved is white and ruddy, the chiefest among ten thousand." Mem = 600, see 155, 98.

אם גלה סודו *em-gawlah sodo*. He reveals his plan [secret]. Mem = 600, see 155.

סנהם *Sanahem*. Lord of triplicity by day for Leo.

Mem = 600, see 155 & *777*, Table IV, Column CXLIV.

716

אדם עלאי *adam Eelo-o*. high man; the celestial or ideal man; the heavenly Adam. The life-power's perfect image of itself. Mem = 600, see 156.

קיום *qiyom, qiyam*. permanence, existence, duration, confirmation. Related to the 23rd path of Mem, the Stable Intelligence. Mem = 600, see 156, 184, 90, 40, 510.

ושתVashti, the queen. In Esther 1:9: "Also *Vashti* the queen made a feast for the women in the royal house which belonged to king Ahasuerus." "The Queen" is one of the titles of Malkuth.

אורה אתכם בוד אל *oreh ethekem be-yao-el*. I will teach by the hand of God; I will teach you concerning the hand of God. Job 27:11: "I will teach you by the hand of God: that which is with the Almighty will I not conceal." Yod is the creative "hand"-it is the fire of spirit behind mental images. See 47, 461, 212.

מטרוניתא *matrona*. mother. See 496, 65, 310.

I. I.Z.Q. Para. 721-722: "And therefore it is said, Genesis 2:3: 'Tetragrammaton blessed the seventh day and hallowed it.' For then, all things are found to exist in the one perfect body. For *Matronitha* [matrona], the mother (i.e., the Inferior Mother) is joined unto the King and is found to form the one body with him. And therefore are there found to be blessing upon the day." [Mathers, 1993, p. 334]

II. I.Z.Q. Para. 746-747: "When Matronitha, the mother, is separated and conjoined with the King face to face in the excellence of the Sabbath, all things become one body. And then the holy one-blessed be He!-sits on his throne, and all things are called the Complete Name, the Holy Name. Blessed be His Name forever, and unto the ages of the ages." [ibid., 1993, p., 337].

III. Rosenroth in K.D.L.C.K. (p.528) says that Binah or the "throne" is thus called, as custodian of the garden (of manifested life). He says that Malkuth also called by this name the lady (*domina*, i.e., Queen) or inferior mother; and Briah, the creative world.

שער הצאן Gate of the Sheep. Nehemiah 2:13

717

זין Letter name of *Zain*. Sword. Nun = 700, see 67.

קהלת יעקב *qehillath vaeqob*. the assembly of Jacob. In Deuteronomy 33:4: "Moses commanded us a law, even the inheritance of the congregation of Jacob." see 551, 1268, 182.

תשחט you shall sacrifice, slaughtered, offering. See Exodus 34:25.

718

חיצים *khitziyim*. arrows. Mem = 600, see 158.

תבשיו and he rested [The Elohim on the seventh day]. See Genesis 2:2.

ישבתו cease. Part of God's promise after the flood. In Genesis 8:22: As long as the earth endures, seedtime and harvest, cold and heat, summer and winter, day and night will never cease.

Χλοη *phloe*. ripeness. "The word suggests that which has been produced from below in the operations of Nature: the high mark of development: great productiveness. A synonym is *phloe*, which implies great generative power. In the following, the word *ichthys* (fish) is to be understood symbolically." [Omikron, 1942, pp. 264-265.]

719 (prime)

ושחתה and he will destroy it, and he destroys her. See Exodus 21:26.

תקטיר you shall burn [an offering]. See Numbers 18:17.

והשבתו and you shall restore it, then you shall give back to him. See Deuteronomy 22:2.

της γης. *tes gehs*. Of the ground. Septuagint translation of האדמה (55) in Genesis 2:6: "But a mist came up from the earth and watered the whole surface of the ground" Note the connection between the earth and the passional nature. See 11.

720

שכל שלם *Saykel Shalom*. Perfect Intelligence, the 8th Path of Wisdom. Shalom means "whole, uninjured, full, complete, well peaceful, happy.

"The meaning 'full' refers to completeness in number, measure and weight. Thus, the name of the 8th path indicates a kind of consciousness that brings forms to completion by applying mathematics principles to accurate measurement. What performs these functions is the human intellect, personified by Thoth in Egypt, by Nebo in Chaldea, by Hermes among the Greeks, and by Mercury in the Roman pantheon. Related to what, in our time concept is the future view of the Life-power's activities. As the Sphere of Mercury, it relates to the self-של conscious process of forming plans to transform desires into realities, as in Key 1, The Magician. Every advance toward a greater perfection is but the utilization, the unveiling of this primordial treasure. Gedulah, or Chesed, is the Life-power's unfailing beneficence. The root of all future blessings is the Life-powers loving provision for our every need through our clear patterns. This word is the root of the Hebrew proper name שלמה, Shelomoh or Solomon." [Case, 1985, pp. 188-190.] see 1431 & Appendix 12.

יין *yayin*. wine. See 70.

נעם *noam*. delight, sweetness, beauty, to be lovely, splendor. See 160

צלם *zehlem, tzelem*. image; God's image, or mental self-representation. A likeness; shadow. Mem = 600, see 160.

קים *qayam*. stable, lasting, enduring. The intelligence of Mem attributed to Water. From a root meaning "to rise" or "to raise from below," i.e., the serpent power. [קימה rising, raising, erection, putting up]. See 160.

כן *ken*. thus, so, just so, such, so much; honest. Nun = 700, see 70.

שררך *shawrerek*. the navel. The root of this is שרר, twisting, to twist, and suggest the double movements involution-evolution." [Paul Case: the Flaming Cube: Light of the Chaldees, p.2] see 700.

σπορος *sporos*. Seed; spore. In Luke 8:11: "Now the parable is this: the seed is the word of God." In the New Testament, *sporos* and *sperma* are equivalent and are interchangeable. See 426, 790, 796, 451 (Greek), 50, 64 (Lt), 1728.

η μητηρ αληθης. *heh meter alethes*. The true mother; i.e., Binah.

μητηρ αληθειας. *meter alethetas*. Mother of truth. Binah manifests the word of God, which is the seed of truth.

εναδιος οικος. *enadios Oikos*. In the Holy temple. The deity's house is in the temple of human personality, grown and nourished by the true mother and completed by the perfect intelligence.

ιερευς. *hiereus*. A priest, sacrificer. See 969, 1480, 1584.

721

נקדה ראשונה *nequdah rashunah*. the First, or Primordial Point, a title of Kether and the number 1. See 599, 620.

אדם עילאה *Adam Illah*. Heavenly Man.

אטתך your wife. See Genesis 3:17.

ונשתרה and secretly, and she is undetected. See Numbers 5:13.

המערות The caves. See Judges 6:2.

תושיה Sound judgment, advice, wisdom, insight, understanding, help, support. See Proverbs 18:1.

722

יריבך *yeribeka*. your adversary. See 242.

כבשת ewe-lambs. See Genesis 21:28.

שכבת a layer, flow, emission of [semen]. See Leviticus 15:16.

723

השחית had corrupted, he corrupted. See Genesis 6:12.

וזרעתם and you shall sow, so you can plant. See Genesis 47:23.

תשחטו you shall slaughter. See Leviticus 22:28.

והשבתי and I will cause to cease, and I will remove. See Leviticus 26:6.

724

עמדים *ammudim*. the pillars. The state of perfect equilibrium is understood as the support or pillars of existence. Mem = 600, see 164.

דיין *diin*. leader, chief, judge (variant spelling). Nun = 700, see 74, 64.

דכן *dikkane*. this, the same, this specifically. An

Aramaic demonstrative pronoun suggesting a particular identity. Has the connotation of exact and specific identification: "this" and no other. Thus it implies knowledge. Nun = 700, see 74.

הגיון *higgayon*. meditation, thought, musing, resounding music, reading, recitation of the text, logic. See 74.

גיהון *Gihon*. A stream, the name of the 2nd river of Eden, is associated with water. Nun = 700, see 74, 77.

725

כהן *kohen*. priest. See 75.

תקטירו you shall [may] burn. See Leviticus 2:11.

הוא שמי + שדי אל חי *hua shaymi + shaddai* El chai. My name is Hua, or that is my name + Lord of Life. The cause of the tree and the garden is that No-thing or Lord of the universe. See 362, 363.

הדד בן בדד *Hadad ben-Bedad*. Hadad, son of Bebad. A king of Edom, associated with Tiphareth in Genesis 36:35. Note that Edom signifies unbalanced force and that the Qlippoth of Tiphareth is the "Hagglers." Nun = 700, see 75, and 45, 1081.

726

דם ענב *dam-aynahb*. blood of the grape. See 166.

ויתריעל VITRIOL. Acronym (rendered into Hebrew letters) for the alchemical *formula Visita interiora terrae rectificando invenies occultum lapiden*, "Visit the interior of the earth; by rectification, you shall find the hidden stone." A reference to the Ego. See 94, 570 (Lt).

אגב + יין *beg + yin*. by, through, employing + wine; i.e., delight. The spirit within the blood; then "the kingdom of spirit is embodied in my flesh." see 720, 6.

μετ ειρηνης *met eirenehs*. In peace. Septuagint translation of בשלום [378] in Genesis 26:29: "That you will do us no harm, as we have not touched you, and as we have done to you nothing but good, and have sent you away in peace: you are now the blessed of the Lord. See 378, 938.

Ο Μεσσιας. The Messiah.

727 (prime)

נקודה ראשונה *nequdah rashunah*. the Primordial Point. See 721

ואשתך and your wife. See Genesis 6:18.

ראש דברך all of your words. In Psalm 119:160: "All your words are true; all your righteous laws are eternal." Resh section of the Psalm. In the Hebrew text, it is written with a small Resh, thus ראש דבבך, indicating the importance of "the beginning, the head." see 1168, 501, 226.

פרכת + בכה *paroketh + bawkah*. curtain, veil, + to drop, distill, to flow down in drops. The first cause's fiery influence is hidden by the veil that separates the holy of holies, or primordial point from the temple's outer sanctuary, or manifested form. See 700, 27.

אור מופלא + זרע אלהים *aur mopeleh + zerao Elohim*. Hidden light + a godly seed. The first point is the seed of this hidden light, or Kether, the "illumination material." see 363, 364.

728

תשכח *tashakach*. suggest a combination of תש weakness + כח power. K.D.L.C.K. (p.506) refers to the closeness of 728 to 729 = "to rend Satan," which see. It also refers to פנים face, countenance; anger, wrath, one's own person, appearance, way, manner. See 180.

מרחפת *merahepeth*. hovering, moving over, brooding. In Genesis 1:2: "Now the earth was formless and empty, darkness was over the surface of the deep, and the Spirit of God was hovering over the waters."

"מרחפת pregnantly-moving. Moses, by a turn of phrase frequently adopted by him, uses here, to express that action of the breath [spirit], of which he was about to speak, a verb which is derived from the same root; which is always attached to the word רוה, [214] and which depicts an expansive and quickening movement. The sign פ, which terminates it now, adds the idea of an active generation of which it is the hieroglyphical symbol. The Samaritan makes use of the word whose root is the same as that of the Hebrew נשף [to blow, breath upon], gives is the sense of agitation with a vital movement, of *animating*. Finally, the Hebraic verb רהוף is the same as בורה, with the sole difference of the character פ being substituted for the character ב: it signifies, *to dilate, to expand, to agitate prolifically*." [d'Olivet, 1976, p. 32.]

מרחפת hovered [over the surface of the waters]. See Genesis 1:2.

חשכת withheld. See Genesis 22:12.

תשכח it shall be forgotten, she will be forgotten. See Deuteronomy 31:21.

729

I. (27 x 27) or 3^6

גן יהוה *gan Jehovah*. garden of God. Nun = 700, see 79.

יאחין *Yachin*. Jakin; one of the pillars in the temple of Solomon, corresponding to the masculine side or pillar of Mercy on the Tree of Life. Nun = 700, see 79, 90.

לא תרצח thou shall not kill. The sixth of ten commandments revealed to Moses by God, in Exodus 20:13. For other commandments, see 2296, 696, 1506, 1026, 2942, 2397, 1837, 1888, 928, 1282, 563; 486, 2002, 1522, 483.

The Zohar [III: 90A] Comments: "We have a mandate that the first five commandments include by implication the other five as well: in other words, in the first five, the second five are engraved, five within five. How? Take the first commandment: 'I am the Lord your God.' Does it not include the firsts of the second five. Indeed it does, for the murderer diminishes the likeness and image of his master, man having been created 'in the image of God,' and it is also written: "And upon the likeness of the throne was the likeness as the appearance of a man upon it.' [Ezekiel 1:26] said Rabbi Hiya: "It is written: 'who so sheds man's blood, by man shall his blood be shed; for in the image of God made he man' [Genesis 9:6]. He who sheds the blood of a fellow man is considered as diminished the divine archetype of man. Thus the first commandment, "I am the Lord your God,' contains the motive for the sixth, 'thou shall not murder.'" (p.277).

730

רך + אביטוב *roke + abitob*. tenderness + father of goodness. The Lord of all things manifests creation through tender love and for the purpose of goodness. אבא (Abba) father. This is a name for the Sephirah חסד Chesed or Mercy, sphere of cosmic memory. The tender father comes from the universal memory of the source. See 4, 700, 30.

כסילים *kesilim*. "thick ones," hence fools. Also strong ones, giants, hence the constellation Orion [the Hunter], conceived of by the ancient as a giant bound upon the sky; constellations generally. Mem = 600, see 170.

מועדים *moadim*. seasons. See 170.

נ + ל Nun + Lamed. *Nun + Lamed*. fish + ox-goad. Imaginative Intelligence is connected with death and change; Faithful Intelligence is connected with the directive power, which guides and regulates the expression of the forces represented by Aleph. See 700, 30.

מה שהיה + יהוה יגמר בעבי *mah shehaiah + IHVH igemer beadi*. The thing that has been + the Lord will accomplish that which concerns me. That which has been being that which shall be in eternity for the great work's performance. See 365.

וישתחו and they bowed down. See Genesis 27:29.

עכרתם you have troubled, you brought trouble. See Genesis 34:30.

כשית you are covered with fat, sleek. See Deuteronomy 32:15.

731

The total length of the visible paths when the Aleph line is 26 units long.

בית השטה *Beth ha-Shittah*. House of the Acacia [Judges 7:22]. Acacia is the special symbolic plant of Freemasonry as well as the sacred wood of the Israelites. Refers to the length of the visible paths of the Tree. Shittah, the sacred wood, was made into the symbolic furniture of the tabernacle and temple representing man; and is a symbol of immortality.

In Judges 7:22: "And the three hundred blew the trumpets, and the Lord set every man's sword against his fellow, all throughout the host: and the host fled to beth-shittah in Zererath, and to the border of Abelmeholah, unto Tabbath." Inman: "It is generally said that this word means 'house of the Acacia,' שתה, Shitah and that it represents a locality where Acacia trees were common. However, the word represents a shrine, house or temple, it is probably derived from שת, *shat*, plural *shathim*, which signifies 'columns' or 'pillars,' in which case the meaning is 'the temple of the pillars.' [Ancient Faiths, Volume 1, pp. 363-364] Both explanations suggest the F∴M∴ lodge.

גבעה האלהים *gibeah ha-Elohim*. Hill of the Elohim. An ancient name for Bethel, The House of God, where Jacob had his dream of the ladder.

This ladder is a symbol for the Tree of Life. Mem = 600, see 171.

כאין *Camio*. Goetia demon by night of the 2nd decan of Virgo associated with the 9 of Pentacles in the Tarot minor arcana. See 81.

קראתיך I called [summoned] you. See Numbers 24:10.

שאלת you did desire, you asked. See Deuteronomy 18:16.

חזיון vision. Nun = 700, see 81.

732

לבן *laban*. white, whiteness; white of the eye, silver coin. With different pointing: *loben*. Whiteness; semen. Nun = 700, see 82.

צלם דהבא *tzelem dahava*. golden image.

רישא חוורא *reshaw chavvura*. the white head, a title of Kether (variant spelling, see 736). See 620 (Kether).

The Kabbalah (p.158): "The mere idea of being, of the absolute, considered from the point to view which we take, constituted a complete form, or to use the usual term, a head, a face; they call it the white head *reeshoh havroh*, because all colors, that is to say, all ideas, all determined modes are blended in the form.

In K.D.L.C.K. (p.680): "Before the white-washing of changes," also attributed to כתר Kether.

לשבת that they may dwell, to stay. See Genesis 13:6.

תבשל you shall cook, boil. See Exodus 23:19.

733 (prime)

בארצתם in their lands [territories]. Genesis 10:5.

ריֹשא הוורה *ha-Risha Havurah*. The White Head. A title of Kether. See The Kabbalah Unveiled (p. 23).

734

ד + שם שמים *Shem ha-shamaim* + *Daleth*. The name of the heavens, i.e., God's name + the door. Creative imagination through the doorway of desire reveals the name of God in all manifested things. See 730, 4.

ותכחש then denied so she lied. See Genesis 18:15.

ותחשך and was darkened, she was black. See Exodus 10:15.

735

קל אדם *kol Adam*. the voice of Adam. In Daniel 8:16: "And I heard a man's voice between the banks of Ulai, which called, and said, Gabriel, make this man understand the vision." [Metathesis of קדמאל *kamael*, the spirit of Venus]. Mem = 600, see 175, 130, 45.

לב אבן *Laib ehben*. heart of the stone. See 85

במרצתג *Bemaratzteg*. Tiphareth, 42-fold name in Yetzirah, the formative world [Crowley, 1977, p. 59]. See 1081.

רצלטות *Retzeloth*. The sixth hell, gates of death, corresponds to Chesed and the Moslem Jahim, reserved for pagans and idolaters.

736

ריֹשא חוורה *Resha Chavvurah*. the White Head. A title of Kether and the number 1. (note spelling difference between (733). See 837, 620, 222.

ארון חדת *Aron ha-edeth*. Ark of the Testimony. An alternate spelling is העדות, see 742, 1386, 3793 (Greek).

עקלקלות *ekalekalloth*. tortuous ways, perverseness. From עקלקל crooked, winding; zig-zag. Suggest the spiral motion of spirit in the macrocosm (whirling in Kether) and microcosm (the serpent-power).

Written עקלקלותם in Psalm 125:5: (4) "Do Good, O Lord, to these who are good, to those who are upright in heart. (5) But those who turn to crooked ways, the Lord will banish with the evildoers."

מלכות כל עלמים *malkuth kawl-olamim*. an everlasting kingdom. In Psalm 145:13: "Your kingdom is an everlasting kingdom, and your dominion endures throughout all generations." The kingdom of spirit embodied in the flesh brings Kether into Malkuth. See 636, 516.

לעולם *le-olahim*. forever, to eternity. Psalm 110:4. Mem = 600, see 176.

737

שלהבת Flame.

לאשתו of his wife. See Genesis 26:7.

ולשאת and for a rising [swelling]. See Leviticus 14:56.

738

גפרית אדם *Gawfriyth Adam*. Sulphur Adam.

חלצים *khalatzim*. loins, lower part, strength.

לשחת to destroy. See Genesis 6:17.

ανδροβασμος. Hero's Progress. "The Narrow Way. The quest of the *aner* [159]. The path of the heroic *mystics*." [Omikron, 1942, p. 249.]

739 (prime)

שכל מוגשם *Sekhel Mughsham*. Corporeal or Incarnating Intelligence. The 29th Path of Qoph. Connects the field of desire (Venus, Netzach) to sensation (Earth, Malkuth). It is the consciousness that shapes bodies and is associated with the "back of the head" (Medulla Oblongata). The law of suggestion controls subconscious forces, resulting in actual cell adaptation of brain cells and body chemistry. This whole process is the work of the Holy Guardian Angel (Ego). The practice of meditation brings changes to the structure of the human body. This path's main work perfects each personality's special characteristics while sharing the spirit's upward vision. Changes in the organism are brought about by efforts to overcome seemingly adverse conditions and are manifest in the "New Creature." see 389, 343, 180, 186, 100, 414, 259, 59.

"I am the Natural Intelligence, completing and perfecting all change beneath the starlight of eternal knowledge." [Meditations on the Paths of Wisdom]

שמש ומגן *shemesh vu-mawgen.* sun and shield. In Psalm 84:11: "For the Lord God is a sun and shield: the Lord will give grace and glory: no good thing will he uphold from then that walk uprightly." see 1589, 640, 93.

שמעון בר יונה *Shimeon bar-jona.* hearing, son of the dove. In John 1:42: ."... thou art Simon the son of Jonah: thou shall be called Cephas, which is... the stone." Simeon is from שמע sound, sonority + שמע report, fame; meaning, sense; hearing capacity. שמע hear, is part of the confession of the unity of God. יונה "dove" is feminine of the masculine יון "dove" and יונה Jonah, who was swallowed by a whale. Note that the dove is a symbol of Venus, ruler of Taurus (intuition, inner hearing, Key 5) = the tribe of Simeon (Gemini-alchemical fixation, 446). Inner hearing is part of the body-building process. See 410, 466, 273, 202, 71.

נצח + הוד + יסוד + מלכות *Netzach + Hod + Yesod + Malkuth.* The great lower triangle of the Sephiroth with יסוד at the center: Victory (Venus, desire), Splendor (Mercury, intellect), Foundation (Moon, astral body) and Kingdom (Elements, physical body). See 148, 15, 80, 496.

יכין *Jakin.* the pillar of Mercy, the white pillar on the Tree of life. Nun = 700, see 90.

בל האבן *liab ha-ehben.* the heart of the stone, the stoney heart. The "stoney heart" symbolizes the sense of separateness pictured by the tower in Key 16. See 90.

מן *mahn, manna.* who? What? a chord. Literally "whatness." With different pointing: *men.* a portion. See 90.

ספר ת *Sepher Tav.* Book of Tav. The planet Saturn, the Lord of time, is attributed to the letter Tav or T. Thus, book T is a record of all time, written upon the flesh of the human body, within and without.

In the Fama, The Book T as the greatest treasure 'next unto the Bible.' Book T is described as a parchment, which is written in the long Latin *Elogium.*

Parchment is the skin of a sheep prepared for writing. A lambskin in connected with Brother C.R. . (The Lamb) and Damcar (Blood of the Lamb). This intimates that Book T is a symbol rather than an actual book. The book described in Revelation is described as being sealed with seven seals. James Pryse says: 'The scroll is a mysterious document that has taken the God eons to write, a Bible which, when rightly read, discloses cosmic and divine mysteries. It is simply the human body, and its seals are the force-centers wherein radiate the Logos' formative force. These seals are the same as the seven Societies and the seven lamp-stands. The expression 'written inside and on the back' refers to the cerebral-spinal axis and the great sympathetic system.'

השפרים השפר *ha-sepher ha-sepherim.* the Book of Books. The microcosm.

דיונסים *Dionsim,* The last 7 letters of the 22-letter name of God." [Godwin. 1999, p. 594.] see 180.

מצרית Egyptian. See Genesis 16:1.

תשם be desolate, she is desolate. See Genesis 47:19.

שמת names of. See Exodus 28:11.

שתם is opened, seeing clearly of. See Numbers 24:3.

תשפר you shall number [count]. See Deuteronomy 16:9.

κτισις. *kteisis*. Creation, formation. building, creation, creature, ordinance. [Strong's Bible Dictionary]

KYKLOE. Cycle.

HΘEPMOΘE. Heat (vibratory force).

ΑΙΘΕΡΟΕΜΕΛΟΕ. Music of the Spheres.

ο επι πασι θεος. *ho epi pasi Theos*. The god over all. Deity creates using the pairs of opposites; Kether emanates Chokmah (Jachin) and Binah (Boaz). See 284 (Greek)

αιμα Ιησου. *haima iesou*. Blood of Jesus. This is the blood of redemption, for "Christ" is created in the blood by receptivity. See 52, 688 (Greek), 888. [1 John 1:7]; 1620, 2220, 2228.

Αιδονευς. *Aidponeus*. Sun of Egypt-Greek worship; hades, the God (of death = Nun = Change = reproductive power).

Αγιασμα Θεου. *Agiasma theou*. Sanctuary of God.

741

I. Σ38 = 741

אמן *Amen*. So be it, to support, be firm, nurture; artificer, artist, master workman. A title of Kether. See 91.

אב לאבן *Ab lebehn*. Father of Fathers.

אמשת *amasmath*. The 4 letters of the elements, hence comprising a concealed IHVH, Aleph = Air, Mem = Water Shin = Fire and Tav = Earth. See 1, 40, 300, 400.

לראיך *Leraik. Leake.* Goetia demon by day of the 2nd decan of Leo. See 91.

ותרעינה and they fed [grazed]. See Genesis 41:2.

ο αρτος. *ho artos*. the bread.

742

מלאך האלהים *Melakh ha-Elohim*. Messenger of God. See 182

משבת to dwell [remain]. See Genesis 36:7.

בשמת in names, by names. See Numbers 32:38.

שבתם and are turned back, away. See Numbers 14:43.

743 (prime)

מגן *mawgen*. shield; defense, to deliver. Nun = 700, see 93.

והלבשת and you shall dress, clothe. See Exodus 28:41.

לשחתה to destroy it [her]. See Genesis 19:13.

מגשת to come near. See Exodus 34:30.

מגן *miggane*. to deliver up, deliver to. See 93.

ולאשתו and for his wife. See Genesis 3:21.

744

הוא ירעה אותם *Hu yire-eh otawm.* He shall feed them. In Ezekiel 34:23: "And I will set up one shepherd over them, and the shepherd shall feed them, even my servant David." see 270, 288.

כח קיום *kach-qiyom.* The power of permanence. See 184

Μαρια αγιοτης. *Maria hagiotes.* Holy Mary. See 592.

παρθενος + ο ανηρ. *parthenos + ho aner.* Virgin + the man; i.e., the resurrected Christ, born of the "virgin."

745

זבלון Tribe of *Zebulon.* "habitation." A tribe of Israel associated with Cancer by Case. Godwin says this tribe is associated with Capricorn. See 95.

המצרית the Egyptian. Genesis 16:3.

משתה a feast, a meal. See Genesis 19:3.

המן *hahman.* to be turbulent. To rage. Nun = 700, see 95.

746

ממונים *mammonim.* chiefs, commander. The governing powers of the individual soul are contained in the One Ego seated in men's hearts. Mem = 600, see 186.

מקום *maqom.* place, locality, dwelling-place. The Book of Concealed Mystery says: "The balance hangs in the מקום (place) which is אין (not). Mem = 600, see 186.

בתל שדי *Tzale Shaddai.* In the shadow of the Almighty. Psalm 91:1: "He who dwells in the shelter of the Most High will rest in the shadow of the Almighty. See 541.

משתאה astonished, watching. See Genesis 24:21.

Ευιλατ. *Evilat.* Havilah, the "land" where there is gold. Septuagint translation of חוילה (59), in Genesis 2:11: "The name of the first [river of Eden] is Pison: it winds through the land of Havilah, where there is gold."

εξ απειρα Θεου. *heks apiera Theou.* Six boundaries of God, i.e., those which form the cube of manifested space.

Χαραγμα *charagma.* A mark, stamp or sign; engraving. See 400, 2886 (Greek).

εξουσια. *eksousia.* Authority.

747

בן אדם *Ben Adam.* Son of man. Nun = 700, see 97, 657, 1307, 2198 (Greek).

אמון *amon.* artificer, master-workman, architect, designer. Variant spelling of אמן. Nun = 700, see 97.

אמון is also the day demon of the 1st decan of Gemini, ruled by Mercury.

אופנים *Ophanim.* Wheels. Choir of angels of Chokmah. See 187

משה איש האלהים *Moshe aish ha-Elohim.* Moses, a man of God, or Moses, a man of the Elohim. In Deuteronomy 33:1: "And this is the blessing, wherewith Moses the Man of God blessed the children of Israel before his death." Moses is linked with the name IHVH and with inner tranquility. It is water (Mem), spirit (Shin) and vision (Heh). The children of Israel are those who rule as God. See 345, 541.

The Zohar [Prologue 6B] says this name implies that he was "The husband, as it were of the divine glory, leading it where so he would go on earth. A privilege no other man has ever employed." see 311.

משחת you anoint. See Genesis 31:13.

שלחתי I sent, I had put forth. See Genesis 38:23.

חמשת five, five of. See Numbers 3:47.

טיט חיון *tit-ha-yaven*. miry clay; clay of death; One of the seven infernal mansions. The infernal abode corresponding to Geburah. Godwin says Tiphareth. Nun = 700, see 99, 28, 74, 102.

ישוע המשיח *Yeshua ha-mawshiyah*. Jesus, the messiah. This spelling of Jesus shows Shin, the letter of Fire, combined with Yod, Tav and Ayin, assigned to the earthy signs Virgo, Taurus, and Capricorn. The Messiah is the anointed one or king, assigned to Tiphareth. Attainment of the oil of illumination is to master the powers of the serpent-power on the physical plane. See 386, 358.

ושלחתה and you shall let her go. See Deuteronomy 21:14.

I. (2 x 3 x 5³)

מדון *mahdone*. contest, quarrel, exertion; contraction; extension, length, height. Nun = 700, see 100.

מין *min*. species, kind. See 100.

לשכל *lishekawth*. chambers, cells; compartments; rooms connected with sanctuary. In 2 Kings 23:11: "And he took away the horse that the kings of Judah had given to the sun, at the entering in of the house of the Lord, by the chambers of Nathan Melech the chamberlain, which was in the suburbs, and burned the chariots of the sun with fire." see Ezekiel 40:44.

שתים two. Genesis 5:8.

מחשבת thoughts. Genesis 6:5. "And all things we have made in pairs [שתים], so that you may give thought." [Koran] With different pointing: מחשבת means: work, workmanship.

עפרת *ophereth*. lead. Short spelling. Saturn's metal is lifted up by alchemical practice or transmuted into Gold Tiphareth via tNun'senergy See 756, 400, 713, 406, 806, 746.

I. *Aesch Mezareph*: "Ophereth, in the Doctrine of Natural things, is referred to Wisdom, for a great Treasure of Wisdom lies hid here. And hither is referred the quotation Proverbs, 3:19. The Lord in Wisdom hath founded the earth; I say, the Earth, concerning which Job speaks, 28:6, which has Dust of Gold. Where, take notice of the Word Ophereth, i.e., Lead. By a Mystical Name, this Lead is called Chol [כל, the all, 50], because therein lies the System of the whole Universe. For its Figure[12] has below a Circle, the Sign of Universal Perfection, and over the circle is a cross formed of four Daleths, whose Angles meet in one Point; so you may know, that all Quaternity lies here, and the Quaternions of Quaternity: whether you refer to the Elements, or Cortices, or Letters or Worlds.

And in this Lead of the Wise Men, four Elements are hidden, i.e., Fire, or the Sulphur of the Philosophers; Air, the Separator of the Waters; the dry Water; and the Earth of the Wonderful Salt.

There are also hidden in it the four Cortices, described in Ezekiel, 1:4, for in the Preparation of it there will occur to thee the Whirlwind, a great Cloud, and a fire enfolding itself, and at length, the desired Splendor [a brightness as the color of amber] breaks forth.

Also, the Natural Sephira of the Tetragrammaton, and the Metal thereof, occurs to thee here. And you will naturally travel through four Worlds in the very Labor; when after the Faction and Formation, laborious enough, there will appear the wonderful creation: after which thou shall have the Emanation of the desired Natural Light.

And note, that the word Chol [כל], whose Number is 50, multiplied by 15, according to the Number of the Sacred Characteristic Name[14] in the Sephira of Wisdom, will produce the Number of Ophereth, i.e., 750." [Westcott, 1997, pp. 34-35]

II. "CHOKMAH, in the Metallic Doctrine, is the Sephira of Lead, or Primordial Salt, in which the Lead of the Wise Men lies hid. But how is so high a Place attributed to lead which is so Ignoble a Metal, and of which there is so seldom Mention made in the Scripture?

But here lies Wisdom! Its several Degrees are kept very secret; hence there is very little mention made of it. But yet here will not be wanting examples of the particular Sephiroth.

For may not that which, in Zechariah 5:7, is called a Lifted up Talent of Lead, and brought from the deep, represent the grade of Kether? And that which in the same Chapter, v. 8, is spoken concerning the Stone of Lead[3] it sets before itself the Letter Yod, which is in Chokmah.

Then Ezekiel, 27:12, Lead is referred to the place of the congregation, of which type is Binah." [ibid, p. 33]

שלכת *shalleketh.* a casting off of leaves; the name of one of the gates of the temple, in 1 Chronicles 26:16: "To Shuppim and Hosah the lot came forth westward, with the gate Shalle-cheth, which is made in the road that goes up, watch opposite watch."

751 (prime)

איש תם *Iysh toom.* a perfect man. See 311, 440, 1351, 1000.

נתדוריאל *Nathdorinel*; Lord of triplicity by night for Pisces. Pisces is the Corporeal Intelligence, connected with body cells' organization during sleep and with alchemical multiplication. This name suggests the reproductive power (Nun) in limited use (Tav), guided by the image and desire (Daleth) of the inner teacher (Vav) who links the cells with solar regenerative force (Resh) in harmony with divine will (Yod) and sprouts seed of change (Nun) into new spiritual expression (Aleph), goaded into balanced activity within the body (Lamed), during repose. See 259.

Χιραμ. Chiram. *Haram Abiff.* Name of the central figure in the legend of Freemasonry, connected with the Christos. The pattern of perfect righteousness and the idea of immortality is symbolized here. Septuagint translation of חורם (254) in 2 Chronicles 2:13: "I am sending you Hurah-Abi, a man of great skill." Hiram Abiff was the chief designer and craftsman of the temple of Solomon.

Manly Hall: "To the initiated builder, the name Chiram Abiff signifies 'my father, the universal spirit, one, in essence, three in aspect.' Thus the murdered master is a type of the cosmic martyr-the crucified spirit of good, the dying God-whose mystery is celebrated throughout the world... To the mystic Christian Mason, Chiram represents the Christ who, in three days (degrees), raised the temple of his body from its earthly sepulcher... thus considered Chiram becomes the higher nature of man and the murderers are ignorance, superstition and fear. The indwelling Christ can express himself in this world only through man's thoughts, feelings, and actions...

Sufficient similarity exists between the Masonic Chiram and the Kundalini of Hindu mysticism to warrant the assumption that Chiram may also be considered a symbol of the Spirit Fire moving through the sixth ventricle of the spinal column. The exact science of human regeneration is the Lost Key of Masonry, for when the Spirit Fire is *lifted up* through the thirty-three degrees, or segments of the spinal column, and enters into the domed chamber of the human skull, it finally passes into the pituitary body (Isis), where it invokes Ra (the pineal gland) and demands the Sacred Name. Operative Masonry, in the fullest meaning of that term, signifies the process by which the Eye of Horus is opened. Wallis Budge has noted that in some papyri illustrating the entrance of the dead souls into the judgment hall of Osiris, the deceased person has a pine cone attached to the crown of his head. The Greek mystics also carried a symbolic staff, the upper end being in the form of a pine cone called the *thyrsus* of Bacchus. In the human brain, a tiny gland called the pineal body, which is the ancients' sacred eye, corresponds to the Cyclops' third eye. Little is known concerning the function of the pineal body, which Descartes suggested (more wisely than he knew) might be the abode of the spirit of man. As its name signifies, the pineal gland is the sacred pine cone in man-the *eye single*, which cannot be opened until Chiram (the Spirit Fire) is *raised* through the sacred seals, which are called the Seven Churches in Asia. [Secret Teaching of All Ages: pp.78, 79, 95] see 254, 273 [Hebrew], 1351 (Greek), 2270, 634.

752

וילון *vilon, wilon*. veil; the 1st Heaven of 7 correspondings to Yesod, the astral and Malkuth, the physical plane. Nun = 700, see 102.

בשות in the year of. See Genesis 7:11.

לשבתך you to dwell in. See Exodus 15:17.

בנקרת in a cleft. See Exodus 33:22.

753

גנן *gawnan*. to hedge about, protect, shield. Nun = 700, see 103.

מגדון *Megiddon*. rendezvous. The place of the battle of Armageddon in the Apocalypse. Nun = 700, see 103, 222, 958; 247 (Greek).

αναστας. *anastas*. Having arisen, arise in Acts 10:13. From a root meaning: make to stand up, raise up, set up: to raise from sleep, and from the dead: to set up, build, build up again; to rouse to action. To rise, to go, set out. Luke 15:18.

754

צדק מלכי מלך שלם *Malchi-zedek Melek Shelem*. Melek Shelem. King of Salem (Melchizedek).

מדין *Midian*; one of the sons of Abraham by

Keturah; later one of several tribes in NW Arabia Nun = 700, see 104.

אבן + *Lapis. Eben + Lapis*. This combination of the Hebrew and Latin words for Stone often occurs in the Western tradition's secret writings. Nun = 700, see 104.

755

πετρος. *petros*. A stone, a rock.

I. "Greek, *petros*, a rock, a boulder, Chaldaic, *kephas*, a rock. Here, a word-play upon the Semitic *peter* means an interpreter, illuminator, and hierophant in the Mysteries being so-called. The arcane rites were celebrated in caves and rock-temples; the stone receptacle in which the sacred symbols were kept was called the petroman, the same name being given to the double stone tablet from which the hierophant expounded (hence the fable, which rests on a mere pun, about Petros being in Rome). Many words referring to the oracles are derived from *petra* (rock); thus, Pataros, a son of the oracle-god Apollon, was said to have founded the oracle city of Patara. Philo Jodaeus calls the Logos a rock; and Paulos in 1 Corinthians 10:1-4 gives a purely mystical interpretation of the myth of the 'Rock in the desert': 'Our fathers were all under the cloud, and all passed through the sea, and all were baptized unto Moses in the cloud and in the sea; and all ate the same pneumatic [spiritual] food and drank the same pneumatic drink, for they drank from a pneumatic Rock accompanying them, and that rock was the anointed." Psycho-physiologically, the rock is the 'philosopher's stone,' the 'third eye' of the seer, as clearly shown in Matthew 16:18-19: 'You are a rock (*Petros*), and on this rock (*petra*) I will build my society, and the gates of Hades shall not prevail against it. And I shall give you the keys of the Ruling of the Skies' [kingdom of heaven]. The 'gates of hades' are the generative powers, as opposed to the 'gate (or door) of Iesous'; and the 'ruling of the skies' (*Basileia ton ouranon*) is the controlling of the seven brain centers by the breath (pneuma), and thus attaining seership on the sidereal planes." [Pryse, 1967, pp. 86-87.] see πετρς (#486).

II. "Literally a stone. As a symbol, the word is connected with the preceding [πετρα, rock], and it implies a pupil of rapid progress, one who solves spiritual enigmas and arrives at intimate knowledge: one who can be built into a living house of exacted service. [Omikron, 1942, p. 262.]

III. Mackey adds that the word Cephas, the Greek rendering of this word (ΚηΦας, 729), is used in the degree of royal master, and there alludes to the stone of foundation. [Encyclopedia of Freemasonry, p.154] see 2521.

756

אבן שאבת *ehben shebeth*. lode-stone, magnet. See 762.

הוא נהרי דחכמתא *hu nehiryu de-chokhmatha*. That is the light of wisdom [Lesser Holy Assembly]. Refers to the "place of beginning." [הוא is read as "that."]

והאבן גדלה *ve-ha-ehben gedolah*. and a great stone. Nun = 700, see 106.

כי שפע ימים יינקו *ki shefa yammim yinaqu*. For they will suck the abundance of the seas [Deuteronomy 33:19]. Said of Zebulun, attributed to the Old Testament passage relating to the Path of Cheth. The field (Cheth) of speech where the distinction between appearance and essence is made for the habitation ("Zebulun") of deity. "Seas" are mental substances; "sand" is spiral, twisting motion directly connected with sound and with thought; root of Havilah, the land where there is "gold," i.e., Tiphareth. See 95, 100, 44.

נון Letter name *Nun*. fish, to grow or multiply. See 106, 50, 700.

סערת יהוה *sa'arath IHVH*. Whirlwind (storm) of Tetragrammaton [Jeremiah 23:19].

ספירות *Sephiroth*. Countings, emanations, spheres, numbers. The ten divine emanations in the Qabalah. [The singular is ספירה, sephirah] The Sephiroth fundamental activity is a whirling motion, running out and returning to its source. Essentially they are all one, but in the process of out-going and returning, they undergo various transformations or changes of aspect. This is the basic idea relating to נון [Nun] and to the corresponding Tarot Key 13. See 1326.

עולמים *olamim*. ages; worlds. See 196.

עופרת *ophereth*. lead (alternate spelling). Saturn's metal is lifted up by alchemical practice or transmuted into gold (Tiphareth) via Nun's energy. "Ophereth, in the doctrine of natural things, is referred to wisdom (Chokmah), for a great treasure of wisdom is hid here." [*Aesch Mezareph* Chapter 6] Refers to Proverbs 3:19: "The Lord is wisdom has founded the earth." see 750.

שנות *shenath*. years. Transmutation takes years of practice.

Χειραμ. *Cheram*. Hiram (from the Septuagint). Old Testament name associated with Masonry. See 50, 120, 54, 372.

757 (prime)

אב + אמיא + בן The sum of *Ab* (3), *Aima* (52) and *Ben* (52), the names of the Qabalistic Trinity: Father (Chokmah), Mother (Binah), and Son (Tiphareth). See 107.

מגן דוד *Mawgen David*. Shield of David, or Shield (or star) of Love. Refers to the hexagram. Nun = 700, see 107.

אונן *onawn*. Onan; probably a clan, of Canaanite origin, that lost its identity in the amalgamation of clans incidental to the growth of the tribe of Judah (Sun, Leo. Nun = 700, see 107.

ותנשא and they shall be exalted. See Numbers 24:7.

ותקראן and they called, and they invited. See Numbers 25:2.

נחשת *nahkhawshah*. serpents; filthiness, harlotry; copper, brass (vessels). The Rosicrucian allegory refers to the memorial table, cast of Brass, which brother N.N. discovered while making repairs in his building. The table was attached to the wall with a nail. When it was pulled out, it took out a stone, which revealed a hidden door. Note the table was made of brass and allow of copper and zinc. Copper is the metal of Venus. And the emerald tablet of Hermes is made from the gem of Venus. Venus is connected with desire and creative imagery. Desire opens the door to the higher life, but untransmuted, it can bring lower imagery's filthiness. See 100.

I. By rearranging the letters נחש serpent, spells שרת the number 6 (*sheth*, see 700) the number of Tiphareth. Six is the number of Vav, meaning "nail." It also spells Seth, meaning: replacement or compensation. This is the reward of those who master the serpent-power; they become united with the son in Tiphareth. The word *Nekosheth* is a formula for the vault of Brother C.R.C. See 358, 700, 6, 12, 1171, 1266.

II. *Aesch Mezareph*: "Amongst the Planets Nogah, Venus corresponds to it. A necessary Instrument to promote the Metallic Splendor. Yet it hath more the part of a Male than Female. For do not deceive thyself, to believe a white Splendor is promised to thee, as the word Nogah infers. But Hod ought to receive a Geburah Influence and gives it also. O, how great is this Mystery. Learn therefore to lift the Serpent up on high, which is called *Nechushtan*, 2 Kings, 18:4, if thou wouldst cure infirm Natures after the Example of Moses." [Westcott, 1997, p. 32]

משחות *mashchith*. destructive, destruction, literally a snare, trap. [Strong's Bible Dictionary]

ותגשן and they came near [approached]. See Genesis 33:6.

והשלחתי and I will send. See Leviticus 26:22.

והשחתם and shall deal corruptly, if you become corrupt. See Deuteronomy 4:25.

כנפים *kanawfeem*. wings. Mem = 600, see 200, 1005 (Greek).

כתר + חכמה + בינה *Kether + Chokmah + Binah*. Crown + Wisdom + Understanding. The names of the three sephiroth composing the supernal triad on the Tree of Life. See 620, 73, 67.

מקביל ומתקבל *maqebiyil ve-mathqabal*. both active and passive said in Qabalah concerning the sephiroth. [Ancient Faiths VI. pp.221-222] Refers to Elohim as having male and female connotations.

קרעשמן *Qaroshaman*. Yesod, 42-fold name in Yetzirah and with Chesed. Yetzirah is the astral plane in the world of formation, the foundation of the physical plane.

בת בבל השדודה *bath babel ha-shedudah*. daughter of Babylon, who are to be destroyed. In Psalm 137:8: "O daughter of Babylon, who are to be destroyed; happy he be, that rewards you as you have served us." see 402, 34, 436.

עצם *Etzem*. bone, body, substance, essence, life. See 200.

קסם *qesem*. divination, witchcraft. See 200.

דמיון *dimyon*. Resemblance, image, like. See 560.

שכלתי I am bereaved. See Genesis 43:14.

תרעץ dashed to pieces, she shattered. See Exodus 15:6.

צרעת leprosy, skin disease. See Leviticus 13:2.

761 (prime)

אבן חן *ehben khane*. precious stone. See 111

אשכילך + מספר *asekilekaw + misepawr*. I will instruct thee + number. The secret wisdom of Egypt and of occult science is "hid in number" [Book of Tokens, Teth] "Number" here is the "thick darkness" which veils the power of the Elohim. See 380, 381.

נשאתי I have lifted up, I will grant. See Genesis 19:21.

והשמתי and I will bring desolation, and I will lay waste. See Leviticus 26:32.

762

אבן שואבת *ehben shebeth*. lode-stone, magnet. Property of the letter Nun as in the Hebrew dictionary. See 756, 53.

תקברני bury me. See Genesis 47:29.

η κυβικη εκκληια. *heh kubikeh ekklesia*. the cubic church.

η οθονη μεγαλη κυβικη. *heh othoneh megaleh kubikeh*. the cubic "great sheet."

763

נשחתה it [she] was corrupt. See Genesis 6:12.

המשחית the destroyer, the one destroying. See Exodus 12:23.

הנחשת brass, brazen, the bronze. See Exodus 35:16.

μεσιτης. mespes., mediator.

764

חמישתו its fifth, fifth of him. See Leviticus 5:16.

תנחשו divination, you practice divination. See Leviticus 19:26.

ותקרבון and you came near. See Deuteronomy 1:22.

התושבים the strangers, the temporary residents. See Leviticus 25:45.

765

שכל הקדוש *Saykel ha-Qodesh*. Sanctifying Intelligence. The 3rd Path of Binah. From a root meaning: to make pure, to set apart, to consecrate. Selection for specific purposes combined with perfection. Implies something which operates to bring about the best expression of the Life-power's potencies, in from fully adequate for such expression. The Rosicrucian grade of Master of the Temple. These are perfected human beings, set apart from the rest of Humanity by a superior personal development that enables them to exercise unusual mental and spiritual powers. The third path is called firmness of faith and mother of faith because the experience of being in touch with something higher and practical demonstration that mental patterns do actually take form builds confidence. Binah is called the "root of your mother" because it is the root of the material basis of every person's experience-our mother, the great womb of nature from which we are all born. See 67, 52, 86, 112, 199, 265, 395, 415, 450, 410.

"It is the Sanctifying Intelligence the foundation of primordial wisdom and the creator of faith. [Meditations of the Paths of Wisdom]

ויברך אתם אלהים *va-yebarekh otham Elohim*. And God [Elohim] blessed them. In Genesis 1:22: "And the Elohim blessed them [the creatures of water and fowl of the air], saying, be fruitful, and multiply, and fill the waters in the seas, and let fowl multiply in the earth." Elohim is the divine name of Binah, the great sea.

השתחוי לו *hesawttahayvei-lo*. worship thou him.

In Psalm 45:11: "So shall the king greatly desire your beauty; for his is your Lord, and worship (do homage unto) thou him." The path to Tiphareth (Beauty) is filled with worship and sanctification of consciousness's personal vehicles. See 776.

אדני היא חכמה *yereath Adonai heia Chokmah.* "The fear of the Lord that is wisdom." In Job 28:28: "And unto man he said, behold, the fear [reverence] of the Lord, that is wisdom [Chokmah]; and to depart from evil is understanding [Binah]. Reverence prepares the way to the sanctifying or "departing from evil."

766

מכון *makhon.* emplacement; fixed place, foundation, institute, institution. Name of the 7th Heaven corresponding to Chesed. With different pointing: a kind of tool, vise. See 566.

מכון *mekuawn.* in a line; a corresponding; exact, precise. The benevolent lines of heaven (Jupiter) are connected with the foundation (Moon) of the earth (Chesed and Yesod). Nun = 700, see 116.

767

את שם יהוה *eth-shem IHVH.* The essence of Tetragrammaton's name [Psalm 135:1]. Grammatically, את is the sign of the accusative. See 366.

זקנים *Zaqenim.* The Elders. Refers to a state of preexistence. See 207.

תבל וישבי בה The world and they that dwell therein [Psalm 24:1]. This pair of numerical correspondences intimates that the mystical meaning of זקנים has to do, not only with states of being before manifestation but also with the idea that whatever exists, including the world and its inhabitants, is actually a projection of the essence designated by the "name" IHVH. See 3638 (Greek)

מזיקים *mezziqim.* Demons; injurers. [Godwin. 1999, p. 597.] Mem = 600, see 207.

ויקח יעקב אבן וירימה מצבה *va-yekkach yawrekob ehben ve-yerimeah may.zay.bah.* and Jacob took a stone and set it up for a pillar [Genesis 31:45]. (Jewish translation: "for a memorial pillar") Jacob means "supplanter"; the stone is *Ehben* (53); the pillar is *Jakin* [90], "firm one, the strong one," alluding to Chokmah, where the essence of Life-force of IHVH, is to be found.

ארורה האדמה בעבורך *ayrurawh hawaydamah ba-aybusake.* Genesis 3:17: To Adam, he said, 'Because you listened to your wife and ate from the tree about which I commanded you, you must not eat of it, Cursed is the ground because of you; through painful toil, you will eat of it all the days of your life." Humanity (אדם) has lost the vision (Heh) of the true meaning of the physical plane (אדמה) or ground, and of its "essence." See 2800.

גאמיגין *Goetia* demon #4 by day of the 1st decan of Taurus [Mathers, 1995, p. 127]. Also spelled המיגין, *Hamigin.* Please note that Godwin spells it without the first Aleph. See 768 & Appendix 11.

768

נחשתי *necheshethi.* coppery, brassy. In Lamentations 3:7: "He has hedged me about [i.e., God], that I cannot escape; he has made by brassy chains heavy." Copper and brass are connected with Venus; a brass tablet led to discovering the vault of C.R.C. See 758.

שת + הבונה *shath + ha-boneh.* foundation, basis + the builder, founder. The foundation is one name for alchemical quicksilver or mercury of the sages at the white stage. These are the builders of the Stone. See 700, 68.

אבה + בחן + גופריתא *abah + be-khane + gophritha.* to desire + to breathe + after, want, need + in grace, by grace, favor + Sulphur, the alchemical principle attributed to Chokmah, Wisdom. Wisdom is sought after through desire and through the grace of God. The stone is the father (Ab) union or Chokmah and son (Ben) or Tiphareth. See 700, 60, 8.

אני בינה לי גבורה + בעברך + ידע *aeni binah li Geburah + baebureka + yawdah.* I am understanding, I have strength + for your sake + to know. It is meant for man to know understanding (Saturn) and strength (Mars) for the sake of the divine plan of evolution. This plan is based on the foundation stone. See 384.

המיגין *hamigin. Goetia* demon by day of the 1st decan of Taurus. Nun = 700, see 118, 767 (alternate spelling).

769 (prime)

ומזרקתיו and its basins [sprinkling bowls]. See Exodus 27:3.

770

ינין *yenin.* shall be continued. Nun = 700,. See 120.

מכין *mawkheen.* strengthening, renewal. See Keys 8, 14. Nun = 700, see 120.

עקורת *aeqweeth.* unfruitful, barren. In Psalm 113:9: "He makes the barren woman to keep house, and to be a joyful mother of children."

נפלים *Nephilim.* Nephilites, distinguished, illustrious noblemen. Translated "giants" in Genesis 6:4. Mem = 600, see 210.

תשע the number nine (9). Genesis 5:5 and 5:27. See 775 for commentary.

771

שעיר אנפין *Seir Anpin.* The Bearded Countenance; a title of Microprosopus or Tiphareth. See 1421, 1081.

שלתיאל *Shelathiel.* Angel of Virgo.

והנשתרים and those that are hidden and the ones hiding. See Deuteronomy 7:20.

772

שבעת seven, seven of. See Genesis 8:10.

שבעת the oath, oath of. See Exodus 22:10.

משלבת joined, paralleling. See Exodus 26:17.

773 (prime)

כהן הגדול *kohen ha-godhol.* the high priest. Nun = 700, see 75, 43, 123.

774

עדן *Eden.* Delight, pleasure, time. Nun = 700, see 124.

מעדנם *maadannim.* delicacies, delights, fetters. Mem = 600, see 214.

בת שבע *bath* (maiden, daughter) – sheba (plenty, full). Rosenroth in K.D.L.C.K. (p.220-221) calls this *fillia* [maiden] *septenarii* [seven] and says it is so-called "when seven sephiroth illuminate within her nature." He says the Zohar refers this name to Geburah, which is said to be the name אלישבע, and that Binah moreover, in another section is so-called.

775

הנפלים *ha-nephilim.* the mighty men. See 780, 652 (Greek). Mem = 600, see 210, 215.

תשעה the number nine (9) [feminine form]. Numbers 1:23. For other numerals, see 13, 400, 636, 273, 348, 600, 372, 395, 570, 441.

תשע nine. I. "The root שע, which signifies literally, *lime, cement*, draws with it all ideas of cementation, consolidation, restoration, conservations, etc. The verb שׂוע, which comes from it, expresses cementing, plastering, and closing carefully. Therefore the name of this number, being visibly composed of this root שע, governed by this sign of reciprocity ת, should be understood as cementation, as mutual consolidation. It maintains a very intimate relation with number three, containing like it, ideas of preservation and salvation." [d'Olivet, 1976, p. 154.]

II. Paul Case writes: "The last numerical symbol, 9, represents the following ideas: completion, attainment, fulfillment, the goal of endeavor, the end of a cycle of activity. Yet, because 8 indicates rhythm as part of the creative process, completion is not absolute cessation. The end of one cycle is the beginning of another. This fact is the basis of all practical occultism. Nobody ever comes to the end of his tether. Nobody ever reaches a point where nothing more remains to be hoped for, where nothing remains to be accomplished. In Qabalah, therefore, 9 is called basis or foundation, and corresponds to the mode of consciousness named Pure of Clear Intelligence, because the completion of any process is the pure, clear, unadulterated expression of the intention or idea which initiated that process." [The Tarot, pp.13-14]

776

מלון *Mahlon*. lodging, inn, night quarters. See 126.

עון *aoon* or *ahvon*. to lie down, rest; to dwell; to move, agitate; guilt, iniquity, punishment, sin, crime, cohabit. Nun = 700, see 126, 160.

סיון *Sivan*, the 9th month of the Hebrew year, corresponding to June-July, and thus to Cancer. Nun = 700, see 95, 126, 418 (Cheth), 1360.

תעשו you shall make, you do. See Genesis 19:8.

777

עולם הקליפות *Olahm ha-Qlippoth*. The World of Shells or Demons. Another name for Assiah, the material world or the world of action. It is the world of matter, made up of the grosser elements of the other three worlds. (Feminine singular קליפה, Qlipah, "peeling, scaling.") In it also is the abode of the evil spirits, called shells by the Qabalah. See 626, 536, 385.

אחת רוח אלהים חיים *Achath Ruach Elohim Chayyim*. One is the Spirit of the Living God.

מתושאל *Methusael*, father of Lamech [Genesis 4:18]. The name is Babylonian, meaning "man of God."

Fabre D'Olivet translates Methusael as "death's fathomless pit," or "abyss of death" (i.e., שאל Sheol).

He comments: This noun comes from two distinct roots. The first מות designates death: the second שאה characterizes every emptiness, every yawning void, every gulf opened to swallow up. In the hieroglyphic formation of the word מתושאל, the convertible sign of the first root ו has been transposed to serve as a liaison with the second, to which has been joined by contraction, the syllable אל [strength, power, might, a name of God. [Hebrew Tongue Restored pp. 138-139]

בעיון הר קדשי *be-tzion har-qawdeshey*. In Zion, my holy mountain. In Joel 3:17: "So shall ye know that I am the Lord your God dwelling in Zion, my holy mountain: then shall Jerusalem be holy, and there shall be no strangers pass through her anymore." On the physical place, "Zion" corresponds to the pineal gland's area in the brain-it is the adytum or holy place. Jerusalem means "abode of peace," and peace comes when the truth of recognizing the unity of God in man is established. See 2117 (Greek).

ברקיע השמים *beraykeyaw ha-shamaim*. in the firmament of the heavens [Genesis 1:14].

τα ενουτα. *ta enouta.* "[of] the things which are within" In Luke 11:41: "But give in alms the things within, and behold, all things are pure to you."

η προθεσις η μεγαλη. *heh prothesis heh megaleh.* The great purpose. Mentioned in Romans 8:28: "And we know that all things work together for good to those who love God-to those being invited according to a purpose."

οι κλητοι βασιλεια. *hoi kletoi basileia.* Those called to the kingdom. See 259 (Greek).

Ηλιος Βασιλειας. *helios basileas.* sun of the kingdom.

778

שלחתם you sent. See Genesis 45:8.

תשבעו you shall be filled. See Exodus 16:12.

תשבעו you shall swear. See Leviticus 19:12.

779

ιλαστηριον. *hilasterion.* The lid, cover. In the Septuagint, it describes the cover of the Ark. In the English Bible, "Mercy Seat." Described by the Hebrew word כפרת, Kapporeth. See 700, 180.

780

I. Σ39 = 780

איש מכאבות *Ish makoboth.* A man of sorrow. In Isaiah 53:3: "He is despised and rejected of men; a man of sorrows, and acquainted with grief: and we hid as it were our faces from him; he was despised, and we esteemed him not." Interpreted by the Christian tradition as a reference to Christ. [The Hebrew translation is "a man of pains," for כאבות is the feminine plural of כאב pains].

מלין *milayin.* decrees; prophetic sayings; words, commands, things (Aramaic). Nun = 700, see 130.

עין Letter name *Ayin*, eye as an organ of sight. Look, face, appearance, color; fountain; investigate; balance. See 130.

מאסו הבונים *mahasu ha-bonim.* Refused by the builders [Psalm 118:22]. Refers to the stone, and thus to Christ and the Masonic Hero, Hiram Abiff. Mem = 600, see 220, 273, 53

שפת *shawfath.* to set, place, to put the pot over the fire; to ordain, establish. By placing spirit (Shin) as the one reality over matter, one becomes illuminated (Peh) and thereby establishes dominion (Tav).

שפת *shepath.* language, speech, words, lips, border, edge, margin, rim, shore, bank. Dominion over the power of speech brings one to the edge of the ocean of consciousness and the realization of a new conception of life, liberation from bondage. See 358, 830, 17.

שכנתי *shawkanithi.* I dwell, have dwelt. In Proverbs 8:12: "I wisdom (אני חכמה), dwell with prudence, and find out knowledge of witty inventions."

I.R.Q. Para. 1122: "I wisdom, have dwelt with prudence;" read it not שכנתי, *Shekenethi*, I have dwelt; but שיכנתי, *Shekeneth-i,* My Shechinah or my Presence. [Mathers, 1993, p. 250]

ומלאו את הארץ *vu-melayau eth ha-eretz.* And fill the earth. In Genesis 1:28: "And God blessed them [humanity], and God said unto them, be fruitful, and multiply, and replenish [fill] the earth, and subdue it: and have dominion over the fish of the sea, and over the fowl of the air, and over every living thing that moves upon the earth." see 1974 (Greek).

ספלים *shfalim.* cups. The suit of cups in the Tarot minor arcana corresponds to Briah. Mem = 600, see 220.

פן *pen.* a removing, hence, that not, "lest" (as a warning) in Genesis 3:22. Nun = 700, see 130.

שלמית *shelomith.* peaceableness. The liberating

stone gives peach (Shalom). See 376

עשתי eleven [one and ten]. See Exodus 26:7.

οφις. *ophis*. Serpent, snake. This Greek word has a definite connection with the whole mystery of which "the Devil" symbolizes. See 358.

781

ועשתה and do, and she does. See Leviticus 5:17.

σοφια. *Sophia*. Wisdom. Either worldly or spiritual. See 1000.

παυλος. *Paulos*. Paul. Saul's mystery name. "single-minded in wisdom." In Acts 13:9: "Then that Saul, also called Paul, being filled with the holy spirit, looking intently on him..." see 901 (Greek), 701 (Greek).

πραυς. *praus*. Meek, humble, mild, gentle. Spelled πραος in Matthew 11:29: "Take my yoke upon you, and be taught by me; for I am meek and lowly in heart, and your lives will find a resting place." In Matthew 21:5: "Say to the daughter of Zion, behold your king comes to thee, lowly, being seated on an ass, even on a colt of a laboring beast."

η δικαιοσυνη. *heh dikaiosuneh*. Righteousness. In Romans 10:6: "But the righteousness from faith thus speaks, 'say not in your heart, 'Who shall ascend into heaven?' That is, to bring Christ down." see 1453, 1962, 2292, 2010, 1850, 2233 and 2 Corinthians 9:9; Galatians 3:21.

782

אלהי אברהם אלהי יצחק ואלהי יעקב *Elohi Abraham Elohi Itzchaq ve-Elohi Yaaqob*. The God of Abraham, the God of Isaac, and the God of Jacob.

בעשתי the eleventh [in one and ten]. See Deuteronomy 1:3.

בשמתם by their names. See Genesis 25:13.

783

גפן *gefen*. the vine, grapevine. A mystical term used by Jesus ("I am the vine and you are the grapes"). Also, the vine from which comes the "blood of the grape." Nun = 700, see 133.

גדעון *Gideon*; "hewer" or "feller"; the fifth judge of Israel in Judges 8:22. Nun = 700, see 133.

784

I. (28 x 28) or 2^4 x 7^2

מתושלח *Methuselah*. See Genesis 5:22.

שיחרירון *Sihariron*. Qlippoth of Cancer. This sign is ruled by the Moon and suggest subconscious imbalance and obsession by negative entities.

785

נרית אדם *neperith Adam*. The separation of Adam. One of the Alchemical names of the Red Stone. See 157, 738.

תעשה [she] shall be made. See Exodus 25:31.

תפשה shall spread abroad, she spread. See Leviticus: 13:7.

786

אש מן השמים *esh min ha-shamaim*. Fire from heaven [2 Kings 1:10]. An ancient title of the letter Peh (Key 16). Refers to lighting. The holy influence is of the same nature as lighting - the electrical constitution of matter. See 78, 899, 395, 503.

ממון *mammon*. Wealth, value; money; fines; penalties. Nun = 700, see 136.

יסוד עולם *Yesod Olam*. Eternal Foundation of the World, a title of Yesod. See 226.

פשות *peshut*. smooth. the smooth point is a name of Kether, the spiritual sun and origin of the "fire of heaven." See 559.

שלומית *shelomith*. peaceableness (variant spelling). To be in harmony with the celestial fire brings peaceableness. See 780.

ארון עצי שטים *aeron etzei shitim*. an ark of Acacia wood. In Exodus 25:10: "And they shall make an ark of acacia wood; two cubits and a half its length, and a cubit and a half its breadth, and a cubit and a half its height." The ark housed the tablets of the law revealed to Moses by God. See 257, 160, 314.

פורך *Phurk*. *Goetia* demon by night of the 2nd decan of Leo. A fallen angel; a renowned president or duke of hell. Kaph = 500, see 306.

את הרקיע *eth ha-raqia*. the firmament. The expanse. In Genesis 1:7: "So God made the expanse and separated the water under the expanse from the water above it. And it was so. " It could be that את here means "essence," thus linking it with the fiery water of Mezla, manifest as lighting. The firmament's essence can be seen as the mind working on the archetypal plane or Atziluth of the Qabalists. Where the prefix Lamed is used instead of Heh and without את. See 1821 (Greek), 380, 410, 1451 (Greek).

I. "את הרקיע, *that-selfsameness-of-the-rarefying*... It was doubtless seen in the first verse of the chapter, that I gave according to the occasion, a particular meaning to the designative preposition, את [401] having rendered את השמים word for word by the *self-sameness (objectivity) of the heavens*; it is true... that this preposition often expresses more than a simple designative inflection, and that it characterizes, especially when it is followed by the determinative article ה, as in the instance the substance itself, the ipseity, the objectivity, the self-sameness of the thing which it designates." [d'Olivet, 1976, pp. 37-38.]

II. F.J. Mayers: "The Hebrew word is 'rakia.' The root of the word is 'rak' [רק], which means anything which expands, extends, dilates, etc. In Arabic, the root denotes something volatile, which spreads out like the scent of a flower or an odor. the meaning of this ancient root is still preserved in our expression: 'to reek of,' and in the Scotch word 'reek,' 'smoke.' 'Rak' is allied to the word רוח (Rauch-spirit or breath) [214], but is rather harder and more materialistic. (It has the heard 'k' instead of the soft Ch]. The word 'rakia' denotes something 'stretching out,' an 'expanse.' It is spiritual in its nature (and therefore, in verse 8 is called 'heaven'), but it linked both with the spiritual and the material. It is said to be in the midst of the waters and 'divide the waters from the waters.' Perhaps, we can best arrive at some understanding of the real nature and purpose of this 'firmament' if we remember that the constitution of 'man' is in close correspondence with the cosmos' constitution. In ourselves, we may find the clue we need... now, is there anything within ourselves - any portion of our being, which seems to correspond with what is told us of the firmament? Is there anything which holds a midway position between our physical being and our spiritual being- which is a link between the two- and which is acted upon and has activities in both.' The writer believes that there is just such a plane of being in that fixed, permanent center of our human consciousness which we call the 'Ego,' the 'I,' which lives, feels, thinks and initiates all our activities." [The Unknown God, pp.35-36]

III. "Symbol of the higher mental plane as the firm foundation of creation, and as a central plane of consciousness dividing the upper planes of reality from the lower planes of illusion... and the supreme now establishes the higher mental plane which shall be a plane of consciousness dividing the Reality from the Mayaic. The mental plane shall divide the Buddhic plane (waters above) of the higher emotions from the astral plane (waters below) of the desires. And to the higher nature, the name of Heaven is given." [Gaskell, 1981, pp. 277-278.]

787 (prime)

אופן *ophan*. Wheel; circle; manner, way. "Identified by the ancient sages as the angel Sandalphon." [Davidson, 1971, p. 213.] Nun = 700, see 137, 280.

חזון מיהוה *khozon mi-Jehovah.* visions from Jehovah. See 137.

788

חכמה נסתרה *Chokmah Nisetarah.* Secret Wisdom. i.e., the Qabalah. See 58, 111, 708.

שפחת handmaid of, servant of. See Genesis 16:8.

למשחית to destroy. See Exodus 12:13.

789

תשפט you shall judge. See Leviticus 19:15.

790

צן *tzen.* thorn. In plural צנים in Proverbs 22:5: "In the paths of the wicked lie thorns and snares, but he who guards his soul stays far from them. Nun = 700, see 140.

נשמת breath of. See Genesis 2:7.

שמנת eight (8) of. See Genesis 17:12.

שדפות blasted, and ones being scorched off. See Genesis 41:23.

במושבתם in their dwellings. See Exodus 10:23.

Κυρος. *Kyros.* Cyrus, king of Persia. Septuagint translation כרש (520) in Ezra 1:2: "This is what Cyrus, king of Persia says: "the Lord, the God of heaven, has given me all the kingdoms of the earth and he has appointed me to build a temple for him at Jerusalem in Judah." Jerusalem (586) means "Abode of peace"; Judah (30) means "praised, celebrated" and is connected with the Sun and with Leo and alchemical digestion. See 520.

791

נאמן *ne'eman.* Faithful, firm, loyal. Part of the title of the 22nd Path. Nun = 700, see 141

כוס תרעלה staggering cup. In Isaiah 51:22: "This is what your Sovereign Lord says, your God, who defends his people: See, I have taken out of your hand the cup that made you stagger; from that cup the goblet of my wrath, you will never drink again." כוס = cup, goblet; תרעלה = reeling, staggering, poison. See 86.

שנאתם you have hated, you were hostile. See Genesis 26:27.

התפרקו let them take (it) off. See Exodus 32:24.

792

אל האבן הגדולה *El ha-ehben ha-gedolah..* On the Great Stone. See 142

ותפשו then they shall lay hold. See Deuteronomy 21:19.

793

עץ החיים *etz ha-chaim*. Tree of Life. Mem = 600, see 233, 228, 1603, 1625 (Greek).

אבצן *Ibzan*, the ninth judge of Israel. Nun = 700, see 143 and Judges 12:18-10.

שפחתה her handmaid [maidservant]. See Genesis 16:3.

794

ושפחת and maidservants. See Genesis 12:16.

ושמחתם and you shall rejoice. See Leviticus 23:40.

חצצרת trumpets, trumpets of. See Numbers 10:2.

795

מטמון *matmon*. treasure; hidden or secret thing.

שפתיה her lips. See Numbers 30:7.

התשיעי the ninth. See Numbers 7:60.

Κεστος. *Kestos*. Literally, stitched, embroidered. Latin *cestus*. A girdle, especially the girdle of Aphrodite (Venus), gave the wearer the power to exiting love.

796

משנתו out of his sleep. See Genesis 28:16.

תקצור you shall reap, you reap. See Leviticus 25:5.

בחצצרות on the trumpets. See Numbers 10:8.

797 (prime)

עצם הכבוד *etzem ha-kabode*. essence of glory, referring to the 13th Path. Mem = 600, see 237

גמל מים למד Letter-name *Gimel-Mem-Lamed* spelled in full. See 237

שמים + גאה + חפשי *shamaim* + *gaw'ah* + *hawphyshiy*. the heavens + to grow, increase, be lifted up + free. The lifting of one's consciousness to the higher planes, symbolized by the heavens, through the path of Gimel is what sets us free. See 398, 399.

798

חלם ישודת *Cholom yesodoth*. Breaker of the foundations; name attributed to the sphere of the elements, i.e., Malkuth (Variant spelling). חלם means breaker, to bind, to dream, see the visions. Suggest the breaking up of mental complexes portrayed in Key 16 and the awakened inner vision that can emerge. See 564, 496, 78.

אמאימון *Amaimon*. According to the Goetia, Demon king of the element Earth and the North, the Demon King of the East [Godwin, 1999, p. 18]. Nun = 700, see 148 & Appendix 11.

משחיתם I will destroy them, destroying them. See Genesis 6:13.

שפחתי my handmaid. See Genesis 16:2.

ושבצת and you shall weave.

799

השפחות the handmaids. See Genesis 33:1.

Section 8

Numbers 800-899

800

ף Mouth (as an organ of speech). Value of the letter Peh is its final form. The letter of Mars is pictured in Key 16 as the lighting-struck tower. Connects Netzach (Venus) and Hod (Mercury) as the Exciting Intelligence path on the Tree of Life. The human body designates the Mars center or alchemical "metal," which stimulates the reproductive organs. In Yoga, this center, called by the Hindus Svadistthana chakra, is the seat of the apas tattva, the tattva of Water. See 80, 85, 899.

קשת archer, bowman; bow, rainbow, penis (as a Mishnaic or Talmudic word), arc, arch, violin bow. Hebrew for Sagittarius. Symbolizes the differentiation of light's vibratory activity into color, when the "water" of consciousness has been mingled with the "fire" of cosmic Life-breath. The rainbow colors are those of the seven planetary centers brought into harmonious activity by the occult use of color and sound to bring opposites to bear on one another. They correlate with the solar spectrum's bow - the sun's white light divided into 7 primary colors (connects with the Greek myth of Iris, the feminine messenger of the Gods). Thus the perfect coordination of the 7 principles of human personality is the interior stars' balanced activity.

I. "A symbol of the higher mental plane forms a bridge between the higher and lower natures (heaven and earth). The rainbow is a peculiarly appropriate symbol of the 'bridge of heaven,' caused as it is by the reflection of the sun (the self) in the water-drops (truth) forth pouring from the cloud (Buddhi) to the earth (lower nature). When the lower nature full reflect, the higher, then the 'bridge' may be transverse the victorious Egos returning to their home above." [Gaskell, 1981, pp. 609-610.]

II. Jacob Boehme: "The rainbow is the sign and token of this covenant, that man has created out of three principles into an image, and that he should live in all three. For the rainbow has the color of all the three principles; viz. the color of the first principle is red and darkish brown, which betokens the dark and fire world, that is the kingdom of God's anger. The second principle's color is white and yellow, signifying a type of the holy word of God, love. The third principle color is green and blue; blue form the chaos, and green form the water or saltpeter... This bow is a figure of the last judgment showing how the inward perpetual world will again manifest itself and swallow up the outward world of four elements." [Mysterium Magnum, p.207]

שרש *shoresh*. a root (of a plant), source, origin; stock, race, genus. Bottom, lowest part; the stem of a word. Indicates that whatever significance there may be in the word קשת "the bow" will lead to a better understanding of the root or fundamental reality from which spring all forms of growth and development. The rootless root concentrates the Limitless Light and sets up the double activity of that restrictive, boundary-setting phase of the Life-power symbolized by Saturn. See 60, 850, 37.

תת *Tath*. Profuse. A title of Kether-The Profuse Giver (לז תת). See 837.

שך *soke*. abode, dwelling, booth, pavilion. With different pointing: thorn. The first two letters of שכל, intelligence. Kaph = 500, see 320.

רם *ram*. High One, lofty, elevated, exalted. Applied to the spirit of brother C.R. Mem = 600, see 240, 340.

לרקיע שמים *la-rawqiya shamaim*. firmament of heaven. In Genesis 1:8: "And Elohim called the firmament heaven." (When Lamed is used as a preposition, it means: to, into, at, near; regarding, in regard to; belonging to, of; according to, after, by; towards, against, during.) Heaven is literally "what is heaved up" and means "names" - the creative name or word (IHVH). It is composed of the union of fire with the waters, or Chokmah and Binah. God is here translated Elohim, the creative powers of strength. See 90, 390.

לו זהב עפרת *aferoth zawhab lo*. It has dust of gold [Job 28:6]. The opening verses where this is found are invested with great occult significance. One of the clues to the hidden meaning is the word ארץ, Eretz, Earth. See 291, 78, 14.

לבבכם ערלות *awreloth lebabikem*. foreskins of your heart. In Jeremiah 4:4: "Circumcise yourself with IHVH, and take away the foreskins of your heart." This should explain the phallic coloring of Qesheth.

קן *qen*. cell, chamber, room, nest. Mem = 700, see 150.

תשמדון you will be destroyed. See Deuteronomy 4:26.

η δυναμις μεγαλη. *he dynamis megaleh*. The great power. In Acts 8:10: "To whom they all gave-heed from the least to the greatest, saying, this man is the great power of God." The name was given Simon Magus by the Samaritans. His name (Simon) means "hearing."

Furthermore, he was converted, and though he fell into an error, for which he was rebuked by Peter in Acts 8:20-3: ("But Peter said to him, 'May your silver go to destruction with thee because thou has thought to buy the gift of God with money; for I see that thou art in the gall of bitterness, and in the bond of wickedness.") He accepted the rebuke and asked for Peter's prayers. Later traditions which make out that Simon Magus was an opponent of Christians, have no scriptural basis. See 466, 1480.

Κυριος. *Kurios*. Lord. One of the titles of Jesus. Used throughout the Septuagint translation of the Old Testament for IHVH. In the New Testament [Mark 13:36 and elsewhere], it is also frequently used in the same way. See 644, 1000 (Greek) 1768, 656, 1480, 1408, 1844.

πιστις. *pistis*. Faith; expectant confidence, trust in others, belief; persuasion of a thing; assurance, good faith, faithfulness, honesty. Also: credit, trust; that which gives trust or confidence, an assurance, pledge of good faith, warrant. A means of persuasion, an argument, proof. Not to be confused with belief or creeds, or even with belief in a teacher's sincerity and dependability. Faith, as St. Paul says, is the substance of things hoped for. It is expectant confidence, founded on repeated experimental verifications of the basic principles of knowledge and wisdom. In Ephesians 4:5 ("One Lord, one faith, one immersion."), kupios and pistis are brought into immediate juxtaposition. See 1304, 1581, 1628.

Κοσυου. World.

801

אתת *othoth*. signs; tokens.

אף *ahf*. anger, wrath, passion. Also: nose, nostrils. In Proverbs 22:24: "Make no friendship with a man of anger, and with a man given to wrath, you shall not go." Unbalanced Mars (Peh) through speech is suggested here. Peh = 800, see 81.

A + ω *Alpha and Omega*. The first and last letters of the Greek alphabet. They express the ideas of basis and completion, necessary for the Great Work in which all students of occultism seek to participate. A name for Christ Revelations 1:8. See 1480, 9, 324, 419, 1, 900.

802

בנימן *Benjamin*. a tribe of Israel associated with Scorpio. Nun = 700, see 152.

תבת An ark, as of Noah. In Genesis 6:14: "So make yourself an ark of cypress wood; make rooms in it and coat it with pitch inside and out." see 407 (תבה) for commentary.

נקם ברית *tehebath*. Vengeance for the covenant. In Leviticus 26:25: "and I will bring a sword upon you, which shall avenge the breaking of the covenant; and you shall flee to your cities; I will send pestilence among you, and you shall be delivered into the hand of the enemy." The covenant is that between God, Abraham and Moses, regarding spiritual Israel. See 612.

213

803

גף *gaf.* back, top; body, person. Peh = 800, see 93.

באתת by signs. See Deuteronomy 4:34.

ומשנאתב because he hated. See Deuteronomy 9:28.

804

אגף *Aqaf.* troop, squadron; shut a door. See 84.

תשמטנה you shall let it rest [the land unplowed on the seventh year]. See Exodus 23:11.

משתחוים were bowing down. See Genesis 37:9.

805

דיד נאמן *Dode neheman.* faithful friend. See 155.

הקשת the bow, the rainbow. See Genesis 9:14.

קשתה cruel. See Genesis 49:7.

806

עדן כבוד *Eden Kabode.* Eden (paradise) of glory. Applied to the 16th Path of Vav. Nun = 700, see 156, 177, 124, 32.

עין יהוה *ayin Jehovah.* the eye of Tetragrammaton. Nun = 700, see 156.

ציון *Zion*, the holy of holies. Nun = 700, see 156, 105.

שותק *shotheq.* silent; the condition of gaining inner receptivity, i.e., intuition. See 815.

רום *rom.* unicorn. With different pointing: *room*: height, loftiness, pride; to rise up, on high, a title of Kether. Mem = 700, see 246.

את בל ארץ החועלה *eth ha-havilah.* The whole land of Havilah. In Genesis 2:11: "The name of the first [river] is Pishon: that is it which compasses the whole land of Havilah, where there is gold." see 804, 59, 291, 50, 401.

נושנת old. See Leviticus 13:11.

קשות jars, jars of. See Numbers 4:7.

807

ראום *Raum. Goetia* demon by night of the 1st decan of Taurus. Mem = 600, see 247.

סמן זית *shemen zayith.* olive oil. In Exodus 27:20: "and you shall command the children of Israel, that they bring you pure olive oil beaten for the light, to cause the lamp to burn always." see 390.

תאות the utmost bound. See Genesis 49:26.

תתאו you shall mark out. See Numbers 34:7.

אותת signs. See Deuteronomy 6:22.

808

נחשתן *Nehushtan.* the bronze serpent. Name given by Hezekiah to the brazen serpent of Moses. In 2 Kings 18:4: He broke into pieces the bronze serpent Moses had made. For unto that time, the Israelites had been burning incense to it. (It was called Nehushtan). See 358.

תחת *tachath.* Under.

אברהם *Abraham.* Father of many Nations, referring to Abraham. "Nations" esoterically are the million of body cells not directly concerned with the control the functions of the body, as are the more highly specialized cells known as the twelve tribes. Mem = 600, see 248, 59, 248.

חף *Chaf.* pure, innocent. Peh = 800, see 88.

חשך *Choshekh, kheshek.* darkness, adversity.

Also, the 9th of the ten plagues against Egypt. Kaph = 500, 328, 444, 924, 380, 541.

מאזנין *mozenin.* scales, balances [Chaldean]. Refers to the zodiacal sign Libra, corresponding to Justice (Key 11) in Tarot. Nun = 700, see 158.

בציון *be-Tzion.* in Zion. Nun = 700, see 158, 156, 513.

רחם *racham.* carrion bird; vulture. Mem = 600, see 248.

קול יהוה אלהיך *kol IHVH Elohekah.* the voice of Tetragrammaton. Mem = 600, see 248.

809 (prime)

גוף *guf.* The physical body, person, substance, essence, or one of the four elements. Peh = 800, see 89.

הדף *hadaf.* To cast out, to drive out, eject. See 89.

טף *taf.* children. Peh = 800, see 89.

תבראת the fruits, the increase crops of [the land]. See Leviticus 23:39.

810

אל חי העולמים *El Chai Ha-Olahmim.* Living God of Ages. Mem = 600, see 250.

באברהם *be-Abraham.* by or through Abraham. See 250.

הב בראם *beh bawreahm.* He created them with Heh (ה). See 250.

ב׳הבראם *behibawream.* When they were created. Heh is raised to hint that it represents the second Heh in IHVH, called "the upper, or superior Heh." This corresponds to the Sephirah Binah, to the element Water, and Briah, the creative world. Mem = 600, see 250, 813 (Greek).

דרום *dawrom.* south, south wind; killed by the beast. See 250.

סימן *simahn.* mark, sign, omen; symptom, paragraph. Nun = 700, see 160.

אנטימן *Antiman.* Antimony. The metal of the earth. It is a cleansing and purifying agent. Nun = 700, see 160.

קין *Qahyin.* Cain; a lance or spear; that which is pointed. Nun = 700, see 160.

מכל עץ הגן אכל תאכל *mee.kol atz ha-gen ah.cok to.kayl* you are free to eat from any tree of the garden. See Genesis 2:16.

I. "אכול תאכל *feeding thou-mayest-feed-upon...* Here is a word, which, as the result of contraction, has become very difficult to understand, on account of the resemblance that it has acquired with certain different words that come from another root, and with which it can easily be confused. Its proper root must be sought for carefully, for Moses has attached great importance to this point. One can see by the pains that he has taken to repeat twice the same verb, first, as continued facultative, and afterward, as temporal future.

This root is עול, elementary matter, unknown substance, symbolized here by the universal convertible sign place between those of physical sense and expansive movement. This root, which is conserved wholly in the Greek νλη, was famous among the Egyptians who made it play an important role n their mythology. One finds in Ethiopic the word *achal* signifying *substance, essence, matter, nourishment.* Element and aliment hold to this through their common root.

Furthermore, this root is used in Hebrew only in a restricted sense, *to nurse an infant,* to give it its first nourishment. One finds עולל to designate an infant at the breast. When the Chaldaic punctuation materializes this root in making consonantal the mother vowel ו, it develops ideas of injustice, crime and perversity.

But if, instead of materializing the vowel, the character of the physical sense ע, is softened by substituting the sign of assimilated life כ; then this root wrote thus, כול, expresses ideas of apprehension, of violent shock; of measure, of substantiation; if it is reduced to the single character כל, one obtains by this contraction, the analogous ideas of assimilation, of substance, and of consummation, whether one considers the action of consummation or of consuming. At this point, Moses has taken it and giving it the exalted meaning he conceived, he has made it rule by the sign of the power א. In this state, the verb אכול which is formed has signified *to feed upon*, that is to say, *to assimilate to one's self elementary matter as food.*

It must be remembered that the root עול of which we are speaking is precisely the same as that which the Samaritan translator used to render the substance called עץ, by Moses, and the objects of alimentation expressed by the verb אכול." [d'Olivet, 1976, pp. 82-84.]

II. Swedenborg affirms that "to 'eat of every tree,' is to know from perception what is good and true; for, as before observed, a 'tree' signifies perception." [Arcana Coelestia, p.61]

III. The Zohar [I:35B]: "Of all the trees of the garden thou shall surely eat. This means that he was permitted to eat them all together, for, as we see, Abraham ate, Isaac and Jacob ate, and all the prophets ate and remained alive. However, this tree was a tree of death, so far that he who ate by itself was bound to die since he took poison. Hence it says, in the day that thou eats thereof thou shall surely die because thereby he would be separating the shoots." (p.133)

IV. Gaskell, commenting on verse 16 + 17: "And instruction by intuition is delivered to the mind (man) that experience is to be acquired through the activities of the lower nature. But it is not through the intuitive sense of absolute right and truth in self-guidance that the main's earlier evolution is to be promoted, for this is impossible to the lower mind. At the period (day) when the soul ultimately arrives at a perfect knowledge of Truth, the lower mind (man) will cease to exist.

The natural course is otherwise, for at the stage when the fall of the ego into matter is accomplished, the direct perception of truth will cease from consciousness." [Gaskell, 1981, p. 767-768.]

קשתי my bow. See Genesis 9:13.

I. Gaskell: the bow in the cloud is "a symbol of the higher mind as the bridge between the higher nature and the lower... between the divine nature and the soul there is to be a channel, or bridge, for purposes of conscious intercommunication, which is to extend from the cloud (truth, wisdom) downwards; and this is the constitute the connection between the personality (earth) and Me, the Individuality, or the lower nature and the Higher." [Gaskell, 1981, p. 123.]

811 (prime)

שבט *Shebet*. rod, stick, staff or scepter. See 311.

בתבואת as the in gatherings, at the harvest. See Genesis 47:24.

IAΩ(O). Mystery term used by Greeks. Many ancient writers, it is believed to represent the Hebrew divine name IHVH, Tetragrammaton. In the Pistis Sophia, it is said: IOTA (I) because the universe hath gone forth; Alpha (A), because it will turn back again; Omega, because the completion of all completeness will take place." Lydus, in De Mensibus, says IAO is Phoenician and relates it to Dionysus and to Sabaoth. The Eleusinian name for Dionysus was Iacchus. It IAO be regarded as a Greek spelling of a Phoenician word, its letters stand, without question, for יהו, Yahoo. This special divine name is so important in the *Sepher Yetzirah*, directly related to the Cube of Space. See 901.

812

בנימין Tribe of *Benjamin*. "son of the right hand." Sagittarius. Nun = 700, see 162.

בהקתה when she was having difficulty. See Genesis 35:17.

האתות the signs.

משבתיכם your habitations, your dwellings. See Exodus 35:3.

813

אראריתא *Ararita*. a name of God; acronym for Achad Rosh Achdotho Rosh Ichudo Temurahzo Achad, "one is His Beginning, one is His individuality, His permutation is one."

ויבדל אלהים בין האור ובין החשך The Elohim separated the light from the darkness.

I. "ויבדל, *and-he-made-a-division*... The verb דבל springs from the two contracted roots בד דל. By the first בד, should be understood every idea of individuality, of isolation, of solitary existence: by the second בל, every kind of division, of opening, of disjunction. The verb here alluded to signifies the act of particularizing literally, isolating one from another, making a solution of things, distinguishing them, separating them, etc. Moses employs it here according to the intensive form to give it more force." [d'Olivet, 1976, p. 34.]

II. The Zohar [I:160] says: "And God divided: he put away strife, so that the whole was in perfect order" (p.70); and in [32A, p.121] "As for the words, 'And God divided the light from the darkness,' this means that he prevented distinction between them.' Said Rabbi Isaac: 'Up to this point, the male principle was represented by light and the female by darkness; subsequently, they were joined together and made one'... Rabbi Simeon said: 'the world is created and established based on a covenant, as it is written, 'if not for my covenant with the day and night, I had not appointed the ordinances of heaven and earth.' [Jeremiah 33:35]. This covenant is the Zaddik (righteous one), the world's foundation [i.e., Yesod]. Therefore the world is established on the covenant of day and night together, as stated in our text, the "ordinances of heaven' being those which flow and issue forth from the celestial Eden.' Also, in [46A p.142-143], "The expression, 'God saw the light that it was good' means really 'God decided that the light should be only good,' that is, that it should never be an instrument of wrath (cf. 'that it was good in the eyes of the Lord to bless Israel,' (Number 24:1); and this is proved by the end of the verse, 'and God divided the light from the darkness.' He afterward united light and darkness, yet this light continued to emanate from the supernal radiance, and through that radiance to bring gladness to all. This also is the right hand through which the most deeply graven letters [יהו of the sacred name] are crowned... The treasuring up of the primal light is referred to in verse, 'how great is your goodness which thou has laid up for them that fear thee, which thou has wrought for them that trust in thee' [Psalm 31;20]."

III. F.J. Mayers: "As a man may look in upon himself and consider the capabilities and qualities of his own mental prowess, so we are told, did God look upon himself... saw that it was 'good' suited to carry out his purpose and power for the task. So he set it in opposition to the 'darkness,' separated it absolutely from the darkness as a 'being of light' to shine into the darkness. Thus the divine intelligence becomes, within chaos, a separative, selective, ordering force. It draws forth from the 'deep' all he needs (and as he requires it) for the 'realization of his every purpose.' Thus universal 'intelligence' was the first manifestation of the deity." [The Unknown God, p.30]

ויאמר אלהים יהי אור ויהי אור and God [Elohim] said, "let there be light." Genesis 1:3.

According to Fabre D'Olivet ויאמר, *and-he-said*... It can be seen by etymology that it signifies not only *to say* but, according to the occasion, it can attain a signification much more exalted. Now, is the occasion more important than that in which beings manifest their creative will? To understand it in the literal sense only is to degrade it and is detrimental to the writer's thought. It is necessary to spiritualize this word's sense and guard against imagining any sort of speech. It is an act of the will and, as is indicated by the hieroglyphic compositions of the verb אמֹר, a power which declares, manifests and reflects itself without, upon the being which it enlightens. See 207 for D'Olivet commentary on אור, light and 31 for his commentary on ויהי, *and-there (shall be)-became.*

βριαρυς. Weight.

814

אבן אפל *ehben ophel*. the concealed (hidden) stone. Stone of thick darkness. Nun = 700, see 164.

אבן פלא *ehben pehleh*. the wonderful stone. Nun = 700, see 164.

חיצון *khitzon*. outer, external, exoteric. Nun = 700, see 164.

חורם *Churam*. Chiram or Hiram Abiff. The personification of the Christos in the Roman allegory. Analyzed as רוח, whiteness, and רם *ram*, height. The spelling of Hiram is used in 2 Chronicles. Mem = 600, see 254.

שכל תמידי *Seykel temidiy*. Perpetual Intelligence. The 21st Path of Shin. Connects the sphere of Mercury (Intellect) to that of the Earth (Sensation). This path's power works to perfect every one of its personal vehicles by providing them with the new creature's spiritual body-a physical body freed from the necessity for birth and death. Then the physical vehicle can be "laid down" and taken up again. Gabriel, another aspect of the Ego, is the angel working here to bring 4-dimensional consciousness into the personality level- the truth that one already has eternal life. This is the path of the Holy letter of "The Life-breath of the Creative Powers" (Elohim). It is the fiery and electric prana, the energy source of all conscious activity, the center of the One Self. The possessor of this path learns to direct the Life-breath through the creative use of imagery and sound. He knows that human life, even now, extends beyond the limits of the physical world because he has directly experienced it. See 454, 478, 360, 300, 86, 464.

רחום *Rachum*. merciful, compassionate. Mem = 600, see 254.

וחשך *ve-kheshek*. and darkness. Kaph = 500, see 334, 1389.

η θεια σοφια. *heh thela sophia*. The divine wisdom.

ο ενεργης λογος. The powerful word.

815

בעל אדמת נכל in a strange land.

שתיקה *shethiqah*. silence.

התקדשו sanctify yourself. See Numbers 11:18.

Μακαριοι οι ειρηνοποιοι. *makarioi hoi eirehnopoio*. "blessed are the peacemakers"; one of the beatitudes. Matthew 5:9: "blessed are the peacemakers; because they will be called sons of God." Recall that inner peace is שלום. See 370, 376, 745, 181 (Greek), 987.

816

מעון *mahown*. dwelling place, temple, lair, den. Nun = 700, see 166.

עליון *oliun, elyon*. the Most High; the Supreme, title of Kether. See 166.

דברים *devarim*. words; Hebrew title of Deuteronomy, the 5th book of the Bible. Mem = 600, see 256, 345.

שועתם their cry (for help) see Exodus 2:23.
ושמעת and hear, and you will obey. See Deuteronomy 4:30.

817

חרטם *chartom.* magician, sage. Mem = 600, see 257.

פורלאך *Phorlakh, Phorlak.* Ruling angel of element Earth. Kaph = 500, see 337.

אורים *Urim.* lights; one half of a priestly divinatory device. Mem = 600, see 257.

אסימון *Asimon.* The unnamable one; a demon, associated with the north-west. Nun = 700, see 167, 767.

818

חירם *Chiram.* Hiram: 1. King of Tyre; 2. architect of the Temple of Solomon. See 258.

ובקשתי and with the bow. See Genesis 48:22.

מושבתיכם your habitations (dwellings). See Exodus 12:20.

819

נטשתי suffer me, allow (let) me. See Genesis 31:28.

820

I. Σ40 = 820

ורדים *veradim.* roses. 260.

כרם *kerem.* vineyard. 260.

כף Letter name *Kaph.* Rock, hand. See 100.

תשעים *tishim.* ninety (90). Value of מים, water and Tzaddi fishhook. Genesis 6:7.

ניסן *Nisan.* Nisah, the 1st month of the Jewish calendar [or seventh, if counting from the new year]. Corresponding to March-April and is

similar to the period ruled by Aries in the zodiac. Nun = 700, see 170.

821 (prime)

והשקית you shall give her to drink. See Numbers 20:8.

ο αληθινος λογος. *ho alethinos logos.* The true logos.

822

חדרים *khadarim.* secret places, conclaves; chambers. Mem = 600, see 262, 367 (Greek), 825.

יכין + שבלת *shibboleth + yawchin.* a flowing stream (i.e., custom, habit) + he will establish, firm one, i.e., the creative power of the one thing, which is the royal secret (silence) of the Life-power's reign. See 732, 90.

שבלת מים waterflood. In Psalm 69:15: "Let not the waterflood overflow me, neither let the deep swallow me up, and let not the pit shut her mouth upon me." see 732, 90.

שבעתים sevenfold, seven times. See Genesis 4:15.

αφθαρσια. *athanatos.* Immorality, eternal existence. 1 Corinthians 15:53, 54: "For this corruptible must put on incorruption, and this mortal must put on immortality. So when this corruptible shall have put on incorruption, and this mortal shall have put on immortality, then shall be brought to pass the saying that is written, death is swallowed up in Victory." see 1 Timothy 6:16.

823 (prime)

תחתיה in its place. See Leviticus 13:23.

דם כר *Dam-Car*. Blood of the lamb. The locale of R.C. See 264.

אדרא רבא קדישא *Idra Rabba Qadish*. Greater Holy Assembly.

ויתחת in his stead, place. See Genesis 36:33.

תתחטאו purify yourselves. See Numbers 31:19.

הקדמוני ים *yawm ha-qadmoni*. the primordial sea. A Title of Binah, the great deep or abyss of chaos, whose root is in the אין *Ain* or unmanifest. Mem = 600. See 265.

לאבן הלבנה *ha-lebanah le-ehben*. Brick for stone. See 175.

בועז יכין *Jahkin-Boaz*. The two pillars. See 175.

נעשתה being done. See Numbers 15:24.

ο πετρος. *ho petros*. The stone (Peter).

עונן *aoon*. to conjure, do magic, soothsay. See 176.

נסיון *nisyon*. trial, temptation.

צמצום *tzimtzum*. contraction.

התבודדות *hitbodedut*. meditation.

גן עדן *Gan Eden*. Garden of Eden. Nun in גן = 500, See 177.

משפחת clans of. See Genesis 10:32.

וכתבת and imprints, and marking off. See Leviticus 19:28. Translated, and you shall write in Deuteronomy 27:3.

כתבואת as the increase of, the product of [the threshing floor]. See Numbers 18:30.

תבואתך of your produce, increase. See Deuteronomy 14:28.

האדרא רבא קדישא *Ha Idra Rabba Qadisha*. The Greater Holy Assembly. One of the 3 books in The Kabbalah Unveiled by Mathers. It is also abbreviated I.R.Q.

יששכר Tribe of *Issachar*. He will bring a reward [Genesis 49:14]. Associated with Capricorn and alchemical fermentation (Godwin associates this with Cancer). Fermentation involves the process of leavening the personal subconscious with the idea that the Life-power is the universal solvent. When the leaven of superconscious has been received, through suspension of personal identification with events and actions which occur through, rather than by, it begins to operate subconsciously. It agitates and excites through the Saturn center at the base of the spine, and its energy is combined with the force of the Mars center. Human nature is intensified at this stage, but proper self-conscious attention applies to seeing through the outer world's mixtures of appearance. Renewal of the mind is thus effected. According to Jacob's blessing, "Issachar is a sturdy ass, lounging among the ravines; he saw that settled life was good, and that the land was pleasant; so he offered his shoulder to bear burdens, and became a gang-slave." The predominance of Earthy imagery in these lines is made clear by the American Translation. Furthermore, one of the ancient symbols of the sign Capricorn is the ass. See 7, 95, 30, 570, 50, 54, 331, 358, 708.

"The 26th path is called the Renewing Intelligence because thereby God... blessed by He!... renews all things that are begun afresh in the creation of the world." [Yetziratic Text]

תלת telahth. three, third (Aramaic). Suggest that the spirit, as ox-goad (Lamed), is the third principle working between the soul (the 1st Tav or divine soul as world-dancer in Key 21) and the body (the 2nd Tav as representing Saturn and the physical form). In this interpretation, Lamed, though work or action, is the "flying serpent." See 430.

בריחים beriyakhim. bars, bolts, latches; axes, clavicles, shoulder-blades, flying serpents. Mem = 600, see 270.

יהוה בקרבך IHVH be-qirebbek. Tetragrammaton is the midst of thee. Kaph = 500, see 350.

פשתים linens. See Leviticus 13:47.

נפשת body, person. Leviticus 21:11.

υε κυε hye kye. An esoteric term in Eleusinian rites. Hippolytus is his refutation of all heresies, says, "This is the Christ who in all who have been generated is the portrayed son of man from the unportrayable Logos. This is the Great unspeakable mystery of the Eleusinian rites-Hye Kye." Here Hippolytus gives an account of the Nasseri's doctrines, a sect of Christian Gnostics, who worshiped the Logos under the serpent's name and image. Their name is itself from נחש, Nahkhash. See 130, 780, 358, 17.

831

אלף letter-name Aleph. Ox; family, clan, cattle; to teach or instruct. The ox or bull of solar fire. See 111.

לאתת le-oththo. for signs [Genesis 1:14] Also, with different vowel points: to moisten grain.

η μεστης. he mesotes. The mean, middle or midst. A mean between two extremes. Christian Gnostic designation of the Ogdoad [Thrice Greatest Hermes, 2:25] is also called "Jerusalem above."

μακροκοσμος. Makrokosmus. Macrocosm. See 901.

πυραμις. pyramis. Pyramid. An Egyptian (Greek) word. Means "fire in the middle" and is a proper late Aleph symbol, the spiritual fire in initiation. See 901.

φαλλος. Phallus. membrum virile. Inman: The ancient emblem of creation was usually made of the wood of the fig tree, under the name Φαλης. He was considered an inferior deity and companion of Bacchus. His name survives, as palus in Latin, pfahl in German, and pole in English. The May-pole was one of his emblems, and he was frequently adorned with bells. The word may take its origin in the Phoenician, in some such word as פלש, palash, or פלש palas, 'he breaks through, or presses into;' or we may derive it from the Greek παλλω, pallo, 'to brandish preparatory to throwing a missile,' etc., Pallas, or Minera, coming from the same root. In the Sanskrit, we have phal signifies 'to burst,' 'to produce,' 'to be fruitful'; phala is 'a plowshare,' and is also a name of Siva; and phul signifies 'to blossom;' all covering the idea of fully ripe fruit or pod, ready to eject the seed which it contains. [Inman, 1942, Vol. 2., pp. 472-473]

832

יהוה איש מלחמה יהוה שמו IHVH Ish Milchamah IHVH Shemo. The Lord is a man of war; IHVH is His Name (Exodus 15:3).

מציון מכלל יפי + קדושו mi-Tzion mikelahl-yophi + qedosho. Out of Zion, the perfection of beauty + his holy one. The divine shines from the holy center within. It is the power of desire that transforms the "child of the earth" into "his holy one." See 416.

לבנת ספיר *lebenath sephir. albedo crystalls*, the whiteness of crystals. The crystalline structure in the brain is the adytum or Zion. Rosenroth in K.D.L.C.K. (p.497) says that this is one of the names given to Malkuth and is also attributed to the seven palatal or double letters attributed to the planets. He cites Exodus 24:10: "And they [Moses, Aaron, and the 72 elders] saw the God of Israel; and there was under his feet as it were a paved work of sapphire stone, clear as the color of the sky."

בשפתים with lips. See Leviticus 5:4.

833

חיות הקדש *Chayoth ha-Qadosh*. Holy Living Creatures; Angelic Choir associated with Kether. These are the Cherubim of Ezekiel's vision in Ezekiel 1:1 to 24. The four creatures of the apocalypse, shown in the four quarters of the arms of Freemasonry. They are Taurus, Leo, Scorpio, and Aquarius. This choir of angels is particularly referred to as Kether in Assiah. In attribution to the 4 letters of Tetragrammaton, they are Taurus: Heh; Aquarius: Vav, Scorpio Heh; and Leo: Yod. In alchemy, Leo is digestion, Scorpio putrefaction, Aquarius, dissolution, Taurus, congelation. These 4 signs are the 2nd, 5th, 8th, 11th (totaling 26), or IHVH. On the arms of Masonry, the Living Creatures indicate חורם אביו (Churam Abiv[1]). The motto on the arms is: קדש ליהוה [460], "holiness to the Lord" (833 +460 = 1293) see 460, 1293, 26, 78, 61, 32, 73, 31, 63, 620.

[1] Khurum Abiv, or Hiram Abiff. The name of the central figure in the legend of Freemasonry. See 273.

I. The Sepher Yetzirah says their course is like the "lightning-flash." Theirs is not a going forth in time as man perceives time or movement in space as man measures space. In its end and beginning are one, and the place thereof is That-which-is not. The mind of Adam falls from the center, which is Eden, into the semblance of the circumference, where he labors with pain. This exile is not forever. The gate shall not be guarded forever with the two-edged flaming sword. The sword is also the lightening-flash, and what is hidden is the return of that outgoing power to the source from where it proceeds. That is why it is written that the living creatures ran and returned.

II. These creatures are the elemental powers, which are the powers of the four letters of Tetragrammaton. They are the Holy Living Creatures seen by the prophet Ezekiel. They come into form by their appearance is the Glory of God which is the true substance of all things, and also the Holy Influence which descends through the paths of the Tree, and ascends again to be swallowed up in the abyss of radiant darkness for which Ain אין is the first veil." see C.23.

III. S.D.: Ch. I:33: "'And the Living Creatures rush forth and return.' this is what is said in Ezekiel 1:14 concerning the living creature, which it is accustomed to being said concerning those letters of the Tetragrammaton, which sometimes holds the last place and sometimes the first; as when Yod, rushes forth to the last place, and when it returns to the beginning again; and so also the letter Heh. Likewise, the Living Creatures are also said to rush forth when the Tetragrammaton is written with the final *Heh* because then the whole system of emanations is exhausted. But they are said to return when the Tetragrammaton is written with the final *Yod*, so that the sense may be collected in such a manner as to return from the last path of the queen into the penultimate of the foundation, which is designated י, *Yod*...." [Mathers, 1993, p. 56]

IV. "The Qabalists by the term חיות הקדש, the Holy Living Creatures, understand the letters of the Tetragrammaton. Concerning the 'letters of the Tetragrammaton, which sometimes holds the last place, and sometimes the first,' the following are two examples-namely, as in the form יהוי, Yod, Heh, Vav, Yod, the letter Yod, is both at the beginning and the end of the word; and in the form which is more usual IHVH, Yod, Heh, Vav, Heh, the letter Heh, is in the second and last place." [ibid., 1993. p., 56].

עובה על רפשע avebah ahl raphasho. transiens super prevarications. Crossing over deviation from truth, or "overcoming falsehood." The deviation or lie is the false illusion of separation.

834

ועובר על פשע va-ghober ghal peshang. passing-over transgressions. IRQ (365): "What does this phrase teach 'passing over transgression'? שפע shepha, influence, it teaches, if Shin is placed before the Peh..." Note: This refers to the 3rd part of the bread of the Macroprosopus. The word פשע transgression, is the metathesis of שפע, influence, emanation, abundance. "300+ 80= ע+ ש+ פ + 70 = 450 = תן than, the dragon. Ergo, according to the exegetical rule of gematria, the dragon will be the symbol of the transgression. But 450 is also the numeration of פשע, influence: therefore, the dragon is also a symbol of influence and power. But this influence passes over into Microprosopus; now one of Pistorius's Qabalistical axioms is paradise is the sephirotic tree. In the midst thereof, the great Adam is Tiphereth.' Therefore the influence passing over into Microprosopus is also the serpent entering into the Garden of Eden." see 450.

תלדת generations, lines of. See Genesis 25:12.

835

לתתה to give her.

תעשינה shall [may] be done. See Leviticus 4:2.

ושפטתם and you shall judge. See Deuteronomy 1:16.

836

את גיד + חטאת eth-giyd + chattawth. The "sinew" with the creative essence + sin, punishment, a mist. The sinew is an esoteric reference to the diversion of nerve-currents of the Mars-force from the lower to the higher centers. The same word meaning "sin" also means the sacrifice which atones for it. [חטא to sin, miss the target].

See 418. חטא

האלף Halphas, i.e., ה-אלף ("the spirit"); Goetia demon by night of the 2nd decan of Aries. Peh = 800. See 116.

נפשות souls, members of. See Genesis 36:6.

837

תת זל Tayth Zal. the Profuse Giver. Kether and the number 1. See 736, 397, 620.

לסרבה lamarbah. for multiplying.

אלוף aluph. chief, duke (as the dukes of Edom, 51); head of a family or tribe; friend, intimate companion; tame, docile; a champion in a game; guide. Peh = 800, see 117 and Genesis 36:15.

פאימון Paimon. "tinkling sound"; demon King of Fire The Goetia demon by day the 3rd decan of Gemini. Nun = 700, see 187.

כי אם גלה סודו אל עבדיו הנביאים + אחבת kiy im-gawlah sodo el-aebawdawyou ha-naybiayim + ahabethaw. But he reveals his secrets (counsel) unto his servants the prophets + thou shall love. See 408.

838

כרובים Kerubim. Cherubim; "the strong" or "the mighty ones." Angelic Choir associated with Malkuth (some sources Yesod) and of Binah of Briah. Mem = 600, see 278, 272.

עולם המוטבע Olam ha-Mevetbau. Natural world.

בריחים + אהב beriyachim + awhab. flying serpents + to live, affection, desired, beloved. Serpents are connected with the "crooked serpent," also called Leviathan, the reproductive force. This must be transmuted into the beloved through love, which is the higher self-expression. See 830, 8.

בתולת a virgin of. See Deuteronomy 22:19.

839 (prime)

שלמים + אחרות *acheduth* + *shilemim*. unities + perfection, wholeness, peaceable. The 13th Path of Gimel, assigned to Key 2, the High Priestess, is the Uniting Intelligence. To this letter is assigned the pair of opposites, strife and peace. The memory of who and what we are brings wholeness and perfection. See 370, 376, 419, 420, 13.

צדקה שמש *shemesh tzedaqah*. Sun of righteousness; an epithet of Christ. In Malachi 4:2: "but for you who revere my name, the sun of righteousness will rise with healing in his wings..." see 640, 199, 1291 (Greek)

840

כנען *Canaan*, flat, low. Ham's son (הם, warmth, heat) and the Land of Palestine's original name, home-land of Israel. Nun = 500, see 190, 54, 160.

יהוה בקרבך *Jehovah be-qirebbek*. Jehovah in the midst. See 360.

צור ילבך *Tzoor yelawdekah*. Rock that begat thee. See 360.

שמך shemkah. your name. see 360.

פנין *Panin*. Pearl; one of the titles of Malkuth, the Kingdom. Nun = 700, see 190, 496.

מף *Moph*. Memphis, the capital of Egypt. A variant name-see 850. See 120.

לממשלת to rule, for-governing-of. in Genesis 1:16: "God made two great lights-the great light to govern the day and the lesser to govern the night."

I. "לממשלת, *for-a-symbolical-representation*... The Hellenist has translated this εις αρΧας, which is the most restricted interpretation; for, in short, it is evident that the sun and moon rule over the day and night. Indeed Moses would be but little understood if one were to stop at an idea so trivial. The verb שמול means, *to be ruler, judge*, or *prince*, but it signifies much oftener *to be the model, the representation, the symbol of something; to speak in allegories, in parables, to present a similitude, an emblem, a figure*. This verb is from the root שו which, containing in itself every idea of parity, similitude and representation, is joined to the signs מ and ל, to express its exterior action and its relative movement in the phrase with which we are occupied, this verb is used according to the intensive form, and consequently invested with the continued facultative of the sign מ, which doubles the force of its action." [d'Olivet, 1976, p. 46-47.]

II. F.J. Mayers: "Then we have the word translated by 'to rule,' 'memesheleth'? the basic word is 'meshol,' it means, sometimes 'to preside,' 'to be a judge,' 'to rule,' but much more often it means 'to be a model,' a 'representative,' a 'symbol' of anything; 'to speak in allegories or parables,' to present a 'similitude, or emblem, or figure of anything.' To go still a little farther into detail, the actual root of the word 'meshol' is 'sho,' which indicates ideas of 'parity,' similitude,' representation, etc. all this makes it quite clear that 'memesheleth' actually means 'symbolic representations of things to be.' [The Unknown God, p.52] see 641.

תמת let die. See Numbers 23:10.

משכנתיך your dwellings. See Numbers 24:5.

πνευμα αληθειας. Spirit of Truth.

841

I. (29 x 29) or 29^2

אפין *Anpin*. face, countenance.

AMΩ *amo*. The Latin word for (1) Love, in Greek characters. "A" corresponds to the tetrahedron, or Fire, M to the Octahedron, or Water and Ω to the cube and Air, suggesting the 3 mother letters of the Hebrew alphabet (see 341).

η πλινθος εις λιθου. *heh plinthos eis lithon*. Brick instead of stone. Septuagint translation of הלבנה לאבן (825) in Genesis 11:3: "And they had brick for stone, and slime had them for mortar." This refers to the substitution of the irrational desires of the animal nature for the impulses from above. The result is the disaster of the tower of Babel, pictured in Key 16. See 175, 825.

842

אראלים *Aralim*. Thrones. The choir of angels associated with Binah. See 282.

ארח חיי למעלה למשכיל *Awrach chaieh lemalelah le-maskil*. Proverbs 15:24: The way of life is above for the wise, (that he may depart from hell beneath). Note: *maskil*, wise, erudite, is a title of Yesod. See 400.

עמוד אש + כשוייעיה *ammud esh + kashuiyah*. a pillar of fire + the angel ruling Capricorn, the sign of the Savior. Capricorn is ruled by Saturn, the restrictor; the pillar of fire guides Israel by night. To depart from "hell," we must overcome the limitations of appearance. See 541, 421.

מכפירים יחידיתי *me-kephirim yechidawthi*. my darling from the lions. In Psalm 35:17: "Lord, how long will you look on? Rescue my soul from their destructions, my darling from the lions." [Jewish translation: "My only one from the lions"] In Psalm 34:10 רפירים is translated 'young lions." יחירה means the only one and is an epithet of the soul, of life, of Israel. יחירה means solitariness, loneliness, privacy, unity, oneness. See 300, 310, 37.

תשופנו shall bruise, you will strike him [the serpent, הנחש]. See Genesis 3:15.

843

צור ילדך + אב *tzur ye lawdekaw + ab*. the rock that begat thee + father. "The rock" is a title of God; it is identical to the life-force in Chokmah. See 840, 3, 296.

אריך אנפין + חזות *arikay ahnepin + hawzuth*. The vast or great countenance, title of Kether, + vision, revelation. The center of intention is the source of memory; the vision implies Beth as an image of cosmic memory in Kether. See 421, 422.

844

הכחות השלכים *ha-kachoth ha-Sekhelim*. intellectual virtues. Refers to all powers of consciousness are concentrated in Netzach, and the "Brilliant Splendor of all the intellectual power, which are beheld by the eye of faith. See 710, 1060, 660.

באר אלים *bar elim*. well of the Gods. Mem = 600, see 284.

כי לעולם חסדו *kay le-olahm ha-saeddu*. for his mercy endures forever. Mem = 600, see 284.

845

נפטון *Neptun*. Neptune.

תהמת the deeps, deep waters. Exodus 15:5,8.

846

וכנה אשר נטעה ימינך *ve-kanawh aesher-nateaw yaymiehnekaw*. the root your right hand has planted. In Psalm 80:15: " The root your right hand has planted, the son [branch] you have raised up for yourself." see 130, 610, 260. [כנה = plant, shoot; stand, ruler. As a verb כבה, give a name, give a title; to surname, nickname; to express by a substitute.]

תולדות *thuledoth*. generations, spelled in full. In Genesis 2:4: "These were the generations of the heavens and of the earth when they were created, in the day that the Lord God made the earth and the heavens." In Ruth 4:18: "Now these are the generations of Pharez: Pharez begat Hezron." Pharez means "a breach."

מורם *Murum. Murmus.* Goetia demon by night of the 3rd decan of Virgo. Mem = 600, see 286.

ותתם and was ended when she ended. See Genesis 47:18.

847

אל עליון *El Elyon.* Most High God.

עצם הבריאה + תהו בהו *etzem ha-briah + tohu-bohu.* essence of creation + without form and void. The essence of creation signifies the paternal force's essential nature, concentrated primarily in Kether, becoming the radiant Life-force in Chokmah. The blackness of the Abyss of the No-thing is only a veil hiding the most dazzling whiteness. See 423, 424.

848

הר אלהים הר בשן *Har-Elohim Har-Bashan.* The mountain of God (is) the mountain of Bashan [Psalm 68:15]. See 291, 352, 86.

ארבעה עשר *arba'ah-asar.* Fourteen (14); the number of the Tarot Key corresponding to Samekh, Temperance, Sagittarius, the Holy Guardian Angel, Michael, alchemical incineration and verification through test and trial. Mentioned as the measurement of the seat of the altar in the temple, in Ezekiel 43:17: "And the seat shall be 14 cubits long and 14 broad in its four squares, and the border about it shall be half a cubit, and the base of it shall be a cubit round about; and its steps shall look toward the east." see 60, 120, 162, 168.

מתחת *metahhat.* from under, below, which were under. Genesis 1:7. See 140 (from above).

849

מלאך המשחית *Malakh ha-Maschith.* Angel of Destruction.

אמונה אמון *Emunah Amen.* Creation of Faith, Firmness of Faith, Basis of Faith. See 199.

אמתחת sacks. See Genesis 44:1.

σχημα. *schema.* A form scene. In 1 Corinthians 7:31: "And those who are using this world, as not using it; for the form of this world is passing away."

μη ψοβεισθε. *meh phobeisthe.* Be not afraid. The words of Jesus to the disciples when walking on water in Mark 6:50: "For they all saw him and were terrified. And immediately he spoke with them, saying 'take courage, it is I; be not afraid.'" see 2352, 1053 (Greek).

Ωμεγα *omega.* Omega spelled in full, meaning: the last, the end. Spelled Ω in Revelations 21:6: "And he said to me, 'they have been done. I am the Alpha and the Omega, the beginning and the end. To the thirsty one I will freely give water from the fountain of life." see 800, 1, 532, 1443, 1536, 2072, 2257, 1998.

μεγας κοσμος. *megas kosmos.* Great cosmos. Cosmos is the universe-the intelligible world or order of all things, including the intelligible word or reason. See 600 (Greek).

η μονας εν τριαδι. *heh monas entriadi.* the one in three.

η τριας εν μοναδι. *heh trias en monadi.* The three in one. The last two phrases suggest the supernal triad of Kether, Chokmah, and Binah. See *A Preliminary Investigation into the Cabala*, pp. [43, 45].

נשרש *nesharash*. Radical, root (race). The 5th Path of Geburah. "So-called because it is akin to the primary force of the Archetypal Binah, which itself is enclosed within the strength of the Primordial Wisdom." The first 3 letters spell נשר, *nasher*, the noun meaning "eagle" and the last 3 form the noun שרש, *sharash*, "a root." Therefore, Radical Intelligence is the "Root of the Eagle." see 800, 1200, 216, 64, 92, 95, 297.

תכלת *tekheleth*. a violet tint (translated as blue). The Zohar (3:135A) says, "Tekeleth, corresponds to Passover, which established the dominance of the true object of faith, symbolized by the color blue, which would predominate after the punishment of the first-born of Egypt was accomplished, so all colors seen in dreams are of good omen, except blue." In Heraldry, blue is Jove or Jupiter, corresponding to the Egyptian Gon Amun, whose body was painted blue. In Freemasonry, and in the National arms of the U.S., blue represents Justice (דין). See 64 and Exodus 26:4.

כלף *kelef*. to clap or strike; a hammer. Peh = 800, see 130.

קדמון *qadmon*. ancient, old; archetypal. The epithet of God. Nun = 700, see 200, 86 (Greek).

מרים *Miriam*. Mary, sister of Moses, signifying "rebellion, perversity, antagonism. Mem = 600, see 290.

ללשנתם according to their tongues. Genesis 10:20.

תמתי *temathi*. my perfect one. In Canticles 5:2: it is written תאומתי "my twin sister." "I sleep, but my heart wakes: it is the voice of my beloved that knocks, saying, open to me my sister, my love, my dove, my undefiled: for my head is filled with dew and my locks with the drops of the night." Continuous redirecting the eagle upward establishes within the brain centers (Moon and Mercury) a tremendous reserve of the precious dew. Hod, sphere of Mercury is called the Perfect Intelligence. Thus this 'perfect one" has established the guidance of the angel as in Key 6 over self and sub-conscious modes of the personality-the heart are opened by Vav (assigned to Tiphareth or 6), and the "dove" (Venus), being purified and undefiled can hear the "voice" of the beloved, or higher self." "My sister" is Gimel or Memory, as the lesser Chokmah or wisdom. See 857.

ο οφις *ho ophis*. The serpent. A symbol of the evil and destructive aspects of the 5th Path of Geburah. See Revelation 12:9 & 15.

Ων *On*. On, an Egyptian God. It is declared of on that he "is, and never knew the beginning." In Genesis, Joseph married Asenath, daughter of the Egyptian priest of On and that Ephraim and Manasseh were children of that marriage. See 581.

אפיקי מים *Aphiqi mayim*. torrents of Water. See 291.

הר אלהים *har-Elohim*. Hill (or mountain) of God. See 291.

נשמתהון *neshemothon*. souls; mentions in IRQ [1052-1055]: in connection with the placing of Cain by God in the mouth of the great abyss or great sea: "And from that body descend the souls, *neshemothon*, of the impious, of the sinners, and of the hardened in spirit. From them, both at once, does thou think? No, but one flows down from one side and another from the other. Blessed are they just, whose *neshemothon*, souls are drawn from the holy body called Adam, which includes all things; the place, as it were, wherein all the crowns and the diadems are associated together, arrayed in the equilibrium of balance. Blessed are they just because all these are holy words which are comprehended; the spirit in whom the supernals and inferiors are collected together (otherwise, whom the supernals and inferiors hear)."

אמרים *amorim*. Amorites; the early inhabitants of

Palestine. Mem = 600, see 291 and Genesis 14:7.

ותהמת and depths, and springs. See Deuteronomy 8:7.

τε λεσται. *telestia*. Complete, fulfilled, mysterious. Generally, any religious ceremony, a solemnity, especially of marriage. See 800.

ΑΜΩ. The Beginning Alpha, the Middle Mu, and the End Omega. See 671.

η παναρχια. *heh panarchia*. The all-powerful; an epithet of deity.

μια πιοτις. *mia pistis*. One-faith. Ephesians 4:5: "One Lord, one faith, one immersion." see 800

παστος. *pastos*. A bridal chamber or bridal bed; a shrine. Related to the Rosicrucian mysteries.

Θεοτης + βασλεια. *theotes + basileia*. godhead + kingdom. "The kingdom of spirit is embodied in my flesh." see 592, 259 (Greek).

852

בן קשת *ben qesheth*. arrow, literally, "son of the bow. Spoken concerning Leviathan (496) in Job 41:28: "The arrow does not make him flee, sling stones are like chaff to him." Also designates a dart. Note that the primitive form of Beth, which denotes the "house" of personality, as well, like attention, concentration and self-consciousness, was an arrowhead and that the bow is connected with Samekh, Sagittarius and the Holy Guardian Angel, as "son" is with Tiphareth. " see 52, 800.

תוך + מושיע *moshiyah + tawvek*. Savior, deliverer; a title of Tiphareth + middle, center, midst; interior, inside. The son, says the Zohar, liberates the Shekinah from exile. This is affected by knowledge of man's true nature, the anointed, and the kingdom (Malkuth). Transformed into Israel or true rulership by the enlightened Ego, he can put new and better conditions in former ones. See 426.

η αγαπη πατρος . The father's love.

853 (prime)

נגף *negef*. plague. Peh = 800, see 133.

שכה תפוחים *sedeh tappuchim*. orchard of apples, or apple orchard. Rosenroth in K.D.L.C.K.(p.706) says that this fundamentally refers to Tiphareth; which is composed of three colors: red, white and golden yellow, corresponding to the likeness of apples: which are to two kinds, some inclined to Chesed, and others of Geburah-he cites several references throughout the Zohar.

החתמת the signet. Genesis 38:25.

854

אלהי אברהם *Elohi Abrham*. The God of Abraham.

נחש לויתן *Leviathan nachash*. Dragon, the sea-serpent [Isaiah 27:1]. See 496, 358.

מלכות משיח *Malkuth Mahshiah*. The Kingdom, Messiah.

ומתחת and underneath. See Deuteronomy 33:27.

855

וייצר יהוה אלהים + שלמים + דבא *vayi-yetzer IHVH Elohim + shilemim + dobeh*. "And IHVH Elohim formed (man out of the dust of the ground) + perfection, wholeness + strength, affluence, rest, quite. The "new creature" is formed by the cosmic father and mother working in the physical vehicle. A whole and perfect body of light give strength to the soul, permeated with inner rest. See 427, 428; 420, 7.

תמלא הארץ חמם *thimawlea ha-aretz hawmam*. The earth was filled with violence. In Genesis 6:11: "The earth also was corrupt before God, and the earth was filled with violence." These events took place before the great flood and Noah's ark. See 861.

תהלתך your glory, your praise. See Deuteronomy 10:21.

לא על הלחם לבדו יחיה האדם כי על כל מוצא פי יהוה יחיה האדם
Man does not live on bread alone but on every word that comes from the mouth of the Lord. See Deuteronomy 8:3.

856

ותתן and she gave. See Genesis 3:6.

תשפכנו you shall pour it out. See Deuteronomy 12:16.

857 (prime)

אלהים גבור *Elohim Gebur*. Literally, "Creative Powers of Strength," God the strong, God of battles. Mem = 600, see 297.

תהומות depths. Proverbs 3:19.

יהיו לאתת *yehawyou leothoth*. and let them before signs. In Genesis 1:4: "And God [Elohim] said, Let there be lights in the firmament of the heaven to divide the day from the night, and let them be for signs, and for seasons, and for days, and years."

אלה הדורים *Eleh ha-devarim*. "These be the words"; Hebrew title of the book of Deuteronomy. See 297.

ארך האבר + מני חשך *ereck ha-ebar + minni-khishek*. long pinions + out of the darkness. The overshadowing wings of spirit bring man's consciousness out of the darkness of ignorance into the light of truth. See 428, 429.

Λογος Θεου. *Logos theou*. Word of God.

858

אתה גבור לעולם אדני *Ateh Gibor le-Olam Adonai*. Thou art mighty forever, O Lord; "Your is the power of the eons, O Lord." In magical manuscripts, we often find the "name" אגלא, Agla as a Notariqon (shorthand) for the above. See 65, 76, 406, 1445, 1418, 211, 176.

בצלם אלהים ברא אתו *be-tzelem Elohim bara othu*. In the image of God created them.

רחמים *Rachamim*. Compassion, a title of Tiphareth. Mem = 600, see 298.

נשמת חיים *neshemath chaiim*. the breath of life. In Genesis 2:7: "And the Lord God formed man of the dust of the ground and breathed into his nostrils the breath of life, and man became a living soul. See 395, 68, 18.

I. "A being exalted, an essence of the lives," and comments: נשמת, a-being-exalted... The verb חושם, whose root שם expresses that which is exalted, employed according to the enunciative form, passive movement, as continued facultative, feminine construction." [d'Olivet, 1976, p. 75.] see 340.

II. The Zohar [I:49A] comments: "And he breathed into his nostrils the breath of life. The breath of life was enclosed in the earth, made pregnant with it like a female impregnated by the male. So the dust and the breath were joined, and the dust became filled with spirits and souls. And the man became a living soul. At this point, he attained his proper form and became a man to support and nourish the living soul." (P.156)

III. "A symbol of the spiritual essence-the divine spark, atma-buddhi, which is immortal… And into this lower mind, or astro-mental body was projected the divine spark, and thence the *man* (manasic being) became a creature capable of responsible, independent existence." [Gaskell, 1981, p. 126.]

IV. "We see that the letter Peh appears in 'dust' 'breathes,' 'nostrils' and that Shin appears in 'breath.' The result of the operation is Adam becoming a living *Nefesh*. Eighty [Peh] stands for all the undeveloped strata of energy. It is given life in *Adam* by *Shin* (300), the cosmic metabolism...

The truth is that this Genesis, this creation of a complete Adam, has not yet taken place-although it may now be in the process of becoming. We can begin to understand this allegory when-rather than imagining it as a mere myth of our remote past-we see that potentially, the complete Adam can come into being within us *now*. Adam is seeking birth, but we stifle it every day in its womb." [Suraes, 1992, p. 105.]

ואת המות *ve-eth ha-haweth*. and death. In Deuteronomy 30:15: "See, I have set before you this day life and good, and death and evil..." Life and death are the pair of opposites assigned to Mercury, which rules Gemini, or Key 6. Raphael symbolizes Mercury. The Tree of the Knowledge of Good and Evil is close to the woman, or sub-consciousness receptive to the angel. See 3760, 932 (Greek).

תחתים lower, lower ones. See Genesis 6:16.

ממישביכם out of your dwellings. See Leviticus. 23:17.

שכל רגוש *Saykel Regash*. Disposing Intelligence. Variant spelling without Heh (the), see 863.

נתבות *nethboth*. Paths, trodden paths. Variant spelling, see 868.

גיהון *Gihon*. The second river in the Garden of Eden is the Gihon; it winds through the entire land of Chush." Nun = 700, see 77, 446, 142, 680; 1560, 623, 1514 (Greek) and Genesis 2:13.

859 (prime)

η υπαρξις *heh uparksis*. Existence, subsistence, substance, goods, possessions. A technical term of the Gnosis. Thus Jesus word: "All that the Father hath is mine," explains the root-meaning

of the Chaldean Oracles: "Containing all things in the one summit of his own Hyparxis, he exists wholly beyond. See 1500, 801 and Hebrews 10:34.

Γετελεσται. *getelestai*. It is finished [John 19:30]. The last statement was made by Jesus on the cross after he had drunk the vinegar.

η ανω. *he ano*. the on high. In Galatians 4:26: "But the Jerusalem which is above [on high] is free, which is the mother of us all." This refers to the ogdoad-the spiritual state of praising God. See 831 (Greek).

φατνη. *phatne*. Manger, cave or grotto. The place where the infant Jesus was born in Luke 2:7, 12, 16. These two words, "It is finished" and "manger," refer to the alchemical death and initiation into the mysteries and to the place of the birth of the Christ-child. The cave is also the alchemical laboratory, where the Virgin's Milk is extracted and utilized. See Luke 2:7, 12, 16.

860

רוח אלהים *Ruach Elohim*. The Life-Breath of the Gods. The breath on the Mighty Ones, the Spirit of God. Mem = 600, see 300.

סף *saf*. sill, threshold, entrance. Peh = 800, see 140.

שפרפר *shepharefhar*. aura, dawn (Chaldean). Written בשפרפרא [at dawn, in the morning] in Daniel 6:19: "Then the king arose very early in the morning, and went in haste unto the den of lions." The last Peh here is the largest letter and the first Peh the smallest letter. See 863.

משענת *misheahnethey*. staff. In Psalm 23:4: "Yea, though I walk through the valley of the shadow of death, I will fear no evil: for you are with me; your rod and your staff they will comfort me." see, 880, 442 (Greek) and Key 9.

אשר שם הזהב *aesher shawm ha-zahab*. where there is gold. In Genesis 2:11: "The name of the first [river of Eden] is Pison: that is it which compasses the whole land of Havilah, where there is gold." see 126, 446, 59, 2825 (Greek).

מעמקים *ma'aemaqim*, depths. Mem = 600, see 300.

Ιησου Ναζαρηε. *Iesou Nazarehe*. Jesus, Nazarene. In Luke 4:34: (the obsessed man cried) "Saying, Let us alone; what have we to do with thee, thou Jesus of Nazareth? Art thou come to destroy us? I know thee who thou art; the holy one of God."

σκοτος. *skotos*. Darkness. Septuagint translation of חשך (328) in Isaiah 45:7: "I form the light and create darkness; I make peace and create evil-I the Lord, do all these things." see 328, 1740, 1753, 925.

αναζαω. *anazao*. To revive, to live again; of sin, to gain strength. See Romans 7:9 & 14:9.

861

שפרפרא *shaypharefara*. dawn. The definite or emphatic form of שפרפר, the Chaldean word for Dawn. See 860, 963, 990 (Greek).

אסף *ahsaf*. to collect, put away, store. See 141.

υτοπια. *Utopia*. Utopia.

τελεια μου. *telia mou*. My flawless one. Septuagint translation of תמת (850) in Canticles 5:2: "I slept, but my heart was awake: it is the voice of my beloved that knocks, saying 'open to me, my sister, my love, my dove, my perfect one: for my head is filled with dew, and my locks with the drops of the night." see 850.

Αποφις. *Apophis*. The destroying aspect of deity corresponding to A. in the mystery name IAO. Represents the elemental forces of the subconscious that aid personality evolution. Corresponding to Typhon, the terrestrial and material envelope of Osiris. See 70 (Lt), 203, 1871 (Greek).

αεωμ. *Eon*. World, universe; a billion years. Written αιωνιον in John 3:15: (14) "And as Moses elevated the serpent in the desert, so must the Son of man be placed on high; (15) that everyone believing into him may have aeonian life."

"Greek, *aion*, a period of time; a manifestation of life in time, a period of evolution; lifetime (from the Sanskrit root, 'to go,' the concept of time being inseparable from that of motion, and time is measured by the motion of the heavenly bodies in space). The God alone is Eternal or Boundless Duration; everything manifested has limits in time and space. The highest *aion* is the lifetime of the manifested universe, considered a conscious divine being. Each evolutionary cycle is the lifetime of the planetary system, of the earth, of a human race-is also an *aion* and collectively a being. The sidereal body (*soma pheumatikon*) of man endures throughout the life-cycle of the cosmos. So after the mystic birth 'from above,' his consciousness is continuous throughout all the lesser cycles of reincarnations, racial periods, etc. Which constitutes the great On-going or Day of the Gods." [Pryse, 1967, pp. 96-97.]

862

תבנית pattern, likeness. See Exodus 25:9.

863 (prime)

שכל שגרהה *Sekhel ha-Hergesh*. Disposing Intelligence. The 17th Path of Zain. Connects the divine soul of Binah to the Ego in Tiphareth. Gives the ability to know true discrimination based on accurate knowledge of reality-faith expressed by action. This is an intense, flaming Mercury activity, the "sword" as the narrow way of attainment. Discrimination is the fruit of love, which conquers death and gives immortality. Its source is the power of the divine soul. In alchemy, discrimination is used between the solar and lunar currents in the body to become a free channel for the cosmic Life-force. See 508, 513 and Appendix 12.

I. The Zain's path is called "the Foundation of Beauty in the place of the Supernals." The foundation is *Yesod*, the 9th Sephirah, the seat of the automatic consciousness and vital soul (Nephesh). Beauty is *Tiphareth*, the seat of the Ego-consciousness. The supernals are *Kether*, *Chokmah* and *Binah* and are part of the archetypal world (Fire). In this connection, note that Zain connects Binah to Tiphareth.

II. The path of Zain, Disposing Intelligence, suggests its name the supernal Binah's operation, Understanding, separating the creatures produced by the Constituting Intelligence (Heh) into species and classes. The fundamental separation is sex. And in this connection, the Path of Zain is Key 6, The Lovers, in the Tarot.

III. "I am the Disposing Intelligence, choosing with discrimination each step towards the one light which alone is pure in beauty." [Meditations on the Paths of Wisdom].

וירא אלהים *Va-ya-re Elohim*. and God saw.

תחתיהם was under them. See Numbers 16:31.

864

קדוש קדשים *Qadosh Qadeshim*. Holy of Holies.

שמש וירח *shemesh ve-yerach*. Sun and Moon; two important parts of the great work of regeneration. They correspond to the solar and lunar currents and their centers at the heart and pituitary microcosm. In Deuteronomy 4:19: "And when you look up to the sky and see the sun, the moon and the stars-all the heavenly array-do not be enticed into bowing down to them and worshiping things the Lord you God has apportioned to all the nations under heavens." see 640.

מתחתיו from his place. Exodus 10:23.

Ιερουσαλημ. *Ierousalem*. Jerusalem.

ο ναος αθανασιας. *ho naos athanasias*. Temple of immortality, and of the resurrection of the spiritual body. See 321.

οικος εκκλσιας. *oikos ekklesias*. House of the church. See 370, 294.

η πολις απειρος. *heh polis apeiros*. the city of the ignorant. See 390.

κοσμος αληεις. *kosmos aletheias*. true world or order. See 600, 264.

αθανασια σαρκος. *athanasia sarkos*. Immortality of the body. See 273.

προθευς. *protheus*. The most profitable [*Fama Fraternitatis*].

Κυριος δεμει. *kurios demei*. The Lord builds his tabernacle.

αγιων. *hagion*. Sanctuary. Septuagint translation of מקדש (444) in Ezekiel 44:1: "Then the man brought me to the outer gate of the sanctuary, the one facing east, and it was shut. (2) The Lord said to me, 'This gate is to remain shut. It must not be opened; no one may enter through it. It is to remain shut because the Lord, the God of Israel, has entered through it. (3) The prince himself is the only one who may sit inside the gateway to eat in the presence of the Lord. He is to enter by way of the portico of the gateway and go out the same way.'" The prince is the messiah or Christos. The sanctuary is the outer holy place and not the holy of holies. See 444.

865

נתתיה I give it, I give her. See Genesis 23:11.

תבואתנו our increase, our crops. See Leviticus 25:20.

סוף *Suph*. end, close, to limit, to perish. Peh = 800, see 146.

נקיון *niqqayone*. cleanliness, innocence. See 216.

שדי התפוחים Referred to in the Greater Holy Assembly or I.R.Q. (paragraph 553) concerning the dew from the skull of Macroprosopus. "And that dew, which distills, distills daily upon the field of apples, in color white and red." The apple תפוח is connected with the serpent-power (Shin) with Mars and with knowledge. See 494, 39.

ירכתי צפון *yarekethi tzafon*. Rosenroth in K.D.L.C.K. (p.457) gives: *latera aquionis* (sides of the eagle) and cites Psalm 48:3: "It is beautiful in its loftiness, the joy of the whole earth, is mount Zion on the sides of the north, the city of the great king." He says that some call these Netzach and Hod, for the influence from Geburah is called the North.

תשמעון you shall hear, hearken. See Deuteronomy 1:17.

משענתו his staff. See Exodus 21:19.

η μετανοια + ειρηνης. *heh metanoia + eirenes*. The repentance, reformation, change of mind plus peace, concord. See 381, 485.

Αδωναι. *Adonai*. Lord. Greek spelling of the Hebrew name of God.

בית השפע *Beth ha-shepha*. House of Influence, House of overflowing, House of Abundance. The intelligence of Cheth, the 18th Path. Beth, mercurial outpouring-the Life-power provides itself with a house' Yod, the Life-power unites all through will; Tav, this power is the dance of Life. Cheth, the whole universe is Life's definition of itself. Shin, the overflowing abundance of the 18th Path is fiery, the Life-breath of the creative powers; Peh. It is martian and disruptive, yet curbed and directed utilizing the saturnine power

of Limitation; Ayin, to travel the 18th Path of the way of return is suggested by reversing the letters of השפע thus: עפשה. See 1217, 414, 418, 95, 319, 450.

אלהי אביך אלהי אבארהם אלהי יצחק ואלהי יעוקב *Elohay abikaw Elohay Abraham Elohay yitzoq ve-Elohay Jacob*. The God of your father, the God of Abraham, the God of Isaac and the God of Jacob. Spelled אבתיכם (aebothekem) in Exodus 3:15: "And God said moreover unto Moses, Thus shall thou say unto the children of Israel, the Lord God of our fathers, the God of Abraham, the God of Isaac and the God of Jacob, has sent me unto you: this is my name forever, and this is my memorial unto all generations." see 1301, 248, 208, 182.

תנואתי my displeasure, my opposition. See Numbers 14:34.

נתיבות *nitivoth*. Paths, trodden paths [Proverbs 3:17]. English like the noun "ways," a synonym for stages, measures, degrees, states, modes, phases or categories. Refers to the 10 sephiroth and 22 sacred letters, the 32 paths of wisdom, modes or phases of the manifestation of Chokmah. These are 1. the power of the fixed stars and zodiacal signs; 2. the power of the cosmic life-force (Chiah). See 350, 73.

Rosenroth in K.D.L.C.K. (p.601) gives: *semitae*, and says they are 32, referring to wisdom, which is called פליאות (mysterious) because they are hidden channels.

מים שין חית Mem-Shin-Cheth. The spelling of משח, oil, in plenitude. This word is the root of messiah, the anointed. See 348, 358, 390, 90, 360, 418.

חסף clay. With different pointing 1. revelation; laying bare. 2. reveal; draw water. Peh = 800, see 148.

סחף to withdraw, retire - with different pointing: to sweep, or scrape, away; to bear down, to cast down. See 148.

יהוה אלהי ישועתי God of my salvation. In Psalm 88:1: "O Lord God of my salvation, I have cried day and night before thee." According to their comprehension of its laws, the power of life causes both joy and misery to those who trod its paths. See 2991 (Greek).

והתאויתם and shall mark out. See Numbers 34:10.

δομος Θεου. *domos theou.* Abode (house) of God.

869

ועץ הדעת טוא ורע and the knowledge of good and evil. In Genesis: and the Lord God made all kinds of trees grow out of the ground-tress that were pleasing to the eye and good for food. In the middle of the garden were the tree of life and the tree of the knowledge of good and evil."

"Let us consider now the phrase (in Genesis 2, verse 9), *the tree of knowledge of Tov and Raa,* translated good and evil. All the Hebrew words relating to this tree (such as *gan, beeden, meqaddam)* convey intense movement. In fact, it is a whirlwind destroying all that is obsolete and all accumulations, which must constantly be swept away by the totality of life that is creative and always new. This concept becomes clear to us when we realize that, in reading the Bible as we know it, the word *Tov,* according to its letter-numbers *(Tav-Vav-Vayt:* 400.6.2), expresses the continuity of existence to which we cling as 'good,' and the word *Raa (Raysh-Ayn:* 200.70) that which upsets our static habits of living is translated 'bad.'" [Suraes, 1992, p. 108.]

תגרירון *Tageriron.* The hagglers; Qlippoth of Tiphareth. Also called Tagaririm (Mathers), Togarini (Waite), Tagiriron (Regardie) and Thagiriron (Crowley). See 620, 1519. The contending forces of disunity and hate. See 1599; 1303, 653.

αλμαζω. *akmazo.* To be at the highest point, to be in full bloom or vigor, to flourish, in the New Testament, to be fully ripe, as fruits in their best state. See Revelations 14:18.

"The second of the two reapers is the Second Logos, and he reaps the dynamic spiritual nature, which on the plane of creative forces corresponds to the fivefold noetic group. The 'vine' of this conquest is identical with the 'river Euphrates' of the three other conquests. Physiologically, it is the spinal cord, the path of the five *pranas,* of life-winds, which are now... metamorphosed into bunches of grapes. These solar forces, permeating and energizing the aura (the wine-vat *outside* the city), produce a return current to the *chakras* of the four somatic divisions... and into the solar body... it is a process analogous to the nutrition of the *fetus in utero.*" [Pryse, 1965, p. 175.]

870

כנף *Kanaf.* wing, skirt; winged. Peh = 800, see 150.

אור הכוכבים *Aur ha-Kokabim.* Light of the Stars, Astral Light; The Great Magical Agent see 300.

התהלכתי I had walked (followed), I walk. See Genesis 24:40.

Η Κυριος. *Ho Kurios.* The Supreme Lord. In Matthew 21:40: "When, therefore, the owner of the vineyard comes, what will he do to those occupants?"

Κυπρος. *Cypros.* Cyprus, the island in the Fama, where brother P.A.L. is said to have "died." Cyprus supplied copper, the metal of Venus, to the ancient world.

In occult symbology and alchemy, death is a symbol of transmutation (see Key 13). P.A.L is an anagram for *Aleph* (see 111) and implies that the superconscious (*Aleph*) impulse is transmuted in the Venus (Cyprus) center. Aleph means bull or ox. The bull is the symbol of Taurus, which rules the neck. Aleph is shown on Key 0, The Fool, with a white sun in the background. This is the central spiritual sun, which our Sun derives its radiance. Thus Brother P.A.L. represents the metaphysical power of the spiritual sun. In Cyprus, he dies, meaning that the sun center's superconscious impulse is changed into the Venus center's awakened functioning.

Venus is associated with the direction east, the place of dawn, the womb of light, and the beginning of spiritual illumination. The Venus center is located in the throat. It is the link between the lower 4 chakras in the body and the higher two in the head. It is associated with creative imagination and emotional responses, and this is the secret to the transmutation. Vivid mental image fueled by intense desire combined with the power of the spiritual solar energy is a method of transmuting the physical vehicle into an adept's body. See 87 (Lt), 111 (P.A.L), 434, 4; 358 (note).

αιματιτης. *Haematites*. Hematite, a reddish-brown stone, attributed to Aries, Mars; "the bloodstone" was the first jewel on the high priest's breastplate. In Exodus 28:17: "And you shall set it in settings of stones, four rows of stones; the first row shall be a hematite, an emerald and a marble." see 45, Adam, oden; 52 (Greek).

871

מאלף *Malf. Malfas Goetia* demon by night of the 3rd decan of Aries. Peh = 800, see 151.

872

ונתתיו and I will make him. See Genesis 17:20.

תתעב you [shall] abhor. See Deuteronomy 23:8.

עבתת (wreathen) chains. See Exodus 28:24.

αγιαων. *agiazon*. Sanctifies. In Hebrews 2:11: "For both he that sanctifies and they that are sanctified are all of one; for which cause he is not ashamed to call them brethren." see 942 (Greek).

873

געף *Gaap. Goetia* demon # 33 by day of the 3rd decan of Aquarius [Mathers, 1995, p. 130]. Peh = 800, see 153 & Appendix 11.

874

ממשפחתו of his family. See Leviticus 25:49.

עתדת things that are to come [dooms]. See Deuteronomy 32:35.

875

I. (5 x 5 x 5 x 7) or 5^3 x 7

אדם רע *Adam Roa*. evil man. Mem = 600, see 315.

הכתנת the coat, tunic. See Genesis 37:31.

876

תכונת *tekunath*. treasure, dwelling place. From a root meaning: to arrange, to measure, to design, to plan. Refers to Hod, Perfect Intelligence, linked to Beth (house-mercury). The introduction of the personal factor of human intellectual activity brings out, arranges, cultivates latent potencies. See 1431.

מלכות ערפל *Malkuth Arawfel*. Kingdom of darkness. A Qabalistic technical term relating to the Malkuth as the ultimate point of descent from the White Brilliance of Kether the Crown. See 496, 380.

עוף *oof*. to cover with wings, to fly, fly away; to flicker. With different pointing: fowl, bird, winged creature. Peh = 800, see 156.

יוסף *Joseph*. Multiplier, addition. Peh = 800, see 156.

ערום *orem*. subtle. Mem = 600, see 316.

צפון tzafon. north, dark, hidden, north-wind. Nun = 700, see 226.

שקוץ שמם *shikkutz shomame*. abomination of desolation. In Daniel 12:11: "And from the time that the daily sacrifice shall be taken away, and the abomination that makes desolate be set up, there shall be a thousand two hundred and ninety days." Compare with Malkuth Arawfel. The word שקוץ is numerically equivalent to מלכות, and שמם = ערפל. The abomination which makes desolate is the substitution of the "Kingdom of Darkness" for the "Rule of Light." It is materialistic reliance on the physical in place of the spiritual. The "abomination of desolation: is darkness for those without the eyes to see. The spirit is our redeemer. It is the power collected in the solar radiance, the water of mediation that nourished our kingship and the light that rules over the physical. See 80, 85, 549, 226, 95, 921, 496.

סר שלום *Sar-Shalom*. Prince of Peace [Isaiah 9:6]. A name of Kether. See 111, 157, 507, 620, 589.

877 (prime)

זעף *zahaef*. anger, wrath. See 157.

גלות + אבן שלימה *gawluth + ehben shelaymah*. exile, banishment, captivity + the whole (perfect) stone. The energy of regeneration is exiled in the ignorant man; the wise man uses the same energy to build the stone of the wise. See 438, 439.

878

תועבת *thabath*. abomination. In Proverbs 15:8,9: "The sacrifice of the wicked is an abomination to the Lord: but the prayer of the upright is his delight. The way of the wicked is an abomination unto the Lord: but he loves him that follows after righteousness." see also Genesis 46:34.

ממשפחתי of my kindred, my clan. See Genesis 24:40.

879

בזעף with rage. See Isaiah 30:30.

בזרעם Their descendants. See Deuteronomy 10.15.

880

כסף *Kehsef*. Silver, alchemically the Moon. Peh = 800, see 160.

נתתיך have I made you, permitting you. See Genesis 17:5.

881 (prime)

דברי הימים *Debere ha-yamim*. "Events of the days," Hebrew title of Chronicles.

ותמלא הארץ חמס *va-thimmawlea ha-aretz hamas*. and the earth was filled with violence. In Genesis 6:11: "The earth also was corrupt before God, and the earth was filled with violence." see 2552, 291.

התעשקו they contended [disputed]. See Genesis 26:20.

αλων. *halon*. A threshing floor.

882

I. (2 x 3 x 3 x 7 x 7) or $2 \times 3^2 \times 7^2$

שכל מנהיג האחדות *Sekhel Manhig ha-Achdoth*. Uniting Intelligence or Inductive Intelligence of Unity (literally "Driver (or Leader) of the Unities.") The 13th Path of Gimel represents the manifestation of the subconsciousness of Yekhidah, the Cosmic Self, as the basis for manifesting the One Ego. Last of the Paths of the Tree with 2-directional movement-outward and downward from above, and inward and upward from below. See 237, 73, 3, 532.

"The thirteenth [path], Gimel, brings beauty into

activity and thus begins to be active before Mercy and Severity. As in creation, the beauty of visible nature was manifest before creatures to whom Mercy and Severity could be shown were brought forth." [32 Paths of Wisdom]

"I am the Uniting Intelligence, linking all opposites together with the bonds of perfect peace." [Meditations of the Paths of Wisdom]

יברים Hebrews. Mem = 600, see 322.

לברמים *Lebarmem*. Lesser assistant angel of Sagittarius; Lord of triplicity by night, Mem = 600, see 322 & Key 14.

883 (prime)

ארבעים *arbaim, arebawyim*. forty (40). Mem = 600, see 323, 541, 190.

התועבת the abominations. See Leviticus 18:26.

884

בנאים הדביר *Bonaim Ha-Debir*. Builders of the Adytum. See 324.

885

אפסי ארץ + בתולה *aphesay-eretz + betulah*. the ends of the earth + a virgin maid. Virginity has to do with the spiritual force, working as Mercury in Virgo in the microcosm's alchemical process. The "earth" is translated or raised in vibration by treading righteousness paths, personality transmutation. See 442, 443.

886

שכל שפע נבדל *Sekhel Shepha Nivdal*. The intelligence of the Mediating Influence. The 6th Path of Tiphareth. See 1081.

ונתתיך and I will make of you. See Genesis 17:6.

ותתכס and she covered herself. See Genesis 24:65.

תלונת the murmurings [grumblings]. See Exodus 16:12.

887

אשפוך I will pout out. See Ezekiel 8:7.

888

חפף *chapaf, chawfaf. aesoth IHVH Elohim*. to cover, protect; to enclose, surround. Peh = 800, see 168.

עשות יהוה אלהים *aesoth IHVH Elohim*. "IHVH Elohim made. In Genesis 2:4: These are the generations of the heavens and of the earth when they were created, in the day that the Lord God [IHVH Elohim] made the earth and the heavens." see 86, 26.

משה + אהיה אשר אהיה *Moshe + eheieh asher eheieh*. Moses + "I am that I am." משה is water (Mem), Fire (Shin) and vision (Heh). He was the great initiate who preceded Jesus and is linked here with the I AM as his illumination source. אשר is also the tribe of Israel connected with alchemical sublimation under the sign Libra, suggesting that equilibrium brings illumination from above, into the head-and heart. See 345, 501, 21, 543, 1648 (Greek).

תפתח you shall engrave. See Exodus 28:11.

תפתח you shall open. See Deuteronomy 15:8.

פתחת you have freed. See Psalm 116: 16.

Ιησους. *Iesous*. Jesus. From the beginning, the church has set apart 8, as the Dominical number, or a number of the Lord, referring to Jesus as One with the Father," who, as IHVH (26) is also 8. See 971, 1844, 1988, 1480, 2368, 644, 1768, 800, 656, 1408, 496, 1776, 688, 326.

I. "The root meaning of this word is side to be 'To Save" or rather To Make Whole. In conjunction with Khristos, the name Iesous refers to the act of (Christ) entering into the body of an *anthropos*." [Omikron, 1942, p. 256.] See under Christos [1480].

II. "For Jesus is a name arithmetically symbolical consisting of six letters, and is known by all those that belong to the called." [Irenaeus].

ο οικδομος αληθειας. *ho oikodomos aletheias*. The architect of truth, or the builder of truth; epithet of Christ.

αληθευομενος. *aletheuomenos*. The one who is fulfilled, the fulfiller.

νικη κοσμου. *nikeh kosmou*. The victory of the world. See 1 John 5:4: "Because all that has been begotten by God overcomes the world; and this is the victory which overcomes the world-our faith."

Κυριος νικη. Victorious Lord.

Λογος εστι. *Logos esti*. He is the word, a reference to Christ.

Λεγων. *Legion*. Legion; variant spelling of legion in Mark 5:9: "And he [Jesus] asked him [the possessed man] 'What is your name? and he says to him [Jesus], "My name is Legion; for we are many."' see 1244, 2209, 970 (Greek).

889

וארבעים And forty. See Genesis 7:4

העדרים The flocks. See Genesis 29:2.

התועבות The detestable things, the abominations. See Jeremiah 7:10.

890

מתנת gifts. See Genesis 25:6.

צררת being bound up. See Exodus 12:34.

תמימת complete, full ones. See Leviticus 23:15.

Εναυλον Διος. *enaulon dios*. Divine Abode. Mount Olympus was considered by the ancient Greeks to be the home of Gods.

891

אפרים *Ephraim*. double fruit. The Tribe of Israel (Taurus). See 331.

ο λογος ο αληθνος *ho logos ho alethinos*. The true word. Appears only in the plural in Revelation 19:9: "And he says to me, 'write; blessed are those who have been invited to the marriage supper of the lamb.' He also said to me, 'these are the true words of God.'" (οι λογοια ληθινοι). Note: the second "ο" has been inserted for numerical purposes. Otherwise, the value would be 821.

ο υρανια βασιλεια. *ourania basileia*. heavenly kingdom. See 1477.

ο κυριακος. *ho kuriakos*. The church. The word also means "pertaining to the Lord."

διδαχη αληθειας. *didache aletheias*. The teaching of truth.

υπερασπιει *hyperaspieth*. Shield. Septuagint translation of מגן (93, 743) in Deuteronomy 33:29: "Blessed are you, O Israel! Who is like you, a people saved by the Lord? He is your shield and helper and your glorious sword. Your enemies will cower before you, and you will trample down their high places." see 93, 743.

Ουρανος. *Ouranos*. Uranos. Uranus; heaven sky. A Titan in Greek myth. In Qabalah, the higher octave of the planet Mercury, symbolized in Tarot by the Fool. In other words, Uranus = spirit. In Revelations 21:1: "And I saw a new heaven and a new earth; for the former heaven and the former earth were gone, and the sea is no more.'" see 902, 961.

αυρανια βασιλεια. *ourania Basileia.* Heavenly Kingdom.

892

והיכן בחסד כסא *ve-hukan ba-chesed kissay.* And in mercy shall the throne be established. Nun = 700, see 242., 3111 (Greek).

אפראים *Ephraim.* a double fruit. Mem = 600, see 331, 332.

שפע אלהות *Shepha elohuth.* Divine Influence. Relates to the 21st Path of Kaph. A Rabbinical term. The descending current of מזלא, the general influence which is the active principle in the Tree of Life. See 78, 636, 183.

893

ומעשה ידיו מגיד הרקיע *uma'aeseh yawdayu maggid ha-rawqia.* and the firmament shows his handiwork. In Psalm 19:1: "The heavens declare the glory of God, and the firmament shows his handiwork." see 318.

צבא + ערלות לבבכם to go forth in a body (to war), to assemble, to mass + the foreskins of your heart. The sword of the spirit is the word of God, the verb "to love." When the desire is purified and perfected, it is transmuted into love. Venus is the ancient personification of the unfailing power of love. Circumcision of the heart is the result of self-purification. See 800, 93.

איעצה עליך עיני + אמות *yaeotzah awlayka eyini + amuth.* "I will guide you with mine eye + mothers. The mother letters represent the three fundamentals, or elements of Air, Water and Fire, out of which the earth or physical universe is formed.

894

פ + צ + ד *Peh + Tzaddi + Daleth.* mouth + fish + door. The occult use of speech transmutes reproductive energy. This is furthered by the practice of meditation and completed by the desire for perfection. Peh = 800, see 800, 90, 4.

מערת המכפלה + אבא *mayawrath ha-makpelah + abba.* cave of duplicity + father. The cave symbolizes the lower nature of the soul, immersed in the physical plane's duplicity or appearance. It cannot perceive that bodes are formed by the power of the father or Chokmah. See 890, 4.

ותפתח and she opened (it). See Exodus 2:6.

ופתחת and you shall engrave. See Exodus 28:9.

תתנחלו you shall inherit, you shall distribute. See Numbers 33:54.

895

אדם קדמון *Adam Qadom.* the archetypal of heavenly man; protogonos. Represented by the ten sephiroth in their totality and unity. קדמון means eastern, ancient, old; epithet of God. Nun = 700, see 245, 200.

יסודות הקדש *yesodoth has-qadosh.* the foundations. Said of Daleth, the 14th Path of the Luminous Intelligence, the "instructor in the secret foundations of holiness and perfection" [Yetziratic Text]. The path is also the "instructor of arcana." See 486, 404.

אשכלות + צמח *shkoloth + tzemakh.* clusters, bunches of grapes + the branch. The "clusters" refers to Hod הוד and נצח Netzach, and this value of 757 equals כתם אופיר gold of Ophir. The "branches" is the name of the Messiah, i.e., he builds the temple of the Lord. Netzach and Hod are the spheres of desire and intellect, balanced by the higher self's guidance. See 757, 138.

דמלכות השמים *de-malkuth ha-shamaim.* The

kingdom of the heavens; the kingdom of heaven. Hebrew version of Greek in Matthew 13:11: "He answered and said unto them, 'because it is given unto you to know the mysteries of the kingdom of heaven, but to them, it is not given." see 1456.

ο υιος Αβρααμ. *ho huios Habraam*. The son of Abraham; epithet applied to Jesus in the genealogy of Matthew: appears as υιου Αβρααμ (son of Abraham) in Matthew 1:1: "A register of the lineage of Jesus Christ, son of David, son of Abraham."

ο αμην ο Μεσσιας. *ho amen ho Messias*. The amen: the Messiah. Epithets of Christ. See 2368, 91, 656, 258.

pater, filius, spiritus sanctus, natura divina, Deus + anima, corpus, spiritus, natura humana, homo (Lt). Father, Son, Holy Spirit God + soul, body, spirit, human nature, man. Sum of the two phrases in [Secret Symbols]

896

אש מים רוח ארץ *esh-mayim-ruach-eretz*. Fire + Water + Air + Earth. The 4 elements, completed by spirit, the Quintessence, depicted in the pentagram's uppermost point. These elements are those of the personality, corresponding to desire, intellect, astral and physical bodies, or the four lower sephiroth from Netzach to Malkuth. See 301, 90.

רפדוני נתפוחים *raphiduniy bathaphuchim*. comfort me with apples. In Canticles 2:5: "Stay me with flagons, comfort me with apples; for I am sick of love."

צוף *tzup*. overflow. Peh = 800, see 176.

תמתון you [will] die [if you eat of the Fruit of good and evil]. See Genesis 3:3.

צררות bundles, tied, pouches. See Genesis 42:35.

נפשתינו our souls, ourselves. See Numbers 31:50.

תמונת form, an image of [an idol]. See Deuteronomy 4:16.

897

את לחת האבן *eth-luchoth ha-ehben*. tables of stone. In Exodus 24:12: "And the Lord said unto Moses, 'come up to me into the mount, and be there: and I will give you tablets of stone, and a law, and commandments which I have written; that you may teach them." see 450, 53.

שרש + בן אדם *soresh + ben adam*. root, stock + son of man. The root, or fundamental reality from which spring all forms of growth and development is the Life-power, expressed through the Mars force. Man becomes the son when he understands how divine grace becomes manifest through correct apprehension of the desire nature. See 800, 97.

נפש חי + בהר יהוה יראה *Nephesh chai + behar IHVH yirayeh*. breath of life + in the mount of Tetragrammaton it shall be provided. The breath of life is the vital soul or field of subconscious mental activity. The mount is the adytum, or Mercury, center in the brain, where self-consciousness is attained by obeying the law. See 448, 449.

פרזים *Perizzim* Perizzites; one of the races in Canaan which the Israelites were expected to displace. Mem = 600, see 237.

תוצאת the ends. See Numbers 34:8.

Επιστατα. *epistata*. "Master," an epithet applied to Jesus. In Luke 5:5: "and Simon answering, said: 'Master, we have labored through the whole night, and have caught nothing; yet, at your word, I will let down the nets.'" see Luke 8:24; 8:45; 9:33; 9:49 and 17:13.

αι ξ εντη Ασια εκκλησιαι *hai z enteh Asia ekklesia*. The 7 churches in Asia; identical to the 7 interior stars of alchemy. Mentioned in Revelations 1:4: "John to those seven congregations in Asia; favor and peace to you from God the one who is, and the one who was, and the one who is coming; and from the seven spirits which are before his throne." Asia is עשיה Assiah, the word of action or the material world of the Qabalists. See 809, 979, 1987, 4303.

898

שרים לכב הארץ *sawrin be-kawl ha-aretz*. Princes in all the earth, Princes throughout the land. In Psalm 45:16: "Your sons will take the place of your fathers; you will make them princes throughout the land. The "earth" is the manifested world or Malkuth. See 550, 500, 50, 291.

כסף חי *kesef chai*. Living silver; Quicksilver, the Mercury of the sages. Peh = 800, see 178, 570, 949.

למשפחתם by their families. Genesis 10:5.

Ευτερπη. *Euterpe*. The muse of music, mainly Dionysiac; patroness of joy and pleasure, and of flute-players. A Pythagorean name for 8. "Because it is the most mutable (μαλιστα ευτερπτος) of all the numbers within the decad, being evenly-even... it can be divided by 2 as far as to unity." [Thomas Taylor: Theoretic Arithmetic, p.200]

οι ζ αστερες. *hoi zeta-z-asteres*. the 7 stars. Written οι επτα αστερες in Revelation 1:20: "As for the secret of the seven stars which you saw in my right hand, and the seven golden lampstands; the seven stars are messengers (angels) of the seven congregations, and the seven lampstands are the seven congregations." see 897, 979, 1987, 4303. Note that 7 + 1 (Christ) = 8.

899

שכל מורגש *Seykel Moragash*. Exciting or Active Intelligence. The 27th Path of Peh. Joins the field of desire (Venus) to that of intellect (Mercury) on the Tree of life. On the Cube of Space, Peh is assigned the northern face.] see 549, 503, 91, 474, 84, 786, 90, 395, 80, 85, 696 and Appendix 12.

The letter Peh is called the mouth as an organ of speech. There is a connection between consciousness, which forms itself into speech and electrical energy, which is the basis of all activity of the Exciting Intelligence. Life and this universe were created from the "Word of Life," the whirling breath that emanates and returns like a lighting-flash. Peh is the Mars-force, an electrical, fluidic Water of the Alchemist. Thus the Word is made manifest through the Water of the Alchemist. Thus Geburah, the sphere of Mars, is a Watery Sephiroth. The Bible says that man does not live by bread alone but by what comes from the mouth of Tetragrammaton. This is the mouth that speaks the silent word in the darkness of the North. It is a feminine mouth.

1. "The 27th Path is called the Exciting or Active Intelligence because thence is created the spirit of every creature under the supreme orb and the assemblage of them all." The possessor of this path is said "to foresee all future events which do not depend on a superior free will, or an all undiscernible cause" [Eliphas Levi]

2. "The Path of Peh, which joins Victory to Splendor, is analogous to the paths of Daleth and Teth. The Exciting Intelligence follows the Renewing Intelligence because of the sense of limitation sooner or later gives way to the conviction that this limitation is not permanent. This conviction is man's chief incentive to the kinds of activities that will lead to freedom. It originates in an inanimate perception that man's spirit is one with the universal spirit which, as we have seen, must necessarily succeed in carrying out the great purpose of which it projects itself in a universe. This intuitive perception comes suddenly like a lighting-flash and usually overthrows the whole conception of the meaning

of a life held previously by him to whom it comes. This is an experience, not only of a single person but also to whole races at certain stages of their development. It is the great influence which affects sweeping changes in the thought and work of the world." [32 Paths of Wisdom]

3. "I am the Exciting Intelligence, breaking down all structures of error and false knowledge." [Meditations on the Paths of Wisdom]

מטמני מסתרים *matemeni masettawrim*. riches stored in secret places. In Isaiah 45:3: "And I will give you the treasures of darkness, and riches stored in secret places, so that you may know that I am the Lord, the God of Israel, who summons you by name." These "hidden riches" are linked to the use of the power of Peh. [Listed with the connective Vav, under 905.]

הביטו אל צור חצבתם *ha-beytu el tur chutzbethem*. Look to the rock from which you were cut. In Isaiah 51:1: "Listen to me, you who pursue righteousness and who seek the Lord: Look to the rock from which you were cut and to the quarry from which you were hewn;" The "rock" is a title of God, connecting it with Key 4 and the Stone of the wise, which is completed by Mars. See 296, 836.

נר אלהים *nare Elohim*. lamp of God. Mem = 600, see 336.

Section 9

Numbers 900 – 999

900

I. (30x30) or 2^2 x 3^2 x 5^2

ץ Final *Tzaddi*. A trap, snare, "fishhook." Tzaddi is assigned the function of meditation, which is the basis of alchemical sublimation, the process whereby the wise attain conscious union with the Life-power via the water of consciousness, which is the "mute dark mirror." Tzaddi consists of a Nun (fish) surmounted by a Yod (Hand), representing the male and female creation principles. Using the fishhook Tzaddi via meditation raises Nun, the "fish," out of the "water" of subconsciousness into the region of self-conscious awareness; it also raises the Scorpio force to awaken the higher brain centers. See 90, 395.

שם *Sham*. there, then. With different pointing: Shem. Location, sign, token, memorial, son of Noah. Often used in Qabalistic writing to designate the divine name IHVH. Mem = 600, see 340.

רן *ron*. shout, rejoicing; ringing cry. The plural in [Psalm 32:7] "You are my hiding place; you will protect me from trouble and surround me with songs (i.e., cries) of deliverance. Selah." [Nun = 700] see 250.

פרי עץ + הזחלת *peree-etz + ha-zo-hehelth*. the fruit of the tree + the serpent. The serpent power is rightly directed through meditation, which makes man the "fruit of the tree." See 450.

תרש *tarash*. to be strong, hard, firm. Root to תרשיש, Tarshish, the place where Solomon got his Gold for the temple. The allusions are to strengthen and direct the Mars energy through meditational practices to reach the "Sun" or Tiphareth. See 1210.

תשר *tawshar*. to make a gift or to present A Mishnaic or Talmudic word. It is the gift of the profuse giver or spirit, and its promise is the "rainbow." See 600, 120, 186, 162.

ותתים I have given them Numbers 18:8.

תך *tokh*. Oppression. See 420.

901

ארן *Oren*. The pine, fir or cedar; strength. See 251.

ארן *Aron*. Ark (of the covenant).

תשאר shall be left behind, she may be left. See Exodus 10:26.

תארש you shall betroth [pledge]. See Deuteronomy 28:30.

περιστερα. *peristera*. The dove. The dove is the symbol of the Holy Spirit or Ruach. Also a symbol of spiritual Israel. See 71, 214.

Ιακχος. *Iaccus*. Dionysus. The Eleusinian mystery name for Dionysus. See 811.

Ο Μακροκομος. Ho Makrokosmos. The Macrocosm, universe.

ο πυραμις. *ho pyramis*. The pyramid. An Egyptian word. The pyramid was regarded as a geometrical symbol of the Macrocosm.

ο φαλλος. *ho phallos*. The phallus, i.e., creative power symbolized in India by the Shiva-lingam. See 831.

902

היכל לבנת השפיר *Hekel Lebanath ha-saphir*. Palace of the Pavement of Sapphire Stone, Heavenly Mansion corresponding to Yesod & Malkuth.

תשבר you shall break in pieces. See Exodus 23:24.

בץ whitish clay, mire. See 92.

903

גשם gawsham. to rain violently; a hard shower. See 343.

ויאמר אלהים vay-yomer Elohim. And God said. Mem = 600, see 343.

גרשת drove out. See Genesis 4:14.

904

בתבניתם after their pattern. See Exodus 25:40.

905

השם Ha-Shem. The Name, Tetragrammaton.

השרת the ministry. See Numbers 4:12.

התלעת the worm. See Deuteronomy 28:39.

תהפכת perverse. See Deuteronomy 32:20.

906

קוף Letter name Qoph. Back of head; ape. Peh = 800, see 186.

מוסף musawf. Increase or addition; attachment. See 186.

תוך tavek. Middle, center, midst. Kaph = 500, see 426.

תורש you come to poverty, you will be destitute. See Genesis 45:11.

תולעת scarlet. See Exodus 28:5.

907

ארון chest of. Refereeing to the construction of the ark. See Exodus 25:10.

908

חץ chez. arrow, lighting; punishment; wound. With different pointing: choz: Out! Avaunt! Go away! Tzaddi = 900.

תשברו you shall break, smash. See Deuteronomy 7:5.

909

ראובן Tribe of Reuben. "see, a son." Paul Case says it's associated with Pisces. Godwin says Aquarius. See 259.

שרטת cuttings, cut. See Leviticus 21:5.

910

וירא אלהים כי טוב va-ya-re Elohim ki tov. And God saw that it was good. Mem = 600, see 350.

מתכנת the count, amount, number of. See Exodus 5:8.

ירשת who possesses, inheriting. See Numbers 36:8.

ודרשת and you shall inquire. See Deuteronomy 13:15.

911 (prime)

אשים Ishim. "The fiery ones," the flames. The choir of angles associated with Malkuth. Mem = 600, see 351.

ראשית rashith. First, beginning, primal, chief, first-fruit, choice, best, magistracy, office, choicest. See 913, בראשית & Genesis 10:10.

באר שחת *bar shachoth*. Pit of decay. Pit of destruction. One of the 7 infernal mansions, The 5th Hell, corresponding to Geburah. See 337, 57, 99, 1026, 566, 108, 291.

שארית a remnant. See Genesis 45:7.

χαρις. *kharis*. grace. "Kindred with this word is *kar*, whose root-meaning is strength, maturity, preeminence: the from *khar* suggest an intensification of the same ideas. As a synonym for *kharis* we may note *terpsis*-the act of cultivation and beautifying: enriching in power, sweetness, and efficiency. The Graces, *Kharitides*, were the assistants of heavenly Aphrodite, who inspired and fostered influences that ripened and refined Earthly Being. *Terpsichore* was the most winsome of all the Muses, and as she strung her golden lyre, she thrilled the whole Aetherial Realm. Only those who had the power of this inner Grace, *Kharis*, could awaken it in others. Hence the word connotes a gift from the greater to the lesser: a power awakened: fruition forwarded: and even a magical charm or endowment. But it also implies that the gift made was an award from progress already achieved. The 'Grace' of God extends to all Nature and to all Mankind, but its award is in keeping with the great psychic law 'To him that has it shall be given.'" [Omikron, 1942, pp. 263-264.]

912

ברקים *bawrahqim*. lighting. Mem = 600, see 352.

אהרון *Aaron*. Lofty; the name of Moses' brother and spokesman. See 262.

בת שר *bath shir*. song-maiden; muse.

Προμηθευς *Prometheus*. A Titan in Greek mythology that brought fire to man.

913

בראשית *Bereshith*. In the Beginning, in principle. Genesis 1:1 Hebrew title of Genesis. Reduces to

13. Thus the beginning is indicated as being love and unity. See 13.

"*Bereshit:* Containers of existences, existences in their containers. Universe containing the existences, containing its own existence. (Movement of the Universe.) Upspringing of life, intermittent pulsation invisible, not thinkable; life always new, always present, never present.

Creation! Vertiginous movement, immeasurable movement, a movement that transcends all conception. In the hidden depths of movement is the secret of existence. And this movement is the custodian of all possible possibilities. Existence, projection of life, the negation of existence. (Everything that exists must cease to exist.) Apparent betrayal of life. Revelation! Life-death is One. And the collision, the shock of passive resistance of the mass, the hard, the dry, the stones: blessed resistance! Without resistance, there could be no birth. This is becoming.

Thus are introduced the two partners playing against each other: *Aleph* springing from its containers, and *Yod* smitten by the "breath" of *Sheen* pressing against all that resists it to contain it." [Suraes, 1992, p. 78.]

תוצאתיו it ends, it's going out. See Numbers 34:5.

914

אט אביך *Eth Abika*. The essence of your Father. see 434.

שדים *shedim*. Demons. Mem = 600, see 354.

915

אמתחתינו our sacks. See Genesis 43:21.

916

ובחרשת and in cutting, carving. See Exodus 31:5.

917

וראשית the first (fruits). See Genesis 49:3.

במתכנתה according to its composition [formula]. See Exodus 30:37.

מתזנתך was your prostitution not enough? Literally: from-prostitutions-of-you. See Ezekiel 16:20.

918

דביר היכל אולם debir-haikal-ulam. Adtum-temple-vestibule. See 358.

919 (prime)

וגרשתי and I will drive out. See Exodus 33:2.

Μελχισεδεκ. Melchizedek. King of Salem. Greek spelling of Old Testament Name.

920

ישים Ishim. The Flames, Fiery Ones. See 360.

רעמים Rahamim. Thunders. See 360.

שכם Skekem. shoulder-blades; Old Testament city. See 360.

921

וירשתה and you shall possess it, and you possess her [the land of the Lord]. See Deuteronomy 17:14.

922

תורישו you will drive out. See Numbers 33:55.

923

זרע אלהים Zera Elohim. a godly seed, a seed of God or offspring of God. See 363.

924

חשך אפלה khoshek-afilah. thick darkness. See 444.

ויברא אלהים את האדם בצלמו vay-yi-vera Elohim eth ha-adham be-tzalmu. So God created man in his own image.

ובמתכנתו and according to its composition [formula]. See Exodus 30:32.

925

πωλει polei. Sells.

926

תלונתם their murmurings.

927

ο ζων. ho zon. The living one.

928

כבד את אביך ואת אמך kabedh eth-abika ve-eth-immeka. Honor your father and your mother.

מפתחת engraved. See Exodus 39:6.

תתעבנו you shall hate it. See Deuteronomy 7:26.

929 (prime)

עולם הבריאה Olahm Ha Briah. World of Creation. See 269.

היכל קדוש קדשים Hekel Qadesh Qadeshim. Palace

246

of the Holy of Holies; Heavenly Mansion corresponding to the Supernals.

930

The number of years Adam lived (Genesis 5:5).

שלם *shalom*. Whole, complete, healthy; to complete, to be safe, peace, perfect. See 370.

סנדלפון *Sandalphon*. Archangel is associated with Malkuth. Nun = 700, see 280.

לנפשתיכם of your lives, to yourself. See Genesis 9:5.

לרשת to possess [inherit]. See Leviticus 20:24.

931

רוח הרוחות הלבנה *Ruach ha-Ruachoth ha-Lebanah*. "Spirit of the Spirits of the Moon (a literal Hebrew translation." [Godwin. 1999, p. 613.] see 3321.

932

כבשים young lambs. See 372.

עץ הדעת בוט ורע Tree of the Knowledge of Good and Evil.

933

אלהי העברים *Elohi ha-Ibrim*. God of the Hebrews. Mem = 600, see 373.

934

The total unit length of the Invisible paths on the Tree of Life if the Aleph line is considered 26 unit lengths.

כשׁים *Kasdim*. Chaldees (a reference to Astrology).

935

הנערים The men. See Genesis 14:24.

הסרסים The court officials, see Jeremiah 34:19.

936

שולם *shalom*. Peace, health, prosperity, friend. See 376.

תקל ופרסין *tekel upharsin*. Weighed and divided. Part of the handwriting on the wall [Daniel 5:25]. Use to indicate that Belshazzar failed to come up to the standards of the divine order.

נה שם הם יפת *Noah-Shem-Ham-Japheth*. Noah (rest, cessation) is cessation from action or Pralaya. The rest-period between cycles of active manifestation. Shem (name, location); everything manifest has a name and a place or location. Ham (heat, warmth); when a cycle of manifestation begins, the concentration of energy sets up whirling motion, which generates heat. Hapheth (expansion); its diffusion makes it assume a vast number of forms. Thus Noah and his sons are linked to the idea of renewal symbolized by the number 8. (There were 8 persons in the ark, and the Rosicrucian Order was founded by 8 persons.) see 58, 340, 48, 490, 676.

תנופת an [wave] offering. See Exodus 35:22.

κεκρυπται *kekruptai* (Greek). (is) Hid. The verb in the sentence: "Your life is hidden with Christ in God." Colossians 3:3. From the same root as the English noun "crypt." In Rosicrucian symbolism, it is connected with the vault or sepulcher or brother C.R. The vault, like the ark, is a symbol of man, the Microcosm. As in Noah's ark, hidden things were needful for the complete revival of the Rosicrucian wisdom.

937 (prime)

זרח בן יובב *Yobab ben Zerah*. Hobab, son of Zerah; a King of Edom associated with Chesed.

938

ובנערים And the servants. See Job 1:16.

וזהירין And take care, be careful. See Ezra 4:22.

939

חברה זרח בקר אור *Chevrah Zerach Boqer Aur.* "Society of the Shining Light of Dawn"; official Hebrew name of the Hermetic Order of the Golden Dawn.

והתנחתם and you shall inherit them, and you can will. See Leviticus 25:46.

ο μονογενης λογος. *ho monogenes* Logos. The only-begotten son.

940

מצרים *Mizraim.* Name given to Egypt by the Jews. See 380.

מץ *motz.* chaff.

הקול מתוף החשך the voice from out of the darkness. See Deuteronomy 5:22.

תרמש that will crawl, she moves [on the ground]. See Genesis 9:2.

משרת dipping, liquor, soaking, juice of [the grape]. See Numbers 6:3.

941

אמתך Your maidservant. See Genesis

אספרם I should count them. See Psalm 139:18.

942

וישרתוך and minister unto you, and they may assist you. See Numbers 18:2.

943

באשמרת in the watch. See Exodus 14:24.

944

דלתיך Your doors. See Isaiah 26:20.

ארגמן Purple. See Numbers 4:13.

945

הרמשת that moves, creeps, the moving. See Genesis 1:21.

התעללתי I have mocked, I heave dealt harshly. See Exodus 10:2.

נקדה פשות The Smooth Point, a title of Kether. See The Kabbalah Unveiled (p. 23).

946

תשמרו you shall keep, observe; be mindful of. See Genesis 17:10.

תתצון you shall break down [the alters]. See Exodus 34:13.

ופתלתל and crooked. See Deuteronomy 32:5.

947 (prime)

ארמון *armon.* fortress, castle, citadel. See 297.

שבעה עשר *shivah-asar.* seventeen (17).

948

ושברתם and dash in pieces [smash]. See Deuteronomy 12:3.

מגושם *megusham*. magician, sorcerer. See 389.

מוגשם *mogashem*. Corporeal, incarnating, realized, materialized. See 389.

גפרית כסף חי מלך *gawphriyth, keseph, khai, melakh*. Sulphur, Mercury (literally Living silver), Salt. The constituents of the Stone. See 389, 57, 259.

περιτομη καρδιασ *peritomeh kardias*. Matter (circumcision) of the heart. In Romans 2:29: "The real Jew is the man who is one inwardly, and real circumcision is a matter of the heart, a spiritual, not a literal thing." This circumcision of the heart is an apt figure of speech for the purpose and method of the Great Work. It is a work involving the purpose of making the stone. Yesod and the letter Yod represent the part of man's body affected by the symbolic rite. See 613.

ספרים *sepharim*. letters. See 390.

שמים *shamaim*. Heavens, firmament, sky. "what is heaved up." see 390.

נץ *netz*. flower; hawk.

המתהפכת which turned every way, the one flashing around [the sword of the cherubim]. See Genesis 3:24.

לרשתך that you may inherit. See Genesis 28:4.

שכרתיך I hired you. See Genesis 30:16.

תלנתיכם your murmurings [grumblings]. See Exodus 16:7.

מרשית from the beginning. See Deuteronomy 11:12.

צדק ילין בה *tzedeq yahin bah*. Justice abides in her. See 301.

אמיץ *ammitz*. strong, mighty; strength, might. Tzaddi = 900, see 141.

שמע ישראל Shema Israel. "Hear, O Israel."

רום מעלה *Rom Maalah*. The Inscrutable Height, a title of Kether.

ישראלית *Israelite*. See Leviticus 24:10.

מראשית of the first. See Numbers 15:21.

ראשיתם the first part [fruit] of them. See Numbers 18:12.

והתעלמת and hide yourself, and you ignore. See Deuteronomy 22:1.

שבילים *shevilim*. Paths.

וזנתך and your lewdness. See Ezekiel 23:29.

וישאלום and granted their request. See Exodus 12:36.

מפתח בית דוד *Maftayakh Beth David*. "Key of the house of David. In Isaiah 22:22: "And the Key of the House of David will I lay upon his shoulder; none shall open." This is the key to the knowledge of immortality. "And that House is the temple, not made with hands, eternal in the heavens." The key is the secret that gives the power to open the temple.

955

השמים *ha shamaim.* the heavens. See 395.

וגרשתמו and you shall drive them out. See Exodus 23:31.

956

ספר התורה *Sepher ha-Torah.* Book of Law.

הנשארת which remains. See Exodus 10:5.

957

מראשתיו under his head. See Genesis 28:11.

958

נחץ *nakhatz.* to press, to urge; to be urgent, to require haste. See 148.

חמשים *chamishim.* fifty (50). Mem = 600, see 398.

תשברון you shall dash into pieces. See Exodus 34:13.

Sanguinalis animala rosa hierichuntis spiritualis. Lucida, argentea, lactea-stillata ex candida lilia in valle Josophat (Lt). [Secret Symbols, page 13]. Animal blood, the spiritual roe of Jericho. Shining, silvery, distilled in milk from which comes the lily of truth in the valley of Jehoshaphat. See 478.

959

וגדולתיך Awesome works. See Psalm 145:6.

והלחשים And the charms. And the amulets. See Isaiah 3:20.

960

תרשיש *medorin.* Ruler of Water.

מדורין *shenaim.* habitations. See 310.

שנים *shenaim.* two, double. See 400.

שכלים *sekhelim.* Intelligences.

נשים *nashim.* Women, wives.

לצמתת in perpetuity, irredeemably, to permanence. See Leviticus 25:23.

מתנתיכם that is given by you. See Numbers 18:29.

תדרשנו you seek [look for] him. See Deuteronomy 4:29.

961

ואשמידם So I may destroy them. Deuteronomy 9:14.

והמיתך And he will put you to death. See Isaiah 65:15.

962

איש האלהים *Ish ha-Elohim.* Man of God; Husband of God (Glory). See 402.

עין יעקב *ayin Jacob.* the fountain (eye) of Jacob. Nun = 700, see 312.

הראשנות the first. See Genesis 41:20.

μαθησις εκκλησιας. *methesis ekklesias.* The teaching of the Church.

η πετρα η κυβικη. *heh petra heh kubike.* The cubic stone.

μεγεθη κυβου. *megethe Kubou.* Dimensions of the cube

963

החמשים the fiftieth [year.] see Leviticus 1:25.

המשחים the ones being anointed. See Numbers 3:3 & 403.

זנותך your prostitution. See Jeremiah 13:26.

נגרשתי I was banished. See Jonah 2:5.

ירזמון they flash, wink. See Job 15:12.

αναστασις. *anastasis*. Rising again; resurrection. An esoteric term. The "dead" are those who are caught in the web of the world's illusion. See 971.

"Anastenia is-to leap upwards upon a certain accomplishment: while *enerthenai* is-to be awakened from sleep. 'The Resurrection of Christ' is the regeneration of the Reasonable Nature from our mortality into Immortality: and from ignorance to an Undeceivable Wisdom." [Omikron, 1942, p. 248.]

τεχνη. *techne*. Art, craft, skill, technique. The "rising again" is not a natural process. The alchemical fire must be controlled and directed by art or "artificial means" (Vaughan). See 301.

964

מטטרון *Metatron*. The Archangel of Kether. See 314.

תחרשון shall hold your peace, you be still. See Exodus 14:14.

965

שם המפרש *Shem ha-Mephorash*. The Divided Name. Name of Extension. A name of God, consisting of 72 three-letter roots, suffixed the termination with AL or IH to complete the names. Each of these 72 words thus formed is attributed to one of the quinaries (a division of 5 degrees) of the zodiac. See 72.

שמנה עשר *shemonah-asar*. eighteen (18).

966

כמוץ *Kamotz*. Angel of 1st decan of Scorpio. Tzaddi = 900, see 156.

מתנותיכם your gifts. See Leviticus 23:38.

והתחזקתם and be of good courage, and do your best. See Numbers 13:20.

967 (prime)

ומשארתך and your kneading dough. See Deuteronomy 28:5.

968

I. (8 x 1 1x 11) or 2^3 x 11^2

בנות שיר *banoth shir*. Song maidens; muses.

969

מכון באמצץ *makuam be-emehtza*. standing in the midst. See 319.

סרטן *Sartain*. The Crab, the sign Cancer. See 319.

970

עץ *etz*. a tree, wood, gallows. See 160.

שנים עשר *shenaim-Asar*. twelve (12).

תרשיס *Tharsis*. Ruler of Water.

שערת hairy. Genesis 27:23.

נפתלתי have I wrestled. See Genesis 30:8.

משכרתי my wages. See Genesis 31:7.

לצמיתת in perpetuity, for the permanence. See Leviticus 25:30.

רשעת you shall tithe. See Deuteronomy 14:22.

971 (prime)

ברשעת in wickedness. Deuteronomy 9:5.

η αναστασις. *heh anastasis*. The resurrection. Refers to Christ. See 1844, 1988, 888, 1480, 644, 1768, 800, 656, 1408, 326, 963.

972

I. (4 x 3 x 3 x 3 x 3 x 3) or 2^2 x 3^5

ספרא דצניעותא *Sephra Dtenioutha*. Book of Concealed Mystery.

973

את יהוה אלהיך *Eth Jehovah Elohekah*. the Lord, your Lord. See 493.

αρχη αληθειας. Beginning of truth.

Ο Θεοπλαστης. *ho theoplastes*. The Divine Creator.

974

מקור חיים *maqor chaiim*. fountain of lives. See 414.

משוטטים *mashottim*. goings forth. See 414.

מיטטרון *Metatron*. The angle of God's presence. See 324.

975

התנפלתי I fell down. See Deuteronomy 9:25.

976

כל עשב זרע זרע *kal esev zorea zara*. Every herb bearing seed.

ושמרתיך and I will keep you. See Genesis 28:15.

תתקעו you shall blow, you shall sound [trumpets]. See Numbers 10:7.

כתועפת like the strength. See Numbers 23:22.

רשעתו his wickedness [crimes]. Deuteronomy 25:2.

977 (prime)

שכאנום *Shakanom*. a title of Tiphareth.

978

מתלקחת flashing up. See Exodus 9:24.

979

ממשפטיך from your laws. See Psalm 119:102.

980

I. (4 x 5 x 7 x 7) 2^2 x 5 x 7^2

בית לחם + תמים *beth-lechem* + *tawmim*. the "house of bread" + perfect, faultless; whole complete, entire. Bethlehem, the birth-place of Christ, called Jesus ("reality liberates"), corresponds to the Virgo area in the human body where food assimilation is carried out. The result is the perfect, immortal body of light of the adept, who has brought the rainbow into full function. See 419.

משכרתך your wages. See Genesis 29:15.

שרפת burning. See Numbers 19:6.

981

משארתם their kneading troughs. See Exodus 12:34.

982

שבעים *shivim*. Seventy, (70).

983 (prime)

עצם הבריאה *etzem ha-briah*. essence of creation, creative force. See 324.

984

בשבעים *Sodom ve-Amorah*. as seventy. See Deuteronomy 10:22.

יחסרון They lacked. See Genesis 18:28.

985

סדם ועמרה Sodom & Gomorrah.

העשרתי enriched. See Genesis 14:23.

986

שכל החפץ המבוקש *Saykel ha-khayfetz ha-meboqash*. Desirous Quest's intelligence, Intelligence of Conciliation, Rewarding Intelligence of Those Who Seek, or Desired and sought Consciousness. The 21st Path of Kaph. Desirous Quest (literally, "the inclination to seek") is from a root word *meboqash* meaning "emptiness," and has a meaning akin to the English nouns "hunger" and "thirst." In Man's quest for abundance, he responds to the life-power's descending influence like his other personal activities. We seek because what we seek is really within us, and whatever we gain is actually a recollection of what the One Identity already has in store for us. Kaph links memory (Chesed) and desire (Netzach).

One part of the secret of this path has to d with radical transformation in the physical body. Perseverance in right desire, meditation, and courage to face difficulties and learn to solve problems are required. Desire is the motive-power that leads to grasping the law of rotation and cyclicity (circulation of the universal Life-breath or "Wheels with Wheels." Through this path of Jupiter, we receive the divine influence and partake of the blessing, which it distributes to all modes of being. It must permeate subconsciousness through the practice of recollection. Recognition of the Ego's identity in man with cosmic Self changes the alchemical metals with the celestial gold of spiritual enlightenment. This is the "Great Reward" of the possessor of this path. See 448, 100, 194, 477, 20, 178, 636.

ותתעלף and wrapped [disguised] herself. See Genesis 38:14.

ותשרף and let her be burned [for prostitution]. But she was not because she was more righteous than Judah. See Exodus 12:10.

ושמרתם and you shall observe [celebrate]. See Exodus 12:17.

תקופת at the turn of. See Exodus 34:22.

ונתצתם and you shall break down. See Deuteronomy 12:3.

987

רבעיהן Their faces. See Ezekiel 1:17.

988

חפץ *khahfatz*. desire, love; to bend, serve. Tzaddi = 900, see 178.

חשמלים *chashmalim*. The Merciful Ones. Angelic Choir attributed to Chesed. Mem = 600, see 428.

989

סמנגלוף *Semangelof.* One of the 3 angels invoked against Lilith. Peh = 800, see 269.

990

I. Σ44 = 990

מספרים *mesaperiym.* declare, are telling. See 430.

ספר מים *Sepher Mem.* Book of Moses. See 430.

פרקים *phereqim.* joints, parts, members. See 430.

משמרתי my charge [requirements]. Genesis 26:5.

צדיק יסוד עולם *Tzadiq-Yesod-Olam.* The Righteous Is the Foundation of the World, a title of Yesod. See 420.

991 (prime)

אשפים *Ashpim.* Men wise in astrology and music. See 431.

אוצרות חשך treasures of darkness. See 889 and Isaiah 45:3.

992

בעדותיך to your statues. See Psalm 119:31.

993

החפץ *hakhahfatz.* to bend or curve. See 183.

וענוים יירשו ארץ *enaeim yeyereshu aretz.* "The meek shall inherit the earth." see 999, 176, 526, 291, 484.

τελειος λογος. *teleios logos.* perfect word.

994

השמים לט *tal ha-shamaim.* dew of heaven. Mem = 600. See 434.

גופה + תשר *thawshar + guphaw.* to present, to make a gift + body, corpse. The physical body is a gift from the divine. See 900, 94.

995

השרצת that swarms, the ones moving. See Leviticus 11:46.

996

רצון *ratzon.* delight, favor, will. Name of the 20th path. See 346.

עתיקא קדישא *Atiqa Qadisha.* The Most Holy Ancient One, a title of Kether.

תשמרון you shall keep, observe. See Deuteronomy 6:17.

997 (prime)

ונשארתם you shall be left [survive]. See Deuteronomy 4:27.

Κορη Κοσου. *Kore Kosmou.* "Virgin of the World." This last is the title of one of the Greco-Egyptian occult books ascribed to Hermes and refers to Isis-Sophia, the Virgin Bride who reveals the book's instruction.

νυμφη. *Nymph.* Bride. Refers to Malkuth, the "Holy City." Also, the world-dancer in Key 21 (Tav). See 476, 406, 55.

"The word connotes that which is or enfolds, a new development. The Muses were *Nymphai*: the Mother of Zeus was a *Nymphe*: so, too, was *Amaltheia* of the skies. The calyx that embraced the coming rosebud was a *nymph*, and also the web that shielded the winged creature emerging from the grub. And among human relations, the newly married maiden (*Kore*) was a *nymphe*. Hippolytus records a notable paragraph concerning the 'Mystic Bride' and her Offspring- her own Spiritualized Self.

This [Greater Myserion] is Heaven's Gate, and this is the House of God where the Good God, the Everlasting One, dwells: into which there shall enter none who is impure, or of the nature of the human soul or of the body; but it is kept for those only who are of the nature of the Spirit. [A House] where those entering must need cast their robes: and [where] all must become Bridegrooms [draped in the seamless robe] having been made *Andres* [compare *tetelesmenos* = androgynous] by virtue of the Virginal Spirit. For this is the Virgin who, receiving in her womb, both conceives and bears a Son, not psychical, nor physical, but a blessed Immortal - a Fruit of Ages. The Savior spoke clearly concerning these [*Andres*]. 'Narrow and steep is the Way that leads [speedily] unto Life Itself and FEW are they who enter upon it. But broad and spacious is the Way that leads into the Everchangeable and MANY are they who pass on by it.'" [Omikron, 1942, pp. 258-260.]

שפטים *shofetim.* judges. Mem = 600, see 439.

Ιερευσ Εαλημ. *Hiereus Salem.* Priest of Salem.

1000

א Large *Aleph*. The Fool. See 1, 61, 111.

תם *Tome*. Inmost point, center. Formed of Mem (Key 12) and Tav (Key 21), whose numbers mirror each other. Their paths are united at the interior center of the cube of space. With different pointing: *tam*. Whole, complete; simple, pious, innocent, sincere, mild, perfect. Mem = 600, see 440, 600.

קץ *qetz*. End. Tzaddi = 900, see 190.

שמנים *Shemonim*. eighty. See 430.

שן *Shen*. *Shen*. Tooth, fang. See 350.

תשקר deal falsely. See Genesis 21:23.

ששת six. See Exodus 16:26.

Κυριου. *Kuriou*. Lord. See 800.

1001

הרצון *ha ratzone*. Will, good pleasure. The 20th Path of Yod. See 351.

1002

בשן *Bashan*. soft, rich soil; Old Testament location. See 352.

קרבן *qarebahn*. offering, sacrifice; a form of vow. See 352.

בעל שם *Baal Shem*. "Master of the Name," a Jewish magician. See 442.

1003

תתגר contend you provoke. See Deut. 2:9.

1004

דם שק *Dam sack*. blood sack. See 444.

פרי עץ זרע זרע *Peri etz zorea zora*. The fruit of a tree yielding seed.

1006

תורת *Torath*. Laws. The kingdom of Malkuth, the manifested world, is the Law in Expression. One form of the Hebrew noun for "Law." see Exodus 13:9.

קוץ *Qotz*. Thorn.

ותקשר and bound, and she tied. See Genesis 38:28.

תותר the excellency, you will excel. See Genesis 49:4.

η νυμφη. *he nymphe*. The bride. See 998.

Η Κορη Κοσμου. *He kore kosmou*. The Virgin [of the] world. Title of an ancient Hermetic Book of Initiation-treats of the creation of the world-order, and the formation of the microcosm (human personality), which is the expression, in the space-time framework of the physical plane, of the whole range of cosmic forces. In tarot, the Virgin of the World is symbolized by the Dancer in Key 21, the true center or Self (I am). See 55, 543, 496, 998, 1776 (Greek).

1008

בן אשה *Ben-isah*. Son of a woman [1 Kings 7:14]. Refers to Hiram Abiff. Ben-eshah, "Son of Fire," is the archetypal of Grand Man, the Architect of the universe, the Tree of Life, the Logos or Word. Nun = 700, see 254, 273, 358.

כשן *Khoshen*. Breastplate of the High Priest. With different vowel points Choshen, Angel of Air. See 358.

תרבות a brood. See Numbers 32:14.

1009

שטן *Satan*. Adversary, accuser, archdemon of Kether.

תתגרו you contend, you make war. See Deuteronomy 2:5.

1010

ירושלים הקדשה *Ierusalaim ha-qodesh*. Jerusalem the Holy. Engraved on the Copper (Venus) ring of a magical wand. See 470, 1480, 414, 596.

כשפים *Keshaphim*. Witchcrafts, sorceries.

קיץ *Qayitz*. Summer.

שין Letter name *Shin*. Flame, tooth, fang. See 360.

למשמרת to be put away kept, care for. See Exodus 12:6.

ירקרקת greenish, greenish ones. See Leviticus 14:37.

φερομενη πνοη βιαια. A mighty rushing wind.

1011

את האדם *eth ha-adam*. essence of man. Genesis 1:27. See 451.

תהום *Tehom*. the abyss of the waters, great deep Genesis 1:2. See 451.

שנאנים *Shinanim*. Angelic Choir is sometimes associated with Tiphareth.

התורת the laws. See Exodus 18:20.

1014

חשון *Cheshvan*. The 2ⁿᵈ month of the Jewish calendar.

1015

הלך *ha.lak*. to go, depart, disappear; traveler. See 535.

השין *Ha-shin*. The tooth. Nun = 500.

1016

ותקעתם and you shall blow. See Numbers 10:5.

1018

שחקים *Sechchaqim*. Clouds; the 3ʳᵈ Heaven corresponding to Netzach. See 458.

יתבששו ashamed, they felt shame. See Genesis 2:25.

ותרבית and increase, or usury. See Leviticus 25:36.

1020

תכרת perish, she will be ruined. See Genesis 41:36.

תכרת you shall cut off. See Exodus 23:32.

1021

αποστολος. apostle. "A general sent for an undertaking: or, as a leader of the way up to a certain point of progress of responsibility. And, in particular, a Herald." - Omikron, 1942, pp. 250-251.

1024

I. (32 x 32) or 2^{10}

תדגת הים *bi-degath ha-yawm*. over fish of the sea. See 464.

זרזיף *Zarziyf*. Showers [Psalm 72:6]. A Qabalistic allusion to the descent of the secret power of the "Son of Fire: who is also the "Son of a Woman"- Hiram Abiff. Represented by the hidden paths of the Tree with Basic (Aleph) measure of 26. The descent of the powers of Ain Soph Aur through the Tree. Peh = 800, see 304, 1008.

1026

שכל מתנוצץ *Sekhel Mitnotze*. Resplendent Intelligence. The 10th Path of Malkuth is called the Resplendent Intelligence. It is so-called because it is exalted above every head and sits on the throne of Binah. It illuminates all the lights' splendor and causes the flowing forth influence from the Prince of Countenances.

Resplendent is from a root nawtzatz נעץ to glitter, to bloom, to flower. Mitnotze and Galgalim גלגלים, are numerically equal. Galgalim means whirlings or whirling motion and is a term for the sum total of the manifestations of the cosmic forces which have their beginning in Kether. The Path of Malkuth is always a receptacle for the total forces and activities expressed by that word.

ומשמרתם and their charge. See Numbers 3:31.

וישלח את הערב Genesis 8:7: And he sent forth the raven. See 1032.

שכון *shawkoon*. living, dwelling, inhabited, establishment, as a masculine noun, *Shikkoon*: realization, execution, repose, rest, provision of houses.

שערי מות *Shaari Mawveth*. Gates of Death. One of the 7 infernal mansions, the 3rd Hell, corresponding to Netzach. Psalm 9:14: "Thou that lift me up from the gates of death." Isaiah 38:10, it is "Gates of Sheol." see 337, 57, 911, 99, 566, 108, 291.

עולם היצירה *Olahm ha-Yetzirah*. world of formation (466).

תורתך your Law.

עשרים ושנים *Esrim u-Shenaim*. Twenty-two (22).

לא תעשה לך פסל *lo tha'aseh-leka pesel*. you shall not make graven images.

1028

במשמרותם According to their responsibilities. See 2 Chronicles 31:16.

ותורתיו. His laws. See Psalm 105:45.

Psalm 94:11. The Lord (IHVH) knows the thoughts of man; he knows that they are in vain (futile, fleeting). This verse adds to 1028.

וחידתם and their riddles (of the wise). See Proverbs 1:6. Mem = 600.

1030

שלשת three. See Genesis 30:36.

כריתת divorce. See Deuteronomy 24:1.

1032

ראשית הגלגלים *Rashith ha-galgalim*. The Beginning of the Whirling. Title of the Mundane chakra (sphere of activity of) Kether (Crown). Result of compression of energy at a center, causing rotation-Intention. Initial movement outward. The sphere of the first motion, Kether, is the beginning of all activity, whose nature is whirling or twisting. See 21, 37, 620, 676, 116.

צדק ושלום נשקו *Tdedek ve-shalom na.sha.ku*. "Righteousness and peace have kissed each other [Psalm 85:10]. צדק is the name of the planet Jupiter, whose quality of expression is the 1st letter (Kaph) in Kether. שלום, shalom is completeness, fullness, at the end or limit of a cycle (ת in כתר). כת are, therefore, "righteousness and peace." Expansion and contraction, complementary opposites are combined in the "Beginning of the Whirling Motion," which originates in Kether. See 860, 1892, 194, 376.

תורת יהוה *Torath Tetragrammaton*. The law of the Lord [Psalm 19:7]. According to the next word in the Psalm cited, this is the law, "perfect." It brings about the harmonious balance or equilibration, or opposite but complementary forces. It is the law of correlated expansion and contraction whereby motion is initiated, producing radiation and light extension. See 495.

ותורתך *ve-Torathkah*. and your law [Psalm 119:14]. See 1026.

וישלח את הערב *va-yeshalach eth ha-oreb*. And he sent forth the Raven [Genesis 8:7]. See 1026, 157, 21, 12.

ויעש אלהים *va-ya-as Elohim*. And God made

1034

זכר ונקבה ברא אתם *zakhar u-neqevah bara otham*. male and female created he them.

1035

והיה ליהוה לאות עולם *vehehyeh la yod-heh-wah-heh leoth olahm*. It shall be for the Lord for a name, for an everlasting sign [Isaiah 55:13]. The creative process's goal is to manifest the divine name, the complete expression and actual representation (sign) of all that is expressed by IHVH, "what was, what is, what will be." The Great Work conclusion is the perfect manifestation of God's idea of Himself, and when completed, it is perfected forever. See 45, 1480, 26, 351, 9, 18, 27, 36, 45, 54, 63, 72, 81, 90.

1039

שלטן *Shuletawn*. Rulership, dominion, sultan. Nun = 700, see 389.

1040

שמן *Shemen*. oil.

נצץ *natzatz*. to sparkle, gleam.

1044

משפטיהם *mishpatiham*. their judgments; their laws. See 484.

תאנטיפצת *Thantifaxath*. The Sentinel of the 32nd Path (Tunnel) of Tav on the Inverse Tree of Life.

I. The 32nd tunnel is under the aegis of Thantifaxath, whose number is 1040, which is the number of the Temenos (the precinct of a temple), and of Choros, which, according to *The Canon* (p. 195), was a dance by which the earliest worshippers invoked the deity, moving with measured steps around the altar'.
In this *Kala* is resumed the entire range of macro- and microcosmic *Kalas*. Sixteen *Kalas* are allotted to the macrocosm, and sixteen to the microcosm. The 32nd *Kala* is, in a sense, the *second* 16th and, as such pertains to Earth, typified by the altar. The sigil of Thantifaxath thus forms the earth or base of the entire series of *Kalas,* and the anode and cathode are linked or earthed to the *Tau* [i.e., the phallic current] that has its origin in the subconsciousness.

The sigil includes the geomantic figure of Acquisitio, which is attributed to the number nine and which, in this instance, is informed by the fiery Sagittarius - hence the electrical nature of Thantifaxath and its earthing in the hidden chthonian cells. These are typified by the forces of restriction and incarceration symbolized by Saturn.

The magical *siddhi* of this *Kala* comprises Works of Malediction and Death and the sickle of

Saturn - The Great One of the Night of Time -is the supreme emblem of this Tunnel, which is the resort of ghouls and larvae of the pit lit by the lurid phosphorescent glare of corpse candles.

The Ash and Cypress, the Nightshade, the Elm, and the Yew are the trees of darkness in whose shadows the tunnel disappears into the earth's deepest cells. Yet this tunnel has affinities with the ocean of space through its association with Set, the child of the Goddess of the Seven Stars whose planetary vehicle is Saturn.

Sebek, the crocodile, is the zoomorphic emblem of this tunnel, and Mako, - a name of Set as the son of Typhon and the powers of darkness, - is the secret deity of this nethermost cell. The God Terminus also belongs here, for this outpost of the cosmic system is truly the end of the cosmic vibrations, which, from this point, return to their source in the stars. This Kala's disease is arteriosclerosis, the hardening of the small arteries that adjunct of senility and the final rigor's onset.

The 32nd Path transmits the astral energies of Yesod to the sphere of Malkuth, thereby affecting the final 'earthing' of all the Kalas and influences streamed through Pluto's tunnels (Kether) to Earth (Malkuth). But at this utmost and final earthing of the cosmic current, a sudden reversal occurs; and this is the formula of Magick itself, that the Current having earthed itself in Malkuth now turns back upon itself and streaks up the Tree to dissolve in its source in the transcosmic centers of energy represented by Kether. [Grant, 1994, p. 253-255.]

1045

תהלים *tehillum*. Psalms.

השמן *ha-shahmen*. the oil.

1046

תרומת offering, gift. See Exodus 30:14.

וקשרתם and you shall bind (tie) them. See Deuteronomy 6:8.

1048

רצון הקדם *Ratzone ha-qadom* + זרע היהודים *Zeroh Hayehudim*. The Primal Will + the seed of the Jews. See 346, 144, 691, 277, 75, 357.

1050

תשמיש *tashemish*. Coition. Attributed to Yod, the hand, as the organ of touch. The sense of touch is associated with Yesod and the animal soul. See 80, 1022, 1119.

בית לחם *Beth-lechem*. House of bread; Bethlehem (490).

מפרין (the) books. See 400.

1051

המקשרות the stronger. See Genesis 30:41.

1052

רוץ עולמים *tsore olahmim*. Everlasting Rock. Everlasting Strength (492).

1054

המתטרת *Hemethterith*. The sentinel of the 15th Path (tunnel) of Heh on the inverse Tree of Life.

I. The 15th tunnel is illuminated by the *Kala* of the Star, known in the Book of Thoth as the 'Daughter of the Firmament; the Dweller between the waters.' She is also the Mother-aspect of *Kala* 13, the Virgin, and *Kala* 14, the Whore. The letter assigned to both Mother and Daughter is Heh, the number 5, and the Pentagram is her seal. The two waters are respectively the blood of the virgin daughter and the milk of the *enceinte* mother.

The Guardian of this Pylon is Hemethterith. Her number is 1054, which is that of the Greek word

Naos, meaning a 'ship' or 'ark,' also the 'navel' and hence the womb. Her sigil suggests a face above three equal-armed crosses arranged in a descending triangle with two serpentine forms dividing the crosses.

The relevant vesicle of 231 reads: Now riseth Ra-Hoor-Khuit, and dominion is established in the Star of Flame.

This is a reference to the child Horus manifesting in Ra-Hoor-Khuit as the Mother's son. The animal sacred to this *Kala* is the peacock, one of the sacred symbols of the Yezidi who worship Shaitan under this form. The peacock is also the *vahana* of Kartikeya, the Hindu Mars, born of the element fire.

In alchemical terms, the 15th *Kala* is that of Sulphur purifying by fire; in other words, the Mother is redeemed by the son's birth. Note that Path 15 links Chokmah, the Sphere of the Magus, with Tiphareth, the Sphere of the Sun.

Chokmah, the Sphere of the Stars, thus pours down its *Kalas* along the 15th Path into the power-zone of the Sun-Son, Ra-Hoor-Khuit (i.e., Tiphereth).

The magical *siddhi* associated with this *Kala* is Astrology, which - on the other side of the Tree - has a very different connotation to that which it usually obtains, for it is there the stars' genuine science or *Kalas*. It differs from the popular conception of astrology, as does the Tarot from the vulgar playing-card game.

The stellar energy that flashes its light through this tunnel is symbolized by the Dog Star, Sothis, and the nature of the child born in this cell of Hemethterith is satanic in the sense that it is procreated by a magical method involving the use of the Eye of Set.

The *Behemiron*, meaning the 'bestial,' are the Qliphoth of this *Kala*, and their name refers to this magical formula. [Grant, 1994, pp. 181-185.]

1056

הדם הוא הנפש *Ha-dam hu ha-nefesh*. Blood is the life. See 496.

ופרסין *upharsin*. divided. See 406.

כשלון *kishshawlon*. a fall. See 406.

תרומתי my offering. See Exodus 25:2.

1057

תאומים *Teomim*. Twins; Gemini.

1060

שכל נסתר *saykel nisetar*. Hidden or Occult Intelligence. The 7th path of Netzach. From the verb *sawther* סתר, to hide, to veil, to cover, to conceal. This veiling has to do with the way desire manifests in human consciousness. We begin our journey toward adeptship while still deluded by the dream of personal separateness caused by the illusions of embodied consciousness. When we desire something, we want it, which means we seem to lack whatever we want. To the eye of sense, there is no visible evidence that we really possess what we desire. However, when we understand that the whole creation is mental, we realize that the desires rising into our personal consciousness are intimations of what is already prepared for us. In the Briatic world, all strong desires are actualities.

משכן *mishkan*. tabernacle.

1061 (prime)

היכל רוצן *Hekel Ratzon*. Place of Delight, Heavenly Mansion corresponding to Tiphareth.

הנותרת the remainder, the ones remaining. See Leviticus 10:12.

1062

צמר לבו *zehmer lahban*. white wool. See 412.

סמן הטוב *shem ha-tobe*. precious oil (or ointment). See 412.

1063

בית האלהים *Beth-ha-Elohim*. The House of God. See 503.

1064

עין אל יהוה יראיו *ayin Jehovah al-yeraia*. The eye of Jehovah is on them that fear him. King James translation. See 414.

1065

זאויר אנפין *Zauir Anpin*. The Lesser Countenance, a title of Tiphareth.
"The One from the Egg, the Six and the Five, give the number 1065, the value of the first-born." [Blavatsky, 1967, p. 47]

1066

רעה צאן a shepherd of flocks. See 416.

יוד סמך וו דלת *Yesod*. Basis, Foundation, spelled in full. See 507.

המאור הקטן *ha-maor ha-qaton*. the lesser light.

פרצופים *partzuphim*. faces. Persons.

כתרומת as that which is set aside, an offering of. See Numbers 15:20.

מתורתך your Torah. See Psalms 119:18.

תסתרו your will be sheltered (hidden).

1067

בעלי השמים *daali ha-shamaim*. Masters of the heavens, astrologers. See 507.

הנותרות that remain, the ones remaining. See Leviticus 27:18.

1070

שכל קיים *Sakhel Qayyum*. Stable intelligence. 23rd path of Mem. See 510.

משלשת three years old. See Genesis 15:9.

1073

אורכא דאנפין *Arika Danpin*. Vast Countenance, one of the titles of Kether. See 423.

ο Θεος της γης. *ho Theos tes ges*. The God of the earth.

1075

שיר השירים *shir ha-shirim*. The Song of Songs.

1076

εταυρος. cross. "Generally, this word implies merely an upright, that is, a standard: symbolically, it suggests a lofty aspiration. The addition of a transom, considered from left to right, adds the suggestion of progress: that is, breath and height of development. The Tau T is a suitable ideogram for human aspiration and effort. When the upright and the transom bisect each other at right angles, we have the 'Cross of the Resurrection,' which signifies the completion of the Soul's aionian labors, that is, the *Anastasis*. Compare [Jesus said to His Apostles] 'HE who has Crucified the world is he who has found My Word, and has fulfilled it according to the Will of Him Who sent Me.'" [Omikron, 1942, pp. 262-263.]

1080

מעשרתיכם your tithes. See Numbers 18:28.

η θυρα ανεωγμενη. *he thrua aneogmene.* The open door.

1081

I. Σ46 = 1081

תפארת *Tiphareth.* Beauty, the 6th Sephirah. The seat of the Creative Word or Logos. Sphere of the sun. the "Intelligence of separated influence" or "Intelligence of parted or allotted outflow." Sometimes "Intelligence of Mediating Influence." Microprospus or lesser countenance. A reservoir, into which flow, by the various letters' channels, influences the 5 sephiroth above it on the Tree. The principle of rulership-the "King" (Melek) who wears the crown (Kether). Tiphareth is the active manifestation of the Cosmic Self as the Ego through the path of Gimel (High Priestess-Memory), which projects *Mezla* [78], the holy influence, from Kether. Represent the formative world of Imagination (Ruach, רוח). At this point, the universal life-breath's power manifests itself as the active principle at the core of our personalities, or "I AM," the Primal Will (Eheyeh or Yekhidah). The consciousness of Lesser Adept in Rosicrucian Initiation. See 45, 52, 67, 80, 311, 528, 1370, 640, 548, 536, 90, 281, 666, 281.

The 6th Sephirah is also חמה, Khammaw, or שמש, Shemesh, the Sphere of the Sun. Sun-gods are gods of justice and its administration. Thus Apollo, among the Greeks, was the rewarder and punisher and patron of the arts, especially music. The Egyptian deity Osiris is also a dispenser of rewards and punishments, a god of fertility, and a sun-god. In the New Testament, the "Son of Man" is a judge, a king, a fertility Source (for from him flows the water of life), and is called "Sun of righteousness."

נוטריקון *Notariqon.* The cabalistic theory of acronyms. See 431.

לך אותרות חשך *Lekah Otzeroth Khoshek.* To thee the treasures of darkness [Isaiah 45:3]. The "darkness" is the primordial state of matter. Its treasures are those of the unmanifest, potential state of being, as limitless now as at any time past.

רכב רבתים אלהים רבתים אלפי *rekeb Elohim ribothaim alifiy.* "The chariots of God are 20,000." "Chariots" are to be understood as vehicles of manifestation, and the number 20,000 may be expressed in Hebrew by a large Kaph (Kaph). The "Chariots" are the wheels of manifestation.

והשתתרתי and I will hide. See Deuteronomy 31:17.

1082

בן עיש *Ben Ayish.* Son of Ayish; Ursa Minor.

ותרועת trumpet blast, and shout of. See Numbers 23:21.

1085

ערז אברהם *zerah Abraham.* seed of Abraham. See 525.

1090

הרמש הרמש *ha-remes ha-romes.* The creeping thing that creeps.

צרף *tzaraf.* to refine, melt together, connect, combine; also to try, to examine. See 370.

1091 (prime)

והעתרתי and I will entreat [pray]. See Exodus 8:25.

ΦιλαδελΦια. *Philadelphia.* Brotherly love. See 1099.

לחם תמיד *lekhem tawmid*. Perpetual bread. See 532.

1094

בכורות מכת *makath be-khoroth*. The Slaying of the Firstborn.

1096

עולם העשיה *Olahm ha-Assiah*. The World of Action or the Material World. See 536.

מקום ספיר *maqom-saphir*. place of sapphires. See 536.

ספר ספירות *Sepher Sephiroth*. Book of the Sephiroth (numbers, emanations).

פישון *Pison*. A river of Eden associated with Fire.

1098

לרכב בשמי שמי קדם *larokeb beshemi shemi-qedem*. Who rides upon the heavens, the heavens of ancient days – Psalm 68:33.

שני המארת הגדלים *shene ha-meoroth ha-gedholim. Tan*. Two great lights.

1099

η φιλαδελφια. *heh Philadelphia*. Brotherly Love. See 1091.

1100

שוכן עד *shoken ad*. dwelling in eternity. See 450.

תן *Tan*. sea-serpent or monster; jackal. See 450.

רץ *ratz*. piece.

תשת you shall drink. See Leviticus 10:9.

1101

ארץ *Aretz*. Earth. One of the 4 elements, one of the 7 earths corresponding to the Supernals. See 291.

אשף *Ashshaf*. astrologer, enchanter, a magician.

1102

עולם מושכל *Olam Mevshekal*. Intellectual World.

תשבת you shall rest. See Exodus 23:12.

שבתת *Sabbaths*. See Leviticus 23:38.

1104

ותצא הארץ דשא *va-totze ha-aretz deshe*. and the earth brought forth grass.

1105

השתרר ruling, prince. See Numbers 16:13.

תשתה drinks, she drinks. See Deuteronomy 11:11.

1106

תרומתכם your gift, Terumah. Numbers 18:27.

1107

אתון *Attun*. furnace. See 457.

1108

תשחת destroy. See Deuteronomy 9:26.

בשררות in the stubbornness. See Deuteronomy 29:18.

1110

מצפץ *Matz-Patz.* a name of God by Temurah. See 300.

תתעמר you shall treat as a slave. See Deuteronomy 21:14.

το αιμα Ιησου. *to haima Yesou.* The blood of Jesus.

υιος μονος. Only son.

οι κεκλημενοι της αληθειας. *Hoi keklemenoi tes aletheasm.* Those called of truth.

1111

והתמכרתם and you shall be sold, and you will sell yourself. Part of the "Curses for Disobedience" from Chapters 15 to 28 (Chapter 29 starts the renewal of the covenant) Eleven is *dahab*, gold in Aramaic. Also *zad*, proud, arrogant, insolent, presumptuous and ode, the fire of the magic light, firebrand, and the magic power (see Aleph, 111). 101 is *Jah Elohim*, Divine name of Daath; *awsam*, a storehouse, rich harvest; *belahatahem*, by their secret enchantments; *qea*, vomit and *alo*, swallowed, destroyed. This suggests that the curse of disobedience is the practice of magic in a way that perverts the rich abundance of that same light. See Deuteronomy 28:68.

1112

תשבית shall you suffer, to be lacking, you leave out. See Leviticus 2:13.

1114

ותשחת and [she] was corrupted. See Genesis 6:11.

1115

הנסתרת the secret things. See Deuteronomy 29:28.

1116

כתר מלכות *Kether Malkuth.* The Crown of Kingdom. Refers to Kether, the Crown (620) in Malkuth (496) and Malkuth in Kether [Book of Esther]. An affirmation that the end is in the beginning and the beginning in the end. "I am the Alpha and the Omega." [Book of Revelation].

שמעין *Simeon.* A tribe of Israel associated with Pisces.

1117 (prime)

ולתפארת and for beauty, honor, glory. See Exodus 28:2.

1118

שמע ישראל יהוה אלהינו יהוה אחד *Shema Israel IHVH Elohenu IHVH Echad.* Hear, O Israel: The Lord our God is one Lord. Deuteronomy 6:4.

מנא מנא תקל ופרסין *mena mena tekel pharsin.* numbered, numbered, weighed and divisions; the handwriting on the wall. *Mena*, means part of, number, ordain, set; *tekel*: to balance, be weighted; *pharsin*: is from the root פרס, meaning to break in pieces, split, distribute, deal, divide (usually without violence). See Daniel 5:25.

תשחית you shall mar, destroy, clip off [hair]. See Leviticus 19:27.

1119

תשתחוה shall bow down. See Exodus 20:5.

1120

כשף *Kashaf.* witch, a magician. See 400.

שתיתי drank. See Deuteronomy 9:9.

καρπος μητρας. *karpos metras.* Fruit of the womb.

1121

נחש הנחשת *nachash ha-nechsheth*. brazen serpent.

1124

ויהי האדם לנפש חיה *vayehi ha-Adam le-nefesh chaiah*. And man became a living soul. See 564 & Genesis 2:7.

חלם יסודות *Kholem Yesodoth*. Breaker of the Foundations. The Sphere of the Elements. See 564.

1125

I. Σ49 = 1125. The theosophic extension of the Kamea of Netzach.

דעתיקים עתיקא *Authiqa-de-Athiqin*. The Ancient of Ancients.

1126

מנה מנה תקל ופרסין *mene mene tekel upharsin*. Numbered, numbered, weighed and divisions; the handwriting on the wall.

כשוף *kishshoof*. magic, sorcery, witchcraft. See 406.

1128

זעיר אנפין *Zauir Anpin*. Lesser Countenance. See 478.

1131

אדיריריך *Adiryaron*. The Mighty One sings; a title of Tiphareth.

1134

חצר עינון *Hretzar enon*. Enclosure of the Fountains. A point near Dan on the ideal N.E. boundary of Cannan. Has alchemical significance. Nun = 700, see 484, 993, 190, 54.

1135

ויאמר אלהים יהי אור *vayomer Elohim yehi aur*. "And the Elohim said, 'Let there be light.'" see 575.

הקדוש ברוך הוא *ha-Qodosh Barukh Hu*. The Holy One, blessed be he.

והשתחוית and you will bow down/worship. See Deuteronomy 4:19.

1141

אור כשדים *ur Kasdim*. light of the Chaldees (astrology). See 581.

אמרתך *emrawthaka*. your word. See 661.

שכל נאמן *Sekhel Ne'eman*. Faithful Intelligence. 22nd Path of Lamed. See 491.

1145

צבאות אלהים *Elohim Tzabaoth*. God of Armies, Creative Powers of Hosts. The Divine Name attributed to Hod, Water, the West. See 585.

1146

ירושלם *Jerusalem*. (older spelling) abode of peace, or founded in peace. See 586.

לויטן *Leviathan* the dark serpent, Dragon. See 496.

1147

παρθενος ουρανια. Heavenly virgin.

יהוה בחכמה יסד ארץ כונן שמים בתבונה "By wisdom, the Lord laid the earth's foundations, by understanding he set the heavens in place;" see Proverbs 3: 19 & 3467 (value with Great Numbers).

1148

בתשומת pledge, in the placing, about something left. See Leviticus 5:21.

1149

להשתחות to bow down. See Genesis 37:10.

1150

נשף *nahshaf.* to blow, to breathe, evening twilight see 430.

נתן *Nathan.* to give.

1153

יש יהוה במקום הזה ואנכי לא ידעתי The Lord was in this place, and I was not aware of it. Said of Jacob after he had the dream of the ladder. See Genesis 28:16

1156

Τετελεσιαι. *Tetelestai.* It is finished. See 859.

1157

תתנשאו you do raise yourself up, to set yourselves. See Numbers 16:3.

1160

תנין *Tanniyn.* serpent, dragon, whale. See 510.

1161

ארץ נוד *Eretz Nod.* The land of Nod. Old Testament place name. See 351.

1164

תשחתון you deal corruptly, you become corrupt. See Deuteronomy 4:16.

1165

ארץ תחתונה Nethermost Earth.

1166

יסוד התפארת *Yesod ha-Tiphareth.* Foundation of Beauty.

1171 (prime)

הארץ אדני *Adonai Ha-Eretz.* Lord of Earth (Malkuth). Divine name associated with Malkuth, Earth and the North. See 361.

1174

תשחיתון you will become corrupt. See Deuteronomy 31:29.

1175

ששה ישר *Shishshah Asar.* sixteen (16).

והשתחויתם and you worshipped them. See Exodus 24:1.

1176

פרצוף partzuf. person, face.

1178

μυστηριον. *mysterion*. mystery. "Literally "For the guarding of things learned in secret.' A *Mysterion* was a school, a sodality, or a mode of practice conducted in secrecy. The imitations and shadows of the FEW Great Mysteries were probably numerous, but of these FEW, the practices and aims were never divulged. Hypothetically, they may be said to have led their severally tested entrants into the far reaches of the Evolution of the Soul: to have stimulated them, prematurely, to the Second Birth-that is, to the Awakening of the Spiritual Consciousness in the womb of the pure Soul. Your *mystai* eventually attained to True Wisdom-the Practical Knowledge of That Which Is." [Omikron, 1942, p. 258.]

1180

שערים *shawrim*. gates. See 620.

רשעים *rawshawim*. wicked men. See 620.

עשרים *esrim*. twenty (20).

ותשתוין and they bowed down. See Genesis 33:6.

1181

στοματος. Mouth. See Revelations 12:15.

1182

אבן החכמות *eheben ha-chokmoth*. stone of the wise. See 532.

1184

η αληθινη διαθηκη Κυριου. *heh alethine diatheke kuriou*. The true covenant of the Lord.

1186

בית עדן *Beth-Eden*. House of Eden. See 536.

1188

אין ברוחו רמיה *ayin beruacho remiyah*. In his spirit there is no guile. See 538.

1190

שרפים *Seraphim*. Angelic Choir associated with Geburah.

1192

עולם יסודות *Olam Yesodoth*. The World of Foundation; the Sphere of the Elements; the part of the material world corresponding to Malkuth.

1194

ο αστηρ εν τη ανατολη. The star in the east.

1195

התנשמת the horned [white] owl. See Leviticus 11:18.

1196

מלכות האדם *Malkuth Awlam*. and everlasting kingdom. See 636.

פעלות האדם *Pehulloth ha-adam*. the works of man. See 636.

1197

ותתפשהו and she caught him [Joseph, by the cloak]. See Genesis 39:12.

1198

בית יוד נון הה *Binah* spelt in full. See 548.

1199

עשרים ואחד *Esrim ve-Achad*. twenty-one (21).

1200

כוס תנחומים *Kos tankhumim*. cup of consolation. See 640.

שכל נשרש *Sekhel Nesharash*. Radical Intelligence. The 5th Path of Geburah. Derived from a noun meaning "root." The first three letters of נשרש (*Nesharash*) spell נשר *Nasher*, meaning "Eagle" and its last three letters from שרש *Sharash*, "A root." Thus, Radical Intelligence is the "Root of the Eagle," which is Scorpio, ruled by Mars. The root or basis of those activities linked with Scorpio, when the Scorpio has been transformed into the Eagle. The root of physical existence becomes purified into the highest powers of creative imagination, constructive reasoning and foresight. The animal reproductive (Mars) force is "Set up for the ruin of many, and for the salvation of the few" at present. See 216, 92, 64, 850.

תו שין וו בית הה *Tav-Shin-Vav-Beth-Heh*. Letter-name values for *Teshubah*, Return. The secret value of תשובה is the number of the 12 tribes of Israel combined with the three-fold multiplication of the number of Yod, and also the number of Malkuth, or 12x10x10x10 = 1200. The tribes are the powers of Adam. See 713.

שרשת chains. See Exodus 28:22.

1201

והתנשמת and the chameleon, and the horned owl. See Leviticus 11:30.

1206

תקון *Tiqqun*. restoration.

וקשקשת and scales (as on a fish). See Leviticus 11:9.

1207

ראשון *Rashun*. first, former, primary. See 557.

1208

בשקתות in the troughs. See Genesis 30:38.

1210

שישרת *Tarshish*. Blackness. Also, the name of the angel of Geburah of Briah. In Exodus 28:20, an emerald.

I. Paul Case" "It is the name of a precious stone, derived from 900= תרש, to be strong, firm, hard. Josephus identifies this stone with chrysolite or Topaz. In the Authorized Version, it is rendered as Beryl. Others think it is Amber. The last is probably the real derivation since it agrees with other Alchemical symbolism. Note, however, that blackness is not the true Hebrew meaning." [Paul Case of D.D. Bryant's Philosophers Stone, V]. Solomon's gold to adorn his temple was said to come from Tarshish [1 Kings 10:22, 22:48].

II. Beryl is linked with Venus and with Leo. Geburah of Briah is Mars in the creative world, Venus is connected with creative imagination (Key 3). Remember that "Brass (i.e., Venus) is molten out of the stone" and that Gold comes from the North (Mars). The Beryl crystal contains a hexagonal pattern linking it with Tiphareth and the heart (Sun) center [Amber is a yellowish, translucent resin, which becomes strongly electric by friction.] "Blackness" suggests the state of the alchemical first matter during the sage of putrefaction (Scorpio). Jehoshaphat means "God has Judged" and is connected with

Geburah, sphere of Mars. See 54, 345, 410, 478, 900.

שפתתיך *sef.toh.tah.eech.* Your lips. Song of Songs 4:3.

1212

תשוקתו his desire. See Genesis 4:7.

1215

שהם יקר The precious onyx. See 665.

1217

שכל בית הקדוש *Sekhel Beth ha-Shepha.* The intelligence of the House of Influence. The title of the 18th Path of Cheth. Connects Binah, the great sea, with the source of volition in Geburah. Represents the field (fence) or personality and is related to the quality of water. It is the channel of the abundant overflow of the fiery activity of the Life-power, taking form as objects, both "thing" and "creatures." This path's possession is to overcome these limitations' elusive power by learning how to use them. The perception of reality wakes consciousness into the stage where no good and perfect gift is withheld. Those who make themselves receptive to the One Will manifest Willpower. This state of being is called the alchemical Philosopher's Stone. It is found in the Holy of Holies, the Adytum of the inner temple of super-consciousness. The field of mastery is that of speech, both thought and vibratory combinations of sound vibrations. See 450, 100, 867, 414.

1218

תחתית the depth, below. See Deuteronomy 32:22.

1219

ιχθυς. *Ichthys.* Fish. The Greek equivalent for the Hebrew letter-name Nun (נון). This word forms the Greek sentence's initials meaning "Jesus Christ, son of God, Savior." Note that 1219 is 23 (the number of חיה, Chaiah, the Life-force) times 53 (*Ehben*, stone). The stone is the Elixir of Immortality. As a proper name, Nun means perpetuity and eternality. Note that the name Jesus is a variant of Joshua, Moses's successor, whose father was named Nun. See 106, 700.

1220

בתחתית at the foot of (the mountain). See Exodus 19:17.

1221

תורה האדם *Torah ha-Adam.* The law of Adam (Humanity). See 661.

מלאך האלהים *Melakh ha-Elohim.* Messenger of God. See 181.

βασιλεια Θεοτητος. Kingdom of the Godhead.

1223

AZΩת *Azoth.* Beginning and end. An alchemical term relating to the first matter, the Quintessential (see 158 Latin), or the 5th essence, akin to the Akasha of Hinduism. See 1, 400, 800, 801, 22.

The word Azoth is formed from the 1st letter of the Hebrew alphabet, Aleph, and the second, third and fourth letters as the last letters of the Latin, Greek and Hebrew alphabet. This Azoth symbolizes the Great Work's completion by passing out of the limitations of time into timelessness (eternity).

"Azoth is a mystical and cabalistic word used principally by the Alchemist of medieval times... in one sense it, therefore, signifies the beginning and the end, or that which is contained within these limits, otherwise, "The essence of all things." In harmony with this, it is used to denote 'the Astral Light' and in Alchemy signifies the philosophical Mercury, the root of all metals, or the divine essence brought own into the operation, which it completes." [Micheal Whity, The meaning of Azoth, Azoth Magazine, July 1920, page 6]. See 11, 414.

1225

I. Σ49 = 1225. 175 x 7 = 1225. The total value of the numbers in a magic square of Venus.

עתיקא דעתקין *Athiqa de-Authiqin*. The Ancient of the Ancient Ones, a title of Kether, the Crown. See 620, 49, 175.

המפתן the threshold. See 1 Samuel 5:4.

היתרים the thongs, ropes. [that bind Sampson]. See Judges 16:9.

ואשחיתך and I will destroy you. Jeremiah 15:6.

והתגדלתי and I will magnify myself. Ezekiel 38:23.

המעשרים those who collect tithes. Referring to the Levites. See Nehemiah 10:38.

חרבתיהם their swords. See Micah 4:3.

ויהי בשלם סכו ומעונתו בציון Psalm 76:3: His tent is in Salem, his dwelling place in Zion.

ירעם הים ומלאו תבל וישבי בה Psalm 98:7: Let the sea resound and everything in it, the world, and all who live in it [her].

1226

שמש יהוה *Shemesh-Jehovah*. Sun of IHVH (Tiphareth). See 666.

תשוקתך your desire. See Genesis 3:16.

1230

וערפל חתלתו and-thick-darkness, wrapping-of-him. See Job 38:9.

1231

גברורתכם *geburathekem*. your strength [Isaiah 30:15] Mem = 600, see 671, 216.

1223

טמירא דטמירין *Temira De-Temirin*. the Concealed of the Concealed (a title of Kether). See 583.

פלאיה דעת ינמם נשגבה לא אוכל לה Such knowledge is too wonderful for me, too lofty for me to attain." see Psalm: 139:6.

1239

כבוד ראשון *Kabodh Rishon*. First Splendor, Primal Glory, a title of Kether. See 589.

1240

τροφος. *trophos*. Nurse.

1242

אפיסת הרעיות Defective thoughts, thinking. A source of sorrow, sin, and the illusion of separateness. See 691, 551.

1255

עולם מורגש *Olam Morgash*. Moral World. See 695.

והתקדשתם and sanctify [consecrate] yourselves. See Leviticus 11:44.

1256

אש השמים *Esh ha-shamaim*. Fire of Heaven (Key 16). See 696.

1258

תתחתן shall marry.

κεκλημενοι κυριου. *keklemenoi kuriou.* The Lord's chosen.

ο παρακλητος. The true comforter.

1260

פרי עץ *Periy etz.* the Fruit of the Tree. See 450.

1263

γνωσις. *Gnosis.* Inner knowledge that is revealed through contact with the divine.

1266

חרש נחשת *Khoresh nekhosheth.* A worker of brass [1 Kings 7:14]. Refers to the Father of Hiram Abiff. Brass is the symbolic metal of Venus, creative imagination. He who is a worker in brass excels in creative imagination. See 636.

כי עמך מקור חיים באורך נראה אור For with thee is the fountain of life (and) through your light do we see light. Psalm 36:9.

1269

Δειπνον Κυριου. *Depinon Kuriou.* The Lord's Supper.

1271

σταυρος. *stauros.* Cross. Latin *Crux.* Relates to the letter Tav as the cross (Saturn) at the center of the cube. Some say Stauros is derived from its standing erect with its arms horizontal. Three forms of the cross are 1. the Tau cross, shaped like the capital letter T; 2. the cross formed from an opened out cube, called the cubical cross; and 3. the St. Andrew's cross, formed like a capital X.

The X is the early form of Tav, as shown in the 9th century B.C. inscription of Debon. See 406, 713, 126, 291, 400, 58 Latin.

η γνωσις. *heh gnosis.* The wisdom, i.e., chokmah, The secret wisdom, is the Qabalah (Reception). See 294, 137, 1378, 73 & *True and Invisible* [p. 41]

he kleronomia hagion. The sacred inheritance. Greek spelling unknown.

1272

η γεδμετρια. *he gedmetria.* the geometry.

1274

אלהים חיים *Elohim Khayim.* Elohim of Lives, Living God. See 154.

שקערורת penetrating streaks, depressions. See Leviticus 14:37.

1278

מים חיים *mem chaeem.* living waters. See 158.

1280

שכל שלם *saykel shalom.* Perfect Intelligence. See 720.

1286

κερατιων Husks, shells. See Luke 15:15, the story of the prodigal son.

בהתעטף Ebb away. In Jonah 2:8, "when my life was ebbing away…"

ישועתך Your salvation. See Psalms 67:3.

תפלשון Mete out (to give out by measure). In Psalms 58.3: No, in your heart, you devise injustice, and your hands mete out violence on the earth."

1290

עתיקין *Atiqin*. Ancient Ones.

צפייתן *tzephiyathan*. Their appearance (Sephiroth). See 640.

1295

πνευμα της γης. *Pneuma tes ges*. Spirit of the earth.

1298

גפרית אדם *Gawfriyth Adam*. Sulfur Adam. See 738.

1299

שכל מוגשם *Sekhel Mughshan*. Corporeal or Incarnating Intelligence. The 29th Path of Qoph. See 739.

1300

שרף *Seraph*. Fiery Serpent. Ruler of Fire; one of the Seraphim. See 580.

1309

שין בית תו אלף יוד *Shin-Beth-Tav-Aleph-Yod*. The secret number of שבתאי *Shabbathai* or Saturn, meaning "Rest." See 713, 1200.

This number is the perfection of the Tribes of Israel (1309). Note that the active tribes are 11, not 12, because Aaron's sons are Levites, separate from the rest. See *C.31*.

1311

איש תם *Aish Toom*. A perfect man. Mem = 600, see 311, 440, 751, 1000.

1313

ευλογεω. *eulogia*. Eulogy, a blessing. Also, the blessed and consecrated bread of the early Christian Eucharist. See 93 Latin.

1303

מסתגף a hermit (lit., "a hidden body"). See 583.

1304

הוא ירעה אותם *Hu yire-eh otawm*. He shall feed them. See 744.

υδωρ. Water. See Revelations 12:15.

1305

השרף *ha-seraf*. the fiery serpent, fiery angels. See 585.

לחוף אנית "For a haven of ships." see 585.

1306

שקוץ *shiqqootz*. disgusting, filthy, an abomination, an idol. See 496.

1310

ανθρωπος *Anthropos*. man. "For *aner* [159] means, par excellence, someone distinguished for a certain virtue, while *anthropos* means someone who is not distinguished for anything in particular. The word *aner* indicates the hero, the leader, the expert, it is said to be akin to ανυω, I complete, while the noun ανυσις means directing, a leading-up to the Above. Both the words *anthropos* and *aner* may be of the common gender." [Omikron, 1942, pp. 249-250.]

תתפתל you-show-yourself-shrewd. See Psalm 18:26.

1313

אבן האדם Ehben ha-Adam. the Stone of Adam. See 103.

1316

נרון קסר Nero Caesar. See 666.

1317

שמנלמאור shemen le-mawaur. oil for lighting. See 667.

1320

מים יוד מים Mem-Yod-Mem. The letter-name Mem, spelled in plentitude. See 200.

שמעתיך I have heard you. See Genesis 17:20.

1321

ותהרין they (Lots daughter's) became pregnant. See Genesis 19:36.

1327

את שם יהוה Eth-shem Jehovah. The essence of God's name. See 767.

1336

דם ענבים Dam enabim. Blood of grapes. See 216.

1337

עולם הקליפות Olahm ha-Qlippoth. The World of Shells or Demons. Assiah. See 777.

1344

את הכרבים ואת להט החרב Cherubim + a flaming sword. Genesis 3:24: "After he drove the man out, he placed on the east (front) side of the Garden of Eden Cherubim and a flaming sword flashing back and forth to guard the way to the Tree of Life."

להט שרף Lat serf. Magic serpent. Lahat means to burn as well as to hide; hence to use occult or magic arts. Seraph is the Serpent on Numbers 21:8 that was placed on a pole that all who gazed on it was cured of snake bite.

1346

מצפון זהב יהתה Gold comes from the north. See 696.

1348

בן אלהים Ben Elohim. Son of God. See 138.

1349

גן אלהים Gan Elohim. Garden of Elohim. Rabbi Gikatalla: "… the children of Israel, will inherit upper Eden, which is Binah." Binah is associated with the Divine name Elohim. See 139. [Gikatalla, 1994, p. 231.]

1351

κρυσταλλος. crustallos. Clear ice, ice, rock crystal.

1352

סוד הפעולות הרוחניות Sod ha-pehulloth ha-rauchnioth. The secret of all spiritual activities. The 19th Path of Teth. See 1702.

1354

חכם בני ושמח לבי ואשיבה חרפי דבר Be wise, my son, and bring joy to my heart; then I can answer anyone who treats me with contempt (reproaches me). See Proverbs 27:11 & 1914 (value with Great Numbers).

1355

μονοκερως *monokeros*. Unicorn.

1356

ετελειωσα. *Eteleiosa*. [I have] finished, literally perfecting. See John 17:4. See 1984, 859 Greek.

1358

ψυχη. *pshcye*. *Psyche*, personality; Rauch [רוח].

ψυχη. *Pneuma*. The divine soul, or Neshamah, connected with Binah. Always in contact as the divine presence, Shekinah, with psyche. See 1708, 395, 710, 214.

εικων λογου. Image of the word.

η μεγαλη γνωσις . The great gnosis.

1359

אבן מאסו הבונים התיה לראש פנה Psalm 118:22. "The stone, the builders, rejected is become the chief corner-stone." See 151, 273.

1360

לוקיע שמים la-*rawqiya shamaim*. Firmament of Heaven. See 800.

ערלום לבבכם *awreloth lebabikem*. Foreskins of your heart. See 800.

1362

η πνοη πνευματος. The breath of the spirit.

1364

לחם ויין *lekhem va-yahyin*. Bread & Wine. See 154.

1369

ο επι-ιερευς Θεου. *ho epi-ierus theou*. High-priest of God.

1370

עשתרת *Ashtoreth*. The Hebrew name of the Goddess Aphrodite, whose birthplace was Cyprus, where copper was mined. With Astarte or Ishtar, she is identified with the great mother whose worship was introduced in Cyprus by the Phoenicians and from Sidon, and which the Romans identified with Venus.

כי אעלה ארכה לך וממכותיך ארפאך נאם יהוה But it will restore you to health and heal your wounds,' declares the Lord…. See Jeremiah 30:17

1376

עשתרות *Astaroth*. Goetia demon #29 by day of the 2nd decan of Capricorn. See Appendix 11.

Goetia: "He is a mighty, strong, duke, and appears in the form of a hurtful angel riding on an infernal beast like a dragon, and carrying in his right hand a viper. Thou must in no wise let him approach too near unto thee, lest he do thee damage by his noisome breath. Wherefore the magician must hold the magical ring near his face, and that will defend him. He gives true answers of things, past, present, and to come, and can discover all secrets. He will declare witting how the spirits fell if desired and the reason for his own fall. He can make men wonderfully knowing in all liberal sciences. He rules 40 Legions of Spirits." [Mathers, 1995, p. 41]

ועשתרת and the flocks. Deuteronomy 7:13.

חכמה גבורה תפארת *Chokmah-Geburah-Tiphareth*. The sum of the Hebrew names for Wisdom, Strength and Beauty. These are the Sephiroth corresponding to the zodiac, the Life-force, Mars and volition and the Sun and the central Ego. The intimation is that the power of Venus, represented by Ashtoreth, is the key that unlocks the door to these levels of consciousness. See 870 Greek, 87 Latin, 73, 216, 1081.

1375

τελειος πετρος. *telios petros*. perfect stone.

1378

I. Σ52 = 1378. The Theosophic extension of 52 is 1378. Jehovah spelled in plentitude in the world of Assiah (see Appendix 7) is also 52 (יוד הה וו הה). Therefore, 1378 represents the full manifestation of the power of the name Jehovah on the physical plane.

II. The birthdate of Brother C. R. C. Note that *Melek Shelomah* (King Solomon, 465), *Khurram Melek Tsore* (Hiram King of Tyre, 640), and *Khurum Abiv* (Hiram Abiff. 273) add tp 1378. These are the names of the 3 original Master Masons.

1380

משמתם from their names. Exodus 28:10.

עשיתם I made them. Genesis 6:7.

שפתם their language. Genesis 11:7.

תשעים ninety (90). Genesis 5:9.

1395

Παλαιος Ημερων. Ancient of Days.

1400

לך יהוה הגדלה והגבורה והתפארת והנצח וההוד *Lekah Jehovah ha-Gedullah, ve-ha-Tiphareth, ve-ha-Netzach, ve-ha-Hod.* Your Oh Lord are the Greatness, and the Beauty, and the Victory, and the Splendor.

שרשרת chains. Exodus 28:14.

1406

η ζωσα πολις. Heh Sosa polis. The living city.

εικων ναου. eikon naou. image of the temple.

ο πυθαγορικος λογος. ho Pythagorikos Logos. the formula of Pythagoras.

1408

Σωτηρ. *Sotehr*. Savior. One of the titles of Jesus. See 644, 1756, 1480, 656, 1844, 1988, 888.

1426

ופלשתים Philistines. See Judges 15:14

והחיות רצוא ושוב כמראה הבזק And the living creatures ran and returned like the appearance of a flash of lightning. See Ezekiel 1:14.

תשכון you will live [in safety, Jerusalem]. See Jeremiah 33:16.

1428

לשמר את דרך עץ החים To guard the way to the Tree of Life. See Genesis 3:24.

1429

ο οικος επι την πετραν. ho oikos epi ten petran. The house upon the rock.

1431

תכונת הקדמות *Tekunath ha-qadmuth*. "dwelling place of the Primordial" or the Treasure of the Primordial." The Perfect Intelligence of the Eighth Path, Hod. Tekunath is from a root meaning: to arrange, to measure, disposition, preparation, things prepared, treasures, fixed place, dwelling-place, quality, characteristic. Every advance toward a greater perfection is the utilization, development and unveiling of this "Primordial Treasure." see 15, 876, 550, 481

אש מתרף *Esh metzaref.* A refiner's fire [Malachi 3:2]. See 711, 301.

1441

σπερμα ζωης. *Sperma zoes.* The seed of life.

1443

אני לדודי ועלי תשוקתו I belong to my lover, and his desire is for me. Song of Songs 7:11.

אני שלום וכי אדבר המה למלחמה I am a man of peace; but when I speak, they are for war. Psalms 120:7

ברח יראתם וחרב אביא עליכם נאם אדני יהוה You fear the sword, and the sword is what I will bring against you, declares the Sovereign Lord. Ezekiel 11:8.

1445

לשאירית נחילתי *Leshairith Nachalton.* The remnant of his heritage.

אתה מלכות וגבורה וגדולה לעולם אמן *Ateh Malkuth ve-Geburah ve-Gedulah le-Olam amen.* "The thee, Kingdom and the Power and the Majesty, throughout endless ages, Amen." The formula of the Qabalistic Cross, used in the lesser ritual of the pentagram. See 858, 1406, 496, 216, 48, 176, 91.

1452

ושמותן and their names. See Ezekiel 23:4

ושקמותם and their sycamore trees.

אלהי הושיעני יהוה כחסדך עזרני Help me, O Lord my God: save me by your love. See Ps. 109:26.

1459

The year that "The Chemical Wedding of Christan Rosenkrutz" was written.

1477

κυβικος πετρος. *kubikos petros.* cubic stone.

1480

שבע שבתות Literally, "7 Sabbaths." Seven periods of 7 days are 49 or 7x7. Related to the powers of Venus (Netzach), important in practical occultism. See 1010, 470.

ο πανδοχευς. *ho phandocheus.* The host (of an inn).

τελεσφορπς. *telesphorphus.* Ripener, perfecter, finisher.

Χριστος. *Khristos.* Christ, the anointed. One of the 7 names of Jesus beside his own, 8 in all. A technical term whereby even exoteric creeds designated the Logos "by whom all things were made" [John 1]. Logos is the basis of manifestation and the power to bring the creative process to a successful conclusion. Thus Christ is called "our foundation" and is also the "Pinnacle Stone," the pyramid's capstone symbolizing a new world order. Christ is called the "author and finisher of our faith," the basis and completion of the words alpha and Omega. They combine to 801, which reduces to 9. Used in 1st Thessalonians 3:13, it implies the completeness, which is one of the ideas inseparable from the meaning of the letter 9. See 80, 324, 9, 1222. See 644, 8, 1768, 800, 656, 1408, 971, 1844, 1988, 888.

I. "The word *Khristos* is the Greek word for Anointed and connotes a king or other anointed leader. Speaking of Jesus the Christ, He is said to be an intermediate between God and Mankind. The description '*Khristos*' must be understood to include both God and Man: while 'Jesus' refers to the act of (Christ) entering into the body of an *anthropos* [1310](*enanthropesis*). The word *Kyrios* (Lord) includes, at times, the idea of Godhood. 'And the *Khristos* is indeed a Lord Divine, by the Anointing of His Manhood in Godhood.'" [Omikron, 1942, p. 265.]

Lithos [λοθος] *trisepapeiros*. Stone of the 3 boundless dimensions. Given without spelling in *True and Invisible*. See below.

"1480 is the value of the Greek words *Mathesis spharas* (Doctrine of the Sphere), *Kaine philosophia* (the New Philosophy), *He aneogmene thura* (the Open Door) and *Lithos trisepapeiros* (Stone of the Three boundless dimensions). That these are all appropriate descriptions of the mystical Christos is evident. But they are also mentioned directly in the *Fama*, which proclaims a *new philosophy* that compares to a globe or circle ('the axiomata, which he know would direct them, like a globe or circle') is truly a *doctrine of the sphere*. This doctrine is hidden in a vault, and the *open door* of the vault is compared to a door which shall be opened in Europe. And the whole secret doctrine is summed up in the occult meaning of the cube, or *stone of three boundless dimensions*." [Case, 1985, pp. 121-122.] see 2368 Greek.

η αναστασις εκ Θεου. The resurrection from God.

η θυρα ανεωγμενη. *he thrua aneogmene*. The open door.

ο αστηρ της αγαπης. *ho astertes agapes*. The star of love.

ο αληθινος υιος Μαριας. *ho alethinos huios Marias*. The true son of Mary.

θρονος σοφιας. Throne of Wisdom.

η αγιωσυνη. The Holiness.

η αγαθωσυνη. The goodness.

αιτιος της ειρηνης. author of peace.

ο παις του ισηλ. The child (or servant) of Israel.

Παις του Δαυιδ. Son of David.

κτισις εκ παρθενου. Creation from a virgin.

1484

Psalm 103:10. "He does not treat us as our sins deserve or repay us according to our iniquities."

Psalm 118:20. "This is the gate of the Lord through which the righteous may enter."

Job 15:22. "Before his time, he will be paid in full, and his branches will not flourish."

1500

תשתרר you shall rule. See Numbers 16:13.

יזרעו וסופתה יקצרוי רוח כי Indeed, they sow the wind, and they reap the whirlwind. Hosea 8:7.

φως. *phos*. Light. Written with letters which are variant of the Hebrew Peh, Ayin and Shin. The mouth or utterer Phi), the seer (Omega, literally, "Great O" or "Great Eye") and the devourer (Shin, tooth, or Epsilon, associated with Fire). "Knowledge of Light," in the Chaldean Oracles, is a technical term of the Mysteries. See 851, 801 Greek, 441, 207.

ενδυμα Κυριου. *endyma Kyriou*. The robe of the Lord. See 801.

Σιων Ορος. Mount Sion.

1502

ο αστηρ εν τη ανατολη. The star in the east.

1512

αποκαλυψις. unveiling. "A making evident. A first-hand knowledge before speaking. A fuller unfoldment of the essential nature. The Fuller Presence of [or Unfoldment by] the Christ." [Omikron, 1942, p. 250.]

1513

התחתן son in law. See 1 Samuel 18:22.

כתועבתיהם with their detestable practices.

1517

Θεια χληδων (theia chledon, Greek). The Sacred Voice.

1520

λιθον ϛωντα. Living Stone." a title of Christ see 1 Peter 2:4.

1516

Ιησους η θυσια. Jesus, the offering.

1543

αλς κυβος τελειος. hals kubos teleios. Perfect salt-cube.

1547

ο κυβικος πετρος. ho kubikos Petros. the cubic stone.

1552

אריך אנפין The Greater Countenance, or Macroprospus. A title of Kether and the name of the number one. See 422, 620, 1346.

1554

I. Total summation of the lines of the magic square of the sun.

παν δωρημα τελεον. *pan dorhema teleion*. Every perfect gift [James 1:17]. The context says every such gift "is from above, and comes down from the father of lights, with whom there is no variableness, neither shadow of turning.: The total summation of the Magic square refers, therefore, to the influx of spiritual powers into Tiphareth, from the Sephiroth above; and indicates clearly to what man should turn for supply for every need. See 666.

Αναστασις σαρκος. *anastasis sarkos*. The resurrection of the body.

αλας κυβομορφον. *halas Kubomorphon*. salt cube.

η αιωνια προθεσις. The eternal purpose.

επιφανεια κυβου. *epiphaneia kubou*. Superficies of the cube.

1570

η πνοη πνευματος. Heh pnoe pneumatos. The breath of the spirit.

1574

אלהים לנו מחסה ועז עזרה בצרות נמצא מאד God is our refuge and strength, an ever-present help in trouble. See Psalm 46:2.

1577

אין סוף *En Sof*. the Limitless, no boundary. Nun = 700, Peh = 800, see 207.

1583

אני אמרתי אלהים אתם ובני עליוך כלכם Psalms 82:6 I have said you are gods; you are all sons [children] of the Most High. With great numbers, 3913.

1591

πας ανθρωπος. All Humanity.

1618

Κυριος Εαβαωθ. *Kurios Sabaoth.* Lord of Hosts. The Greek version of יהוה צבאות. See 525, 800, 1013 Greek and Romans 9:29.

1627

Ευχαριστια. Eucharist.

1628

κεφαλη γωνιας. *kephale uonias.* The head of the corner.

1642

Ο Κυριος της αληθειας. The Lord of Truth.

1654

το εργον ετελειωσα. *To oergon eteleiosa.* The work I have finished. See John 17:14 and 1356, 859 Greek.

1701

ενοικητηριον Κυριου. The dwelling of the Lord.

1702

שכל סוד הפעולות הרוחניות *Saykel sod ha-pehulloth ha-rauchnioth.* The Intelligence secret of all spiritual activities. The 19th Path of Teth. Links the Reciptacular Intelligence (Chesed, cosmic memory) to the Radical Intelligence (Geburah, volition). The prime secret of this path is that whatever exists is a form of spiritual energy and that every form of this energy is subject to the direction and control of the form above it. By controlling the subconscious production of mental images man-as a synthesis and vehicle of universal life, can "pen the Lion's mouth" (In Key 8, the woman (Empress) tames the Lion because she has been instructed by the Hierophant). Another secret is that human life extends beyond the physical world man's limits is immortal. He "enjoys the universal medicine" when his body-cell consciousness has been harmonized with the central indwelling self. Comprehending this secret, he is filled with Joy-he has nothing to acquire-he performs the Great Work by eliminating prejudices, hates, dislikes, and faulty opinions. See 667, 206, 409, 380, 358, 661.

ζωη εις το διηνεκες. Eternal Life.

η βασιλεια κατα γνωσιν. The kingdom according to the gnosis.

1724

ο λοθος ακρογωνιαιος. *ho Lithos Akrogoniaios.* the corner-stone

1755

קדוש קדוש קדוש יהוה צבאות *qadosh, qadosh, qadosh, Jehovah Tzabaoth.* Holy, Holy, Holy, Jehovah of Hosts [Isaiah 6:3]. It is also the burden of the *Sanctus* in the Catholic celebration of the Eucharist. The total of the visible and invisible paths of the Tree. The whole manifested universe is the Body of God. This is the body of Messiah, son of a woman, son of Fire, a seed of the Jews, Shiloh. See 1090, 358, 345.
1768 (8x221)

ο Κυριος ημυν. *Ho Kurios hemon.* Our Lord. One of the titles of Jesus. See 644, 800, 656, 1480, 1408, 1844, 1988, 888.

1771

γνωσις της σοφιας. *gnosis tes sophias.* Knowledge of Wisdom.

1776

η σωτηρια Ισραελ. *He soteria Isreal.* The salvation of Israel. The number on the bottom course of the pyramid on the reverse of the Great Seal of the US. The new world order, begun in 1776, was the first to admit Jews and Gentiles' political, social and economic equality. Esoterically, it has several profound meanings, one of which refers to the liberation of those who constitute the true spiritual Israel. The doctrine of the Holy Trinity is concealed in this phrase. It represents the three Godheads, being 3x592 or The others.

Ιησους εστι λογος. Iesous esti Logos. Jesus is the Word.

η κορη του κοσμου. The Virgin of the World.

1832

Proverbs 20.27: The lamp of the Lord searches for the spirit of the man; it searches out his inmost being.

1836

שכל מתנוצץ *Saykel Mitnotzetz.* Resplendent Intelligence. Title of Malkuth. *Mitnotzetz* shows that every human personality is absolutely dependent upon the universal existence, Tav that the universe is an orderly, rhythmic manifestation of Life, determined by fixed laws, Nun that the dissolution of physical bodies is necessary and beneficent, but not the end of self-conscious existence, Vav that the Self of man includes a consciousness above his personal intellectual level and guidance from this level is man's birthright, Tzaddi that nature unveils herself to man when man practices right meditation. See 656, 496, 1026, 676.

1844

εγω ειμι η αναστασις. *Ego ehimi heh anastasis.* I am the Resurrection. Jesus' own words. See 971, 1988, 888, 1480, 644, 1768, 800, 656, 1408 & John 11:25.

1911

ברוך יהוה אלהים אלהי ישראל עשה נפלאות לבדו Praise the Lord God, the God of Israel, who alone does marvelous deeds. See Psalms 72:18 & 2951 (value with Great Numbers).

1914

שפתי חכמים יזרו דעת ולב כסילים לא כן The lips of the wise spread knowledge; not so the hearts of fools. See Proverbs 15:7 & 3684 (with Great Numbers).

1920

τω πανοχευς. *to phandochei.* The host (of an inn). See 1480.

1940

נפש ברכה תדשן ומרוה גם הוא יורא Proverbs 11:25: A generous man will prosper; he who refreshes others will himself be refreshed.

לא יגרע מצדיק עיניו ואת מלכים לכסא וישיבם לכסא וישבם לנצח ויגבהו Job 35: 7: He does not take his eyes off the righteous; he enthrones them with kings and exalts them forever.

1988

αναστασις νεκρων. *anastasis nekron.* The resurrection of the dead. See 971, 1844, 888, 1480, 644, 1768, 800, 656, 1408 and 1 Corinthians 15:12.

2035

χριστος εν υμιν. *christos en humin.* Christ in you.

2050

Τυφων. *Typhon.* A serpent god.

"One meaning of *Typhon* is… a kind of comet… Another form is either *Typhoeus* or *Typhos* and specifically refers to the youngest son of Gaia, who was also of the three fifty-headed monsters and Garamas. *Typhos* means 'smoke, vapor,' and 'conceit, vanity [הבל, 37] (because it clouds or darkens a man's intellect)'. *Typhos* means 'blind' and specifically 'in the sense of misty, darkened.' The verb *Typhoō* means 'to blind, make blind' or 'to blind, baffle.' It also means 'to wrap in smoke.'

Since Typhon is specifically said to be the father of Sirius (Orthrus) and one of its unexplained definitions is a description of a moving star. Its son has fifty heads. I take all the references to obscurity and invisibility to mean that Typhon represents Sirius B, the dark companion of Sirius and invisible to us. In other words, we are *typhlos* (blind) to *Typhon* because it seems as if it were obscured or *typloo'd* (vapor, smoke), and we are baffled, blind (thyhlos) in the sense of the subject being darkened (*typhoō*).

Typhon's possible origin may be the Egyptian word *tephit* or *teph-t,* both of which have the meaning of 'cave, cavern, hole in the ground.' This Egyptian word describes the chasm perfectly at Delphi in which Python was supposed to lie rotting, his corpse giving off the fumes out of the earth. And, as we have seen, Python was equated with Typhon in early times." [Temple, 1987, p. 163]

2063

עשיר ברשים ימשול ועבד לוה לאיש מלוה The rich rule over the poor and the borrower (לוה, to be joined) is servant to the lender. See Proverbs 22:7.

2080

I Σ64 = 2080 (theosophical extension)

תפתרתרת *Taphthartharath.* Spirit of Mercury and is often related to the destructive or evil manifestations of Mercurial force or human intellect. Actually, none of the planetary spirits are really evil. They do have to do with the disintegrative expressions of the forces we call planetary. These destructive or disintegrative expressions of natural phenomena were called "evil" or "malefic" by primitives because they interfered with his peace and comfort and caused him to fear them. Thus in Ageless Wisdom, the word "evil" is a term that expresses man's reaction to, and interpretation of, the aspects of cosmic life which appear inimical to him. The first two letters and the last two are identical with those of תפארת (Tiphareth, 1081). The middle letters תרת (1000), the value of Aleph, written large. Also, one of the many meanings of the word Aleph, אלף (111). The Spirit of Mercury is really the master power seated in the 6th Sephirah. This power can dominate for good uses, even the most hostile among the universe's disintegrative forces. To invoke Taphthartharath is to realize in oneself the uplifted white wand in the Magician's right hand. See 260.

חכמים וחידתם יראת יהוה ראשית דעת the wise, and their riddles. The fear of the Lord is the beginning of knowledge. See Proverbs 1:6-7.

2096

בשומי ענן לבשו וערפל ותלתח When I made the clouds as garment and wrapped it in thick darkness. See Job 38:9.

2109

ο ενσωματος λογος. *ho ensomatos logos.* The incarnate word. Refers to Jesus.

2142

אם תבקשנה ככסף ורמטמנים תחפשנה Proverbs 2:4: "If you look for her as Silver, and search for her as for hidden treasure." Refers to understanding. Silver is the Moon's metal or subconsciousness; "Her" is the divine soul, Neshamah in Binah. The treasures are those of wisdom, which is spirit, Life and light. Understanding is the Key that unlocks the "door" (Path of Daleth) to Wisdom (Chokmah). See 67, 73, 434, 23, 68. See 2368.

2145

אחד ראש אחדותו ראש יחוד תמורהזו אחד One is his beginning. One of his individuality, His permutation, is one. The Divine Name of 7 Letters. [Zalewski, 2002, pp. 133-134]

2281

הון ועשר בביתו וצדקתו עמדת לעד
Psalms 112:3: Wealth and Riches are in his house, and his righteousness (fairness) endures forever.

2304

ο νομος της συμμετριας. *Ho nomos tes symmetrias*. The law of symmetry.

2311

το πυρ το αιωνιον. *To phur to alonion*. The fire everlasting. See 1571, 23, 11 and Matthew 25:41.

2335

כי לא מחשבותי מחשבותיכם ולא דרכיכם דרכי נאם יהוה

For my thoughts are not your thoughts, neither are your ways my ways, says the Lord. Isaiah 55:8.

2349

ביךך אפקיד רוחי פדיתה אותי יהוה אל אמת Into your hands I commit my spirit; redeem me, O Lord, the God of truth. See Psalms 31:5. Kaph = 500.

2357

יהוה ישמר צאתך ובואך מעתה ועד עולם Psalm 121.7: "The Lord will keep you from all harm, he will watch over your life.

2368

2368 is Jesus Christ in Greek. Note that 2368 = 37 x 64. Or the multiplication of truth.

αληθεια *alethela*, by the powers of Yekhidah יחידה, (a title of Kether, 620), The Indivisible One.

Also, note that the ratio of 2368 (Jesus Christ) to 1480 (Christ) is the same as 8 to 5 (1.6:1), which is the ratio of length to the height of the Vault of Brother C.R.C.

In *The Apostolic Gnosis* by Frederick Bond and Thomas Lea, 500 names and titles relating to Jesus is given from pages 66 to 106. The following is a selection from this book:

1. Ιησους [888]; Χριστος [1480]. Jesus Christos. Jesus Christ. The manifestation of the universal principle (Christ) through an incarnate human being. See 1480 Greek.

2. Ιησους [888]; Υιος [680]; Κυριος [800]. Jesus, Son. Lord.

3. Ιησους [888]; η αληθεια [72]; σωτηρ [1408]. Jesus. The truth. Savior.

4. Ιησους [888]; η αναστασις εκ Θεου [1480]. Jesus; the resurrection from God.

6. Ιησους [888]; Αλφα [532] Ωμεγα [849] Αμημ [99]. Jesus-Alpha-Omega-Amen. Jesus; first and last; amen.

20. Ιησους [888]; θρονος σοφιας [1480]. Jesus; Throne of Wisdom.

21. Ιησους [888]; η θυρα ανεωγμενη [1480]. *Jesus, he thrua aneogmene*. Jesus; the open door.

22. Ιησους [888]; η αγιωσυνη [1480]. Jesus; the Holiness.

23. Ιησους [888]; η αγαθωσυνη [1480]. Jesus; the goodness.

24. Ιησους [888]; ο αστηρ της αγαπης [1480]. Jesous, ho astertes agapes. Jesus; the star of love.

26. Ιησους [888]; Jesous; heh eirene. hlios Dikaiosuehe. Jesus, peace, the sun of righteousness.

27. Ιησους [888]; αιτιος της ειρηνης [1480]. Jesus; author of peace.

28. Ιησους [888]; ο παις του ισηλ [1480]. Jesus; the child (or servant) of Israel.

29. Ιησους [888]; Παις του Δαυιδ [1480]. Jesus; Son of David.

31. Ιησους [888]; κτισις εκ παρθενου. Jesus; creation from a virgin [1480].

32. Ιησους [888]; ο αληθινος υιος Μαριας [1480]. Jesous ho alethinos huios marias. Jesus; the true son of Mary.

45. αιμα Ιησου [740]; η αγαπη [101]; η αληθης γνωσις [1527]. Hiama Iesus, heh agape, heh alethes gnosis. Blood of Jesus, love, the true Gnosis.

47. αγιασμα Θεου [740]; κεφαλη γωνιας [1628]. Agiasma theou, kephale uonias. Sanctuary of God, the head of the corner.

54. το αιμα Κησου[1110]; η εξουσια Θεου [1238]. Haima Yesou, heh eksousia theou. The blood of Jesus, the power of God. This adds to 2348.

63. βασιλεια [259], ο ενσωματος λογος. [2109]. Basileia, ho ensomatos logos. Kingdom, the incarnate word.

85. η ελπις [333]; χριστος εν υμιν [2035]. heh elpis, christos en humin. the hope, Christ in you.

122. η θυρα [518]; Ιερουσαλημ επουρανιος [1851]. Heh thura, Ierousalem epouranios. The gate, the heavenly Jerusalem. This adds to 2369.

145. ο λογος εν ιδεα [518]; πνευμα αληθειας [840]; φερομενη πνοη βιαια [1010]. The word in idea; Spirit of Truth; a rushing mighty wind.

159. η εκκλησια η πασα [592]; η κορη του κοσμου [1776]. The Whole Church; the Virgin of the World.

161. η εκκλησια η πασα [592]; η σωτηρια Ισραηλ [1776]. heh ekklesia he pasa; heh soteria Israel. The whole church, the salvation of Israel.

171a. Θεοτης [592]; η σωτηρια Ισραηλ [1776]. Theotes, heh soteria Israel. Godhead; the salvation of Israel.

173. Θεοτης [592]; Ηλιος [318]; εικων λογου [1358]. Godhead; Sun; image of the word.

182. αγιοτης [592]; Μελχισεδεκ [919]; λογος Θεου [857]. Hagiotes, Melchsedek, Logos theou. Holiness, Melchizedek, Word of God.

190. λογος αγαπης [666]; ο μονογενησ λογος [939]; μεσιτης [763]. Logos agapes, ho monogenes Logos mespes. Word of Love, the only-begotten son, mediator.

201. λογος αγαπης [666]; η βασιλεια κατα γνωσιν [1702]. Word of Love; the kingdom according to the gnosis.

203. λογος αγαπης [666]; ζωη εις το διηνεκες [1702]. Word of Love; Eternal Life.

217. ο αγιος Ισραηλ [703]; εξουσια [746]; Μελχισεδεκ [919]. ho agios Israel, eksousia, melchsedek. The holy one of Israel, authority, Melchizedek.

224. αγιασμα Θεου [740]; ο εξαγωνος λιθος. [1578]. hagiasma Theou, ho eksagonos Lithos. Sanctuary of God, the hexagonal stone (Metacube). This adds to 2318.

234. οι κλητοι βασιλεια [777]; πας ανθρωπος [1591]. The Called to the Kingdom; All Humanity.

250. ο ενεργης λογος [814]; η αιωνια προθεσις [1554]. The powerful word; the eternal purpose.

260. η θεια σοφια [814]; αλας κυβομορφον [1554]. *heh thela sophia, halas Kubomorphon.* The divine wisdom, the salt cube.

281. η αληθινη μαθησις [592]; η σωτηρια Ισραηλ [1776]. h*eh alethine mathesis, heh soteria Israel.* The true teaching, the salvation of Israel. See 1776.

288. η πνοη πνευματος [1362]; η νυμφη [1006]. The breath of the spirit. The Bride.

289. η πνοη πνευματος [1362]; η κορη κοσμου [1006]. *Heh pnoe pneumatos, hehe kore kosmou.* The breath of the spirit, Virgin [of the] World. See 1776.

291. τελεια αγαπη [471]; η επιφανεια του Θεου [1924]. Perfect Love; the manifestation of God. This adds to 2395.

295. η Θεια δυναμις Αγιου Πνευματος. The divine power of the Holy Spirit.

297. Ειων ορος [1500]; δομος Θεου [868]. domos theou. Mount Sion; abode of God.

300. η οικοδομια εν Χριστω. *he oikodomia en Christo.* The building in Christ.

301. ο λιθος ακρογωνιαιος [1724]; Εμμανουηλ [644]. *ho Lithos Akrogoniaios, emmanouel.* the corner-stone; Immanuel.

302. Η Πολις Χρυσους. He Polis Chrusous. The Golden City.

305. η κυβικη εκκλησια [762]; η μορφη Υιου [1606]. *to kubos; heh morphe huiou.* The cubic church; the form of the Son.

310. μεγεθη κυβου [962]; εικων ναου [1406]. *megethe Kubou; eikon naou.* Dimensions of the cube, image of the temple.

312. η πετρα η κυβικη [962]; η ζωσα πολις [1406]. *heh petra heh kubike, heh zosa polis.* The cubic stone; the living city.

318. κυβικα προσωπα Θεου. Cubic faces of God.

321. αληθεια [64]; ο νομος της συμμετριας [2304]. *Alethela, ho nomos tes symmetrias.* Truth, the law of symmetry.

322. αλς κυβος τελειος [1543]; ο Πετρος [825]. *hals kubos teleios, ho petros.* Perfect salt-cube, the stone (Peter).

329. η καλη πολις Θεου ζωντος. The beautiful city of the living God.

330. ο κυβιδος πετρος [1547]; ο αληθινος λογος [821]. *ho kubikos Petros, ho alethinos logos.* The cubic stone, the true logos.

332. η θεια σοφια [814]; επιφανεια κυβου [1554]. *Heh thela sophia, epiphaneia kubou.* The divine wisdom, superficies of the cube.

333. ο κυβικος πετρος κυριακος. *ho kubikos petros kuriakos.* the cubic stone of the Lord.

337. τελειος λογος [993]; τελειος πετρος [1375]. *teleios logos, telios petros.* perfect word, perfect stone.

339. ουρανια βασιλεια [891]; κυβικος πετρος [1477]. *ourania Basileia, kubikos petros.* Heavenly Kingdom, cubic stone.

341. τελειος λιθος [939]; ο οικος επι την πετραν [1429]. *teleios lithos, ho oikos epi ten petran.* Perfect stone, the house upon the rock.

346. μαθησις εκκλησιας [962]; ο πυθαγορικος λογος [1406]. *methesis ekklesias, ho*

Pythagorikos Logos. The teaching of the Church, the formula of Pythagoras.

359. Ιερευς Σαλημ [999]; ο επι-ιερευς Θεου [1369]. *Hiereus Salem; ho epi-ierus theou.* Priest of Salem, high-priest of God.

378. ο Θεος της γνς [1073]; πνευμα της γης [1295]. *ho theos tes ges, pneuma tes ges.* The God of the earth, the spirit of the earth.

383. οι κεκλημενοι της αληθειας [1110]; κεκλημενοι κυριου [1258]. *Hoi keklemenoi tes aletheasm keklemenoi kuriou.* Those called of truth, the Lord's chosen

386. υιος μονος [1110]; ο παρακλητος αληθινος [1258]. Only son; the true comforter.

398. παρθενος ουρανια [1147]; βασιλεια Θεοτητος [1221]. Heavenly virgin; the kingdom of the Godhead.

403. αρχη αληθειας [973]; Παλαιος Ημερων [1395]. Beginning of truth; Ancient of Days.

404. Ο Θεοπλαστης [973]; Παλαιος Ημερων [1395]. *ho theoplastes, palaios hemeron.* The Divine Creator, The Ancient of Days.

408. ηλιος [318]; Αδωναι [866]; αγγελος της ημερας [1174]. *hlios, Adonai, aggelos tes hemeras.* The sun, Adonai (Lord), the messenger of the day. Adds to 2358.

409. ο λογος [443]; ο αρτος [741]; η αληθινη διαθηκη Κυριου [1184]. ho logos, ho artos, heh alethine diatheke kuriou. The word, the bread, the true covenant of the Lord.

413. το Αγιον Αγιων Κυριου. *to agion agion agathon kuriou.* The Holy of Holies of the Lord.

419. γνωσις της σοφιας [1771]; η αγκυρα [533]. *gnosis tes sophias, heh agkura.* Knowledge of Wisdom, the anchor.

428. καρπος μητρας [1120]; Μεσσιας [656]; Θεοτης [592]. *karpos metras, messias, theotes.* Fruit of the womb, messiah, Godhead.

429. καρπος εκ μητρας της παρθενου. Fruit of the virgin's womb.

439. Θειος λογος [667]; ενοικητηριον Κυριου [1701]. Divine logos; the dwelling of the Lord.

440. λογια του Θεου Κυριου. Sayings of the Lord God.

448. Ο Μεσσιας [726]; ο Κυριος της αληθειας [1642]. The Messiah; the Lord of Truth.

452. η μεγαλη γνωσις [1358]; φερομενη πνοη βιαια [1010]. The great gnosis; a mighty rushing wind.

455. κλεις της πισεως. Key of the faith.

462. φως [1500]; Δομος Θεου [868]. phos, domos theou. Light, house of God.

463. Αδωναι [866]; ο αστηρ εν τη ανατολη [1502]. Adonai; the star in the east.

465. Αγιος Αγιων [1148]; Οικος Κυριου [1370]. Holy of Holies; the Lord's House. Adds to 2518.

468. το Θελημα του Θεου Πατρος. The will of God the Father. Adds to 2,468

469. η αγαπη πατρος [852]; Ιησους η θυσια [1516]. The father's love; Jesus the offering.

483. ο αρτος ζωης αθανατος. *ho artos zeos athanatos*. The immortal bread of Life. Adds to 2388.

485. Ευχαριστια [1627]; ο αρτος [741]. *Eucharistia, ho artos*. Eucharist, the bread.

487. Δειπνον Κυριου [1269]; η φιλαδελφια [1099]. *Depinon Kuriou, heh philadelphia*. The Lord's Supper, brotherly Love.

490. ο ζων [927]; σπερμα ζωης [1441]. *ho zon, sperma zoes*. The living one, seed of Life.

492. η μεγαλειοτης Κυριου Ιησου. The majesty of the Lord Jesus.

2436

בדעתו תהומות נבקעו ושחקים ירעפו טל "By Knowledge the deeps (depths) were divided, and the clouds let drop the dew." see Proverbs 3: 20 & 2996 (value with Great Numbers).

2676

ואתה יהוה מגן בעדי כבורי ומרים But you are a shield around me, O Lord, my Glorious One, who lifts up my head. See Psalm 3:4.

2809

I. (53x53) or 53^2

II. The area of the face of a cube, having lines of 53, is the cube of stone. Reduces to 19 (הוח, Havah, Eve) and 10 (Malkuth, the Kingdom). Thus each face represents the power of the mother, which is the power of manifestation. Yet this power of the mother essentially that of the physical plane. See 53, 496, 16, 854, 148, 877.

III. Psalm 74:20. "Have regard for your covenant because haunts of violence fill the dark places of the land." This verse adds to 2080.

2945

אחד ראש אחדותו ראש יחודותו תמורתו אחד
Echud rosh, echudotho rosh yechudotho, temuratho echud. "One (His) beginning; one principle his individuality; his permutation one." It refers to the white brilliance of Kether, to the divine name Hu, and to Yekhidah, the indivisible one seated in Kether. The initials of each word of this sentence form the notariqon Ararita. [Talismans & Evocations of the Golden Dawn, Ch 5, p. 135] see 13, 501, 37, 620, 12, 25, 57.

3015

כי גדול אתה ועשה נפלאות אתה אלהים לבדך
Psalm 86:10: For you are great, and you do wondrous (אלף) things, you alone are God. 1975 without great numbers.

3030

ο υιος του ανθρωπου. Son of Man. Jesus called himself this epithet 37 times in the New Testament. See 37 and Matthew 13:37.

3138

שמרה נפשי כי חסיד אני הושע עבדך אתה אלהי הבוטח אליך
Psalm 86:2: Guard my life, for I am devoted to you. You are my God; save your servant who trusts in you. Without great numbers, this is 2178.

3321

Σ81 = 3,321.

מלכא בתרשישים עד ברוח שחרים "The Intelligence of the Intelligence of the Moon." Mem = 600, see 369, 9, 1050, 2201, 41.

I. "Queen among the Tarshishim (a choir of angels assigned to the 5th Sephirah in Briah) forever, in the spirit of the Dawning (Ones)." A title attributed to the Moon. In all printed texts, the Hebrew is corrupt. This rendering is from a manuscript source. Some of the printed versions add up correctly, but the words make no sense." [Soror A.L., 1995, p.113.]

שד רב שמעת השרתתן This is not often spelled correctly. The very corrupt late Hebrew may be translated: "Destruction, son of Shimath ('what is announced') Chief of the Howling Ones." Shad also means the female breast. Nun = 700, see 2571.

נהם ככפיר זעף מלך וכטל על עשב רצונו A King's rage is like the roar of a lion, but his favor is like dew on the grass. Proverbs 19:12.

ως εν ουρανω και επι της γης. *Hos en ourano kai epi tis gehs.* In Matthew 6:10: On earth as it is in Heaven. Literally, as in Heaven, also on the earth. This is the hermetic axiom, "As above, so below," As it is phrased in the Lord's prayer. Note the principle of reflection related to the sphere of the Moon.

3394

ο κρυπτος της καρδιας ανθρωπος. *Ho kruptos tehs kardias anthropos.* The hidden man of the heart. In 1 Peter 3:3,4: "Whose decoration, let it not be that external one, of braiding the hair, and putting on of gold chains, or wearing of apparel; but decorate *the hidden man of the heart.*" A reference to Tiphareth. See 666, 336, 1170, 136, 1310 Greek.

3690

אז תלך לבטח דרכך ורגלך לא תגוף Then you will go on your way in safety, and your foot will not stumble. See Proverbs 3:23.

4000

אשר שננו כחרב לשונם דרכו חצם דבר מר Psalm 64:3. "Who sharpen their tongues like swords and aim their words like deadly arrows."

5000

ה *Heh.* Synthesizes the full expression of Binah, בינה, or the successive multiplication of the values of its letters (2x10x50x5 = 5,000). See 250, 4, 14, 104, 67.

5050

Σ100 = 5,050.

6887

εγω ειμι το Α και το Ω, αρχη και τελος, ο πρωτος και ο εσχατος. Ego to Alpha to Omega, Ho parotos Kai Ho Eschatos, heh arche kai to Jelos (Greek) [2]. "I am the Alpha and Omega, the beginning and the end, the first and the last." see 859, 1, 800 Greek and Revelations 22:13.

7381

Σ121 = 7,381.

16,854

The total area of the 6 faces of a cube of 53 or 6x2809 (2809 = 53x53). The final reduction is 6, the number of Tiphareth, which relates the cube's surface to the idea of Beauty. See 2809, 148,877.

31,415

3.1415 the value of Pi (π). The ratio of the circumference of a circle to its radius.

"The Three, the One, the Four, the One, the Five (in their totality – twice seven) represent 31415 – the numerical hierarch of the Dhyan-Chohans or various orders, and of the inner or circumscribed world. When placed on the boundary of the great circle of 'pass not' (see Stanza V.) also called the Dhyanipasa, the 'Rope of the Angels,' the 'rope' that hedges off the phenomenal from the noumenal Kosmos… 31415 anagrammatically and Kabbalistically, being both the number of the circle and the mystic Svastika [a Jaina cross inside a circle]…" [Blavatsky, 1967, p. 47]

144,000

A number of the redeemed souls in Revelation, chapter 14. 100 = Qoph, back of the head, the source of material, or spiritual awareness. 40 = Mem = Water or spirit. 4 = Daleth = the crossing of a threshold. 1,000 = association of advancement. The Biblical statement can be read: Those who succeed in advancing their consciousness from the state of material awareness (back of the head) to the forehead (the location of the 3rd eye or anga chakra, which, when opened, gives spiritual awareness) are the ones who shall redeem themselves (gain the freedom of their divine nature). [The Quantum Gods - J. Love, page 59].

148,877

The volume of a cube of 53. Reduces to 9 as its least number and refers to Yesod, the Foundation. See 80, 2809, 16,854.

1,366,560

I. $2^5 \times 3^2 \times 5 \times 13 \times 73$

The number associated with the birth date of Venus in the Mayan Dresden Codex.

Appendix 1 - Gematria Tables

Hebrew Letters and Numbers								
1	2	3	4	5	6	7	8	9
Aleph[1]	Beth	Gimel	Daleth	Heh	Vav	Zain	Cheth	Teth
א	ב	ג	ד	ה	ו	ז	ח	ט
10	20	30	40	50	60	70	80	90
Yod	Kaph	Lamed	Mem	Nun	Samekh	Ayin	Peh	Tzaddi
י	כ	ל	מ	נ	ס	ע	פ	צ
100	200	300	400	20 & 500	40 & 600	50 & 700	80 & 800	90 & 900
Qoph	Resh	Shin	Tav	Final Kaph	Final Mem	Final Nun	Final Peh	Final Tzaddi
ק	ר	ש	ת	ך	ם	ן	ף	ץ

[1] When Aleph is written large א, its value is 1000.

Qabalah of the 9 chambers is a method where the number is reduced to the smallest single digit. This is called Theosophic Reduction For Example: $800 = 8 + 0 + 0 = 8$

The Qabalah of the 9 Chambers										
Shin	Lamed	Gimel		Resh	Kaph	Beth		Qoph	Yod	Aleph
ש	ל	ג		ר	כ	ב		ק	י	א
300	30	3		200	20	2		100	10	1
Final Mem	Samekh	Vav		Final Kaph	Nun	Heh		Tau	Mem	Daleth
ם	ס	ו		ך	נ	ה		ת	מ	ד
600	60	6		500	50	5		400	40	4
Final Tzaddi	Tzaddi	Teth		Final Peh	Peh	Cheth		Final Nun	Ayin	Zain
ץ	צ	ט		ף	פ	ח		ן	ע	ז
900	90	9		800	80	8		700	70	7

Greek Table								
1	2	3	4	5	6	7	8	9
Alpha	Beta	Gamma	Delta	Epsilon		Zeta	Eta	Theta
A	B	Γ	Δ	E		Z	H	Θ
α	β	γ	δ	ε		ζ	η	θ
10	20	30	40	50	60	70	80	90
Iota	Kappa	Lambda	Mu	Nu	Xi	Omicron	Pi	
I	K	Λ	M	N	Ξ	O	Π	
ι	κ	λ	μ	ν	ξ	o	π	
100	200	300	400	500	600	700	800	
Rho	Sigma	Tau	Upsilon	Phi	Chi	Psi	Omega	
P	Σ	T	Y	Φ	X	Ψ	Ω	
ρ	σ, ς	τ	υ	Φ	χ	ψ	ω	

Roman Letters in Qabalah Simplex										
#	1	2	3	4	5	6	7	8	9	10
	A	B	C	D	E	F	G	H	I (J)	L
	11	12	13	14	15	16	17	18	19	20
	M	N	O	P	Q	R	S	T	V (U)	X
	21	22								
	Y	Z								

I have seen several methods to derive the numerical values of English letters. This is the simplest and makes the most sense.

English Letters in Qabalah Simplex									
1	2	3	4	5	6	7	8	9	10
A	B	C	D	E	F	G	H	I	J
11	12	13	14	15	16	17	18	19	20
K	L	M	N	O	P	Q	R	S	T
21	22	23	24	25	26				
U	V	W	X	Y	Z				

The Cabala Simplex of the 9 Chambers									
A	J	S		B	K	T		C	L	U
1	10	19		2	11	20		3	12	21
D	M	V		E	N	W		F	O	X
4	13	22		5	14	23		6	15	24
G	P	Y		H	Q	Z		I	R	
7	16	25		8	17	26		9	18	

Hebrew Letters Spelled in Full (Miliui method)						
Hebrew	Spelled in Full	#		Hebrew	Spelled in Full	#
א	אלף	111		ל	למד	74
ב	בית	412		מ	מים	90
ג	גמל	73		נ	נון	106
ד	דלת	474		ס	סמך	120
ה	הא	6		ע	עין	130
ו	וו	12		פ	פא	91
ז	זין	67		צ	צדי	104
ח	חית	418		ק	קוף	186
ט	טית	419		ר	ריש	510
י	יוד	20		ש	שין	360
כ	כף	100		ת	תו	406

Appendix 2 - The Nature of Numbers

The following is an excerpt from the *Cube of Space* by Kevin Townley. This passage relates the different characteristics of numbers to the four worlds of the Cabala.

Consider the **Point,** the three geometrical forms, the triangle, the hexagram, and the enneagram [9 sided figure]. The point and these three forms are representative of the first sphere Kether, the third sphere Binah, the sixth sphere Tiphareth, and the ninth sphere of Yesod. These forms and, hence, their numbers bring us to a very important consideration concerning creation.

Jah created the universe using numbers, letters and sounds. Ayin Soph Aur contains 9 letters, *Ayin Soph* contains 6, and *Ayin* contains 3 letters. When taking these three numbers, 9, 6, and 3, we find that they hold a special function in creating the universe. In fact, there are only four real numbers: 1, 3, 6, and 9. This, of course, sounds absurd at first, yet if we look beyond the surface of appearance, we find this to be true. All other numbers are different expressions of 1, 3, 6, and 9.

Indeed, everything is One because all things come from One, as the Emerald Tablet states. The All is One. One is the undifferentiated and infinite possibility, and its reflection gives rise to the expression of the Father, the Number Two.

The All is three because the One Life always expresses itself through the Trinity or the Supernal Triad. The union of One and its reflection, 2, takes us from the negative veils of undifferentiated potential to the world of differentiated potential. This gives rise to the idea of the Trinity, 1+2=3, and the Mother's vehicle, the vital ingredient for manifestation. The union of these forces is 1+2+3=6, which brings us to the third of the four numbers of creation, 6.

The All is six, as it expresses itself through the Divine Mother and the Divine Father's agencies, where the six directions of the Cube of Space are sealed, bringing forth a new generation, the **Son/Sun.** Furthermore, it is through the process of separation, or division, that manifestation comes into being. If we were to take the number 3, the number of the Divine Mother and sphere of Saturn, and divide it by .5, we find the number 6, the Divine Son/Sun sphere.

The All is nine, for there are nine letters in the third veil of Negative Existence and nine is also the number that completes the cycle of numbers. Nine is also the product of the Magic Square of the Divine Mother, 3x3=9. After nine, we return again to the number one, and the cycle begins all over again and continues on infinitely

At this point, we have become familiar with the basic cycle of numbers from one to nine. In esoteric sciences, the numbers from one to nine are used for mystical studies. There are other areas in the study of numbers that speak to the Ayin Soph Aur's creative process and the numbers 1, 3, 6, and 9.

Kether is the tenth aspect in relation to the *Ayin Soph Aur,* which is the line of demarcation between negative existence and positive existence. This begins the cycle of numbers at a new level of expression.

Now let's consider the statement that there are only four real numbers, 1, 3, 6 and 9 and that all other numbers are expressions of one of these four numbers. As there are four worlds in the Qabalah, there are four levels in which numbers manifest. They are called: apparent, reduced, extended, and root numbers.

Apparent numbers are quite simply the numbers we use on a day-to-day basis and are symbolic of the world of *Assiah*. This is exemplified in the Tarot by the suit of Pentacles, and Key Fifteen, The Devil, a sign of cardinal earth. The hand of the Devil is in a position that says, "What you see is all the reality there is." We need to look beyond the surface of appearance to gain the whole truth of a matter, just as we must maneuver a cube to see all its sides.

Any number being dealt with has an apparent value. This explanation is not an attempt to disregard apparent numbers but alert us to the fact that much more lies beneath the surface.

Reduced numbers are symbolic of the world *Yetzirah* and are mostly used in the science of numerology. This is the reduction of any multi-digit number to a single digit. This reduces otherwise complex digits to a common ground to understand the basic quality of the otherwise infinite. For example, the number 358, reduces to 3+5+8=16, 1+6=7. Through reduction, the number 358 can be expressed as number 7. This process is called **Theosophical Reduction.**

Extended numbers, symbolic of the *Briatic* world, allow us to examine the greater relationships between numbers. Extending numbers is called **Theosophical Extension.** We can see the total influence within a number and its underlying relationship between different numbers and words of the same value through theosophical extension. This process is used most extensively in the science of gematria, where relationships of letters and numbers are explored. An example of this can be seen in the number 4 - , adding number fours total value, we find that the number 4 extended has the value of 10, 1+2+3+4=10, and 10= 1+0=1. This tells us that the numbers 4 and 10 have a profound relationship with each other, and they express a unique quality of the number 1, just as each center of expression manifests the essence of the One.

A couple of formulae allow the student to find the extended value of any size number and reversing the process to discover what a particular number is an extension of. To find the extension of a given number, use the following formula:

$$n(n + 1)/2 = \text{extension}$$

We will use the example of 31, the value of EL, Lamed + Aleph, the divine name given to the fourth sphere on the Tree of Life, Chesed. The name means God.

$n = 31$, $n + 1 = 32$

$(31 \times 32)/2 = 992/2 = 496$

496 is the extension of 31 and the value of Malkuth [מלכות].

This tells us that the extension of 31 is the extension of God's creative powers, manifesting in the earth's sphere, Malkuth, 496.

Root numbers associated with the *Atziluthic* World tell us that there is an underlying unity in all things and that the One has three basic modes of expression. The following numerical. chart reveals the four types of numbers.

Assiah	Apparent	1	2	3	4	5	6	7	8	9	10	11	12	13
Yetzirah	Reduced	1	2	3	4	5	6	7	8	9	1	2	3	4
Briah	Extended	1	3	6	10	15	21	28	36	45	55	66	78	91
Atziluth	Root	1	3	6	1	6	3	1	9	9	1	3	6	1

Each number in the last horizontal row results from an extension and then reduces a number, which reveals 1, 3, 6, or 9. In the first two rows, the numbers remain identical from one through nine. Once they go beyond single digits, the apparent numbers take on their own form while their reduced value brings them back within the one through nine number cycle.

The third row takes these numbers and shows their quantitative value, and expresses them in a multi-digit form when it applies. The final value in the last row takes the quantitative value and reduces it to a single digit which, reveals series *1-3-6-1-6-3-1-9-9*. This series goes on infinitely. Now, if we take this one step further and break the series into its trinitarian expression (1-3-6), (1-6-3), (1-9-9), then add the sum of each group, we find that the trinity always expresses the one, *1+3+6=10, 1+0=1, 1+9+9 = 19 = 1]*. Each of the three groups reduces to one and, the One expresses itself through *3*.

$$(1+3+6)=10, \ (1+6+3)=10, \ (1+9+9)=10$$
$$1 \quad + \quad 1 \quad + \quad 1 = 3$$

"All things are from One by the mediation of One, and all things have their birth from this one thing by adaptation." The One Life is the root of all existence and is continually expressed through the Trinity

Cube of Space (Chapter 2, pp. 39-42)

Appendix 3 - Theosophic Extensions[1]

Theosophic Extensions from 1 to 120							
#	Σ	#	Σ	#	Σ	#	Σ
1	1	31	496	61	1,891	91	4,186
2	3	32	528	62	1,953	92	4,278
3	6	33	561	63	2,016	93	4,371
4	10	34	595	64	2,080	94	4,465
5	15	35	630	65	2,145	95	4,560
6	21	36	666	66	2,211	96	4,656
7	28	37	703	67	2,278	97	4,753
8	36	38	741	68	2,346	98	4,851
9	45	39	780	69	2,415	99	4,950
10	55	40	820	70	2,485	100	5,050
11	66	41	861	71	2,556	101	5,151
12	78	42	903	72	2,628	102	5,253
13	91	43	946	73	2,701	103	5,356
14	105	44	990	74	2,775	104	5,460
15	120	45	1,035	75	2,850	105	5,565
16	136	46	1,081	76	2,926	106	5,671
17	153	47	1,128	77	3,003	107	5,778
18	171	48	1,176	78	3,081	108	5,886
19	190	49	1,225	79	3,160	109	5,995
20	210	50	1,275	80	3,240	110	6,105
21	231	51	1326	81	3,321	111	6,216
22	253	52	1,378	82	3,403	112	6,328
23	276	53	1,431	83	3,486	113	6,441
24	300	54	1,485	84	3,570	114	6,555
25	325	55	1,540	85	3,655	115	6,670
26	351	56	1,596	86	3,741	116	6,786
27	378	57	1,653	87	3,828	117	6,903
28	406	58	1,711	88	3,916	118	7,021
29	435	59	1,770	89	4,005	119	7,140
30	465	60	1,830	90	4,095	120	7,260

[1] In mathematics, the theosophic extension is called the summation and is represented by the Greet letter Σ. Therefore the summation of 6 is Σ6= 1+2+3+4+5+6 = 21.

Appendix 4 - Prime Numbers From 1 to 5,000

Prime Numbers From 1 – 2,521								
2	181	431	683	977	1,277	1,567	1,877	2,207
3	191	433	691	983	1,279	1,571	1,879	2,213
5	193	439	701	991	1,283	1,579	1,889	2,221
7	197	443	709	997	1,289	1,583	1,901	2,237
11	199	449	719	1,009	1,291	1,597	1,907	2,239
13	211	457	727	1,013	1,297	1,601	1,913	2,243
17	223	461	733	1,019	1,301	1,607	1,931	2,251
19	227	463	739	1,021	1,303	1,609	1,933	2,267
23	229	467	743	1,031	1,307	1,613	1,949	2,269
29	233	479	751	1,033	1,319	1,619	1,951	2,273
31	239	487	757	1,039	1,321	1,621	1,973	2,281
37	241	491	761	1,049	1,327	1,627	1,979	2,287
41	251	499	769	1,051	1,361	1,637	1,987	2,293
43	257	503	773	1,061	1,367	1,657	1,993	2,297
47	263	509	787	1,063	1,373	1,663	1,997	2,309
53	269	521	797	1,069	1,381	1,667	1,999	2,311
59	271	523	809	1,087	1,399	1,669	2,003	2,333
61	277	541	811	1,091	1,409	1,693	2,011	2,339
67	281	547	821	1,093	1,423	1,697	2,017	2,341
71	283	557	823	1,097	1,427	1,699	2,027	2,347
73	293	563	827	1,103	1,429	1,709	2029	2,351
79	307	569	829	1,109	1,433	1,721	2,039	2,357
83	311	571	839	1,117	1,439	1,723	2,053	2,371
89	313	577	853	1,123	1,447	1,733	2,063	2,377
97	317	587	857	1,129	1,451	1,741	2,069	2,381
101	331	593	859	1,151	1,453	1,747	2,081	2,383
103	337	599	863	1,153	1,459	1,753	2,083	2,389
107	347	601	877	1,163	1,471	1,759	2,087	2,393
109	349	607	881	1,171	1,481	1,777	2,089	2,399
113	353	613	883	1,181	1,483	1,783	2,099	2,411
127	359	617	887	1,187	1,487	1,787	2,111	2,417
131	367	619	907	1,193	1,489	1,789	2,113	2,423
137	373	631	911	1,201	1,493	1,801	2,129	2,437
139	379	641	919	1,213	1,499	1,811	2,131	2,441
149	383	643	929	1,217	1,511	1,823	2,137	2,447
151	389	647	937	1,223	1,523	1,831	2,141	2,459
157	397	653	941	1,229	1,531	1,847	2,143	2,467
163	401	659	947	1,231	1,543	1,861	2,153	2,473
167	409	661	953	1,237	1,549	1,867	2,161	2,477
173	419	673	967	1,249	1,553	1,871	2,179	2,503
179	421	677	971	1,259	1,559	1,873	2,203	2,521

Prime Numbers to 4,999							
2,531	2,833	3,191	3,529	3,851	4,201	4,547	4,919
2,539	2,837	3,203	3,533	3,853	4211	4,549	4,931
2,543	2,843	3,209	3,539	3,863	4,217	4,561	4,933
2,549	2,851	3,217	3,541	3,877	4,219	4,567	4,937
2,551	2,857	3,221	3,547	3,881	4,229	4,583	4,943
2,557	2,861	3,229	3,557	3,889	4,231	4,591	4,951
2,579	2,879	3,251	3,559	3,907	4,241	4,597	4,957
2,591	2,887	3,253	3,571	3,911	4,243	4,603	4,967
2,593	2,897	3,257	3,581	3,917	4,253	4,621	4,969
2,609	2,903	3,259	3,583	3,919	4,259	4,637	4,973
2,617	2,909	3,271	3,593	3,923	4,261	4,639	4,987
2,621	2,917	3,299	3,607	3,929	4,271	4,643	4,993
2,633	2,927	3,301	3,613	3,931	4,273	4,649	4,999
2,647	2,939	3,307	3,617	3,943	4,283	4,651	
2,657	2,953	3,313	3,623	3,947	4,289	4,657	
2,659	2,957	3,319	3,631	3,967	4,297	4,663	
2,663	2,963	3,323	3,637	3,989	4,327	4,673	
2,671	2,969	3,329	3,643	4,001	4,337	4,679	
2,677	2,971	3,331	3,659	4,003	4,339	4,691	
2,683	2,999	3,343	3,671	4,007	4,349	4,703	
2,687	3,001	3,347	3,673	4,013	4,357	4,721	
2,689	3,011	3,359	3,677	4,019	4,363	4,723	
2,693	3,019	3,361	3,691	4,021	4,373	4,729	
2,699	3,023	3,371	3,697	4,027	4,391	4,733	
2,707	3,037	3,373	3,701	4,049	4,397	4,751	
2,711	3,041	3,389	3,709	4,051	4,409	4,759	
2,713	3,049	3,391	3,719	4,057	4,421	4,783	
2,719	3,061	3,407	3,727	4,073	4,423	4,787	
2,729	3,067	3,413	3,733	4,079	4,441	4,789	
2,731	3,079	3,433	3,739	4,091	4,47	4,793	
2,741	3,083	3,449	3,761	4,093	4,451	4,799	
2,749	3,089	3,457	3,767	4,099	4,457	4,801	
2,753	3,109	3,461	3,769	4,111	4,463	4,813	
2,767	3,119	3,463	3,779	4,127	4,481	4,817	
2,777	3,121	3,467	3,793	4,129	4,483	4,831	
2,789	3,137	3,469	3,797	4,133	4,493	4,861	
2,791	3,163	3,491	3,803	4,139	4,507	4,871	
2,797	3,167	3,499	3,821	4,153	4,513	4,877	
2,801	3,169	3,511	3,823	4,157	4,517	4,889	
2,803	3,181	3,517	3,833	4,159	4,519	4,903	
2,819	3,187	3,527	3,847	4,177	4,523	4,909	

Appendix 5 - Perfect Numbers

The study of perfect numbers is ancient. The first recorded instance of their study was by Pythagoras and his followers. Their interest was in their mystical properties.

A perfect number is a number that is the sum of its divisors. A divisor was called an 'aliquot parts' of a number by the ancients. For example, the aliquot parts of 10 are 1, 2 and 5. Note that $1 = {}^{10}/_{10}$; $2 = {}^{10}/_5$; and $5 = {}^{10}/_2$. 10 is not an aliquot part of 10 since it is not a proper quotient (The number obtained by dividing one quantity by another) is a quotient different from the number itself.

The four perfect numbers 6, 28, 496 and 8128 were known from ancient times. There is no record of these discoveries. There are:

$6 = 1 + \mathbf{2} + \mathbf{3}$; $2 \times 3 = 6$
$28 = 1 + 2 + 4 + 7 + 14 = 28$; $1 + 2 + \mathbf{4} = \mathbf{7}$; $4 \times 7 = 28$
$496 = 1 + 2 + 4 + 8 + 16 + 31 + 62 + 124 + 248 = 496$; $1 + 2 + 4 + 8 + \mathbf{16} = \mathbf{31}$; $16 \times 31 = 496$

$8128 = 1 + 2 + 4 + 8 + 16 + 32 + \mathbf{64} + \mathbf{127} + 254 + 508 + 1016 + 2032 + 4064$

The first recorded mathematical result concerning perfect numbers which is known occurs in Proposition 36 of Book IX of Euclid's *Elements* written around 300BC.

Simply stated if $1 + 2 + 4 = 7$ which is prime. Then (the sum) $\times$ (the last) $= 7 \times 4 = 28$, which is a perfect number. Also, $1 + 2 + 4 + 8 + 16 = 31$ which is prime. Then $31 \times 16 = 496$ is a perfect number.

If we restate Euclid's rigorous proof in modern form:

If $1 + 2 + 4 + ... + 2^{n-1} = 2^n - 1$.

If, for some $n > 1$, $2^n - 1$ is prime then $2^{n-1}(2^n - 1)$ is a perfect number.

However, this did not stand the test of time. It was discovered later that if a number was of this form, it may be a candidate to be a perfect number but not always.

Please note that prime numbers of the form $2^n - 1$ are called Mersenne Primes after Marin Mersenne, a French priest.

The next significant study of perfect numbers was made by Nicomachus of Gerasa. Around 100 C.E., Nicomachus wrote *Introductio Arithmetica,* which gives a classification of numbers based on the concept of perfect numbers. Nicomachus divides numbers into three classes, the superabundant numbers (the sum of the divisors [aliquot parts] is greater than the number, deficient numbers (the sum of the aliquot parts is less than the number), and perfect numbers (that the sum of their aliquot parts is equal to the number). He states:

Among simple even numbers, some are superabundant, others are deficient: these two classes are as two extremes opposed to one another; as for those that occupy the middle position between the two, they are said to be perfect. And those to be opposite each other, the superabundant and the deficient, are divided in their condition, which is inequality, into them too much and the too little.

Note the moral terms that Nicomachus describes there three sets of numbers:

Too much produces excess, superfluity, exaggerations, and abuse; in too little, it produces wanting, defaults, privations, and insufficiencies. And those found between the too much and the too little, that is in equality, are produced virtue, just measure, propriety, beauty and things of that sort - of which the most exemplary form is that type of number called perfect.

Perfect numbers had a religious significance, namely that 6 is the number of days taken by God to create the world. It is said that God chooses this number because it was perfect, and the next perfect number is 28, the number of days it takes the Moon to travel around the Earth. Saint Augustine (354-430) writes in *The City of God*:-

Six is a number perfect in itself, and not because God created all things in six days; rather, the converse is true. God created all things in six days because the number is perfect...

Nicomachus goes on to describe certain results concerning perfect numbers. I will list those that stood the test of time are:

1. All perfect numbers are even.
2. All perfect numbers end in 6 and 8.
3. There are infinitely many perfect numbers.

The next step forward came in 1603 when Cataldi was able to show that $2^{17}- 1$ and $2^{19} - 1$ are prime and therefore derived the 6th and 7th perfect numbers (see table below).

In 1732 Euler found the 8th perfect number (the first in 125 years). He also proved that every even perfect number must be from $2^{p-1}(2^p - 1)$. And that every even perfect number must end in either 6 or 8. Euler also tried to make some headway on the problem of whether odd perfect numbers existed.

As of 2003, 39 perfect numbers are known. It is not known if there are any odd perfect numbers. It has been shown that there are no odd perfect numbers in the interval from 1 to 10^{50}.

	List of Perfect numbers base on Euler's formula: $2^{n-1}(2^n - 1)$		
	Perfect Number	Value of n	Formula
1	6	2	$2^1(2^2-1)$
2	28	3	$2^2(2^3-1)$
3	496	5	$2^4(2^5-1)$
4	8128	7	$2^6(2^7-1)$
5	33550336	13	$2^{12}(2^{13} - 1)$
6	8589869056	17	$2^{16}(2^{17} - 1)$
7	137438691328	19	$2^{18}(2^{19} - 1)$
8	2305843008139952128	31	$2^{30}(2^{31} - 1)$
9	2658455991569831744465… …4692615953842176	61	$2^{60}(2^{61} - 1)$

Appendix 6 - The Divine Proportion

The Divine Proportion is also called the Golden Mean, Golden Section, Golden Cut or extreme and mean proportion.

One unique point exists that divides a line into two unequal segments so that the whole is to the greater as, the greater is to the lesser.

Consider the line segment A + B. If we divide it in just the right spot, we find that the length of the entire segment (A + B) is to the length of segment A as the length of segment A is to the length of segment B. If we calculate these ratios, we see that we get an approximation of the Golden Ratio.

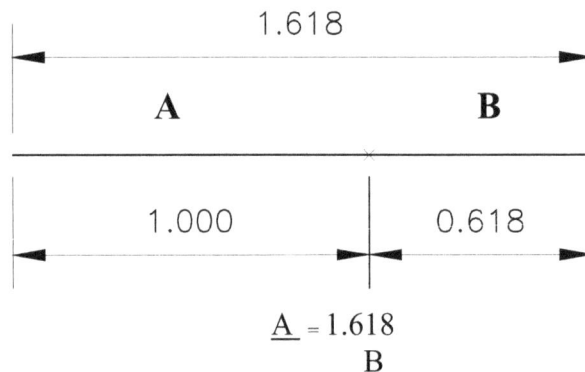

$$\frac{A + B}{A} = 1.618 \qquad\qquad \frac{A}{B} = 1.618$$

Please note that 1.618 is only an approximation of the golden ratio. The Golden Ratio is an irrational number. An irrational number has no *exact* decimal equivalent, although 1.618 is a good approximation. In mathematics, the Golden Ratio number is called *Phi* (ϕ). For the sake of convenience, I will use the term *Phi* (ϕ) exclusively.

Phi has many unique properties. IT IS THE ONLY NUMBER, WHICH, WHEN, SUBTRACTED FROM ONE (1), BECOMES ITS OWN RECIPROCAL.

$$\phi - 1 = 1/\phi$$

$$\text{or} \qquad \phi^2 - \phi - 1 = 0$$

When solving this equation we find that the roots are

$$\phi = \frac{1 + \sqrt{5}}{2} \sim 1.618... \quad \text{or} \quad \phi = \frac{1 - \sqrt{5}}{2} \sim -0.618...$$

[~ means approximately equal to]

If we define $1/\phi$ as ϕ', we have interesting solutions.

$$\phi + \phi' = 1 \qquad\qquad \phi\phi' = -1.$$

What does this mean? *Phi* is the only number added to itself is ONE, and the only number multiplied by itself is negative ONE.

One more point, and I will stop talking a foreign language.

Leonardo Fibonacci posed the following problem in his book, *Liber Abaci*: How many pairs of rabbits will be produced in a year, beginning with a single pair, if in every month each pair bears a new pair which becomes productive from the second month on?

The solution is 1, 1, 2, 3, 5, 8, 13, 21... Take the number 1 in the series. Add to it the previous number 0, and you get the next number in the series (1). Then take the previous number 1 plus the current number (1) and get the next number (2). Then the previous number (1) plus the current number (2) is equal to three (3). This is how you derive this series. To describe this in terms of math, we have:

$$U_{(n+1)} = U_n + U_{(n-1)}$$

This is called the Fibonacci series. Constructing the following table, we see that the ratio of these numbers approaches the irrational number *Phi*. The Fibonacci series approximates *Phi*.

1/1	=	1
2/1	=	2
3/2	=	1.5
5/3	=	1.66
8/5	=	1.6
13/8	=	1.62
21/13	=	1.615

As the series continues, this ratio approaches the number *Phi*.

The number *Phi* and its approximation, the Fibonacci series, is the pattern of life. Organisms (whether plants, humans and solar systems) organize their structures in relation to the number *Phi*. The most well known is the Nautilus shell.

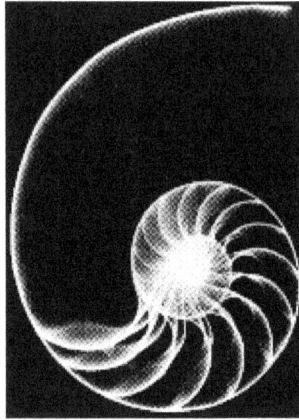

We can generate an approximation of the Nautilus shell by using another figure. A rectangle constructed from the *Phi* (φ) ratio. It is called the Golden Rectangle. This particular rectangle has sides A and B that are in proportion to the Golden Ratio. It has been said that the Golden Rectangle is the most pleasing rectangle to the eye. It is said that any geometrical shape with the Golden Ratio is the most pleasing to look at those types of figures.

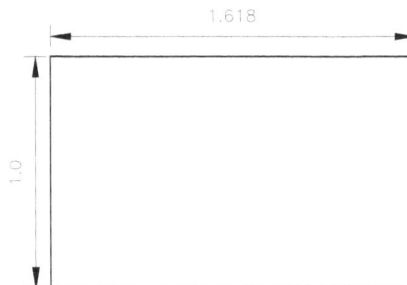

If we take the Fibonacci series and construct a series of rectangles, we get the following shape.

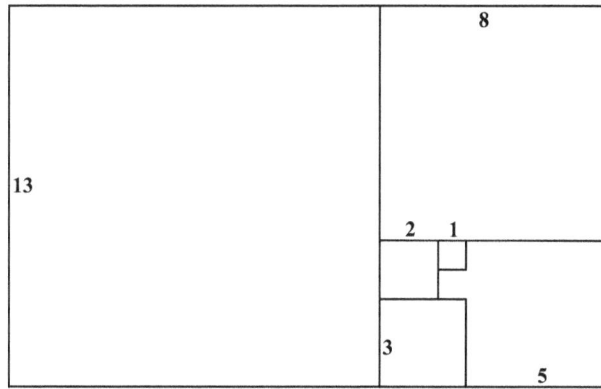

We can generate a shape that APPROXIMATES the Logarithmic spiral or Nautilus shell by connecting the points.

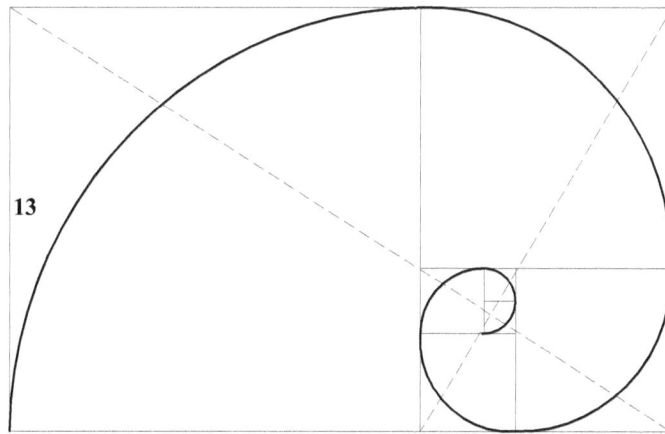

Another shape that is generated is called the Golden Triangle.

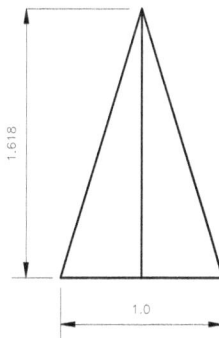

It can also generate an approximation to the Logarithmic spiral by dividing the line segments by 0.618.

305

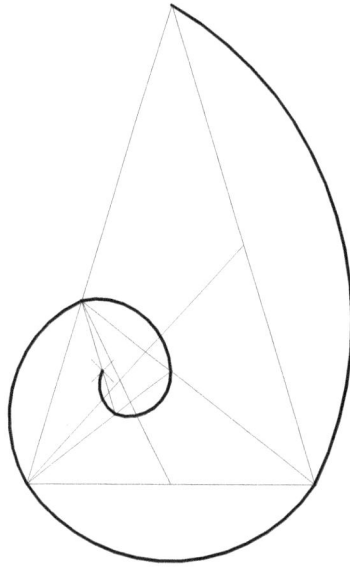

And the Golden Ellipse:

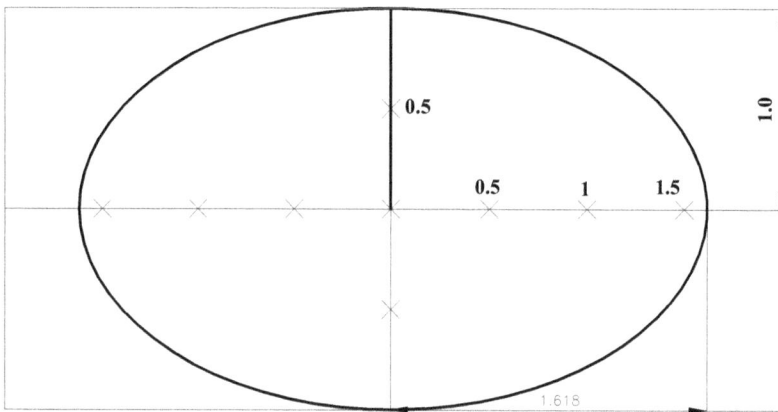

The Golden Vesica Pisces

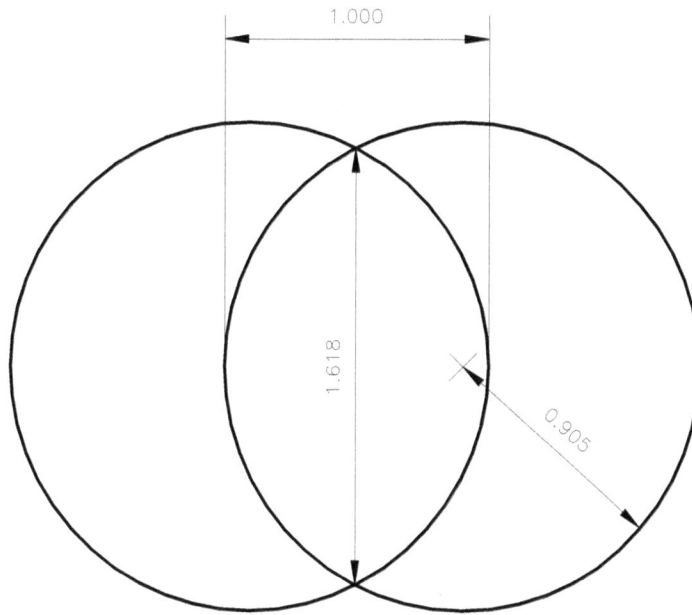

To construct this figure, use these dimensions.

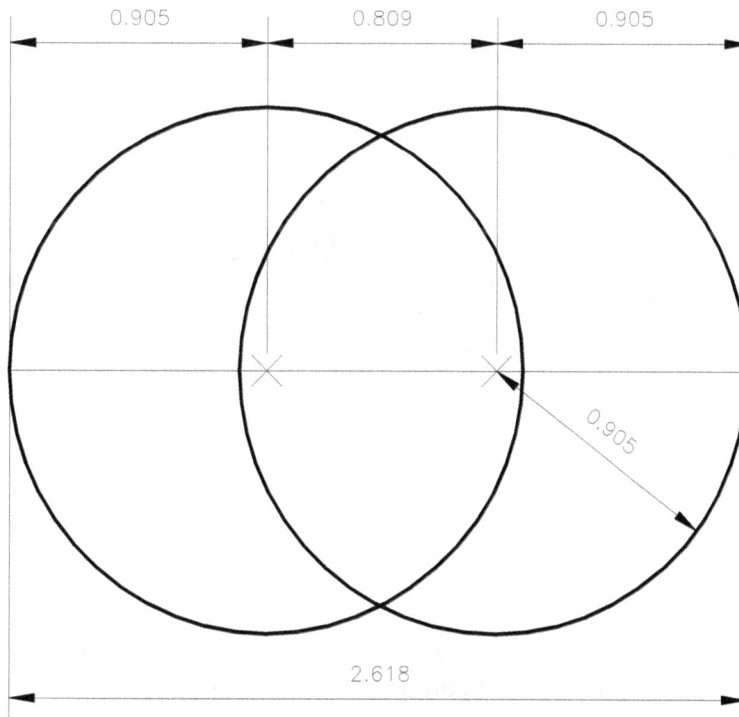

The Golden Mean of the Pentagram

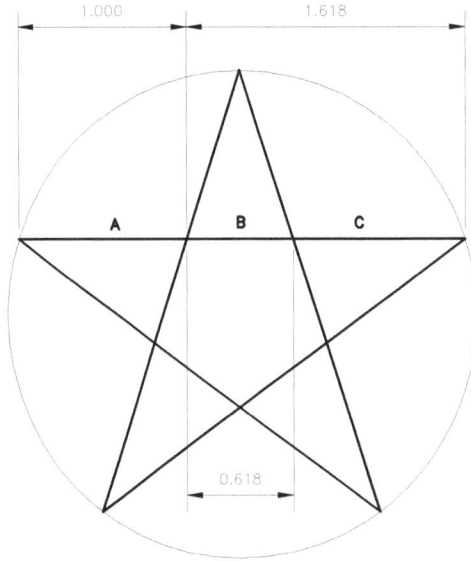

Draw a pentagram with the line segment A =1.

Then line segment B + C = 1.618 (ϕ). Line segment B = 0.618 (1/ ϕ).

What does this all mean? Many life patterns are built from this shape, from plants' growth patterns to the bones of a human body are built on this pattern. It is a pattern of beauty. It is the pattern of existence. It is a symbol of Life.

							Properties
1.1.2	=	א	א	ב	=	4	
1.2.3	=	א	ב	ג	=	6	S3 = 6 The first perfect number
2.3.5	=	ב	ג	ו	=	10	S4 = 10
3.5.8	=	ג	ו	ח	=	16	358 is Nachash & Messiah.
5.8.13[1] (584)	=	ו	ח	נ	=	64	

[1] Key 13, Death is associated with Nun (נ).

In gematria, we can see the pattern of life in the Hebrew letters' pattern of numbers. The interested student could look up these numbers, research correlations, etc. Good hunting.

How to Draw a Phi Ratio Vesica Pisces.

Draw a line with the lengths shown ($\phi/4 = 0.809$).

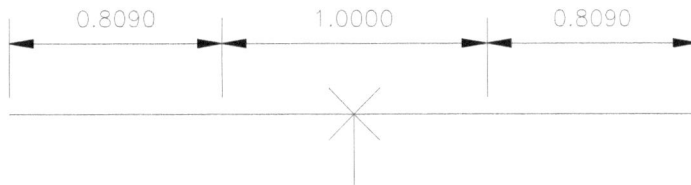

From the center shown, draw a circle with a diameter Phi/4 (0.045).

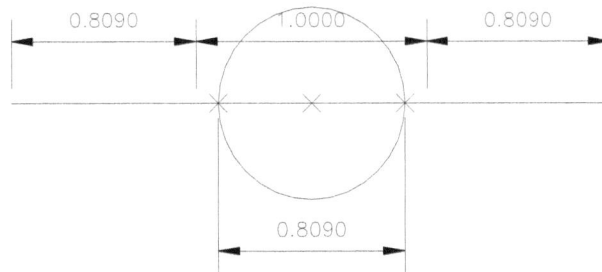

From these two endpoints, draw circles are shown.

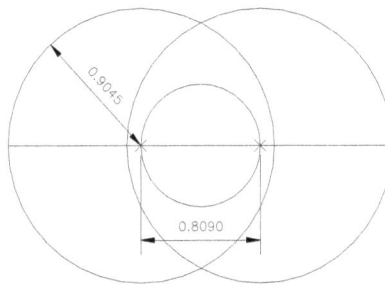

This figure draws a Vesica Pisces that is very close to the phi ratio.

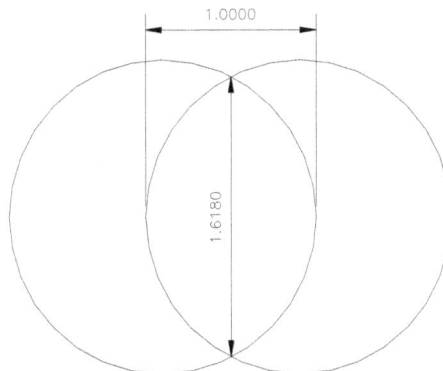

Appendix 7 - Magic Squares

A magic square is an arrangement of the numbers from **1** to n^2 in an **nxn** matrix, with each number occurring exactly once, and have the following properties:

1. Every row adds up to the same number
2. Every column adds up to that same number
3. Both diagonals add up to that number

The simplest magic square is the **1x1** magic square whose only entry is number **1**.

1

The next simplest is the **3x3** magic square (There are no 2 by 2 magic squares).

4	3	8
9	5	1
2	7	6

The sum of all the numbers in a magic square is also called the *Theosophic Extension*. This property is called a summation in calculus and is represented by the Greek Letter Epsilon (Σ).

In a 3 by 3 magic square, there are **9** cells. The theosophic extension can be represented as:

Theosophic Extension = Σ9 = 1+2+3+4+5+6+7+8+9 = 45.

For larger order magic squares, this can be cumbersome to add up all the numbers. The following formula describes a quick method for determining the *Theosophic Extension* or *Summation* of a magic square:

n(n+1)/2   **Where n = the number of cells**

In the above example of a 3 by 3 square **n** = 9, so the equation is:

9(9+1)/2 = 9(10)/2 = 45

For a 11 by 11 square the formula is:

121(121 + 1)/2 = 121(122)/2 = 7381.

Since each Sephiroth has a corresponding number on the Tree of Life, a magic square is attributed to each Sephiroth based on this number.

Planetary/Sephirah Numbers						
Sephirah/Planet	#	# of cells	Sum of any line[1]	Sum of square	Sum of the Perimeter of Square[2]	Sum of 4 corner cells
Binah/Saturn	3	9	15	45	40	20
Chesed/Jupiter	4	16	34	136	102	34
Geburah/Mars	5	25	65	325	208	52
Tiphareth/Sun	6	36	111	666	370	74[2]
Netzach/Venus	7	49	175	1,225	600	100
Hod/Mercury	8	64	260	2,080	910	130
Yesod/Moon	9	81	369	3,321	1,312	164
Malkuth [3]	10	100	505	5,050	1,818	202
Daath/Pluto	11	121	671	7,381	2,440	244

[1] Horizontal, vertical or diagonal; also called the magic constant

[2] I found one exception in one Magic Square of The Sun.

[3] Traditionally, there is no magic square attributed to the sphere of Malkuth. However, a 10 by 10 magic square does exist.

Magic Squares of Saturn

Agrippa's Kamea				Hebrew		
4	9	2		ד	ט	ב
3	5	7		ג	ה	ז
8	1	6		ח	א	ו

Magic Squares of Jupiter

Agrippa's Kamea				Hebrew			
4	14	15	1	ד	די	וט	א
9	7	6	12	ט	ז	ו	בי
5	11	10	8	ה	אי	י	ח
16	2	3	13	זט	ב	ג	גי

MATLAB Square				Tamori's Square			
16	5	9	4	1	14	15	4
2	11	7	14	8	11	10	5
3	10	6	15	12	7	6	9
13	8	12	1	13	2	3	16

Magic Squares of Mars

Agrippa's Kamea						Agrippa's Kamea in Hebrew				
11	24	7	20	3		אי	דכ	ז	כ	ג
4	12	25	8	16		ד	בי	הכ	ח	וי
17	5	13	21	9		זי	ה	גי	אכ	ט
10	18	1	14	22		י	חי	א	די	בכ
23	6	19	2	15		גכ	ו	טי	ב	הי

Note that the magic constant or sum of any row is equal to 65, which is the sum of two different squares.

$$1^2 + 8^2 = 65;$$
$$4^2 + 7^2 = 65$$

The sum of all the numbers is 325, which is the sum of three different squares.

$$1^2 + 18^2 = 325;$$
$$6^2 + 17^2 = 325;$$
$$10^2 + 15^2 = 325.$$

Magic Squares of the Sun

Agrippa's Kamea					
6	32	3	34	35	1
7	11	27	28	8	30
19	14	16	15	23	24
18	20	22	21	17	13
25	29	10	9	26	12
36	5	33	4	2	31

Agrippa's Kamea in Hebrew					
ו	בל	ג	דל	הל	א
ז	אי	זכ	חכ	ח	ל
טי	די	וי	הי	גכ	דכ
חי	כ	בכ	אכ	זי	גי
הכ	טכ	י	ט	כו	בי
ול	ה	גל	ד	ב	אל

Paul Case's Kamea					
3	2	1	36	35	34
31	32	33	4	5	6
15	13	23	19	20	21
22	24	14	18	17	16
12	11	10	27	26	25
28	29	30	7	8	9

Magic Squares of Venus

Agrippa's Kamea

22	47	16	41	10	35	4
5	23	48	17	42	11	29
30	6	24	49	18	36	12
13	31	7	25	43	19	37
38	14	32	1	26	44	20
21	39	8	33	2	27	45
46	15	40	9	34	3	28

Agrippa's Kamea in Hebrew

וכ	זמ	זט	אמ	י	הל	ד
ה	גכ	חמ	יז	דמ	אי	טכ
ל	ו	דכ	טמ	טי	ול	בי
גי	אל	ז	הכ	גמ	טי	זל
חל	די	בל	א	וכ	דמ	כ
אכ	טל	ח	לג	ב	זכ	המ
ומ	וט	מ	ט	דל	ג	חכ

The magic constant or summation of a row, column or diagonal is 175, equal to $1^2 + 7^2 + 5^2$. The sum of all the numbers of the square is $1225 = 35^2$.

Agrippa's Mercury Magic Square

8	58	59	5	4	62	63	1
49	15	14	52	53	11	10	56
41	23	22	44	48	19	18	45
32	34	35	29	28	38	39	25
40	26	27	37	36	30	31	33
17	47	46	20	21	43	42	24
9	55	54	12	13	51	50	16
64	2	3	61	60	6	7	57

Agrippa's Kamea in Hebrew

ח	טג	טנ	ה	ד	בס	גס	א
טמ	הי	די	בן	גנ	אי	י	ונ
אמ	גכ	בכ	דמ	המ	טי	חי	חמ
בל	דל	הל	טכ	חכ	חל	טל	המ
מ	וכ	זכ	זל	ול	ל	אל	גל
זי	זמ	ומ	כ	אכ	גמ	במ	דכ
ט	הג	דנ	בי	גי	אן	נ	וי
דס	ב	ג	אס	ס	ו	ז	זנ

Benjamin Franklin's Mercury Square

52	61	4	13	20	29	36	45
14	3	62	51	46	35	30	19
53	60	5	12	21	28	37	44
11	6	59	54	43	38	27	22
55	58	7	10	23	26	39	42
9	8	57	56	41	40	25	24
50	63	2	15	18	31	34	47
16	1	64	49	48	33	32	17

Magic Squares of the Moon

Agrippa's Kamea								
37	78	29	70	21	62	13	54	5
6	38	79	30	71	22	63	14	46
47	7	39	80	31	72	23	55	15
16	48	8	40	81	32	64	24	56
57	17	49	9	41	73	33	65	25
26	58	18	50	1	42	74	34	66
67	27	59	10	51	2	43	75	35
36	68	19	60	11	52	3	44	76
77	28	69	20	61	12	53	4	45

Agrippa's Kamea in Hebrew								
זל׳	חע	טכ	ע	אכ	בס	גי	דנ	ה
ו	חל׳	טע	ל	אע	בכ	גס	די	ומ
זמ	ז	טל	פ	אל	בע	גכ	הנ	הי
וי	חמ	ח	מ	אפ	בל	דס	דכ	ון
זנ	זי	טמ	ט	אמ	גע	גל׳	הס	הכ
וכ	חנ	חי	נ	א	במ	דע	דל׳	וס
זס	זכ	טנ	י	אנ	ב	גמ	הע	הל׳
ול׳	חס	טי	ס	אי	בנ	ג	דמ	וע
זע	חכ	טס	כ	אס	בי	גנ	ד	ה

317

Magic Square of Malkuth

10 by 10 MATLAB Square									
92	98	4	85	86	17	23	79	10	11
99	80	81	87	93	24	5	6	12	18
1	7	88	19	25	76	82	13	94	100
8	14	20	21	2	83	89	95	96	77
15	16	22	3	9	90	91	97	78	84
67	73	54	60	61	42	48	29	35	36
74	55	56	62	68	49	30	31	37	43
51	57	63	69	75	26	32	38	44	50
58	64	70	71	52	33	39	45	46	27
40	41	47	28	34	65	66	72	53	59

10 by 10 Tamori's Square									
1	92	3	94	5	6	97	98	99	10
20	89	18	87	16	15	84	13	82	81
21	72	23	74	25	76	77	28	79	30
40	69	38	67	35	36	64	33	62	61
41	52	43	44	56	55	57	48	59	50
51	42	58	54	46	45	47	53	49	60
70	39	68	37	66	65	34	63	32	31
80	22	73	24	75	26	27	78	29	71
90	19	88	17	86	85	14	83	12	11
91	9	93	7	95	96	4	8	2	100

Magic Square of Daath										
56	117	46	107	36	97	26	87	16	77	6
7	57	118	47	108	37	98	27	88	17	67
68	8	58	119	48	109	38	99	28	78	18
19	69	9	59	120	49	110	39	89	29	79
80	20	70	10	60	121	50	100	40	90	30
31	81	21	71	11	61	111	51	101	41	91
92	32	82	22	72	1	62	112	52	102	42
43	93	33	83	12	73	2	63	113	53	103
104	44	94	23	84	13	74	3	64	114	54
55	105	34	95	24	85	14	75	4	65	115
116	45	106	35	96	25	86	15	76	5	66

11 by 11 Tamori's Square										
56	55	43	31	19	7	116	104	92	80	68
69	57	45	44	32	20	8	117	105	93	81
82	70	58	46	34	33	21	9	118	106	94
95	83	71	59	47	35	23	22	10	119	107
108	96	84	72	60	48	36	24	12	11	120
121	109	97	85	73	61	49	37	25	13	1
2	111	110	98	86	74	62	50	38	26	14
15	3	112	100	99	87	75	63	51	39	27
28	16	4	113	101	89	88	76	64	52	40
41	29	17	5	114	102	90	78	77	65	53
54	42	30	18	6	115	103	91	79	67	66

Appendix 8 - Gematria of יהוה in the Four Worlds

The Name of Tetragrammaton in the Four Worlds[1]						
						#
Qabalistic World	Secret Name	Yod י	Heh ה	Vav ו	Heh ה	26
Atziloth	עב Aub (72)	יוד	הי	ויו	הי	72
Briah	סג Seg (63)	יוד	הי	ואו	הי	63
Yetzirah	מה Mah (45)	יוד	הא	ואו	הא	45
Assiah	בן Ben (52)	יוד	הה	וו	הה	52

[1] Derived from page 33 [plate 5] of Kabbalah Unveiled – Rosenroth adds on page 32 of Mather's translation:

68. Now, there are four secret names referred to the four worlds of Atziluth, Briah, Yetzirah, and Asiah; and again, the Tetragrammaton is said to go forth written in a certain manner in each of these four worlds. The secret name of Atziloth is *Aub*; that of Briah is *Seg*, that of Yetzirah is *Mah*, and That of Assiah is Ben (meaning son).

69. These names operate together with the Sephiroth through the '231 gates,' as the various combinations of the alphabet are called; but it would take too much space to go fully into the subject here.

The value of all four names is 232.

The Four Cabalistic Worlds				
World		#	Meaning	Sephiroth
Atziluth	אצילות	537	Archetypal Emanation	Kether, Chokmah & Binah
Briah	בריאה	218	Creation creative	Chesed, Geburah & Tiphareth
Yetzirah	יצירה	315	Formative Formation	Netzach, Hod and Yesod
Assiah	עשיה	385	Manifestation physical	Malkuth

Secret Names of the World Worlds

The secret name of the World of Atzilut: *Aub*, (OB, עב, 72).

Isaiah 14.14: I will ascend above the tops of the clouds (OB), I will make myself like the Most High.

Gesenius: An architectural term, thresholds, steps, by which one goes up to a porch. Darkness, especially of a cloud. A dark thicket of wood.

The secret name of the World of Briah, *Seg* (SG, סג, 63).

Psalm 53.4: Everyone has turned away (SG, he turned away). They have together become corrupt; no one does good.

סיג SIG: the refuse created by the refinement of metals.

סוג, SVG: to go away from, to depart. One who draws back in the heart (from God).

The secret name of the World of Yetzirah, *Mah* (MH, מה, 45).

Meaning what. Indefinite pronoun, anything, something, whatever. Wherefore, why, how, how much (an exclamation), in what manner?

The secret name of the World of Assiah: (Ben (BN, בן, 52).

A son. Children of both sexes. A youth denotes a person or thing, whether born or appearing in that time, or as having existed during that time. "A son of 22 years." "A son of Old Age," followed by a genitive denoting virtue, vice or condition of life; a denotes a man who has that virtue or vice or has been brought up in that condition. "A son of Strength," "son of wickedness."

Appendix 9

The Gematria of the Shem ha-Mephorash

The Shem ha-Mephorash, Schemhamphoras [שם המפרש], or the Divided Name, is derived from the Book of Exodus[1], chapter 14, verses 19, 20, and 21. Each verse is composed of 72 letters (in the original Hebrew). If one writes these three verses' one above the other, the first from right to left, the second from left to right, and the third from right to left (as the ox plows), one will get 72 columns of three-letter names of God. The 72 names are divided into four columns of eighteen names each. Each of the four columns falls under one of the letters of the Tetragrammaton, יהוי and the four Cabalistic Worlds.

י

V19	כ	ל	ה	ה	מ	י	ה	ל	א	ה	כ	א	ל	מ	ע	ס	י	ו
V20	ל	א	ק	ר	ב	ז	ה	א	ל	ז	ה	כ	ל	ה	ל	י	ל	ה
V21	י	ו	מ	י	ה	ל	ע	ו	ד	י	ת	א	ה	ש	מ	ט	י	ו
	18	17	16	15	14	13	12	11	10	9	8	7	6	5	4	3	2	1

ה

V19	מ	כ	ל	י	ו	ל	א	ר	ש	י	ה	נ	ח	מ	י	נ	פ	ל
V20	נ	ו	ה	ח	ש	כ	ו	י	א	ר	א	ת	ה	ל	י	ל	ה	ו
V21	ד	ק	ח	ו	ר	ב	מ	י	ה	ת	א	ה	ו	ה	י	כ	ל	ו
	36	35	34	33	32	31	30	29	28	27	26	25	24	23	22	21	20	19

ו

V19	נ	נ	ע	ה	ד	ו	מ	ע	ע	ס	י	ו	מ	ה	י	ר	ח	א
V20	י	נ	מ	ח	נ	ה	י	ש	ר	א	ל	ו	י	ה	י	ה	ע	נ
V21	ת	א	מ	ש	י	ו	ה	ל	י	ל	ה	כ	ה	ז	ע	מ	י	
	54	53	52	51	50	49	48	47	46	45	44	43	42	41	40	39	38	37

ה

V19	מ	ה	י	ר	ח	א	מ	ד	מ	ע	י	ו	מ	ה	י	נ	פ	מ
V20	ו	י	ב	א	ב	י	נ	מ	ח	נ	ה	מ	צ	ר	י	מ	ו	ב
V21	מ	י	מ	ה	ו	ע	ק	ב	י	ו	ה	ב	ר	ח	ל	מ	י	ה
	72	71	70	69	68	67	66	65	64	63	62	61	60	59	58	57	56	55

Exodus 14:

(19) And the angel of God, which went before the camp of Israel, removed and went behind them; and the pillar of the cloud went from before their face, and stood behind them.

(20) And it came between the camp of the Egyptians and the camp of Israel, and it was a cloud and darkness to them, but it gave light by night to these: so that the one came not near the other all night.

(21) And Moses stretched out his hand over the sea, and the Lord caused the sea to go back by a strong east wind all that night, and made thee dry sea land, and the waters were divided.
The Pronunciation of these God names (Mathers style) are as follows:

Heh		Vau		Heh		Yod	
Assiah		Yetzirah		Briah		Atziluth	
55	Mabeh	37	Ani	19	Levo	1	Vehu
56	Poi	38	Chaum	20	Pah	2	Yeli
57	Nemem	39	Rehau	21	Nelak	3	Sit
58	Yeil	40	Yeiz	22	Yiai	4	Aulem
59	Harach	41	Hahah	23	Melah	5	Mahash
60	Metzer	42	Mik	24	Chaho	6	Lelah
61	Vamet	43	Veval	25	Nethah	7	Aka
62	Yehah	44	Yelah	26	Haa	8	Kahath
63	Aunu	45	Sael	27	Yereth	9	Hezi
64	Mechi	46	Auri	28	Shaah	10	Elad
65	Dameb	47	Aushal	29	Riyi	11	Lav
66	Menaq	48	Miah	30	Aum	12	Hahau
67	Aiau	49	Vaho	31	Lekab	13	Yezel
68	Chebo	50	Doni	32	Vesher	14	Mebah
68	Raah	51	Hachash	33	Yecho	15	Heri
70	Yebem	52	Aumem	34	Lehach	16	Haqem
71	Haiai	53	Nena	35	Keveq	17	Lau
72	Moum	54	Neith	36	Menad	18	Keli

By adding לא (Masculine, Severity, Justice aspect of God), הי (Feminine, Mercy, aspect), we get the names of the Angels.

Presidency	Choir of Angles	#	God Name		Angelic Name	# God Name	# Angel Name
P r e s i d e n c y	1st Choir Seraphim	1	והו	הי	Vahaviah	17	32
		2	ילי	לא	Yelayiel	50	81
		3	טיס	לא	Saitel	79	110
		4	מלע	הי	Olmiah	140	155
		5	שהמ	הי	Mahashiah	345	360
		6	הלל	לא	Lelahel	65	96
		7	אכא	הי	Akaiah	22	37
		8	תהכ	לא	Kehethel	425	456
י	2nd Choir Kerubim	9	יזה	לא	Haziel	22	53
		10	דלא	הי	Aldaiah	35	50
		11	ואל	הי	Laviah	37	52
		12	עהה	הי	Hihaayah	80	95
		13	לזי	לא	Yeyalel	47	78
		14	הבמ	לא	Mebahael	47	78
		15	ירה	לא	Harayel	215	246
		16	מקה	הי	Hoqamiah	145	160
ה	3rd Choir Thrones	17	ואל	הי	Laviah	37	52
		18	ילכ	לא	Keliel	60	91
		19	וול	הי	Livohyah	42	57
		20	להפ	הי	Phehilyah	115	130
		21	כלנ	לא	Nelokhiel	100	131
		22	ייי	לא	Yeyayiel	30	61
		23	הלמ	לא	Melohel	75	106
		24	והח	הי	Chahaviah	19	34
	4th Choir Dominions	25	התנ	הי	Nithahiah	455	470
		26	אאה	הי	Haeyoh	7	22
		27	תרי	לא	Yirthiel	610	641
		28	האש	הי	Sahayoh	306	321
		29	ייר	לא	Reyayel	220	251
		30	מוא	לא	Evamel	47	78
		31	בכל	לא	Lekabel	52	83
		32	רשו	הי	Veshiriah	506	521
	5th Choir Powers	33	וחי	הי	Yechavah	24	39
		34	חהל	הי	Lehachah	43	58
		35	קוכ	הי	Kevequiah	126	141
		36	דנמ	לא	Mendiel	94	125

P	Choir of Angles	#	God Name		Name	# God Name	# Angel Name
r		37	לא	ינא	Eniel	61	92
e	5th	38	הי	מעה	Chaamiah	118	133
s	Choir	39	לא	עהר	Rehaaiel	275	306
i	Powers	40	לא	זיי	Yeyeziel	27	58
d		41	לא	ההה	Hehihel	15	46
e		42	לא	כימ	Michael	70	101
n	6th	43	הי	לוו	Vaveliah	42	57
c		44	הי	הלי	Yelahiah	45	60
y	Choir	45	הי	לאס	Saliyah	91	106
		46	לא	ירע	Aariel	280	311
	Virtues	47	הי	לשע	Aslayah	400	415
		48	לא	הימ	Mihel	55	86
ן		49	לא	והו	Vaho	17	48
		50	לא	ינד	Deneyel	64	95
	7th	51	הי	שחה	Hechachyah	313	328
		52	הי	ממע	Aamemiah	150	165
	Choir	53	לא	אננ	Nanael	101	132
		54	לא	תינ	Nithael	460	491
	Principalities	55	הי	הבמ	Mibalaiah	47	62
		56	לא	יופ	Payiel	96	127
		57	הי	ממנ	Nemamiah	130	145
		58	לא	ליי	Yeyalel	50	81
	8th	59	לא	חרה	Herachiel	213	244
		60	לא	רצמ	Mitzreel	330	361
	Choir	61	לא	במו	Vemibael	48	79
		62	לא	ההי	Yahohel	20	51
	Archangels	63	לא	ונע	Aaneval	126	157
ה		64	לא	יחמ	Mockael	58	89
		65	הי	במד	Demaiah	46	61
		66	לא	קנמ	Menqel	190	221
	9th	67	לא	עיא	Ayael	81	112
		68	הי	ובח	Chabeuyah	16	31
	Choir	69	לא	האר	Rahael	206	237
		70	הי	מבי	Yebomayah	52	67
	Angels	71	לא	ייה	Hayeyel	25	56
		72	הי	מומ	Mevimayah	86	101

Mathers assigns these the Angels of the decans and the Zodiac quintic, beginning with Leo's sign. There are 2 for every 10 degrees (decans). The Angel in the first 5 degrees (quinance) of the decan is considered the "day" angel and the last 5 degrees of the "night" Angel. The night angels are shown bold (darker) under the decan column.

#	Hebrew	Name	Sign	Planet	Minor Arcana	Decan	Quinance
1	היוהו	Vahaviah	♌	☉	5 of W	1	1
2	לאילי	Yelayiel				**1**	2
3	לאטיס	Saitel		♃	6 of W	2	3
4	הימלע	Olmiah				**2**	4
5	הישהמ	Mahashiah		♂	7 of W	3	5
6	לאללה	Lelahel				**3**	6
7	היאבא	Akaiah	♍	☿	8 of P	1	1
8	לאתהכ	Kehethel				**1**	2
9	לאיזה	Hazayel		♄	9 of P	2	3
10	הידלא	Aldaiah				**2**	4
11	היואל	Laviah		♀	10 of P	3	5
12	היעהה	Hihaayah				**3**	6
13	לאלזי	Yeyalel	♎	♀	2 of S	1	1
14	לאהבמ	Mebahael				**1**	2
15	לאירה	Harayel		♄ & ♅	3 of S	2	3
16	הימקה	Hoqamiah				**2**	4
17	היואל	Laviah		☿	4 of S	3	5
18	לאילכ	Keliel				**3**	6

#	Hebrew	Name	Sign	Planet	Minor Arcana	Decan	Quinance
19	היוול	Livohyah	♏	♇ & ♂	5 of C	1	1
20	הילהפ	Phehilyah				**1**	2
21	לאבלנ	Nelokhiel		♆ & ♃	6 of C	2	3
22	לאייי	Yeyayiel				**2**	4
23	לאהלמ	Melohel		☽	7 of C	3	5
24	היוהח	Chahaviah				**3**	6
25	היהתנ	Nithahiah	♐	♃	8 of W	1	1
26	היאאה	Haeyoh				**1**	2
27	לאתרי	Yirthiel		♂	9 of W	2	3
28	היהאש	Sahayoh				**2**	4
29	לאייר	Reyayel		☉	10 of W	3	5
30	לאמוא	Evamel				**3**	6
31	לאבכל	Lekabel	♑	♄	2 of P	1	1
32	הירשו	Veshiriah				**1**	2
33	היוחי	Yeshavah		♀	3 of P	2	3
34	היחהל	Lehachah				**2**	4
35	היקוכ	Kevequiah		☿	4 of P	3	5
36	לאדנמ	Mendiel				**3**	6

#		Name	Sign	Planet	Minor Arcana	Decan	Quinance
37	לאינא	Eniel	♒	♄ & ♅	5 of S	1	1
38	הימעח	Chaamiah				**1**	2
39	לאעהר	Rehaaiel		☿	6 of S	2	3
40	לאזיי	Yeyeziel				**2**	4
41	לאההה	Hehihel		♀	7 of S	3	5
42	לאכימ	Michael				**3**	6
43	הילוו	Vaveliah	♓	♆ & ♃	8 of C	1	1
44	היהלי	Yelahiah				**1**	2
45	הילאס	Saliyah		☽	9 of C	2	3
46	לאירע	Aariel				**2**	4
47	הילשע	Aslayah		♇	10 of C	3	5
48	לאהימ	Mihel		♂		**3**	6
49	לאוהו	Vahoel	♈	♂	2 of W	1	1
50	לאינד	Deneyel				**1**	2
51	הישחה	Hechachyah		☉	3 of W	2	3
52	הימםע	Aamemiah				**2**	4
53	לאאנג	Nanael		♃	4 of W	3	5
54	לאתינ	Nithael				**3**	6

#		Name	Sign	Planet	Minor Arcana	Decan	Quinance
55	מבהיה	Mibalaiah		♀		1	1
56	פויאל	Payiel			5 of P	**1**	2
57	נממיה	Nemamiah		☿		2	3
58	ייליא	Yeyalel	♉		6 of P	**2**	4
59	הרחאל	Herachiel		♄		3	5
60	מצראל	Mitzreel			7 of P	**3**	6
61	ומבאל	Vemibael		☿		1	1
62	יההאל	Yahohel			8 of S	**1**	2
63	ענואל	Aaneval		♀		2	3
64	מחיאל	Mockael	♊		9 of S	**2**	4
65	דמביה	Demaiah		♄		3	5
66	מנקאל	Menqel			10 of S	**3**	6
67	איעאל	Ayael		☉		1	1
68	חבויה	Chabeuyah			2 of C	**1**	2
69	ראהאל	Rahael		♇ & ♂		2	3
70	יבמיה	Yebomayah	♋		3 of C	**2**	4
71	הייאל	Hayeyel		♆ & ♃		3	5
72	מומיה	Mevimayah			4 of C	**3**	6

Appendix 10 – Gematria of the Goetia Demons

#	Hebrew	Gematria	English	Sign	Decan	Planet
			Goetia Day Demons in Astrological Order			
1	לאב	33	Bael	♈	1	☉
2	ראגא (שאראגא)	205 (506)	Agares (Agreas)		2	♀
3	וגאשו	316	Vassago		3	♃
4	זיגימג (זיגמאג)	116 & 766 (107) & (757)	(Gamigin) Samigina	♉	1	☽
5	בראמ (שבראמ)	243 (543)	Marbas		2	☿
6	רפלאו (רהפלאו)	317 (322)	Valefor		3	♀
7	זומא	97 & 747	Amon	♊	1	☽
8	שוטברב	519	Barbatos		2	♀
9	זומיאפ	187 & 837	Paimon		3	☉
10	ראוב	209	Buer	♋	1	☿
11	זויסוג	135 & 785	Gusion		2	♀
12	ירטיש	529	Sitri		3	♃
13	תאלב	433	Beleth (Bileth, Bilet)	♌	1	☉
14	דיארל	261 & 741	Leraje (Leraie, Lerakha)		2	☽
15	שוגילא	350	Eligos		3	♀
16	רפאז	288	Zepar	♍	1	♀
17	שיטוב	327	Botis		2	♂ & ☿
18	זיתאב	463 & 1,113	Bathin		3	♀
19	שולאש	637	Sallos (Saleos)	♎	1	♀
20	זושרופ	642 & 1,292	Purson		2	☉
21	זאראמ (סאראמ)	332 & 1,142 (302)	Marax		3	♂ & ☿
22	שופי	396	Ipos	♏	1	♂ & ♃
23	םיא	51	Aim		2	♀
24	רבנ (שוירבנ)	252 (568)	Naberius		3	☽

#	Hebrew	English	Gematria	Sign	Decan	Planet
25	לובלסאלג (שלו-בל-איסאלג)	Glasya Labolas	162 (473)		1	♂ & ☿
26	ביס	Bune (Bime, Bim)	52 & 612	♐	2	♀
27	ויניר (וונור)	Roneve	272 268		3	♂ & ☽
28	ברית	Berith, Beale, Beal, Bofry, Bolfry	612		1	♀
29	תורתשא (תוראטשא)	Astaroth	1307 (917)	♑	2	♀
30	שאנרופ (שואנרוהפ)	Forneus	637 (648)		3	☽
31	שארופ	Foras	587		1	☿
32	יאדומסא (ידומסא)	Asmoday (Asmodai)	122 (121)	♒	2	☉
33	געף (פאאג)	Gaap	153 & 873 (85) & (805)		3	☿ & ♉
34	רופרופ (רוהפרוהפ)	Furfur	572 (582)		1	♂
35	מרחוש (שאישוחרמ)	Marchosias	554 (865)	♓	2	☽
36	שוטלוש (שוטלושי)	Stolos (Istolos)	651 (661)		3	♉

			Goetia Night Demons in Astrological Order			
#	Hebrew	English	Gematria	Sign	Decan	Planet
37	צנאפ (סינאפ)	Phenex (Pheynix)	221 & 1031 (201)	♈	1	☽
38	הלאה (שואנרוהפ)	Halphas Malthus, Malthas)	116 & 836 (648)		2	♂
39	מאלתׁ (שתלאמ)	Malphas	151 & 871 (771)		3	☿
40	ראומ	Raum	247 & 807	♉	1	♂
41	פוכלור (פהורכלור)	Focalar (Forcalor, Furcalor)	324 (547)		2	♀
42	ופאר	Vepar (Vephar)	287		3	♀
43	שבניד (שבנוד)	Sabnock (Savnok)	382 & 862 (378) & (858)	♊	1	☽
44	שיצ (שאז)	Shax (Shaz, Shass)	390 & 1,200 (308)		2	☽
45	ויני	Vine (Vinea)	57		3	☉ & ♂
46	ביפרו (ביפהרונש)	Bifrons (Bifrous, Bifrous)	298 (653)	♋	1	♂
47	אואל (לאוו)	Uvall (Vual, Voval)	38 (43)		2	♀
48	העגנת (האגנטי)	Haagenti	528 (78)		3	☿

		Goetia Night Demons in Astrological Order				
#	Hebrew	English	Gematria	Sign	Decan	Planet
49	לכורכ	Crocell (Crokel)	276	♌	1	♀
50	דרופ (שכרהפ)	Furcas	306 & 786 (605)		2	♄
51	םלעב (םאלאב)	Balam (Balaam)	142 & 702 (74) & (634)		3	☉
52	דולא (סאכולא)	Alloces (Alocas)	57 & 537 (118)	♍	1	♀
53	ויאכ (וימאכ)	Camio (Caim)	81 & 731 (77)		2	☿
54	םרומ (סומרומ)	Murmur (Murmus, Murmux)	286 & 846 (352)		3	♀ & ♂
55	בוארוא (שבורו)	Orobas	216 (514)		1	♃
56	רומג (ירומג)	Gremory (Gamori)	249 (259)	♎	2	♀
57	ושו	Ose (Oso, Voso)	312		3	☿
58	ואז (שנוא)	Amy (Avnas)	57 & 707 (357)		1	☿
59	ואירז (סאירו)	Oriax (Orias)	307 (1,117) (277)	♏	2	☽
60	לופנ (אלופנ)	Vapula (Naphula)	166 (167)		3	☿

#	Hebrew	English	Gematria	Sign	Decan	Planet
		Goetia Night Demons in Astrological Order				
61	זגאז (זאגאז)	Zagan	61 & 711 (62) & (712)	♐	1	☉ & ☿
62	לאו (ולאו)	Volac (Valak, Valu, Ualac)	37 (43)		2	☿
63	רדנא (שארדנא)	Andras	255 (556)		3	☽
64	רואה (שארואה)	Hauras, Havres, Flauros	212 (513)	♑	1	♀
65	פלארדנא (שוהפלארדנא)	Andrealphus	366 & 1,086 (677)		2	☽
66	רואמיכ (שיראמיכ)	Cimejes, Cimeies, Kimaris	277 (581)		3	☽
67	דודמא (שאיכודמא)	Amdusias (Amdukias)	71 & 551 (382)	♒	1	♀
68	לאילב	Belial	73		2	☉
69	בארואכד (איבראכד)	Decarabia	234 (238)		3	☽
70	ראש	Seere (Sear, Seir)	501	♓	1	♃
71	לאתנד (זוילאתנד)	Dantalion[1]	485 (551), (1,201)		2	♀
72	לאמורדנא (שוילמורדנא)	Andromalius	332 (647)		3	♂

[1] Spelled with a ת instead of a ט in Godwin's Cabalistic Encyclopedia.

#	Path	Name	Hebrew	Gematria
		Appendix 11		
		Sentinels of the Tunnels of Set		
11	א	Amprodias	סידורפמא	401
12	ב	Baratchial	לאיחטרב	260
13	ג	Gargophias	ץאיפוגרג	393, 1203
14	ד	Dagdagiel	לאיגדגד	55
15	ה	Hemethterith	תרטתמה	1054
16	ו	Uriens	סנהירע	395
17	ז	Zamradiel	לאידרמז	292
18	ח	Characith	תיכאראח	640
19	ט	Temphioth	תעיפמאט	610
20	י	Yamatu	עטאמאי	131
21	כ	Kurgasiax	זטיסגרוכ	315
22	ל	Lafcursiax	ץאיצרעקפל	671, 1481
23	מ	Malkunofat	טאפענוכלאמ	307
24	נ	Niantiel	לאיטנינ	160
25	ס	Saksaksalim	םילסכסכס	300, 860
26	ע	A'ano'nin	ןינאונע	237, 887
27	פ	Parfaxitas	סאטיחאפראפ	450
28	צ	Tzuflifu	ופילפוצ	302
29	ק	Qulielfi	יפלילוק	266
30	ר	Raflifu	ופילפר	406
31	ש	Shalicu	עקלש	500
32	ת	Thantifaxath	תצפיטנאת	1040

The spelling of sentinels of the tunnels is taken from Godwin's Cabalistic Encyclopedia.

#	Sephiroth	God Name (Atziluth)	Archangel (Briah)
1	Kether כתר	Eheih אהיה	Metatron מטטרון
2	Chokmah חכמה	IH or IHVH יה or יהוה	Raziel רזיאל
3	Binah בינה	IHVH Elohim יהוה אלהים	Tzaphqiel צפקיאל
4	Chesed חסד	Al, El אל	Tzadqiel צדקיאל
5	Geburah גבורה	Elohim Gibor אלהים גובר	Kamael כמאל
6	Tiphareth תפארת	IHVH Eloah va-Daath יהוה אלוה ודעת	Raphael רפאל
7	Netzach נצח	IHVH Tzabaoth יהוה תואבצ	Haniel האניאל
8	Hod הוד	Alohim Tzabaoth אלהים תואבצ	Michael מיכאל
9	Yesod יסוד	Shaddai El Chai שדי אל חי	Gabriel גבריאל
10	Malkuth מלכות	Adonai Ha Aretz אדני הארץ	Sandalphon סנדלפון
11	Daath דעת	IHVH Elohim יהוה אלהים	Mesukiel מסוכיאל

Appendix 12 - Names Attributed to the Sephiroth

Appendix 12 - Names Attributed to the Sephiroth

#	Sephiroth	Choir of Angels (Yetzirah)	Planet or Sphere of Activity (Assiah)
1	Kether כתר	Chayoth ha-Qadesh Holy Living Creatures חיות הקדש	Rashith ha-Gilgalim Beginning of the Whirlings The Prime Moble ראשית הגלגלים
2	Chokmah חכמה	Ophanim (Wheels) אופנים	Mazloth (Zodiac) תולזם
3	Binah בינה	Aralim (Mighty Ones) אראלים	Shabbathai (Saturn) שבתאי
4	Chesed חסד	Chashmalim Merciful Ones חשמלים	Tzedek (Jupiter) צדק
5	Geburah גבורה	Seraphim (Flaming Serpents) שרפים	Madim (Mars) מאדים
6	Tiphareth תפארת	Melekim (Kings) מלכים	Shemesh (The Sun) שמש
7	Netzach נצח	Elohim אלהים	Nogah (Venus) נוגה
8	Hod הוד	Beni Elohim בני אלהים	Kokab (Mercury) כוכב
9	Yesod יסוד	Kerubim (Cherubs) כרובים	Lebanah (The Moon) לבנה
10	Malkuth מלכות	Eshim (Flames) אשים	Olam Yesodoth (World of Foundations) יסודות עולם
11	Daath דעת		Esrim עשירם

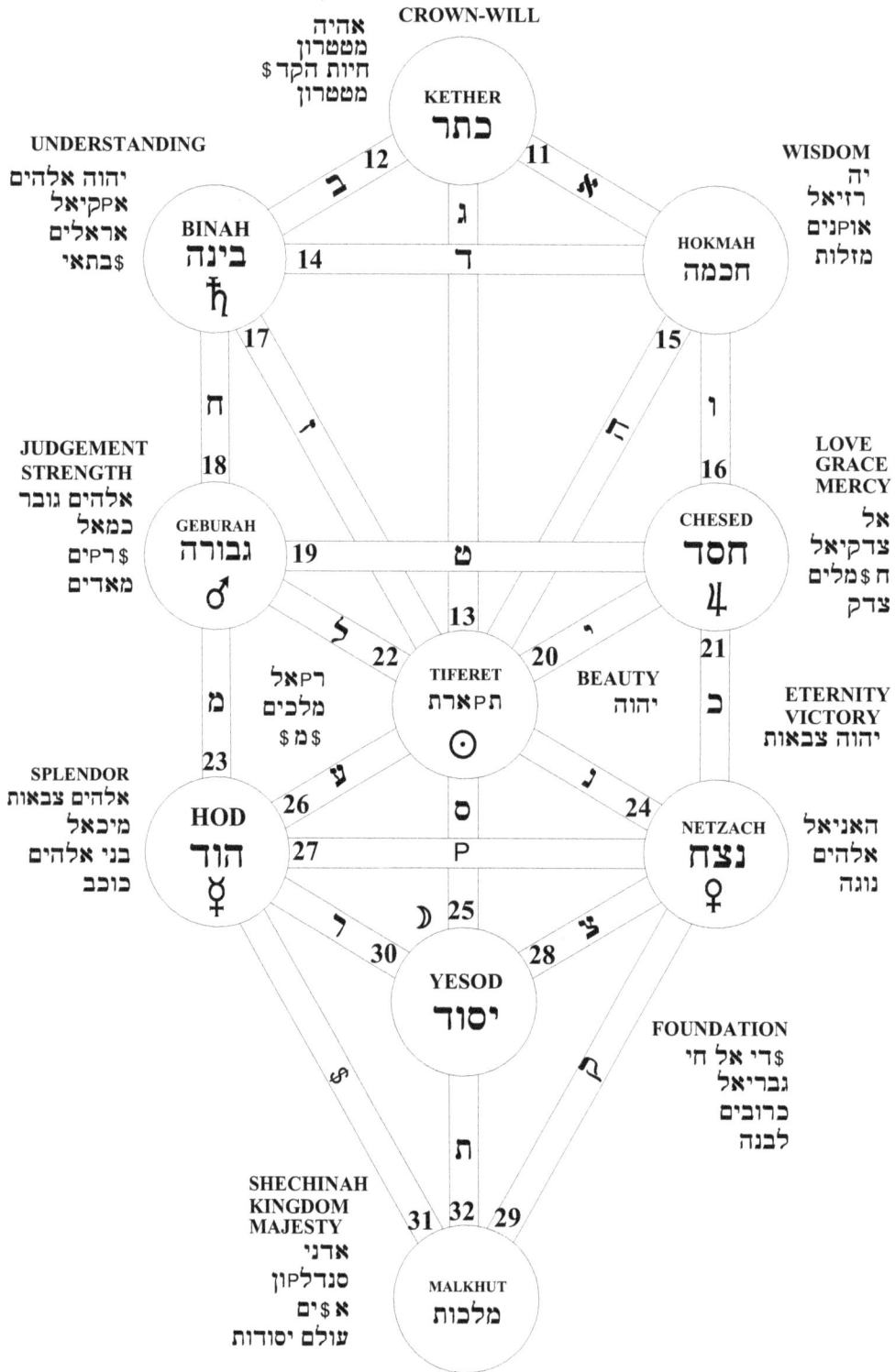

אור אין סוף

CROWN-WILL

KETHER
כתר

אהיה
מטטרון
חיות הקד $
מטטרון

UNDERSTANDING

יהוה אלהים
אPקיאל
אראלים
$בתאי

BINAH
בינה
♄

WISDOM

יה
רזיאל
אוPנים
מזלות

HOKMAH
חכמה

JUDGEMENT STRENGTH

אלהים גובר
כמאל
$רPים
מאדים

GEBURAH
גבורה
♂

LOVE GRACE MERCY

אל
צדקיאל
ח $מלים
צדק

CHESED
חסד
4

TIFERET
תPארת
☉

רPאל
מלכים
$מ $

BEAUTY
יהוה

ETERNITY VICTORY
יהוה צבאות

SPLENDOR

אלהים צבאות
מיכאל
בני אלהים
כוכב

HOD
הוד
☿

NETZACH
נצח
♀

האניאל
אלהים
נוגה

YESOD
יסוד

FOUNDATION
$די אל חי
גבריאל
כרובים
לבנה

SHECHINAH KINGDOM MAJESTY

אדני
סנדלPון
א $ים
עולם יסודות

MALKHUT
מלכות

Paths: 11 א · 12 ב · 13 · 14 ד · 15 · 16 · 17 ח · 18 · 19 ט · 20 · 21 כ · 22 ל · 23 מ · 24 נ · 25 ☽ · 26 ע · 27 P · 28 · 29 P · 30 ר · 31 · 32 ת

Appendix 14 - The 32 Paths of Wisdom Attributions

The thirty-two Paths of Wisdom consist of the ten sephiroth and the twenty-two Tarot keys that connect the paths (see figure above). The following table and commentary are derived from Dr. Paul Foster Case's *The Thirty-two Paths of Wisdom*.

	Hebrew	Transliteral	English	#
1	שכל מופלא	Sekhel Mopla	Admirable or Wonderful Intelligence	507
2	שכל מזהיר	Sekhel Mazohir	Illuminating or Radiant Intelligence	608
3	שכל הקודש	Sekhel Ha Qodesh	Sanctifying Intelligence	765
4	שכל קבוע	Sekhel Qavua	Measuring, Arresting or Receptacular Intelligence	528
5	שכל נשרש	Sekhel Nesharash	Radical Intelligence	1,200
6	שכל שפע נבדל	Sekhel Shepha Nivdal	Intelligence of Separative Influence	886
7	שכל נסתר	Sekhel Nisetar	Occult or Hidden Intelligence	1060
8	שכל שלם	Sekhel Shalom	Perfect Intelligence	720 or 1,280
9	שכל טהור	Sekhel Tahur	Pure Intelligence	570
10	שכל מתנוצץ	Sekhel Mitnotzetz	Resplendent Intelligence	1,836 or 2,646
11	שכל מצוחצח	Sekhel Metzochtzoch	Scintillating or Fiery Intelligence	592
12	שכל בוער	Sekhel Bahir	Intelligence of Transparency	567

	Hebrew	Transliteral	English	#
13	שכל האחדות מנהיג	Sekhel Menhig ha-Achdoth	Uniting Intelligence	882
14	שכל מאיר	Sekhel Meir	Luminous Intelligence	601
15	שכל מעמיד	Sekhel Maamid	Constituting Intelligence	514
16	שכל נצחי	Sekhel Nitzchi	Triumphant or Eternal Intelligence	508
17	שכל ההרגש	Sekhel ha-Hergesh	Disposing Intelligence	863
18	שכל בית השפע	Sekhel Beth ha-Shepha	Intelligence of the House of Influence	1,217
19	שכל סוד הפעולות הרוחניות	Sekhel Sod ha-pauloth ha-Ruachnioth	Int of Secret of all Spiritual Activities	1,702
20	שכל הרצון	Sekhel ha-Ratzon	Intelligence of Will	701 or 1351
21	שכל החפץ המבוקש	Sekhel h'Chaphutz ha-Mevupash	Intelligence of Desirous Quest	986 or 1796
22	שכל נאמן	Sekhel Ne'eman	Faithful Intelligence	491 or 1,141
23	שכל קיום	Sekhel Qayyam	Stable Intelligence	510 or 1,070
24	שכל דמיוני	Sekhel Dimyoni	Imaginative Intelligence	470

Path	Hebrew	Transliteral	English	#
25	שכל נסיוני	Sekhel Nisyoni	Intelligence of Probation or Trial	536
26	שכל מחודש	Sekhel Mechudash	Renewing Intelligence	708
27	שכל מורגש	Sekhel Morgash	Exciting or Active Intelligence	899
28	שכל מורגש	Sekhel Motba	Natural Intelligence	477
29	שכל מוגשם	Sakyel Mughsham	Corporeal Intelligence	739 or 1299
30	שכל כללי	Sekhel Kelali	Collective Intelligence	440
31	שכל תמידי	Sekhel Temidi	Perpetual Intelligence	814
32	שכל נעבד	Sekhel Ne'evad	Serving or Administrative Intel	476

Appendix 15 - The 32 Paths of Wisdom

1st Path is *Sekhel Mopla*

The 1st Path (Kether, the 1st Sephirah) is called the Admirable or Wonderful Intelligence, the Supreme Crown. It is the light of the Primordial Intelligence, and this is the Primary Glory. Among all created beings, none may attain its essential reality.

Mopla, a variant of פלא, *pehleh*, is used in Isaiah 9:6: "For a child will be born to us, a son will be given to us, and the government will rest on His shoulders; And His name will be called Wonderful Counselor, Mighty God, Eternal Father, Prince of Peace [שר שלום]."

The Wonderful Intelligence is the light of the Primordial Intelligence, a Conscious, Radiant Energy. In whatever world we find it manifest, we are dealing with living, conscious light.

On all planes, the Kether [כתר, 620] point is a contraction of power (כ), at a point of condensation (ת), which, concerning the successive stages of manifestation, becomes a point of radiation (ר). It is the Limitless Light's primary condensation into a point which is a center of whirling, vertical motion.

This is also called the Primary Glory, [כבוד ראשון, 589] *kabode rashun*, and the noun *kabode*, though translated as "glory" has for its primary meaning "weight."

The radiating energy projected from Kether is named [מזלא, 78], *mezla*, meaning "influence." The root of this term is [מזל, which is the singular form of the noun מזכות, *masloth*, literally, the "wanderers," and meaning the "planets." Thus the force proceeding from the first Sephirah is identified with planetary influences. Remember that planets, like the moon, do not shine by their own light but reflect the sun's light around which they revolve. That sun is the Kether of their World-system.

Mezla is a whirling force, and in its physical expression is the spiraling, electro-magnetic energy which, is the substance from which the atoms of the physical universe are constructed.

The real presence of Kether is at the innermost center of human personality. Though this knowledge does not include (and does not need to include) intellectual comprehension of the essential reality of the Life-power, it does include an ever-increasing grasp of the possibilities for bringing to bear the limitless potencies of this real presence, to effect transformations in human personality itself, and, through human personality, in human society and the physical conditions of the human environment.

2nd Path is *Sekhel Mazohir*

The 2nd Path (Chokmah, the 2nd Sephirah) is called the Illuminating or Radiant Intelligence. It is the Crown of Creation, and the Splendor of Unity, to which it is the most nearly approximate. In the mouths of the Masters of the Qabalah, it is called the Second Glory.

The Illuminating suggests radiance. The Light in Chokmah reflects the original light of Kether, it is considered as the source of illumination for everything below it on the Tree of Life. Chokmah is thus often referred to as the Kether of Briah, the Crown of Creation. It is the starting point for the entire creative series from Chokmah to Malkuth.

Chokmah is called the "Splendor of Unity" [הוד האחדות, 439]. Note the plural ending on Unity [ות] to indicate the general aspect of something or quality. Thus the plural form of *Unities* suggests that unity is not empty and abstract, but a fullness.

The whirling Life and Light force attributed to Chokmah is Chaiah חיה. The Qabalistic conception of life is inseparable from that of consciousness. The heavens' order is mental, and the energy manifested in that order is radiant, conscious and vital.

From our human point of view, the conscious energy of Chokmah is super-conscious. It is the Life-power's own knowledge of its own nature and powers, transcending every human mental state. In one sense, it is the Life-power's awareness of itself before the beginning of a creative activity cycle. Creation is a continual process going on now, just as surely as it did millions of years ago.

Chokmah in relation to Kether is to be thought of as the Life-power's eternal awareness of itself, and in this sense, Chokmah is said to be feminine. It is the mirror of Kether. It is the universal consciousness, turned inward and upward toward *Yekhidah* [37].

3rd Path is *Sekhel Ha Qodesh*

The 3rd Path (Binah, the 3rd Sephirah) is called the Sanctifying Intelligence. It is the foundation of Primordial Wisdom, termed Firmness of Faith, and Root of your Mother. It is the Mother of Faith, for the power of Faith emanates from it.

Ha Qodesh is from a root adjective: "to make pure, to set apart, to consecrate." This is the purifying, consecrating aspect of Binah, the seat of the Divine Soul, *Neshamah*. The Divine Soul is called The Untouchable Glory of God in Latin. No matter how humanity may "sin," the Divine Soul is the well-spring that cannot be touched by humanity's misinterpretations of reality.

Binah is the field of separative activity whereby the infinite possibilities of Life-power manifest in a diversity of finite, specialized forms. Thus the idea of multiplication associated with the number 3 is really connected with subdivision. The One Reality does not lose its unity through the creative process of subdivision or specialization, which, results in manifold cosmic possibility behind any class of specific forms is One. However, many variations may result from it.

This power of specialization is personal as well as universal. The Pattern on the Trestleboard says each of us is *filled* with Understanding, and by that, Understanding is guided, moment by moment. Until we reach a certain measure of ripeness, we are not aware of this guidance. We believe ourselves to be autonomous, self-directed beings, gifted with personal free-will.

Careful self-examination will convince you that whatever understanding of these truths you now possess began as an intuitive perception. You didn't manufacture it. It *came* to you from something deeper and higher than your personal intellect. That higher and deeper something is the Sanctifying Intelligence, as made manifest through *Neshamah*, the Divine Soul. This is the *single* Divine Soul that never ceases to be ONE, though its omnipresence makes it dwell simultaneously in all personal souls, incarnate and discerned, human and non-human.

As we begin to experience the truth that we are in touch with something higher, and as we have a practical demonstration that our mental patterns actually take form, we grow in confidence. This is why the 3rd Path is said to be Firmness of Faith and Mother of Faith. Faith is more than assurance. It is a power that can produce psychological and physiological manifestations. Faith cures ailing bodies and minds. Faith heals diseased circumstances. Faith enables those who have attained full ripeness, to the full expression of the Sanctifying Intelligence, to perform works of power far beyond average men and women's accomplishments. Every one of these works of power is accomplished as a fulfillment of the law, and faith is the power that makes these works possible.

The 3rd Path is said to be "Root of your Mother." These words emphasize the idea that Binah is the root of the material basis of every person's experience. Binah is our mother, the great womb of nature, from which we are all born.

It is the universal subconsciousness, having the same qualities, on the universal scale, that we associate with our personal subconscious activity. Our personal subconsciousness is one with the universal (or collective) subconsciousness, as a bay or inlet is continuous with the ocean. Thus Binah is known as the Great Sea and is called Aima [62], the Mother.

4ᵗʰ Path is *Sekhel Qavua*

The 4th Path (Chesed or Gedulah) is called the Measuring, Arresting or Receptacular (קְבוּעַ) Intelligence. It is so-called because from thence is the origin of all beneficent power of the subtle emanations of the most abstract essences that emanate one from another by the Primordial Emanation's power.

These are powers of Chokmah, powers of the universal light-force, which is also the life-force of mankind. They are beneficent powers and are symbolized in Key 5, corresponding to the path of Vav, which carries the influence of the Illuminating Intelligence *from* Chokmah *to* Chesed.

These beneficent powers emanate from one another by the power of the Primordial Emanation, which is Kether. The power of Kether is carried from the 1ˢᵗ Sephirah to Chokmah through the Path of Aleph. They are said to be "abstract essences" because they are subdivisions or specializations of the life-force, like waves in an ocean, or currents within it, though not really separate from the whole expanse and depth of the sea.

Chesed is the seat of memory, both cosmic and personal memory. The Life-power's perfect recollection of itself and its potentialities and the entire sequence of events in the creative process is the continuity of the cosmic order. We call "laws of nature" rooted in this cosmic recollection, and the dependability of these laws has its basis in this cosmic memory.

The 4ᵗʰ Path marks the beginning of the differentiation and distribution of special powers. These emanate by way of "subtlety." This noun signifies "fineness, minuteness." Thus from Chesed emanate an exceedingly fine, corpuscular substance having actual mass and weight. It is projected by those who have entered into a full understanding of this 4ᵗʰ Path.

Benevolent thought and speech have actual weight and set up the real movement of actual substance. The blessings that one of the Chasidim showers on those entering into relation with him are no abstractions. They are projections of real substance.

The 4ᵗʰ Sephirah is said to rise like a boundary, and on this account is called the Arresting Intelligence. Here we have the ideas of a specific form, of definite limitation, of the marking out of boundaries. The suggestion reminds us of Binah, the Sphere of Saturn.

The Saturn force is the spiral moving toward a center and winding up energy. Psychologically this Saturnine influence tends to make one self-contained and self-centered. The Jupiter force is also a spiral, but it moves away from a center, diffusing energy.

The psychological influence of Jupiter is centrifugal. It makes one expansive and manifests as an interest in the welfare of others. Thus it corresponds to the fundamental characteristic of the Chasidim. They give freely and abundantly of themselves and of their possessions. They are never self-centered. They enter into the lives of their fellows.

But the 4th Sephirah is called the Measuring Intelligence to show that although those motivated by its influence give freely, they also impart their beneficences wisely. Although their generosity is measured, it is never stingy. They know they have access to an inexhaustible supply of whatever may be needed to fill the special circumstance requirements they may have to deal with.

The way to keep in contact with Eternal Supply is to act as if you were perfectly sure of it. To give freely of your time, your knowledge, your interest, your possessions. Freely, yet not wasteful. To give as intelligently as you can, where the gift fills a real need. To let go of whatever you have given, leaving the recipient of your benevolence to use the gift as he sees fit. He learns this fine art becomes one of the Chasidim, having free access to Eternal Supply's limitless treasure.

5th Path is *Sekhel Nesharash*

The 5th Path (Pachad, Geburah or Deen, the 5th Sephirah) is called the Radical (נשרש) Intelligence. It is so-called because it is the very substance of Unity, within the substance of that Binah, which itself emanates from within the depths (literally, "from within the enclosure") of the Primordial Wisdom.

The first 3 letters of *nesharash* spell נשר *nasher*, eagle and the last three שרש, *sharash*, a root. Therefore, Radical Intelligence is the "Root of the Eagle." The eagle stands for Scorpio, Key 13. The letter Shin (Pluto) co-rules Scorpio. Study these Keys together, and you can see that the conscious immortality symbolized by Key 20 is a direct consequence of the direction of the force, which, is the active principle symbolized by Key 13. This force is closely connected with the feeling of personal will.

The cosmic life-force, seated in Chokmah, is the immediate source of the feeling of "personal will." Our feeling of willpower is due to tensions set up in our bodies as the cosmic life-force plays through them. All personal activity is due to various types of resistance that the human organism offers to the life-force's flow. Our bodies (physical bodies and finer bodies) perform their various functions because they are so arranged that they offer specific types of resistance to the flow of the current of Life-power.

Radical Intelligence is the "very substance of Unity." Unity here means Kether. The force of the 5th Path is the same *Mezla*, the primary whirling motion concentrated in Kether. This one Conscious Energy is the substance of all things.

The Radical Intelligence is said to be within Binah's substance to bring out the truth that the ten Sephiroth are not separate entities but rather 10 ways in which the human mind conceives a single reality.

The substance of Binah, within which the Radical Intelligence is enclosed, itself emanates from within the depths of the Primordial Wisdom. This shows that what we are concerned about within the 5th Path is the life force, *Chaiah*, which has its seat in Chokmah. In Geburah, the life-force is specialized as Mars, which is the basis of our will-power feeling.

6th Path is *Sekhel Shepha Nivdal*

The 6th Path (Tiphareth) is called the Intelligence of Separative Influence (שפע נבדל). It is so-called because it gathers together the archetypal influence's emanations and communicates them to all those blessed ones who are united to its essence.

Mediating or Separative is from a root, nivdal נבדל, meaning: to be divided, separated, set apart; similar to the English "to distinguish." Separative Intelligence is a mode of consciousness that acts in man as the discriminative power that classifies various objects of experience. In the plane of creative thinking, this discriminative quality of the Ego is the power that classifies various objects of thought and imagination. In Briah, the image-generating faculty of Tiphareth within us gives shape and diversity to the archetypal principles flowing into our field of awareness from above. To make this image-generating, transforming power work toward our further growth and illumination, we must act intentionally and consciously as transmitters of power that descends from above.

Thus the name for Tiphareth is "The Intelligence of Separated Influence," or "Intelligence of Parted or *Allotted* Outflow," or "Intelligence of Mediating Influence." All 3 names for this path are derived from the central position of Tiphareth, and from the fact that it collects at one point the descending powers from above, and from that same point distributes those powers through the channels which are below.

Tiphareth is like a reservoir into which are poured the influences of the five Sephiroth above it, and from which flow, by way of the paths of the letters Nun, Samekh and Ayin, the influences active in man's desire nature, man's intellect, and the Vital Soul which man shares with the rest of terrestrial organic life. Hence the 6th Path of wisdom is called the Intelligence of the Mediating Influence.

The 6th Path is said to gather together the emanations of the archetypal influence. The powers of the archetypal world are outside the limits of time. The EGO in all of us is also outside those limits. The One Ego exercises dominion over everything below the egoic level because it is free from the delusions rooted in the common idea that the past *was* and the future *is to be*, while only the present is actual and real.

To establish the dominion over circumstances, which is the main work of a Lesser Adept associated with the 6th Path, we must act on the assumption that we do not understand. Still, because it is a correct assumption, we speedily accumulate a store of experience, which teaches them the value of adopting this mental attitude. Thus we rid ourselves of impatience. We are free from hurry, of whom it is written: "He that believes shall not make haste."

Tiphareth is the point on the Tree of Life, symbolizing the EGO center in the heart of man. At this point, we feel the influx of cosmic radiance, which is the source of all personal activity. If we mistake what we feel and suppose it to be some power of our own, independent and self-originated, we fall into all the consequences of this error. When we truly understand ourselves, or as the parable of the prodigal phrases it, "come to ourselves," from then on, we are in direct communication with the cosmic dynamo. No longer do we try to live by using up the energy of our personal storage batteries. We recharge them continually from the reservoir of universal vital energy. Then do we begin to discover the hitherto unimaginable potencies present within us. We begin to live radiant, beautiful lives. The burden is shifted from our personal shoulders. The Universal Life manifests itself through us with ever-increasing power and freedom. We find that we are children of the Spiritual Sun, possessing the sacred inheritance of strength and knowledge, enabling us to be administrators of the perfect laws at work in even the least details of the Life-power's self-manifestation. We are the Sons of God.

7th Path is *Sekhel Nisetar*

The 7th Path (Netzach) is called the Occult or Hidden (נסתר) Intelligence. It is so-called because it is the brilliant splendor of all the intellectual powers which are beheld by the eye of understanding and by the thought of faith.

Hidden or Occult is from the verb *sah.tar* סתר, to hide, veil, cover, and conceal. This veiling has to do with the way desire manifests in human consciousness. We begin our journey toward adeptship while still deluded by the dream of personal separateness caused by the illusions of embodied consciousness. When we understand that the whole creation is mental, we realize that the desires rising into our personal consciousness are intimations of what is already prepared. In the Briatic world, all strong desires are actualities.

The whole creation is mental. The condensation of the invisible, intangible powers of mind into the visible, tangible things of the physical plane is always a projection of the Life-power through mental images. The eye of understanding and the thought of faith see our desires as something rising into our personal consciousness because Life-power makes them rise. Our desires are intimations of what is already prepared for us.

The powers of this path are to be thought of as being hidden from the eye of sense, for it says the 7th Path is "the brilliant splendor of all the intellectual powers which are beheld by the eye of faith."

Intellectual powers is הכחות השכליים *ha-kakhoth ha-saykelim*, and the second of these two words is the plural of שכל Sekhel, which we translate "intelligence." What is intimated here is that all the powers of consciousness are concentrated in the 7th Path.

An old Latin commentary on the 7th Path says: "It is called Hidden because it is not to be comprehended by intellectual reckonings only; yet we distinguish it from the 1st Path, because the latter is truly incomprehensible, whereas this may be comprehended; and this path is also called that of intellectual substance." Insight into the 7th Path requires both self-conscious intellectual knowledge and the operation of an intuitive realization. There is nothing in the surface appearances which are the basis of man's "intellectual reckonings" which enables us to see with the "eye of understanding," and think with the "thought of faith." We must be taught from within.

The "eye of understanding" is a Qabalistic psychological term symbolized by the eye in a triangle that forms part of the United States' national arms. This is the -seeing Eye. The opening of the "eye of understanding" is a stage of spiritual unfoldment. It is the awakening of the pineal gland in the human brain. This is accomplished by the force's operation, described as "the brilliant splendor of all the intellectual powers." What this force actually is, is clearly indicated by Qabalistic analysis of the word *Netzach* [נצח, 148]. Which is the magical reproductive force [נ], Meditational practices of balancing the interior stars [צ], and realization of the true value of personality and its relation to the Rider of the Chariot [ח].

8th Path is *Sekhel Shalom*

The 8th Path (Hod, the 8th Sephirah) is called the Perfect (שלם) Intelligence. It is so-called because it is the dwelling-place of the Primordial. It has no root in which it may abide other than the recesses of Gedulah whence its essence emanates.

Shalom means: perfect, whole, uninjured, full, complete, sound, healthy. Full refers to completeness in number, measure and weight. The 8th Path indicates a kind of consciousness that brings forms to completion by applying mathematics principles to accurate measurement. The Perfect Intelligence is the "dwelling place of the Primordial" or the Treasure of the Primordial" [תכונת הקדמות, 1,431] *Tekunath ha-qadmuth*. *Tekunath* is from a root meaning: to arrange, to measure. Through the powers of arrangement and discrimination, a man brings nature's products from their wild state into the perfection of those symbolized by the cultivated flowers in the Magician's garden. All advancement in civilization is the unveiling of Primordial Treasure. All magical practices partake of the knowledge which assumes that the objective to be reached is already existing reality. It simply has not yet appeared to the eye of sense.

The Perfect Intelligence of Hod is said to have no root "other than the recesses of Gedulah, whence its essence emanates." This is the unfailing beneficence of Chesed, which is diametrically opposite to Hod on the Tree. It is the simple declaration that the desirable perfection of things to come is already provided for. True, we must make clear patterns of our objectives, but as we progress in our practice of the Magic of Light, we understand that the patterns are truly shown. They are gifts from above and from within. Thus the Path of Mem symbolizes the consciousness, "I do nothing of myself." Thus *Mem* activates Hod with the Will force from Geburah.

Hod is a focal point in which the will force from Geburah, the image-making power of the Ego in Tiphareth, and the desired force from Netzach are mingled. It is man's growing intellectual awareness of the essential perfection of the cosmic order. This combination of forces in the 8th Path is in Qabalistic psychology connected with the concentrating, intellectual human self-consciousness operations.

Because man can measure, he is the form of existence that makes possible the completion of the Life-power's other modes of expression. Because man can arrange the elements of his environment in various kinds of order not spontaneously provided by nature, man is charged with finishing the Great Work. Because man can rearrange the forms composing his mental, emotional and physical existence, he may cultivate his personality as he cultivates plants and modifies animals. By such self-cultivation, he may advance beyond the natural man's limits and become a new species member.

In Binah, the Universal Mind contemplates what must follow from what it is in itself, and this great pattern of life-expression is held in the perfect memory of Chesed. Thus the essence of man's intellectual ability is the Life-power's perfect memory of what it is in itself (Chesed) and of what it foresees as the inevitable result of what it knows itself to be (Binah).

9th Path is *Sekhel Tahur*

The 9th Path (Yesod, the 9th Sephirah) is called the Pure (טהור) Intelligence. It is so-called because it purifies the essence of the Sephiroth, proves and preserves their images, and prevents them from losing their union with itself.

The adjective *tahoor* means clean or pure. It gives the lie to all those false notions which put the stigma of impurity and uncleanness on those powers of organic life, which are truly basic in evolution.

Yesod is the Vital Soul seat, [430, נפש] *Nefesh*, the light and life force common to man and all forms of being below him. In the mineral kingdom, the Vital Soul expresses itself as the force which binds electrons together to form atoms and results in the electric, magnetic and, chemical phenomena of that kingdom. In the vegetable kingdom, this energy's vital quality is more fully expressed in the power of reproduction, which is the main characteristic of organic, distinguished from inorganic matter. Plants have senses and rudiments of desire and volition, which are more fully displayed through animal forms' ascending scale. From the lowest mineral to the highest animal forms, the whole range of powers is recapitulated in man. These powers are present in the Vital Soul's automatic consciousness.

Our text says the Pure Intelligence is what purifies the essence of the Sephiroth. The *Nefesh* in Yesod is, in some respects, like a filter or like a distilling apparatus. In our human personality, the Vital Soul is the active agency of subconsciousness. The sphere of the Moon is the field in which power is at work in shaping, maintaining, and transforming our bodies. Through this work at the Vital Soul's subconscious level are carried on all the operations of heredity. These do not include the transmission from generation to generation of a single personal incarnation's acquired characteristics and habits. It is only the *essence* of the Sephiroth, which is concentrated in Yesod. The accidental details of our various personal lives are filtered out.

The 9th Path "proves the images of the Sephiroth." This suggests its function is to test and try the fitness of every human personality. The word translated as "images" is a form of a Hebrew noun that signifies "form, model, pattern." Deep in subconsciousness are the patterns for every cell and every organ of our bodies. Sometimes, during gestation, the shaping of the physical body is interfered with just as crystals' development is sometimes conditioned by the circumstances in which they are formed. Yet, the fundamental types are always present in subconsciousness. They are standards, and when the EGO selects personalities for entry into the Fifth Kingdom.

10th Path is Sekhel Mitnotzetz

The 10th Path (Malkuth) is called the Resplendent Intelligence. It is so-called because it is exalted above every head and sits on the throne of Binah. It illuminates all the lights' splendor and causes the flowing forth influence from the Prince of Countenances.

Resplendent is from a root nawtzatz [210, נעץ], to glitter, bloom, or flower. Malkuth is called the flower of the Tree. The number of *Mathanutzatz* 656 is the same as Galgalim [גלגלים, 676], whirlings or whirling motion. Galgalim is a term for the sum total of the manifestations of the cosmic forces. The Path of Malkuth in any world is always a receptacle for the total forces and activities expressed by that word.

The 10th Path is said to be "exalted above every head, and sits on the throne of Binah." Thus Malkuth is really identical with the 3rd Sephirah, Binah. The world of things we see surrounding us appears to be full of darkness and opacity. This is because we have not yet learned how to see *into* it. When we do, we find that it is all light and brightness. Analysis of the physical world's nature makes all things appear as forms of the manifestation of scintillating energy, which is [אור, 207], *Aur*, meaning Light.

Malkuth is to Kether as is the fruit of a tree to its root. It is the point at which all the influences which descend from Kether finally converge and the point from which, on the Way of Return, man's consciousness begins its ascent.

The root of the word [מלכות, 496], *Malkuth*, is [מלך, 90], *Melek*, King, which is one of the names for Tiphareth. Thus the essential idea behind the 10th Sephirah is that of the manifestation or expression of power to rule, derived from the EGO, or the Christos.

The temple of God is a house not made with hands, eternal in the heavens, and that temple is MAN... embodied man. Saint Paul said, "Know you are the temple of God, and that the Spirit of God dwells in you?"
That temple is already eternal in the heavens. The power that made the world, and rules everything in the universe, has its dwelling in this temple NOW. We do not have to wait until we are dead to know this. Nor do we have to do anything to establish the embodiment of the Kingdom of Spirit in our flesh.

Malkuth, Kingdom, is the physical world, the seat of sensation and the physical body (guph). It is also the Sphere of the Elements, called [564, יסודות חלם] *Cholom Yesodoth*, "The Breaker of the Foundations," because it is the field in which the fundamental unity of cosmic substance appears to be broken up into the four great classifications, designated as Fire, Water, Air and Earth.

11th Path is *Sekhel Metzochtzoch*

The 11th Path (Aleph, joining Kether to Chokmah) is called the Scintillating or Fiery Intelligence. It is the veil's essence before the dispositions and order of the superior and inferior causes. He who possesses this path is in the enjoyment of great dignity, for he stands face to face with the Cause of Causes.

Scintillating or Fiery is a root word meaning brightness, clearness, splendor. Thus the 11th Path is the channel for the first outpouring from Kether, the concentrated white brilliance of the Limitless Light.

Through the Path of Aleph, the Kether power is transmitted to Chokmah. Because all powers associated with Chokmah are above the human intellectual level, the Fool is the Tarot symbol of super-consciousness.

The 11th Path is the "essence of the veil placed before the dispositions and order of the superior and inferior causes." This indicates that the Divine Self-expression veils its inner nature in its outpouring, utilizing Name and Form's illusions, which produce the phenomenal universe. A Qabalistic aphorism suggests the same thing when it says: "The Spirit clothes itself to come down."

The powers and privileges corresponding to Aleph are that the adept "beholds God face to face without dying, and converses familiarly with the 7 genii who command the entire celestial army." The 7 inferior causes are the 7 genii, and the text ends with the statement that he who possesses this path "stands face to face with the cause of Causes."

In the state of super consciousness, which may be experienced while yet we are incarnate on the physical plane, one does stand face to face with the glory of the Supreme Crown. For this reason, in our version of the Fool, he looks upward toward the left side of the Key so that if the Key is placed on the Path of Aleph in the Tree of Life, the Fool faces upward toward Kether. Yet, to show that he comes from Kether, a white sun is behind him. This is to say that the goal toward which he turns his eager gaze is the same as the source whence he came. Waite says: "The sun, which shines behind him, knows whence he came, whither he is going, and how he will return by another path after many days. He is the spirit in search of experience."

The 11th Path represents the vision of the cosmic SELF, which comes to those who experience super consciousness. It is the link between *Yekhidah*, the Cosmic Self and *Chaiah*, the life-force.

12th Path is *Sekhel Bahir*

The 12th Path (Beth, joining Kether to Binah) is called the Intelligence of Transparency because it is the image of that phase of Gedulah (literally, of that wheeling of Gedulah) which is the source of vision in those who behold apparitions.

The adjective Transparency or Light *Bahir* [בהיר, 217] means clear, bright, transparent, lucid. Light in Hebrew is אור, *Aur*. This light is universally diffused. The Hebrew account of creation says light manifested before the formation of luminaries, suggesting that Beth's self-conscious attentive power is necessary to concentrate these units of diffused power into a central focus. Note that *Bahir*, has the same numerical value of word אויר, meaning, fiery.

The activity of Beth is said to be penetrative, specializing and, particularizing. *Through* expresses the idea that Beth's path has something to do with an agency that carries power from above to below. The word *into*, which is related to Beth, expresses that this path carries a force that descends into a field prepared to receive it.

On the Tree of Life, this power from above is Kether, and Beth carries its force into Binah's field. Beth is a symbol of self-consciousness and is the mediating influence between Binah, the universal subconsciousness, and Kether, super-conscious. Thus the Intelligence of Transparency serves as a transparent medium for the passage of light.

The 12th Path is said to be the "image (body, or substance) of that wheeling of *Gedulah,* which is called [חזחזית, 440], *Chachazith.*" It is derived from the same root as [חזות, 421] *chazoth,* signifying vision or revelation.

The mode of consciousness associated with the 12th Path is said to be a phase of *Gedulah. Gedulah* is the 4th Sephirah, the seat of memory. Vision requires memory. We do not really see anything until we recognize it. Yet, on the Tree of Life, we find *Gedulah* at a lower level than the 12th Path. This indicates that a phase of *Gedulah* is in the first Sephirah. This is per the Qabalistic doctrine that every Sephirah contains within itself a whole Tree of Life.

This is said that the 12th Path is "the source of vision in those who behold apparitions." "Apparitions" are not limited to ghosts or to other phantasms. The power we are concerned with here is the power to perceive even ordinary sense appearances.

We designate the higher and truer vision by the term insight is the real power at work in the 12th Path. Superficial, careless, or lazy observers are never gifted with true insight. One must look attentively at appearances to develop the ability to see into them. Just as a competent builder must know the ground where he intends to raise his house, the qualities and strength of the materials for his building, so must he who seeks to develop insight make himself thoroughly acquainted with the nature of the appearances surrounding him.

13th Path is *Sekhel Menhig ha-Achdoth*

The 13th Path (Gimel, joining Kether to Tiphareth) is called the Uniting Intelligence, or Inductive Intelligence of Unity because it is essence of glory and the perfection of the truths of spiritual unities.

Uniting Intelligence is literally: "Driver of Unities." The noun [מנהיג, 108], *menahig*, driver, is from the verb מנהג, *minhag*, to drive (as a chariot). Note that the study of the Tree of Life and its relationships is often called "The Work of the Chariot."

This path is said to be the essence of glory, [עצם הכבוד, 237], *etzem ha-kabode*. *Etzem*, adds up to 200, the number of the letter Resh, the Sun. Ha-kabode adds to 37, the word *Yekhidah*, which designates the cosmic SELF in Kether. Furthermore, *ha-kabode* has the primary significance of **weight** and is the Hebrew for **gravitation**. Thus the Gematria of *etzem ha-kabode* indicates that the "essence of glory" is really the gravitational force of the radiant energy which is, the first Sephirah. This glory is a radiance, shining forth from the light-source. The total value of *etzem ha-kabode* is 237, the value of the letter-name Gimel, spelled in full, [גמל מים דמל']. This is a direct correspondence between the name of the letter and what is said concerning the 13th Path.

The 13th Path is the "perfection of the truths of spiritual unities." From an old Latin commentary, it says: "All the paths, when they are united with the Supreme Unity, are joined thereto through this 13th Path, for אחד, *echad*, unity, resolved into a number, gives 13."

Through the path of Gimel, the influence from Kether passes to Tiphareth. The 6th Sephirah is the seat of the Ego of the entire human race. It is the Son who is "one with the Father (Chokmah)" and equally "one with the Mother (Binah)." Its link with the universal SELF (*Yekhidah*) is the perfect memory which SELF has of itself throughout eternity. Because memory is the fundamental quality of subconsciousness, the Tarot High Priestess completes the expression of the power of Kether. Thus the 13th Path may be said to be the manifestation of the subconsciousness of *Yekhidah*, the cosmic SELF, as the 11th is the manifestation of *Yekhidah's* super-consciousness, and the 12th the manifestation of its self-consciousness. This subconscious, eternal self-recollection is the basis of *Yekhidah's* manifestation in the One Ego activity of all humanity, seated in the Tiphareth.

The power of recollection is basic in the 13th Path. In the symbolism of the High Priestess, it is represented by her scroll, which is inscribed with the word TORA, the Hebrew for law, to show that what we call the "laws of nature" are really the Life power's perfect memory of the orderly sequences of its self-expression. Fundamental in all manifestations of Life-power is the electromagnetic radiant energy operation, called *Aur*, Light.

14th Path, *Sekhel Meir*

The 14th Path (Daleth, joining Chokmah to Binah) is called the Luminous Intelligence because it is the essence of that which is the instructor in the secret foundations of holiness and perfection.

The adjective, *mowayir* [מאיר, 251], indicates a **derived** luminosity. This path originates in the Illuminating Intelligence of Chokmah, and Chokmah is the source of its light. Chokmah is the dynamo, and the Luminous Intelligence is the light-bulb glowing with incandescence.

The 14th Path is said to be called Luminous Intelligence "because it is the essence of that *Khashmal,* which is the instructor in the secret foundations of holiness and perfection." The noun [חשמל, 378], *Khashmal*, is a derivative from the noun נחש [358], which is the Hebrew name for copper, the metal of Venus. Note also that the noun יסודות [486], *Yesodoth*, foundations, is the plural of Yesod, the name of the 9th Sephirah, attributed the reproductive activities of both microcosm and macrocosm.

A Latin commentary on the 14th Path terms *Khashmal* "establishes the mysteries" and is called "the path of the hidden things of nonexistent creation." The 14th Path is the pattern-forming power of creative imagination that shapes mind-stuff into form before the externalization of such mental patterns into things that exist at the level of physical, tangible manifestation.

In the 14th Path, we are dealing with the activity whereby the creative male life-force, which is identical with the energy streaming through space from the fixed stars, passes into the field of differentiation and specialization represented by Binah. This activity is the generation, multiplication and development of the paternal seed (*Chaiah* in Chokmah) and its mental imagery expression. This activity is both cosmic and personal. Life-power brings the universe into being by creative imagination. We, utilizing the same power, shape our world and its circumstances in the image of "holiness," which is really completeness, or perfection.

Chiah, the life-force attributed to Chokmah, is projected through the Path of Daleth into Binah to complete the activator of the 3rd Sephirah. Daleth shows a woman crowned with 12 stars, typifying the zodiac. Yet she is pregnant to indicate that concealed within her is the paternal power of Chokmah, the Father. She is a symbol of the outcome of the Path of Daleth's activity, as manifested in Binah. Note also the symbolism of the waterfall (male) and the pool (female) in the picture of the Empress. Daleth, Key 3 corresponds to the number of אב *Ab*, the Father, as well as and Binah, the Mother. Again, at the Empress's feet is a field of grain representing the multiplication (really subdivision) which is), of the ideas connected in occultism to 3.

The 14th Path of Daleth joins Chokmah to Binah. The central point of this path, where it crosses the 13th of Gimel, is *Da'ath* [דעת, 474], Knowledge, for all knowledge has its root in the Divine contemplation of the perfect primal Beauty. Daleth is the first of the reciprocal paths that cross the Tree of Life, a bridge linking Mercy's Pillar to Severity's Pillar.

15th Path is *Sekhel Maamid*

The 15th Path (Heh, joining Chokmah to Tiphareth) is called the Constituting Intelligence because it constitutes creative force (or, the essence of creation) in pure darkness. According to masters of contemplation, this is that darkness mentioned in Scripture: "Thick darkness a swaddling-band for it."

The adjective *Maamid* [מעמיד, 164] is derived from a verb meaning "to rise, to stand erect." The phallic significance is confirmed by the attribution of the sign Aries. Since Mars is the ruler of Aries, the dominant power in the 15th Path is the Mars-force, the active generative principle in nature. The universal creative force, *Chaiah*, is identical to the procreative power of living organisms.

The "creative force" is *etzem ha-briah* [עצם הבריאה, 423], literally "essence of creation." The word *etzem* is closely related to the word *etz*, signifying tree. Like the *Hyle* of the Gnostics, its primary meaning is "wood," but *etzem* is also translated in the English Bible as "body, bone, life, and substance." By its numeration (200), *etzem* is closely related to radiant energy, Resh, corresponding to the Sun.

The second-word *ha-briah*, adds to 223. The value of the mysterious word *abreach* [אברך], which means, "tender father" or "father of tenderness." It is also the value of the noun Kabzeel [קבצאל], "gathering of God." This word represents the concentration of the Limitless Light in the 1st Sephirah.

The creative force is "made to rise" in "pure darkness." The word translated "pure" is tahoor [טהור, 219]. This intimates that the creative force is reproductive energy associated with the 9th Path. It is the archetypal Adam's generative forces seat, and this Adam is the EGO seated in Tiphareth. Furthermore, the name of the 9th Sephirah, Yesod, is said by Qabalists to signify Sod Yod, "Secret of Yod," Yod symbolizes the phallus. In this instance, the word secret has a double meaning: something kept hidden or known only to a few, which remains beyond explanation or understanding.

The pure darkness in which the creative force is made to rise is the obscurity of the universal subconscious plane of life-activity represented by the 9th Path. Subconsciousness is the basis or foundation of all that makes its appearance in manifestation. It is the plane wherein the creative force is set in motion by the Constituting Intelligence. It is the "great womb" into which the seed of creation is cast. Hence, in the background of Key 4, on a level below that where the Emperor sits, flows a river which symbolizes the stream of subconscious activity... the stream of the cosmic creative force, or Water of Life.

The Hebrew noun translated "darkness" is awrawfel [ערפל, 380]. The uninitiated regard the darkness as a thing of terror, mystery and evil. It is the devil of exoteric dogmatism (Ayin). Initiates perceive it to be radiant darkness behind which they see the liberating, regenerative power (Resh). They understand that this creative force is represented as a flash of lightning (Peh), which tears down the prison of false science in which personal consciousness is immured. Finally, they know that this radiant darkness is the source of the power of adjustment, which, preserves balance preserving forces in action throughout the universe (Lamed).

Heh is the 2nd Path from Chokmah, symbolized by the Emperor. It carries the influence from Chokmah to the 6th Sephirah. The characteristic of this path is the function of Sight. In this connection, consider this passage from the 11th chapter of the Gospel, according to St. Matthew:

"Everything has been handed over to me by my Father, and no one understands the Son but the Father, nor does anyone understand the Father but the Son and anyone to whom the Son chooses to reveal him."

16th Path is *Sekhel Nitzchi*

The 16th Path (Vav, joining Chokmah to Chesed) is called the Triumphant or Eternal Intelligence because it is the delight of glory, the glory of *Ain*, the No-Thing, veiling the name of Him, the Fortunate One, and it is also called the Garden of Eden, prepared for the compassionate.

The Hebrew for "Triumphant" is *Netzachiy* [נצחי, 158]. It also means enduring, eternal and sure. This adjective is derived from the noun [נצח] Victory, the seventh Sephirah. What the Hierophant represents is a mode of consciousness that invariably results in triumphant or victory. This is because, in dealing with every problem of human experience, it provides those who open their interior hearing to the Voice of the Master an absolute certainty based on eternal principles.

Vav joins Wisdom to Mercy, for when creatures begin to exist, Mercy becomes active. This is the passage of Wisdom into the Divine Spirit's self-impartation, through the self-contemplation of His (or Its) limitless possibilities as an eternal Spirit of Life.

This path is the consciousness of the life-power's victorious quality and shows us also its freedom from all limitations of time. Through the letter Vav, this path is associated with intuition. Intuition is communication of the Life-power's own knowledge of itself to the personal consciousness of a human being.

Life-power always knows that it is engaged in a work that is bound to succeed. It always knows that it is subject to no limitation of past, present or future. It imparts this knowledge to us through the channel of memory, the specific function assigned to the 4th Sephirah.

The Hierophant is attributed to Taurus, which is another association with memory. Taurus is ruled by Venus, the planet assigned to Daleth, and Venus is the planet that corresponds to the cosmic activity of creative imagination. Whether it be cosmic or personal, all imagination is elaborating and developing ideas preserved by memory. Additionally, the Moon (Key 2) is exalted in Taurus. The High Priestess symbolizes subconsciousness as the recorder of experience, and her scroll typifies memory. It is the Book of Cosmic Experience.

Gan Ayden, Garden of Eden. Literally, "garden of delight." The garden grows the lilies and roses at the Magician's feet and wherein the Empress sits. Because *gan* [גן], garden, and *ehben* [אבן], stone, stand for the same state of conscious identification of the EGO with the cosmic, or universal SELF. They represent the state of Consciousness from which human personality is driven when it falls into the delusion of separateness resulting from eating the fruit of the Tree of Knowledge.

From Chokmah proceeds the Path of Vav. The Hierophant represents the Divine Wisdom, while the ministers at his feet, typifying knowledge (lilies) and desire (roses) stand for the Receptacular or Measuring Intelligence of the 4th Path of wisdom. The Triumphant and Eternal Intelligence, symbolized by Key 5, is the heavenly order's direct expression. As intuition makes us aware of that perfect correlation of forces, we are struck by its magnificence and made conscious of its beneficence.

The 16th Path is called "the delight of glory, the glory of *Ain*, the No-Thing, because, when at last we do hear, the message of the Inner Voice has to do with the mystery of the Divine Radiance, termed "glory." Thus whatever we learn from the Hierophant may be understood to be some aspect of the science of cosmic radiation, some portion of the universal truth concerning the One Power, which is, in its physical manifestation, not only electromagnetism and gravitation but also the stuff from which everything we sense is made. When we receive the instruction, we are filled with joy, and our joy is the emotion inspired by our realization that the Self within is none other than the eternal I AM, whose very essence is the *Ain*, or No-Thing. This we have in mind when we say: "All the power that ever was, or will be, is here now." Hence every communication we receive from the Inner Voice reveals some fresh truth concerning the ONE POWER Which Hindus call "Existence-Knowledge-Bliss Absolute."

The text says the 16th Path "veils the name of Him, the Fortunate One." This is because the letter-name, Vav וו, has the value 12, as the Divine Name [הוא], *Hu*, or *Hoa*, "He," a third personal pronoun, one of the titles of Kether. Thus the Hierophant may be considered a symbol for the Cosmic SELF, Yekhidah, acting as the Inner Teacher of mankind.

17th Path is *Sekhel ha-Hergesh*

The 17th Path (Zain, joining Binah to Tiphareth) is called the Intelligence of Sensation (or the Disposing Intelligence). It establishes the faith of the compassionate, clothes them with the Holy Life-Breath, and is called the Foundation of Tiphareth in the plane of the Supernals.

The adjective *ha-regash* is from a noun signifying feeling or sensation and an adjective derived from a verbal root meaning to rage, to be violently agitated. This connects the letter-name Zain, sword, and the idea of violent activity.

Long before we wake from our nightmare of separateness, our Mother prepares us. She is like a woman who hears her child crying in the night and finds the little one struggling in the throes of a bad dream. Gently she wakes us and comforts us, and shows us there is really nothing whatever to fear. Years before any person knows that he is interested in the higher knowledge, the Great Mother, the Divine Soul, is gently nudging him to wake him from his tortured dream. While we still sleep, her endeavors to arouse us are incorporated into our nightmares. Yet it is only the Mother, full of compassion, bringing him to realization.

While we remain in the grip of the dream, her touch frightens us the more. We believe it to be a tiger of disease, a wolf of poverty, a lion of oppression, a serpent of sin. The experiences which will finally liberate him are then interpreted as being all manner of dangers and miseries. When the dream is at an end, then we know that the Mother was only shaking him into wakefulness so that he might be released from his pain and terror.

When we wake, she takes us by the hand and guides us in her ways. This sense of contact with reality is what is said in our text to "establish the faith of the compassionate." Theirs is faith expressed by action, as shown in Tarot Key 11. It says "Amen," or "So be it," to all experience because it understands every event's meaning.

Disposing Intelligence is called the "Foundation of Tiphareth in the plane of the Supernals." The power active in this path is the power of the Divine Soul, symbolized by Raphael in Key 6. The plane of the Supernals consists of Kether, Will; Chokmah, Wisdom; Binah, Understanding. Of these three, Binah is the Yesod, or Foundation, of Tiphareth, because without Understanding the EGO in Tiphareth would have no firm basis.

In Key 6, Zain, the angel Raphael (God the Healer) stands for the descent of Kether through the Path of Beth, whereby the One SELF is manifest in Binah as *Neshamah*, the Divine Soul. The woman represents the Great Mother, Binah, as the agency whereby the One SELF's power is communicated to the Ego in Tiphareth. The man is Adam, the Ego in Tiphareth.

We read that the Great Work is performed in alchemical books employing the Sun and Moon with Mercury's aid. This is illustrated by the symbolism of Key 6. The man is the Sun, the woman, the Moon. The angel is Raphael, the angel of Mercury.

These symbols represent two aspects of the Life-Breath, Prana. The positive, male aspect is *Surya*, the sun. The negative, female aspect is *Rayi*, the moon. *Surya* is the hot, driving, violent current of Prana. *Rayi* is the cool, responsive lunar current, and what chiefly distinguishes it is *impressibility*.

These two currents, solar and lunar, work through two halves of the human body, chiefly along the sympathetic system's nerves. The solar current works through the right half, which is called *Pingala*. The lunar current works through the left half named *Ida*.

When the solar and lunar currents of the Life-power are rightly perceived, rightly discriminated, and when their operation is kept in proper order, the personality of the man engaged in this practice becomes a free, unobstructed channel for the outpouring of the cosmic life-force. Thus our text says the Disposing Intelligence clothes the compassionate with the Holy Life-Breath.

Zain is the first path projected from Binah, which it joins to Tiphareth. Thus it is the link connecting the Divine Soul with the EGO. The Path of Zain suggests by its name the Supernal Understanding operation *in separating the creatures produced* by the Constituting Intelligence into species, classes etc. The fundamental separation is that of sex, and hence this path is indicated by Zain the Sword and by the Lovers.

The text says, 'disposes the righteous to faithfulness,' or establishes the compassionate faith. The righteous are those who have brought their thought, feeling and actions into harmony with the universal order. And the faithfulness to which they are disposed is symbolized by Key 11 (the Faithful Intelligence). Those disposed to faithfulness are 'clothed with the Holy Life-Breath.' In Key 6, this is symbolized by the nude figures. They hide nothing. There are clothed with Spirit, which is synonymous with the element *Air*. Thus they are clothed with the Life-Breath (Key 0) and given powers unknown to ordinary human beings.

18th Path is *Sekhel Beth ha-Shepha*

The 18th Path (Cheth, joining Binah to Geburah) is called the Intelligence of the House of Influence; and from the interior walls of its perfections, the arcana flow down, with the hidden meanings concealed in their shadow, and therefrom is union with the **in**nermost reality of the Most High.

The noun "influence" suggests the notion of water. The Hebrew *shefah* occurs once in the Old Testament, where it is translated as "abundance." "They shall suck the abundance of the seas." Here the idea of abundance is directly connected with water. In this passage, there is also an occult reference to time because the word for *seas* is *yomim* [ימים, 100] identical in spelling with a noun which signifies *days*.

The 18th Path is related to water or an activity like that of water when it says the arcana "flows down." The flowing motion having its origin at an inner source, which is also superior, is what the phrasing suggests. The arcana, or hidden powers of super-consciousness, do flow down the personal field, but this same super-consciousness is the *depth*, the Great Within. It is the Holy of Holies, the Adytum of the Inner Temple. From this source, power flows down into our daily experience.

The power is truly like water, as intimated by Cheth corresponding to Cancer. The power comes in waves. It runs in currents. It ebbs and flows. It is purifying, and in it, all forms are held, either in suspension or in solution. Often it is compared to a great ocean. Thus Binah, the source of the 18th Path, is called the Great Sea and the Great Mother.

In Key 7, the background houses refer to Beth's Path, which joins Kether to Binah. The walled city refers to Binah, for the "Holy City," which is symbolic for Binah and the Sanctifying Intelligence. With many other details of the design, the chariot and the charioteer give a martial aspect to this Tarot Key. Thus, the background of the picture relates to the Sephirah from which the Path of Cheth begins, while what is in the foreground relates to the Sphere of Mars, the seat of Volition, in which the Path of Cheth is completed.

Thus the consciousness developed by a Greater Adept is dependent on his adopting the interpretation of human personality as being the vehicle or instrument of the Divine Soul. This is symbolized by Key 7, carrying the influence from the third Sephirah to the fifth.

Not until this separating influence has projected the power of Understanding into Beauty can the activity of Severity be manifest through the Path of Cheth, which, setting off definite fields of operation, and so in a sense circumscribing the expression of the Divine Understanding, brings into actual effect the Radical Intelligence of Geburah.

19th Path is *Sekhel Sod ha-pauloth ha-Ruachnioth*

The 19th Path (Teth, joining Chesed to Geburah) is called the Intelligence of the Secret of all Spiritual Activities because of its influence from the supreme blessing and the supernal glory.

The prime secret of the 19th Path is that whatever exists is a form of spiritual energy. Every form of spiritual energy is subject to the direction and control of the form above it. The conscious imagery of man is a form of spiritual energy. All forms below this level are subject to its direction. It, in turn, is subject to the influence which descends from super-conscious levels. This flows down into subconscious levels through the agency of man's mind, which is the mediator between that above and below.

Man is the synthesis of all cosmic activities. Human intelligence gathers together all the various threads of the Life-power's self-manifestation. By the operation of the law pictured in Key 8, human intelligence can carry the cosmic life-expression into manifestations beyond anything which could come into existence apart from man and his intelligence. By controlling the subconscious production of mental images, man can "open the lion's mouth" and bring subhuman forces under the direction of thought systems appraised in words.

The power at work in the 19th Path proceeds from the 4th Sephirah. Which, in turn, receives the Wisdom of Chokmah through the Path of Vav. One part of the secret is that the woman tames the lion because she has been instructed by the Hierophant.

The dominant influence in the 19th Path is recollection, and remembrance is part of the secret. Through contact with the deeper, more interior levels of memory, it is possible to discover that the cosmic order is not merely a mechanism. When we learn how to listen, it speaks to us. On the mechanism of nature are written characters we may learn to read. Within us is a point of contact with a principle of knowledge that reveals all experience's meaning. No matter what may be the appearance of an event, it has a meaning for us, and one which may be put to effective use in what we think, say and, do.

Another part of the secret is that even now, human life extends beyond the physical world's limits. Man *is* a 4-dimensional, immortal being. Thus one of the practical consequences of attaining that mastery of subhuman powers, pictured by Key 8, is the liberation of man into conscious awareness of immortality.

Individual knowledge and experience of immortality are achieved by those who learn how to direct and control the Mars-force utilizing mental imagery. This is another aspect of the secret of the 19th Path.

At this point, the Spirit's full realization of its power as a limitless self-imparting Principle manifested in limited forms of expression unites the potencies of Mercy to those of Severity, thought the Path of the letter Teth. This path is also called Intelligence of the Secret because the Great Arcanum is based upon the fact that Limitless Life expresses Itself in limited forms. Therein you may discover the great secret of all magical operations, the Arcanum of the equilibrium between Severity and Mercy.

Notice also that this path crosses that of Gimel. The central point of the magical equilibrium is the realization that the **Primal Will** eternally projects Itself in Beauty; and this Path of Gimel being that of the Uniting Intelligence, the implication is that the true equilibrium can only be attained utilizing the conscious self-identification of the personal will with the Universal Self-direction toward the realization of Beauty.

20th Path is *Sekhel ha-Ratzon*

The 20th Path (Yod, joining Chesed to Tiphareth) is called the Intelligence of Will because it forms all patterns, and to know this Intelligence is to know all the reality of the Primordial Wisdom.

Rawtzone, Will, by its four letters, represent radiant energy or fire (Resh); air (Tzaddi); earth (Vav); and water (Nun). The occult significance of the word relates to the idea of a synthesis of the four elements, which synthesis is none other than the One Reality, the Ancient of Days represented by the Hermit, and customarily designated by the Divine Name Jehovah.

Men feel in their very bodies as the power called "will" is the surge of the light-force through the bloodstream and nerve and tissue.

The Path of Yod's possessor is truly "acquainted with the laws of perpetual motion" because this path leads to perfect identification with the One Conscious Energy and to a profound knowledge of its eternal laws. The infinite whirling motion of the Limitless Light is the true perpetual motion. They who know the secret of the Intelligence of Will possess full knowledge of this energy and its laws.

Thus they can demonstrate, or make manifest in their control of circumstance, their perfect union with the **One Will Power**. This pure spiritual will is the perfect circle of Divine Life. He who is in union with it appraises the perfect order in all that he does. That order is symbolized by the number 4 and the square. It is the perfect order of the Measuring Intelligence of the Chesed descending into Tiphareth through the 20th Path of wisdom.

Of this path, it is said that "it forms *all* patterns, and to know this intelligence is to know all the reality of the Primordial Wisdom." Yod carries the influence of the cosmic memory seated in Chesed into the EGO in Tiphareth concentrated in a complete realization of the cosmic purpose, indicated by the Path's name, Intelligence of Will. The Hermit, looking down and back over a path that his own footsteps have made, is clearly related to memory. He illustrates the masculine expression of Beneficence through Yod, the letter of the Father. Yet there are feminine concepts in this Key, notably in its relation to the sign Virgo.

21st Path is *Sekhel ha-Chaphutz ha-Mevupash*

The 21st Path (Kaph, joining Chesed to Netzach) is called the Intelligence of Desirous Quest because it receives the divine influence, which it distributes as a blessing to all modes of being.

Desirous Quest (literally, "the inclination to seek") is from a root word *meboqash* meaning "emptiness," and has a meaning akin to the English nouns "hunger" and "thirst." In Man's quest for abundance, like his other personal activities, is a response to the descending influence of the Life-power. We seek because what we seek is really within us, and whatever we gain is actually a recollection of what the One Identity already has in store for us.

When we first enter the Path of Desirous Quest, we have vague notions concerning what we seek. We feel an aching emptiness of mind and heart. At the very beginning, we are prone to think that if only we possessed certain things, if only we could find ourselves in different circumstances, all would be well. After a while, we begin to get brief flashes of the Inner Light, and in time these make us realize that the essence of all right desire is the longing to *be*, rather than the wish to have. Ultimately we come to understand that the desire to be is the Life-power's way of revealing to us what we really are. The Way to Liberation is the path of discovery, leading to a full perception of the true nature of the SELF.

One of the Path of the Desirous Quest's secrets is our interior stars' balance through meditation. Nobody ever succeeds in meditation, which was lukewarm in his desire for freedom. Meditation, especially in its early stages, is hard work. It must be persisted in for some time before any striking results are attained. We must hunger and thirst after righteousness and be steadfast in meditation before we taste its fruits.

Another secret is courage. To develop this, we must face difficulties and learn to solve problems. To affirm the "goodness of ALL" is to speak truly enough. Still, our human problems need that affirmation for just one reason - to give us the strength to face our problems boldly because we are confident we have at our disposal a power adequate to turn these very problems into magnificent opportunities. To stop with the affirmation, to turn ourselves into talking-machines that do nothing but repeat such affirmations, is to be guilty of the sin of vain repetition. What we need most is to use daily that day's "sufficient evil."

This means keeping awake now. It means interpreting the experiences of the present as being particular dealings of the Divine Spirit with our souls. Day after day it subjects us to tests. To dread the future is supremely unintelligent. To refuse to face the appearances of evil in the present is even worse.

The illumined mind lives in eternity, and the only human word which truly designates this eternity is **now**. **Now** is truly the acceptable time. **Now** is truly the day of liberation. Guidance comes **now**, or not at all. Or it would probably be more accurate to say that although every human being is always under guidance, whenever he is truly aware of it, he knows it to be active **now**.

The Path of Desirous Quest is associated through the letter Kaph with the planet Jupiter. Thus it is pictured in Key 7 of Tarot by the wheels of the chariot. There are two wheels to symbolize that so that the influence of the 21st Path is made effective in human life, it must be felt subconsciously as well as consciously. It is not enough to have an intellectual perception of the truth that through this path, we receive the divine influence and partake of the blessing it distributes to all modes of being. Such perception is necessary, but it is not sufficient. It must permeate our subconsciousness and be built by subconscious activities into the personal vehicle's entire structure. This is one reason for the emphasis placed on meditation. Truth must be printed indelibly on subconsciousness so that we never forget its principles. Thus only may it bear fruit in our lives.

This final path from Chesed ends in Netzach, the 7th Sephirah, seat in man of the desire nature. The static manifestation of Beauty is not effected until after the Path of Kaph, or Conciliating Intelligence has brought Netzach into activity by the projection of the influence of Chesed because Karma does not begin to operate until the turning wheel of manifestation has brought into the field of the unfolding universal self-consciousness a definite conception of the victorious end towards which it's self-impartation is directed. Karma cannot be supposed to work without an objective, and the nature of Spirit assures us that Its objective must be the successful outcome of the creative process. Hence Lamed and the 22nd Path follow Kaph and the 21st.

22nd Path is *Sekhel Ne'eman*

The 22nd Path (Lamed, joining Geburah to Tiphareth) is called Faithful Intelligence because it is increased by its spiritual powers. All dwellers on earth are under its shadow.

The psychological drive in this 22nd Path is volition. It is fiery and Martian in quality, but it is also what a Hindu would call "Pranic force," partaking of the spiritual power which is associated with air or breath.

Its urge is toward increase, and because increase is growth, we may understand the power of the 22nd Path to be related to the reproductive drive, which ensures the continuation of species.

When we will, we aim invariably at change. Every strong volition is a practical demonstration of the misconception that any human is an independent, separate personality. The magical will is not the false self-will of those who seek to impose their "own way" on other people or on circumstances. It is what Eliphas Levi calls the "will of intelligent beings." They are the true adepts, whose will is the law because it is perfectly identified with Geburah's absolute Justice.

Man is never, as a personal being, the thinker, the speaker, or the actor. Every thought, word, and deed is the operation of the sum-total of universal powers and laws, known and unknown, taking form through the instrumentality of a human being or other active center of expression for the One Life. This is not fatalism. It is simply the right discrimination between the personality and the **Self**. The **Self** is the Indivisible One, the sole originating Principle of the universe. Personality is dependent, conditioned, determined. The Self is absolutely free and is the conditioner and determiner of the functions and activities of personality.

In consequence of right instruction and right practice, he who sees the truth of reality and has an intuitive perception of its inner significance can make new combinations through the exercise of creative imagination. Man is the instrument for the modification of the cosmos in which he finds himself. Human personality is the indispensable agency whereby Life-power completes the Great Work. All work, including the "Great Work," is related to the 22nd Path. By looking at Key 11, one knows the ancient dictum, "Equilibrium is the secret of the Great Work."

This equilibrium is effected in human life through the agency of subconsciousness. Thus the central figure in Key 11 is the same as the High Priestess. The pomegranates on the veil behind the High Priestess are symbols of **increased spiritual powers,** mentioned in the text. They are symbols of the Sephiroth on the Tree because the Sephiroth do summarize all spiritual powers.

Though subconsciousness is the immediate agency whereby the transformations and transmutations of the Great Work are brought about, the work itself is under the supervision of Key 4. In the tableau, Key 4 stands above Key 11, indicating that the Great Work's success must be well grounded in theory before attempting to practice. Poor reasoners never succeed in the operations of the 22nd Path.

Thus the transformations of personality that constitute the alchemist's primary work of the alchemist are accomplished under the direction of self-consciousness. They are the results of clear and definite intention, and of long-continued practice.

In the sign Libra, corresponding to this path, Saturn is exalted. In the Great Work, the serpent-power is exalted or lifted up by the process of sublimation. Thus the hilt of the sword of Justice is a T-cross, symbolizing the Saturn force at the base of the spine. It is shown raised up to indicate its sublimation and combination with the Mars force.

The Greater Adept becomes a conscious administrator of cosmic justice. He begins with himself and trains himself to regard all his actions and work as his own but merely personal expressions of universal laws. He enters with all his powers of mind and body into action, but, through meditation and reflection, makes habitual the thought that whatever he thinks or says or does is accomplished *through* his personality, rather than *by* it. He looks on his life as being devoted to making manifest the operation of Divine Justice.

Thus Key 11 represents this mental attitude, showing a feminine figure reminiscent of the High Priestess, but having yellow hair like the Empress and the chariot's driver in Key 7. This symbolism is intended to show that Key 11 represents a *habitual* attitude, one which is maintained consistently because it has been made subconscious.

Lamed is the link between the Sphere of Mars, the seat of volition, and the Sphere of the Sun, the seat of the EGO. It shows a feminine influence in Faithful Intelligence's activity, which perfects or completes Beauty's static manifestation through equilibrated Action or Work (Karma).

23rd Path is *Sekhel Qayyam*

The 23rd Path (Mem, joining Geburah to Hod) is called the Stable Intelligence because it is the power of permanence in all the Sephiroth. The Path of Mem descends from Geburah and participates in the influence carried from Chesed to Geburah through the Path of the letter Teth. The Hebrew adjective translated "stable" is from a verbal root meaning "to rise," or "to raise from below," This has to do with the controlling, and raising or sublimating the serpent-power, Kundalini.

The 23rd Path is "the power of permanence in all the Sephiroth." This power of permanence is related to rhythmic, controlled vibration. The Hebrew term is *kach qiyom* [כח קיום, 184], the power of: "duration," or "existence," as well as by "permanence." It also means "confirmation."

The Hanged Man is a synthesis of the whole Tarot, and Mem is placed with Tav at the center of the Cube of Space. These two letters from the word *toom* [440, תם], signifying the ultimate attainment and ultimate perfection. This is a central, permanent, and directly connected power in the cube symbolism with the Palace or Temple of Holiness in the midst supporting all things. Samadhi leads to complete identification with the ONE POWER. This is no more intellectual apprehension. It makes a tremendous difference in the man or woman who experiences it.

The Hanged Man has white hair, like the Hermit and the Emperor. The state of perfect stability of mind he symbolizes cannot be arrived at without reasoning, nor can it be attained without the secret operations over which the Hermit presides -the subtle changes in the body's chemistry, which occur in the region governed by the sign Virgo. The main thing achieved in the seedless Samadhi pictured by Key 12 is the high vision of which the Tarot Fool is one of the principal emblems.

The 23rd Path is the third in the descent from Kether along the north side of the Tree of Life. Thus it is a consequence of what Tarot pictures by the Magician. A seer in Samadhi does not for a moment lose self-consciousness. He can descend into ordinary modes of human life at will. He may abstract his attention from the phantasmagoria of sensation, but whenever he wills to do so, he can resume his place among ordinary human beings who do not share his vision.

Concentration is the beginning of the practical work, which makes one a possessor of the 23rd Path. The absolute impersonality suggested by Key 12 is a direct consequence of the seer's realization that his personality is what is pictured by Key 7. Only as a consequence of prolonged concentration can the ordinary notion that a human being is a person separate from others, and possessed of autonomous free will, be completely reversed so that it is replaced by the attitude of complete dependence symbolized by the Hanged Man.

The associative functions of subconsciousness are limited by concentration. Therefore, the Hanged Man (suspended mind) is supported by a gallows in the form of the letter Tav, associated with Saturn, an astrological representative of limitation. The Hanged Man is the adept bound by his engagements." The engagements are like those of one wheel with another in a piece of machinery, like engaging the clutch in an automobile. This is a consequence of a definite *intention* on the part of the person who practices control of the mind-stuff fluctuations.

In the earlier stages of the work, this intention has continually to be recollected. A continuous flow of knowledge in a particular object is impossible unless the object is remembered and kept in mind.

The path connecting Severity (will) and Splendor (intellect) is the letter Mem. Key 12 is the last path passes the influence of Geburah to Hod. The Hanged Man is merely a further development of what is shown by Key 11. The Greater Adept suspends all ordinary notions of personal activity. He is certain he does nothing of or by himself. He rests securely in his knowledge that the universal life and law support him. He is "the adept bound by his engagements" because even the least details of the personal activity are seen by him to be "engaged" to the other activities of the cosmos, just as a wheel in a watch is "engaged" to the rest of the works, and moved by the power of the mainspring.

Note that the Hanged Man is pictured as being a pendulum. This symbolism was intended to suggest the very "clockwork" simile we have just employed in this paragraph.

The fixed unwavering self-contemplation proceeding primarily from the supernal Understanding is associated with Mem because of the Creator's self-understanding. When this state of the universal consciousness finds expression through a personal form, the complete realization of the divine Splendor is made actual.

24ᵗʰ Path is *Sekhel Dimyoni*

The 24ᵗʰ Path (Nun, joining Tiphareth to Netzach) is called the Intelligence of Resemblance (or, Imaginative Intelligence) because it constitutes the similarity in all created beings' likenesses.

The work of the 24ᵗʰ Path has to do with modifications of the blood. Note that the first two letters of *Dimyoni* are דם, the Hebrew noun for blood. The rest of the world יוני, is numerically equivalent to a Hebrew noun חביון, meaning "hidden treasure." The secret of the 24ᵗʰ Path has something to do with the valuable occult properties of blood.

We may understand Key 13 as a symbol of the will-to-live, and this will enable us to see why this path is the link between the EGO and the desire nature. All our desires are but variants of the will-to-live. No matter what forms our desires may take, what we all want is more abundant life. When we grasp the truth that our desires are intimations that we already possess what we seem to lack, then we arrive at the state of freedom from desire.

The 24ᵗʰ Path is when the Ego's power to project mental images is the fundamental activity. Desires inevitably tend to take form in some sort of physical activity, and every physical action is a little death. The work of practical occultism tends to put out the fires of desire and end the generation of a diversity of mental images leading to action.

When we realize that human personality never acts of itself, the chariot comes to a standstill. When one is truly fully absorbed, through Samadi, with the One Self, one is identified with the Actionless. The one becomes like the sphinx in Key 10. The wheel of manifestation turns, but the SELF remains immobile. There is nothing to want because we realize our perfect union with the Possessor of ALL. Then we can say, "All power is given me of my Father."

Note well that present tense. The will-to-live ceases when we find within ourselves the fountain of Limitless Life. Tasting of that, we thirst no more. This is by no means sterile indifference to living. It realizes Limitless Life to the full. To get rid of the will-to-live is not to lose interest in living. It is to put a plus sign for a minus

We kill our own bodies by our restless struggles to acquire what, if only we knew it, we already have. When life flows through us unobstructed, the balance of metabolism is maintained. We find we never were born. We know we shall never die. We learn that we are four-dimensional, not three-dimensional, beings, and enter into a realm of power and joy for which there are no words. The possessor of the 24ᵗʰ Path has this awareness, and his subconsciousness weaves the realization into the very cells of his body.

Through Nun descends the influence from Tiphareth to Netzach. It is the link between the Ego and the desire nature between the Sun and the Sphere of Venus. The Path Nun is the first manifestation of the dynamic or projective aspect of Tiphareth (as contrasted with the static or receptive aspect). It is called "Imaginative Intelligence" because the primary activity of Beauty works through imagination in bringing about new modes of expression. This involves the passing away of the forms which are supplanted by those which imagination calls into existence.

New forms are developments of the old. This is suggested by the nature of the harvest gathered by the Reaper in Key 13. The result is the perfection of Netzach, for, through the transformations wrought by the power of Beauty, the final Victory is attained.

25th Path is *Sekhel Nisyoni*

The 25th Path (Samekh, joining Tiphareth to Yesod) is called the Intelligence of Probation or Trial because it is the first test whereby the Creator tries the compassionate.

The adjective is derived from *nisawyun* [נסיון,176], meaning "trial, temptation, test, experiment, experience." Probation or Trial signifies the testing of the ideas and innovations suggested by the imagination. It joins Beauty to Foundation because only by experiments, trials and tests can the harmony of Tiphareth become actualized in term Foundation.

This path's work is described as the "first test whereby the Creator tries the compassionate." They to whom this test is applied are the Chasidim, who is active in the spirit of mercy derived from the 4th Sephirah.

The Chasidim do nothing of themselves. The One Ego symbolized by Michael, the Angel of Jehovah, is the real Actor in all personal thinking, speaking or doing. With them, this is an ever-present recollection. This state of mind is established in one who has gained the Grade of Exempt Adept by practice, and the practice is shown by Key 5, which symbolizes the essential meaning of Key 14.

The difference between the two Keys and their corresponding paths is that Key 5 has to do with *receiving* instruction, while Key 14 has to do with *testing* the instruction in the fires of actual experience.

Then, this practice's object is not to put an end to this condition of a flux of the mental stream, which would be impossible; but to <u>direct that stream always in a sense we desire to progress.</u> And the method advocated consists in constantly observing, in standing apart and watching and noting accurately just what we are doing all through our daily life; combined, on the one hand, with a constant effort to cast out the Self-concept from our consciousness as they arise; and, on the other hand, with keeping before us all the time the recollection of our high aim; that we are doing all this to reduce the suffering of life.

And so with whatsoever, you may be engaged on, you sit apart, as it were, and intently watch, down to the minutest detail, what you are doing; you suppress as far as possible all idea that it is *you* that do these things.

The flow of power from above or within produces the *feeling* of "egoity." The error of supposing each of us *owns* a "self" is what makes all the trouble. The truth is the reverse. Every single human personality is "owned" by the Ego in Tiphareth.

The simple terms of the Rosicrucian vow to look upon every circumstance as a particular dealing of God with one's soul provide a clear pattern for right recollectedness. Sooner or later, it will dawn upon us that even our decision so to regard every event, and our mental effort to keep the vow, are just as much part of God's particular dealings as anything else. Then the difficulties vanish, and we find that the "royal yoga" is veritably the "easy yoke."

In Key 14, we see a crown in the background, symbolizing Kether. The Path in Key 14 stands for the two paths above Yesod, and the pool at its lower end is the ninth Sephirah, the seat of the Vital Soul. On one side is an eagle, to indicate Scorpio and the Path of Nun. On the other is a lion, the "roaring lion," one of the devil's symbols, the Path of Ayin, Key 15.

Key 14 shows the Ego as the Holy Guardian Angel, tempering and modifying the Vital Soul and communicating to it the direct influence from Tiphareth. The angel is Michael, representing the powers of the sixth Sephirah, the Sphere of the Sun. For the Holy, Guardian Angel is none other than the Ego which, Ego the, Actor and Knower, manifesting its consciousness and energy through the personal awareness and activity of innumerable human beings. When a student devotes all his personal actions to this Holy Guardian Angel's direction, there is a modification of the Vital Soul activities and its automatic consciousness. The practice of completely devoting all personal action, both mental and physical, to the SELF brings about the purification of the automatic consciousness. The inevitable result is an alteration of the habitual, subconscious time concept.

Jupiter, the Wheel of Fortune, rules Sagittarius. Thus, the 25th Path's work is concerned with our daily testing by Spirit to see whether we interpret our experiences correctly as being cosmic events, just as truly as they are personal activities. Notice that we do not have to deny that they are personal activities that really occur. What we get from our steady watchfulness is the comprehension that what we call a "personal activity" is that something more, and the something more is it's being a special manifestation, in our personal field of time and space, of forces and laws which flow into that field and out of it but never originate in it.

26th Path is *Sekhel Mechudash*

The 26th Path (Ayin, joining Tiphareth to Hod) is called the Renewing Intelligence because thereby God -blessed be He- renews all things which are begun afresh in the creation of the world.

The root of this adjective is akin to the verb in Psalm 51:10: "Create in me a clean heart, O God; and *renew* a right spirit within me." The same verb appears in Psalm 104:30: "Thou sends forth your spirit, they are created: and thou *renews* the face of the earth." Of similar import is the passage in Revelation 21:5: "Behold, I make all things new."

Life-power is not only the Creator and the Preserver, but also the great Renewer. In the process of renovation, old things pass away, and the unenlightened, clinging to familiar forms, distrust and fear these changes. This is why ignorant misunderstanding hates innovations and looks upon new movements' leaders as inspired by the devil.

This path's work is concerned with man's conscious, personal grasp of the meaning of his daily experience. The development of this conscious comprehension requires that persons be brought face to face with problems. For the ignorant, these problems are evils, caused by some principle of malice, working in external nature and in human nature, to bring about various natural disasters and various types of human wickedness. Out of their own enlightenment, the wise learn better. They come to recognize the Ego as being the only Actor. They know that their past "sins" are wholly forgiven, being the inevitable imperfections of human thought and behavior expressed through unenlightened persons' lives.

They look back over the panorama of their personal lives (for full enlightenment brings memory of other incarnations) and see that all their "personal" activities were part of the Work of the Chariot. They find plenty of imperfections but see how they were inevitable at the various stages of development. *They find nothing to condemn.*

From their own experience, they are taught that there is nothing to condemn in the life of any human being. There are many imperfections, but the person who sins and fails is simply a vehicle which the Life-power has not yet completed, and the Life-power does not condemn even the least of its unfinished instruments.

This does not open a door for sentimental condoning of ineffective, ill-judged, or false ideas or actions. *Actions* may be rightly judged (but only by those truly God-taught) as being "missings of the mark." *Persons* fall under no condemnation.

An enlightened man sees how the Ego works through humanity's total expression to achieve its end, and that end is the liberation of all. Thus, the wise believe in democracy, believe in the good results of enduring in political affairs, by the majority's expressed will. For they have the first-hand experience to teach them that no matter how blind and ignorant persons may be, there is true "a Destiny which shapes our ends, rough-hew them how we will."

That Destiny is the Ego, the Son in perfect union with the Father, the Anointed Liberator in Tiphareth. Angel of Death, to make the Great Work possible. Angel of Guidance, to set our feet upon the Way of Peace. Angel of Temptation, misunderstood by the ignorant as the Devil when he is the Eternal Renovator forever making all things new.

The 26th Path of wisdom carries the power of Ruach in Tiphareth down to Hod. It is the link between the Sphere of the Sun and the Sphere of Mercury, between imagination and intellect, and between the Egoic Body and the Mental Body. This path has to do with the means whereby the EGO in Tiphareth effects changes in man's personal intellect, which corresponds to Hod at the lower end of the Path of Ayin.

The Path of Ayin is perhaps the most obscure of all. The "Renewing Intelligence" completes the dynamic expression of Beauty (Tiphareth) by the union it to Splendor (Hod) on the side of the Pillar of Severity. The key to the mystery of this path is the word *limitation*. Renewing Intelligence is the source of human consciousness of limitation, incompleteness, lack, and bondage. Our sense of bondage reflects our intuitive knowledge of the freedom of That, which is the essential Self of every man. When we consider the small extent of our personal achievements, the One Self's essential perfection seems to be an unattainable ideal. The sense of bondage, however, is what drives humanity to seek freedom. Thus it leads at last to the Splendor, which is the consequence of the strict justice of Geburah and the outcome of the dynamic impulse toward Beauty, which pervades creation. At the same time, this Splendor is the reflection of Victory (Netzach).

The skeleton in Key 13, the angel in Key 14, and the devil in Key 15 are not three different things. They are three aspects of the One Ego, as that Ego appears to personal consciousness. In dealing with Key 15, we understand that the devil is really Master of the Game. He represents the way the Ego appears to the ignorant. He typifies what seems to be the threatening lion of Key 14. Yet he really is what brings about man's intellectual development, and for this reason, the symbol of Mercury is a prominent detail of Key 15. It is by meeting and solving problems which threaten him that man develops intellectual power. So long as man accepts his environment's superficial appearances at face value, his intellect does not evolve. So long as he believes in evil spirits or in a single Lord of Evil, he cannot catch a glimpse of the Eternal Splendor corresponding to the 8th Sephirah.

27th Path is *Sekhel Morgash*

The 27th Path (Peh, joining Netzach to Hod) is called the Exciting or Active Intelligence because thence is created the spirit of every creature under the supreme orb, and the assemblage of them all.

From a verbal root meaning "to be noisy, to be tumultuous, to rage." Thus the 27th Path assigned to Mars may be considered to partake of the nature of Geburah. It is as if the current descending from Geburah through Tiphareth to Netzach were reflected back to Hod through this path.

The first path flowing from Netzach is Peh, symbolizing the overthrow of "common sense" by spiritual intuition. It also stands for the Mars force active in Geburah and finds expression in the activities pictured by the Emperor and by Death. The force works in a man's brain to give him a higher vision, which sees things instead of just looking *at* them. It is the force that is the means whereby man's physical life is reproduced in his posterity and the power that enables him to reproduce himself in new of circumstance.

There are two ancient titles for Key 16, "The House of God" and the "The Fire of Heaven."

"The Fire of Heaven," *esh min-ha-shamaim* אש מן השמים [786], refers to lighting in 2 Kings 1:10. Lighting is the Holy Influence called *Mezela* [78]. It descends through the Tree of Life and the 32 Paths. It is symbolized by the lighting-flash in Key 16. *Mezela* is the radiating energy projected from Kether whereby all things are brought into existence. It is a whirling force, and in its physical expression is the spiraling, electro-magnetic energy which, is the substance from which the atoms of the physical universe are constructed.
Additionally, the "water" of the alchemists is fiery. Electricity is often described as being fluid. The Mars-force and this electrical fluid are identical.

Beth ha-Elohim בית האלהים means "House of God" and is numerically 503 as well as *gawrash* [גרש], and the phrase *yekhavah-da'ath* [יחוה דעת].

Gawrash, a verb meaning "to drive, to thrust, to cast out, to expel, to put forth fruit." The Tower's symbolism in Key 16, with its falling figures and toppling crown, is in agreement. Since Mars presided over the fertility of fields and herds and the active force in reproduction, "to put forth fruit" is also understandable.

As a noun, *geresh* signifies "a fruit, a product of the earth, produce." The letters of the word are clues to a deeper meaning. They are Gimel (Moon), Resh (Sun) and Shin, the Fire and Quintessence of the Alchemist and the symbol of *Prana*. Thus the word is a symbol for Moon, Sun and Fire, and since it also means "a product of the earth," it is a symbol for that most precious fruit, the Stone of the Wise, compounded by Moon, Sun and Fire from the elements composing the earth.

The phrase *yekhavah da'ath* means "shows knowledge," from Psalm 19:2, "Night unto night shows knowledge." Note that night shows knowledge tonight, while day utters speech today. This phrase is directly associated with Peh, the mouth as the organ of speech.

Some ancient Tarot Keys show the lightning-bolt issuing from a sun disk's mouth with a human face. Genesis says "night" is the name for darkness, and for Binah the Mother. The womb of night brings forth the day. The night is the time we associate with generation and conception, and *da'ath*, knowledge, is known to mean what the Bible intimates when it says: "And Adam knew his wife, and she conceived."

"House of God" is part of a New Testament statement: "What, do you not know that your body is a temple of the Holy Spirit that is within you, which you have received from God? (1 Corinthians, 6:19)." Thus the tower is a symbol for the human body.

The magical power attributed to the 27th Path is: "To foresee all future events that do not depend on a superior free will or an all undiscernible cause." The choice of words here is subtle. No event depends on any *personal* "superior free will" because all events depend on the One Will, which finds expression through every living creature. It is what excites every creature into action and constitutes its essential life.

This One Will, which seems to be an "all undiscernible cause," is an indwelling *Presence*. Its light of direct knowledge, like a lightning-flash and overthrows the whole conception of the meaning of a life held previously. This perception destroys the delusion of personal autonomy and isolation. It gives both insight and foresight. Then we see truly what the SELF is and the real meaning and purpose of human personality. This is an experience of a single person and whole races at certain stages of their development. It is the great influence that affects sweeping changes in the thought and work of the world.

The reciprocal path of Peh joins Victory to Splendor, the field of desire to that of intellect. It is the "Exciting Intelligence," and it follows the Renewing Intelligence because the sense of limitation sooner or later gives way to the conviction that this limitation is not permanent. This conviction is man's chief incentive to the kinds of activities that will lead to freedom. This conviction is an intuitive perception that the Spirit of man is one with the Universal Spirit, which as we have seen must necessarily succeed in carrying out the great purpose for which it projects Itself in a universe.

28th Path is *Sekhel Motba*

The 28th Path (Tzaddi, joining Netzach to Yesod) is called the Natural Intelligence because it is perfected the nature of all things under the orb of the sun.

As a verb *Tawbah* [טבע, 81] means: to press in, to impress, to sink. As a noun, it means nature. This word's meanings imply that nature is like the impression made on wax by a signet ring. Closely related is the occult doctrine that nature is impressed with characters written by the Hand of God. This is a figurative way of stating what is strictly true. One needs only to pay close attention to events and things to read their inner meaning.

The second path proceeding from Netzach is Tzaddi, associated with meditation. Meditation carries the thought of faith into man's subconsciousness, where it begins to influence the Vital Soul's activities. In the highest ranges of practical occultism, meditation is employed to evolve the etheric pattern of the new creature. The truth that a new organism result from the desire for a new function is here in evidence. We must want to be more than we seem to be. We must dwell on our image of the new creature. Meditation transfers that image to the Vital Soul or automatic consciousness field. The latter then proceeds to set in motion the activities that bring the new creature into actual manifestation. Our conscious part in this is to meditate on the image, and this image gets clearer and clearer as we meditate.

In Key 17, the Star, the nude woman kneeling symbolizes the Ego because the Ego, though usually termed by Qabalists the Son, is really androgyny. Meditation is a function of the Ego, which raises to the conscious level the powers of the automatic consciousness in Yesod, symbolized by the pool. He who seeks to enter the Fifth Kingdom must meditate. However much it may seem to us at first that meditation is a personal activity, when we really succeed in meditation, we discover that what happens is not what we meditate, but rather that we are *meditated*.

We experience the peace of illumination during quiet meditation after the storm and conflict of our early awakenings have passed. A man in meditation surrenders himself to the indwelling *Shekinah,* the "Light of Wisdom," who is the "Daughter of the Seven." He makes an appointment with Her. He seeks Her out, and to her faithful lover, She unveils.

The "building" is the secret place of the Most High. It is within the brain of the illuminated adept and is what we call the "Adytum." In an unenlightened man, it is in the same condition as the Temple at the time of David. The materials are gathered but cannot be erected into a temple by David, the warrior and man of blood. They must wait for Solomon, whose name signifies "peaceful."

The Path of Tzaddi joins Netzach, sphere of the desire nature, to the automatic consciousness. The sudden inspiration in Key 16 is followed by the calmer influence of the Tzaddi, called the "Natural Intelligence." This path represents the gradual unfoldment of man's intuitive knowledge of the truth. This knowledge begins to find expression in his thought as soon as he realizes that he is not the bondslave of external conditions. It is the projection of Victory, which recognizes as inevitable, which is the root of all human hopes.

29th Path is *Sakyel Mughsham*

The 29th Path (Qoph, joining Netzach to Malkuth) is called the Corporeal Intelligence because it marks out the forms of all bodies which are incorporated under every revolution of the zodiac, and is what constitutes the arrangement and the disposition thereof.

Corporeal means Incarnating. The adjective *mogashem* is derived from a verb [גשם, 343], *gawsham*, meaning "to rain violently," or as a noun: "a hard shower." Key 18 pictures a shower of 18 Yods. Yod is 10, so 10 x 18 = 180, the number of degrees in a semicircle. Because the sun follows the apparent path of a semicircle from east to west during a day, 180 is a symbol of the "day," or incarnation period of a personality.

As the Intelligence which "informs everybody," it is that which affects all structural transformations. It is the immediate agency of evolution. The word is employed in its archaic meaning, "to form, vitalize, make or inspirit."

The main work of the Corporeal Intelligence has to do with the marking out of the bodies peculiar to the 12 zodiacal types, as our text intimates when it says the Corporeal Intelligence "marks out the forms of all bodies which are incorporated under every revolution of the zodiac." Illumination is not a loss of personal identity. It does not erase the special characteristics which make, say, a Taurean clearly distinguishable from a Libran. Thus the symbol of the Holy City in the Apocalypse has 12 gates and 12 foundations. Illumination does not do away with personal identity or personality. It enlightens and liberates.

Corporeal Intelligence is that mode of consciousness that builds the soul's physical vehicle. The consciousness has its bodily location in the head's back, in the cerebellum and the medulla oblongata. The medulla consciousness is active at all times, even when the higher brain-centers are asleep, for it controls all the principle vital functions.

Qoph joins Netzach (the Supreme Spirit's hidden knowledge of Its limitless potentialities, which must find expression sooner or later in the perfect manifestation of Itself implied by the noun Victory) to Malkuth, the field of desire to that of sensation. This path begins the operation of the tenth Sephirah. Malkuth is connected to man's physical body. During sleep, the desires we formulate clearly are impressed on the cell structure.

The Corporeal Intelligence acts in response to desire, even in the lowest forms of living organisms. All structural changes in the evolution of higher types of life from lower ones are brought about by efforts to gratify some desire felt by the entity in whose organism repeated action directed towards some definite end brings about such changes. In man, these changes occur only, or at least principally, within the range of the nervous organism, by the transformation so wrought--during natural sleep, that the latent powers of man find expression. The higher faculties hid, or occult, in the masses of humanity, are brought forth into adepts' supernormal powers.

Eliphas Levi's states that the magical power of a possessor of the Path of Qoph is "To triumph over adversities." This is a concise summary of the entire process of embodiment which, is the work of the Corporeal Intelligence. The changes in the human organism, which are brought about by endeavors to overcome seemingly adverse conditions, and the great change from the natural man to the new creature, are direct consequences of the work connected with the 29th Path.

30th Path is *Sekhel Kelali*

The 30th Path (Resh, joining Hod to Yesod) is called the Collective Intelligence because thence astrologers, by the judgment of the stars and the zodiac, derive the perfection of their knowledge of the revolution of ruling principles.

Kellawliy is derived from [כלל, 80], *kellawl*, signifying "whole, complete." The 30th Path has to do with completing the Great Work in the production of the new creature, evolved from the natural man by the Life-power, working through the mental, emotional and physical activities of a human personality.

The personality is the instrument or vehicle through which the Life-power evolves the new creature. The active transforming power does <u>not originate in the personality</u>, though it does dwell within it. Key 14 pictures as the Holy Guardian Angel are shown in Key 19 as a sun with a human face. It is the one EGO, the Christos.

The EGO utilizes to bring about the new creature's evolution: the cosmic life-force, or Chaiah, seated in Chokmah. *Chiah* is the universal radiant energy. Thus it is associated in our text with the stars and the zodiac.

An individual who possesses the power of this path belongs to that small minority described in our text by the term [בעלי שמים, 507], *baali ha-shamaim*, masters of the heavens. Do not confuse them with exoteric astrologers. Besides knowing and interpreting external celestial forces' influences, they have become masters of their *interior* stars. This mastery is one consequence of the meditation symbolized by Key 17.

These individuals know how to solve their problems and have behind them a record of success, giving them confidence. They approach their problems with joy. Their work is not labor, but, in the truest and best sense of the word, recreation.

Thus the little children in Key 19 stand with one foot in the fairy ring's inner circle and one foot in the outer circle. This means that they have yet to do some work. This stage of unfoldment is but preliminary to the two which come after it, and these are connected with the 31st and 32nd Paths of wisdom.

Resh is the first path proceeding from Hod, which it joins to Yesod, thus being the link between the Sphere of Mercury and the Sphere of the Moon, and between intellect and the automatic consciousness. In Key 19, the boy is on the side corresponding to Hod and the girl on the side corresponding to Yesod, but they are linked by their joined hands.

Resh is the compliment or reflection of Natural Intelligence. It is called the Collecting Intelligence because this path corresponds to the Sun, a great storage battery of cosmic and spiritual fire. This fire is collected in the sun and there lowered in vibratory speed so that it becomes perceptible to our gross senses in the phenomena of light and heat. The cosmic energy itself is actively manifest in the Absolute or Perfect Intelligence of Hod. The fundamental principle of the universe is consciousness. Activity, whether fine or gross, is inherently mental in quality. This fact is the scientific basis of magic.

Resh carries the patterns arranged by intellectual activity (which is cosmic energy collected or focussed as solar force) to the Vital Soul level. In Key 19, the sun at the top of the picture stands for the Hod. The Sphere of Mercury is to be carefully distinguished from the planet Mercury. Our day-star is a concentration of the Life-power's self-conscious energy, and that self-conscious energy is the Mercury of the Sages concentrated in the EGO in Tiphareth.

The Path of Resh represents the early stages of man's conscious awareness that he is actually becoming a new creature. It is a picture of something which occurs at both conscious and subconscious levels. The two children symbolize these two modes of personal consciousness, and the sun behind them is like the angel of Key 14. They are personal embodiments of what some have called the "solar consciousness." Their dance in a fairy ring is a manifestation at the personal level of the EGO's conscious energy in Tiphareth, symbolized by the daystar overhead with its human face.

31st Path is *Sekhel Temidi*

The 31st Path (Shin, joining Hod to Malkuth) is called the Perpetual Intelligence because it rules the movements of the sun and moon according to their constitution and perfects all the powers of all the revolutions of the zodiac and the arrangement (or, form) of their judgments.

Temidiy [תמידי, 510] is derived from [תמיד, 454], *tawmeed*, signifying continuance, or indefinite extension, and often referring in ancient Hebrew to perpetual time.

The Path of Qoph is that which is chiefly concerned with the corporeal pattern and form. It carries our desire for nature into the sphere of physical sensation. Its opposite, the 31st Path of Shin, carries into the physical organism the influences descending from Kether through the side of Geburah on the Tree. The whole series of paths on the pillar of severity has to do with activities which, from the ordinary human standpoint, are concerned with the future, with the elaboration of the consequences of what the One Self knows itself to be, into forms of expression which make that knowledge manifest in actual states of realization.

It is for this reason that Key 20, corresponding to the 31st Path, is a symbol of a state of human personality, which is the "future" for the majority of human beings.

Note that the last word of the text concerning the 31st Path is "judgments," in this instance written משפטיהם, *mishpatiham*, "their judgments." The "revolutions of the zodiacs" are the cycles of successive incarnation. The form of their judgments is a veiled reference to the completion of the incarnation cycle by the "resurrection" from what St. Paul calls "the body of this death" (Romans 7:24). This is the "natural body," the body of sin, dominated by the vital soul and not yet perfected by the EGO.

Yet this "body of death" or "natural body" is the seed of the spiritual body, which is finally evolved after the creative process. What raises it from corruption is the spiritual fire that enters it through the channel of the 31st Path.

The angel in Key 20 is Gabriel, whose name is from the same root as Geburah. Gabriel is the Divine Presence manifested as the irresistible strength of volition. He is the sounder of the last trump, and Key 20 shows that sound is active in the process, raising the new creature from the "death" of the delusion of separateness.

Seven rays extend from the angel's trumpet to show that the powers of all seven Elohim are combined in the sound, which brings the resurrected figures from their floating stone coffins. This sound is also the Voice, and by Greek geometry, the word for "voice" or "sound" is equivalent to the Greek for "the full (exact, perfect) knowledge," and the Greek for "Robe of Adonai." The Robe of Adonai is the perfected body of the new creature, and it is because he has this new body that he enters into the perfect knowledge of his Divine Selfhood.

Until this final consummation of the Great Work, we seem to be directing it from the field of intellectual, self-conscious awareness. We make plans. We concentrate. We study and practice. Yet, the final liberation is a call from above. It is not our work but the operation of the fiery Spirit.

The Perpetual Intelligence is the spiritual power that, without a single break in the continuity of its operation, works to perfect every one of its personal vehicles by providing each of them with the new creature's spiritual body. This is a body incarnate on the physical plane, but it is freed from the necessity for birth and death. It begins its final incarnation as a natural body but ends that incarnation transmuted into the immortal vehicle of the liberated adept. This is the completion of the evolutionary cycle, hence its title, the Judgment.

Perpetual Intelligence is even now at work within you. It is even now preparing you for the event pictured by the symbols of Key 20. Perhaps that event may seem to you to be far in the future, but remember that both "past" and "future" are terms belonging to our natural time-sense. They are meaningless to a human being who has risen from the grave of error into the light of the acute knowledge which, knowledge the, fruition of the Great Work whereby the EGO brings its personal vehicles to completion as new creatures.

32nd Path is *Sekhel Ne'evad*

The 32nd Path (Tav, joining Yesod to Malkuth) is called the Serving, or Administrative Intelligence because it directs all the seven planets' operations and concurs therein.

Tav is called the Serving, aiding, or Administrative Intelligence. It is the only path proceeding from Yesod, joining the Sphere of the Moon to the Sphere of the Elements, the automatic consciousness field and the vital soul to sensation and physical embodiment. Without the propagative power of Yesod, the Resplendent Intelligence of Malkuth would be barren and unproductive.

The number of the letter-name Tav [תו] is 406. Note that the theosophic extension of 7 is 28, and 406 is the extension of 28. Hence, Tav may be considered as being the full development of what is symbolized by Zain, Key 6, the 17th Path of wisdom. Furthermore, the extension of 6 is 21, the number of the Tarot Key for Saturn.

Thus the 32nd Path is, in some sense development of ideas related to the 17th Path. The Path of Zain conducts the Holy influence from Binah, the Sphere of Saturn, down to Tiphareth, the Sphere of the Sun, and the EGO seat. This suggests a strong Saturn influence at work in the 17th Path.

Right discrimination, pictured by Key 6, uses this same Saturnine quality to make the sharp distinctions between conscious and subconscious functions necessary to establish balance in our personal manifestations of these two modes of consciousness. You will remember the occult dictum that "above" and "within" are synonyms. The highest is the innermost. Consequently, the mountain peak in the background of Key 6, and the angel to whom the woman lifts her eyes, are both symbols of the *central* Spiritual Presence. Union with that Presence is the goal of spiritual attainment, and this goal is the mountain peak. The top of the mountain is comparable to the single point at the apex of a pyramid, and this is the *Central Point*.

In the Cube of Space, the Central Point is innermost. This is the "Palace of Holiness in the midst," the Holy Temple that stands at the center. *The Book of Formation* says this temple or palace corresponds to Tav.

Hence our text says the Administrative Intelligence "directs all the seven planets' operations and concurs therein." This central presence is what is symbolized in the Apocalypse by the "Lamb." The Lamb is the light of the city. The Lamb, in union with the Lord God Almighty, constitutes the inner temple of the city. The throne of God and the Lamb is amid this crystalline, golden cube, and from the throne flows the river of living water, clear as crystal.

The Holy City is also called the Bride, the Qabalistic term for Malkuth, the tenth Sephirah. She is the world-dancer of Key 21. Her Hebrew name [55, כלה], *Kallah*, is usually translated "bride" or "spouse," but means literally "crowned one," and is derived from the root [50, כלל], *kallal*, complete, perfect.

This city's foundation is the vital soul seated in Yesod when that vital soul is impregnated with the EGO's power. The EGO is the "Lamb." The EGO is the LIGHT. The EGO is manifested in the Administrative Intelligence, the greatest of all because it is all servant.

Appendix 15

A Dissertation Concerning the 32 Paths of Wisdom

The Paths of the Tree of Life indicate the order of manifestation after the ten Sephiroth powers' primary expression, indicated by the Lighting-flash. Not until the paths of the letters are manifested do the Sephiroth come into full expression. Before this, they are like unrealized ideas. The paths of the letters make them active.

Now consider the order of the paths. The 11th (Aleph, א) brings *Wisdom* (*Chokmah*) into activity; the 12th (*Beth*, ב) *Understanding* (*Binah*); the 13th (*Gimel*) *Beauty* (*Tiphareth*), and thus *Beauty* begins to be active before *Mercy* (*Chesed*) and *Severity* (*Geburah*), as in creating the beauty of the visible nature was manifest before creatures to whom mercy or severity could be shown, were brought forth.

Beauty being established, the 14th Path (*Daleth*) unites *Wisdom* and *Understanding*; and the central point of this path, where it crosses the 13[th,] is Da'ath (דעת) in Hebrew Knowledge, for all knowledge, has its root in the Divine contemplation of the perfect primal *Beauty*. *Wisdom* or *Chokmah*, which includes the idea of skill in construction, then projects the path of Constituting Intelligence (15th Path) *Heh* (ה), and through this path *Beauty*, which hitherto has received only the influx of power from Kether, the Crown of Primal Will, now receives the influence of the Illuminating Intelligence of the Father *Chokmah*

The Constitution Intelligence is the letter *Heh* "with which creation took place," hence the next path, that of *Vau* (ו) joins *Wisdom* to *Mercy*, for when creatures begin to exist, *Mercy* becomes active. This is the passage of *Wisdom* (*Chokmah*) into the Divine Spirit's self-impartation, through the self-contemplation of His (or Its) limitless possibilities as an eternal Spirit of Life.

Mercy (*Chesed*) is before *Severity* (*Geburah*) for reasons that will appear shortly. Do not confuse this sequential manifestation of the Sephiroth with the instantaneous one indicated by the Lightning-Flash, which brings them into potential, but not actual expression simultaneously.

The path of *Zain* (ז), Disposing Intelligence, suggests by its name the Supernal Understanding (Binah) operation in separating the creatures produced by the Constituting Intelligence into species, classes, etc. The fundamental separation is that of sex, and hence this path is indicated by *Zain* the Sword and by the Lovers in the Tarot.

Not until this separating influence has projected the power of *Understanding* into *Beauty*, can the activity of Severity be manifest through the path of *Cheth* (ח), which, setting off definite fields of operation, and so in a sense circumscribing the expression of the Divine *Understanding*, brings into actual effect the Radical Intelligence of *Geburah*.

At this point, the Spirit's full realization of its power as a limitless self-imparting Principle manifested in limited forms of expression, unites Mercy's potencies to those of *Severity*, thought the path of the letter *Teth* (ט), called Intelligence of all Spiritual Activities. This path is also called Intelligence of the Secret because the Great Arcanum is based upon the fact that Limitless Life expresses Itself in limited forms. Therein you may discover the great secret of all magical operations, ----- the Arcanum of the equilibrium between *Severity* and *Mercy*.

Notice also that this path crosses that of *Gimel* (ג). The central point of the magical equilibrium is realizing that the Primal Will (*Kether*) eternally projects Itself in *Beauty*. This path of *Gimel* is that of Uniting

Intelligence. The implication is that the true equilibrium can only be attained through the conscious self-identification of the personal will with the Universal Self-direction toward the realization of *Beauty*.

Now comes the path of *Yod* (י), which carries Mercy's influence into *Beauty*, concentrated in a complete realization of the cosmic purpose, indicated by the path's name, Intelligence of Will. In the Tarot, the Hermit, far from being a conventional type of Prudence, illustrates beneficence's masculine expression (*Chesed*) through *Yod*, the Father's letter. This will be clear upon examination of the 9th Key of the Tarot.

The path of the letter *Lamed* (ל) by contrast, shows a feminine influence (that of the ruler of the sign Libra, the feminine planet Venus) in the activity of Faithful Intelligence, which perfects or completes the static manifestation of *Beauty* through equilibrated Action or Work (Karma).

But this static manifestation of *Beauty* is not effected until after the path of *Kaph* (כ) or Conciliating Intelligence has brought *Netzach* into activity by the projection of the influence of *Chesed* because Karma does not begin to operate until the turning wheel of manifestation has brought into the field of the unfolding universal self-consciousness a definite conception of the victorious end towards which IT's self-impartation is directed. Karma cannot be supposed to work without an objective, and the nature of Spirit assures us that Its objective must be the successful outcome of the creative process. Hence *Lamed* and the 22nd path follow *Kaph* and the 21st.

The static expression of *Beauty* being realized, *Severity* projects *Splendor* (*Hod*) to balance *Splendor* (Netzach). You will observe that Understanding, *Severity*, and *Splendor* are reflections of Wisdom, *Mercy*, and Victory, respectively). The path connecting *Severity* and *Splendor* is *Mem* (מ), called "Stable Intelligence." The fixed unwavering self-contemplation proceeding primarily from the supernal Understanding is associated with *Mem* because of the Creator's self-understanding. This path refers to a condition of human consciousness.

In the Tarot, the Hanged Man, i.e., the "suspended mind," or *manas* in the state of freedom from activity, which the Hindus compare to a perfectly calm body of water. When this state of the universal consciousness finds expression through a personal form, the complete realization of the divine *Splendor* is made actual.

The path *Nun* (נ) is the first manifestation of the dynamic or projective aspect of *Tiphareth* (as contrasted with the static or receptive aspect). It is called "Imaginative Intelligence" because the primary activity of *Beauty* works through imagination in bringing about new modes of expression. This involves the passing away of the forms which are supplanted by those which imagination calls into existence.

The passing away of supplanted forms is indicated in the symbol is of the Tarot Key entitled Death. The fact that the new forms are developments of the old is suggested by the Reaper harvest in the picture. The result is the perfection of *Netzach*, for, through the transformations wrought by the power of *Beauty*, the final Victory is attained.

The path of the "Intelligence of Probation or Trial," attributed to the letter *Samekh* (ס), because it signifies the testing of the ideas and innovations suggested by the imagination. It joins *Beauty* to *Foundation* (*Yesod*) because only by experiments, trials and tests can the harmony of *Tiphareth* become actualized in term *Foundation*. (Note that Foundation is the propagative Sephirah, and you will have a clue to many problems.)

The path of *Ayin* (ע) is perhaps the most obscure of all. The "Renewing Intelligence" completes the dynamic expression of *Beauty* by the union it to *Splendor*, on the side of the Pillar of Severity. The key to the mystery of this path is the word <u>limitation</u>. Renewing Intelligence is the source of human consciousness of limitation, incompleteness, lack, and bondage. Our sense of bondage, after all, is the reflection of our intuitive knowledge of the freedom of THAT, which is the essential SELF of every man. When we consider the small extent of our personal achievements, the essential perfection of the ONE SELF seems to be an unattainable ideal. Millions of people personify this ideal as an external deity. It's opposite, to which they attribute limitation of all kinds, they personify as a hostile and malignant agency, the devil. The sense of bondage, however, is what drives humans to seek freedom. Thus it leads at last to the Splendor, which is the consequence of the strict justice of Geburah and the outcome of the dynamic impulse toward Beauty, which pervades creation. At the same time, this *Splendor* is the reflection of *Victory*.

The path of Peh (פ), which joins *Victory* to *Splendor*, is analogous to the paths of *Daleth* and *Teth*. It is the "Exciting Intelligence," and it follows the Renewing Intelligence because the sense of limitation sooner or later gives way to the conviction that this limitation is not permanent. This conviction is man's chief incentive to the kinds of activities that will lead to freedom.

It originates in an intuitive perception that the Spirit of man is one with the Universal Spirit, which we have seen must necessarily succeed in carrying out the great purpose it projects Itself in a universe.

This intuitive perception comes suddenly, like a Lightning Flash, and usually overthrows the whole conception of the meaning of a life held previously by him to whom it comes. This is an experience of a single person and whole races at certain stages of their development. It is the great influence that affects sweeping changes in the thought and work of the world.

This sudden inspiration is followed by the calmer influence of the next path, attributed to the letter *Tzaddi* (צ), called the "Natural Intelligence." This path represents the gradual unfoldment of man's intuitive knowledge of the truth. This knowledge begins to find expression in his thought as soon as he realizes that he is not the bondslave of external conditions. It is the projection of *Victory*, which recognizes as inevitable, which is the root of all human hopes.

The next path is that of the letter *Qoph* (ק), in Hebrew, the meaning of this word *Qoph* is somewhat obscure. Usually, it is given as "the back of the head," and there is no doubt that this agrees with the occult tradition and certain facts. But the word *Qoph* is also translated "ape" and is apparently of obscure foreign derivation. If it means "ape" in the alphabet, it suggests a knowledge of the evolution of the part of Qabalists antedating the theories of Darwin by some thousands of years; for the path of *Qoph* is that of "Corporeal Intelligence," "which informs everybody in the influence of the solar orb, and is the root of all growth." (The word <u>informs</u> as here employed, has the sense, now obsolete, of to form, vitalize, make or inspirit.")

Corporeal Intelligence is that mode of consciousness that builds the soul's physical vehicle. The consciousness has its bodily location in the back of the head, in the cerebellum and the medulla oblongata. In the latter particularly, consciousness is active at all times, even when the higher brain-centers are asleep, for it controls all the principle vital functions.

The letter *Qoph* is associated with sleep in the Book of Formation, hinting that the Corporeal Intelligence remains active even in sleep. Furthermore, as the Intelligence which informs everybody, it affects all structural transformations, and thus it is the immediate agency of evolution.
Hence the Corporeal Intelligence unites the "Occult Intelligence" of Netzach (the Supreme Spirit's hidden knowledge of Its limitless potentialities, which must find expression sooner or later in the perfect manifestation of Itself implied by the noun Victory) to the "Resplendent Intelligence" of *Malkuth*. Note also that this path corresponds to the zodiacal sign Pisces, which rules the feet, and that it ends in *Malkuth*, wherein are placed the feet of the Grand of Macrocosmic Man.

This Corporeal Intelligence acts in response to desire, even in the lowest forms of living organisms. All structural changes in the evolution of higher types of life from lower ones, as Lamark long ago pointed out, are brought about by efforts to gratify some desire felt by the entity in whose organism repeated action directed towards some definite end brings about such changes. In man, these changes occur only, or at least principally, within the range of the nervous organism. By the transformation so wrought--during natural sleep, be it observed-- that human's latent powers find expression. In other words, the higher faculties hidden, or occult, in the masses of humanity, are brought forth into the supernormal powers of adepts, who have become partakers in the Heavenly Kingdom (*Malkuth*) through powers constitute Resplendent Intelligence of *Malkuth*.

The next path is Resh (ר), the compliment or reflection of the "Natural Intelligence." It is called the "Collecting Intelligence" because this path corresponds to the Sun, a great storage battery of cosmic and spiritual fire. This fire is collected in the sun and there lowered in vibratory speed so that it becomes perceptible to our gross senses in the phenomena of light and heat. The cosmic energy itself is actively manifest in the "Absolute or Perfect Intelligence" of *Hod*. The sages unite in declaring that the universe's fundamental principle is consciousness, whence it follows that the activity, whether fine or gross, is inherently mental in quality. This fact is the scientific basis of magic.

The cosmic energy is collected or focussed as a solar force in the path of *Resh*, which communicates this force to the ninth Sephira, *Yesod*.

The next path is that of *Shin* (ש), joining the Perfect Intelligence of *Hod* to the Resplendent Intelligence of *Malkuth*. It is called "Perpetual Intelligence" because it is subject to no change. Thus it is in direct contrast to the ever-changing Corporeal Intelligence attributed to the letter *Qoph*. Since this path is attributed to Shin, the third Mother-letter, it also refers to the Primal Fire. This path communicates the influence of the Pillar of *Severity* to *Malkuth*. Perpetual Intelligence persists through the series of incarnations, as the spark or core of individuality around which the successive personalities are built.

The last path is that of the letter *Tau* (ת), the "Administrative or Assisting Intelligence," which communicates to the Resplendent Intelligence of *Malkuth*, the propagative power of *Yesod*, without which the Resplendent Intelligence would be barren and unproductive.

Compare this path with that of the Renewing Intelligence and those of *Lamed* (ל) and *Tzaddi* (צ). The point in common is the influence of Saturn, which rules Capricorn (*Ayin*) and Aquarius (*Tzaddi*), and is exalted in Libra (*Lamed*). The power of Saturn is double. Thus the alchemists say that their Saturn (Lead) is corrosive externally and Lunar internally. It combines the from-destroying power of corrosion with the perfect reflecting power that the alchemists call the Moon.

The corrosive power predominates in Capricorn or Renewing Intelligence. The reflective power is active in Natural Intelligence. This Natural Intelligence through the letter *Tzaddi* is associated with meditation. The path of *Lamed* represents the equilibration of the corrosive and reflecting powers.

These correspondences are shown in Key 11, Justice, a female figure, like her who kneels in the picture called The Star, holds the sword of corrosion and the scales, which symbolize the equilibrium attained through meditation. *Lamed* moreover corresponds to Work and is thus allied to the Assisting Intelligence, which, as pictured by The World in the Tarot, represents Saturnine nature's perfection.

The Assisting Intelligence completes the sequential manifestation of the Sephiroth. Human consciousness is expressed as self-identification with the Supreme Spirit and the dedication of the whole personal life to the Great Work's furtherance.

Received in 1919 by the two Brothers who first recovered the outline of the Book of Tokens.

#	Key	Letter	Meaning	Color	Note	Astro
			Appendix 16 – Tarot Attributions			
1	The Fool	Aleph	bull	Yellow	E	♅
2	The Magician	Beth	house	Yellow	E	☿
3	The High Priestess	Gimel	camel, foot	Blue	G#	☽
4	The Empress	Daleth	door	Green	F#	♀
5	The Emperor	Heh	window	Red	C	♈
6	The Hierophant	Vav	hook	Red-Orange	C#	♉
7	The Lovers	Zain	sword	Orange	D	♊
8	The Chariot	Cheth	fence	Orange- Yellow	D#	♋
9	Strength	Teth	clay basket (serpent)	Yellow	E	♌
10	The Hermit	Yod	open hand	Yellow-Green	F	♍
11	The Wheel of Fortune	Kaph	palm of hand	Violet	A#	♃

Appendix 16 – Tarot Attributions					
#	Key	Letter	Meaning	Color	Note	Astro
12	Justice	Lamed	ox goad	Green	F#	♎
13	The Hanged Man	Mem	water	Blue	G#	♆
14	Death	Nun	fish	Blue-Green	G	♏
15	Temperance	Samekh	prop, thorn	Blue	G#	♐
16	The Devil	Ayin	eye	Blue-Violet	A	♑
17	The Tower	Peh	mouth	Red	C	♂
18	The Star	Tzaddi	fish-hook	Violet	A#	♒
19	The Moon	Qoph	sun at the Horizon	Violet-Red	B	♓
20	The Sun	Resh	head	Orange	D	☉
21	Judgement	Shin	tooth	Red	C	♇
22	The World	Tav	mark	Blue-Violet	A	♄

Appendix 17

The Correlation Between Sound and Color

Many esoteric schools have correlations between sound and color in their healing and chanting work. This appendix is based on the *premise* that the correlation between sound and color is based on the octave. That is, we double the frequency of sound to the point that it becomes light. Before we begin, sound, octave and light must be defined.

Sound is vibration carried through the Air. The frequency range that a human ear can perceive is between 20 to 20,000 vibrations per second (or Hertz, abbreviated Hz). The human ear is very sensitive to changes in pitch (change in frequency). Music theory describes sound with great detail. I will cover the very basics.

The Pythagorean Music Scale

Pythagoras (570-504 BCE) is credited with discovering that vibrating strings of whole number proportion create "pleasing" sounds. Consider a single-stringed instrument with a moveable bridge, Pythagoras noted that a string's pitch (frequency) was exactly one octave lower than the pitch created when the string's length was halved. For example, if the string produced an A (440 Hz) note when plucked, then moving the bridge to the string's midpoint would cause it to produce one octave above (880 Hz). He then experimented with the sounds produced when two strings of different lengths are plucked simultaneously (a cord). He discovered that when two strings of length L and $(2/3)L$ are plucked together, the resulting frequencies created a pleasing sound.

Additionally, strings that are one octave apart that are played together also create a pleasing sound. For example, if a pitch of 440 Hz simultaneously with a pitch of 880 Hz, the result is a smooth blending of the two. Therefore in the Pythagorean scale, the octave (2:1 ratio) and the 5th (3:2 ratio) create pleasing sounds.

Pythagoras built his musical scale around the octave, firstly, and then around the fifth (3:2). Additionally, the interval from the fifth to the octave is the ratio 4:3. The ratio from the fourth to fifth is 9:8.

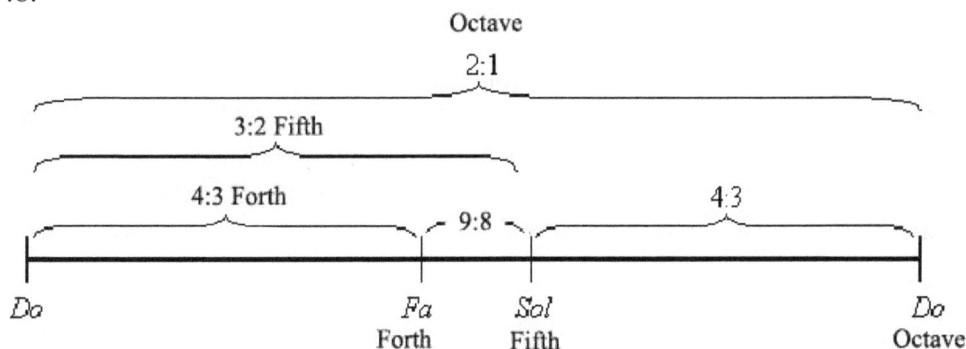

So what does this all mean? I will skip a few steps and show the whole numbers from the notes for a seven-step scale.

Pythagorean Whole Number Seven-Step Scale							
C	D	E	F	G	A	B	C
1	9/8	81/64	4/3	3/2	27/16	243/128	2

If you look at the scale visually, you can see that the steps.

$$1 \quad 9/8 \quad \frac{81}{64} \quad \frac{4}{3} \quad \frac{3}{2} \quad \frac{27}{16} \quad \frac{243}{128} \quad 2$$

Do Ra Me Fa So La Te Do

Pythagorean 7 Step Scale

The Pythagorean scale creates pleasing harmonies. But it is not suited for modern instruments, like a keyboard. Changing Keys (which is too long to explain here) requires retuning the musical instrument. To play in any Key without retuning your instrument, the "Equal Tempered Scale" was developed.

The Equal Tempered Scale

Several tempered (meantone, just tone, well tempered, etc.) scales were developed over the centuries as a compromise between harmonic balance and ease of play. The true equal temperament scale was not available to musicians had to wait until the 1870s until the development of scientific tuning and measurement.

The equal-tempered scale was developed for keyboard instruments to be played equally well (or badly) in any key. It is a compromise tuning scheme. The equal-tempered system uses a constant frequency multiple between the notes of the chromatic scale. The chromatic scale is divided into 12 equal steps: the number of piano keys between octaves. On the equal-tempered scale, each semitone is equal to the twelfth root of 2 or 1.059.

The following table shows a comparison between the Pythagorean scale and the temperate scale:

Note	Temperate Scale		Pythagorean Scale		%
	Power	Value	Fraction	Value	Difference
C	$2^{0/12}$	1.000	1/1	1.000	0
C#	$2^{1/12}$	1.059			
D	$2^{2/12}$	1.122	9/8	1.125	6
D#	$2^{3/12}$	1.189			
E	$2^{4/12}$	1.260	81/64	1.266	0.44
F	$2^{5/12}$	1.335	4/3	1.333	0.15
F#	$2^{6/12}$	1.414			
G	$2^{7/12}$	1.498	3/2	1.500	0.13
G#	$2^{8/12}$	1.587			
A	$2^{9/12}$	1.682	27/16	1.688	0.36
A#	$2^{10/12}$	1.782			
B	$2^{11/12}$	1.888	243/128	1.898	0.55
C	$2^{12/12}$	2.000	2/1	2.000	0

We can also visually compare the scales.

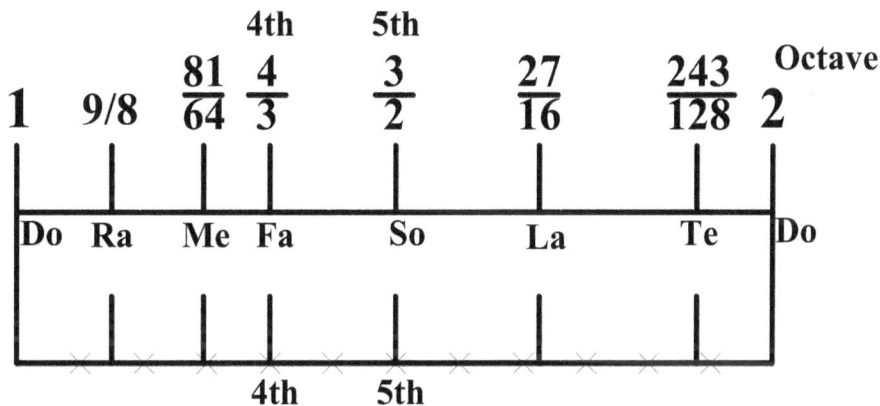

The "x" marks show the 12 equal divisions. Note that the 4th and 5th are good approximations of each other on both scales. However, the human ear can still discern the difference.

Pythagoras scale is based on whole numbers, the equal-tempered scale is based on the irrational number $2^{1/12}$. In Pythagorean times they knew the existence of irrational numbers, but they kept this knowledge secret from the general public. They felt the average human mind was not yet developed enough to handle the concept that a number could not be precisely defined.

Fabre D'Olivet (1767-1825), in his book *The Secret Lore of Music*, had nothing but contempt for "modern" music. He was a firm believer in the Pythagorean mode of music. However, without the different tempered scales, we would be without the music of Bach (1685-1750), Mozart (1756-

1791), Beethoven (1770-1827) and Chopin (1810-1849).

Musical Pitch Standard

There are two accepted musical pitch standards, the American Standard pitch, which takes A in the fourth piano octave (A4) to have a frequency of 440 Hz, and the older International pitch standard, which takes A4 to have the frequency of 435 Hz. The following table is the frequency based on the American Standard Pitch.

Notes	Frequency (octaves) of the American Standard Pitch				
A	55.00	110.00	220.00	440.00	880.00
A#	58.27	116.54	233.08	466.16	932.32
B	61.74	123.48	246.96	493.92	987.84
C	65.41	130.82	261.64	523.28	1046.56
C#	69.30	138.60	277.20	554.40	1108.80
D	73.42	146.84	293.68	587.36	1174.72
D#	77.78	155.56	311.12	622.24	1244.48
E	82.41	164.82	329.64	659.28	1318.56
F	87.31	174.62	349.24	698.48	1396.96
F#	92.50	185.00	370.00	740.00	1480.00
G	98.00	196.00	392.00	784.00	1568.00
Ad	103.83	207.66	415.32	830.64	1661.28

Sound is vibration in Air. When it is a pure tone, it can be described as a *Note* that can be played on a musical instrument. An Octave is a doubling (or halving) of a musical Note.

Frequency of Light vs. Perceived Color

Light is an electromagnetic wave, which is a coupling of an electric and magnetic field. Light can also be described as a discrete particle having zero mass, no electric charge, and an indefinitely long lifetime.

Electromagnetic Wave

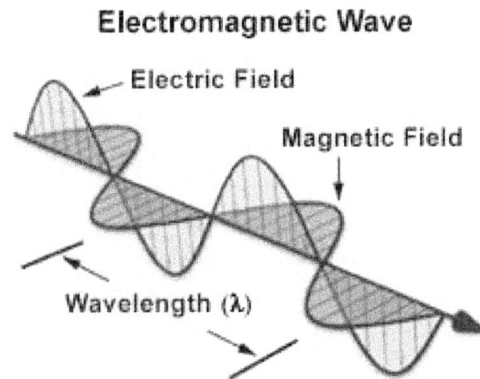

Electric Field

Magnetic Field

Wavelength (λ)

The only thing you need to understand for this paper is light is a wave or vibration that we perceive with our eyes, and sound is a wave that we perceive with our ears.

Visible Light Wavelength and Perceived Color		
Wavelength Range (nanometers) 10^{-9}	Frequency in Terahertz (10^{14})	Perceived Color
340-400	8.8 – 7.5	Near Ultraviolet (UV; Invisible)
400-430	7.5 – 6.9	Violet
430-445	6.9 – 6.7	Blue-Violet
445-482	6.7 – 6.2	Blue
482-500	6.2 – 6.0	Blue-Green (Cyan)
500-538	6.0 – 5.6	Green
538-560	5.6 – 5.3	Yellow-Green
560-595	5.3 – 5.0	Yellow
595-620	5.0 – 4.8	Yellow-Orange
620-645	4.8 – 4.6	Orange
645-690	4.6 – 4.3	Red-Orange
690-730	4.3 – 4.1	Red
Over 730	less than 4.1	Near-Infrared (IR; Invisible)
Frequency = C/wavelength or Wavelength = C/Frequency where C = The speed of light 299,392,458 meters / second		

The Correlation of Sound to Color

Esoteric schools state there is a correlation between sound and color. If we double the frequency of sound by a factor of 40 to 41 octaves, we have a correlation between sound and color. The following table shows the results of this logic:

Note	Frequency (Hz)	multiplied by the octave		Frequency in Terahertz (10^{14})	Color
C	261.62	x	2^{41}	5.7	Green
C#	277.18	x	2^{41}	6.1	Blue-Green
D	293.67	x	2^{41}	6.5	Blue
D#	311.13	x	2^{41}	6.8	Blue-Violet
E	329.63	x	2^{41}	7.2	Violet
F	349.23	x	2^{41} or 2^{40}	3.8	Red-Violet[1]
F#	369.99	x	2^{40}	4. 1	Red
G	392.00	x	2^{40}	4.3	Red-Orange
G#	415.30	x	2^{40}	4.6	Orange
A	440.00	x	2^{40}	4.8	Yellow-Orange
A#	466.16	x	2^{40}	5.1	Yellow
B	493.88	x	2^{40}	5.4	Yellow-Green
[1] near Ultra-Violet if multiplied by 2^{41} and near Infrared if multiplied by 2^{40}.					

In Paul Case's Work, *Correlations of Sound and Color* (1931), as well as *The Highlights of the Tarot* (1931), the following is a summary of the correspondence between sound and color:

Note	Corresponding Color	Color Complement
C	red	green
C#	red-orange	green-blue
D	orange	blue
D#	yellow-orange	blue-violet
E	yellow	violet
F	green-yellow	red-violet
F#	green	red
G	blue-green	red-orange
G#	blue	orange
A	blue-violet	yellow-orange
A#	violet	yellow
B	red-violet	green-yellow

Using the well-tempered chromatic scale, note that the *color complement appears to correspond* to the sound and color correlation used by Paul Foster Case.

Please be aware that color is subjective, and my choice of frequency and wavelength may differ from others. Additionally, the frequency of notes changes depending on which standard you use. I hope this stimulates thought and discussion. Perhaps a more musically trained individual may add to this work.

Except for Metatron and Sandalphon, the meaning of the Sephiroth angels' names are derived from the Hebrew. Note that the AL (אל) at the end of the word means in this context "of God." אל means strong, mighty, a mighty one, a hero. It is the divine name associated with Chesed.

	Table 1 – Spelling & Meaning of Angels of the Sephiroth			
	Sephiroth	Angel	Hebrew	Meaning
1	Kether	Metatron	מטטרון	
2	Chokmah	Raziel	רזיאל	Secret of God
3	Binah	Tsaphqiel	צפקיאל	Watcher of God
4	Chesed	Tzadqiel	צדקיאל	Righteousness of God
5	Geburah	Kamael	כמאל	Longing (desire) of God
6	Tiphareth	Michael	מיכאל	Who is as God (IS)
7	Netzach	Haniel	האניאל	Grace of God
8	Hod	Raphael	רפאל	Whom God has healed Healing of God
9	Yesod	Gabriel	גבריאל	Strength of God
10	Malkuth	Sandalphon	סנדלפון	

Note that I have spelled Haniel, with a Cheth (ח) instead of the Heh (ה) as it is customarily written. Table 2 notes that *Kan* (חן), meaning grace and favor, is spelled with a Cheth (ח).

The change of spelling to a Heh was probably a transcribing error. Before the ballpoint pen and the word processor, the manuscript was handwritten by dipping your pen in ink well. A slight skip of the pen and a Cheth (ח) turns into a Heh (ה).

I also listed under Netzach other words that begin with Heh that are similar to the spelling of Haniel. Neither of these words suggests grace or favor, which is the meaning of Haniel.

	Sephiroth	Root	Meaning
			Table 2 – The Etymology of the Names of the Angels
2	Chokmah	רז	a secret. A mystery.
3	Binah	צפף	to twitter, pip, or chirp, as a bird. Isaiah 10.14: As one reaches into a next, so my had reached for the nations' wealth; as men gather abandoned eggs, so I gathered all the countries; not on flapped a wing, or opened its mouth to **chirp**.
		צפצפה	A Willow (Tree).
		צף	1. to shine, to be bright. 2. To look out, to view. A metaphor used of prophets, who, like watchmen, declares future events as divinely revealed to them by visions. 3. to observe accurately. 4. overlay with gold or silver.
		צפו	watch-tower. a son of Elpphaz, see Genesis 36:11, 15.
4	Chesed	צדק	Righteousness. What is right and just. What is so or ought to be so. Justice. Liberation, welfare, felicity.

	Sephiroth	Root	Meaning
			Table 2 – The Etymology of the Names of the Angels
5	Geburah	כמה	To pine with longing for anything. To become pale form longing. See Psalms 63:2.
		סמל	Likeness. An image, a figure, the statue of the figure, a carved idol.
6	Tiphareth	מי	Who?
		כ	A preposition, meaning: like, as.
7	Netzach	חן	Grace, favor, goodwill. Supplication, prayer.
		הא	Behold! Look! See!
		הן	Feminine plural pronoun, meaning: they those.
8	Hod	רפא	to sew together to mend, to heal, to restore to pristine happiness. To be healed.
9	Yesod	גבר	To be strong, to prevail. The primary power is that of binding, to bind anything broken, to make firm. A virile man. A hero, soldier.

The names Metatron and Sandalphon do not appear to be derived from Hebrew words. However, Both names appear in rabbinic literature (Talmud). Metatron appears in the medieval Jewish mystical texts The Book of Enoch. Metatron occurs in two forms in rabbinic literature one written with six letters, מטטרון, and the other with seven letters, מיטטרון.

Metatron may be derived from MTR, מטר, meaning: to rain, to pour down rain. It is applied to other things that God pours down from heaven in great abundance. In this connection, one of the titles of Kether is "Profuse Giver."

The last three letters RVN (רון) means: to conquer, to overcome. This suggests the same meaning as the addition of the letters אל to the end of angelic names.

You could also the word RNN, רָנַן: to emit a tremulous and strident sound. 1. of the tremulous sound of a mast or tall pole shaken by the wind. 2. as a verb, it is to vibrate the voice (trillern), shout for joy, and lift up joyful outcries.

The name sounds like Greek words *meta* and *tron*. However, it seems unlikely that medieval Rabbis would borrow words from another language to make a Hebrew name. However, the meaning of these words are interesting and worth exploring.

Meta (μετά) in Greek means: after, beyond, among, with, adjacent. Thus suggesting this angel is "with" or very close to God. In English, meta means 1. later in time. 2. situated behind. 3. change, transformation. 4. Beyond; transcending; more comprehensive. At a higher stage of development. 5. Having gone through a metamorphosis.

Meta is from another root word *me*, meaning: 1. to measure, mark, appoint a time, time for eating, meal. 2. Latin *metir*, to measure. 3. From Greek, *metis*, wisdom, skill. 4. From Greek *Metron*, measure, rule. 4. length, proportion. Hence the concept of rulership through the ability to weigh and measure.

Tron in Greek refers to an instrument, a scale (which weighs and measures).

From the perspective of Metatron being a Greek name, it suggests an instrument (Of God) that weighs and measures. This is an aspect of the mind. One of the Names of Kether is "The Light of the Primordial Intelligence."

Sandalphon

Sandalphon does not appear to be derived from a Hebrew word. However, Sandalphon (סנדלפון) appears in the mystical literary traditions, notably in the Midrash and the Talmud and early Christianity. Traditionally she is female and described as the "Twin Brother" of Metatron. Ezekiel 1:15 was interpreted in The Babylonian Talmud *Hagigah* 13b says Sandalphon's head reaches Heaven, which is also said of the Greek giant Typhon (Τυφῶν).

Ezekiel 1:15. "As I looked at the living creatures (החיות, *hayot*), I saw a wheel (אופן, *Ophan*) on the ground beside each creature with its four faces." Note that *Hayot* is part of the Divine Name associated with Kether (חיות הקדש). And אופנים is the Choir of angels attributed to Chokmah, the sphere of the zodiac. Traditionally the wheel described in Ezekiel is Sandalphon.

I found no word SND (סנד) or NDL (נדל) in *Gesenius Hebrew-Chaldee Lexicon to the Old Testament*. I did find DLP (דלף), 1. to drop, to drip (through a roof). 2. to weep, to shed tears (from the eye). In Job: "my eye sheds tears to God." In Psalms: "my soul weeps." In Aramaic: to pour out, to flow. I also found PVN (פון), which means: 1. to set (as the sun) and darkened. 2, to be perplexed, distracted.

Sandalphon in Greek is Σανδαλφών. It may come from the Greek *sandalion*, meaning "sandal"; or "one who wears sandals." It is also possibly derived from the Greek prefix *sym* or *syn*, meaning "together," and *adelphos*, meaning "brother"; thus, approximately meaning "co-brother." This probably refers to its relationship with Metatron. Additionally, the Greek suffix *phon* means voice, and it is said that Sandalphon is a master of heavenly song.

Bibliography

Atwood, Mary Anne. *A Suggestive Inquiry into the Hermetic Mystery with a Dissertation on the More Celebrated of the Alchemical Philosophers being an attempt towards the recovery of the Ancient Experiment of Nature.* With an Introduction by Walter Leslie Wilmshurst. Belfast: William Tait, 1918.

Blech, Benjamin. *The Secrets of the Hebrew Words.* Photos by Gill Aron. New Jersey: Jason Aronson, 1991.

Böhme, Jacob. *Mysterium Pansophicum: Theosophisch-pansophische Schriften.* Freiburg: Aurum Verlag, 1980.

Bond, Frederick Bligh and Thomas Simcox Lea. Gematria: *a Preliminary Investigation of the Cabala.* London, England: Research into Lost Knowledge Organization, 1977.

___. *Materials for the Study of the Apostolic Gnosis: A Pioneering Elucidation of a Purposeful Mathematical Symbolism for the Mysteries of Faith in the Greek Scriptures.* Two volumes. London: Research into Lost Knowledge Organization, Vol. I, 1979; Vol. II, 1985.

Case, Paul Foster and J. Craik Patten. *The Flaming Cube of the Chaldees.* Los Angeles, CA: BOTA Chapter document, 1930.

___. *Notebook of Questions and Answers from Day to Day.* Typed Manuscript. Private collection. Page 1 (20 October 1914).

___. '*The Secret Doctrine of the Tarot,*' printed in *The Word*, New York: Theosophical Publishing Company, June 1917.

___. *The True and Invisible Rosicrucian Order: An Interpretation of the Rosicrucian Allegory and An Explanation of the Ten Rosicrucian Grades.* York Beach, ME: Samuel Weiser, Inc., 1985.

Crowley, Aleister. *777 and Other Qabalistic Writings: including Gematria and Sepher Sephiroth.* Introduction by Israel Regardie. York Beach, ME: Samuel Weiser, Inc., 1977.

Davidson, Gustav. *Dictionary of Angels: Including the Fallen Angels.* New York: Random House, Inc, 1971.

d'Olivet, Fabre. *The Hebrew Tongue Restored and the True Meaning of the Hebrew Words Re-established and Proved by their Radical Analysis.* Translated by Nayán Louise Redfield. York Beach, ME: Samuel Weiser, Inc., 1976.

[Feldman, Daniel Hale.] *Gematria Handbook: A Qabalistic Tool.* n.p.: AIN Center Publications, 1974.

Gaskell, G.A. *Dictionary of All Scriptures & Myths.* New Jersey: Gramercy Books, 1981.

Gesenius, H.W.F. *Gesenius' Hebrew-Chaldee Lexicon to the Old Testament.* Grand Rapids, Michigan. Baker Book House., 1992.

Gikatilla, Joseph. *Gates of Light, Sha'are Orah.* Translated by Avi Weinstein. California: AltaMira Press, 1994.

Ginsburg, Yitzchak. *The Alef Beit.* Northvale, New Jersey: Jason Aronson Inc., 1995.

Godwin, David. *Godwin's Cabalistic Encyclopedia: Complete Guidance to Both Practical and Esoteric Applications.* Third revised and enlarged edition. St. Paul, MN: Lewellyn Publications, 1999.

Grant, Kenneth. *Nightside of Eden.* London, England: Skoob Books, 1994.

Hall, Manly P. *Secret Teachings of All Ages: An Encyclopedic Outline of Masonic, Hermetic, Qabbalistic and Rosicrucian Symbolical Philosophy.* Illustrations by J. Augustus Knapp. Los Angles, CA: Philosophical Research Society, 1994.

Inman, Thomas. *Ancient Faiths Embodied in Ancient Names.* 2 Volumes. London and Liverpool: Privately printed for the Author, 1868.

Kaplan Aryeh. *Sefer Yetzirah: the Book of Creation in Theory and Practice.* York Beach, ME: Weiser Books, 1997.

Kohlenberger III, John R. *The Interlinear NIV Hebrew-English Old Testament.* Michigan: Zondervan Publishing House, 1987.

Locks, Gutman. *Spice of Torah-Gematria.* New York: Judica Press, 1985.

Mathers, S.L. MacGregor. *The Book of the Sacred Magic of Abra-Melin the Mage.* Wellingborough, Northamptonshire: The Aquarian Press, 1976.

___. *The Goetia: The Lesser Key of Solomon the King.* Edited with an Introduction by Aleister Crowley. York Beach, ME: Samuel Weiser, 1995.

___. *The Kabbalah Unveiled; Containing the following Books of the Zohar: The Book of Concealed Mystery, The Greater Holy Assembly, The Lesser Holy Assembly.* York Beach, Maine, Samuel Weiser, 1993.

___. *The Key of Solomon the King.* Foreword by Richard Cavendish. York Beach, ME: Samuel Weiser, 1972.

Omikron. *Letters from Paulos, a Leader in Wisdom, to His Pupils in Korinthos.* London: Kegan Paul, Trench, Trubner, 1920.

Papus [Gérard Encausse]. *The Qabalah.* York Beach, ME: Samuel Weiser, Inc., 1977.

Pike, Albert. *Morals and Dogma of the Ancient and Accepted Scottish Rite.* Charleston, NC: L.H. Jenkins, 1947.

Pryse, James. *The Apocalypse unsealed: Being an Esoteric Interpretation of the Initiation of Ioannes, commonly called the Revelation of St. John.* London: John M. Watkins, 1925.

___. *The Magical Message of Ioannes commonly called the Gospel According to St. John.* London, England: Theosophical Publishing Company, 1909.

Simpson, D.P. *Cassell's Latin Dictionary.* Indianapolis, IN: Macmillian Publishing Company, 1968.

Soror A.L. *Western Mandalas for Transformation.* St. Paul, MN: Llewellyn Publications, 1995.

Strong, James. *The New Strong's Complete Dictionary of Bible Words.* Thomas Nelson Publishers, 1996.

___. *Strong's Exhaustive Concordance of the Bible.* World Bible Publishers, 1980.

Suraes, Carlo. *The Cipher of Genesis.* York Beach, ME: Samuel Weiser under agreement from Shambhala Publications, 1992.

Townley, Kevin. *The Cube of Space.* Boulder, CO: Archive Press, 1993.

Troward, Tomas. *Bible Mystery and Bible Meaning.* New York: Dodd, Mead & Company, 1942.

Waite, A.E. *The Brotherhood of the Rosy Cross: Being Records of the House of the Holy Spirit in its Inward and Outward History.* New Hyde Park, New York: University Books, [1961].

___. *The Hermetic Museum: Containing Twenty-two Most Celebrated Chemical Tracts.* York Beach, ME: Samuel Weiser, 1995.

___. *The Holy Kabalah.* Carol Publishing Group, 1992.

Westcott, William Wynn. *Aesch Mezareph or Purifying Fire.* New York, NY: The Occult Research Press, n.d.

___. *Sepher Yetzirah: the Book of Formation with the Fifty Gates of Intelligence and the Thirty-two Paths of Wisdom.* York Beach, ME: Samuel Weiser, 1980.

Wilson, William. *Wilson's Old Testament Word Studies.* Kregel Publications, 1987.

Young, Robert. *Young's Analytical Concordance to the Bible.* Thomas Nelson Publishers, 1980.

www.ingramcontent.com/pod-product-compliance
Lightning Source LLC
Chambersburg PA
CBHW081143270326
41930CB00014B/3018